COLLEGE ALGEBRA I

CUSTOM EDITION FOR KAPLAN UNIVERSITY

Taken from:

Beginning and Intermediate Algebra, Second Edition
by John Tobey, Jeffrey Slater, and Jamie Blair

Taken from:

Beginning and Intermediate Algebra, Second Edition
by John Tobey, Jeffrey Slater, and Jamie Blair
Copyright © 2006, 2002 by Pearson Education, Inc.
Published by Prentice Hall
Upper Saddle River, New Jersey 07458

This special edition published in cooperation with Pearson Custom Publishing.

Printed in the United States of America

10 9 8 7 6 5 4 3 2 1

ISBN 0-536-50894-1

2007420546

RG

Please visit our web site at *www.pearsoncustom.com*

PEARSON CUSTOM PUBLISHING
501 Boylston Street, Suite 900, Boston, MA 02116
A Pearson Education Company

Contents

CHAPTER 1

Prealgebra Review   1

1.1   **Simplifying Fractions**   2
1.2   **Adding and Subtracting Fractions**   11
1.3   **Multiplying and Dividing Fractions**   22
     How Am I Doing? Sections 1.1–1.3   30
1.4   **Using Decimals**   31
     Chapter 1 Organizer   *43*
     Chapter 1 Review Problems   *44*
     How Am I Doing? Chapter 1 Test   46

CHAPTER 2

Real Numbers and Variables   49

2.1   **Adding Real Numbers**   50
2.2   **Subtracting Real Numbers**   61
2.3   **Multiplying and Dividing Real Numbers**   66
2.4   **Exponents**   76
2.5   **The Order of Operations**   80
     How Am I Doing? Sections 2.1–2.5   84
2.6   **Using the Distributive Property to Simplify Algebraic Expressions**   85
2.7   **Combining Like Terms**   90
2.8   **Using Substitution to Evaluate Algebraic Expressions and Formulas**   95
2.9   **Grouping Symbols**   103
     Chapter 2 Organizer   *108*
     Chapter 2 Review Problems   *109*
     How Am I Doing? Chapter 2 Test   113

CHAPTER 3

Equations, Inequalities, and Applications   115

3.1   **The Addition Principle of Equality**   116
3.2   **The Multiplication Principle of Equality**   122
3.3   **Using the Addition and Multiplication Principles Together**   128

3.4   Solving Equations with Fractions   135
How Am I Doing? Sections 3.1–3.4   143
3.5   Translating English Phrases into Algebraic Expressions   144
3.6   Solving Inequalities in One Variable   150
Chapter 3 Organizer   162
Chapter 3 Review Problems   164
How Am I Doing? Chapter 3 Test   168

CHAPTER 4

Graphing and Functions   171

4.1   The Rectangular Coordinate System   172
4.2   Graphing Linear Equations   184
4.3   The Slope of a Line   194
How Am I Doing? Sections 4.1–4.3   205
4.4   Writing the Equation of a Line   207
Chapter 4 Organizer   212
Chapter 4 Review Problems   213
How Am I Doing? Chapter 4 Test   215

CHAPTER 5

Systems of Linear Equations and Inequalities   217

5.1   Systems of Linear Equations in Two Variables   218
How Am I Doing? Section 5.1   232
Chapter 5 Organizer   234
Chapter 5 Review Problems   235
How Am I Doing? Chapter 5 Test   240

CHAPTER 6

Exponents and Polynomials   241

6.1   The Rules of Exponents   242
6.2   Negative Exponents and Scientific Notation   251
How Am I Doing? Sections 6.1–6.2   258
Chapter 6 Organizer   260
Chapter 6 Review Problems   260
How Am I Doing? Chapter 6 Test   262

Glossary   G-1

Appendix A: Foundations for Intermediate Algebra   A-1
  A.1: Integer Exponents, Square Roots, Order of Operations, and Scientific Notation   A-1
  A.2: Polynomial Operations   A-13
  A.3: Factoring Polynomials   A-20
  A.4: Special Cases of Factoring   A-30
  A.5: The Point–Slope Form of a Line   A-38

Appendix B: Using the Mathematics Blueprint for Problem Solving   A-43

Appendix C: Practice with Operations of Whole Numbers   A-50

Appendix D: Tables   A-52
  Table D-1: Table of Square Roots   A-52
  Table D-2: Exponential Values   A-53

Appendix E: Determinants and Cramer's Rule   A-54

Appendix F: Solving Systems of Linear Equations Using Matrices   A-62

Appendix G: Sets   A-67

Solutions to Practice Problems   SP-1

Answers to Selected Exercises   SA-1

Applications Index   I-1

Subject Index   I-3

1

Have you ever thought about the large lakes that cover the earth? What is the largest lake that you have visited? Some of them are more than 30,000 square miles in area. Turn to page 42 and see if you can solve some mathematical problems involving some of the larger lakes.

Prealgebra Review

1.1   SIMPLIFYING FRACTIONS   2

1.2   ADDING AND SUBTRACTING FRACTIONS   11

1.3   MULTIPLYING AND DIVIDING FRACTIONS   22

HOW AM I DOING? SECTIONS 1.1–1.3   30

1.4   USING DECIMALS   31

CHAPTER 1 ORGANIZER   43

CHAPTER 1 REVIEW PROBLEMS   44

HOW AM I DOING? CHAPTER 1 TEST   46

Student Learning Objectives

After studying this section, you will be able to:

 1 Understand basic mathematical definitions.

2 Simplify fractions to lowest terms using prime numbers.

3 Convert between improper fractions and mixed numbers.

4 Change a fraction to an equivalent fraction with a given denominator.

Chapter 1 is designed to give you a mental "warm-up." In this chapter you'll be able to step back a bit and tone up your math skills. This brief review of prealgebra will increase your math flexibility and give you a good running start into algebra.

① Understanding Basic Mathematical Definitions

Whole numbers are the set of numbers 0, 1, 2, 3, 4, 5, 6, 7, ... They are used to describe whole objects, or entire quantities.

Fractions are a set of numbers that are used to describe parts of whole quantities. In the object shown in the figure there are four equal parts. The *three* of the *four* parts that are shaded are represented by the fraction $\frac{3}{4}$. In the fraction $\frac{3}{4}$ the number 3 is called the **numerator** and the number 4, the **denominator.**

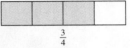

$$\frac{3}{4}$$

$$3 \leftarrow Numerator \text{ is on the top}$$
$$4 \leftarrow Denominator \text{ is on the bottom}$$

The *denominator* of a fraction shows the number of equal parts in the whole and the *numerator* shows the number of these parts being talked about or being used.

Numerals are symbols we use to name numbers. There are many different numerals that can be used to describe the same number. We know that $\frac{1}{2} = \frac{2}{4}$. The fractions $\frac{1}{2}$ and $\frac{2}{4}$ both describe the same number.

Usually, we find it more useful to use fractions that are simplified. A fraction is considered to be in **simplest form** or **reduced form** when the numerator (top) and the denominator (bottom) can both be divided exactly by no number other than 1, and the denominator is greater than 1.

$$\frac{1}{2} \text{ is in simplest form.}$$

$$\frac{2}{4} \text{ is } not \text{ in simplest form, since the numerator and the denominator can both be divided by 2.}$$

If you get the answer $\frac{2}{4}$ to a problem, you should state it in simplest form, $\frac{1}{2}$. The process of changing $\frac{2}{4}$ to $\frac{1}{2}$ is called **simplifying** or **reducing** the fraction.

② Simplifying Fractions to Lowest Terms Using Prime Numbers

Natural numbers or **counting numbers** are the set of whole numbers excluding 0. Thus the natural numbers are the numbers 1, 2, 3, 4, 5, 6, ...

When two or more numbers are multiplied, each number that is multiplied is called a **factor.** For example, when we write $3 \times 7 \times 5$, each of the numbers 3, 7, and 5 is called a factor.

Prime numbers are all natural numbers greater than 1 whose only natural number factors are 1 and itself. The number 5 is prime. The only natural number factors of 5 are 5 and 1.

$$5 = 5 \times 1$$

The number 6 is not prime. The natural number factors of 6 are 3 and 2 or 6 and 1.

$$6 = 3 \times 2 \qquad 6 = 6 \times 1$$

The first 15 prime numbers are

$$2, 3, 5, 7, 11, 13, 17, 19, 23, 29, 31, 37, 41, 43, 47.$$

Any natural number greater than 1 either is prime or can be written as the product of prime numbers. For example, we can take each of the numbers 12, 30, 14, 19, and 29 and either indicate that they are prime or, if they are not prime, write them as the product of prime numbers. We write as follows:

$12 = 2 \times 2 \times 3$ $30 = 2 \times 3 \times 5$ $14 = 2 \times 7$

19 is a prime number.   29 is a prime number.

To reduce a fraction, we use prime numbers to factor the numerator and the denominator. Write each part of the fraction (numerator and denominator) as a product of prime numbers. Note any *factors* that appear in both the *numerator* (top) and *denominator* (bottom) of the fraction. If we divide numerator and denominator by these values we will obtain an equivalent fraction in *simplest form.* When the new fraction is simplified, it is said to be in **lowest terms.** Throughout this text, to *simplify* a fraction will always mean to simplify the fraction to lowest terms.

EXAMPLE 1   Simplify each fraction.   **(a)** $\dfrac{14}{21}$ **(b)** $\dfrac{15}{35}$ **(c)** $\dfrac{20}{70}$

Solution

(a) $\dfrac{14}{21} = \dfrac{\not{7} \times 2}{\not{7} \times 3} = \dfrac{2}{3}$ We factor 14 and factor 21. Then we divide numerator and denominator by 7.

(b) $\dfrac{15}{35} = \dfrac{\not{5} \times 3}{\not{5} \times 7} = \dfrac{3}{7}$ We factor 15 and factor 35. Then we divide numerator and denominator by 5.

(c) $\dfrac{20}{70} = \dfrac{2 \times \not{2} \times \not{5}}{7 \times \not{2} \times \not{5}} = \dfrac{2}{7}$ We factor 20 and factor 70. Then we divide numerator and denominator by both 2 and 5.

Practice Problem 1   Simplify.   **(a)** $\dfrac{10}{16}$ **(b)** $\dfrac{24}{36}$ **(c)** $\dfrac{36}{42}$

Sometimes when we simplify a fraction, all the prime factors in the top (numerator) are divided out. When this happens, we must remember that a 1 is left in the numerator.

EXAMPLE 2   Simplify each fraction.   **(a)** $\dfrac{7}{21}$ **(b)** $\dfrac{15}{105}$

Solution   **(a)** $\dfrac{7}{21} = \dfrac{\not{7} \times 1}{\not{7} \times 3} = \dfrac{1}{3}$ **(b)** $\dfrac{15}{105} = \dfrac{\not{5} \times \not{3} \times 1}{7 \times \not{5} \times \not{3}} = \dfrac{1}{7}$

Practice Problem 2   Simplify.   **(a)** $\dfrac{4}{12}$ **(b)** $\dfrac{25}{125}$ **(c)** $\dfrac{73}{146}$

NOTE TO STUDENT: Fully worked-out solutions to all of the Practice Problems can be found at the back of the text starting at page SP-1

If all the prime numbers in the bottom (denominator) are divided out, we do not need to leave a 1 in the denominator, since we do not need to express the answer as a fraction. The answer is then a whole number and is not usually expressed as a fraction.

EXAMPLE 3   Simplify each fraction.   **(a)** $\dfrac{35}{7}$ **(b)** $\dfrac{70}{10}$

Solution   **(a)** $\dfrac{35}{7} = \dfrac{5 \times \not{7}}{\not{7} \times 1} = 5$ **(b)** $\dfrac{70}{10} = \dfrac{7 \times \not{5} \times \not{2}}{\not{5} \times \not{2} \times 1} = 7$

Practice Problem 3   Simplify.   **(a)** $\dfrac{18}{6}$ **(b)** $\dfrac{146}{73}$ **(c)** $\dfrac{28}{7}$

Sometimes the fraction we use represents how many of a certain thing are successful. For example, if a baseball player was at bat 30 times and achieved 12 hits, we could say that he had a hit $\frac{12}{30}$ of the time. If we reduce the fraction, we could say he had a hit $\frac{2}{5}$ of the time.

EXAMPLE 4   Cindy got 48 out of 56 questions correct on a test. Write this as a fraction.

Solution   Express as a fraction in simplest form the number of correct responses out of the total number of questions on the test.

$$48 \text{ out of } 56 \rightarrow \frac{48}{56} = \frac{6 \times 8}{7 \times 8} = \frac{6}{7}$$

Cindy answered the questions correctly $\frac{6}{7}$ of the time.

Practice Problem 4   The major league pennant winner in 1917 won 56 games out of 154 games played. Express as a fraction in simplest form the number of games won in relation to the number of games played.

NOTE TO STUDENT: Fully worked-out solutions to all of the Practice Problems can be found at the back of the text starting at page SP-1

The number *one* can be expressed as $1, \frac{1}{1}, \frac{2}{2}, \frac{6}{6}, \frac{8}{8}$, and so on, since

$$1 = \frac{1}{1} = \frac{2}{2} = \frac{6}{6} = \frac{8}{8}.$$

We say that these numerals are *equivalent ways* of writing the number *one* because they all express the same quantity even though they appear to be different.

SIDELIGHT: The Multiplicative Identity
When we simplify fractions, we are actually using the fact that we can multiply any number by 1 without changing the value of that number. (Mathematicians call the number 1 the **multiplicative identity** because it leaves any number it multiplies with the same identical value as before.)

Let's look again at one of the previous examples.

$$\frac{14}{21} = \frac{7 \times 2}{7 \times 3} = \frac{7}{7} \times \frac{2}{3} = 1 \times \frac{2}{3} = \frac{2}{3}$$

So we see that

$$\frac{14}{21} = \frac{2}{3}.$$

When we simplify fractions, we are using this property of multiplying by 1.

3 Converting Between Improper Fractions and Mixed Numbers

If the numerator is less than the denominator, the fraction is a **proper fraction.** A proper fraction is used to describe a quantity smaller than a whole.

Fractions can also be used to describe quantities larger than a whole. The following figure shows two bars that are equal in size. Each bar is divided into 5 equal pieces. The first bar is shaded in completely. The second bar has 2 of the 5 pieces shaded in.

The shaded-in region can be represented by $\frac{7}{5}$ since 7 of the pieces (each of which is $\frac{1}{5}$ of a whole box) are shaded. The fraction $\frac{7}{5}$ is called an improper fraction. An **improper fraction** is one in which the numerator is larger than or equal to the denominator.

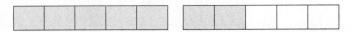

The shaded-in region can also be represented by 1 whole added to $\frac{2}{5}$ of a whole, or $1 + \frac{2}{5}$. This is written as $1\frac{2}{5}$. The fraction $1\frac{2}{5}$ is called a mixed number. A **mixed number** consists of a whole number added to a proper fraction (the numerator is smaller than the denominator). The addition is understood but not written. When we write $1\frac{2}{5}$, it represents $1 + \frac{2}{5}$. The numbers $1\frac{7}{8}, 2\frac{3}{4}, 8\frac{1}{3}$, and $126\frac{1}{10}$ are all mixed numbers. From the preceding figure it seems clear that $\frac{7}{5} = 1\frac{2}{5}$. This suggests that we can change from one form to the other without changing the value of the fraction.

From a picture it is easy to see how to *change improper fractions to mixed numbers*. For example, suppose we start with the fraction $\frac{11}{3}$ and represent it by the following figure (where 11 of the pieces, each of which is $\frac{1}{3}$ of a box, are shaded). We see that $\frac{11}{3} = 3\frac{2}{3}$, since 3 whole boxes and $\frac{2}{3}$ of a box are shaded.

Changing Improper Fractions to Mixed Numbers   You can follow the same procedure without a picture. For example, to change $\frac{11}{3}$ to a mixed number, we can do the following:

$$\frac{11}{3} = \frac{3}{3} + \frac{3}{3} + \frac{3}{3} + \frac{2}{3} \qquad \text{By the rule for adding fractions (which is discussed in detail in Section 1.2)}$$

$$= 1 + 1 + 1 + \frac{2}{3} \qquad \text{Write 1 in place of } \frac{3}{3}, \text{ since } \frac{3}{3} = 1.$$

$$= 3 + \frac{2}{3} \qquad \text{Write 3 in place of } 1 + 1 + 1.$$

$$= 3\frac{2}{3} \qquad \text{Use the notation for mixed numbers.}$$

Now that you know how to change improper fractions to mixed numbers and why the procedure works, here is a shorter method.

> **TO CHANGE AN IMPROPER FRACTION TO A MIXED NUMBER**
>
> 1. Divide the denominator into the numerator.
> 2. The result is the whole-number part of the mixed number.
> 3. The remainder from the division will be the numerator of the fraction. The denominator of the fraction remains unchanged.

We can write the fraction as a division statement and divide. The arrows show how to write the mixed number.

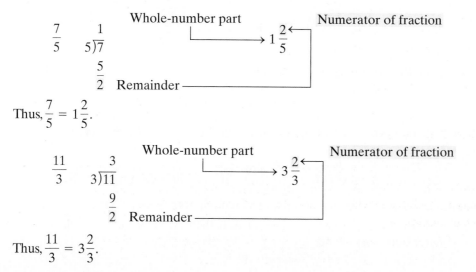

Thus, $\frac{7}{5} = 1\frac{2}{5}$.

Thus, $\frac{11}{3} = 3\frac{2}{3}$.

Sometimes the remainder is 0. In this case, the improper fraction changes to a whole number.

EXAMPLE 5   Change to a mixed number or to a whole number.

(a) $\dfrac{7}{4}$

(b) $\dfrac{15}{3}$

Solution

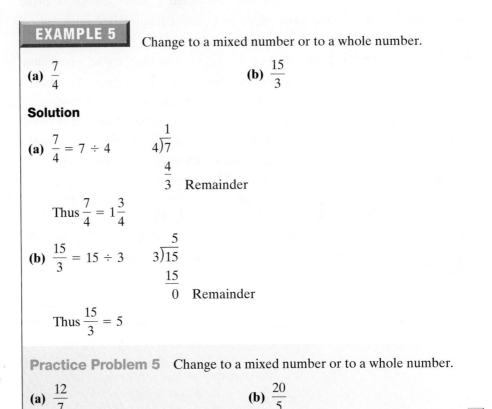

(a) $\dfrac{7}{4} = 7 \div 4$

$$4\overline{)7} \\ \underline{4} \\ 3 \quad \text{Remainder}$$

with quotient 1.

Thus $\dfrac{7}{4} = 1\dfrac{3}{4}$

(b) $\dfrac{15}{3} = 15 \div 3$

$$3\overline{)15} \\ \underline{15} \\ 0 \quad \text{Remainder}$$

with quotient 5.

Thus $\dfrac{15}{3} = 5$

NOTE TO STUDENT: Fully worked-out solutions to all of the Practice Problems can be found at the back of the text starting at page SP-1

Practice Problem 5   Change to a mixed number or to a whole number.

(a) $\dfrac{12}{7}$

(b) $\dfrac{20}{5}$

Changing Mixed Numbers to Improper Fractions   It is not difficult to see how to change mixed numbers to improper fractions. Suppose that you wanted to write $2\frac{2}{3}$ as an improper fraction.

$$2\dfrac{2}{3} = 2 + \dfrac{2}{3} \qquad \text{The meaning of mixed number notation}$$

$$= 1 + 1 + \dfrac{2}{3} \qquad \text{Since } 1 + 1 = 2$$

$$= \dfrac{3}{3} + \dfrac{3}{3} + \dfrac{2}{3} \qquad \text{Since } 1 = \frac{3}{3}$$

When we draw a picture of $\frac{3}{3} + \frac{3}{3} + \frac{2}{3}$, we have this figure:

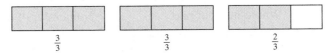

$$\frac{3}{3} \qquad\qquad \frac{3}{3} \qquad\qquad \frac{2}{3}$$

If we count the shaded parts, we see that

$$\dfrac{3}{3} + \dfrac{3}{3} + \dfrac{2}{3} = \dfrac{8}{3}. \qquad \text{Thus} \quad 2\dfrac{2}{3} = \dfrac{8}{3}.$$

Now that you have seen how this change can be done, here is a shorter method.

TO CHANGE A MIXED NUMBER TO AN IMPROPER FRACTION

1. Multiply the whole number by the denominator.
2. Add this to the numerator. The result is the new numerator. The denominator does not change.

EXAMPLE 6   Change to an improper fraction.

(a) $3\frac{1}{7}$ **(b)** $5\frac{4}{5}$

Solution

(a) $3\frac{1}{7} = \frac{(3 \times 7) + 1}{7} = \frac{21 + 1}{7} = \frac{22}{7}$

(b) $5\frac{4}{5} = \frac{(5 \times 5) + 4}{5} = \frac{25 + 4}{5} = \frac{29}{5}$

Practice Problem 6   Change to an improper fraction.

(a) $3\frac{2}{5}$ **(b)** $1\frac{3}{7}$ **(c)** $2\frac{6}{11}$ **(d)** $4\frac{2}{3}$

Changing a Fraction to an Equivalent Fraction with a Given Denominator

Fractions can be changed to an equivalent fraction with a different denominator by multiplying both numerator and denominator by the same number.

$$\frac{5}{6} = \frac{5}{6} \times 1 = \frac{5}{6} \times \frac{2}{2} = \frac{5 \times 2}{6 \times 2} = \frac{10}{12} \qquad \frac{3}{7} = \frac{3}{7} \times 1 = \frac{3}{7} \times \frac{3}{3} = \frac{3 \times 3}{7 \times 3} = \frac{9}{21}$$

So $\frac{5}{6}$ is equivalent to $\frac{10}{12}$. $\frac{3}{7}$ is equivalent to $\frac{9}{21}$.

We often multiply in this way to obtain an equivalent fraction with a *particular denominator.*

EXAMPLE 7   Find the missing number.

(a) $\frac{3}{5} = \frac{?}{25}$ **(b)** $\frac{3}{7} = \frac{?}{21}$ **(c)** $\frac{2}{9} = \frac{?}{36}$

Solution

(a) $\frac{3}{5} = \frac{?}{25}$ Observe that we need to multiply the denominator by 5 to obtain 25. So we multiply the numerator 3 by 5 also.

$\frac{3 \times 5}{5 \times 5} = \frac{15}{25}$ The desired numerator is 15.

(b) $\frac{3}{7} = \frac{?}{21}$ Observe that $7 \times 3 = 21$. We need to multiply the numerator by 3 to get the new numerator.

$\frac{3 \times 3}{7 \times 3} = \frac{9}{21}$ The desired numerator is 9.

(c) $\frac{2}{9} = \frac{?}{36}$ Observe that $9 \times 4 = 36$. We need to multiply the numerator by 4 to get the new numerator.

$\frac{2 \times 4}{9 \times 4} = \frac{8}{36}$ The desired numerator is 8.

Practice Problem 7   Find the missing number.

(a) $\frac{3}{8} = \frac{?}{24}$ **(b)** $\frac{5}{6} = \frac{?}{30}$ **(c)** $\frac{2}{7} = \frac{?}{56}$

1.1 Exercises

Student Solutions Manual · CD/Video · PH Math Tutor Center · MathXL®Tutorials on CD · MathXL® · MyMathLab® · Interactmath.com

Verbal and Writing Skills

1. In the fraction $\frac{12}{13}$, what number is the numerator?

2. In the fraction $\frac{13}{17}$, what is the denominator?

3. What is a factor? Give an example.

4. Give some examples of the number 1 written as a fraction.

5. Draw a diagram to illustrate $2\frac{2}{3}$.

6. Draw a diagram to illustrate $3\frac{3}{4}$.

Simplify each fraction.

7. $\frac{18}{24}$ **8.** $\frac{20}{35}$ **9.** $\frac{12}{36}$ **10.** $\frac{12}{48}$ **11.** $\frac{60}{12}$ **12.** $\frac{45}{15}$

13. $\frac{24}{36}$ **14.** $\frac{32}{64}$ **15.** $\frac{30}{85}$ **16.** $\frac{33}{55}$ **17.** $\frac{42}{54}$ **18.** $\frac{63}{81}$

Change to a mixed number.

19. $\frac{17}{6}$ **20.** $\frac{19}{5}$ **21.** $\frac{111}{9}$ **22.** $\frac{124}{8}$ **23.** $\frac{38}{7}$ **24.** $\frac{41}{6}$

25. $\frac{41}{2}$ **26.** $\frac{25}{3}$ **27.** $\frac{32}{5}$ **28.** $\frac{79}{7}$ **29.** $\frac{47}{5}$ **30.** $\frac{54}{7}$

Change to an improper fraction.

31. $3\frac{1}{5}$ **32.** $2\frac{6}{7}$ **33.** $6\frac{3}{5}$ **34.** $5\frac{3}{8}$ **35.** $\frac{72}{9}$ **36.** $\frac{78}{6}$

37. $8\frac{3}{7}$ **38.** $6\frac{2}{3}$ **39.** $24\frac{1}{4}$ **40.** $10\frac{1}{9}$ **41.** $15\frac{2}{3}$ **42.** $13\frac{3}{5}$

Find the missing numerator.

43. $\dfrac{3}{11} = \dfrac{?}{44}$ **44.** $\dfrac{5}{7} = \dfrac{?}{28}$ **45.** $\dfrac{3}{5} = \dfrac{?}{35}$ **46.** $\dfrac{5}{9} = \dfrac{?}{45}$ **47.** $\dfrac{4}{13} = \dfrac{?}{39}$ **48.** $\dfrac{13}{17} = \dfrac{?}{51}$

49. $\dfrac{3}{7} = \dfrac{?}{49}$ **50.** $\dfrac{10}{15} = \dfrac{?}{60}$ **51.** $\dfrac{3}{4} = \dfrac{?}{20}$ **52.** $\dfrac{7}{8} = \dfrac{?}{40}$ **53.** $\dfrac{35}{40} = \dfrac{?}{80}$ **54.** $\dfrac{45}{50} = \dfrac{?}{100}$

Applications

Solve.

55. *Basketball* Charles Barkley of the Phoenix Suns once scored 1560 points during 68 games played during the season. Express as a mixed number in simplified form how many points he averaged per game.

56. *Kentucky Derby* In 2002, 417 horses were nominated to compete in the Kentucky Derby. Only 18 horses were actually chosen to compete in the Derby. What simplified fraction shows what portion of nominated horses actually competed in the Derby?

57. *Income Tax* Last year, my parents had a combined income of $64,000. They paid $13,200 in federal income taxes. What simplified fraction shows how much my parents spent on their federal taxes?

58. *Transfer Students* The University of California system accepted 14,664 out of 18,330 California Community College students who applied as transfers in the fall of 2003. What simplified fraction shows what portion of applications were accepted?

Trail Mix   *The following chart gives the recipe for a trail mix.*

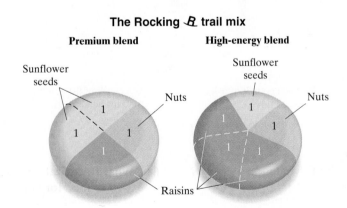

The Rocking *R* trail mix

Premium blend   **High-energy blend**

59. What part of the premium blend is nuts?

60. What part of the high-energy blend is raisins?

61. What part of the premium blend is not sunflower seeds?

62. What part of the high-energy blend does not contain nuts?

Baseball   *The following chart provides some statistics for the North Andover Knights.*

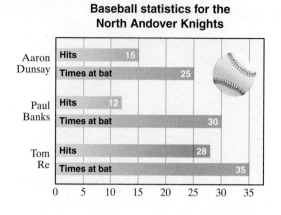

63. Determine how often each player hit the ball based on the number of times at bat. Write each answer as a reduced fraction.

64. Which player was the best hitter?

Fish Catch   *The following chart provides some statistics about the fish catch in the United States.*

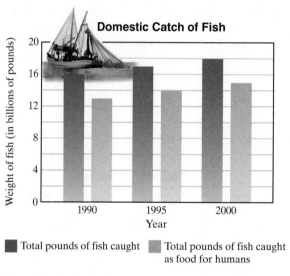

Source: National Marine Fisheries Service

65. What fractional part of the fish catch in 1990 was used as food for humans?

66. What fractional part of the fish catch in 2000 was used as food for humans?

1.2 ADDING AND SUBTRACTING FRACTIONS

① Adding or Subtracting Fractions with a Common Denominator

If fractions have the same denominator, the numerators may be added or subtracted. The denominator remains the same.

> **TO ADD OR SUBTRACT TWO FRACTIONS WITH A COMMON DENOMINATOR**
>
> 1. Add or subtract the numerators.
> 2. Keep the same (common) denominator.
> 3. Simplify the answer whenever possible.

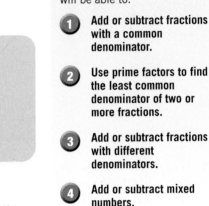

Student Learning Objectives

After studying this section, you will be able to:

① Add or subtract fractions with a common denominator.

② Use prime factors to find the least common denominator of two or more fractions.

③ Add or subtract fractions with different denominators.

④ Add or subtract mixed numbers.

EXAMPLE 1 Add the fractions. Simplify your answer whenever possible.

(a) $\dfrac{5}{7} + \dfrac{1}{7}$ (b) $\dfrac{2}{3} + \dfrac{1}{3}$ (c) $\dfrac{1}{8} + \dfrac{3}{8} + \dfrac{2}{8}$ (d) $\dfrac{3}{5} + \dfrac{4}{5}$

Solution

(a) $\dfrac{5}{7} + \dfrac{1}{7} = \dfrac{5+1}{7} = \dfrac{6}{7}$

(b) $\dfrac{2}{3} + \dfrac{1}{3} = \dfrac{2+1}{3} = \dfrac{3}{3} = 1$

(c) $\dfrac{1}{8} + \dfrac{3}{8} + \dfrac{2}{8} = \dfrac{1+3+2}{8} = \dfrac{6}{8} = \dfrac{3}{4}$

(d) $\dfrac{3}{5} + \dfrac{4}{5} = \dfrac{3+4}{5} = \dfrac{7}{5} = 1\dfrac{2}{5}$

Practice Problem 1 Add.

(a) $\dfrac{3}{6} + \dfrac{2}{6}$ (b) $\dfrac{3}{11} + \dfrac{8}{11}$ (c) $\dfrac{1}{8} + \dfrac{2}{8} + \dfrac{1}{8}$ (d) $\dfrac{5}{9} + \dfrac{8}{9}$

EXAMPLE 2 Subtract the fractions. Simplify your answer whenever possible.

(a) $\dfrac{9}{11} - \dfrac{2}{11}$ (b) $\dfrac{5}{6} - \dfrac{1}{6}$

Solution

(a) $\dfrac{9}{11} - \dfrac{2}{11} = \dfrac{9-2}{11} = \dfrac{7}{11}$

(b) $\dfrac{5}{6} - \dfrac{1}{6} = \dfrac{5-1}{6} = \dfrac{4}{6} = \dfrac{2}{3}$

Practice Problem 2 Subtract.

(a) $\dfrac{11}{13} - \dfrac{6}{13}$ (b) $\dfrac{8}{9} - \dfrac{2}{9}$

NOTE TO STUDENT: Fully worked-out solutions to all of the Practice Problems can be found at the back of the text starting at page SP-1

Although adding and subtracting fractions with the same denominator is fairly simple, most problems involve fractions that do not have a common denominator. Fractions and mixed numbers such as halves, fourths, and eighths are often used. To add or subtract such fractions, we begin by finding a common denominator.

② Using Prime Factors to Find the Least Common Denominator of Two or More Fractions

Before you can add or subtract fractions, they must have the same denominator. To save work, we select the smallest possible common denominator. This is called the **least common denominator** or LCD (also known as the *lowest common denominator*).

The LCD of two or more fractions is the smallest whole number that is exactly divisible by each denominator of the fractions.

EXAMPLE 3   Find the LCD. $\frac{2}{3}$ and $\frac{1}{4}$

Solution   The numbers are small enough to find the LCD by inspection. The LCD is 12, since 12 is exactly divisible by 4 and by 3. There is no smaller number that is exactly divisible by 4 and 3.

NOTE TO STUDENT: Fully worked-out solutions to all of the Practice Problems can be found at the back of the text starting at page SP-1

Practice Problem 3   Find the LCD. $\frac{1}{8}$ and $\frac{5}{12}$

In some cases, the LCD cannot easily be determined by inspection. If we write each denominator as the product of prime factors, we will be able to find the LCD. We will use (·) to indicate multiplication. For example, $30 = 2 \cdot 3 \cdot 5$. This means $30 = 2 \times 3 \times 5$.

PROCEDURE TO FIND THE LCD USING PRIME FACTORS

1. Write each denominator as the product of prime factors.
2. The LCD is a product containing each different factor.
3. If a factor occurs more than once in any one denominator, the LCD will contain that factor repeated the greatest number of times that it occurs in any one denominator.

EXAMPLE 4   Find the LCD of $\frac{5}{6}$ and $\frac{1}{15}$ by this new procedure.

Solution

$$6 = 2 \cdot 3$$
$$15 = \quad 3 \cdot 5$$

Write each denominator as the product of prime factors.

$$LCD = 2 \cdot 3 \cdot 5$$
$$LCD = 2 \cdot 3 \cdot 5 = 30$$

The LCD is a product containing each different prime factor. The different factors are 2, 3, and 5, and each factor appears at most once in any one denominator.

Practice Problem 4   Use prime factors to find the LCD of $\frac{8}{35}$ and $\frac{6}{15}$.

Great care should be used to determine the LCD in the case of repeated factors.

EXAMPLE 5   Find the LCD of $\frac{4}{27}$ and $\frac{5}{18}$.

Solution

$$27 = 3 \cdot 3 \cdot 3$$

Write each denominator as the product of prime factors. We observe that the factor 3 occurs three times in the factorization of 27.

$$18 = \quad 3 \cdot 3 \cdot 2$$

$$\text{LCD} = 3 \cdot 3 \cdot 3 \cdot 2$$
$$\text{LCD} = 3 \cdot 3 \cdot 3 \cdot 2 = 54$$

The LCD is a product containing each different factor. The factor 3 *occurred most* in the factorization of 27, where it occurred *three* times. Thus the LCD will be the product of *three* 3's and *one* 2.

Practice Problem 5   Find the LCD of $\frac{5}{12}$ and $\frac{7}{30}$.

EXAMPLE 6   Find the LCD of $\frac{5}{12}$, $\frac{1}{15}$, and $\frac{7}{30}$.

Solution

$$12 = 2 \cdot 2 \cdot 3$$

Write each denominator as the product of prime factors. Notice that the only repeated factor is 2, which occurs twice in the factorization of 12.

$$15 = \quad 3 \cdot 5$$
$$30 = \quad 2 \cdot 3 \cdot 5$$

$$\text{LCD} = 2 \cdot 2 \cdot 3 \cdot 5$$
$$\text{LCD} = 2 \cdot 2 \cdot 3 \cdot 5 = 60$$

The LCD is the product of each different factor with the factor 2 appearing twice since it occurred twice in one denominator.

Practice Problem 6   Find the LCD of $\frac{2}{27}$, $\frac{1}{18}$, and $\frac{5}{12}$.

---

③ Adding or Subtracting Fractions with Different Denominators

Before you can add or subtract them, fractions must have the same denominator. Using the LCD will make your work easier. First you must find the LCD. Then change each fraction to a fraction that has the LCD as the denominator. Sometimes one of the fractions will already have the LCD as the denominator. Once all the fractions have the same denominator, you can add or subtract. Be sure to simplify the fraction in your answer if this is possible.

TO ADD OR SUBTRACT FRACTIONS THAT DO NOT HAVE A COMMON DENOMINATOR

1. Find the LCD of the fractions.
2. Change each fraction to an equivalent fraction with the LCD for a denominator.
3. Add or subtract the fractions.
4. Simplify the answer whenever possible.

Let us return to the two fractions of Example 3. We have previously found that the LCD is 12.

EXAMPLE 7   Bob picked $\frac{2}{3}$ of a bushel of apples on Monday and $\frac{1}{4}$ of a bushel of apples on Tuesday. How much did he have in total?

Solution   To solve this problem we need to add $\frac{2}{3}$ and $\frac{1}{4}$, but before we can do so, we must change $\frac{2}{3}$ and $\frac{1}{4}$ to fractions with the same denominator. We change each fraction to an equivalent fraction with a common denominator of 12, the LCD.

$$\frac{2}{3} = \frac{?}{12} \qquad \frac{2}{3} \times \frac{4}{4} = \frac{8}{12} \quad \text{so} \quad \frac{2}{3} = \frac{8}{12}$$

$$\frac{1}{4} = \frac{?}{12} \qquad \frac{1}{4} \times \frac{3}{3} = \frac{3}{12} \quad \text{so} \quad \frac{1}{4} = \frac{3}{12}$$

Then we rewrite the problem with common denominators and add.

$$\frac{2}{3} + \frac{1}{4} = \frac{8}{12} + \frac{3}{12} = \frac{8 + 3}{12} = \frac{11}{12}$$

In total Bob picked $\frac{11}{12}$ of a bushel of apples.

NOTE TO STUDENT: Fully worked-out solutions to all of the Practice Problems can be found at the back of the text starting at page SP-1

Practice Problem 7   Carol planted corn in $\frac{5}{12}$ of the farm fields at the Old Robinson Farm. Connie planted soybeans in $\frac{1}{8}$ of the farm fields. What fractional part of the farm fields of the Old Robinson Farm was planted in corn or soybeans?

Sometimes one of the denominators is the LCD. In such cases the fraction that has the LCD for the denominator will not need to be changed. If every other denominator divides into the largest denominator, the largest denominator is the LCD.

EXAMPLE 8   Find the LCD and then add. $\dfrac{3}{5} + \dfrac{7}{20} + \dfrac{1}{2}$

Solution   We can see by inspection that both 5 and 2 divide exactly into 20. Thus 20 is the LCD. Now add.

$$\frac{3}{5} + \frac{7}{20} + \frac{1}{2}$$

We change $\frac{3}{5}$ and $\frac{1}{2}$ to equivalent fractions with a common denominator of 20, the LCD.

$$\frac{3}{5} = \frac{?}{20} \qquad \frac{3}{5} \times \frac{4}{4} = \frac{12}{20} \quad \text{so} \quad \frac{3}{5} = \frac{12}{20}$$

$$\frac{1}{2} = \frac{?}{20} \qquad \frac{1}{2} \times \frac{10}{10} = \frac{10}{20} \quad \text{so} \quad \frac{1}{2} = \frac{10}{20}$$

Then we rewrite the problem with common denominators and add.

$$\frac{3}{5} + \frac{7}{20} + \frac{1}{2} = \frac{12}{20} + \frac{7}{20} + \frac{10}{20} = \frac{12 + 7 + 10}{20} = \frac{29}{20} \quad \text{or} \quad 1\frac{9}{20}$$

Practice Problem 8   Find the LCD and add. $\dfrac{3}{5} + \dfrac{4}{25} + \dfrac{1}{10}$

Now we turn to examples where the selection of the LCD is not so obvious. In Examples 9 through 11 we will use the prime factorization method to find the LCD.

EXAMPLE 9   Add. $\dfrac{7}{18} + \dfrac{5}{12}$

Solution   First we find the LCD.

$$18 = 3 \cdot 3 \cdot 2$$
$$12 = \quad 3 \cdot 2 \cdot 2$$
$$LCD = 3 \cdot 3 \cdot 2 \cdot 2 = 9 \cdot 4 = 36$$

Now we change $\dfrac{7}{18}$ and $\dfrac{5}{12}$ to equivalent fractions that have the LCD.

$$\frac{7}{18} = \frac{?}{36} \qquad \frac{7}{18} \times \frac{2}{2} = \frac{14}{36}$$

$$\frac{5}{12} = \frac{?}{36} \qquad \frac{5}{12} \times \frac{3}{3} = \frac{15}{36}$$

Now we add the fractions.

$$\frac{7}{18} + \frac{5}{12} = \frac{14}{36} + \frac{15}{36} = \frac{29}{36} \qquad \text{This fraction cannot be simplified.}$$

Practice Problem 9   Add. $\dfrac{1}{49} + \dfrac{3}{14}$

EXAMPLE 10   Subtract. $\dfrac{25}{48} - \dfrac{5}{36}$

Solution   First we find the LCD.

$$48 = 2 \cdot 2 \cdot 2 \cdot 2 \cdot 3$$
$$36 = \quad 2 \cdot 2 \cdot 3 \cdot 3$$
$$LCD = 2 \cdot 2 \cdot 2 \cdot 2 \cdot 3 \cdot 3 = 16 \cdot 9 = 144$$

Now we change $\dfrac{25}{48}$ and $\dfrac{5}{36}$ to equivalent fractions that have the LCD.

$$\frac{25}{48} = \frac{?}{144} \qquad \frac{25}{48} \times \frac{3}{3} = \frac{75}{144}$$

$$\frac{5}{36} = \frac{?}{144} \qquad \frac{5}{36} \times \frac{4}{4} = \frac{20}{144}$$

Now we subtract the fractions.

$$\frac{25}{48} - \frac{5}{36} = \frac{75}{144} - \frac{20}{144} = \frac{55}{144} \qquad \text{This fraction cannot be simplified.}$$

Practice Problem 10   Subtract. $\dfrac{1}{12} - \dfrac{1}{30}$

EXAMPLE 11 Combine. $\dfrac{1}{5} + \dfrac{1}{6} - \dfrac{3}{10}$

Solution First we find the LCD.

$$5 = 5$$
$$6 = \quad 2 \cdot 3$$
$$10 = 5 \cdot 2$$
$$\text{LCD} = 5 \cdot 2 \cdot 3 = 10 \cdot 3 = 30$$

Now we change $\frac{1}{5}, \frac{1}{6}$, and $\frac{3}{10}$ to equivalent fractions that have the LCD for a denominator.

$$\dfrac{1}{5} = \dfrac{?}{30} \qquad \dfrac{1}{5} \times \dfrac{6}{6} = \dfrac{6}{30}$$

$$\dfrac{1}{6} = \dfrac{?}{30} \qquad \dfrac{1}{6} \times \dfrac{5}{5} = \dfrac{5}{30}$$

$$\dfrac{3}{10} = \dfrac{?}{30} \qquad \dfrac{3}{10} \times \dfrac{3}{3} = \dfrac{9}{30}$$

Now we combine the three fractions.

$$\dfrac{1}{5} + \dfrac{1}{6} - \dfrac{3}{10} = \dfrac{6}{30} + \dfrac{5}{30} - \dfrac{9}{30} = \dfrac{2}{30} = \dfrac{1}{15}$$

Note the important step of simplifying the fraction to obtain the final answer.

NOTE TO STUDENT: *Fully worked-out solutions to all of the Practice Problems can be found at the back of the text starting at page SP-1*

Practice Problem 11 Combine. $\dfrac{2}{3} + \dfrac{3}{4} - \dfrac{3}{8}$

4 Adding or Subtracting Mixed Numbers

If the problem you are adding or subtracting has mixed numbers, change them to improper fractions first and then combine (add or subtract). As a convention in this book, if the original problem contains mixed numbers, express the result as a mixed number rather than as an improper fraction.

EXAMPLE 12 Combine. Simplify your answer whenever possible.

(a) $5\dfrac{1}{2} + 2\dfrac{1}{3}$ **(b)** $2\dfrac{1}{5} - 1\dfrac{3}{4}$ **(c)** $1\dfrac{5}{12} + \dfrac{7}{30}$

Solution

(a) First we change the mixed numbers to improper fractions.

$$5\dfrac{1}{2} = \dfrac{5 \times 2 + 1}{2} = \dfrac{11}{2} \qquad 2\dfrac{1}{3} = \dfrac{2 \times 3 + 1}{3} = \dfrac{7}{3}$$

Next we change each fraction to an equivalent form with a common denominator of 6.

$$\dfrac{11}{2} = \dfrac{?}{6} \qquad \dfrac{11}{2} \times \dfrac{3}{3} = \dfrac{33}{6}$$

$$\dfrac{7}{3} = \dfrac{?}{6} \qquad \dfrac{7}{3} \times \dfrac{2}{2} = \dfrac{14}{6}$$

Finally, we add the two fractions and change our answer to a mixed number.

$$\frac{33}{6} + \frac{14}{6} = \frac{47}{6} = 7\frac{5}{6}$$

Thus $5\frac{1}{2} + 2\frac{1}{3} = 7\frac{5}{6}$.

(b) First we change the mixed numbers to improper fractions.

$$2\frac{1}{5} = \frac{2 \times 5 + 1}{5} = \frac{11}{5} \qquad 1\frac{3}{4} = \frac{1 \times 4 + 3}{4} = \frac{7}{4}$$

Next we change each fraction to an equivalent form with a common denominator of 20.

$$\frac{11}{5} = \frac{?}{20} \qquad \frac{11}{5} \times \frac{4}{4} = \frac{44}{20}$$

$$\frac{7}{4} = \frac{?}{20} \qquad \frac{7}{4} \times \frac{5}{5} = \frac{35}{20}$$

Now we subtract the two fractions.

$$\frac{44}{20} - \frac{35}{20} = \frac{9}{20}$$

Thus $2\frac{1}{5} - 1\frac{3}{4} = \frac{9}{20}$.

Note: It is not necessary to use these exact steps to add and subtract mixed numbers. If you know another method and can use it to obtain the correct answers, it is all right to continue to use that method throughout this chapter.

(c) Now we add $1\frac{5}{12} + \frac{7}{30}$.

The LCD of 12 and 30 is 60. Why? Change the mixed number to an improper fraction. Then change each fraction to an equivalent form with a common denominator.

$$1\frac{5}{12} = \frac{17}{12} \times \frac{5}{5} = \frac{85}{60} \qquad \frac{7}{30} \times \frac{2}{2} = \frac{14}{60}$$

Then add the fractions, simplify, and write the answer as a mixed number.

$$\frac{85}{60} + \frac{14}{60} = \frac{99}{60} = \frac{33}{20} = 1\frac{13}{20}$$

Thus $1\frac{5}{12} + \frac{7}{30} = 1\frac{13}{20}$.

Practice Problem 12 Combine.

(a) $1\frac{2}{3} + 2\frac{4}{5}$ **(b)** $5\frac{1}{4} - 2\frac{2}{3}$

▲ **EXAMPLE 13**   Manuel is enclosing a triangular-shaped exercise yard for his new dog. He wants to determine how many feet of fencing he will need. The sides of the yard measure $20\frac{3}{4}$ feet, $15\frac{1}{2}$ feet, and $18\frac{1}{8}$ feet. What is the perimeter of (total distance around) the triangle?

Solution

Understand the problem. Begin by drawing a picture.

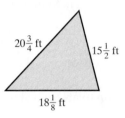

We want to add up the lengths of all three sides of the triangle. This distance around the triangle is called the **perimeter.**

$$20\frac{3}{4} + 15\frac{1}{2} + 18\frac{1}{8} = \frac{83}{4} + \frac{31}{2} + \frac{145}{8}$$

$$= \frac{166}{8} + \frac{124}{8} + \frac{145}{8} = \frac{435}{8} = 54\frac{3}{8} \text{ feet}$$

He will need $54\frac{3}{8}$ feet of fencing.

NOTE TO STUDENT: Fully worked-out solutions to all of the Practice Problems can be found at the back of the text starting at page SP-1

▲ **Practice Problem 13**   Find the perimeter of a rectangle with sides of $4\frac{1}{5}$ cm and $6\frac{1}{2}$ cm. Begin by drawing a picture. Label the picture by including the measure of *each* side.

Developing Your Study Skills

Class Attendance

A student of mathematics needs to get started in the right direction by choosing to attend class every day, beginning with the first day of class. Statistics show that class attendance and good grades go together. Classroom activities are designed to enhance learning and you must be in class to benefit from them. Vital information and explanations that can help you in understanding concepts are given each day. Do not be deceived into thinking that you can just find out from a friend what went on in class. There is no good substitute for firsthand experience. Give yourself a push in the right direction by developing the habit of going to class every day.

Class Participation

People learn mathematics through active participation, not through observation from the sidelines. If you want to do well in this course, be involved in classroom activities. Sit near the front where you can see and hear well and where your focus is on the instruction process and not on the students around you. Ask questions, be ready to contribute toward solutions, and take part in all classroom activities. Your contributions are valuable to the class and to yourself. Class participation requires an investment of yourself in the learning process, which you will find pays huge dividends.

Verbal and Writing Skills

1. Explain why the denominator 8 is the least common denominator of $\frac{3}{4}$ and $\frac{5}{8}$.

2. What must you do before you add or subtract fractions that do not have a common denominator?

Find the LCD (least common denominator) of each pair of fractions. Do not combine the fractions; only find the LCD.

3. $\frac{7}{15}$ and $\frac{11}{21}$

4. $\frac{13}{25}$ and $\frac{29}{40}$

5. $\frac{7}{10}$ and $\frac{1}{4}$

6. $\frac{3}{16}$ and $\frac{1}{24}$

7. $\frac{5}{18}$ and $\frac{7}{54}$

8. $\frac{7}{24}$ and $\frac{5}{48}$

9. $\frac{1}{15}$ and $\frac{4}{21}$

10. $\frac{11}{12}$ and $\frac{7}{20}$

11. $\frac{17}{40}$ and $\frac{13}{60}$

12. $\frac{7}{30}$ and $\frac{8}{45}$

13. $\frac{2}{5}, \frac{3}{8}$, and $\frac{5}{12}$

14. $\frac{5}{6}, \frac{9}{14}$, and $\frac{17}{26}$

15. $\frac{1}{7}, \frac{3}{14}$, and $\frac{9}{35}$

16. $\frac{3}{8}, \frac{5}{12}$, and $\frac{11}{42}$

17. $\frac{1}{2}, \frac{1}{18}$, and $\frac{13}{30}$

18. $\frac{5}{8}, \frac{3}{14}$, and $\frac{11}{16}$

Combine. Be sure to simplify your answer whenever possible.

19. $\frac{3}{8} + \frac{2}{8}$

20. $\frac{2}{9} + \frac{5}{9}$

21. $\frac{5}{14} - \frac{1}{14}$

22. $\frac{9}{20} - \frac{3}{20}$

23. $\frac{3}{8} + \frac{5}{6}$

24. $\frac{7}{10} + \frac{8}{15}$

25. $\frac{5}{7} - \frac{2}{9}$

26. $\frac{7}{8} - \frac{2}{3}$

27. $\frac{1}{3} + \frac{2}{5}$

28. $\frac{2}{7} + \frac{1}{3}$

29. $\frac{7}{18} + \frac{1}{12}$

30. $\frac{3}{10} + \frac{3}{25}$

31. $\frac{11}{15} - \frac{31}{45}$

32. $\frac{21}{12} - \frac{23}{24}$

33. $\frac{16}{24} - \frac{1}{6}$

34. $\frac{11}{28} - \frac{1}{7}$

35. $\frac{3}{8} + \frac{4}{7}$

36. $\frac{7}{4} + \frac{5}{9}$

37. $\frac{2}{3} + \frac{7}{12} + \frac{1}{4}$

38. $\frac{4}{7} + \frac{7}{9} + \frac{1}{3}$

39. $\frac{5}{30} + \frac{3}{40} + \frac{1}{8}$

40. $\frac{1}{12} + \frac{3}{14} + \frac{4}{21}$

41. $\frac{1}{3} + \frac{1}{12} - \frac{1}{6}$

42. $\frac{1}{5} + \frac{2}{3} - \frac{11}{15}$

43. $\dfrac{5}{36} + \dfrac{7}{9} - \dfrac{5}{12}$

44. $\dfrac{5}{24} + \dfrac{3}{8} - \dfrac{1}{3}$

45. $4\dfrac{1}{3} + 3\dfrac{2}{5}$

46. $3\dfrac{1}{8} + 2\dfrac{1}{6}$

47. $1\dfrac{5}{24} + \dfrac{5}{18}$

48. $6\dfrac{2}{3} + \dfrac{3}{4}$

49. $7\dfrac{1}{6} - 2\dfrac{1}{4}$

50. $7\dfrac{2}{5} - 3\dfrac{3}{4}$

51. $8\dfrac{5}{7} - 2\dfrac{1}{4}$

52. $7\dfrac{8}{15} - 2\dfrac{3}{5}$

53. $2\dfrac{1}{8} + 3\dfrac{2}{3}$

54. $3\dfrac{1}{7} + 4\dfrac{1}{3}$

55. $11\dfrac{1}{7} - 6\dfrac{5}{7}$

56. $17\dfrac{1}{5} - 10\dfrac{3}{5}$

57. $2\dfrac{1}{8} + 6\dfrac{3}{4}$

58. $3\dfrac{1}{4} + 4\dfrac{5}{8}$

Mixed Practice

59. $\dfrac{7}{9} + \dfrac{5}{6}$

60. $\dfrac{7}{15} + \dfrac{3}{20}$

61. $2\dfrac{1}{7} + 3\dfrac{11}{14}$

62. $4\dfrac{1}{6} + 5\dfrac{11}{12}$

63. $\dfrac{16}{21} - \dfrac{2}{7}$

64. $\dfrac{15}{24} - \dfrac{3}{8}$

65. $5\dfrac{1}{5} - 2\dfrac{1}{2}$

66. $6\dfrac{1}{3} - 4\dfrac{1}{4}$

67. $25\dfrac{2}{3} - 6\dfrac{1}{7}$

68. $45\dfrac{3}{8} - 26\dfrac{1}{10}$

69. $1\dfrac{1}{6} + \dfrac{3}{8}$

70. $1\dfrac{2}{3} + \dfrac{5}{18}$

71. $8\dfrac{1}{4} + 3\dfrac{5}{6}$

72. $7\dfrac{3}{4} + 6\dfrac{2}{5}$

73. $32 - 1\dfrac{2}{9}$

74. $24 - 3\dfrac{4}{11}$

Applications

75. *Inline Skating* Jenny and Laura went inline skating. They skated $3\dfrac{1}{8}$ miles on Monday, $2\dfrac{2}{3}$ miles on Tuesday, and $4\dfrac{1}{2}$ miles on Wednesday. What was their total distance for those three days?

76. *Marathon Training* Jomo and Eskinder were training for the New York Marathon. Their coach scheduled them to run $11\dfrac{1}{2}$ miles Monday, $13\dfrac{2}{3}$ miles Wednesday, and $21\dfrac{1}{8}$ miles on Friday, with Tuesday and Thursday reserved for weight training. How many miles did they run this week?

77. *MTV Video* Sheryl has $8\frac{1}{2}$ hours this weekend to work on her new video. She estimates that it will take $2\frac{2}{3}$ hours to lip sync the new song and $1\frac{3}{4}$ hours to learn the new dance steps. How much time will she have left over for her MTV interview?

78. *Aquariums* Carl bought a 20 gallon aquarium. He put $17\frac{3}{4}$ gallons of water into the aquarium, but it looked too low, so he added $1\frac{1}{4}$ more gallons of water. He then put in the artificial plants and the gravel but now the water was too high, so he siphoned off $2\frac{2}{3}$ gallons of water. How many gallons of water are now in the aquarium?

To Think About

Carpentry *Carpenters use fractions in their work. The picture below is a diagram of a spice cabinet. The symbol " means inches. Use the picture to answer exercises 79 and 80.*

79. Before you can determine where the cabinet will fit, you need to calculate the height, *A*, and the width, *B*. Don't forget to include the $\frac{1}{2}$-inch thickness of the wood where needed.

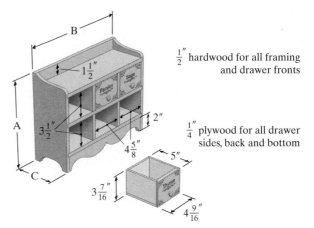

$\frac{1}{2}"$ hardwood for all framing and drawer fronts

$\frac{1}{4}"$ plywood for all drawer sides, back and bottom

80. Look at the close-up of the drawer. The width is $4\frac{9}{16}"$. In the diagram, the width of the opening for the drawer is $4\frac{5}{8}"$. What is the difference? Why do you think the drawer is smaller than the opening?

81. *Putting Green Care* The Falmouth Country Club maintains the putting greens with a grass height of $\frac{7}{8}$ inch. The grass on the fairways is maintained at $2\frac{1}{2}$ inches. How much must the mower blade be lowered by a person mowing the fairways if that person will be using the same mowing machine on the putting greens?

82. *Fairway Care* The director of facilities maintenance at the club discovered that due to slippage in the adjustment lever that the lawn mower actually cuts the grass $\frac{1}{16}$ of an inch too long or too short on some days. What is the maximum height that the fairway grass could be after being mowed with this machine? What is the minimum height that the putting greens could be after being mowed with this machine?

Cumulative Review

83. Simplify. $\dfrac{36}{44}$

84. Change to an improper fraction. $26\dfrac{3}{5}$

Student Learning Objectives

After studying this section, you will be able to:

① Multiply fractions, whole numbers, and mixed numbers.

② Divide fractions, whole numbers, and mixed numbers.

① Multiplying Fractions, Whole Numbers, and Mixed Numbers

Multiplying Fractions During a recent snowstorm, the runway at Beverly Airport was plowed. However, the plow cleared only $\frac{3}{5}$ of the width and $\frac{2}{7}$ of the length. What fraction of the total runway area was cleared? To answer this question, we need to multiply $\frac{3}{5} \times \frac{2}{7}$.

The answer is that $\frac{6}{35}$ of the total runway area was cleared.

The multiplication rule for fractions states that to multiply two fractions, we multiply the two numerators and multiply the two denominators.

TO MULTIPLY ANY TWO FRACTIONS

1. Multiply the numerators.
2. Multiply the denominators.

EXAMPLE 1 Multiply.

(a) $\frac{3}{5} \times \frac{2}{7}$ (b) $\frac{1}{3} \times \frac{5}{4}$ (c) $\frac{7}{3} \times \frac{1}{5}$ (d) $\frac{6}{5} \times \frac{2}{3}$

Solution

(a) $\frac{3}{5} \times \frac{2}{7} = \frac{3 \cdot 2}{5 \cdot 7} = \frac{6}{35}$ (b) $\frac{1}{3} \times \frac{5}{4} = \frac{1 \cdot 5}{3 \cdot 4} = \frac{5}{12}$

(c) $\frac{7}{3} \times \frac{1}{5} = \frac{7 \cdot 1}{3 \cdot 5} = \frac{7}{15}$ (d) $\frac{6}{5} \times \frac{2}{3} = \frac{6 \cdot 2}{5 \cdot 3} = \frac{12}{15} = \frac{4}{5}$

Note that we must simplify this fraction.

NOTE TO STUDENT: Fully worked-out solutions to all of the Practice Problems can be found at the back of the text starting at page SP-1

Practice Problem 1 Multiply.

(a) $\frac{2}{7} \times \frac{5}{11}$ (b) $\frac{1}{5} \times \frac{7}{10}$ (c) $\frac{9}{5} \times \frac{1}{4}$ (d) $\frac{8}{9} \times \frac{3}{10}$

It is possible to avoid having to simplify a fraction at the last step. In many cases we can divide by a value that appears as a factor in both a numerator and a denominator. Often it is helpful to write a number as a product of prime factors in order to do this.

EXAMPLE 2 Multiply. (a) $\frac{3}{5} \times \frac{5}{7}$ (b) $\frac{4}{11} \times \frac{5}{2}$ (c) $\frac{15}{8} \times \frac{10}{27}$

Solution (a) $\frac{3}{5} \times \frac{5}{7} = \frac{3 \cdot 5}{5 \cdot 7} = \frac{3 \cdot \overset{1}{\cancel{5}}}{7 \cdot \cancel{5}} = \frac{3}{7}$ Note that here we divided numerator and denominator by 5.

If we factor each number, we can see the common factors.

(b) $\frac{4}{11} \times \frac{5}{2} = \frac{2 \cdot \overset{1}{\cancel{2}}}{11} \times \frac{5}{\underset{1}{\cancel{2}}} = \frac{10}{11}$ (c) $\frac{15}{8} \times \frac{10}{27} = \frac{\overset{1}{\cancel{3}} \cdot 5}{2 \cdot 2 \cdot \underset{1}{\cancel{2}}} \times \frac{5 \cdot \overset{1}{\cancel{2}}}{\underset{1}{\cancel{3}} \cdot 3 \cdot 3} = \frac{25}{36}$

After dividing out common factors, the resulting multiplication problem involves smaller numbers and the answers are in simplified form.

Practice Problem 2 Multiply. (a) $\frac{3}{5} \times \frac{4}{3}$ (b) $\frac{9}{10} \times \frac{5}{12}$

SIDELIGHT: Dividing Out Common Factors

Why does this method of dividing out a value that appears as a factor in both numerator and denominator work? Let's reexamine one of the examples we have solved previously.

$$\frac{3}{5} \times \frac{5}{7} = \frac{3}{\cancel{5}} \times \frac{\cancel{5}^1}{7} = \frac{3}{7}$$

Consider the following steps and reasons.

$$\frac{3}{5} \times \frac{5}{7} = \frac{3 \cdot 5}{5 \cdot 7}$$ Definition of multiplication of fractions.

$$= \frac{5 \cdot 3}{5 \cdot 7}$$ Change the order of the factors in the numerator, since $3 \cdot 5 = 5 \cdot 3$. This is called the commutative property of multiplication.

$$= \frac{5}{5} \cdot \frac{3}{7}$$ Definition of multiplication of fractions.

$$= 1 \cdot \frac{3}{7}$$ Write 1 in place of $\frac{5}{5}$, since 1 is another name for $\frac{5}{5}$.

$$= \frac{3}{7}$$ $1 \cdot \frac{3}{7} = \frac{3}{7}$, since any number can be multiplied by 1 without changing the value of the number.

Think about this concept. It is an important one that we will use again when we discuss rational expressions.

Multiplying a Fraction by a Whole Number   Whole numbers can be named using fractional notation. $3, \frac{9}{3}, \frac{6}{2}$, and $\frac{3}{1}$ are ways of expressing the number *three*. Therefore,

$$3 = \frac{9}{3} = \frac{6}{2} = \frac{3}{1}.$$

When we multiply a fraction by a whole number, we merely express the whole number as a fraction whose denominator is 1 and follow the multiplication rule for fractions.

EXAMPLE 3   Multiply.

(a) $7 \times \frac{3}{5}$

(b) $\frac{3}{16} \times 4$

Solution

(a) $7 \times \frac{3}{5} = \frac{7}{1} \times \frac{3}{5} = \frac{21}{5} = 4\frac{1}{5}$

(b) $\frac{3}{16} \times 4 = \frac{3}{16} \times \frac{4}{1} = \frac{3}{4 \cdot \cancel{4}} \times \frac{\cancel{4}}{1} = \frac{3}{4}$

Notice that in (b) we did not use *prime* factors to factor 16. We recognized that $16 = 4 \cdot 4$. This is a more convenient factorization of 16 for this problem. Choose the factorization that works best for each problem. If you cannot decide what is best, factor into primes.

Practice Problem 3   Multiply.

(a) $4 \times \frac{2}{7}$

(b) $12 \times \frac{3}{4}$

Multiplying Mixed Numbers   When multiplying mixed numbers, we first change them to improper fractions and then follow the multiplication rule for fractions.

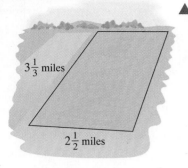

$3\frac{1}{3}$ miles

$2\frac{1}{2}$ miles

NOTE TO STUDENT: *Fully worked-out solutions to all of the Practice Problems can be found at the back of the text starting at page SP-1*

▲ **EXAMPLE 4**   How do we find the area of a rectangular field $3\frac{1}{3}$ miles long by $2\frac{1}{2}$ miles wide?

Solution   To find the area, we multiply length times width.

$$3\frac{1}{3} \times 2\frac{1}{2} = \frac{10}{3} \times \frac{5}{2} = \frac{\cancel{2} \cdot 5}{3} \times \frac{5}{\cancel{2}} = \frac{25}{3} = 8\frac{1}{3}$$

The area is $8\frac{1}{3}$ square miles.

▲ **Practice Problem 4**   Delbert Robinson had a farm that had a rectangular field that measured $5\frac{3}{5}$ miles long and $3\frac{3}{4}$ miles wide. What was the area of that field?

EXAMPLE 5   Multiply. $2\frac{2}{3} \times \frac{1}{4} \times 6$

Solution $2\frac{2}{3} \times \frac{1}{4} \times 6 = \frac{8}{3} \times \frac{1}{4} \times \frac{6}{1} = \frac{\cancel{4} \cdot 2}{\cancel{3}} \times \frac{1}{\cancel{4}} \times \frac{2 \cdot \cancel{3}}{1} = \frac{4}{1} = 4$

Practice Problem 5   Multiply. $3\frac{1}{2} \times \frac{1}{14} \times 4$

② Dividing Fractions, Whole Numbers, and Mixed Numbers

Dividing Fractions   To divide two fractions, we invert the second fraction (that is, the divisor) and then multiply the two fractions.

> **TO DIVIDE TWO FRACTIONS**
>
> 1. Invert the second fraction (that is, the divisor).
> 2. Now multiply the two fractions.

EXAMPLE 6   Divide.

(a) $\frac{1}{3} \div \frac{1}{2}$ (b) $\frac{2}{5} \div \frac{3}{10}$ (c) $\frac{2}{3} \div \frac{7}{5}$

Solution

(a) $\frac{1}{3} \div \frac{1}{2} = \frac{1}{3} \times \frac{2}{1} = \frac{2}{3}$ Note that we always invert the *second* fraction.

(b) $\frac{2}{5} \div \frac{3}{10} = \frac{2}{5} \times \frac{10}{3} = \frac{2}{\cancel{5}} \times \frac{\cancel{5} \cdot 2}{3} = \frac{4}{3} = 1\frac{1}{3}$ (c) $\frac{2}{3} \div \frac{7}{5} = \frac{2}{3} \times \frac{5}{7} = \frac{10}{21}$

Practice Problem 6   Divide.   (a) $\frac{2}{5} \div \frac{1}{3}$ (b) $\frac{12}{13} \div \frac{4}{3}$

Dividing a Fraction and a Whole Number   The process of inverting the second fraction and then multiplying the two fractions should be done very carefully when one of the original values is a whole number. Remember, a whole number such as 2 is equivalent to $\frac{2}{1}$.

EXAMPLE 7   Divide.

(a) $\frac{1}{3} \div 2$ **(b)** $5 \div \frac{1}{3}$

Solution

(a) $\frac{1}{3} \div 2 = \frac{1}{3} \div \frac{2}{1} = \frac{1}{3} \times \frac{1}{2} = \frac{1}{6}$

(b) $5 \div \frac{1}{3} = \frac{5}{1} \div \frac{1}{3} = \frac{5}{1} \times \frac{3}{1} = \frac{15}{1} = 15$

Practice Problem 7 Divide.

(a) $\frac{3}{7} \div 6$ **(b)** $8 \div \frac{2}{3}$

SIDELIGHT: Number Sense

Look at the answers to the problems in Example 7. In part (a), you will notice that $\frac{1}{6}$ is less than the original number $\frac{1}{3}$. Does this seem reasonable? Let's see. If $\frac{1}{3}$ is divided by 2, it means that $\frac{1}{3}$ will be divided into two equal parts. We would expect that each part would be less than $\frac{1}{3}$. $\frac{1}{6}$ is a reasonable answer to this division problem.

In part (b), 15 is greater than the original number 5. Does this seem reasonable? Think of what $5 \div \frac{1}{3}$ means. It means that 5 will be divided into thirds. Let's think of an easier problem. What happens when we divide 1 into thirds? We get *three* thirds. We would expect, therefore, that when we divide 5 into thirds, we would get 5×3 or 15 thirds. 15 is a reasonable answer to this division problem.

Complex Fractions

Sometimes division is written in the form of a **complex fraction** with one fraction in the numerator and one fraction in the denominator. It is best to write this in standard division notation first; then complete the problem using the rule for division.

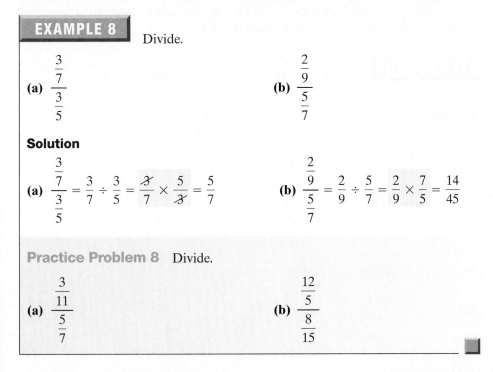

EXAMPLE 8   Divide.

(a) $\dfrac{\frac{3}{7}}{\frac{3}{5}}$ **(b)** $\dfrac{\frac{2}{9}}{\frac{5}{7}}$

Solution

(a) $\dfrac{\frac{3}{7}}{\frac{3}{5}} = \frac{3}{7} \div \frac{3}{5} = \frac{\cancel{3}}{7} \times \frac{5}{\cancel{3}} = \frac{5}{7}$ **(b)** $\dfrac{\frac{2}{9}}{\frac{5}{7}} = \frac{2}{9} \div \frac{5}{7} = \frac{2}{9} \times \frac{7}{5} = \frac{14}{45}$

Practice Problem 8 Divide.

(a) $\dfrac{\frac{3}{11}}{\frac{5}{7}}$ **(b)** $\dfrac{\frac{12}{5}}{\frac{8}{15}}$

SIDELIGHT: Invert and Multiply

Why does the method of "invert and multiply" work? The division rule really depends on the property that any number can be multiplied by 1 without changing the value of the number. Let's look carefully at an example of division of fractions:

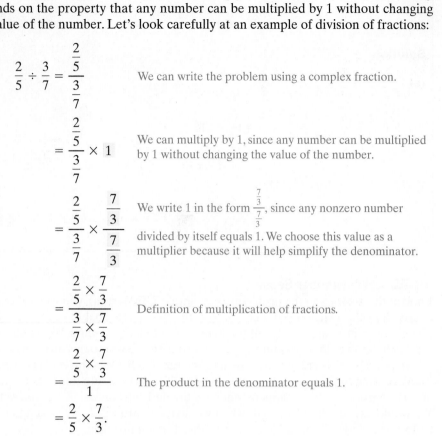

$$\frac{2}{5} \div \frac{3}{7} = \frac{\dfrac{2}{5}}{\dfrac{3}{7}}$$ We can write the problem using a complex fraction.

$$= \frac{\dfrac{2}{5}}{\dfrac{3}{7}} \times \boxed{1}$$ We can multiply by 1, since any number can be multiplied by 1 without changing the value of the number.

$$= \frac{\dfrac{2}{5}}{\dfrac{3}{7}} \times \frac{\dfrac{7}{3}}{\dfrac{7}{3}}$$ We write 1 in the form $\dfrac{\frac{7}{3}}{\frac{7}{3}}$, since any nonzero number divided by itself equals 1. We choose this value as a multiplier because it will help simplify the denominator.

$$= \frac{\dfrac{2}{5} \times \dfrac{7}{3}}{\dfrac{3}{7} \times \dfrac{7}{3}}$$ Definition of multiplication of fractions.

$$= \frac{\dfrac{2}{5} \times \dfrac{7}{3}}{1}$$ The product in the denominator equals 1.

$$= \frac{2}{5} \times \frac{7}{3}.$$

Thus we have shown that $\frac{2}{5} \div \frac{3}{7}$ is equivalent to $\frac{2}{5} \times \frac{7}{3}$ and have shown some justification for the "invert and multiply rule."

Dividing Mixed Numbers

This method for division of fractions can be used with mixed numbers. However, we first must change the mixed numbers to improper fractions and then use the rule for dividing fractions.

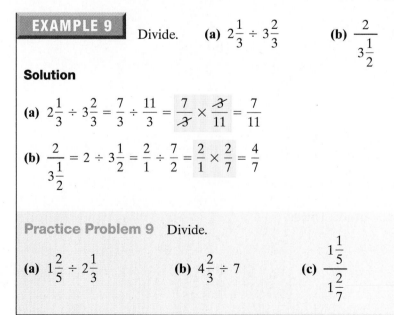

EXAMPLE 9   Divide.   **(a)** $2\frac{1}{3} \div 3\frac{2}{3}$ **(b)** $\dfrac{2}{3\frac{1}{2}}$

Solution

(a) $2\frac{1}{3} \div 3\frac{2}{3} = \frac{7}{3} \div \frac{11}{3} = \frac{7}{\cancel{3}} \times \frac{\cancel{3}}{11} = \frac{7}{11}$

(b) $\dfrac{2}{3\frac{1}{2}} = 2 \div 3\frac{1}{2} = \frac{2}{1} \div \frac{7}{2} = \frac{2}{1} \times \frac{2}{7} = \frac{4}{7}$

Practice Problem 9   Divide.

(a) $1\frac{2}{5} \div 2\frac{1}{3}$ **(b)** $4\frac{2}{3} \div 7$ **(c)** $\dfrac{1\frac{1}{5}}{1\frac{2}{7}}$

NOTE TO STUDENT: Fully worked-out solutions to all of the Practice Problems can be found at the back of the text starting at page SP-1

EXAMPLE 10   A chemist has 96 fluid ounces of a solution. She pours the solution into test tubes. Each test tube holds $\frac{3}{4}$ fluid ounce. How many test tubes can she fill?

Solution   We need to divide the total number of ounces, 96, by the number of ounces in each test tube, $\frac{3}{4}$.

$$96 \div \frac{3}{4} = \frac{96}{1} \div \frac{3}{4} = \frac{96}{1} \times \frac{4}{3} = \frac{\cancel{3} \cdot 32}{1} \times \frac{4}{\cancel{3}} = \frac{128}{1} = 128$$

She will be able to fill 128 test tubes.

Pause for a moment to think about the answer. Does 128 test tubes filled with solution seem like a reasonable answer? Did you perform the correct operation?

Practice Problem 10   A chemist has 64 fluid ounces of a solution. He wishes to fill several jars, each holding $5\frac{1}{3}$ fluid ounces. How many jars can he fill?

Sometimes when solving word problems involving fractions or mixed numbers, it is helpful to solve the problem using simpler numbers first. Once you understand what operation is involved, you can go back and solve using the original numbers in the word problem.

EXAMPLE 11   A car traveled 301 miles on $10\frac{3}{4}$ gallons of gas. How many miles per gallon did it get?

Solution   Use simpler numbers: 300 miles on 10 gallons of gas. We want to find out how many miles the car traveled on 1 gallon of gas. You may want to draw a picture.

10 gallons

Divide. $300 \div 10 = 30$.

300 miles

Now use the original numbers given in the problem.

$$301 \div 10\frac{3}{4} = \frac{301}{1} \div \frac{43}{4} = \frac{301}{1} \times \frac{4}{43} = \frac{1204}{43} = 28$$

This is 28 miles to the gallon.

Practice Problem 11   A car can travel $25\frac{1}{2}$ miles on 1 gallon of gas. How many miles can a car travel on $5\frac{1}{4}$ gallons of gas? Check your answer to see if it is reasonable.

Developing Your Study Skills

Why Is Homework Necessary?

Mathematics is a set of skills that you learn by doing, not by watching. Your instructor may make solving a mathematics problem look very easy, but for you to learn the necessary skills, you must practice them over and over again, just as your instructor once had to do. There is no other way. Learning mathematics is like learning to play a musical instrument, to type, or to play a sport. No matter how much you watch someone else do it, how many books you may read on "how to" do it, or how easy it may seem to be, the key to success is to practice on a regular basis. Homework provides this practice.

Student Solutions Manual   CD/ Video   PH Math Tutor Center   MathXL®Tutorials on CD   MathXL®   MyMathLab®   Interactmath.com

Verbal and Writing Skills

1. Explain in your own words how to multiply two mixed numbers.

2. Explain in your own words how to divide two proper fractions.

Multiply. Simplify your answer whenever possible.

3. $\dfrac{36}{7} \times \dfrac{5}{9}$

4. $\dfrac{3}{8} \times \dfrac{24}{5}$

5. $\dfrac{17}{18} \times \dfrac{3}{5}$

6. $\dfrac{21}{22} \times \dfrac{11}{6}$

7. $\dfrac{4}{5} \times \dfrac{3}{10}$

8. $\dfrac{5}{6} \times \dfrac{7}{11}$

9. $\dfrac{24}{25} \times \dfrac{5}{2}$

10. $\dfrac{15}{24} \times \dfrac{8}{9}$

11. $\dfrac{7}{12} \times \dfrac{8}{28}$

12. $\dfrac{6}{21} \times \dfrac{9}{18}$

13. $\dfrac{6}{35} \times 5$

14. $\dfrac{2}{21} \times 15$

15. $9 \times \dfrac{2}{5}$

16. $\dfrac{8}{11} \times 3$

Divide. Simplify your answer whenever possible.

17. $\dfrac{8}{5} \div \dfrac{8}{3}$

18. $\dfrac{13}{9} \div \dfrac{13}{7}$

19. $\dfrac{3}{7} \div 3$

20. $\dfrac{7}{8} \div 4$

21. $10 \div \dfrac{5}{7}$

22. $18 \div \dfrac{2}{9}$

23. $\dfrac{6}{14} \div \dfrac{3}{8}$

24. $\dfrac{8}{12} \div \dfrac{5}{6}$

25. $\dfrac{7}{24} \div \dfrac{9}{8}$

26. $\dfrac{9}{28} \div \dfrac{4}{7}$

27. $\dfrac{\frac{7}{8}}{\frac{3}{4}}$

28. $\dfrac{\frac{5}{6}}{\frac{10}{13}}$

29. $\dfrac{\frac{5}{6}}{\frac{7}{9}}$

30. $\dfrac{\frac{3}{4}}{\frac{11}{12}}$

31. $1\dfrac{3}{7} \div 6\dfrac{1}{4}$

32. $4\dfrac{1}{2} \div 3\dfrac{3}{8}$

33. $3\dfrac{1}{3} \div 2\dfrac{1}{2}$

34. $5\dfrac{1}{2} \div 3\dfrac{3}{4}$

35. $6\dfrac{1}{2} \div \dfrac{3}{4}$

36. $\dfrac{1}{4} \div 1\dfrac{7}{8}$

37. $\dfrac{\frac{7}{9}}{1\frac{1}{3}}$

38. $\dfrac{\frac{5}{8}}{1\frac{3}{4}}$

39. $\dfrac{\frac{2}{3}}{1\frac{1}{4}}$

40. $\dfrac{\frac{5}{6}}{2\frac{1}{2}}$

Mixed Practice

Perform the proper calculations. Reduce your answer whenever possible.

41. $\dfrac{6}{5} \times \dfrac{10}{12}$

42. $\dfrac{5}{24} \times \dfrac{18}{15}$

43. $\dfrac{5}{14} \div \dfrac{2}{7}$

44. $\dfrac{5}{6} \div \dfrac{11}{18}$

45. $10\dfrac{3}{7} \times 5\dfrac{1}{4}$

46. $10\dfrac{2}{9} \div 2\dfrac{1}{3}$

47. $2\dfrac{1}{8} \div \dfrac{1}{4}$

48. $4 \div 1\dfrac{7}{9}$

49. $6 \times 4\dfrac{2}{3}$

50. $5\dfrac{1}{2} \times 10$

51. $2\dfrac{1}{2} \times \dfrac{1}{10} \times \dfrac{3}{4}$

52. $3\dfrac{1}{3} \times \dfrac{1}{5} \times \dfrac{2}{3}$

53. (a) $\dfrac{1}{15} \times \dfrac{25}{21}$

   (b) $\dfrac{1}{15} \div \dfrac{25}{21}$

54. (a) $\dfrac{1}{6} \times \dfrac{24}{15}$

   (b) $\dfrac{1}{6} \div \dfrac{24}{15}$

55. (a) $\dfrac{2}{3} \div \dfrac{12}{21}$

   (b) $\dfrac{2}{3} \times \dfrac{12}{21}$

56. (a) $\dfrac{3}{7} \div \dfrac{21}{25}$

   (b) $\dfrac{3}{7} \times \dfrac{21}{25}$

Applications

57. *Shirt Manufacturing* A denim shirt at the Gap requires $2\dfrac{3}{4}$ yards of material. How many yards would be needed to make 26 shirts?

58. *Pullover Manufacturing* A fleece pullover requires $1\dfrac{5}{8}$ yds of material. How many yards will it take to make 18 pullovers?

59. *Mountain Biking* Jennifer rode her mountain bike for $4\dfrac{1}{5}$ miles after work. Two-thirds of the distance was over a mountain bike trail. How long is the mountain bike trail?

60. *Cross-Country Racing* Phil ran a cross-country race that was $3\dfrac{3}{8}$ miles long. One-third of that race was on a hilly nature preserve trail. How long is the nature preserve trail?

Cumulative Review

In exercises 61 and 62, simplify each fraction.

61. $\dfrac{116}{124}$

62. $\dfrac{33}{77}$

Write as a mixed number.

63. $\dfrac{22}{7}$

64. $\dfrac{18}{5}$

Write as an improper fraction.

65. $12\dfrac{1}{3}$

66. $9\dfrac{7}{8}$

How are you doing with your homework assignments in Sections 1.1 to 1.3? Do you feel you have mastered the material so far? Do you understand the concepts you have covered? Before you go further in the textbook, take some time to do each of the following problems.

1.1

In exercises 1 and 2, simplify each fraction.

1. $\dfrac{15}{55}$

2. $\dfrac{46}{115}$

3. Write $\dfrac{15}{4}$ as a mixed number.

4. Change $4\dfrac{5}{7}$ to an improper fraction.

Find the missing number.

5. $\dfrac{3}{7} = \dfrac{?}{14}$

6. $\dfrac{7}{4} = \dfrac{?}{20}$

1.2

7. Find the LCD, but do not add. $\dfrac{3}{8}$, $\dfrac{5}{6}$, and $\dfrac{7}{15}$

Perform the calculation indicated. Write the answer in simplest form.

8. $\dfrac{3}{7} + \dfrac{2}{7}$

9. $\dfrac{5}{14} + \dfrac{2}{21}$

10. $2\dfrac{3}{4} + 5\dfrac{2}{3}$

11. $\dfrac{17}{18} - \dfrac{5}{9}$

12. $\dfrac{6}{7} - \dfrac{2}{3}$

13. $3\dfrac{1}{5} - 1\dfrac{3}{8}$

1.3

Perform the calculations indicated. Write the answer in simplest form.

14. $\dfrac{25}{7} \times \dfrac{14}{45}$

15. $2\dfrac{4}{5} \times 3\dfrac{3}{4}$

16. $4 \div \dfrac{8}{7}$

17. $2\dfrac{1}{3} \div 3\dfrac{1}{4}$

18. $\dfrac{\dfrac{6}{25}}{\dfrac{9}{10}}$

19. Ranak owns a rectangular plot of land that measures $3\dfrac{3}{4}$ miles long and $5\dfrac{1}{3}$ miles wide. What is the area of Ranak's land?

Now turn to page SA-1 for the answer to each of these problems. Each answer also includes a reference to the objective in which the problem is first taught. If you missed any of these problems, you should stop and review the Examples and Practice Problems in the referenced objective. A little review now will help you master the material in the upcoming sections of the text.

1. _____
2. _____
3. _____
4. _____
5. _____
6. _____
7. _____
8. _____
9. _____
10. _____
11. _____
12. _____
13. _____
14. _____
15. _____
16. _____
17. _____
18. _____
19. _____

① Understanding the Meaning of Decimals

We can express a part of a whole as a fraction or as a decimal. A **decimal** is another way of writing a fraction whose denominator is 10, 100, 1000, and so on.

$$\frac{3}{10} = 0.3 \qquad \frac{5}{100} = 0.05 \qquad \frac{172}{1000} = 0.172 \qquad \frac{58}{10,000} = 0.0058$$

The period in decimal notation is known as the **decimal point.** The number of digits in a number to the right of the decimal point is known as the number of **decimal places** of the number. The place value of decimals is shown in the following chart.

Hundred-thousands	Ten-thousands	Thousands	Hundreds	Tens	ones	← Decimal point	Tenths	Hundredths	Thousandths	Ten-thousandths	Hundred-thousandths
100,000	10,000	1000	100	10	1	.	$\frac{1}{10}$	$\frac{1}{100}$	$\frac{1}{1000}$	$\frac{1}{10,000}$	$\frac{1}{100,000}$

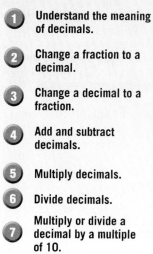

Student Learning Objectives

After studying this section, you will be able to:

① Understand the meaning of decimals.

② Change a fraction to a decimal.

③ Change a decimal to a fraction.

④ Add and subtract decimals.

⑤ Multiply decimals.

⑥ Divide decimals.

⑦ Multiply or divide a decimal by a multiple of 10.

EXAMPLE 1 Write each of the following decimals as a fraction. State the number of decimal places. Write out in words the way the number would be spoken.

(a) 0.6 **(b)** 0.29 **(c)** 0.527 **(d)** 1.38 **(e)** 0.00007

Solution

Decimal Form	Fraction Form	Number of Decimal Places	The Words Used to Describe the Number
(a) 0.6	$\frac{6}{10}$	one	six-tenths
(b) 0.29	$\frac{29}{100}$	two	twenty-nine hundredths
(c) 0.527	$\frac{527}{1000}$	three	five hundred twenty-seven thousandths
(d) 1.38	$1\frac{38}{100}$	two	one and thirty-eight hundredths
(e) 0.00007	$\frac{7}{100,000}$	five	seven hundred-thousandths

Practice Problem 1 Write each decimal as a fraction and in words.

(a) 0.9 **(b)** 0.09 **(c)** 0.731 **(d)** 1.371 **(e)** 0.0005

You have seen that a given fraction can be written in several different but equivalent ways. There are also several different equivalent ways of writing the decimal form of fractions. The decimal 0.18 can be written in the following equivalent ways:

$$\text{Fractional form: } \frac{18}{100} = \frac{180}{1000} = \frac{1800}{10,000} = \frac{18,000}{100,000}$$

$$\text{Decimal form: } 0.18 = 0.180 = 0.1800 = 0.18000.$$

NOTE TO STUDENT: Fully worked-out solutions to all of the Practice Problems can be found at the back of the text starting at page SP-1

Thus we see that *any number of terminal zeros may be added to the right-hand side of a decimal* without changing its value.

$$0.13 = 0.1300 \qquad 0.162 = 0.162000$$

Similarly, *any number of terminal zeros may be removed from the right-hand side of a decimal* without changing its value.

2 Changing a Fraction to a Decimal

A fraction can be changed to a decimal by dividing the denominator into the numerator.

EXAMPLE 2   Write each of the following fractions as a decimal.

(a) $\dfrac{3}{4}$ (b) $\dfrac{21}{20}$ (c) $\dfrac{1}{8}$ (d) $\dfrac{3}{200}$

Solution

(a) $\dfrac{3}{4} = 0.75$ since $\begin{array}{r} 0.75 \\ 4\overline{)3.00} \\ \underline{28} \\ 20 \\ \underline{20} \\ 0 \end{array}$

(b) $\dfrac{21}{20} = 1.05$ since $\begin{array}{r} 1.05 \\ 20\overline{)21.00} \\ \underline{20} \\ 100 \\ \underline{100} \\ 0 \end{array}$

(c) $\dfrac{1}{8} = 0.125$ since $\begin{array}{r} 0.125 \\ 8\overline{)1.000} \\ \underline{8} \\ 20 \\ \underline{16} \\ 40 \\ \underline{40} \\ 0 \end{array}$

(d) $\dfrac{3}{200} = 0.015$ since $\begin{array}{r} 0.015 \\ 200\overline{)3.000} \\ \underline{200} \\ 1000 \\ \underline{1000} \\ 0 \end{array}$

Practice Problem 2   Write as decimals.

(a) $\dfrac{3}{8}$ (b) $\dfrac{7}{200}$ (c) $\dfrac{33}{20}$

NOTE TO STUDENT: Fully worked-out solutions to all of the Practice Problems can be found at the back of the text starting at page SP-1

Calculator

Fraction to Decimal

You can use a calculator to change $\frac{3}{5}$ to a decimal. Enter:

3 ÷ 5 =

The display should read

0.6

Try the following.

(a) $\dfrac{17}{25}$ (b) $\dfrac{2}{9}$

(c) $\dfrac{13}{10}$ (d) $\dfrac{15}{19}$

Answers:

(a) 0.68   (b) $0.\overline{2}$

(c) 1.3

(d) 0.7894737 (Rounded to seven decimal places.)

Sometimes division yields an infinite repeating decimal. We use three dots to indicate that the pattern continues forever. For example,

$$\frac{1}{3} = 0.3333\ldots \qquad \begin{array}{r} 0.333 \\ 3\overline{)1.000} \\ \underline{9} \\ 10 \\ \underline{9} \\ 10 \\ \underline{9} \\ 1. \end{array}$$

An alternative notation is to place a bar over the repeating digit(s):

$$0.3333\ldots = 0.\overline{3} \qquad 0.575757\ldots = 0.\overline{57}.$$

EXAMPLE 3   Write each fraction as a decimal.

(a) $\dfrac{2}{11}$

(b) $\dfrac{5}{6}$

Solution

(a) $\dfrac{2}{11} = 0.181818\ldots$ or $0.\overline{18}$

$$
\begin{array}{r}
0.1818 \\
11\overline{)2.0000} \\
\underline{11} \\
90 \\
\underline{88} \\
20 \\
\underline{11} \\
90 \\
\underline{88} \\
2
\end{array}
$$

(b) $\dfrac{5}{6} = 0.8333\ldots$ or $0.8\overline{3}$

$$
\begin{array}{r}
0.8333 \\
6\overline{)5.0000} \\
\underline{48} \\
20 \\
\underline{18} \\
20 \\
\underline{18} \\
20 \\
\underline{18} \\
2
\end{array}
$$

Note that the 8 does not repeat. Only the digit 3 is repeating.

Practice Problem 3   Write each fraction as a decimal.

(a) $\dfrac{1}{6}$

(b) $\dfrac{5}{11}$

Sometimes division must be carried out to many places in order to observe the repeating pattern. This is true in the following example:

$$\frac{2}{7} = 0.285714285714285714\ldots \qquad \text{This can also be written as } \frac{2}{7} = 0.\overline{285714}.$$

It can be shown that the denominator determines the maximum number of decimal places that might repeat. So $\frac{2}{7}$ must repeat in the seventh decimal place or sooner.

③ Changing a Decimal to a Fraction

To convert from a decimal to a fraction, merely write the decimal as a fraction with a denominator of 10, 100, 1000, 10,000, and so on, and simplify the result when possible.

EXAMPLE 4   Write each decimal as a fraction.

(a) 0.2   (b) 0.35   (c) 0.516   (d) 0.74   (e) 0.138   (f) 0.008

Solution

(a) $0.2 = \dfrac{2}{10} = \dfrac{1}{5}$

(b) $0.35 = \dfrac{35}{100} = \dfrac{7}{20}$

(c) $0.516 = \dfrac{516}{1000} = \dfrac{129}{250}$

(d) $0.74 = \dfrac{74}{100} = \dfrac{37}{50}$

(e) $0.138 = \dfrac{138}{1000} = \dfrac{69}{500}$

(f) $0.008 = \dfrac{8}{1000} = \dfrac{1}{125}$

Practice Problem 4   Write each decimal as a fraction and simplify whenever possible.

(a) 0.8   (b) 0.88   (c) 0.45   (d) 0.148   (e) 0.612   (f) 0.016

All repeating decimals can also be converted to fractional form. In practice, however, repeating decimals are usually rounded to a few places. It will not be necessary, therefore, to learn how to convert $0.\overline{033}$ to $\frac{11}{333}$ for this course.

4 Adding and Subtracting Decimals

Last week Bob spent $19.83 on lunches purchased at the cafeteria at work. During this same period, Sally spent $24.76 on lunches. How much did the two of them spend on lunches last week?

Adding or subtracting decimals is similar to adding and subtracting whole numbers, except that it is necessary to line up decimal points. To perform the operation $19.83 + 24.76$, we line up the numbers in column form and add the digits:

$$\begin{array}{r} 19.83 \\ +\ 24.76 \\ \hline 44.59 \end{array}$$

Thus Bob and Sally spent $44.59 on lunches last week.

> **ADDITION AND SUBTRACTION OF DECIMALS**
>
> 1. Write in column form and line up decimal points.
> 2. Add or subtract the digits.

EXAMPLE 5   Perform the following operations.

(a) $3.6 + 2.3$ **(b)** $127.32 - 38.48$

(c) $3.1 + 42.36 + 9.034$ **(d)** $5.0006 - 3.1248$

Solution

(a) $\quad\begin{array}{r} 3.6 \\ +2.3 \\ \hline 5.9 \end{array}$ **(b)** $\begin{array}{r} 127.32 \\ -\ 38.48 \\ \hline 88.84 \end{array}$ **(c)** $\begin{array}{r} 3.1 \\ 42.36 \\ +\ 9.034 \\ \hline 54.494 \end{array}$ **(d)** $\begin{array}{r} 5.0006 \\ -\ 3.1248 \\ \hline 1.8758 \end{array}$

NOTE TO STUDENT: *Fully worked-out solutions to all of the Practice Problems can be found at the back of the text starting at page SP-1*

Practice Problem 5   Add or subtract.

(a) $3.12 + 5.08 + 1.42$ **(b)** $152.003 - 136.118$

(c) $1.1 + 3.16 + 5.123$ **(d)** $1.0052 - 0.1234$

SIDELIGHT: Adding Zeros to the Right-Hand Side of the Decimal

When we added fractions, we had to have common denominators. Since decimals are really fractions, why can we add them without having common denominators? Actually, we have to have common denominators to add any fractions, whether they are in decimal form or fraction form. However, sometimes the notation does not show this. Let's examine Example 5(c).

Original Problem   We are adding the three numbers:

$$\begin{array}{r} 3.1 \\ 42.36 \\ +\ 9.034 \\ \hline 54.494 \end{array}$$

$3\frac{1}{10} \quad + 42\frac{36}{100} \quad + 9\frac{34}{1000}$

$3\frac{100}{1000} + 42\frac{360}{1000} + 9\frac{34}{1000}$

$3.100 + 42.360 + 9.034$ This is the new problem.

Original Problem   *New Problem*

3.1	3.100
42.36	42.360
+ 9.034	+ 9.034
54.494	54.494

We notice that the results are the same. The only difference is the notation. We are using the property that any number of zeros may be added to the right-hand side of a decimal without changing its value.

This shows the convenience of adding and subtracting fractions in decimal form. Little work is needed to change the decimals so that they have a common denominator. All that is required is to add zeros to the right-hand side of the decimal (and we usually do not even write out that step except when subtracting).

As long as we line up the decimal points, we can add or subtract any decimal fractions.

In the following example we will find it useful to add zeros to the right-hand side of the decimal.

EXAMPLE 6   Perform the following operations.

(a) $1.0003 + 0.02 + 3.4$ **(b)** $12 - 0.057$

Solution   We will add zeros so that each number shows the same number of decimal places.

(a)
1.0003
0.0200
+ 3.4000
4.4203

(b)
12.000
− 0.057
11.943

Practice Problem 6   Perform the following operations.

(a) $0.061 + 5.0008 + 1.3$ **(b)** $18 - 0.126$

---

5 Multiplying Decimals

MULTIPLICATION OF DECIMALS

To multiply decimals, you first multiply as with whole numbers. To determine the position of the decimal point, you count the total number of decimal places in the two numbers being multiplied. This will determine the number of decimal places that should appear in the answer.

EXAMPLE 7   Multiply. 0.8×0.4

Solution

0.8	(one decimal place)
×0.4	(one decimal place)
0.32	(two decimal places)

Practice Problem 7   Multiply. 0.5×0.3

Note that you will often have to add zeros to the left of the digits obtained in the product so that you obtain the necessary number of decimal places.

EXAMPLE 8   Multiply. 0.123×0.5

Solution

$$
\begin{array}{r}
0.123 \quad (\text{three decimal places}) \\
\times \quad\ 0.5 \quad (\text{one decimal place}) \\
\hline
0.0615 \quad (\text{four decimal places})
\end{array}
$$

Practice Problem 8   Multiply. 0.12×0.4

Here are some examples that involve more decimal places.

EXAMPLE 9   Multiply.

(a) 2.56×0.003

(b) 0.0036×0.008

Solution

(a)
$$
\begin{array}{r}
2.56 \quad (\text{two decimal places}) \\
\times\ 0.003 \quad (\text{three decimal places}) \\
\hline
0.00768 \quad (\text{five decimal places})
\end{array}
$$

(b)
$$
\begin{array}{r}
0.0036 \quad (\text{four decimal places}) \\
\times\ 0.008 \quad (\text{three decimal places}) \\
\hline
0.0000288 \quad (\text{seven decimal places})
\end{array}
$$

NOTE TO STUDENT: Fully worked-out solutions to all of the Practice Problems can be found at the back of the text starting at page SP-1

Practice Problem 9   Multiply.

(a) 1.23×0.005

(b) 0.003×0.00002

SIDELIGHT: Counting the Number of Decimal Places

Why do we count the number of decimal places? The rule really comes from the properties of fractions. If we write the problem in Example 8 in fraction form, we have

$$
0.123 \times 0.5 = \frac{123}{1000} \times \frac{5}{10} = \frac{615}{10,000} = 0.0615.
$$

6 Dividing Decimals

When discussing division of decimals, we frequently refer to the three primary parts of a division problem. Be sure you know the meaning of each term.

The **divisor** is the number you divide into another.
The **dividend** is the number to be divided.
The **quotient** is the result of dividing one number by another.

In the problem $6 \div 2 = 3$ we represent each of these terms as follows:

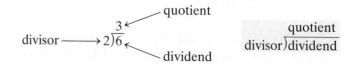

When dividing two decimals, count *the number of decimal places* in the divisor. Then *move the decimal point to the right* that *same number of places* in both *the divisor* and *the dividend*. Mark that position with a caret ($_\wedge$). Finally, perform the division. Be sure to line up the decimal point in the quotient with the position indicated by the caret in the dividend.

EXAMPLE 10 Four friends went out for lunch. The total bill, including tax, was $32.68. How much did each person pay if they shared the cost equally?

Solution   To answer this question, we must calculate $32.68 \div 4$.

$$
\begin{array}{r}
8.17 \\
4\overline{)32.68} \\
\underline{32} \\
6 \\
\underline{4} \\
28 \\
\underline{28} \\
0
\end{array}
$$

Since there are no decimal places in the divisor, we do not need to move the decimal point. We must be careful, however, to place the decimal point in the quotient directly above the decimal point in the dividend.

Thus $32.68 \div 4 = 8.17$, and each friend paid $8.17.

Practice Problem 10   Sally Keyser purchased 6 boxes of paper for the inkjet printer. The cost was $31.56. There was no tax since she purchased the paper for a charitable organization. How much did she pay for each box of paper?

Note that sometimes we will need to place extra zeros in the dividend in order to move the decimal point the required number of places.

EXAMPLE 11 Divide. $16.2 \div 0.027$

Solution

$$0.027\overline{)16.200}$$

There are **three** decimal places in the divisor, so we move the decimal point **three places** to **the right** in the **divisor** and **dividend** and mark the new position by a caret. Note that we must add two zeros to 16.2 in order to do this.

three decimal places

$$
\begin{array}{r}
600. \\
0.027\overline{)16.200} \\
\underline{16\,2} \\
000
\end{array}
$$

Now perform the division as with whole numbers. The decimal point in the answer is directly above the caret in the dividend.

Thus $16.2 \div 0.027 = 600$.

Practice Problem 11   Divide. $1800 \div 0.06$

Special care must be taken to line up the digits in the quotient. Note that sometimes we will need to place zeros in the quotient after the decimal point.

EXAMPLE 12   Divide. $0.04288 \div 3.2$

Solution

$$3.2\overline{)0.0\overset{\wedge}{4}288}$$

There is **one** decimal place in the divisor, so we move the decimal point **one place** to **the right** in the **divisor** and **dividend** and mark the new position by a caret.

one decimal place

$$\begin{array}{r} 0.0134 \\ 3.2\overline{)0.0\overset{\wedge}{4}288} \\ \underline{32} \\ 108 \\ \underline{96} \\ 128 \\ \underline{128} \\ 0 \end{array}$$

Now perform the division as for whole numbers. The decimal point in the answer is directly above the caret in the dividend. Note the need for the initial zero after the decimal point in the answer.

Thus $0.04288 \div 3.2 = 0.0134$.

NOTE TO STUDENT: Fully worked-out solutions to all of the Practice Problems can be found at the back of the text starting at page SP-1

Practice Problem 12   Divide. $0.01764 \div 4.9$

SIDELIGHT: Dividing Decimals by Another Method

Why does this method of dividing decimals work? Essentially, we are using the steps we used in Section 1.1 to change a fraction to an equivalent fraction by multiplying both the numerator and denominator by the same number. Let's reexamine Example 12.

$$0.04288 \div 3.2 = \frac{0.04288}{3.2}$$

Write the original problem using fraction notation.

$$= \frac{0.04288 \times 10}{3.2 \quad \times 10}$$

Multiply the numerator and denominator by 10. Since this is the same as multiplying by 1, we are not changing the fraction.

$$= \frac{0.4288}{32}$$

Write the result of multiplication by 10.

$$= 0.4288 \div 32$$

Rewrite the fraction as an equivalent problem with division notation.

Notice that we have obtained a new problem that is the same as the problem in Example 12 when we moved the decimal one place to the right in the divisor and dividend. We see that the reason we can move the decimal point as many places as necessary to the right in divisor and dividend is that this is the same as multiplying the numerator and denominator of a fraction by a power of 10 to obtain an equivalent fraction.

⑦ Multiplying and Dividing a Decimal by a Multiple of 10

When multiplying by 10, 100, 1000, and so on, a simple rule may be used to obtain the answer. For every zero in the multiplier, move the decimal point one place to the right.

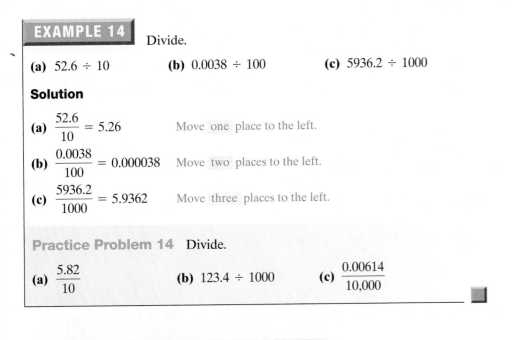

EXAMPLE 13 Multiply.

(a) 3.24×10 **(b)** 15.6×100 **(c)** 0.0026×1000

Solution

(a) $3.24 \times 10 = 32.4$ One zero—move decimal point one place to the right.

(b) $15.6 \times 100 = 1560$ Two zeros—move decimal point two places to the right.

(c) $0.0026 \times 1000 = 2.6$ Three zeros—move decimal point three places to the right.

Practice Problem 13 Multiply.

(a) 0.0016×100 **(b)** 2.34×1000 **(c)** $56.75 \times 10,000$

The reverse rule is true for division. When dividing by 10, 100, 1000, 10,000, and so on, move the decimal point one place to the left for every zero in the divisor.

EXAMPLE 14 Divide.

(a) $52.6 \div 10$ **(b)** $0.0038 \div 100$ **(c)** $5936.2 \div 1000$

Solution

(a) $\dfrac{52.6}{10} = 5.26$ Move one place to the left.

(b) $\dfrac{0.0038}{100} = 0.000038$ Move two places to the left.

(c) $\dfrac{5936.2}{1000} = 5.9362$ Move three places to the left.

Practice Problem 14 Divide.

(a) $\dfrac{5.82}{10}$ **(b)** $123.4 \div 1000$ **(c)** $\dfrac{0.00614}{10,000}$

Developing Your Study Skills

Making a Friend in the Class

Attempt to make a friend in your class. You may find that you enjoy sitting together and drawing support and encouragement from one another. Exchange phone numbers so you can call each other whenever you get stuck in your study. Set up convenient times to study together on a regular basis, to do homework, and to review for exams.

You must not depend on a friend or fellow student to tutor you, do your work for you, or in any way be responsible for your learning. However, you will learn from one another as you seek to master the course. Studying with a friend and comparing notes, methods, and solutions can be very helpful. And it can make learning mathematics a lot more fun!

1.4 EXERCISES

Student Solutions Manual | CD/Video | PH Math Tutor Center | MathXL®Tutorials on CD | MathXL® | MyMathLab® | Interactmath.com

Verbal and Writing Skills

1. A decimal is another way of writing a fraction whose denominator is _____.

2. We write 0.42 in words as _____.

3. When dividing 7432.9 by 1000 we move the decimal point _____ places to the _____.

4. When dividing 96.3 by 10,000 we move the decimal point _____ places to the _____.

Write each fraction as a decimal.

5. $\dfrac{5}{8}$ **6.** $\dfrac{6}{25}$ **7.** $\dfrac{3}{15}$ **8.** $\dfrac{12}{15}$ **9.** $\dfrac{7}{11}$ **10.** $\dfrac{2}{3}$

Write each decimal as a fraction in simplified form.

11. 0.8   **12.** 0.5   **13.** 0.25   **14.** 0.15   **15.** 0.625   **16.** 0.475

17. 0.06   **18.** 0.08   **19.** 2.6   **20.** 4.8   **21.** 5.5   **22.** 1.8

Add or subtract.

23. $1.71 + 0.38$ **24.** $3.42 + 0.38$ **25.** $2.5 + 3.42 + 4.9$ **26.** $6.31 + 4.2 + 8.5$

27. $46.03 + 215.1 + 0.078$ **28.** $33.01 + 0.38 + 175.401$ **29.** $147.18 - 15.39$ **30.** $131.43 - 86.95$

31. $53.783 - 2.34$ **32.** $48.575 - 5.44$ **33.** $125.43 - 2.8$ **34.** $30 - 0.82$

Multiply or divide.

35. 7.21×4.2 **36.** 7.12×2.6 **37.** 0.04×0.08 **38.** 5.23×1.41

39. 4.23×0.025 **40.** 3.84×0.0017 **41.** $169,000 \times 0.0013$ **42.** $368,000 \times 0.00021$

43. $3.616 \div 64$ **44.** $12.6672 \div 39$ **45.** $7.9728 \div 3.02$ **46.** $6.519 \div 2.05$

47. $0.5230 \div 0.002$ **48.** $0.031 \div 0.005$ **49.** $0.02056 \div 0.08$ **50.** $0.03222 \div 0.09$

Multiply or divide by moving the decimal point.

51. 3.45×1000 **52.** 1.36×1000 **53.** $0.76 \div 100$ **54.** $175,318 \div 1000$

55. $7.36 \times 10,000$ **56.** $0.00243 \times 100,000$ **57.** $73,892 \div 100,000$ **58.** $3.52 \div 1000$

59. 0.1498×100 **60.** $1.931 \div 100$ **61.** $85.54 \times 10,000$ **62.** $96.12 \div 10,000$

Mixed Practice

Perform the indicated calculations.

63. 23.75×0.06

64. 1.824×0.004

65. $1.62 + 2.005 + 8.1007$

66. $1.5 + 3.06 + 4.209$

67. $0.05724 \div 0.027$

68. $77.136 \div 0.003$

69. 0.7683×1000

70. $34.72 \times 10,000$

71. $25.98 - 2.33$

72. $12.1 - 0.23$

73. $153.7 \div 100$

74. $0.0388 \div 1000$

Applications

75. *Measurement* In a recent chemistry lab, Jerome needed to change the measured data from inches to centimeters. If there are 2.54 cm in an inch, and the original measurement was 9.5 inches, what is the measured data in cms?

76. *Hybrid Cars* Hai Hung bought a hybrid electric-gas–powered car because of its great miles per gallon in the city. The car averages 46.2 miles per gallon in the city, and the tank holds 9.7 gallons of gas. How many miles can Hai travel in the city on a full tank of gas?

77. *Curtain Material* Lexi decided that she would need 18.5 yards of material to make curtains. If the material she chose cost $11.50 per yard, what did the material for her curtains cost?

78. *Turkey Weight* The Parkins family is going to order a turkey for Thanksgiving dinner from Ray's Turkey Farm. Mrs. Parkins estimates that she will need 12 pounds of meat to serve all her guests. The turkey farm owner claims that each turkey yields about 0.78 of its weight in meat. If Mrs. Parkins buys a 17.3-pound turkey, will there be enough meat for everyone?

79. *Drinking Water* The EPA standard for safe drinking water is a maximum of 1.3 milligrams of copper per liter of water. A water testing firm found 6.8 milligrams of copper in a 5-liter sample drawn from Jim and Sharon LeBlanc's house. Is the water safe or not? By how much does the amount of copper exceed or fall short of the maximum allowed?

80. *Wages* Harry has a part-time job at Stop and Shop. He earns $8.50 an hour. Last week he worked 19 hours. He had hoped to earn at least $150. Did he reach his goal or not? By how much did he exceed or fall short of his goal?

Cumulative Review

Perform each operation. Simplify all answers.

81. $3\dfrac{1}{2} \div 5\dfrac{1}{4}$

82. $\dfrac{3}{8} \cdot \dfrac{12}{27}$

83. $\dfrac{12}{25} + \dfrac{9}{20}$

84. $1\dfrac{3}{5} - \dfrac{1}{2}$

Putting Your Skills to Work

Bodies of Water: The World's Largest Lakes

Did you know that any body of water surrounded by land is called a lake, even salty bodies of water? Thus, the Caspian Sea in Asia, the Aral Sea in Asia, the Great Salt Lake in the United States, and the Eyre in Australia are all considered lakes. Look at the following information on the largest *freshwater* lakes in the world.

Lake	Location	Area (in 1000 square miles)
Superior	US	31.8
Victoria	Africa	26.6
Huron	United States, Canada	23
Michigan	United States	22.4
Tanganyika	Africa	13.9
Great Bear	Canada	12.3
Lake Baikul	Russia	11.8

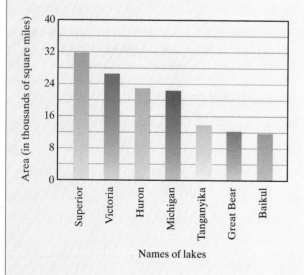

Problems for Individual Investigation and Analysis:

1. How much larger in area is Lake Victoria than Lake Tanganyika?

2. How much larger in area is Lake Superior than Lake Michigan?

Problems for Group Investigation and Cooperative Learning:

3. The smallest Great Lake is Lake Ontario with an area of 7540 sq. mi. About how many times would Lake Ontario fit into Lake Superior?

4. The largest lake in New Hampshire is Lake Winnipesaukee with an area of 72 square miles. About how many times would Lake Winnipesaukee fit into Lake Huron?

Topic	Procedure	Examples
Simplifying fractions, p. 3.	1. Write the **numerator** and **denominator** as a product of prime factors. 2. Use the basic rule of fractions that $$\frac{a \times c}{b \times c} = \frac{a}{b}$$ for any factor that appears in both the numerator and the denominator. 3. Multiply the remaining factors for the numerator and separately for the denominator.	$$\frac{15}{25} = \frac{\cancel{5} \cdot 3}{\cancel{5} \cdot 5} = \frac{3}{5}$$ $$\frac{36}{48} = \frac{\cancel{2} \cdot \cancel{2} \cdot 3 \cdot \cancel{3}}{\cancel{2} \cdot \cancel{2} \cdot 2 \cdot 2 \cdot \cancel{3}} = \frac{3}{4}$$ $$\frac{26}{39} = \frac{2 \cdot \cancel{13}}{3 \cdot \cancel{13}} = \frac{2}{3}$$
Changing improper fractions to mixed numbers, p. 5.	1. Divide the denominator into the numerator to obtain the whole-number part of the mixed fraction. 2. The remainder from the division will be the numerator of the fraction. 3. The denominator remains unchanged.	$\frac{14}{3} = 4\frac{2}{3}$ $\frac{19}{8} = 2\frac{3}{8}$ since $3\overline{)14}$ ... since $8\overline{)19}$
Changing mixed numbers to improper fractions, p. 6.	1. Multiply the whole number by the denominator and add the result to the numerator. This will yield the new numerator. 2. The denominator does not change.	$$4\frac{5}{6} = \frac{(4 \times 6) + 5}{6} = \frac{24 + 5}{6} = \frac{29}{6}$$ $$3\frac{1}{7} = \frac{(3 \times 7) + 1}{7} = \frac{21 + 1}{7} = \frac{22}{7}$$
Changing fractions to equivalent fractions with a given denominator, p. 7.	1. Divide the original denominator into the new denominator. This result is the value that we use for multiplication. 2. Multiply the numerator and the denominator of the original fraction by that value.	$$\frac{4}{7} = \frac{?}{21}$$ $\overset{3}{7\overline{)21}} \leftarrow$ Use this to multiply $\frac{4 \times 3}{7 \times 3} = \frac{12}{21}$
Finding the LCD (least common denominator) of two or more fractions, p. 12.	1. Write each denominator as the product of prime factors. 2. The LCD is a product containing each different factor. 3. If a factor occurs more than once in any one denominator, the LCD will contain that factor repeated the greatest number of times that it occurs in any one denominator.	Find the LCD of $\frac{4}{15}$ and $\frac{3}{35}$. $15 = 5 \cdot 3$ $35 = 5 \cdot 7$ $LCD = 3 \cdot 5 \cdot 7 = 105$ Find the LCD of $\frac{11}{18}$ and $\frac{7}{45}$. $18 = 3 \cdot 3 \cdot 2$ (factor 3 appears twice) $45 = 3 \cdot 3 \cdot 5$ (factor 3 appears twice) $LCD = 2 \cdot 3 \cdot 3 \cdot 5 = 90$
Adding and subtracting fractions that do not have a common denominator, p. 13.	1. Find the LCD. 2. Change each fraction to an equivalent fraction with the LCD for a denominator. 3. Add or subtract the fractions and simplify the answer if possible.	$$\frac{3}{8} + \frac{1}{3} = \frac{3 \cdot 3}{8 \cdot 3} + \frac{1 \cdot 8}{3 \cdot 8} = \frac{9}{24} + \frac{8}{24} = \frac{17}{24}$$ $$\frac{11}{12} - \frac{1}{4} = \frac{11}{12} - \frac{1 \cdot 3}{4 \cdot 3} = \frac{11}{12} - \frac{3}{12} = \frac{8}{12} = \frac{2}{3}$$
Adding and subtracting mixed numbers, p. 16.	1. Change the mixed numbers to improper fractions. 2. Follow the rules for adding and subtracting fractions. 3. If necessary, change your answer to a mixed number.	$$1\frac{2}{3} + 1\frac{3}{4} = \frac{5}{3} + \frac{7}{4} = \frac{5 \cdot 4}{3 \cdot 4} + \frac{7 \cdot 3}{4 \cdot 3}$$ $$= \frac{20}{12} + \frac{21}{12} = \frac{41}{12} = 3\frac{5}{12}$$ $$2\frac{1}{4} - 1\frac{3}{4} = \frac{9}{4} - \frac{7}{4} = \frac{2}{4} = \frac{1}{2}$$
Multiplying fractions, p. 22.	1. If there are no common factors, multiply the numerators. Then multiply the denominators. 2. If possible, write the numerators and denominators as the product of prime factors. Use the basic rule of fractions to divide out any value that appears in both a numerator and a denominator. Multiply the remaining factors in the numerator. Multiply the remaining factors in the denominator.	$$\frac{3}{7} \times \frac{2}{13} = \frac{6}{91}$$ $$\frac{6}{15} \times \frac{35}{91} = \frac{2 \cdot \cancel{3}}{\cancel{3} \cdot \cancel{5}} \times \frac{\cancel{5} \cdot \cancel{7}}{\cancel{7} \cdot 13} = \frac{2}{13}$$ $$3 \times \frac{5}{8} = \frac{3}{1} \times \frac{5}{8} = \frac{15}{8} \text{ or } 1\frac{7}{8}$$

Topic	Procedure	Examples
Dividing fractions, p. 24.	1. Change the division sign to multiplication. 2. Invert the second fraction. 3. Multiply the fractions.	$\dfrac{4}{7} \div \dfrac{11}{3} = \dfrac{4}{7} \times \dfrac{3}{11} = \dfrac{12}{77}$ $\dfrac{5}{9} \div \dfrac{5}{7} = \dfrac{\cancel{5}}{9} \times \dfrac{7}{\cancel{5}} = \dfrac{7}{9}$
Multiplying and dividing mixed numbers, pp. 23 and 26.	1. Change each mixed number to an improper fraction. 2. Use the rules for multiplying or dividing fractions. 3. Change your answer to a mixed number.	$2\dfrac{1}{4} \times 3\dfrac{3}{5} = \dfrac{9}{4} \times \dfrac{18}{5}$ $= \dfrac{3 \cdot 3}{2 \cdot 2} \times \dfrac{\cancel{2} \cdot 3 \cdot 3}{5} = \dfrac{81}{10} = 8\dfrac{1}{10}$ $1\dfrac{1}{4} \div 1\dfrac{1}{2} = \dfrac{5}{4} \div \dfrac{3}{2} = \dfrac{5}{2 \cdot \cancel{2}} \times \dfrac{\cancel{2}}{3} = \dfrac{5}{6}$
Changing fractional form to decimal form, p. 32.	Divide the denominator into the numerator.	$\dfrac{5}{8} = 0.625$ since $8)\overline{5.000}^{\,0.625}$
Changing decimal form to fractional form, p. 33.	1. Write the decimal as a fraction with a denominator of 10, 100, 1000, and so on. 2. Simplify the fraction, if possible.	$0.37 = \dfrac{37}{100}$ $0.375 = \dfrac{375}{1000} = \dfrac{3}{8}$
Adding and subtracting decimals, p. 34.	1. Carefully line up the decimal points as indicated for addition and subtraction. (Extra zeros may be added to the right-hand side of the decimals if desired.) 2. Add or subtract the appropriate digits.	Add. $1.236 + 7.825$ $\begin{array}{r} 1.236 \\ + 7.825 \\ \hline 9.061 \end{array}$ Subtract. $2 - 1.32$ $\begin{array}{r} 2.00 \\ - 1.32 \\ \hline 0.68 \end{array}$
Multiplying decimals, p. 35.	1. First multiply the digits. 2. Count the total number of decimal places in the numbers being multiplied. 3. This number determines the number of decimal places in the answer.	$\begin{array}{r} 0.9 \text{ (one place)} \\ \times\, 0.7 \text{ (one place)} \\ \hline 0.63 \text{ (two places)} \end{array}$ $\begin{array}{r} 0.009 \text{ (three places)} \\ \times\,\, 0.07 \text{ (two places)} \\ \hline 0.00063 \text{ (five places)} \end{array}$
Dividing decimals, p. 36.	1. Count the number of decimal places in the divisor. 2. Move the decimal point to the right the same number of places in both the divisor and dividend. 3. Mark that position with a caret ($_\wedge$). 4. Perform the division. Line up the decimal point in the quotient with the position indicated by the caret in the dividend.	Divide. $7.5 \div 0.6$. Move decimal point one place to the right. $0.6_{\wedge})\overline{7.5_{\wedge}0}^{\,12.5}$ Therefore, $\dfrac{6}{15}$ $7.5 \div 0.6 = 12.5$ $\dfrac{12}{30}$ $\dfrac{30}{0}$

Chapter 1 Review Problems

Section 1.1

In exercises 1–4, simplify.

1. $\dfrac{36}{48}$ **2.** $\dfrac{15}{50}$ **3.** $\dfrac{36}{82}$ **4.** $\dfrac{18}{30}$

5. Write $4\dfrac{3}{5}$ as an improper fraction.   **6.** Write $\dfrac{34}{5}$ as a mixed number.   **7.** Write $\dfrac{39}{6}$ as a mixed number.

Change each fraction to an equivalent fraction with the specified denominator.

8. $\dfrac{5}{8} = \dfrac{?}{24}$ **9.** $\dfrac{1}{7} = \dfrac{?}{35}$ **10.** $\dfrac{5}{9} = \dfrac{?}{72}$ **11.** $\dfrac{2}{5} = \dfrac{?}{55}$

Section 1.2

Combine.

12. $\dfrac{3}{5} + \dfrac{1}{4}$ **13.** $\dfrac{7}{12} + \dfrac{5}{8}$ **14.** $\dfrac{7}{20} - \dfrac{1}{12}$ **15.** $\dfrac{7}{10} - \dfrac{4}{15}$

16. $3\dfrac{1}{6} + 2\dfrac{3}{5}$ **17.** $1\dfrac{1}{4} + 2\dfrac{7}{10}$ **18.** $6\dfrac{2}{9} - 3\dfrac{5}{12}$ **19.** $3\dfrac{1}{15} - 1\dfrac{3}{20}$

Section 1.3

Multiply.

20. $6 \times \dfrac{5}{11}$ **21.** $2\dfrac{1}{3} \times 4\dfrac{1}{2}$ **22.** $1\dfrac{1}{8} \times 2\dfrac{1}{9}$ **23.** $\dfrac{4}{7} \times 5$

Divide.

24. $\dfrac{3}{8} \div 6$ **25.** $\dfrac{\frac{8}{3}}{\frac{5}{9}}$ **26.** $\dfrac{15}{16} \div 6\dfrac{1}{4}$ **27.** $2\dfrac{6}{7} \div \dfrac{10}{21}$

Section 1.4

Combine.

28. $1.634 + 3.007 + 2.560$ **29.** $24.831 - 17.094$ **30.** $47.251 - 17.69$ **31.** $1.9 + 2.53 + 0.006$

Multiply.

32. 0.007×5.35 **33.** 362.341×1000 **34.** $2.6 \times 0.03 \times 1.02$ **35.** $1.08 \times 0.06 \times 160$

Divide.

36. $0.186 \div 100$ **37.** $71.32 \div 1000$ **38.** $0.523 \div 0.4$ **39.** $1.35 \div 0.015$

40. $4.186 \div 2.3$ **41.** $0.19 \div 0.38$ **42.** Write as a decimal: $\dfrac{3}{8}$.

43. Write as a fraction in simplified form: 0.36.

In exercises 1 and 2, simplify.

1. $\dfrac{16}{18}$

2. $\dfrac{48}{36}$

3. Write as an improper fraction. $6\dfrac{3}{7}$

4. Write as a mixed number: $\dfrac{105}{9}$.

In exercises 5–12, perform the operations indicated. Simplify answers whenever possible.

5. $\dfrac{2}{3} + \dfrac{5}{6} + \dfrac{3}{8}$

6. $1\dfrac{1}{8} + 3\dfrac{3}{4}$

7. $3\dfrac{2}{3} - 2\dfrac{5}{6}$

8. $\dfrac{5}{7} \times \dfrac{28}{15}$

9. $\dfrac{5}{18} \times \dfrac{3}{4}$

10. $5\dfrac{3}{8} \div 2\dfrac{3}{4}$

11. $2\dfrac{1}{2} \times 3\dfrac{1}{4}$

12. $\dfrac{\frac{7}{4}}{\frac{1}{2}}$

In exercises 13–18, perform the calculations indicated.

13. $1.6 + 3.24 + 9.8$

14. $7.0046 - 3.0149$

15. 32.8×0.04

16. 0.07385×1000

1. _____

2. _____

3. _____

4. _____

5. _____

6. _____

7. _____

8. _____

9. _____

10. _____

11. _____

12. _____

13. _____

14. _____

15. _____

16. _____

17. $12.88 \div 0.056$

18. $26,325.9 \div 100$

19. Write as a percent. 0.073

20. Write as a decimal. 196.5%

21. What is 3.5% of 180?

22. What is 2% of 16.8?

23. 39 is what percent of 650?

24. What percent of 460 is 138?

25. A 4-inch stack of computer chips is on the table. Each computer chip is $\frac{2}{9}$ of an inch thick. How many computer chips are in the stack?

In exercises 26–27, estimate. Round each number to one nonzero digit. Then calculate.

26. $52,344\overline{)4,678,987}$

27. $285.36 + 311.85 + 113.6$

17. _____

18. _____

19. _____

20. _____

21. _____

22. _____

23. _____

24. _____

25. _____

26. _____

27. _____

CHAPTER

2

Do you have any idea how much the use of the Internet has grown in recent years? Do you think it has spread to farmers and fishermen? Do you have any idea how many people use a computer both at home and at work? Turn to the Putting Your Skills to Work on page 107 and see how good your estimates were.

Real Numbers and Variables

2.1   **ADDING REAL NUMBERS**   50

2.2   **SUBTRACTING REAL NUMBERS**   61

2.3   **MULTIPLYING AND DIVIDING REAL NUMBERS**   66

2.4   **EXPONENTS**   76

2.5   **THE ORDER OF OPERATIONS**   80

       HOW AM I DOING? SECTIONS 2.1–2.5   84

2.6   **USING THE DISTRIBUTIVE PROPERTY TO SIMPLIFY ALGEBRAIC EXPRESSIONS**   85

2.7   **COMBINING LIKE TERMS**   90

2.8   **USING SUBSTITUTION TO EVALUATE ALGEBRAIC EXPRESSIONS AND FORMULAS**   95

2.9   **GROUPING SYMBOLS**   103

       CHAPTER 2 ORGANIZER   108

       CHAPTER 2 REVIEW PROBLEMS   109

       HOW AM I DOING? CHAPTER 2 TEST   113

Student Learning Objectives

After studying this section, you will be able to:

1 Identify different types of numbers.

2 Use real numbers in real-life situations.

3 Add real numbers with the same sign.

4 Add real numbers with opposite signs.

5 Use the addition properties for real numbers.

1 Identifying Different Types of Numbers

Let's review some of the basic terms we use to talk about numbers.

Whole numbers are numbers such as $0, 1, 2, 3, 4, \ldots$

Integers are numbers such as $\ldots, -3, -2, -1, 0, 1, 2, 3, \ldots$.

Rational numbers are numbers such as $\frac{3}{2}, \frac{5}{7}, -\frac{3}{8}, -\frac{4}{13}, \frac{6}{1}$, and $-\frac{8}{2}$.

Rational numbers can be written as one integer divided by another integer (as long as the denominator is not zero!). Integers can be written as fractions ($3 = \frac{3}{1}$, for example), so we can see that all integers are rational numbers. Rational numbers can be expressed in decimal form. For example, $\frac{3}{2} = 1.5$, $-\frac{3}{8} = -0.375$, and $\frac{1}{3} = 0.333\ldots$ or $0.\overline{3}$. It is important to note that rational numbers in decimal form are either terminating decimals or repeating decimals.

Irrational numbers are numbers that cannot be expressed as one integer divided by another integer. The numbers π, $\sqrt{2}$, and $\sqrt[3]{7}$ are irrational numbers.

Irrational numbers can be expressed in decimal form. The decimal form of an irrational number is a nonterminating, nonrepeating decimal. For example, $\sqrt{2} = 1.414213\ldots$ can be carried out to an infinite number of decimal places with no repeating pattern of digits

Finally, **real numbers** are all the rational numbers and all the irrational numbers.

EXAMPLE 1 Classify as an integer, a rational number, an irrational number, and/or a real number.

(a) 5   **(b)** $-\frac{1}{3}$ **(c)** 2.85   **(d)** $\sqrt{2}$ **(e)** $0.777\ldots$

Solution Make a table. Check off the description of the number that applies.

	Number	Integer	Rational Number	Irrational Number	Real Number
(a)	5	✓	✓		✓
(b)	$-\frac{1}{3}$		✓		✓
(c)	2.85		✓		✓
(d)	$\sqrt{2}$			✓	✓
(e)	$0.777\ldots$		✓		✓

NOTE TO STUDENT: Fully worked-out solutions to all of the Practice Problems can be found at the back of the text starting at page SP-1

Practice Problem 1 Classify.

(a) $-\frac{2}{5}$ **(b)** $1.515151\ldots$ **(c)** -8 **(d)** π

Any real number can be pictured on a **number line.**

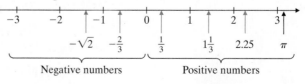

Negative numbers   Positive numbers

Positive numbers are to the right of 0 on the number line.

Negative numbers are to the left of 0 on the number line.

The **real numbers** include the positive numbers, the negative numbers, and zero.

2 Using Real Numbers in Real-Life Situations

We often encounter practical examples of number lines that include positive and negative rational numbers. For example, we can tell by reading the accompanying thermometer that the temperature is 20° below 0. From the stock market report, we see that the stock opened at 36 and closed at 34.5, and the net change for the day was −1.5.

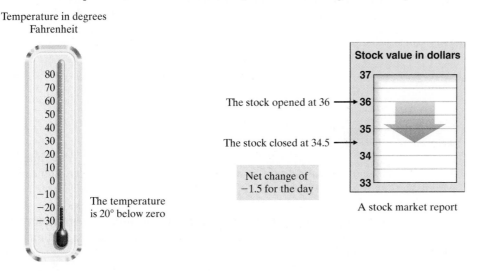

Temperature in degrees Fahrenheit

The temperature is 20° below zero

Stock value in dollars

The stock opened at 36

The stock closed at 34.5

Net change of −1.5 for the day

A stock market report

In the following example we use real numbers to represent real-life situations.

EXAMPLE 2   Use a real number to represent each situation.

(a) A temperature of 128.6°F below zero is recorded at Vostok, Antarctica.

(b) The Himalayan peak K2 rises 29,064 feet above sea level.

(c) The Dow gains 10.24 points.

(d) An oil drilling platform extends 328 feet below sea level.

Solution   A key word can help you to decide whether a number is positive or negative.

(a) 128.6°F *below* zero is −128.6.

(b) 29,064 feet *above* sea level is +29,064.

(c) A *gain* of 10.24 points is +10.24.

(d) 328 feet *below* sea level is −328.

Practice Problem 2   Use a real number to represent each situation.

(a) A population growth of 1259   **(b)** A depreciation of $763

(c) A wind-chill factor of minus 10

In everyday life we consider positive numbers the opposite of negative numbers. For example, a gain of 3 yards in a football game is the opposite of a loss of 3 yards; a check written for $2.16 on a checking account is the opposite of a deposit of $2.16.

Each positive number has an opposite negative number. Similarly, each negative number has an opposite positive number. **Opposite numbers,** also called **additive inverses,** have the same magnitude but different signs and can be represented on the number line.

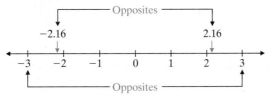

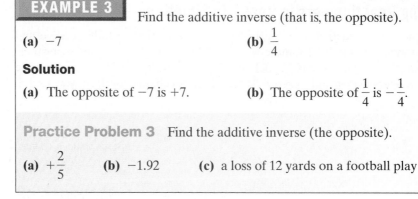

NOTE TO STUDENT: *Fully worked-out solutions to all of the Practice Problems can be found at the back of the text starting at page SP-1*

Practice Problem 3 Find the additive inverse (the opposite).

(a) $+\dfrac{2}{5}$ **(b)** -1.92 **(c)** a loss of 12 yards on a football play

3 Adding Real Numbers with the Same Sign

To use a real number, we need to be clear about its sign. When we write the number three as $+3$, the sign indicates that it is a positive number. The positive sign can be omitted. If someone writes three (3), it is understood that it is a positive three ($+3$). To write a negative number such as negative three (-3), we must include the sign.

A concept that will help us add and subtract real numbers is the idea of absolute value. The **absolute value** of a number is the distance between that number and zero on the number line. The absolute value of 3 is written $|3|$.

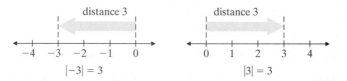

Distance is always a positive number regardless of the direction we travel. This means that the absolute value of any number will be a positive value or zero. We place the symbols $|$ and $|$ around a number to mean the absolute value of the number.

The distance from 0 to 3 is 3, so $|3| = 3$. This is read "the absolute value of 3 is 3."

The distance from 0 to -3 is 3, so $|-3| = 3$. This is read "the absolute value of -3 is 3."

Some other examples are

$$|-22| = 22, \qquad |5.6| = 5.6, \qquad \text{and} \qquad |0| = 0.$$

Thus, the absolute value of a number can be thought of as the magnitude of the number, without regard to its sign.

EXAMPLE 4 Find the absolute value.

(a) $|-4.62|$ **(b)** $\left|\dfrac{3}{7}\right|$ **(c)** $|0|$

Solution

(a) $|-4.62| = 4.62$ **(b)** $\left|\dfrac{3}{7}\right| = \dfrac{3}{7}$ **(c)** $|0| = 0$

Practice Problem 4 Find the absolute value.

(a) $|-7.34|$ **(b)** $\left|\dfrac{5}{8}\right|$ **(c)** $\left|\dfrac{0}{2}\right|$

Now let's look at addition of real numbers when the two numbers have the same sign. Suppose that you are keeping track of your checking account at a local bank. When you make a deposit of 5 dollars, you record it as +5. When you write a check for 4 dollars, you record it as −4, as a debit. Consider two situations.

SITUATION 1: Total Deposit   You made a deposit of 20 dollars on one day and a deposit of 15 dollars the next day. You want to know the total value of your deposits.
   Your record for situation 1.

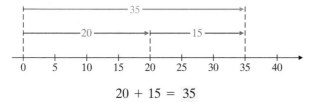

$$20 + 15 = 35$$

   The amount of the deposit on the first day added to the amount of the deposit on the second day is the total of the deposits made over the two days.

SITUATION 2: Total Debit   You write a check for 25 dollars to pay one bill and two days later write a check for 5 dollars. You want to know the total value of debits to your account for the two checks.
   Your record for situation 2.

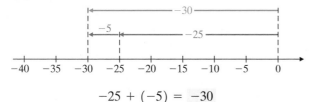

$$-25 + (-5) = -30$$

   The value of the first check added to the value of the second check is the total debit to your account.
   In each situation we found that we added the absolute value of each number. (That is, we added the numbers without regarding their sign.) The answer always contained the sign that was common to both numbers.
   We will now state these results as a formal rule.

ADDITION RULE FOR TWO NUMBERS WITH THE SAME SIGN

To add two numbers with the same sign, add the absolute values of the numbers and use the common sign in the answer.

EXAMPLE 5   Add.

(a) 14 + 16   **(b)** −8 + (−7)

Solution

(a) 14 +   16   Add the absolute values of the numbers.
       14 +   16 = 30   Use the common sign in the answer. Here the common
       14 +   16 = + 30   sign is the + sign.

(b) −8 +   (−7)   Add the absolute values of the numbers.
        8 +   7 = 15   Use the common sign in the answer. Here the common
       − 8 +   (− 7) = − 15   sign is the − sign.

Practice Problem 5   Add.

(a) 37 + 19   **(b)** −23 + (−35)

NOTE TO STUDENT: Fully worked-out solutions to all of the Practice Problems can be found at the back of the text starting at page SP-1

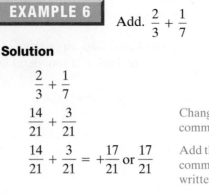

EXAMPLE 6 Add. $\dfrac{2}{3} + \dfrac{1}{7}$

Solution

$$\dfrac{2}{3} + \dfrac{1}{7}$$

$$\dfrac{14}{21} + \dfrac{3}{21} \qquad \text{Change each fraction to an equivalent fraction with a common denominator of 21.}$$

$$\dfrac{14}{21} + \dfrac{3}{21} = +\dfrac{17}{21} \text{ or } \dfrac{17}{21} \qquad \text{Add the absolute values of the numbers. Use the common sign in the answer. Note that if no sign is written, the number is understood to be positive.}$$

Practice Problem 6 Add. $-\dfrac{3}{5} + \left(-\dfrac{4}{7}\right)$

EXAMPLE 7 Add. $-4.2 + (-3.94)$

Solution

$$-4.2 + \qquad (-3.94)$$
$$4.20 + \qquad 3.94 \ = 8.14 \qquad \text{Add the absolute values of the numbers.}$$
$$-4.20 + \ (-3.94) = -8.14 \qquad \text{Use the common sign in the answer.}$$

Practice Problem 7 Add. $-12.7 + (-9.38)$

The rule for adding two numbers with the same signs can be extended to more than two numbers. If we add more than two numbers with the same sign, the answer will have the sign common to all.

EXAMPLE 8 Add. $-7 + (-2) + (-5)$

Solution

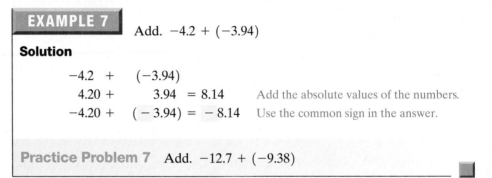

$$-7 + (-2) + (-5) \qquad \text{We are adding three real numbers all with the same sign. We begin by adding the first two numbers.}$$

$$= -9 + (-5) \qquad \text{Add } -7 + (-2) = -9.$$
$$= -14 \qquad \text{Add } -9 + (-5) = -14.$$

Of course, this can be shortened by adding the three numbers without regard to sign and then using the common sign for the answer.

Practice Problem 8 Add. $-7 + (-11) + (-33)$

④ Adding Real Numbers with Opposite Signs

What if the signs of the numbers you are adding are different? Let's consider our checking account again to see how such a situation might occur.

SITUATION 3: Net Increase You made a deposit of 30 dollars on one day. On the next day you write a check for 25 dollars. You want to know the result of your two transactions.

Your record for situation 3.

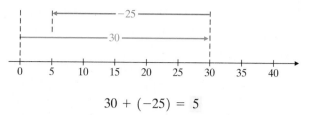

$$30 + (-25) = 5$$

A positive 30 for the deposit added to a negative 25 for the check, which is a debit, gives a net increase of 5 dollars in the account.

SITUATION 4: Net Decrease   You made a deposit of 10 dollars on one day. The next day you write a check for 40 dollars. You want to know the result of your two transactions.

Your record for situation 4.

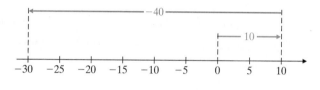

$$10 + (-40) = -30$$

A positive 10 for the deposit added to a negative 40 for the check, which is a debit, gives a net decrease of 30 dollars in the account.

The result is a negative thirty (-30), because the check was larger than the deposit. If you do not have at least 30 dollars in your account at the start of Situation 4, you have overdrawn your account.

What do we observe from situations 3 and 4? In each case, first we found the difference of the absolute values of the two numbers. Then the sign of the result was always the sign of the number with the greater absolute value. Thus, in situation 3, 30 is larger than 25. The sign of 30 is positive. The sign of the answer (5) is positive. In situation 4, 40 is larger than 10. The sign of 40 is negative. The sign of the answer (-30) is negative.

We will now state these results as a formal rule.

ADDITION RULE FOR TWO NUMBERS WITH DIFFERENT SIGNS

1. Find the difference between the larger absolute value and the smaller one.
2. Give the answer the sign of the number having the larger absolute value.

EXAMPLE 9   Add. $8 + (-7)$

Solution

$8 + (-7)$	We are to add two numbers with opposite signs.
$8 - 7 = 1$	Find the difference between the two absolute values, which is 1.
$+8 + (-7) = +1$ or 1	The answer will have the sign of the number with the larger absolute value. That number is $+8$. Its sign is **positive**, so the answer will be $+1$.

Practice Problem 9   Add. $-9 + 15$

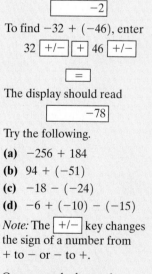

Calculator

Negative Numbers

To enter a negative number on most scientific calculators, find the key marked $\boxed{+/-}$. To enter the number -2, press the key 2 and then the key $+/-$. The display should read

$$\boxed{\qquad -2}$$

To find $-32 + (-46)$, enter

$$32 \boxed{+/-} \boxed{+} 46 \boxed{+/-}$$

$$\boxed{=}$$

The display should read

$$\boxed{\qquad -78}$$

Try the following.

(a) $-256 + 184$
(b) $94 + (-51)$
(c) $-18 - (-24)$
(d) $-6 + (-10) - (-15)$

Note: The $\boxed{+/-}$ key changes the sign of a number from $+$ to $-$ or $-$ to $+$.

On some calculators the negative sign must be entered first, followed by the number.

Answers:
(a) 72   **(b)** 43
(c) 6   **(d)** -1

Using the Addition Properties for Real Numbers

It is useful to know the following three properties of real numbers.

1. *Addition is commutative.*
   This property states that if two numbers are added, the result is the same no matter which number is written first. The order of the numbers does not affect the result.

$$3 + 6 = 6 + 3 = 9$$
$$-7 + (-8) = (-8) + (-7) = -15$$
$$-15 + 3 = 3 + (-15) = -12$$

2. *Addition of zero to any given number will result in that given number again.*

$$0 + 5 = 5$$
$$-8 + 0 = -8$$

3. *Addition is associative.*
   This property states that if three numbers are added, it does not matter which two numbers are grouped by parentheses and added first.

$$3 + (5 + 7) = (3 + 5) + 7$$
$$3 + (12) = (8) + 7$$
$$15 = 15$$

First combine numbers inside parentheses; then combine the remaining numbers. The results are the same no matter which numbers are grouped first.

We can use these properties along with the rules we have for adding real numbers to add three or more numbers. We go from left to right, adding two numbers at a time.

EXAMPLE 10 Add. $\dfrac{3}{17} + \left(-\dfrac{8}{17}\right) + \dfrac{4}{17}$

Solution

$$-\dfrac{5}{17} + \dfrac{4}{17}$$ Add $\dfrac{3}{17} + \left(-\dfrac{8}{17}\right) = -\dfrac{5}{17}$.
The answer is negative since the larger of the two absolute values is negative.

$$= -\dfrac{1}{17}$$ Add $-\dfrac{5}{17} + \dfrac{4}{17} = -\dfrac{1}{17}$.
The answer is negative since the larger of the two absolute values is negative.

NOTE TO STUDENT: Fully worked-out solutions to all of the Practice Problems can be found at the back of the text starting at page SP-1

Practice Problem 10 Add. $-\dfrac{5}{12} + \dfrac{7}{12} + \left(-\dfrac{11}{12}\right)$

Sometimes the numbers being added have the same signs; sometimes the signs are different. When adding three or more numbers, you may encounter both situations.

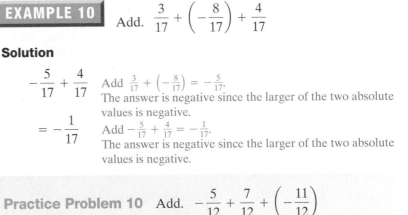

EXAMPLE 11 Add. $-1.8 + 1.4 + (-2.6)$

Solution

$$-0.4 + (-2.6)$$ We take the difference of 1.8 and 1.4 and use the sign of the number with the larger absolute value.

$$= -3.0$$ Add $-0.4 + (-2.6) = -3.0$. The signs are the same; we add the absolute values of the numbers and use the common sign.

Practice Problem 11 Add. $-6.3 + (-8.0) + 3.5$

If many real numbers are added, it is often easier to add numbers with like signs in a column format. Remember that addition is commutative; therefore, real numbers can be added *in any order*. You do *not* need to combine the first two numbers as your first step.

EXAMPLE 12   Add. $-8 + 3 + (-5) + (-2) + 6 + 5$

Solution

$$
\begin{array}{l}
-8 \\
-5 \\
\underline{-2} \\
-15
\end{array}
$$
All the signs are the same.
Add the three negative
numbers to obtain -15.

$$
\begin{array}{l}
+3 \\
+6 \\
\underline{+5} \\
+14
\end{array}
$$
All the signs are the same
Add the three positive
numbers to obtain $+14$.

Add the two results.

$$-15 \ + \ 14 \ = -1$$

The answer is negative because the number with the larger absolute value is negative.

Practice Problem 12   Add. $-6 + 5 + (-7) + (-2) + 5 + 3$

A word about notation: The only time we really need to show the sign of a number is when the number is negative—for example, -3. The only time we need to show parentheses when we add real numbers is when we have two different signs preceding a number. For example, $-5 + (-6)$.

EXAMPLE 13   Add.

(a) $2.8 + (-1.3)$ **(b)** $-\dfrac{2}{5} + \left(-\dfrac{3}{4}\right)$

Solution

(a) $2.8 + (-1.3) = 1.5$

(b) $-\dfrac{2}{5} + \left(-\dfrac{3}{4}\right) = -\dfrac{8}{20} + \left(-\dfrac{15}{20}\right) = -\dfrac{23}{20}$ or $-1\dfrac{3}{20}$

Practice Problem 13   Add.

(a) $-2.9 + (-5.7)$ **(b)** $\dfrac{2}{3} + \left(-\dfrac{1}{4}\right)$

2.1 EXERCISES

Student Solutions Manual | CD/Video | PH Math Tutor Center | MathXL®Tutorials on CD | MathXL® | MyMathLab® | Interactmath.com

Verbal and Writing Skills

Check off any description of the number that applies.

	Number	Whole Number	Rational Number	Irrational Number	Real Number
1.	23				
2.	$-\dfrac{4}{5}$				
3.	π				
4.	2.34				
5.	$-6.666\ldots$				

	Number	Whole Number	Rational Number	Irrational Number	Real Number
6.	$-\dfrac{7}{9}$				
7.	$-2.3434\ldots$				
8.	14				
9.	$\sqrt{2}$				
10.	$3.232232223\ldots$				

Use a real number to represent each situation.

11. Jules Verne wrote a book with the title *20,000 Leagues under the Sea.*

12. The value of the dollar is up $0.07 with respect to the yen.

13. Ramona lost $37\dfrac{1}{2}$ pounds on Weight Watchers.

14. The scouts hiked from sea level to the top of a 3642-foot-high mountain.

15. The temperature rises 7°F.

16. Maya lost the game by 12 points.

Find the additive inverse (opposite).

17. 8

18. $-\dfrac{4}{5}$

19. -2.73

20. 85.4

Find the absolute value.

21. $|-1.3|$

22. $|-5.9|$

23. $\left|\dfrac{5}{6}\right|$

24. $\left|\dfrac{7}{12}\right|$

Add.

25. $-6 + (-5)$

26. $-13 + (-3)$

27. $-17 + (-14)$

28. $-12 + (-19)$

29. $-\dfrac{5}{16} + \dfrac{9}{16}$

30. $-\dfrac{2}{9} + \left(\dfrac{-4}{9}\right)$

31. $-\dfrac{2}{13} + \left(-\dfrac{5}{13}\right)$

32. $-\dfrac{5}{14} + \dfrac{2}{14}$

33. $-\dfrac{2}{5} + \dfrac{3}{7}$

34. $-\dfrac{2}{7} + \dfrac{3}{14}$

35. $-1.5 + (-2.3)$

36. $-1.8 + (-1.4)$

37. $0.6 + (-0.2)$

38. $-0.8 + 0.5$

39. $-5.26 + (-8.9)$

40. $-6.48 + (-3.7)$

41. $-8 + 5 + (-3)$ **42.** $7 + (-8) + (-4)$ **43.** $-3 + 5 + (-7)$ **44.** $-9 + 6 + (-12)$

45. $-\dfrac{4}{5} + \dfrac{8}{15}$ **46.** $-\dfrac{5}{6} + \dfrac{7}{18}$ **47.** $-7 + (-9) + 8$ **48.** $-4 + (-13) + 7$

Mixed Practice

Add.

49. $8 + (-11)$ **50.** $16 + (-24)$ **51.** $-83 + 142$ **52.** $-114 + 186$

53. $-\dfrac{4}{9} + \dfrac{5}{6}$ **54.** $-\dfrac{3}{5} + \dfrac{2}{3}$ **55.** $-\dfrac{1}{10} + \dfrac{1}{2}$ **56.** $-\dfrac{2}{3} + \left(-\dfrac{1}{4}\right)$

57. $4.36 + (-3.6)$ **58.** $4.79 + (-9.1)$ **59.** $4 + (-8) + 16$ **60.** $27 + (-11) + (-4)$

61. $34 + (-18) + 11 + (-27)$ **62.** $-23 + 4 + (-11) + 17$

63. $17.85 + (-2.06) + 0.15$ **64.** $23.17 + 5.03 + (-11.81)$

Applications

65. *Profit/Loss* Holly paid $47 for a vase at an estate auction. She resold it to an antiques dealer for $214. What was her profit or loss?

66. *Temperature* When we skied at Jackson Hole, Wyoming, yesterday, the temperature at the summit was $-12°F$. Today when we called the ski report, the temperature had risen $7°F$. What is the temperature at the summit today?

67. *Home Equity Line of Credit* Ramon borrowed $2300 from his home equity line of credit to pay off his car loan. He then borrowed another $1500 to pay to have his kitchen repainted. Represent how much Ramon owed on his home equity line of credit as a real number.

68. *Time Change* During the winter, New York City is on Eastern Standard Time (EST). Melbourne, Australia is 15 hours ahead of New York. If it is 11 P.M. in Melbourne, what time is it in New York?

69. *Football* On three successive football running plays, Jon gained 9 yards, lost 11 yards, and gained 5 yards. What was his total gain or loss?

70. *School Fees* Wanda's financial aid account at school held $643.85. She withdrew $185.50 to buy books for the semester. Does she have enough left in her account to pay the $475.00 registration fee for the next semester? If so, how much extra money does she have? If not, how much is she short?

71. *Butterfly Population* The population of a particular butterfly species was 8000. Twenty years later there were 3000 fewer. Today, there are 1500 fewer. Study the graph to the right. What is the new population?

72. *Credit Card Balance* Aaron owes $258 to a credit card company. He makes a purchase of $32 with the card and then makes a payment of $150 on the account. How much does he still owe?

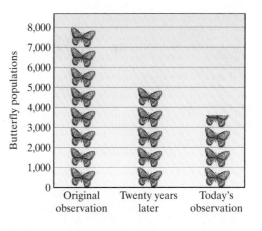

Profit/Loss *During the first five months of 2005 a regional Midwest airline posted profit and loss figures for each month of operation, as shown in the accompanying bar graph.*

73. For the first three months of 2005, what were the total earnings of the airline?

74. For the first five months of 2005, what were the total earnings for the airline?

To Think About

75. What number must be added to -13 to get 5?

76. What number must be added to -18 to get 10?

77. *Football* Vern rushed for 8 yards to his team's 17-yard line in the last quarter of the home football game. On the next play, the quarterback was sacked and lost 4 yards. On the third down, the pass was incomplete. How many yards must the team make on the next play to make first down?

78. *Discount Stores* Filene's Basement Store in Boston is famous for its Automatic Markdown Policy. Each item is dated when it enters the store. If it does not sell after 14 days, the price is reduced by 25%. If it is still there after 21 days, the discount is now 50%. After 28 days, the discount becomes a whopping 75%. If the item has still not sold after 35 days, it is taken from the store and donated to charity. While shopping in Filene's Basement, Heather Bean found two blouses that she liked a lot. The red blouse was originally $87.99 and had been in the store for 22 days. The blue blouse was originally $57.99 but had only been in the store for 19 days. Which one was cheaper? Which one was a better value?

Cumulative Review

Perform the indicated calculations.

79. $\dfrac{3}{7} + \dfrac{5}{21}$

80. $\left(\dfrac{2}{5}\right)\left(\dfrac{20}{27}\right)$

81. $\dfrac{2}{15} - \dfrac{1}{20}$

82. $2\dfrac{1}{2} \div 3\dfrac{2}{5}$

83. $0.72 + 0.8$

84. $1.63 - 0.98$

85. $(1.63)(0.7)$

86. $0.208 \div 0.8$

2.2 SUBTRACTING REAL NUMBERS

1 Subtracting Real Numbers with Like or Unlike Signs

So far we have developed the rules for adding real numbers. We can use these rules to subtract real numbers. Let's look at a checkbook situation to see how.

SITUATION 5: Subtract a Deposit and Add a Debit You have a balance of 20 dollars in your checking account. The bank calls you and says that a deposit of 5 dollars that belongs to another account was erroneously added to your account. They say they will correct the account balance to 15 dollars. The bank tells you that since they cannot take away the erroneous credit, they will add a debit to your account. You want to keep track of what's happening to your account.

Your record for situation 5.

$$20 - (+5) = 15$$

From your present balance subtract the deposit to give the new balance. This equation shows what needs to be done to your account. The bank tells you that because the error happened in the past they cannot "take it away." However, they can add to your account a debit of 5 dollars. Here is the equivalent addition.

$$20 + (-5) = 15$$

To your present balance add a debit to give the new balance. Subtracting a positive 5 has the same effect as adding a negative 5.

> ### SUBTRACTION OF REAL NUMBERS
>
> To subtract real numbers, add the opposite of the second number (that is, the number you are subtracting) to the first.

The rule tells us to do three things when we subtract real numbers. First, change subtraction to addition. Second, replace the second number by its opposite. Third, add the two numbers using the rules for addition of real numbers.

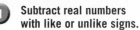

EXAMPLE 1 Subtract. $6 - (-2)$

Solution

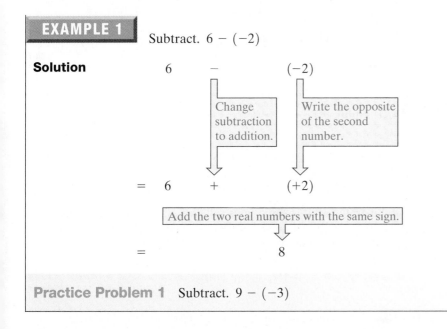

Practice Problem 1 Subtract. $9 - (-3)$

NOTE TO STUDENT: Fully worked-out solutions to all of the Practice Problems can be found at the back of the text starting at page SP-1

Student Learning Objective

After studying this section, you will be able to:

1 **Subtract real numbers with like or unlike signs.**

EXAMPLE 2   Subtract. $-8 - (-6)$

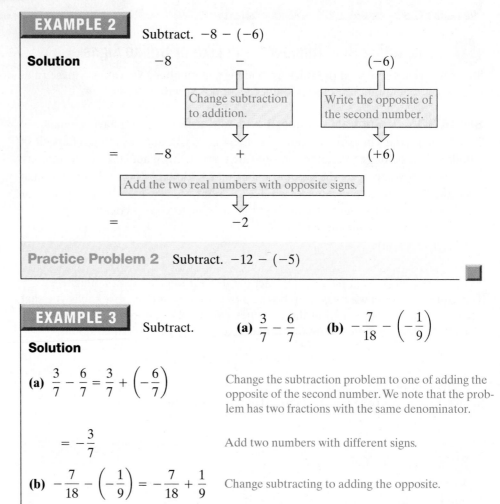

Solution

-8 $-$ (-6)

Change subtraction to addition.

Write the opposite of the second number.

$=$ -8 $+$ $(+6)$

Add the two real numbers with opposite signs.

$=$ -2

NOTE TO STUDENT: Fully worked-out solutions to all of the Practice Problems can be found at the back of the text starting at page SP-1

Practice Problem 2   Subtract. $-12 - (-5)$

EXAMPLE 3   Subtract.   **(a)** $\dfrac{3}{7} - \dfrac{6}{7}$ **(b)** $-\dfrac{7}{18} - \left(-\dfrac{1}{9}\right)$

Solution

(a) $\dfrac{3}{7} - \dfrac{6}{7} = \dfrac{3}{7} + \left(-\dfrac{6}{7}\right)$ Change the subtraction problem to one of adding the opposite of the second number. We note that the problem has two fractions with the same denominator.

$= -\dfrac{3}{7}$ Add two numbers with different signs.

(b) $-\dfrac{7}{18} - \left(-\dfrac{1}{9}\right) = -\dfrac{7}{18} + \dfrac{1}{9}$ Change subtracting to adding the opposite.

$= -\dfrac{7}{18} + \dfrac{2}{18}$ Change $\frac{1}{9}$ to $\frac{2}{18}$ since LCD = 18.

$= -\dfrac{5}{18}$ Add two numbers with different signs.

Practice Problem 3   Subtract.   **(a)** $\dfrac{5}{9} - \dfrac{7}{9}$ **(b)** $-\dfrac{5}{21} - \left(-\dfrac{3}{7}\right)$

EXAMPLE 4   Subtract. $-5.2 - (-5.2)$

Solution

$-5.2 - (-5.2) = -5.2 + 5.2$ Change the subtraction problem to one of adding the opposite of the second number.

$= 0$ Add two numbers with different signs.

Example 4 illustrates what is sometimes called the **additive inverse property.** When you add two real numbers that are opposites of each other, you will obtain zero. Examples of this are the following:

$$5 + (-5) = 0 \qquad -186 + 186 = 0 \qquad -\dfrac{1}{8} + \dfrac{1}{8} = 0.$$

Practice Problem 4   Subtract. $-17.3 - (-17.3)$

EXAMPLE 5   Calculate.

(a) $-8 - 2$ **(b)** $23 - 28$ **(c)** $5 - (-3)$ **(d)** $\dfrac{1}{4} - 8$

Solution

(a) $-8 - 2 = -8 + (-2)$ Notice that we are subtracting a positive 2. Change to addition.

$\qquad\quad = -10$ Add.

In a similar fashion we have

(b) $23 - 28 = 23 + (-28) = -5$

(c) $5 - (-3) = 5 + 3 = 8$

(d) $\dfrac{1}{4} - 8 = \dfrac{1}{4} + (-8) = \dfrac{1}{4} + \left(-\dfrac{32}{4}\right) = -\dfrac{31}{4}$

Practice Problem 5   Calculate.

(a) $-21 - 9$ **(b)** $17 - 36$ **(c)** $12 - (-15)$ **(d)** $\dfrac{3}{5} - 2$

EXAMPLE 6   A satellite is recording radioactive emissions from nuclear waste buried 3 miles below sea level. The satellite orbits the Earth at 98 miles above sea level. How far is the satellite from the nuclear waste?

Solution   We want to find the difference between $+98$ miles and -3 miles. This means we must subtract -3 from 98.

$$98 - (-3) = 98 + 3$$
$$= 101$$

The satellite is 101 miles from the nuclear waste.

Practice Problem 6   A helicopter is directly over a sunken vessel. The helicopter is 350 feet above sea level. The vessel lies 186 feet below sea level. How far is the helicopter from the sunken vessel?

Developing Your Study Skills

Reading the Textbook

Begin reading your textbook with a paper and pencil in hand. As you come across a new definition or concept, underline it in the text and/or write it down in your notebook. Whenever you encounter an unfamiliar term, look it up and make a note of it. When you come to an example, work through it step-by-step. Be sure to read each word and follow directions carefully.

Notice the helpful hints the author provides. They guide you to correct solutions and prevent you from making errors. Take advantage of these pieces of expert advice.

Be sure that you understand what you are reading. Make a note of any of those things that you do not understand and ask your instructor about them. Do not hurry through the material. Learning mathematics takes time.

Verbal and Writing Skills

1. Explain in your own words how you would perform the necessary steps to find $-8 - (-3)$.

2. Explain in your own words how you would perform the necessary steps to find $-10 - (-15)$.

Subtract by adding the opposite.

3. $18 - 35$

4. $16 - 48$

5. $15 - 20$

6. $18 - 24$

7. $-14 - (-3)$

8. $-24 - (-7)$

9. $-52 - (-60)$

10. $-48 - (-80)$

11. $0 - (-5)$

12. $0 - (-7)$

13. $-18 - (-18)$

14. $-24 - (-24)$

15. $-11 - (-8)$

16. $-35 - (-10)$

17. $\dfrac{2}{5} - \dfrac{4}{5}$

18. $\dfrac{2}{9} - \dfrac{7}{9}$

19. $\dfrac{3}{4} - \left(-\dfrac{3}{5}\right)$

20. $-\dfrac{2}{3} - \dfrac{1}{4}$

21. $-\dfrac{3}{4} - \dfrac{5}{6}$

22. $-\dfrac{7}{10} - \dfrac{10}{15}$

23. $-0.6 - 0.3$

24. $-0.9 - 0.5$

25. $2.64 - (-1.83)$

26. $-0.03 - 0.06$

Mixed Practice

Calculate.

27. $\dfrac{3}{5} - 4$

28. $\dfrac{5}{6} - 3$

29. $-\dfrac{2}{7} + 6$

30. $-\dfrac{3}{8} + 5$

31. $34 - 87$

32. $19 - 76$

33. $-25 - 48$

34. $-74 - 11$

35. $2.3 - (-4.8)$

36. $8.4 - (-2.7)$

37. $8 - \left(-\dfrac{3}{4}\right)$

38. $\dfrac{2}{3} - (-6)$

39. $\dfrac{5}{6} - 7$

40. $9 - \dfrac{2}{3}$

41. $-\dfrac{3}{10} - \dfrac{3}{4}$

42. $-\dfrac{11}{12} - \dfrac{5}{18}$

43. $-135 - (-126.5)$

44. $-97.6 - (-146)$

45. $\dfrac{1}{5} - 6$

46. $\dfrac{2}{7} - (-3)$

47. $5 - (-3.162)$ **48.** $7 - (-6.183)$ **49.** $-3 - 2.047$ **50.** $-1.043 - 4$

51. Subtract -9 from -2.   **52.** Subtract -12 from 20.   **53.** Subtract 13 from -35.

One Step Further

Change each subtraction operation to "adding the opposite." Then combine the numbers.

54. $9 + 6 - (-5)$ **55.** $7 + (-6) - 3$ **56.** $8 + (-4) - 10$ **57.** $-10 + 6 - (-15)$

58. $18 - (-15) - 3$ **59.** $7 + (-42) - 27$ **60.** $-4.2 - (-3.8) + 1.5$ **61.** $-6.4 - (-2.7) + 5.3$

62. $-3 - (-12) + 18 + 15 - (-6)$ **63.** $42 - (-30) - 65 - (-11) + 20$

Applications

64. *Sea Rescue* A rescue helicopter is 300 feet above sea level. The captain has located an ailing submarine directly below it that is 126 feet below sea level. How far is the helicopter from the submarine?

65. *Checking Account Balance* Yesterday Jackie had $112 in her checking account. Today her account reads "balance $-$37." Find the difference in these two amounts.

66. *Temperature Change* On June 22, 1943, in Spearfish, South Dakota, the temperature was $-4°F$ at 7:30 A.M. At 7:32 A.M., the temperature was $+44.6°F$. Find the difference in temperature over those two minutes.

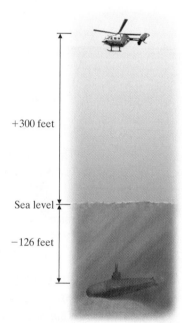

+300 feet

Sea level

−126 feet

67. *Elevation Difference* The highest point in Africa is Mt. Kilimanjaro in Tanzania, which is 5895 meters above sea level. The lowest point in Africa is Lake Assal in Djibouti, which is 156 meters below sea level. What is the difference in elevation between Mt. Kilimanjaro and Lake Assal?

68. *Federal Taxes* In 2004, Rachel had $1815 withheld from her paycheck in federal taxes. When she filed her tax return, she received a $265 refund. How much did she actually pay in taxes?

Cumulative Review

In exercises 69–73, perform the indicated operations.

69. $-37 + 16$ **70.** $-37 + (-14)$ **71.** $-3 + (-6) + (-10)$

72. *Temperature* What is the temperature after a rise of $13°C$ from a start of $-21°C$?

73. *Hiking* Sean and Khalid went hiking in the Blue Ridge Mountains. During their $8\frac{1}{3}$ mile hike, $\frac{4}{5}$ of the distance was covered with snow. How many miles were snow covered?

Student Learning Objectives

After studying this section, you will be able to:

 1 Multiply real numbers.

2 Use the multiplication properties for real numbers.

3 Divide real numbers.

1 Multiplying Real Numbers

We are familiar with the meaning of multiplication for positive numbers. For example, $5 \times 90 = 450$ might mean that you receive five weekly checks of 90 dollars each and you gain $450. Let's look at a situation that corresponds to $5 \times (-90)$. What might that mean?

SITUATION 6: Checking an Account Balance You write a check for five weeks in a row to pay your weekly room rent of 90 dollars. You want to know the total impact on your checking account balance.
Your record for situation 6.

$(+5)$	$\times$	(-90)	$=$	-450
The number of checks you have written	times	negative 90 the value of each check that was a debit to your account,	gives	negative 450 dollars, a net debit to your account.

Note that a multiplication symbol is not needed between the $(+5)$ and the (-90) because the two sets of parentheses indicate multiplication. The multiplication $(5)(-90)$ is the same as repeated addition of five (-90)'s. Note that 5 multiplied by -90 can be written as $5(-90)$ or $(5)(-90)$.

$$(-90) + (-90) + (-90) + (-90) + (-90) = -450$$

This example seems to show that a positive number multiplied by a negative number is negative.

What if the negative number is the one that is written first? If $(5)(-90) = -450$, then $(-90)(5) = -450$ by the commutative property of multiplication. This is an example showing that *when two numbers with opposite signs* (one positive, one negative) *are multiplied, the result is negative.*

But what if both numbers are negative? Consider the following situation.

SITUATION 7: Renting a Room Last year at college you rented a room at 90 dollars per week for 36 weeks, which included two semesters and summer school. This year you will not attend the summer session, so you will be renting the room for only 30 weeks. Thus the number of weekly rental checks will be six less than last year. You are making out your budget for this year. You want to know the financial impact of renting the room for six fewer weeks.
Your record for situation 7.

(-6)	$\times$	(-90)	$=$	540
The difference in the number of checks this year compared to last is -6, which is negative to show a decrease,	times	-90, the value of each check paid out,	gives	$+540$ dollars. The product is positive, because your financial situation will be 540 dollars better this year.

You could check that the answer is positive by calculating the total rental expenses.

Dollars in rent last year	$(36)(90) =$	3240
(subtract) Dollars in rent this year	$-(30)(90) =$	-2700
Extra dollars available this year	$=$	$+540$

This agrees with our previous answer: $(-6)(-90) = +540$.

In this situation it seems reasonable that a negative number times a negative number yields a positive answer. We already know from arithmetic that a positive number times a positive number yields a positive answer. Thus we might see the general rule that *when two numbers with the same sign* (both positive or both negative) *are multiplied, the result is positive.*

We will now state our rule.

MULTIPLICATION OF REAL NUMBERS

To multiply two real numbers with **the same sign,** multiply the absolute values. The sign of the result is **positive.**

To multiply two real numbers with **opposite signs,** multiply the absolute values. The sign of the result is **negative.**

Note that negative 6 times -90 can be written as $-6(-90)$ or $(-6)(-90)$.

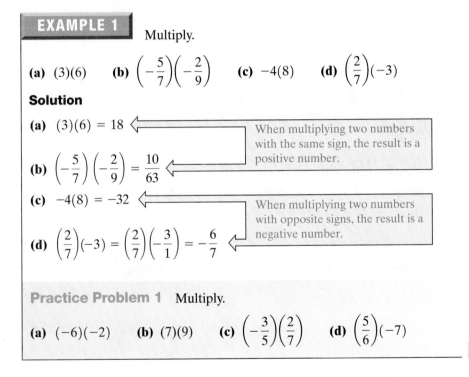

EXAMPLE 1   Multiply.

(a) $(3)(6)$ **(b)** $\left(-\dfrac{5}{7}\right)\left(-\dfrac{2}{9}\right)$ **(c)** $-4(8)$ **(d)** $\left(\dfrac{2}{7}\right)(-3)$

Solution

(a) $(3)(6) = 18$ ⟵

When multiplying two numbers with the same sign, the result is a positive number.

(b) $\left(-\dfrac{5}{7}\right)\left(-\dfrac{2}{9}\right) = \dfrac{10}{63}$ ⟵

(c) $-4(8) = -32$ ⟵

When multiplying two numbers with opposite signs, the result is a negative number.

(d) $\left(\dfrac{2}{7}\right)(-3) = \left(\dfrac{2}{7}\right)\left(-\dfrac{3}{1}\right) = -\dfrac{6}{7}$ ⟵

Practice Problem 1   Multiply.

(a) $(-6)(-2)$ **(b)** $(7)(9)$ **(c)** $\left(-\dfrac{3}{5}\right)\left(\dfrac{2}{7}\right)$ **(d)** $\left(\dfrac{5}{6}\right)(-7)$

NOTE TO STUDENT: Fully worked-out solutions to all of the Practice Problems can be found at the back of the text starting at page SP-1

To multiply more than two numbers, multiply two numbers at a time.

EXAMPLE 2   Multiply. $(-4)(-3)(-2)$

Solution

$(-4)(-3)(-2) = (+12)(-2)$ We begin by multiplying the first two numbers, (-4) and (-3). The signs are the same. The answer is positive 12.

$= -24$ Now we multiply $(+12)$ and (-2). The signs are different. The answer is negative 24.

Practice Problem 2   Multiply. $(-5)(-2)(-6)$

EXAMPLE 3   Multiply.

(a) $-3(-1.5)$ **(b)** $\left(-\dfrac{1}{2}\right)(-1)(-4)$ **(c)** $-2(-2)(-2)(-2)$

Solution   Multiply two numbers at a time. See if you find a pattern.

(a) $-3(-1.5) = 4.5$ Be sure to place the decimal point in your answer.

(b) $\left(-\dfrac{1}{2}\right)(-1)(-4) = +\dfrac{1}{2}(-4) = -2$

(c) $-2(-2)(-2)(-2) = +4(-2)(-2) = -8(-2) = +16 \text{ or } 16$

What kind of answer would we obtain if we multiplied five negative numbers? If you guessed "negative," you probably see the pattern.

Practice Problem 3   Determine the sign of the product. Then multiply to check.

(a) $-2(-3)$ **(b)** $(-1)(-3)(-2)$ **(c)** $-4\left(-\dfrac{1}{4}\right)(-2)(-6)$

NOTE TO STUDENT: Fully worked-out solutions to all of the Practice Problems can be found at the back of the text starting at page SP-1

When you multiply two or more real numbers:

1. The result is always **positive** if there are an **even** number of negative signs.
2. The result is always **negative** if there are an **odd** number of negative signs.

② Using the Multiplication Properties for Real Numbers

For convenience, we will list the properties of multiplication.

1. *Multiplication is commutative.*

   This property states that if two real numbers are multiplied, the order of the numbers does not affect the result. The result is the same no matter which number is written first.

   $$(5)(7) = (7)(5) = 35, \qquad \left(\dfrac{1}{3}\right)\left(\dfrac{2}{7}\right) = \left(\dfrac{2}{7}\right)\left(\dfrac{1}{3}\right) = \dfrac{2}{21}$$

2. *Multiplication of any real number by zero will result in zero.*

   $$(5)(0) = 0, \qquad (-5)(0) = 0, \qquad (0)\left(\dfrac{3}{8}\right) = 0, \qquad (0)(0) = 0$$

3. *Multiplication of any real number by 1 will result in that same number.*

   $$(5)(1) = 5, \qquad (1)(-7) = -7, \qquad (1)\left(-\dfrac{5}{3}\right) = -\dfrac{5}{3}$$

4. *Multiplication is associative.*

   This property states that if three real numbers are multiplied, it does not matter which two numbers are grouped by parentheses and multiplied first.

   $2 \times (3 \times 4) = (2 \times 3) \times 4$ First multiply the numbers in parentheses. Then multiply the remaining numbers.

   $\qquad 2 \times (12) = (6) \times 4$ The results are the same no matter which numbers are grouped and multiplied first.

   $\qquad\qquad 24 = 24$

③ Dividing Real Numbers

What about division? Any division problem can be rewritten as a multiplication problem.

We know that $20 \div 4 = 5$ because $4(5) = 20$.

Similarly, $-20 \div (-4) = 5$ because $-4(5) = -20$.

In both division problems the answer is positive 5. Thus we see that *when you divide two numbers with the same sign* (both positive or both negative), *the answer is positive*. What if the signs are different?

We know that $-20 \div 4 = -5$ because $4(-5) = -20$.

Similarly, $20 \div (-4) = -5$ because $-4(-5) = 20$.

In these two problems the answer is negative 5. So we have reasonable evidence to see that *when you divide two numbers with different signs* (one positive and one negative), *the answer is negative*.

We will now state our rule for division.

> **DIVISION OF REAL NUMBERS**
>
> To divide two real numbers with **the same sign,** divide the absolute values. The sign of the result is **positive.**
>
> To divide two real numbers with **different signs,** divide the absolute values. The sign of the result is **negative.**

EXAMPLE 4   Divide.

(a) $12 \div 4$ **(b)** $(-25) \div (-5)$ **(c)** $\dfrac{-36}{18}$ **(d)** $\dfrac{42}{-7}$

Solution

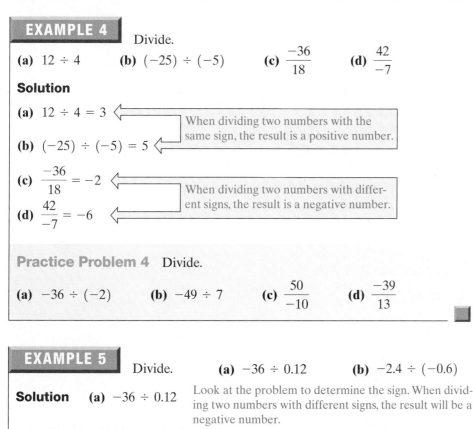

(a) $12 \div 4 = 3$

When dividing two numbers with the same sign, the result is a positive number.

(b) $(-25) \div (-5) = 5$

(c) $\dfrac{-36}{18} = -2$

When dividing two numbers with different signs, the result is a negative number.

(d) $\dfrac{42}{-7} = -6$

Practice Problem 4   Divide.

(a) $-36 \div (-2)$ **(b)** $-49 \div 7$ **(c)** $\dfrac{50}{-10}$ **(d)** $\dfrac{-39}{13}$

EXAMPLE 5   Divide.   **(a)** $-36 \div 0.12$ **(b)** $-2.4 \div (-0.6)$

Solution   **(a)** $-36 \div 0.12$ Look at the problem to determine the sign. When dividing two numbers with different signs, the result will be a negative number.

We then divide the absolute values.

$$0.12_\wedge \overline{)36.00_\wedge} \quad \begin{array}{r} 3\ 00. \\ \hline \underline{36} \\ 00 \end{array}$$

Thus $-36 \div 0.12 = -300$. The answer is a negative number.

(b) $-2.4 \div (-0.6)$ Look at the problem to determine the sign. When dividing two numbers with the same sign, the result will be positive.

We then divide the absolute values.

$$
\begin{array}{r}
4. \\
0.6_\wedge \overline{)2.4_\wedge} \\
\underline{2\ 4}
\end{array}
$$

Thus $-2.4 \div (-0.6) = 4$. The answer is a positive number.

NOTE TO STUDENT: Fully worked-out solutions to all of the Practice Problems can be found at the back of the text starting at page SP-1

Practice Problem 5   Divide.   **(a)** $-12.6 \div (-1.8)$ **(b)** $0.45 \div (-0.9)$

Note that the rules for multiplication and division are the same. When you **multiply** or **divide** two numbers with the **same** sign, you obtain **a positive** number. When you **multiply** or **divide** two numbers with **different** signs, you obtain a **negative** number.

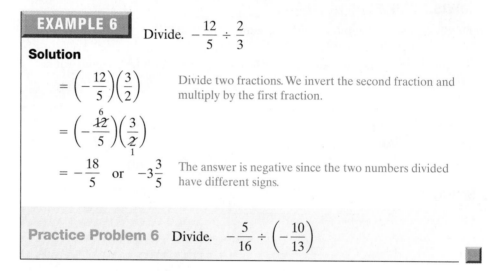

EXAMPLE 6   Divide. $-\dfrac{12}{5} \div \dfrac{2}{3}$

Solution

$$= \left(-\frac{12}{5}\right)\left(\frac{3}{2}\right)$$ Divide two fractions. We invert the second fraction and multiply by the first fraction.

$$= \left(-\frac{\overset{6}{\cancel{12}}}{5}\right)\left(\frac{3}{\underset{1}{\cancel{2}}}\right)$$

$$= -\frac{18}{5} \quad \text{or} \quad -3\frac{3}{5}$$ The answer is negative since the two numbers divided have different signs.

Practice Problem 6   Divide. $-\dfrac{5}{16} \div \left(-\dfrac{10}{13}\right)$

Note that division can be indicated by the symbol $\div$ or by the fraction bar $-$. $\frac{2}{3}$ means $2 \div 3$.

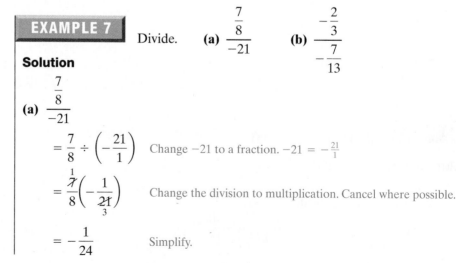

EXAMPLE 7   Divide.   **(a)** $\dfrac{\frac{7}{8}}{-21}$ **(b)** $\dfrac{-\frac{2}{3}}{-\frac{7}{13}}$

Solution

(a) $\dfrac{\frac{7}{8}}{-21}$

$$= \frac{7}{8} \div \left(-\frac{21}{1}\right)$$ Change -21 to a fraction. $-21 = -\frac{21}{1}$

$$= \frac{\overset{1}{\cancel{7}}}{8}\left(-\frac{1}{\underset{3}{\cancel{21}}}\right)$$ Change the division to multiplication. Cancel where possible.

$$= -\frac{1}{24}$$ Simplify.

(b) $\dfrac{-\dfrac{2}{3}}{-\dfrac{7}{13}} = -\dfrac{2}{3} \div \left(-\dfrac{7}{13}\right) = -\dfrac{2}{3}\left(-\dfrac{13}{7}\right) = \dfrac{26}{21}$ or $1\dfrac{5}{21}$

Practice Problem 7   Divide.   **(a)** $\dfrac{-12}{\dfrac{4}{-\dfrac{4}{5}}}$ **(b)** $\dfrac{-\dfrac{2}{9}}{\dfrac{8}{13}}$

---

1. *Division of 0 by any nonzero real number gives 0 as a result.*

$$0 \div 5 = 0, \qquad 0 \div \frac{2}{3} = 0, \qquad \frac{0}{5.6} = 0, \qquad \frac{0}{1000} = 0$$

You can divide zero by $5, \frac{2}{3}, 5.6, 1000$, or any number (except 0).

2. *Division of any real number by 0 is* **undefined.**

$$7 \div 0 \qquad\qquad \frac{64}{0}$$
$$\uparrow \qquad\qquad\quad \uparrow$$

Neither of these operations is possible. **Division by zero is undefined.**

You may be wondering why division by zero is undefined. Let us think about it for a minute. We said that $7 \div 0$ is undefined. Suppose there were an answer. Let us call the answer a. So we assume for a minute that $7 \div 0 = a$. Then it would have to follow that $7 = 0(a)$. But this is impossible. Zero times any number is zero. So we see that if there were such a number, it would contradict known mathematical facts. Therefore there is no number a such that $7 \div 0 = a$. Thus we conclude that division by zero is undefined.

When combining two numbers, it is important to be sure you know which rule applies. Think about the concepts in the following chart. See if you agree with each example.

Operation	Two Real Numbers with the Same Sign	Two Real Numbers with Different Signs
Addition	Result may be positive or negative. $9 + 2 = 11$ $-5 + (-6) = -11$	Result may be positive or negative. $-3 + 7 = 4$ $4 + (-12) = -8$
Subtraction	Result may be positive or negative. $15 - 6 = 15 + (-6) = 9$ $-12 - (-3) = -12 + 3 = -9$	Result may be positive or negative. $-12 - 3 = -12 + (-3) = -15$ $5 - (-6) = 5 + 6 = 11$
Multiplication	Result is always positive. $9(3) = 27$ $-8(-5) = 40$	Result is always negative. $-6(12) = -72$ $8(-3) = -24$
Division	Result is always positive. $150 \div 6 = 25$ $-72 \div (-2) = 36$	Result is always negative. $-60 \div 10 = -6$ $30 \div (-6) = -5$

EXAMPLE 8   The Hamilton-Wenham Generals recently analyzed the 48 plays their team made while in the possession of the football during their last game. The following bar graph illustrates the number of plays made in each category. The team statistician prepared the following chart indicating the average number of yards gained or lost during each type of play.

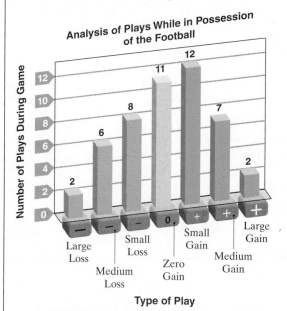

Analysis of Plays While in Possession of the Football

Type of Play	Average Yards Gained or Lost for Play
Large gain	+25
Medium gain	+15
Small gain	+5
Zero gain	0
Small loss	−5
Medium loss	−10
Large loss	−15

(a) How many yards were lost by the Generals in the plays that were considered small losses?

(b) How many yards were gained by the Generals in the plays that were considered small gains?

(c) If the total yards gained in small gains were combined with the total yards lost in small losses, what would be the result?

Solution

(a) We multiply the number of small losses by the average number of total yards lost on each small loss:

$$8(-5) = -40.$$

The team lost approximately 40 yards with plays that were considered small losses.

(b) We multiply the number of small gains by the average number of yards gained on each small gain:

$$12(5) = 60.$$

The team gained approximately 60 yards with plays that were considered small gains.

(c) We combine the results for (a) and (b):

$$-40 + 60 = 20.$$

A total of 20 yards was gained during the plays that were small losses and small gains.

NOTE TO STUDENT: *Fully worked-out solutions to all of the Practice Problems can be found at the back of the text starting at page SP-1*

Practice Problem 8   Using the information provided in Example 8, answer the following:

(a) How many yards were lost by the Generals in the plays that were considered medium losses?

(b) How many yards were gained by the Generals in the plays that were considered medium gains?

(c) If the total yards gained in medium gains were combined with the total yards lost in medium losses, what would be the result?

Verbal and Writing Skills

1. Explain in your own words the rule for determining the correct sign when multiplying two real numbers.

2. Explain in your own words the rule for determining the correct sign when multiplying three or more real numbers.

Multiply. Be sure to write your answer in the simplest form.

3. $5(-4)$

4. $8(-2)$

5. $0(-12)$

6. $0(-150)$

7. $16(1.5)$

8. $24(2.5)$

9. $(-1.32)(-0.2)$

10. $(-2.3)(-0.11)$

11. $0.7(-2.5)$

12. $0.6(-3.5)$

13. $\left(\dfrac{3}{8}\right)(-4)$

14. $(5)\left(-\dfrac{7}{10}\right)$

15. $\left(-\dfrac{3}{5}\right)\left(-\dfrac{15}{11}\right)$

16. $\left(-\dfrac{4}{9}\right)\left(-\dfrac{3}{5}\right)$

17. $\left(\dfrac{12}{13}\right)\left(\dfrac{-5}{24}\right)$

18. $\left(\dfrac{14}{17}\right)\left(-\dfrac{3}{28}\right)$

Divide.

19. $-36 \div (-9)$

20. $0 \div (-15)$

21. $-48 \div (-8)$

22. $-45 \div (9)$

23. $-220 \div (-11)$

24. $240 \div (-15)$

25. $156 \div (-13)$

26. $-0.6 \div 0.3$

27. $-9.1 \div (0.07)$

28. $8.1 \div (-0.03)$

29. $0.54 \div (-0.9)$

30. $-7.2 \div 8$

31. $-6.3 \div 7$

32. $\dfrac{2}{7} \div \left(-\dfrac{3}{5}\right)$

33. $\left(-\dfrac{1}{5}\right) \div \left(\dfrac{2}{3}\right)$

34. $\left(-\dfrac{5}{6}\right) \div \left(-\dfrac{7}{18}\right)$

35. $-\dfrac{5}{7} \div \left(-\dfrac{3}{28}\right)$

36. $\left(-\dfrac{4}{9}\right) \div \left(-\dfrac{8}{15}\right)$

37. $\left(-\dfrac{7}{12}\right) \div \left(-\dfrac{5}{6}\right)$

38. $\dfrac{12}{-\dfrac{2}{5}}$

39. $\dfrac{-6}{-\dfrac{3}{7}}$

40. $\dfrac{-\dfrac{3}{8}}{-\dfrac{2}{3}}$

41. $\dfrac{\dfrac{-2}{3}}{\dfrac{8}{15}}$

42. $\dfrac{\dfrac{5}{12}}{-\dfrac{7}{24}}$

43. $\dfrac{-\dfrac{7}{8}}{-\dfrac{14}{15}}$

Multiply. You may want to determine the sign of the product before you multiply.

44. $-6(2)(-3)(4)$

45. $-1(-2)(-3)(4)$

46. $-2(-1)(3)(-1)(-4)$

47. $-2(-2)(2)(-1)(-3)$

48. $-3(2)(-4)(0)(-2)$

49. $-3(-2)\left(\dfrac{1}{3}\right)(-4)(2)$

50. $60(-0.6)(-0.002)(0.5)$

51. $-3(-0.03)(0.001)(-2)$

52. $\left(\dfrac{3}{8}\right)\left(\dfrac{1}{2}\right)\left(-\dfrac{5}{6}\right)$

53. $\left(-\dfrac{4}{5}\right)\left(-\dfrac{6}{7}\right)\left(-\dfrac{1}{3}\right)$

54. $\left(-\dfrac{1}{2}\right)\left(\dfrac{4}{5}\right)\left(-\dfrac{7}{8}\right)\left(-\dfrac{2}{3}\right)$

55. $\left(-\dfrac{3}{4}\right)\left(-\dfrac{7}{15}\right)\left(-\dfrac{8}{21}\right)\left(-\dfrac{5}{9}\right)$

Mixed Practice

Take a minute to review the chart before Example 8. Be sure that you can remember the sign rules for each operation. Then do exercises 56–65. Perform the indicated calculations.

56. $-5 - (-2)$

57. $-36 \div (-4)$

58. $-3(-9)$

59. $5 + (-7)$

60. $18 \div (-6)$

61. $8 - (-9)$

62. $-6 + (-3)$

63. $6(-12)$

64. $18 \div (-18)$

65. $-37 \div 37$

Applications

66. ***Stock Trading*** Your favorite stock opened the day's trading at $37.20 per share. When trading closed for the day, your stock was priced at $27.30 per share. If you owned 75 shares, what was your profit or loss that day?

67. ***Equal Contributions*** Ed, Ned, Ted, and Fred went camping. They each contributed an equal share of money towards food. Fred did the shopping. When he returned from the store, he had $17.60 left. How much money did Fred give back to each person?

68. ***Student Loans*** Ramon will pay $6480 on his student loan over the next 3 years. If $180 is automatically deducted from his bank account each month to pay the loan off, how much does he still owe after one year?

69. ***Car Payments*** Keith will pay the Ford dealer a total of $15,768 to be paid off in 48 equal monthly installments. What is his monthly bill?

Football *The Beverly Panthers recently analyzed the 37 plays their team made while in the possession of the football during their last game. The team statistician prepared the following chart indicating the number of plays in each category and the average number of yards gained or lost during each type of play. Use this chart to answer exercises 70–77.*

Type of Play	Number of Plays	Average Yards Gained or Lost per Play
Large gain	1	+25
Medium gain	6	+15
Small gain	4	+5
Zero gain	5	0
Small loss	10	−5
Medium loss	7	−10
Large loss	4	−15

70. How many yards were lost by the Panthers in the plays that were considered small losses?

71. How many yards were gained by the Panthers in the plays that were considered small gains?

72. If the total yards gained in small gains were combined with the total yards lost in small losses, what would be the result?

73. How many yards were lost by the Panthers in the plays that were considered medium losses?

74. How many yards were gained by the Panthers in the plays that were considered medium gains?

75. If the total yards gained in medium gains were combined with the total yards lost in medium losses, what would be the result?

76. The game being studied was lost by the Panthers. The coach said that if two of the large-loss plays had been avoided and the number of small-gain plays had been doubled, they would have won the game. If those actions listed by the coach had happened, how many additional yards would the Panthers have gained? Assume each play would reflect the average yards gained or lost per play.

77. The game being studied was lost by the Panthers. The coach of the opposing team said that they could have scored two more touchdowns against the Panthers if they had caused three more large-loss plays and avoided four medium-gain plays. If those actions had happened, what effect would this have had on total yards gained by the Panthers? Assume each play would reflect the average yards gained or lost per play.

Cumulative Review

78. $-17.4 + 8.31 + 2.40$

79. $-\dfrac{3}{4} + \left(-\dfrac{2}{3}\right) + \left(-\dfrac{5}{12}\right)$

80. $-47 - (-32)$

81. $-37 - 51$

82. *Sneaker Production* A sneaker company needs $104\frac{1}{2}$ square yards of white leather, $88\frac{2}{3}$ square yards of neon-yellow leather, and $72\frac{5}{6}$ square yards of neon-red leather to make today's batch of designer sneakers. What is today's required total square yardage of leather?

Developing Your Study Skills

Steps Toward Success in Mathematics

Mathematics is a building process, mastered one step at a time. The foundation of this process consists of a few basic requirements. Those who are successful in mathematics realize the absolute necessity for building a study of mathematics on the firm foundation of these six minimum requirements.

1. Attend class every day.

2. Read the textbook.

3. Take notes in class.

4. Do assigned homework every day.

5. Get help immediately when needed.

6. Review regularly.

Writing Numbers in Exponent Form

In mathematics, we use exponents as a way to abbreviate repeated multiplication.

Long Notation		Exponent Form
$2 \cdot 2 \cdot 2 \cdot 2 \cdot 2 \cdot 2$	$=$	2^6

There are two parts to exponent notation: (1) the **base** and (2) the **exponent.** The **base** tells you what number is being multiplied and the **exponent** tells you how many times this number is used as a factor. (A *factor*, you recall, is a number being multiplied.)

$$2 \cdot 2 \cdot 2 \cdot 2 \cdot 2 \cdot 2 = 2^6$$

The *base* is 2   The *exponent* is 6
(the number being multiplied)   (the number of times 2 is used as a factor)

If the base is a *positive* real number, the exponent appears to the right and slightly above the level of the number as in, for example, 5^6 and 8^3. If the base is a *negative* real number, then parentheses are used around the number and the exponent appears outside the parentheses. For example, $(-2)(-2)(-2) = (-2)^3$.

In algebra, if we do not know the value of a number, we use a letter to represent the unknown number. We call the letter a **variable.** This is quite useful in the case of exponents. Suppose we do not know the value of a number, but we know the number is multiplied by itself several times. We can represent this with a variable base and a whole-number exponent. For example, when we have an unknown number, represented by the variable x, and this number occurs as a factor four times, we have

$$(x)(x)(x)(x) = x^4.$$

Likewise if an unknown number, represented by the variable w, occurs as a factor five times, we have

$$(w)(w)(w)(w)(w) = w^5.$$

EXAMPLE 1   Write in exponent form.

(a) $9(9)(9)$ (b) $13(13)(13)(13)$ (c) $-7(-7)(-7)(-7)(-7)$

(d) $-4(-4)(-4)(-4)(-4)(-4)$ (e) $(x)(x)$ (f) $(y)(y)(y)$

Solution

(a) $9(9)(9) = 9^3$ (b) $13(13)(13)(13) = 13^4$

(c) The -7 is used as a factor five times. The answer must contain parentheses. Thus $-7(-7)(-7)(-7)(-7) = (-7)^5$.

(d) $-4(-4)(-4)(-4)(-4)(-4) = (-4)^6$

(e) $(x)(x) = x^2$ (f) $(y)(y)(y) = y^3$

Practice Problem 1   Write in exponent form.

(a) $6(6)(6)(6)$ (b) $-2(-2)(-2)(-2)(-2)$ (c) $108(108)(108)$

(d) $-11(-11)(-11)(-11)(-11)(-11)$ (e) $(w)(w)(w)$ (f) $(z)(z)(z)(z)$

NOTE TO STUDENT: Fully worked-out solutions to all of the Practice Problems can be found at the back of the text starting at page SP-1

If the base has an exponent of 2, we say the base is **squared.**
If the base has an exponent of 3, we say the base is **cubed.**
If the base has an exponent greater than 3, we say the base is raised **to the (exponent)-th power.**

x^2 is read "x squared." y^3 is read "y cubed."

3^6 is read "three to the sixth power" or simply "three to the sixth."

2 Evaluating Numerical Expressions That Contain Exponents

EXAMPLE 2   Evaluate.   **(a)** 2^5 **(b)** $2^3 + 4^4$

Solution

(a) $2^5 = (2)(2)(2)(2)(2) = 32$

(b) First we evaluate each power.

$2^3 = 8$ $4^4 = 256$

Then we add. $8 + 256 = 264$

Practice Problem 2   Evaluate.   **(a)** 3^5 **(b)** $2^2 + 3^3$

If the base is negative, be especially careful in determining the sign. Notice the following:

$$(-3)^2 = (-3)(-3) = +9 \qquad (-3)^3 = (-3)(-3)(-3) = -27.$$

From Section 2.3 we know that when you multiply two or more real numbers, first you multiply their absolute values.

- The result is positive if there are an even number of negative signs.
- The result is negative if there are an odd number of negative signs.

SIGN RULE FOR EXPONENTS

Suppose that a number is written in exponent form and the base is negative. The result is **positive** if the exponent is **even.** The result is **negative** if the exponent is **odd.**

Be careful how you read expressions with exponents and negative signs.

$$(-3)^4 \text{ means } (-3)(-3)(-3)(-3) \text{ or } +81.$$
$$-3^4 \text{ means } -(3)(3)(3)(3) \text{ or } -81.$$

EXAMPLE 3   Evaluate.

(a) $(-2)^3$ **(b)** $(-4)^6$ **(c)** -3^6 **(d)** $-(5^4)$

Solution

(a) $(-2)^3 = -8$ The answer is negative since the base is negative and the exponent 3 is odd.

(b) $(-4)^6 = +4096$ The answer is positive since the exponent 6 is even.

(c) $-3^6 = -729$ The negative sign is not contained in parentheses. Thus we find 3 raised to the sixth power and then take the negative of that value.

(d) $-(5^4) = -625$ The negative sign is outside the parentheses.

Practice Problem 3   Evaluate.

(a) $(-3)^3$ **(b)** $(-2)^6$ **(c)** -2^4 **(d)** $-(3^6)$

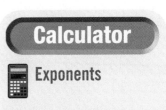

Calculator

Exponents

You can use a calculator to evaluate 3^5. Press the following keys:

$$\boxed{3}\ \boxed{y^x}\ \boxed{5}\ \boxed{=}$$

The display should read

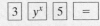

Try the following.

(a) 4^6 **(b)** $(0.2)^5$
(c) 18^6 **(d)** 3^{12}

Answers:

(a) 4096   **(b)** 0.00032
(c) 34,012,224   **(d)** 531,441

The steps needed to raise a number to a power are slightly different on some calculators.

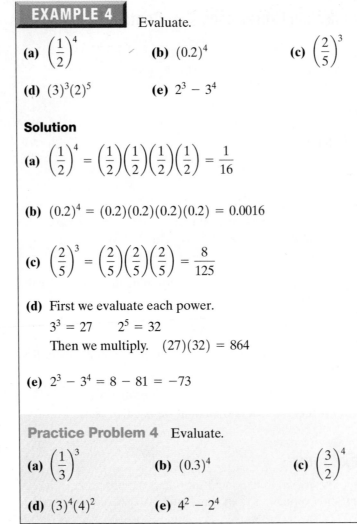

EXAMPLE 4   Evaluate.

(a) $\left(\dfrac{1}{2}\right)^4$ **(b)** $(0.2)^4$ **(c)** $\left(\dfrac{2}{5}\right)^3$

(d) $(3)^3(2)^5$ **(e)** $2^3 - 3^4$

Solution

(a) $\left(\dfrac{1}{2}\right)^4 = \left(\dfrac{1}{2}\right)\left(\dfrac{1}{2}\right)\left(\dfrac{1}{2}\right)\left(\dfrac{1}{2}\right) = \dfrac{1}{16}$

(b) $(0.2)^4 = (0.2)(0.2)(0.2)(0.2) = 0.0016$

(c) $\left(\dfrac{2}{5}\right)^3 = \left(\dfrac{2}{5}\right)\left(\dfrac{2}{5}\right)\left(\dfrac{2}{5}\right) = \dfrac{8}{125}$

(d) First we evaluate each power.
$$3^3 = 27 \qquad 2^5 = 32$$
Then we multiply. $(27)(32) = 864$

(e) $2^3 - 3^4 = 8 - 81 = -73$

NOTE TO STUDENT: Fully worked-out solutions to all of the Practice Problems can be found at the back of the text starting at page SP-1

Practice Problem 4   Evaluate.

(a) $\left(\dfrac{1}{3}\right)^3$ **(b)** $(0.3)^4$ **(c)** $\left(\dfrac{3}{2}\right)^4$

(d) $(3)^4(4)^2$ **(e)** $4^2 - 2^4$

Student Solutions Manual · CD/Video · PH Math Tutor Center · MathXL®Tutorials on CD · MathXL® · MyMathLab® · Interactmath.com

Verbal and Writing Skills

1. Explain in your own words how to evaluate 4^4.

2. Explain in your own words how to evaluate 9^2.

3. Explain how you would determine whether $(-5)^3$ is negative or positive.

4. Explain how you would determine whether $(-2)^5$ is negative or positive.

5. Explain the difference between $(-2)^4$ and -2^4. What answers do you obtain when you evaluate the expressions?

6. Explain the difference between $(-3)^4$ and -3^4. What answers do you obtain when you evaluate the expressions?

Write in exponent form.

7. $(5)(5)(5)(5)(5)(5)(5)$

8. $(7)(7)(7)(7)(7)$

9. $(w)(w)$

10. $(z)(z)(z)$

11. $(p)(p)(p)(p)$

12. $(x)(x)(x)(x)(x)$

13. $(3q)(3q)(3q)$

14. $(6x)(6x)(6x)(6x)$

Evaluate.

15. 3^3

16. 4^2

17. 3^4

18. 8^3

19. 6^3

20. 15^2

21. $(-3)^3$

22. $(-2)^3$

23. $(-4)^2$

24. $(-5)^4$

25. -5^2

26. -4^2

27. $\left(\frac{1}{4}\right)^2$

28. $\left(\frac{1}{2}\right)^3$

29. $\left(\frac{2}{5}\right)^3$

30. $\left(\frac{2}{3}\right)^4$

31. $(1.1)^2$

32. $(1.2)^2$

33. $(0.2)^4$

34. $(0.7)^3$

35. $(-16)^2$

36. $(-7)^4$

37. -16^2

38. -7^4

Evaluate.

39. $5^3 + 6^2$

40. $7^2 + 6^3$

41. $5^3 - 3^2$

42. $4^3 - 2^5$

43. $(-3)^3 - (8)^2$

44. $(-2)^3 - (-5)^4$

45. $2^5 - (-3)^2$

46. $8^2 - (-2)^3$

47. $(-4)^3(-3)^2$

48. $(-7)^3(-2)^4$

49. $8^2(-2)^3$

50. $9^2(-3)^3$

51. 4^{12}

52. 6^{11}

To Think About

53. What number to the third power equals -343?

54. What number to the eighth power equals 256?

Cumulative Review

Evaluate.

55. $(-11) + (-13) + 6 + (-9) + 8$

56. $\frac{3}{4} \div \left(-\frac{9}{20}\right)$

57. $-17 - (-9)$

58. $(-2.1)(-1.2)$

59. Amanda decided to invest her summer job earnings of $1600. At the end of the year she earned 6% on her investment. How much money did Amanda have at the end of the year?

Using the Order of Operations to Simplify Numerical Expressions

It is important to know *when* to do certain operations as well as how to do them. For example, to simplify the expression $2 - 4 \cdot 3$, should we subtract first or multiply first?

Also remember that multiplication can be written several ways. Thus $4 \cdot 3$, 4×3, $4(3)$, and $(4)(3)$ all indicate that we are multiplying 4 times 3.

The following list will assist you. It tells which operations to do first: the correct **order of operations.** You might think of it as a *list of priorities.*

ORDER OF OPERATIONS FOR NUMBERS

Follow this order of operations:

Do first   **1.** Do all operations inside parentheses.

            2. Raise numbers to a power.

            3. Multiply and divide numbers from left to right.

Do last   **4.** Add and subtract numbers from left to right.

Let's return to the problem $2 - 4 \cdot 3$. There are no parentheses or numbers raised to a power, so multiplication comes next. We do that first. Then we subtract since this comes last on our list.

$$2 - 4 \cdot 3 = 2 - 12 \quad \text{Follow the order of operations by first multiplying } 4 \cdot 3 = 12.$$
$$= -10 \quad \text{Combine } 2 - 12 = -10.$$

EXAMPLE 1 Evaluate. $8 \div 2 \cdot 3 + 4^2$

Solution

$$8 \div 2 \cdot 3 + 4^2 = 8 \div 2 \cdot 3 + 16 \quad \text{Evaluate } 4^2 = 16 \text{ because the highest priority in this problem is raising to a power.}$$
$$= 4 \cdot 3 + 16 \quad \text{Next multiply and divide from left to right. So } 8 \div 2 = 4 \text{ and } 4 \cdot 3 = 12.$$
$$= 12 + 16$$
$$= 28 \quad \text{Finally, add.}$$

Practice Problem 1 Evaluate. $25 \div 5 \cdot 6 + 2^3$

Note: Multiplication and division have equal priority. We do not do multiplication first. Rather, we work from left to right, doing any multiplication or division that we encounter. Similarly, addition and subtraction have equal priority.

EXAMPLE 2 Evaluate. $(-3)^3 - 2^4$

Solution The highest priority is to raise the expressions to the appropriate powers.

$$(-3)^3 - 2^4 = -27 - 16 \quad \text{In } (-3)^3 \text{ we are cubing the number } -3 \text{ to obtain } -27.$$
$$\text{Be careful; } -2^4 \text{ is not } (-2)^4!$$
$$\text{Raise 2 to the fourth power and take the negative of the result.}$$
$$= -43 \quad \text{The last step is to add and subtract from left to right.}$$

Practice Problem 2 Evaluate. $(-4)^3 - 2^6$

EXAMPLE 3 Evaluate. $2 \cdot (2 - 3)^3 + 6 \div 3 + (8 - 5)^2$

Solution

$2 \cdot (2 - 3)^3 + 6 \div 3 + (8 - 5)^2$ Combine the numbers inside the parentheses.

$= 2 \cdot (-1)^3 + 6 \div 3 + 3^2$

$= 2 \cdot (-1) + 6 \div 3 + 9$ Next, raise to a power. Note that we need parentheses for -1 because of the negative sign, but they are not needed for 3.

$= -2 + 2 + 9$ Next, multiply and divide from left to right.

$= 9$ Finally, add and subtract from left to right.

Practice Problem 3   Evaluate. $6 - (8 - 12)^2 + 8 \div 2$

EXAMPLE 4 Evaluate. $\left(-\dfrac{1}{5}\right)\left(\dfrac{1}{2}\right) - \left(\dfrac{3}{2}\right)^2$

Solution   The highest priority is to raise $\dfrac{3}{2}$ to the second power.

$\left(\dfrac{3}{2}\right)^2 = \left(\dfrac{3}{2}\right)\left(\dfrac{3}{2}\right) = \dfrac{9}{4}$ Next we multiply.

$\left(-\dfrac{1}{5}\right)\left(\dfrac{1}{2}\right) - \left(\dfrac{3}{2}\right)^2 = \left(-\dfrac{1}{5}\right)\left(\dfrac{1}{2}\right) - \dfrac{9}{4}$

$= -\dfrac{1}{10} - \dfrac{9}{4}$

$= -\dfrac{1 \cdot 2}{10 \cdot 2} - \dfrac{9 \cdot 5}{4 \cdot 5}$ We need to write each fraction as an equivalent fraction with the LCD of 20.

$= -\dfrac{2}{20} - \dfrac{45}{20}$

$= -\dfrac{47}{20}$ Add.

Practice Problem 4   Evaluate. $\left(-\dfrac{1}{7}\right)\left(-\dfrac{14}{5}\right) + \left(-\dfrac{1}{2}\right) \div \left(\dfrac{3}{4}\right)$

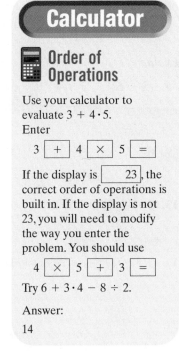

Calculator

Order of Operations

Use your calculator to evaluate $3 + 4 \cdot 5$.
Enter

   3 $\boxed{+}$ 4 $\boxed{\times}$ 5 $\boxed{=}$

If the display is $\boxed{23}$, the correct order of operations is built in. If the display is not 23, you will need to modify the way you enter the problem. You should use

   4 $\boxed{\times}$ 5 $\boxed{+}$ 3 $\boxed{=}$

Try $6 + 3 \cdot 4 - 8 \div 2$.

Answer:

14

Developing Your Study Skills

Previewing New Material

Part of your study time each day should consist of looking over the sections in your text that are to be covered the following day. You do not necessarily need to study and learn the material on your own, but a survey of the concepts, terminology, diagrams, and examples will help the new ideas seem more familiar as the instructor presents them. You can look for concepts that appear confusing or difficult and be ready to listen carefully for your instructor's explanations. You can be prepared to ask the questions that will increase your understanding. Previewing new material enables you to see what is coming and prepares you to be ready to absorb it.

Verbal and Writing Skills

Game Points   *You have lost a game of UNO and are counting the points left in your hand. You announce that you have three fours and six fives.*

1. Write this as a number expression.

2. How many points have you in your hand?

3. What answer would you get for the number expression if you simplified it by
(a) performing the operations from left to right?

(b) following the order of operations?

4. Which procedure in exercise 3 gives the correct number of total points?

Evaluate.

5. $(2 - 5)^2 \div 3 \times 4$

6. $(3 - 7)^2 \div 2 \times 5$

7. $2(3 - 5 + 6) + 5$

8. $3(9 - 2 + 3) + 7$

9. $8 - 2^3 \cdot 5 + 3$

10. $6 - 3^2 \cdot 6 + 4$

11. $4 + 42 \div 3 \cdot 2 - 8$

12. $7 + 36 \div 12 \cdot 3 - 14$

13. $3 \cdot 5 + 7 \cdot 3 - 5 \cdot 3$

14. $2 \cdot 6 + 5 \cdot 3 - 7 \cdot 4$

15. $8 - 5(2)^3 \div (-8)$

16. $11 - 3(4)^2 \div (-6)$

17. $3(5 - 7)^2 - 6(3)$

18. $-2(3 - 6)^2 - (-2)$

19. $5 \cdot 6 - (3 - 5)^2 + 8 \cdot 2$

20. $(-3)^2 \cdot 6 \div 9 + 4 \cdot 2$

21. $\dfrac{1}{2} \div \dfrac{2}{3} + 6 \cdot \dfrac{1}{4}$

22. $\dfrac{5}{6} \div \dfrac{2}{3} - 6 \cdot \left(\dfrac{1}{2}\right)^2$

23. $0.8 + 0.3(0.6 - 0.2)^2$

24. $0.05 + 1.4 - (0.5 - 0.7)^3$

25. $\dfrac{3}{4}\left(-\dfrac{2}{5}\right) - \left(-\dfrac{3}{5}\right)$

26. $-\dfrac{2}{3}\left(\dfrac{3}{5}\right) + \dfrac{5}{7} \div \dfrac{5}{3}$

Mixed Practice

27. $(3 - 7)^2 \div 8 + 3$

28. $\left(\dfrac{3}{5}\right)\left(\dfrac{5}{6}\right) - \dfrac{3}{4} \div 6$

29. $\left(\dfrac{3}{4}\right)^2 (-16) + \dfrac{4}{5} \div \dfrac{-8}{25}$

30. $\left(2\dfrac{4}{7}\right) \div \left(-1\dfrac{1}{5}\right)$

31. $-6.3 - (-2.7)(1.1) + (3.3)^2$

32. $4.35 + 8.06 \div (-2.6) - (2.1)^2$

33. $\left(\frac{1}{2}\right)^3 + \frac{1}{4} - \left(\frac{1}{6} - \frac{1}{12}\right) - \frac{2}{3} \cdot \left(\frac{1}{4}\right)^2$

34. $(2.4 \cdot 1.2)^2 - 1.6 \cdot 2.2 \div 4.0 - 3.6$

Applications

Tiger Woods just completed a round of golf, and created the following scoring table based on his score per hole, compared to par:

Score on a Hole	Number of Times the Score Occurred
Eagle (-2)	3
Birdie (-1)	9
Par (0)	5
Bogey $(+1)$	1

35. Write his score as the sum of eagles, birdies, pars, and bogeys.

36. What was his final score for the round, when compared to par?

37. What answer do you get if you do the arithmetic left to right?

38. Explain why the answers in #36 and #37 do not match.

Cumulative Review

Simplify.

39. $(0.5)^3$

40. $-\frac{3}{4} - \frac{5}{6}$

41. -1^{20}

42. $3\frac{3}{5} \div 6\frac{1}{4}$

43. *Health Drink* An Olympic weight lifter has been told by his trainer to increase his daily consumption of protein by 15 grams. The trainer suggested a health drink that provides 2 grams of protein for every 6 ounces consumed. How many ounces of this health drink would the weight lifter need to consume daily to reach his goal of 15 additional grams per day?

44. $(0.76)(0.9)$

45. $0.324 \div 0.6$

1. _____

2. _____

3. _____

4. _____

5. _____

6. _____

7. _____

8. _____

9. _____

10. _____

11. _____

12. _____

13. _____

14. _____

15. _____

16. _____

17. _____

18. _____

19. _____

20. _____

21. _____

22. _____

How are you doing with your homework assignments in Sections 2.1 to 2.5? Do you feel you have mastered the material so far? Do you understand the concepts you have covered? Before you go further in the textbook, take some time to do each of the following problems.

Simplify each of the following. If the answer is a fraction, be sure to leave it in reduced form.

2.1

1. $3 + (-12)$

2. $-\dfrac{5}{6} + \left(-\dfrac{7}{8}\right)$

3. $0.34 + 0.9$

4. $-14 + 3 + (-2.5) + 6.4$

2.2

5. $-23 - (-34)$

6. $-\dfrac{4}{5} - \dfrac{1}{3}$

7. $4.5 - (-7.8)$

8. $-4 - (-5) + 9$

2.3

9. $(-3)(-8)(2)(-2)$

10. $\left(-\dfrac{6}{11}\right)\left(-\dfrac{5}{3}\right)$

11. $-0.072 \div 0.08$

12. $\dfrac{5}{8} \div \left(-\dfrac{17}{16}\right)$

2.4

Evaluate.

13. $(0.7)^3$

14. $(-4)^4$

15. -2^8

16. $\left(\dfrac{2}{3}\right)^3$

17. $5^3 + (-2)^4$

2.5

18. $12 \div 6(2) + 3$

19. $15 + 3 - 2 + (-6)$

20. $(9 - 13)^2 + 15 \div (-3)$

21. $-0.12 \div 0.6 + (-3)(1.2) - (-0.5)$

22. $\left(\dfrac{3}{4}\right)\left(-\dfrac{2}{5}\right) + \left(-\dfrac{1}{2}\right)\left(\dfrac{4}{5}\right) + \left(\dfrac{1}{2}\right)^2$

Now turn to page SA-3 for the answer to each of these problems. Each answer also includes a reference to the objective in which the problem is first taught. If you missed any of these problems, you should stop and review the Examples and Practice Problems in the referenced objective. A little review now will help you master the material in the upcoming sections of the text.

Using the Distributive Property to Simplify Algebraic Expressions

As we learned previously, we use letters called *variables* to represent unknown numbers. If a number is multiplied by a variable we do not need any symbol between the number and variable. Thus, to indicate $(2)(x)$, we write $2x$. To indicate $3 \cdot y$, we write $3y$. If one variable is multiplied by another variable, we place the variables next to each other. Thus, $(a)(b)$ is written ab. We use exponent form if an unknown number (a variable) is used several times as a factor. Thus, $x \cdot x \cdot x = x^3$. Similarly, $(y)(y)(y)(y) = y^4$.

In algebra, we need to be familiar with several definitions. We will use them throughout the remainder of this book. Take some time to think through how each of these definitions is used.

An **algebraic expression** is a quantity that contains numbers and variables, such as $a + b, 2x - 3$, and $5ab^2$. In this chapter we will be learning rules about adding and multiplying algebraic expressions. A **term** is a number, a variable, or a product of numbers and variables. $17, x, 5xy$, and $22xy^3$ are all examples of terms. We will refer to terms when we discuss the distributive property.

An important property of algebra is the **distributive property.** We can state it in an equation as follows:

> **DISTRIBUTIVE PROPERTY**
>
> For all real numbers a, b, and c,
> $$a(b + c) = ab + ac.$$

A numerical example shows that it does seem reasonable.

$$5(3 + 6) = 5(3) + 5(6)$$
$$5(9) = 15 + 30$$
$$45 = 45$$

We can use the distributive property to multiply any term by the sum of two or more terms. In Section 2.4, we defined the word *factor*. Two or more algebraic expressions that are multiplied are called **factors.** Consider the following examples of multiplying algebraic expressions.

EXAMPLE 1 Multiply. **(a)** $5(a + b)$ **(b)** $-3(3x + 2y)$

Solution

(a) $5(a + b) = 5a + 5b$ Multiply the factor $(a + b)$ by the factor 5.

(b) $-3(3x + 2y) = -3(3x) + (-3)(2y)$ Multiply the factor $(3x + 2y)$ by the
$$= -9x - 6y$$ factor (-3).

Practice Problem 1 Multiply. **(a)** $3(x + 2y)$ **(b)** $-a(a - 3b)$

If the parentheses are preceded by a negative sign, we consider this to be the product of (-1) and the expression inside the parentheses.

NOTE TO STUDENT: Fully worked-out solutions to all of the Practice Problems can be found at the back of the text starting at page SP-1

The area of a circle is given by

$$A = \pi r^2.$$

We will use 3.14 as an approximation for the *irrational number π*.

▲ **EXAMPLE 5**   Find the area of a circle if the radius is 2 inches.

Solution

$A = \pi r^2 \approx (3.14)(2 \text{ inches})^2$ Write the formula and substitute the given values for the letters.

$\quad = (3.14)(4)(\text{in.})^2$ Raise to a power. Then multiply.

$\quad = 12.56 \text{ square inches}$

▲ **Practice Problem 5**   Find the area of a circle if the radius is 3 meters.

The formula $C = \frac{5}{9}(F - 32)$ allows us to find the Celsius temperature if we know the Fahrenheit temperature. That is, we can substitute a value for F in degrees Fahrenheit into the formula to obtain a temperature C in degrees Celsius.

EXAMPLE 6   What is the Celsius temperature when the Fahrenheit temperature is $F = -22°$?

Solution   Use the formula.

$$C = \frac{5}{9}(F - 32)$$

$$\quad = \frac{5}{9}((-22) - 32) \quad \text{Substitute } -22 \text{ for } F \text{ in the formula.}$$

$$\quad = \frac{5}{9}(-54) \quad\quad\quad \text{Combine the numbers inside the parentheses.}$$

$$\quad = (5)(-6) \quad\quad\quad\quad \text{Simplify.}$$

$$\quad = -30 \quad\quad\quad\quad\quad \text{Multiply.}$$

The temperature is $-30°$ Celsius.

NOTE TO STUDENT: Fully worked-out solutions to all of the Practice Problems can be found at the back of the text starting at page SP-1

Practice Problem 6   What is the Celsius temperature when the Fahrenheit temperature is $F = 68°$? Use the formula $C = \frac{5}{9}(F - 32)$.

When driving in Canada or Mexico, we must observe speed limits posted in kilometers per hour. A formula that converts r (miles per hour) to k (kilometers per hour) is $k \approx 1.61r$. Note that this is an approximation.

EXAMPLE 7   You are driving on a highway in Mexico. It has a posted maximum speed of 100 kilometers per hour. You are driving at 61 miles per hour. Are you exceeding the speed limit?

Solution   Use the formula.

$$k \approx 1.61r$$
$$= (1.61)(61) \quad \text{Replace } r \text{ by } 61.$$
$$= 98.21 \quad \text{Multiply the numbers.}$$

You are driving at approximately 98 kilometers per hour. You are not exceeding the speed limit.

Practice Problem 7   You are driving behind a heavily loaded truck on a Canadian highway. The highway has a posted minimum speed of 65 kilometers per hour. When you travel at exactly the same speed as the truck ahead of you, you observe that the speedometer reads 35 miles per hour. Assuming that your speedometer is accurate, determine whether the truck is violating the minimum speed law.

Developing Your Study Skills

Problems with Accuracy

Strive for accuracy. Mistakes are often made as a result of human error rather than from lack of understanding. Such mistakes are frustrating. A simple arithmetic or sign error can lead to an incorrect answer.

These five steps will help you cut down on errors.

1. Work carefully and take your time. Do not rush through a problem just to get it done.
2. Concentrate on one problem at a time. Sometimes problems become mechanical, and your mind begins to wander. You can become careless and make a mistake.
3. Check your problem. Be sure that you copied it correctly from the book.
4. Check your computations from step to step. Check the solution in the problem. Does it work? Does it make sense?
5. Keep practicing new skills. Remember the old saying, "Practice makes perfect." An increase in practice results in an increase in accuracy. Many errors are due simply to lack of practice.

There is no magic formula for eliminating all errors, but these five steps will be a tremendous help in reducing them.

2.8 EXERCISES

Student Solutions Manual | CD/Video | PH Math Tutor Center | MathXL®Tutorials on CD | MathXL® | MyMathLab® | Interactmath.com

Evaluate.

1. $-2x + 1$ for $x = 3$

2. $-4x - 2$ for $x = 5$

3. $\frac{2}{3}x - 5$ for $x = -9$

4. $\frac{3}{4}x + 8$ for $x = -8$

5. $5x + 10$ for $x = \frac{1}{2}$

6. $7x + 20$ for $x = -\frac{1}{2}$

7. $2 - 4x$ for $x = 7$

8. $3 - 5x$ for $x = 8$

9. $3.5 - 2x$ for $x = 2.4$

10. $6.3 - 3x$ for $x = 2.3$

11. $9x + 13$ for $x = -\frac{3}{4}$

12. $5x + 7$ for $x = -\frac{2}{3}$

13. $x^2 - 3x$ for $x = -2$

14. $x^2 + 3x$ for $x = 4$

15. $3x^2$ for $x = -1$

16. $4x^2$ for $x = -1$

17. $-3x^3$ for $x = 2$

18. $-7x^2$ for $x = 5$

19. $-5x^2$ for $x = -2$

20. $-2x^2$ for $x = -3$

21. $2x^2 + 3x$ for $x = -3$

22. $18 + 3x^2$ for $x = -3$

23. $(2x)^2 + x$ for $x = 3$

24. $2 - x^2$ for $x = -2$

25. $2 - (-x)^2$ for $x = -2$

26. $2x - 3x^2$ for $x = -4$

27. $7x + (2x)^2$ for $x = -3$

28. $5x + (3x)^2$ for $x = -2$

29. $3x^2 - 5x$ for $x = -3$

30. $7 - 2x^2$ for $x = -4$

31. $x^2 - 7x + 3$ for $x = 3$

32. $4x^2 - 3x + 9$ for $x = 2$

33. $\frac{1}{2}x^2 - 3x + 9$ for $x = -4$

34. $\frac{1}{3}x^2 + 2x - 5$ for $x = -3$

35. $x^2 - 2y + 3y^2$ for $x = -3$ and $y = 4$

36. $2x^2 - 3xy + 2y$ for $x = 4$ and $y = -1$

37. $a^3 + 2abc - 3c^2$ for $a = 5, b = 9,$ and $c = -1$

38. $a^2 - 2ab + 2c^2$ for $a = 3, b = 2,$ and $c = -4$

39. $\dfrac{a^2 + ab}{3b}$ for $a = -1$ and $b = -2$

40. $\dfrac{x^2 - 2xy}{2y}$ for $x = -2$ and $y = -3$

Applications

▲ **41.** *Geometry* A sign is made in the shape of a parallelogram. The base measures 22 feet. The altitude measures 16 feet. What is the area of the sign?

▲ **42.** *Geometry* A field is shaped like a parallelogram. The base measures 92 feet. The altitude measures 54 feet. What is the area of the field?

▲ **43.** *TV Parts* A square support unit in a television is made with a side measuring 3 centimeters. A new model being designed for next year will have a larger square with a side measuring 3.2 centimeters. By how much will the area of the square be increased?

▲ **44.** *Computer Chips* A square computer chip for last year's computer had a side measuring 23 millimeters. This year the computer chip has been reduced in size. The new square chip has a side of 20 millimeters. By how much has the area of the chip decreased?

▲ **45.** *Carpentry* A carpenter cut out a small trapezoid as a wooden support for the front step. It has an altitude of 4 inches. One base of the trapezoid measures 9 inches and the other base measures 7 inches. What is the area of this support?

▲ **46.** *Signal Tower* The Comcast signal tower has a small trapezoid frame on the top of the tower. The frame has an altitude of 9 inches. One base of the trapezoid is 20 inches and the other base measures 17 inches. What is the area of this small trapezoidal frame?

▲ **47.** *Geometry* Bradley Palmer State Park has a triangular piece of land on the border. The altitude of the triangle is 400 feet. The base of the triangle is 280 feet. What is the area of this piece of land?

▲ **48.** *Roofing* The ceiling in the Madisons' house has a leak. The roofer exposed a triangular region that needs to be sealed and then reroofed. The region has an altitude of 14 feet. The base of the region is 19 feet. What is the area of the region that needs to be reroofed?

▲ **49.** *Geometry* The radius of a circular opening of a chemistry flask is 4 cm. What is the area of the opening?

▲ **50.** *Geometry* An ancient outdoor sundial has a radius of 5 meters. What is its area?

Temperature For exercises 51 and 52, use the formula $C = \dfrac{5}{9}(F - 32)$ to find the Celsius temperature.

51. Dry ice is solid carbon dioxide. Dry ice does not melt, it goes directly from the solid state to the gaseous state. Dry ice changes from a solid to a gas at $-109.3°F$. What is this temperature in C?

52. Ivana was an exchange student from Russia, attending school in Montgomery, Alabama. Her host family told her to take a jacket to school because the temperature was not supposed to rise above 50°. Since Ivana was used to temperatures in Celsius, this made no sense at all, for 50°C is incredibly warm. The host family realized they needed to change the temperature into Celsius for Ivana. What was the temperature in Celsius?

Solve.

▲ **53.** ***Sail Dimensions*** Find the total cost of making a triangular sail that has a base dimension of 12 feet and a height of 20 feet if the price for making the sail is $19.50 per square foot.

▲ **54.** ***Window Coating*** A semicircular window of radius 15 inches is to be laminated with a sunblock coating that costs $0.85 per square inch to apply. What is the total cost of coating the window, to the nearest cent? (Use $\pi \approx 3.14$.)

55. ***Temperature Tolerance*** Some new computers can be exposed to extreme temperatures (as high as 60°C and as low as −50°C). What is the temperature range in Fahrenheit that these computers can be exposed to? (Use the formula $F = \frac{9}{5}C + 32$.)

56. ***Temperature Tolerance*** To deal with extreme temperatures while doing research at the South Pole, scientists have developed accommodations that can comfortably withstand an outside temperature of −60°C with no wind blowing, or −30°C with wind gusts of up to 50 miles per hour. What is the corresponding Fahrenheit temperature range? (Use the formula $F = \frac{9}{5}C + 32$.)

57. ***Sea Level*** Bruce becomes exhausted while on a bicycle trip in Canada. He reads on the map that his present elevation is 2.3 kilometers above sea level. How many miles to the nearest tenth above sea level is he? Why is he so tired? Use the formula $r = 0.62k$ where r is the number of miles and k is the number of kilometers.

58. ***Bicycle Travel*** While biking down the Pacific coast of Mexico, you see on the map that it is 20 kilometers to the nearest town. Approximately how many miles is it to the nearest town? Use the formula $r = 0.62k$ where r is the number of miles and k is the number of kilometers.

Cumulative Review

In exercises 59–60, simplify.

59. $(-2)^4 - 4 \div 2 - (-2)$

60. $3(x - 2y) - (x^2 - y) - (x - y)$

61. ***CD Recording*** A 93-minute-long recordable compact disc is used to record 15 songs. Express in decimal form the average number of minutes available per song.

62. ***Homework Grading*** The economics class lecture session had 214 students. If there were 4 teaching assistants to grade homework, approximately how many homework papers were given to each teaching assistant? (Give in decimal form; then round to the nearest whole number.)

1 Simplifying Algebraic Expressions by Removing Grouping Symbols

Many expressions in algebra use **grouping symbols** such as parentheses, brackets, and braces. Sometimes expressions are inside other expressions. Because it can be confusing to have more than one set of parentheses, brackets and braces are also used. How do we know what to do first when we see an expression like $2[5 - 4(a + b)]$?

To simplify the expression, we start with the innermost grouping symbols. Here is a set of parentheses. We first use the distributive law to multiply.

$$2[5 - 4(a + b)] = 2[5 - 4a - 4b]$$

We use the distributive law again.

$$= 10 - 8a - 8b$$

There are no like terms, so this is our final answer.

Notice that we started with two sets of grouping symbols, but our final answer has none. So we can say we *removed* the grouping symbols. Of course, we didn't just take them away; we used the distributive law and the rules for real numbers to simplify as much as possible. Although simplifying expressions like this involves many steps, we sometimes say "remove parentheses" as a shorthand direction. Sometimes we say "simplify."

Remember to remove the innermost parentheses first. Keep working from the inside out.

EXAMPLE 1 Simplify. $3[6 - 2(x + y)]$

Solution We want to remove the innermost parentheses first. Therefore, we first use the distributive property to simplify $-2(x + y)$.

$$3[6 - 2(x + y)] = 3[6 - 2x - 2y] \quad \text{Use the distributive property.}$$

$$= 18 - 6x - 6y \quad \text{Use the distributive property again.}$$

Practice Problem 1 Simplify. $5[4x - 3(y - 2)]$

NOTE TO STUDENT: Fully worked-out solutions to all of the Practice Problems can be found at the back of the text starting at page SP-1

You recall that a negative sign in front of parentheses is equivalent to having a coefficient of negative 1. You can write the -1 and then multiply by -1 using the distributive property.

$$-(x + 2y) = -1(x + 2y) = -x - 2y$$

Notice that this has the effect of removing the parentheses. Each term in the result now has its sign changed.

Similarly, a positive sign in front of parentheses can be viewed as multiplication by $+1$.

$$+(5x - 6y) = +1(5x - 6y) = 5x - 6y$$

If a grouping symbol has a positive or negative sign in front, we mentally multiply by $+1$ or -1, respectively.

Fraction bars are also considered grouping symbols. Later in this book we will encounter problems where our first step will be to simplify expressions above and below fraction bars. This type of operation will have some similarities to the operation of removing parentheses.

EXAMPLE 2   Simplify. $-2\,[3a - (b + 2c) + (d - 3e)]$

Solution

$= -2\,[3a - b - 2c + d - 3e\,]$ Remove the two innermost sets of parentheses. Since one is not inside the other, we remove both sets at once.

$= -6a + 2b + 4c - 2d + 6e$ Now we remove the brackets by multiplying each term by -2.

NOTE TO STUDENT: *Fully worked-out solutions to all of the Practice Problems can be found at the back of the text starting at page SP-1*

Practice Problem 2   Simplify. $-3\,[2a - (3b - c) + 4a]$

EXAMPLE 3   Simplify. $2\,[3x - (y + w)] - 3\,[2x + 2(3y - 2w)]$

Solution

$= 2\,[3x - y - w] - 3\,[2x + 6y - 4w]$ In each set of brackets, remove the inner parentheses.

$= 6x - 2y - 2w - 6x - 18y + 12w$ Remove each set of brackets by multiplying by the appropriate number.

$= -20y + 10w$ or $10w - 20y$ Combine like terms. (Note that $6x - 6x = 0x = 0$.)

Practice Problem 3   Simplify. $3\,[4x - 2\,(1 - x)] - [3x + (x - 2)]$

You can always simplify problems with many sets of grouping symbols by the method shown. Essentially, you just keep removing one level of grouping symbols at each step. Finally, at the end you add up the like terms if possible.

Sometimes it is possible to combine like terms at each step.

EXAMPLE 4   Simplify. $-3\,\{7x - 2\,[x - (2x - 1)]\}$

Solution

$= -3\,\{7x - 2\,[x - 2x + 1]\}$ Remove the inner parentheses by multiplying each term within the parentheses by -1.

$= -3\,\{7x - 2\,[-x + 1]\}$ Combine like terms by combining $+x - 2x$.

$= -3\,\{7x + 2x - 2\}$ Remove the brackets by multiplying each term within them by -2.

$= -3\,\{9x - 2\}$ Combine the x-terms.

$= -27x + 6$ Remove the braces by multiplying each term by -3.

Practice Problem 4   Simplify. $-2\,\{5x - 3x\,[2x - (x^2 - 4x)]\}$

Developing Your Study Skills

The Night Before Your Exam

With adequate preparation, you can spend the night before an exam pulling together the final details.

1. Look over each section to be covered in the exam. Review the steps needed to solve each type of problem.
2. Review your list of terms, rules, and formulas that you are expected to know for the exam.

3. Take the Practice Test at the end of the chapter just as though you were taking the actual exam. Do not look in your text or get help in any way. Time yourself so that you know how long it takes you to complete the test.
4. Check the Practice Test. Redo the problems you missed.
5. Be sure you have ready the necessary supplies for taking your exam.

Verbal and Writing Skills

1. Rewrite the expression $-3x - 2y$ using a negative sign and parentheses.

2. Rewrite the expression $-x + 5y$ using a negative sign and parentheses.

3. To simplify expressions with grouping symbols, we use the _____ property.

4. When an expression contains many grouping symbols, remove the _____ parentheses first.

Simplify. Remove grouping symbols and combine like terms.

5. $6x - 3(x - 2y)$

6. $-4x - 2(y - 3x)$

7. $2(a + 3b) - 3(b - a)$

8. $4(x - y) - 2(3x + y)$

9. $-3(x + 3y) + 2(2x + y)$

10. $-4(a + 2b) + 5(2b - a)$

11. $2x[4x^2 - 2(x - 3)]$

12. $4y[-3y^2 + 2(4 - y)]$

13. $2[5(x + y) - 2(3x - 4y)]$

14. $-3[2(3a + b) - 5(a - 2b)]$

15. $2(x - 2y) - [3 - 2(x - y)]$

16. $3(x + 2y) - [4 - 2(x + y)]$

17. $5[3a - 2a(3a + 6b) + 6a^2]$

18. $3[x - y(3x + y) + y^2]$

19. $6a(2a^2 - 3a - 4) - a(a - 2)$

20. $7b(3b^2 - 2b - 5) - 2b(4 - b)$

21. $3a^2 - 4[2b - 3b(b + 2)]$

22. $2b^2 - 3[5b + 2b(2 - b)]$

23. $6b - \{5a - 2[a + (b - 2a)]\}$

24. $2a - \{6b - 4[a - (b - 3a)]\}$

25. $3\{3b^2 + 2\,[5b - (2 - b)]\}$

26. $2\{3x^2 + 4\,[2x - (3 - x)]\}$

27. $-4\{3a^2 - 2\,[4a^2 - (b + a^2)]\}$

28. $-2\{x^2 - 3\,[x - (x - 2x^2)]\}$

To Think About

29. *Robot Success* The job of a four-wheeled robot called Nomad, built by the Robotics Institute at Carnegie Mellon University, is to find samples of meteorites in Antarctica. If Nomad is successful in finding meteorites 2.5% of the time, out of four tries per day for six years, estimate the number of successful and unsuccessful meteorite search attempts. Round to the nearest whole number.

30. *Tipping* Grandma and Grandpa Tobey had a tradition of eating out once a week. The average cost of the meal was $20. In Massachusetts there is a 5% state sales tax that is added to the cost of the meal. The Tobeys always left a 15% tip. They continued this pattern for ten years. Mrs. Tobey felt that they should calculate the tip on the total of the cost of the meal including the sales tax. Mr. Tobey felt they should calculate the tip on the cost of the meal alone. How much difference would this make over the ten-year period?

Cumulative Review

31. *Temperature* Use $F = 1.8C + 32$ to find the Fahrenheit temperature equivalent to 36.4° Celsius.

▲ **32.** *Geometry* Use 3.14 as an approximation for π to compute the area covered by a circular irrigation system with radial arm of length 380 feet. $A = \pi r^2$.

▲ **33.** *Marble Flooring* The base of an office building is in the shape of a trapezoid. The altitude of the trapezoid is 400 feet. The bases of the trapezoid are 700 feet and 800 feet, respectively. What is the area of the base of the office building? If the base has a marble floor that cost $55 per square foot, what was the cost of the marble floor?

▲ **34.** *Signal Paint* The Global Media Tower has a triangular signal tester at the top of the tower. The altitude of the triangle is 3.5 feet and the base is 6.5 feet. What is the area of the triangular signal tester? If the signal tester is coated with a special metallic surface paint that costs $122 per square foot, what was the cost of the amount of paint needed to coat one side of the triangle?

35. *Dog Weight* An average Great Dane weighs between 120 and 150 pounds. Express the range of weight for a Great Dane in kilograms. Use the formula $k = 2.205p$ (where k = kilograms, p = pounds).

36. *Dog Weight* An average Miniature Pinscher weighs between 9 and 14 pounds. Express the range of weight for a Miniature Pinscher in kilograms. Use the formula $k = 2.205p$ (where k = kilograms, p = pounds.)

Putting Your Skills to Work

Looking at Computer Usage

NTIA and the Economics and Statistics Administration have published *A Nation Online: How Americans Are Expanding Their Use of the Internet.* This report is based on the September 2001 U.S. Census Bureau's Current Population Survey—a survey of approximately 57,000 households and more than 137,000 individuals across the United States. As such, the data in this study are among the most broad-based and reliable data sets that have been gathered on Internet, broadband, and computer connectivity.

Computer use is expanding ever quicker both at work and at home. Look at the following information gathered for this government report.

Computer Use at Work by Occupation (2001)

Occupation	Employed		Uses computer at main job			Main computer uses (by percent)		
	Total (in 1000s)	Percent women	Total (in 1000s)	Percent of employed	E-mail	Word processing	Spreadsheet database	Calendar, schedule
TOTAL	**115,065**	**46.3**	**65,190**	**56.7**	**41.7**	**38.6**	**35.9**	**30.4**
Professional Managerial	39,412	50.2	31,723	80.5	66.8	63.2	56.5	48.8
Support Staff	31,482	62.9	22,205	70.5	49.2	45.5	43.1	34.7
Precision Production	13,083	8.4	4,152	31.7	19.0	14.8	16.6	14.6
Service	13,678	61.6	3,478	25.4	13.9	14.3	11.8	12.3
Laborers	14,504	24.3	3,006	20.7	9.2	7.6	8.7	7.0
Farming, forestry, fishing	2,905	20.3	625	21.5	14.6	13.0	13.2	9.2

Source: Statistical Abstract of the United States, 2002

Problems for Individual Investigation and Analysis

1. The data shows that 66.8% of computer using professionals use e-mail on a regular basis. How many professionals in the United States use e-mail at their main job?

2. How many more professionals than support staff use computers at their main job?

3. The NTIA estimates that 77% of Americans who use computers at home also use computers at work. How many American do you estimate used computers at home as of September 2001?

4. If computer use grows by 17.5% per year, how many people would you expect used computers at work in 2002, the year after this survey?

Problems for Group Investigation and Cooperative Learning

A number of business professionals feel that the number of people using computers at work in the future can be predicted in the near future by the formula

$$N = 65,190,000 + 4,500,000x,$$

where N is the number of people using computers at work and x is the number of years since 2001. For example, in the year 2003 the value of x would be 2. In the year 2004 the value of x would be 3.

5. Use this formula to estimate the number of people who will use computers at work in the year 2007.

6. Use this formula to estimate the number of people who will use computers at work in the year 2010

Topic	Procedure	Examples
Absolute value, p. 52.	The absolute value of a number is the distance between that number and zero on the number line. The absolute value of any number will be positive or zero.	$\lvert 3 \rvert = 3$ $\lvert -2 \rvert = 2$ $\lvert 0 \rvert = 0$ $\left\lvert -\dfrac{5}{6} \right\rvert = \dfrac{5}{6}$ $\lvert -1.38 \rvert = 1.38$
Adding real numbers with the same sign, p. 53.	If the signs are the same, add the absolute values of the numbers. Use the common sign in the answer.	$-3 + (-7) = -10$
Adding real numbers with opposite signs, p. 55.	If the signs are different: 1. Find the difference between the larger and the smaller absolute value. 2. Give the answer the sign of the number having the larger absolute value.	$(-7) + 13 = 6$ $7 + (-13) = -6$
Adding several real numbers, p. 56.	When adding several real numbers, separate them into two groups by sign. Find the sum of all the positive numbers and the sum of all the negative numbers. Combine these two subtotals by the method described above.	$-7 + 6 + 8 + (-11) + (-13) + 22$ $\begin{array}{cc} -7 & +6 \\ -11 & +8 \\ \underline{-13} & \underline{+22} \\ -31 & +36 \end{array}$ $-31 + 36 = 5$ The answer is positive since 36 is positive.
Subtracting real numbers, p. 61.	Change the sign of the second number (the number you are subtracting) and then add.	$-3 - (-13) = -3 + (+13) = 10$
Multiplying and dividing real numbers, p. 67 and p. 69.	1. If the two numbers have the same sign, multiply (or divide) the absolute values. The result is positive. 2. If the two numbers have different signs, multiply (or divide) the absolute values. The result is negative.	$-5(-3) = +15$ $-36 \div (-4) = +9$ $28 \div (-7) = -4$ $-6(3) = -18$
Exponent form, p. 76.	The base tells you what number is being multiplied. The exponent tells you how many times this number is used as a factor.	$2^5 = 2 \cdot 2 \cdot 2 \cdot 2 \cdot 2 = 32$ $4^3 = 4 \cdot 4 \cdot 4 = 64$ $(-3)^4 = (-3)(-3)(-3)(-3) = 81$
Raising a negative number to a power, p. 77.	When the base is negative, the result is positive for even exponents, and negative for odd exponents.	$(-3)^3 = -27$ but $(-2)^4 = 16$
Order of operations, p. 80.	Remember the proper order of operations: 1. Perform operations inside parentheses. 2. Raise to powers. 3. Multiply and divide from left to right. 4. Add and subtract from left to right.	$3(5 + 4)^2 - 2^2 \cdot 3 \div (9 - 2^3)$ $= 3 \cdot 9^2 - 4 \cdot 3 \div (9 - 8)$ $= 3 \cdot 81 - 12 \div 1$ $= 243 - 12 = 231$
Removing parentheses, p. 85.	Use the distributive property to remove parentheses. $$a(b + c) = ab + ac$$	$3(5x + 2) = 15x + 6$ $-4(x - 3y) = -4x + 12y$

Topic	Procedure	Examples
Combining like terms, p. 90.	Combine terms that have identical letters and exponents.	$7x^2 - 3x + 4y + 2x^2 - 8x - 9y = 9x^2 - 11x - 5y$
Substituting into variable expressions, p. 95.	1. Replace each letter by the numerical value given for it. 2. Follow the order of operations in evaluating the expression.	Evaluate $2x^3 + 3xy + 4y^2$ for $x = -3$ and $y = 2$. $2(-3)^3 + 3(-3)(2) + 4(2)^2$ $\qquad = 2(-27) + 3(-3)(2) + 4(4)$ $\qquad = -54 - 18 + 16$ $\qquad = -56$
Using formulas, p. 97.	1. Replace the variables in the formula by the given values. 2. Evaluate the expression. 3. Label units carefully.	Find the area of a circle with radius 4 feet. Use $A = \pi r^2$, with π as approximately 3.14. $\qquad A = (3.14)(4 \text{ feet})^2$ $\qquad = (3.14)(16 \text{ feet}^2)$ $\qquad = 50.24 \text{ feet}^2$ The area of the circle is approximately 50.24 square feet.
Removing grouping symbols, p. 103.	1. Remove innermost grouping symbols first. 2. Then remove remaining innermost grouping symbols. 3. Continue until all grouping symbols are removed. 4. Combine like terms.	$5\{3x - 2[4 + 3(x - 1)]\}$ $\qquad = 5\{3x - 2[4 + 3x - 3]\}$ $\qquad = 5\{3x - 8 - 6x + 6\}$ $\qquad = 15x - 40 - 30x + 30$ $\qquad = -15x - 10$

Chapter 2 Review Problems

Section 2.1

Add.

1. $-6 + (-2)$

2. $-12 + 7.8$

3. $5 + (-2) + (-12)$

4. $3.7 + (-1.8)$

5. $\dfrac{1}{2} + \left(-\dfrac{5}{6}\right)$

6. $-\dfrac{3}{11} + \left(-\dfrac{1}{22}\right)$

7. $\dfrac{3}{4} + \left(-\dfrac{1}{12}\right) + \left(-\dfrac{1}{2}\right)$

8. $-\dfrac{4}{15} + \dfrac{12}{5} + \left(-\dfrac{2}{3}\right)$

Section 2.2

Add or subtract.

9. $5 - (-3)$

10. $-2 - (-15)$

11. $-30 - (+3)$

12. $8 - (-1.2)$

13. $-\dfrac{7}{8} + \left(-\dfrac{3}{4}\right)$

14. $-\dfrac{3}{14} + \dfrac{5}{7}$

15. $-20.8 - 1.9$

16. $-151 - (-63)$

Section 2.3

17. $87 \div (-29)$

18. $-5(-6) + 4(-3)$

19. $\dfrac{-24}{-\dfrac{3}{4}}$

20. $-\dfrac{1}{2} \div \left(\dfrac{3}{4}\right)$

21. $\dfrac{5}{7} \div \left(-\dfrac{5}{25}\right)$

22. $-6(3)(4)$

23. $-1(-2)(-3)(-5)$

24. $(-5)\left(-\dfrac{1}{2}\right)(4)(-3)$

Mixed Practice

Sections 2.1–2.3

Perform the operations indicated. Simplify all answers.

25. $-5 + (-2) - (-3)$ **26.** $6 - (-4) + (-2) + 8$ **27.** $-16 + (-13)$ **28.** $-11 - (-12)$

29. $-\dfrac{4}{3} + \dfrac{2}{3} + \dfrac{1}{6}$ **30.** $-\dfrac{6}{7} + \dfrac{1}{2} + \left(-\dfrac{3}{14}\right)$ **31.** $-3(-2)(-5)$ **32.** $-6 + (-2) - (-3)$

33. $3.5(-2.6)$ **34.** $-5.4 \div (-6)$ **35.** $5 - (-3.5) + 1.6$ **36.** $-8 + 2 - (-4.8)$

37. $17 + 3.4 + (-16) + (-2.5)$ **38.** $37 + (-44) + 12.5 + (-6.8)$

Solve.

39. *Football* The Dallas Cowboys football team had three plays in which they lost 8 yards each time. What was the total yardage lost?

40. *Temperature Change* The low temperature in Anchorage, Alaska, last night was $-34°F$. During the day the temperature rose $12°F$. What was the temperature during the day?

41. *Elevation Levels* A mountain peak is 6895 feet above sea level. A location in Death Valley is 468 feet below sea level. What is the difference in height between these two locations?

42. *Stock Prices* During January 2000, IBM stock rose $1\frac{1}{2}$ points on Monday, dropped $3\frac{1}{4}$ points on Tuesday, rose 2 points on Wednesday, and dropped $2\frac{1}{2}$ points on Thursday. What was the total gain or loss on the value of the stock over this four-day period?

Section 2.4

Evaluate.

43. $(-3)^5$ **44.** $(-2)^7$ **45.** $(-5)^4$ **46.** $\left(\dfrac{2}{3}\right)^3$

47. -9^2 **48.** $(0.6)^2$ **49.** $\left(\dfrac{5}{6}\right)^2$ **50.** $\left(\dfrac{3}{4}\right)^3$

Section 2.5

Simplify using the order of operations.

51. $5(-4) + 3(-2)^3$ **52.** $20 - (-10) - (-6) + (-5) - 1$ **53.** $(7 - 9)^3 + -6(-2) + (-3)$

Section 2.6

Use the distributive property to multiply.

54. $5(3x - 7y)$ **55.** $2x(3x - 7y + 4)$ **56.** $-(7x^2 - 3x + 11)$ **57.** $(2xy + x - y)(-3y)$

Section 2.7

Combine like terms.

58. $3a^2b - 2bc + 6bc^2 - 8a^2b - 6bc^2 + 5bc$ **59.** $9x + 11y - 12x - 15y$

60. $4x^2 - 13x + 7 - 9x^2 - 22x - 16$

61. $-x + \dfrac{1}{2} + 14x^2 - 7x - 1 - 4x^2$

Section 2.8

Evaluate for the given value of the variable.

62. $7x - 6$ for $x = -7$

63. $7 - \dfrac{3}{4}x$ for $x = 8$

64. $x^2 + 3x - 4$ for $x = -3$

65. $-3x^2 - 4x + 5$ for $x = 2$

66. $-3x^3 - 4x^2 + 2x + 6$ for $x = -2$

67. $vt - \dfrac{1}{2}at^2$ for $v = 24, t = 2$, and $a = 32$

68. $\dfrac{nRT}{V}$ for $n = 16, R = -2, T = 4$, and $V = -20$

Solve.

69. *Simple Interest* Find the simple interest on a loan of \$6000 at an annual interest rate of 18% per year for $\frac{3}{4}$ of a year. Use $I = prt$, where $p =$ principal, $r =$ rate per year, and $t =$ time in years.

70. *Temperature* Find the Fahrenheit temperature if a radio announcer in Mexico City says that the high temperature today was 30°C. Use the formula
$$F = \dfrac{9C + 160}{5}.$$

▲ **71.** *Sign Painting* How much will it cost to paint a circular sign with a radius of 15 meters if the painter charges \$3 per square meter? Use $A = \pi r^2$, where π is approximately 3.14.

72. *Profit* Find the daily profit P at a furniture factory if the initial cost of setting up the factory $C = \$1200$, rent $R = \$300$, and sales of furniture $S = \$56$. Use the profit formula $P = 180S - R - C$.

▲ **73.** *Parking Lot Sealer* A parking lot is in the shape of a trapezoid. The altitude of the trapezoid is 200 feet, and the bases of the trapezoid are 300 feet and 700 feet. What is the area of the parking lot? If the parking lot had a sealer applied that costs \$2 per square foot, what was the cost of the amount of sealer needed for the entire parking lot?

▲ **74.** *Signal Paint* The Green Mountain Telephone Company has a triangular signal tester at the top of a communications tower. The altitude of the triangle is 3.8 feet and the base is 5.5 feet. What is the area of the triangular signal tester? If the signal tester is painted with a special metallic surface paint that costs \$66 per square foot, what was the cost of the amount of paint needed to paint one side of the triangle?

Section 2.9

Simplify.

75. $5x - 7(x - 6)$

76. $3(x - 2) - 4(5x + 3)$

77. $2[3 - (4 - 5x)]$

78. $-3x[x + 3(x - 7)]$

79. $2xy^3 - 6x^3y - 4x^2y^2 + 3(xy^3 - 2x^2y - 3x^2y^2)$

80. $-5(x + 2y - 7) + 3x(2 - 5y)$

81. $2\{x - 3(y - 2) + 4[x - 2(y + 3)]\}$

82. $-5\{2a - b[5a - b(3 + 2a)]\}$

83. $-3\{2x - [x - 3y(x - 2y)]\}$

84. $2\{3x + 2[x + 2y(x - 4)]\}$

Mixed Practice

Simplify the following.

85. $-6.3 + 4$

86. $4 + (-8) + 12$

87. $-\dfrac{2}{3} - \dfrac{4}{5}$

88. $-\dfrac{7}{8} - \left(-\dfrac{3}{4}\right)$

89. $3 - (-4) + (-8)$

90. $-1.1 - (-0.2) + 0.4$

91. $\left(-\dfrac{3}{5}\right)\left(-2\dfrac{1}{2}\right)$

92. $(-4.2) \div (-0.7)$

93. $-14.4 \div (-0.06)$

94. $(-8.2)(3.1)$

95. *Jeopardy* A Jeopardy quiz show contestant began the second round (Double Jeopardy) with $400. She buzzed in on the first two questions, answering a $1000 question correctly, but then giving the incorrect answer to a $800 question. What was her score?

Simplify the following.

96. $(-0.3)^4$

97. -0.5^4

98. $9(5) - 5(2)^3 + 5$

99. $3.8x - 0.2y - 8.7x + 4.3y$

100. *Evaluate.* $\dfrac{2p + q}{3q}$ for $p = -2$ and $q = 3$

101. *Evaluate.* $\dfrac{4s - 7t}{s}$ for $s = -3$ and $t = -2$

102. *Dog Body Temperature* The normal body temperature of a dog is 38.6°C. Your dog has a temperature of 101.1°F. Does your dog have a fever? Use the formula $F = \dfrac{9}{5}C + 32$ to convert normal temperature in Fahrenheit.

103. $-7(x - 3y^2 + 4) + 3y(4 - 6y)$

104. $-2\{6x - 3[7y - 2y(3 - x)]\}$

Simplify.

1. $-2.5 + 6.3 + (-4.1)$

2. $-5 - (-7)$

3. $\left(-\dfrac{2}{3}\right)(7)$

4. $-5(-2)(7)(-1)$

5. $-12 \div (-3)$

6. $-1.8 \div (0.6)$

7. $(-4)^3$

8. $(1.6)^2$

9. $\left(\dfrac{2}{3}\right)^4$

10. $(0.2)^2 - (2.1)(-3) + 0.46$

11. $3(4 - 6)^3 + 12 \div (-4) + 2$

12. $-5x(x + 2y - 7)$

13. $-2ab^2(-3a - 2b + 7ab)$

14. $6ab - \dfrac{1}{2}a^2b + \dfrac{3}{2}ab + \dfrac{5}{2}a^2b$

15. $2.3x^2y - 8.1xy^2 + 3.4xy^2 - 4.1x^2y$

16. $3(2 - a) - 4(-6 - 2a)$

17. $5(3x - 2y) - (x + 6y)$

1. _____

2. _____

3. _____

4. _____

5. _____

6. _____

7. _____

8. _____

9. _____

10. _____

11. _____

12. _____

13. _____

14. _____

15. _____

16. _____

17. _____

18. _____

19. _____

20. _____

21. _____

22. _____

23. _____

24. _____

25. _____

26. _____

In questions 18–20, evaluate for the value of the variable indicated.

18. $x^3 - 3x^2y + 2y - 5$ for $x = 3$ and $y = -4$

19. $3x^2 - 7x - 11$ for $x = -3$

20. $2a - 3b$ for $a = \dfrac{1}{3}$ and $b = -\dfrac{1}{2}$

21. If you are traveling 60 miles per hour on a highway in Canada, how fast are you traveling in kilometers per hour? (Use $k = 1.61r$, where r = rate in miles per hour and k = rate in kilometers per hour.)

▲ **22.** A field is in the shape of a trapezoid. The altitude of the trapezoid is 120 feet and the bases of the trapezoid are 180 feet and 200 feet. What is the area of the field?

▲ **23.** Jeff Slater's garage has a triangular roof support beam. The support beam is covered with a sheet of plywood. The altitude of the triangular region is 6.8 feet and the base is 8.5 feet. If the triangular piece of plywood was painted with paint that cost $0.80 per square foot, what was the cost of the amount of paint needed to coat one side of the triangle?

▲ **24.** You wish to apply blacktop sealer to your driveway, but do not know how much to buy. If your rectangular driveway measures 60 feet long by 10 feet wide, and a can of blacktop sealer claims to cover 200 square feet, how many cans should you buy?

Simplify.

25. $3\left[x - 2y\left(x + 2y\right) - 3y^2\right]$

26. $-3\left\{a + b\left[3a - b\left(1 - a\right)\right]\right\}$

CHAPTER

3

People who own sport fishing boats and charter them out for fishing are often concerned with the cost of fuel. Many outboard boats are equipped with either one or two motors. Having two motors increases realibility and generates a higher speed. However, the added fuel cost may present a problem. Can you analyze exactly how much more fuel will be used if a boat is equipped with two outboard motors instead of one? Turn to the Putting Your Skills to Work on page 161 to find out.

Equations, Inequalities, and Applications

3.1   THE ADDITION PRINCIPLE OF EQUALITY   116

3.2   THE MULTIPLICATION PRINCIPLE OF EQUALITY   122

3.3   USING THE ADDITION AND MULTIPLICATION PRINCIPLES TOGETHER   128

3.4   SOLVING EQUATIONS WITH FRACTIONS   135

     HOW AM I DOING? SECTIONS 3.1–3.4   143

3.5   TRANSLATING ENGLISH PHRASES INTO ALGEBRAIC EXPRESSIONS   144

3.6   SOLVING INEQUALITIES IN ONE VARIABLE   150

     CHAPTER 3 ORGANIZER   162

     CHAPTER 3 REVIEW PROBLEMS   164

     HOW AM I DOING? CHAPTER 3 TEST   168

Using the Addition Principle to Solve Equations of the Form $x + b = c$

When we use an equal sign ($=$), we are indicating that two expressions are equal in value. Such a statement is called an **equation.** For example, $x + 5 = 23$ is an equation. A **solution** of an equation is a number that when substituted for the variable makes the equation true. Thus 18 is a solution of $x + 5 = 23$ because $18 + 5 = 23$. Equations that have exactly the same solutions are called **equivalent equations.** By following certain procedures, we can often transform an equation to a simpler equivalent one that has the form $x =$ some number. Then this number is a solution of the equation. The process of finding all solutions of an equation is called **solving the equation.**

One of the first procedures used in solving equations has an application in our everyday world. Suppose that we place a 10-kilogram box on one side of a seesaw and a 10-kilogram stone on the other side. If the center of the box is the same distance from the balance point as the center of the stone, we would expect the seesaw to balance. The box and the stone do not look the same, but their weights are equal. If we add a 2-kilogram lead weight to the center of weight of each object at the same time, the seesaw should still balance. The weights are still equal.

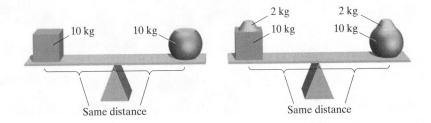

There is a similar principle in mathematics. We can state it in words as follows.

THE ADDITION PRINCIPLE

If the same number is added to both sides of an equation, the results on both sides are equal in value.

We can restate it in symbols this way.

For real numbers a, b, and c, if $a = b$, then $a + c = b + c$.

Here is an example. If $3 = \dfrac{6}{2}$, then $3 + 5 = \dfrac{6}{2} + 5$.

Since we added the same amount, 5, to both sides, the sides remain equal to each other.

$$3 + 5 = \frac{6}{2} + 5$$

$$8 = \frac{6}{2} + \frac{10}{2}$$

$$8 = \frac{16}{2}$$

$$8 = 8$$

We can use the addition principle to solve certain equations.

EXAMPLE 1   Solve for x. $x + 16 = 20$

Solution $x + 16 + (-16) = 20 + (-16)$ Use the addition principle to add -16 to both sides.

$x + 0 = 4$ Simplify.

$x = 4$ The value of x is 4.

We have just found a solution of the equation. A **solution** is a value for the variable that makes the equation true. We then say that the value 4 in our example **satisfies** the equation. We can easily verify that 4 is a solution by substituting this value into the original equation. This step is called **checking** the solution.

Check.

$x + 16 = 20$

$4 + 16 \overset{?}{=} 20$

$20 = 20$ ✓

When the same value appears on both sides of the equal sign, we call the equation an **identity.** Because the two sides of the equation in our check have the same value, we know that the original equation has been solved correctly. We have found a solution, and since no other number makes the equation true, it is the only solution.

Practice Problem 1   Solve for x and check your solution. $x + 14 = 23$

NOTE TO STUDENT: *Fully worked-out solutions to all of the Practice Problems can be found at the back of the text starting at page SP-1*

Notice that when you are trying to solve these types of equations, you must add a particular number to both sides of the equation. What is the number to choose? Look at the number that is on the same side of the equation with x, that is, the number added to x. Then think of the number that is **opposite in sign.** This is called the **additive inverse** of the number. The additive inverse of 16 is -16. The additive inverse of -3 is 3. The number to add to both sides of the equation is precisely this additive inverse.

It does not matter which side of the equation contains the variable. The x-term may be on the right or left. In the next example the x-term will be on the right.

EXAMPLE 2   Solve for x. $14 = x - 3$

Solution $14 + 3 = x - 3 + 3$ Notice that -3 is being added to x in the original equation. Add 3 to both sides, since 3 is the additive inverse of -3. This will eliminate the -3 on the right and isolate x.

$17 = x + 0$ Simplify.

$17 = x$ The value of x is 17.

Check. $14 = x - 3$

$14 \overset{?}{=} 17 - 3$ Replace x by 17.

$14 = 14$ ✓   Simplify. It checks. The solution is 17.

Practice Problem 2   Solve for x and check your solution. $17 = x - 5$

Before you add a number to both sides, you should always simplify the equation. The following example shows how combining numbers by addition—separately, on both sides of the equation—simplifies the equation.

EXAMPLE 3 Solve for x. $1.5 + 0.2 = 0.3 + x + 0.2$

Solution

$$1.7 = x + 0.5 \qquad \text{Simplify by adding.}$$
$$1.7 + (-0.5) = x + 0.5 + (-0.5) \qquad \text{Add the value } -0.5 \text{ to both}$$
sides, since -0.5 is the additive
inverse of 0.5.
$$1.2 = x \qquad \text{Simplify. The value of } x \text{ is } 1.2.$$

Check.
$$1.5 + 0.2 = 0.3 + x + 0.2$$
$$1.5 + 0.2 \overset{?}{=} 0.3 + 1.2 + 0.2 \qquad \text{Replace } x \text{ by } 1.2 \text{ in the original equation.}$$
$$1.7 = 1.7 \;\checkmark \qquad \text{It checks.}$$

Practice Problem 3 Solve for x and check your solution. $0.5 - 1.2 = x - 0.3$

In Example 3 we added -0.5 to each side. You could subtract 0.5 from each side and get the same result. In Chapter 2 we discussed how subtracting a 0.5 is the same as adding a negative 0.5. Do you see why?

Just as it is possible to add the same number to both sides of an equation, it is also possible to subtract the same number from both sides of an equation. This is so because any subtraction problem can be rewritten as an addition problem. For example, $17 - 5 = 17 + (-5)$. Thus the addition principle tells us that we can subtract the same number from both sides of the equation.

We can determine whether a value is the solution to an equation by following the same steps used to check an answer. Substitute the value to be tested for the variable in the original equation. We will obtain an identity if the value is the solution.

EXAMPLE 4 Is 10 the solution to the equation $-15 + 2 = x - 3$? If it is not, find the solution.

Solution We substitute 10 for x in the equation and see if we obtain an identity.

$$-15 + 2 = x - 3$$
$$-15 + 2 \overset{?}{=} 10 - 3$$
$$-13 \neq 7 \qquad \text{The values are not equal. The statement is not an identity.}$$

Thus, 10 is not the solution. Now we take the original equation and solve to find the solution.

$$-15 + 2 = x - 3$$
$$-13 = x - 3 \qquad \text{Simplify by adding.}$$
$$-13 + 3 = x - 3 + 3 \qquad \text{Add 3 to both sides. 3 is the additive inverse of } -3.$$
$$-10 = x$$

Check to see if -10 is the solution. The value 10 was incorrect because of a sign error. We must be especially careful to write the correct sign for each number when solving equations.

NOTE TO STUDENT: Fully worked-out solutions to all of the Practice Problems can be found at the back of the text starting at page SP-1

Practice Problem 4 Is -2 the solution to the equation $x + 8 = -22 + 6$? If it is not, find the solution.

EXAMPLE 5   Find the value of x that satisfies the equation

$$\frac{1}{5} + x = -\frac{1}{10} + \frac{1}{2}.$$

Solution   To be combined, the fractions must have common denominators. The least common denominator (LCD) of the fractions is 10.

$$\frac{1 \cdot 2}{5 \cdot 2} + x = -\frac{1}{10} + \frac{1 \cdot 5}{2 \cdot 5}$$ Change each fraction to an equivalent fraction with a denominator of 10.

$$\frac{2}{10} + x = -\frac{1}{10} + \frac{5}{10}$$ This is an equivalent equation.

$$\frac{2}{10} + x = \frac{4}{10}$$ Simplify by adding.

$$\frac{2}{10} + \left(-\frac{2}{10}\right) + x = \frac{4}{10} + \left(-\frac{2}{10}\right)$$ Add the additive inverse of $\frac{2}{10}$ to each side. You could also say that you are subtracting $\frac{2}{10}$ from each side.

$$x = \frac{2}{10}$$ Add the fractions.

$$x = \frac{1}{5}$$ Simplify the answer.

Check.   We substitute $\frac{1}{5}$ for x in the original equation and see if we obtain an identity.

$$\frac{1}{5} + x = -\frac{1}{10} + \frac{1}{2}$$

$$\frac{1}{5} + \frac{1}{5} \stackrel{?}{=} -\frac{1}{10} + \frac{1}{2}$$ Substitute $\frac{1}{5}$ for x.

$$\frac{2}{5} \stackrel{?}{=} -\frac{1}{10} + \frac{5}{10}$$

$$\frac{2}{5} \stackrel{?}{=} \frac{4}{10}$$

$$\frac{2}{5} = \frac{2}{5} \quad \checkmark$$ It checks.

Practice Problem 5   Find the value of x that satisfies the equation

$$\frac{1}{20} - \frac{1}{2} = x + \frac{3}{5}.$$

Developing Your Study Skills

Why Study Mathematics?

In our present-day, technological world, it is easy to see mathematics at work. Many vocational and professional areas—such as the fields of business, statistics, economics, psychology, finance, computer science, chemistry, physics, engineering, electronics, nuclear energy, banking, quality control, and teaching—require a certain level of expertise in mathematics. Those who want to work in these fields must be able to function at a given mathematical level. Those who cannot will not make it. So if your field of study requires you to take higher-level mathematics courses, be sure to master the topics of this course. Then you will be ready for the next one.

Student Solutions Manual | CD/Video | PH Math Tutor Center | MathXL®Tutorials on CD | MathXL® | MyMathLab® | Interactmath.com

Verbal and Writing Skills

In exercises 1–3, fill in the blank with the appropriate word.

1. When we use the _____ sign, we indicate two expressions are _____ in value.

2. If the _____ _____ is added to both sides of an equation, the results on each side are equal in value.

3. The _____ of an equation is a value of the variable that makes the equation true.

4. What is the additive inverse of -20?

5. Why do we add the additive inverse of a to each side of $x + a = b$ to solve for x?

6. What is the additive inverse of a?

Solve for x. Check your answers.

7. $x + 11 = 15$

8. $x + 12 = 18$

9. $17 = 5 + x$

10. $23 = x + 16$

11. $x - 3 = 14$

12. $x - 11 = 5$

13. $0 = x + 5$

14. $0 = x - 7$

15. $x - 6 = -19$

16. $x - 11 = -13$

17. $-12 + x = 50$

18. $-18 + x = 48$

19. $3 + 5 = x - 7$

20. $8 - 2 = x + 5$

21. $32 - 17 = x - 6$

22. $27 - 12 = x - 9$

23. $4 + 8 + x = 6 + 6$

24. $18 - 6 + x = 15 - 3$

25. $8 - 23 + 7 = 1 + x - 2$

26. $3 - 17 + 8 = 8 + x - 3$

27. $-12 + x - 3 = 15 - 18 + 9$

28. $-19 + x - 7 = 20 - 42 + 10$

In exercises 29–36, determine whether the given solution is correct. If it is not, find the solution.

29. Is $x = 5$ the solution to $-7 + x = 2$?

30. Is $x = 7$ the solution to $-13 + x = 4$?

31. Is -3 a solution to $-18 - 2 = x - 7$?

32. Is -5 a solution to $-16 + 5 = x - 6$?

33. Is -33 the solution to $x - 23 = -56$?

34. Is -8 the solution to $-39 = x - 47$?

35. Is 35 the solution to $15 - 3 + 20 = x - 3$?

36. Is -12 the solution to $x + 8 = 12 - 19 + 3$?

Find the value of x that satisfies each equation.

37. $2.5 + x = 0.7$ **38.** $4.2 + x = 1.3$ **39.** $2.7 + x - 1.4 = 3.8$ **40.** $4.3 + x - 2.6 = 3.4$

41. $x - \dfrac{1}{4} = \dfrac{3}{4}$ **42.** $x + \dfrac{1}{3} = \dfrac{2}{3}$ **43.** $\dfrac{2}{3} + x = \dfrac{1}{6} + \dfrac{1}{4}$ **44.** $\dfrac{2}{5} + x = \dfrac{1}{2} - \dfrac{3}{10}$

Mixed Practice

Solve for x.

45. $3 + x = -12 + 8$ **46.** $12 + x = -7 + 20$ **47.** $5\dfrac{1}{6} + x = 8$ **48.** $7\dfrac{1}{8} = -20 + x$

49. $\dfrac{5}{12} - \dfrac{5}{6} = x - \dfrac{3}{2}$ **50.** $\dfrac{4}{15} - \dfrac{3}{5} = x - \dfrac{4}{3}$

51. $1.6 + 4x - 3.2 = -2x + 5.6 + 5x$ **52.** $0.7 + 3x - 4.2 = 9x + 3.6 - 7x$

53. $x + 0.7513 = 2.2419$ **54.** $x - 0.2314 = -4.0144$

Cumulative Review

Simplify by adding like terms.

55. $x + 3y - 5x - 7y + 2x$ **56.** $y^2 + y - 12 - 3y^2 - 5y + 16$

57. *Quality Control* The Perception Toy Company wishes to cut costs and decides that improving quality control will help. It can do this by reducing the amount of rejected frisbees to 3%. In a recent week, a quality control inspector found that 8 out of 413 frisbees were rejected. Did they meet Perception's goal?

58. *Checking Account Balance* Trevor pays his monthly computer lease bill for $49.99, but forgets to look at his checking account balance before doing so. When he gets his checking account statement at the local ATM, his balance reads −$35.07. How much was in his account before he wrote the check?

59. *Radar Picture* A 90-meter-wide radar picture is taken of a swamp in northern Australia. The radar detects a rock outcrop that is 90 feet above sea level, and a vein of opal (a semiprecious stone) 27 feet below sea level. How far is the top of the rock from the location of the opal?

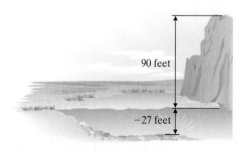

90 feet

−27 feet

Solving Equations of the Form $\frac{1}{a}x = b$

The addition principle allows us to add the same number to both sides of an equation. What would happen if we multiplied each side of an equation by the same number? For example, what would happen if we multiplied each side of an equation by 3?

To answer this question, let's return to our simple example of the box and the stone on a balanced seesaw. If we triple the weight on each side (that is, multiply the weight on each side by 3), the seesaw should still balance. The weight values of both sides remain equal.

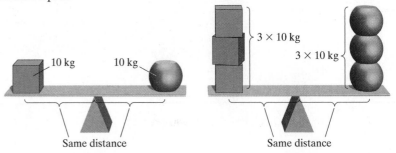

In words we can state this principle thus.

MULTIPLICATION PRINCIPLE

If both sides of an equation are multiplied by the same nonzero number, the results on both sides are equal in value.

In symbols we can restate the multiplication principle this way.

For real numbers a, b, and c with $c \neq 0$, if $a = b$, then $ca = cb$.

It is important that we say $c \neq 0$. We will explore this idea in the To Think About exercises.

Let us look at an equation where it would be helpful to multiply each side by 3.

EXAMPLE 1   Solve for x. $\frac{1}{3}x = -15$

Solution   We know that $(3)\left(\frac{1}{3}\right) = 1$. We will multiply each side of the equation by 3 because we want to isolate the variable x.

$$3\left(\frac{1}{3}x\right) = 3(-15)$$ Multiply each side of the equation by 3 since $(3)\left(\frac{1}{3}\right) = 1$.

$$\left(\frac{3}{1}\right)\left(\frac{1}{3}\right)(x) = -45$$

$$1x = -45$$ Simplify.

$$x = -45$$ The solution is -45.

Check. $\frac{1}{3}(-45) \overset{?}{=} -15$ Substitute -45 for x in the original equation.

$$-15 = -15 \checkmark$$ It checks.

Practice Problem 1   Solve for x. $\frac{1}{8}x = -2$

Note that $\frac{1}{5}x$ can be written as $\frac{x}{5}$. To solve the equation $\frac{x}{5} = 3$, we could multiply each side of the equation by 5. Try it. Then check your solution.

② Solving Equations of the Form $ax = b$

We can see that using the multiplication principle to multiply each side of an equation by $\frac{1}{2}$ is the same as dividing each side of the equation by 2. Thus, it would seem that the multiplication principle would allow us to divide each side of the equation by any nonzero real number. Is there a real-life example of this idea?

Let's return to our simple example of the box and the stone on a balanced seesaw. Suppose that we were to cut the two objects in half (so that the amount of weight of each was divided by 2). We then return the objects to the same places on the seesaw. The seesaw would still balance. The weight values of both sides remain equal.

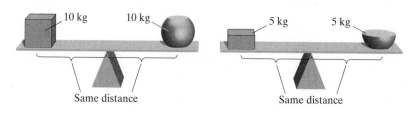

In words we can state this principle thus.

DIVISION PRINCIPLE

If both sides of an equation are divided by the same nonzero number, the results on both sides are equal in value.

Note: We put a restriction on the number by which we are dividing. We cannot divide by zero. We say that expressions like $\frac{2}{0}$ are not defined. Thus we restrict our divisor to *nonzero* numbers. We can restate the division principle this way.

For real numbers a, b, and c where $c \neq 0$,   if $a = b$,   then $\dfrac{a}{c} = \dfrac{b}{c}$.

EXAMPLE 2   Solve for x. $5x = 125$

Solution

$$\frac{5x}{5} = \frac{125}{5}$$ Divide both sides by 5.

$$x = 25$$ Simplify. The solution is 25.

Check.

$$5x = 125$$
$$5(25) \overset{?}{=} 125$$ Replace x by 25.
$$125 = 125 \checkmark$$ It checks.

Practice Problem 2   Solve for x. $9x = 72$

For equations of the form $ax = b$ (a number multiplied by x equals another number), we solve the equation by choosing to divide both sides by a particular number. What is the number to choose? We look at the side of the equation that contains x. We notice the number that is multiplied by x. We divide by that number.

The division principle tells us that we can still have a true equation provided that we divide by that number *on both sides* of the equation.

The solution to an equation may be a proper fraction or an improper fraction.

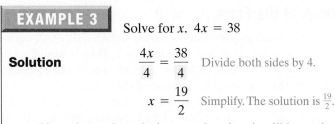

EXAMPLE 3   Solve for x. $4x = 38$

Solution

$$\frac{4x}{4} = \frac{38}{4} \quad \text{Divide both sides by 4.}$$

$$x = \frac{19}{2} \quad \text{Simplify. The solution is } \frac{19}{2}.$$

If you leave the solution as a fraction, it will be easier to check that solution in the original equation.

Check.
$$4x = 38$$
$$\overset{2}{\cancel{4}}\left(\frac{19}{\cancel{2}}\right) \overset{?}{=} 38 \qquad \text{Replace } x \text{ by } \frac{19}{2}.$$
$$38 = 38 \quad \checkmark \quad \text{It checks.}$$

Practice Problem 3   Solve for x. $6x = 50$

NOTE TO STUDENT: Fully worked-out solutions to all of the Practice Problems can be found at the back of the text starting at page SP-1

In Examples 2 and 3 we *divided by the number multiplied by x.* This procedure is followed regardless of whether the sign of that number is positive or negative. In equations of the form $ax = b$ the **coefficient** of x is a. A coefficient is a multiplier.

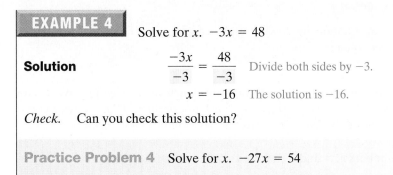

EXAMPLE 4   Solve for x. $-3x = 48$

Solution

$$\frac{-3x}{-3} = \frac{48}{-3} \quad \text{Divide both sides by } -3.$$

$$x = -16 \quad \text{The solution is } -16.$$

Check.   Can you check this solution?

Practice Problem 4   Solve for x. $-27x = 54$

The coefficient of x may be 1 or -1. You may have to rewrite the equation so that the coefficient of 1 or -1 is obvious. With practice you may be able to recognize the coefficient without actually rewriting the equation.

EXAMPLE 5   Solve for x. $-x = -24$.

Solution

$$-1x = -24 \quad \begin{array}{l}\text{Rewrite the equation. } -1x \text{ is the same as } -x. \\ \text{Now the coefficient of } -1 \text{ is obvious.}\end{array}$$

$$\frac{-1x}{-1} = \frac{-24}{-1} \quad \text{Divide both sides by } -1.$$

$$x = 24 \quad \text{The solution is 24.}$$

Check.   Can you check this solution?

Practice Problem 5   Solve for x. $-x = 36$

The variable can be on either side of the equation. The equation $-78 = -3x$ can be solved in exactly the same way as $-3x = -78$.

EXAMPLE 6   Solve for x. $-78 = -3x$

Solution

$$\frac{-78}{-3} = \frac{-3x}{-3}$$ Divide both sides by -3.

$$26 = x$$ The solution is 26.

Check. $-78 = -3x$

$-78 \overset{?}{=} -3(26)$ Replace x by 26.

$-78 = -78$ ✓   It checks.

Practice Problem 6   Solve for x. $-51 = -6x$ ◼

There is a mathematical concept that unites what we have learned in this section. The concept uses the idea of a multiplicative inverse. For any nonzero number a, the **multiplicative inverse** of a is $\frac{1}{a}$. Likewise, for any nonzero number a, the multiplicative inverse of $\frac{1}{a}$ is a. So to solve an equation of the form $ax = b$, we say that we need to multiply each side by the multiplicative inverse of a. Thus to solve $5x = 45$, we would multiply each side of the equation by the multiplicative inverse of 5, which is $\frac{1}{5}$. In similar fashion, if we wanted to solve the equation $\left(\frac{1}{6}\right)x = 4$, we would multiply each side of the equation by the multiplicative inverse of $\frac{1}{6}$, which is 6. In general, all the problems we have covered so far in this section can be solved by multiplying both sides of the equation by the multiplicative inverse of the coefficient of x.

EXAMPLE 7   Solve for x. $31.2 = 6.0x - 0.8x$

Solution

$31.2 = 6.0x - 0.8x$ There are like terms on the right side.

$31.2 = 5.2x$ Collect like terms.

$$\frac{31.2}{5.2} = \frac{5.2x}{5.2}$$ Divide both sides by 5.2 (which is the same as multiplying both sides by the multiplicative inverse of 5.2).

$6 = x$ The solution is 6.

Note: Be sure to place the decimal point in the quotient directly above the caret ($_\wedge$) when performing the division.

$$5.2_\wedge \overline{)31.2_\wedge}$$

$$\begin{array}{r} 6. \\ \underline{31.2} \\ 0 \end{array}$$

Check.   The check is up to you.

Practice Problem 7   Solve for x. $16.2 = 5.2x - 3.4x$ ◼

Developing Your Study Skills

Getting Help

Getting the right kind of help at the right time can be a key ingredient in being successful in mathematics. When you have gone to class on a regular basis, taken careful notes, methodically read your textbook, and diligently done your homework—all of which means making every effort possible to learn the mathematics—you may find that you are still having difficulty. If this is the case, then you need to seek help. Make an appointment with your instructor to find out what help is available to you. The instructor, tutoring services, a mathematics lab, videotapes, and computer software may be among the resources you can draw on.

Once you discover the resources available in your school, you need to take advantage of them. Do not put it off, or you will find yourself getting behind. You cannot afford that. When studying mathematics, you must keep up with your work.

Verbal and Writing Skills

1. To solve the equation $6x = -24$, divide each side of the equation by _____.

2. To solve the equation $-7x = 56$, divide each side of the equation by _____.

3. To solve the equation $\frac{1}{7}x = -2$, multiply each side of the equation by _____.

4. To solve the equation $\frac{1}{9}x = 5$, multiply each side of the equation by _____.

Solve for x. Be sure to reduce your answer. Check your solution.

5. $\frac{1}{9}x = 4$

6. $\frac{1}{7}x = 6$

7. $\frac{1}{3}x = -9$

8. $\frac{1}{4}x = -20$

9. $\frac{x}{5} = 16$

10. $\frac{x}{10} = 8$

11. $-3 = \frac{x}{5}$

12. $\frac{x}{3} = -12$

13. $13x = 52$

14. $15x = 60$

15. $56 = 7x$

16. $46 = 2x$

17. $-16 = 6x$

18. $-35 = 21x$

19. $1.5x = 75$

20. $2x = 0.36$

21. $-15 = -x$

22. $32 = -x$

23. $-112 = 16x$

24. $-108 = -18x$

25. $0.4x = 0.08$

26. $2.1x = 0.3$

27. $-3.9x = -15.6$

28. $-4.7x = -14.1$

Determine whether the given solution is correct. If it is not, find the correct solution.

29. Is 7 the solution for $-3x = 21$?

30. Is 8 the solution for $5x = -40$?

31. Is -6 the solution for $-11x = 66$?

32. Is -20 the solution for $-x = 20$?

Mixed Practice

Find the value of the variable that satisfies the equation.

33. $7y = -0.21$

34. $-3y = 0.42$

35. $-56 = -21t$

36. $34 = -51q$

37. $4.6y = -3.22$

38. $-2.8y = -3.08$

39. $4x + 3x = 21$

40. $5x + 4x = 36$

41. $2x - 7x = 20$

42. $3x - 9x = 18$

43. $-6x - 3x = -7$

44. $y - 11y = 7$

45. $12 - 19 = -7x$ **46.** $36 - 22 = -2x$ **47.** $6x = -18 + 36$ **48.** $11x = -20 + 42$

49. $\frac{2}{3}x = 18$ **50.** $\frac{3}{5}x = 39$ 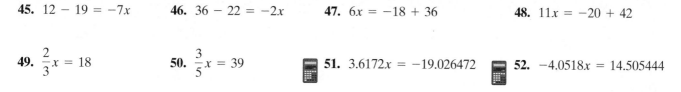 **51.** $3.6172x = -19.026472$ **52.** $-4.0518x = 14.505444$

To Think About

53. We have said that if $a = b$ and $c \neq 0$, then $ac = bc$. Why is it important that $c \neq 0$? What would happen if we tried to solve an equation by multiplying both sides by zero?

54. We have said that if $a = b$ and $c \neq 0$ then $\frac{a}{c} = \frac{b}{c}$. Why is it important that $c \neq 0$? What would happen if we tried to solve an equation by dividing both sides by zero?

Cumulative Review

Evaluate using the correct order of operations. (Be careful to avoid sign errors.)

55. $(-6)(-8) + (-3)(2)$ **56.** $(-3)^3 + (-20) \div 2$ **57.** $5 + (2 - 6)^2$

58. *Discount Merchandise* An off-price clothing store chain specializes in last year's merchandise. Their contact in Hong Kong has purchased 12,000 famous designer men's sport coats for the stores. When the shipment is unloaded, 800 sport coats have no left sleeve. What percent of the shipment is acceptable?

59. *Investments* In January, Keiko invested $600 in a certain stock. In February, the stock gained $82.00. In March, the stock lost $47.00. In April, the stock gained $103.00. In May, the stock lost $106.00. What was Keiko's stock holding worth after the May loss?

60. *Whale Calf Population* In 1995, the humpback whale calf population at Stellwagen Bank, near Gloucester, Massachusetts, was estimated at 12 calves. The population grew by 21 calves in 1996, 18 calves in 1997, and 51 calves in 1998. In 1999, the number of whale calves decreased by 4, and in 2000 it increased by 6. What was the whale calf population at the end of 2000?

61. *Earthquakes* In an average year, worldwide, there are 20 earthquakes of magnitude 7 on the Richter scale. If next year is predicted to be an exceptional year, and the number of earthquakes of magnitude 7 is expected to increase by 35%, about how many earthquakes of magnitude 7 can be expected? (Round off to the nearest whole number.)

Student Learning Objectives

After studying this section, you will be able to:

 1 Solve equations of the form $ax + b = c$.

 2 Solve equations with the variable on both sides of the equation.

3 Solve equations with parentheses.

NOTE TO STUDENT: Fully worked-out solutions to all of the Practice Problems can be found at the back of the text starting at page SP-1

1 ### Solving Equations of the Form $ax + b = c$

Jenny Crawford scored several goals in field hockey during April. Her teammates scored three more than five times the number she scored. Together the team scored 18 goals in April. How many did Jenny score? To solve this problem, we need to solve the equation $5x + 3 = 18$.

To solve an equation of the form $ax + b = c$, we must use both the addition principle and the multiplication principle.

> **EXAMPLE 1** Solve for x to determine how many goals Jenny scored and check your solution.
>
> $$5x + 3 = 18$$
>
> **Solution** We first want to isolate the variable term.
>
> | | |
> |---|---|
> | $5x + 3 + (-3) = 18 + (-3)$ | Use the addition principle to add -3 to both sides. |
> | $5x = 15$ | Simplify. |
> | $\dfrac{5x}{5} = \dfrac{15}{5}$ | Use the division principle to divide both sides by 5. |
> | $x = 3$ | The solution is 3. Thus Jenny scored 3 goals. |
>
> *Check.*
> $$5(3) + 3 \overset{?}{=} 18$$
> $$15 + 3 \overset{?}{=} 18$$
> $$18 = 18 \ \checkmark \qquad \text{It checks.}$$

Practice Problem 1 Solve for x and check your solution. $9x + 2 = 38$

2 ### Solving Equations with the Variable on Both Sides of the Equation

In some cases the variable appears on both sides of the equation. We would like to rewrite the equation so that all the terms containing the variable appear on one side. To do this, we apply the addition principle to the variable term.

> **EXAMPLE 2** Solve for x. $9x = 6x + 15$
>
> **Solution**
>
> | | |
> |---|---|
> | $9x + (-6x) = 6x + (-6x) + 15$ | Add $-6x$ to both sides. Notice $6x + (-6x)$ eliminates the variable on the right side. |
> | $3x = 15$ | Combine like terms. |
> | $\dfrac{3x}{3} = \dfrac{15}{3}$ | Divide both sides by 3. |
> | $x = 5$ | The solution is 5. |
>
> *Check.* The check is left to the student.

Practice Problem 2 Solve for x. $13x = 2x - 66$

In many problems the variable terms and constant terms appear on both sides of the equations. You will want to get all the variable terms on one side and all the constant terms on the other side.

EXAMPLE 3   Solve for x and check your solution. $9x + 3 = 7x - 2$.

Solution   First we want to isolate the variable term.

$9x + (-7x) + 3 = 7x + (-7x) - 2$	Add $-7x$ to both sides of the equation.
$2x + 3 = -2$	Combine like terms.
$2x + 3 + (-3) = -2 + (-3)$	Add -3 to both sides.
$2x = -5$	Simplify.
$\dfrac{2x}{2} = \dfrac{-5}{2}$	Divide both sides by 2.
$x = -\dfrac{5}{2}$	The solution is $-\frac{5}{2}$.

Check.

$$9x + 3 = 7x - 2$$

$9\left(-\dfrac{5}{2}\right) + 3 \overset{?}{=} 7\left(-\dfrac{5}{2}\right) - 2$	Replace x by $-\dfrac{5}{2}$.
$-\dfrac{45}{2} + 3 \overset{?}{=} -\dfrac{35}{2} - 2$	Simplify.
$-\dfrac{45}{2} + \dfrac{6}{2} \overset{?}{=} -\dfrac{35}{2} - \dfrac{4}{2}$	Change to equivalent fractions with a common denominator.
$-\dfrac{39}{2} = -\dfrac{39}{2}$ ✓	It checks. The solution is $-\frac{5}{2}$.

Practice Problem 3   Solve for x and check your solution. $3x + 2 = 5x + 2$

In our next example we will study equations that need simplifying before any other steps are taken. Where it is possible, you should first collect like terms on one or both sides of the equation. The variable terms can be collected on the right side or the left side. In this example we will collect all the x-terms on the right side.

EXAMPLE 4   Solve for x. $5x + 26 - 6 = 9x + 12x$

Solution

$5x + 20 = 21x$	Combine like terms.
$5x + (-5x) + 20 = 21x + (-5x)$	Add $-5x$ to both sides.
$20 = 16x$	Combine like terms.
$\dfrac{20}{16} = \dfrac{16x}{16}$	Divide both sides by 16.
$\dfrac{5}{4} = x$	Don't forget to reduce the resulting fraction.

Check.   The check is left to the student.

Practice Problem 4   Solve for z. $-z + 8 - z = 3z + 10 - 3$

Do you really need all these steps? No. As you become more proficient you will be able to combine or eliminate some of these steps. However, it is best to write each step in its entirety until you are consistently obtaining the correct solution. It is much better to show every step than to take a lot of shortcuts and possibly obtain a wrong answer. This is a section of the algebra course where working neatly and accurately will help you—both now and as you progress through the course.

3 Solving Equations with Parentheses

The equations that you just solved are simpler versions of equations that we will now discuss. These equations contain parentheses. If the parentheses are first removed, the problems then become just like those encountered previously. We use the distributive property to remove the parentheses.

EXAMPLE 5 Solve for x and check your solution.

$$4(x + 1) - 3(x - 3) = 25$$

Solution $4(x + 1) - 3(x - 3) = 25$

$4x + 4 - 3x + 9 = 25$ Multiply by 4 and -3 to remove parentheses. Be careful of the signs. Remember that $(-3)(-3) = 9$.

After removing the parentheses, it is important to collect like terms on each side of the equation. Do this before going on to isolate the variable.

$x + 13 = 25$ Collect like terms.

$x + 13 - 13 = 25 - 13$ Add -13 to both sides to isolate the variable.

$x = 12$ The solution is 12.

Check. $4(12 + 1) - 3(12 - 3) \stackrel{?}{=} 25$ Replace x by 12.

$4(13) - 3(9) \stackrel{?}{=} 25$ Combine numbers inside parentheses.

$52 - 27 \stackrel{?}{=} 25$ Multiply.

$25 = 25$ ✓   Simplify. It checks.

NOTE TO STUDENT: Fully worked-out solutions to all of the Practice Problems can be found at the back of the text starting at page SP-1

Practice Problem 5   Solve for x and check your solution.

$$4x - (x + 3) = 12 - 3(x - 2)$$

EXAMPLE 6   Solve for x. $3(-x - 7) = -2(2x + 5)$

Solution $-3x - 21 = -4x - 10$ Remove parentheses. Watch the signs carefully.

$-3x + 4x - 21 = -4x + 4x - 10$ Add $4x$ to both sides.

$x - 21 = -10$ Simplify.

$x - 21 + 21 = -10 + 21$ Add 21 to both sides.

$x = 11$ The solution is 11.

Check.   The check is left to the student.

Practice Problem 6   Solve for x. $4(-2x - 3) = -5(x - 2) + 2$

In problems that involve decimals, great care should be taken. In some steps you will be multiplying decimal quantities, and in other steps you will be adding them.

EXAMPLE 7   Solve for x. $0.3(1.2x - 3.6) = 4.2x - 16.44$

Solution

$0.36x - 1.08 = 4.2x - 16.44$	Remove parentheses.
$0.36x - 0.36x - 1.08 = 4.2x - 0.36x - 16.44$	Subtract $0.36x$ from both sides.
$-1.08 = 3.84x - 16.44$	Collect like terms.
$-1.08 + 16.44 = 3.84x - 16.44 + 16.44$	Add 16.44 to both sides.
$15.36 = 3.84x$	Simplify.
$\dfrac{15.36}{3.84} = \dfrac{3.84x}{3.84}$	Divide both sides by 3.84.
$4 = x$	The solution is 4.

Check.   The check is left to the student.

Practice Problem 7   Solve for x. $0.3x - 2(x + 0.1) = 0.4(x - 3) - 1.1$

EXAMPLE 8   Solve for z and check. $2(3z - 5) + 2 = 4z - 3(2z + 8)$

Solution

$6z - 10 + 2 = 4z - 6z - 24$	Remove parentheses.
$6z - 8 = -2z - 24$	Collect like terms.
$6z - 8 + 2z = -2z + 2z - 24$	Add $2z$ to each side.
$8z - 8 = -24$	Simplify.
$8z - 8 + 8 = -24 + 8$	Add 8 to each side.
$8z = -16$	Simplify.
$\dfrac{8z}{8} = \dfrac{-16}{8}$	Divide each side by 8.
$z = -2$	Simplify. The solution is -2.

Check.

$2[3(-2) - 5] + 2 \overset{?}{=} 4(-2) - 3[2(-2) + 8]$	Replace z by -2.
$2[-6 - 5] + 2 \overset{?}{=} -8 - 3[-4 + 8]$	Multiply.
$2[-11] + 2 \overset{?}{=} -8 - 3[4]$	Simplify.
$-22 + 2 \overset{?}{=} -8 - 12$	
$-20 = -20 \ \checkmark$	It checks.

Practice Problem 8   Solve for z and check.

$$5(2z - 1) + 7 = 7z - 4(z + 3)$$

3.3 EXERCISES

| Student Solutions Manual | CD/Video | PH Math Tutor Center | MathXL®Tutorials on CD | MathXL® | MyMathLab® | Interactmath.com |

Find the value of the variable that satisfies the equation in exercises 1–22. Check your solution. Answers that are not integers may be left in fractional form or decimal form.

1. $4x + 13 = 21$

2. $7x + 4 = 53$

3. $4x - 11 = 13$

4. $5x - 11 = 39$

5. $7x - 18 = -46$

6. $6x - 23 = -71$

7. $-4x + 17 = -35$

8. $-6x + 25 = -83$

9. $2x + 3.2 = 9.4$

10. $4x + 4.6 = 9.2$

11. $\frac{1}{5}x - 2 = 6$

12. $\frac{1}{3}x - 7 = 4$

13. $\frac{1}{3}x + 5 = -4$

14. $\frac{1}{8}x - 3 = -9$

15. $8x = 48 + 2x$

16. $5x = 22 + 3x$

17. $-6x = -27 + 3x$

18. $-7x = -26 + 6x$

19. $63 - x = 8x$

20. $56 - 3x = 5x$

21. $54 - 2x = -8x$

22. $72 - 4x = -12x$

23. Is 2 the solution for $2y + 3y = 12 - y$?

24. Is 4 the solution for $5y + 2 = 6y - 6 + y$?

25. Is 11 a solution for $7x + 6 - 3x = 2x - 5 + x$?

26. Is −12 a solution for $9x + 2 - 5x = -8 + 5x - 2$?

Solve for the variable. You may move the variable terms to the right or to the left.

27. $14 - 2x = -5x + 11$

28. $8 - 3x = 7x + 8$

29. $x - 6 = 8 - x$

30. $-x + 12 = -4 + x$

31. $0.8y - 0.4 = 0.9 - 0.5y$

32. $0.7y - 0.5 = 1.1 - 0.1y$

33. $5x - 9 = 3x + 23$

34. $9x - 5 = 7x + 43$

To Think About Exercises 35–36

First collect like terms on each side of the equation. Then solve for y by getting all the y-terms on the left. Then solve for y by getting all the y-terms on the right. Which approach is better?

35. $-3 + 10y + 6 = 15 + 12y - 18$

36. $7y + 21 - 5y = 5y - 7 + y$

Remove the parentheses and solve for the variable. Check your solution. Answers that are not integers may be left in fractional form or decimal form.

37. $5(x + 3) = 35$

38. $6(x + 2) = 42$

39. $6(3x + 2) - 8 = -2$

40. $4(2x + 1) - 7 = 6 - 5$

41. $7x - 3(5 - x) = 10$

42. $8x - 2(4 - x) = 14$

43. $0.5x - 0.3(2 - x) = 4.6$

44. $0.4x - 0.2(3 - x) = 1.8$

45. $5(x - 3) + 5 = 3(x + 2)$

46. $3(x - 2) + 2 = 2(x - 4)$

47. $-2(x + 3) + 4 = 3(x + 4) + 2$

48. $-3(x + 5) + 2 = 4(x + 6) - 9$

49. $-3(y - 3y) + 4 = -4(3y - y) + 6 + 13y$

50. $2(4x - x) + 6 = 2(2x + x) + 8 - x$

Mixed Practice

Solve for the variable.

51. $5.7x + 3 = 4.2x - 3$

52. $4x - 3.1 = 5.3 - 3x$

53. $5z + 7 - 2z = 32 - 2z$

54. $8 - 7z + 2z = 20 + 5z$

55. $-0.3a + 1.4 = -1.2 - 0.7a$

56. $-0.7b + 1.6 = -1.7 - 1.5b$

57. $6x + 8 - 3x = 11 - 12x - 13$ **58.** $4 - 7x - 13 = 8x - 3 - 5x$ **59.** $-3.5x + 1.3 = -2.7x + 1.5$

60. $2.8x - 0.9 = 5.2x - 3.3$ **61.** $5(4 + x) = 3(3x - 1) - 9$ **62.** $6(3x - 1) = 4(2x + 5) - 6$

63. $4x + 3.2 - 1.9x = 0.3x - 4.9$ **64.** $3x + 2 - 1.7x = 0.6x + 31.4$

65. $3(x + 4) - 5(3x - 2) = 8$ **66.** $3(2z - 4) - 4(z + 5) = 6$

Solve for x. Round your answer to the nearest hundredth.

67. $1.63x - 9.23 = 5.71x + 8.04$ **68.** $-2.21x + 8.65 = 3.69x - 7.78$

Cumulative Review

Simplify.

69. $2x(3x - y) + 4(2x^2 - 3xy)$ **70.** $2\{x - 3[4 + 2(3 + x)]\}$

71. *Investments* On March 30, 2000, Nancy owned three different stocks: Coca Cola, General Motors and Alcoa. Her portfolio contained the following:

4.0 shares of Coca Cola stock valued at $52\frac{1}{8}$,
3.2 shares of General Motors stock valued at $81\frac{7}{8}$, and
5.2 shares of Alcoa stock valued at $71\frac{7}{8}$.

Find the market value of Nancy's stock holdings on March 30, 2000. (*Note*: In 2000 stock quotes were given in fractional form. Now decimals are used.)

72. *Employee Discount* Bea works for a large department store and obtains a 10% discount on anything she buys from the store. One item Bea wishes to purchase costs $140 and is on sale at a 25% discount.

(a) What is the price if Bea has a total discount of 35%? (Disregard sales tax.)

(b) What is the price if Bea has a 10% discount on the 25% discount price? (Disregard sales tax.)

Student Learning Objective

After studying this section, you will be able to:

 Solve equations with fractions.

1 Solving Equations with Fractions

Equations with fractions can be rather difficult to solve. This difficulty is simply due to the extra care we usually have to use when computing with fractions. The actual equation-solving procedures are the same, with fractions or without. To avoid unnecessary work, we transform the given equation with fractions to an equivalent equation that does not contain fractions. How do we do this? We multiply each side of the equation by the least common denominator of all the fractions contained in the equation. We then use the distributive property so that the LCD is multiplied by each term of the equation.

EXAMPLE 1 Solve for x. $\dfrac{1}{4}x - \dfrac{2}{3} = \dfrac{5}{12}x$

Solution First we find that the LCD $= 12$.

$$12\left(\frac{1}{4}x - \frac{2}{3}\right) = 12\left(\frac{5}{12}x\right)$$ Multiply each side by 12.

$$\left(\frac{12}{1}\right)\left(\frac{1}{4}\right)(x) - \left(\frac{12}{1}\right)\left(\frac{2}{3}\right) = \left(\frac{12}{1}\right)\left(\frac{5}{12}\right)(x)$$ Use the distributive property.

$$3x - 8 = 5x$$ Simplify.

$$3x + (-3x) - 8 = 5x + (-3x)$$ Add $-3x$ to each side.

$$-8 = 2x$$ Simplify.

$$\frac{-8}{2} = \frac{2x}{2}$$ Divide each side by 2.

$$-4 = x$$ Simplify.

Check.

$$\frac{1}{4}(-4) - \frac{2}{3} \stackrel{?}{=} \frac{5}{12}(-4)$$

$$-1 - \frac{2}{3} \stackrel{?}{=} -\frac{5}{3}$$

$$-\frac{3}{3} - \frac{2}{3} \stackrel{?}{=} -\frac{5}{3}$$

$$-\frac{5}{3} = -\frac{5}{3} \checkmark$$ It checks.

Practice Problem 1 Solve for x. $\dfrac{3}{8}x - \dfrac{3}{2} = \dfrac{1}{4}x$

NOTE TO STUDENT: Fully worked-out solutions to all of the Practice Problems can be found at the back of the text starting at page SP-1

In Example 1 we multiplied each side of the equation by the LCD. However, most students prefer to go immediately to the second step and multiply each term by the LCD. This avoids having to write out a separate step using the distributive property.

EXAMPLE 2   Solve for x and check your solution. $\dfrac{x}{3} + 3 = \dfrac{x}{5} - \dfrac{1}{3}$

Solution

$$15\left(\dfrac{x}{3}\right) + 15\,(3) = 15\left(\dfrac{x}{5}\right) - 15\left(\dfrac{1}{3}\right)$$

The LCD is 15. Use the multiplication principle to multiply each term by 15.

$$5x + 45 = 3x - 5$$ Simplify.

$$5x - 3x + 45 = 3x - 3x - 5$$ Add $-3x$ to both sides.

$$2x + 45 = -5$$ Combine like terms.

$$2x + 45 - 45 = -5 - 45$$ Add -45 to both sides.

$$2x = -50$$ Simplify.

$$\dfrac{2x}{2} = \dfrac{-50}{2}$$ Divide both sides by 2.

$$x = -25$$ The solution is -25.

Check.

$$\dfrac{-25}{3} + 3 \overset{?}{=} \dfrac{-25}{5} - \dfrac{1}{3}$$

$$-\dfrac{25}{3} + \dfrac{9}{3} \overset{?}{=} -\dfrac{5}{1} - \dfrac{1}{3}$$

$$-\dfrac{16}{3} \overset{?}{=} -\dfrac{15}{3} - \dfrac{1}{3}$$

$$-\dfrac{16}{3} = -\dfrac{16}{3} \checkmark$$

Practice Problem 2   Solve for x and check your solution.

$$\dfrac{5x}{4} - 1 = \dfrac{3x}{4} + \dfrac{1}{2}$$

NOTE TO STUDENT: Fully worked-out solutions to all of the Practice Problems can be found at the back of the text starting at page SP-1

EXAMPLE 3   Solve for x. $\dfrac{x + 5}{7} = \dfrac{x}{4} + \dfrac{1}{2}$

Solution

$$\dfrac{x}{7} + \dfrac{5}{7} = \dfrac{x}{4} + \dfrac{1}{2}$$

First we rewrite the left side as two fractions. This is actually multiplying $\frac{1}{7}(x + 5) = \frac{x}{7} + \frac{5}{7}$.

$$28\left(\dfrac{x}{7}\right) + 28\left(\dfrac{5}{7}\right) = 28\left(\dfrac{x}{4}\right) + 28\left(\dfrac{1}{2}\right)$$

We observe that the LCD is 28, so we multiply each term by 28.

$$4x + 20 = 7x + 14$$ Simplify.

$$4x - 4x + 20 = 7x - 4x + 14$$ Add $-4x$ to both sides.

$$20 = 3x + 14$$ Combine like terms.

$$20 - 14 = 3x + 14 - 14$$ Add -14 to both sides.

$$6 = 3x$$ Combine like terms.

$$\dfrac{6}{3} = \dfrac{3x}{3}$$ Divide both sides by 3.

$$2 = x$$ The solution is 2.

Check.   The check is left to the student.

Practice Problem 3   Solve for x $\dfrac{x + 6}{9} = \dfrac{x}{6} + \dfrac{1}{2}$

TO THINK ABOUT: Does Every Equation Have One Solution?   Actually, no. There are some rare cases where an equation has no solution at all. Suppose we try to solve the equation

$$5(x + 3) = 2x - 8 + 3x.$$

If we remove the parentheses and collect like terms we have

$$5x + 15 = 5x - 8.$$

If we add $-5x$ to each side, we obtain

$$15 = -8.$$

Clearly this is impossible. There is no value of x for which these two numbers are equal. We would say this equation has **no solution.**

One additional surprise may happen. An equation may have an infinite number of solutions. Suppose we try to solve the equation

$$9x - 8x - 7 = 3 + x - 10.$$

If we combine like terms on each side, we have the equation

$$x - 7 = x - 7.$$

If we add $-x$ to each side, we obtain

$$-7 = -7.$$

Now this statement is always true, no matter what the value of x. We would say this equation has **an infinite number of solutions.**

In the To Think About exercises in this section, we will encounter some equations that have no solution or an infinite number of solutions.

Developing Your Study Skills

Taking Notes in Class

An important part of studying mathematics is taking notes. To take meaningful notes, you must be an active listener. Keep your mind on what the instructor is saying, and be ready with questions whenever you do not understand something.

If you have previewed the lesson material, you will be prepared to take good notes. The important concepts will seem somewhat familiar. If you frantically try to write all that the instructor says or copy all the examples done in class, you may find your notes nearly worthless when you are home alone. Write down *important* ideas and examples as the instructor lectures, making sure that you are listening and following the logic. Include any helpful hints or suggestions that your instructor gives you or refers to in your text.

In exercises 1–16, solve for the variable and check your answer. Noninteger answers may be left in fractional form or decimal form.

1. $\dfrac{1}{2}x + \dfrac{2}{3} = \dfrac{1}{6}$

2. $\dfrac{1}{3} + \dfrac{5}{12}x = \dfrac{3}{4}$

3. $\dfrac{2}{3}x = \dfrac{1}{15}x + \dfrac{3}{5}$

4. $\dfrac{5}{21}x = \dfrac{2}{3}x - \dfrac{1}{7}$

5. $\dfrac{x}{2} + \dfrac{x}{5} = \dfrac{7}{10}$

6. $\dfrac{x}{5} - \dfrac{x}{3} = \dfrac{8}{15}$

7. $20 - \dfrac{1}{3}x = \dfrac{1}{2}x$

8. $15 - \dfrac{1}{2}x = \dfrac{1}{4}x$

9. $2 + \dfrac{y}{2} = \dfrac{3y}{4} - 3$

10. $\dfrac{x}{3} - 1 = -\dfrac{1}{2} - x$

11. $\dfrac{x-3}{5} = 1 - \dfrac{x}{3}$

12. $\dfrac{y-5}{4} = 1 - \dfrac{y}{5}$

13. $\dfrac{x+3}{4} = \dfrac{x}{2} + \dfrac{1}{6}$

14. $\dfrac{x+5}{6} = \dfrac{x}{2} + \dfrac{3}{4}$

15. $0.6x + 5.9 = 3.8$

16. $1.2x - 2.2 = 5.6$

17. Is 4 a solution to $\dfrac{1}{2}(y - 2) + 2 = \dfrac{3}{8}(3y - 4)$?

18. Is 2 a solution to $\dfrac{1}{5}(y + 2) = \dfrac{1}{10}y + \dfrac{3}{5}$?

19. Is $\dfrac{5}{8}$ a solution to $\dfrac{1}{2}\left(y - \dfrac{1}{5}\right) = \dfrac{1}{5}(y + 2)$?

20. Is $\dfrac{13}{3}$ a solution to $\dfrac{y}{2} - \dfrac{7}{9} = \dfrac{y}{6} + \dfrac{2}{3}$?

Remove parentheses first. Then collect like terms. Solve for the variable. Noninteger answers may be left in fractional form or decimal form.

21. $\dfrac{3}{4}(3x + 1) = 2(3 - 2x) + 1$

22. $\dfrac{1}{4}(3x + 1) = 2(2x - 4) - 8$

23. $2(x - 2) = \dfrac{2}{5}(3x + 1) + 2$

24. $2(x - 4) = \dfrac{5}{6}(x + 6) - 6$

25. $0.3x - 0.2(3 - 5x) = -0.5(x - 6)$

26. $0.3(x - 2) + 0.4x = -0.2(x - 6)$

27. $-5(0.2x + 0.1) - 0.6 = 1.9$

28. $0.3x + 1.7 = 0.2x - 0.4(5x + 1)$

Mixed Practice

Solve. Noninteger answers may be left in fractional form or decimal form.

29. $\frac{1}{3}(y + 2) = 3y - 5(y - 2)$

30. $\frac{1}{4}(y + 6) = 2y - 3(y - 3)$

31. $\frac{1 + 2x}{5} + \frac{4 - x}{3} = \frac{1}{15}$

32. $\frac{1 + 3x}{2} + \frac{2 - x}{3} = \frac{5}{6}$

33. $\frac{1}{5}(x + 3) = 2x - 3(2 - x) - 3$

34. $\frac{2}{3}(x + 4) = 6 - \frac{1}{4}(3x - 2) - 1$

35. $\frac{1}{3}(x - 2) = 3x - 2(x - 1) + \frac{16}{3}$

36. $\frac{3}{4}(x - 2) + \frac{3}{5} = \frac{1}{5}(x + 1)$

37. $\frac{4}{5}x - \frac{2}{3} = \frac{3x + 1}{2}$

38. $\frac{4}{7}x + \frac{1}{3} = \frac{3x - 2}{14}$

39. $0.2(x + 3) = 4(0.5x - 0.03)$

40. $0.6(x + 0.1) = 2(0.4x - 0.2)$

To Think About

Solve. Be careful to examine your work to see if the equation may have no solution or an infinite number of solutions.

41. $-1 + 5(x - 2) = 12x + 3 - 7x$

42. $x + 3x - 2 + 3x = -11 + 7(x + 2)$

43. $9(x + 3) - 6 = 24 - 2x - 3 + 11x$

44. $7(x + 4) - 10 = 3x + 20 + 4x - 2$

45. $7x + 6 = 2(3x - 1) + 8$

46. $9x + 10 = 5(4x - 1) + 15$

47. $3(4x + 1) - 2x = 2(5x - 3)$

48. $5(-3 + 4x) = 4(2x + 4) + 12x$

Cumulative Review

49. Add. $\dfrac{3}{7} + 1\dfrac{5}{10}$

50. Subtract. $3\dfrac{1}{5} - 2\dfrac{1}{4}$

51. Multiply: $\left(-3\dfrac{1}{4}\right)\left(5\dfrac{1}{3}\right) =$

52. Divide. $5\dfrac{1}{2} \div 1\dfrac{1}{4}$

53. *Falcon Population* In 1975 there were 40 nesting pairs of the American peregrine falcon nesting in the United States and Canada. Between 1975 and 1985, the peregrine falcon population increased by 20 percent. Between 1985 and 2000, the population increased by 450 percent. How many pairs of peregrine falcons were thriving in 2000? (Source: U.S. Department of the Interior.)

54. *Auditorium Seating* The seating area of an auditorium is shaped like a trapezoid, with front and back sides parallel. The front of the auditorium measures 88 feet across, the back of the auditorium measures 150 feet across, and the auditorium is 200 feet from front to back. If each seat requires a space that is 2.5 feet wide by 3 feet deep, how many seats will the auditorium hold? (This will only be an approximation because of the angled side walls. Round off to the nearest whole number.)

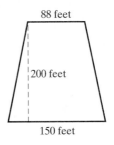

88 feet

200 feet

150 feet

▲ **55.** *Vent Grill* The Newbury Elementary School needs a new air vent drilled into the wall of the maintenance room. The circular hole that is necessary will have a radius of 6 inches. The stainless steel grill that will cover the vent costs \$2 per square inch. How much will the vent cost? Use $\pi \approx 3.14$.

▲ **56.** *Sail Material* Tom Rourke needs to replace the sail on his sailboat. It is in the shape of a triangle with an altitude of 9 feet and a base of 8 feet. The material to make the sail costs \$3 per square foot. How much will the material cost to make a new sail for the boat?

How are you doing with your homework assignments in Sections 3.1 to 3.4? Do you feel you have mastered the material so far? Do you understand the concepts you have covered? Before you go further in the textbook, take some time to do each of the following problems.

Solve for x. If the solution is not an integer, you may express your answer as a fraction or as a decimal.

3.1

1. $5 - 8 + x = -12$

2. $3.6 + x = -7.3$

3.2

3. $-45 = -5x$

4. $12x - 6x = -48$

3.3

5. $-1.2x + 3.5 = 2.7$

6. $9x - 3 = -17x + 4$

7. $14x + 2(7 - 2x) = 20$

8. $0.5(1.2x - 3.4) = -1.4x + 5.8$

9. $3(x + 6) = -2(4x - 1) + x$

3.4

10. $\dfrac{x}{5} + \dfrac{x}{4} = \dfrac{2}{5}$

11. $\dfrac{1}{4}(x + 3) = 4x - 2(x - 3)$

12. $\dfrac{1}{2}(x - 1) + 2 = 3(2x - 1)$

13. $\dfrac{1}{7}(7x - 14) - 2 = \dfrac{1}{3}(x - 2)$

14. $0.2\,(x - 3) = 4\,(0.2x - 0.1)$

Now turn to page SA-5 for the answer to each of these problems. Each answer also includes a reference to the objective in which the problem is first taught. If you missed any of these problems, you should stop and review the Examples and Practice Problems in the referenced objective. A little review now will help you master the material in the upcoming sections of the text.

1. _____

2. _____

3. _____

4. _____

5. _____

6. _____

7. _____

8. _____

9. _____

10. _____

11. _____

12. _____

13. _____

14. _____

Student Learning Objectives

After studying this section, you will be able to:

 Translate English phrases into algebraic expressions.

2 Write an algebraic expression to compare two or more quantities.

1 Translating English Phrases into Algebraic Expressions

One of the most useful applications of algebra is solving word problems. One of the first steps in solving word problems is translating the conditions of the problem into algebra. In this section we show you how to translate common English phrases into algebraic symbols. This process is similar to translating between languages like Spanish and French.

Several English phrases describe the operation of addition. If we represent an unknown number by the variable x, all of the following phrases can be translated into algebra as $x + 3$.

English Phrases Describing Addition	Algebraic Expression	Diagram
Three *more than* a number		
The *sum of* a number and three		
A number *increased by* three	$x + 3$	
Three is *added to* a number.		
Three *greater than* a number		
A number *plus* three		

In a similar way we can use algebra to express English phrases that describe the operations of subtraction, multiplication, and division.

CAUTION Since subtraction is not commutative, the order is essential. A number decreased by five is $x - 5$. It is not correct to say $5 - x$. Use extra care as you study each example. Make sure you understand the proper order.

English Phrases Describing Subtraction	Algebraic Expression	Diagram
A number *decreased by* four		
Four *less than* a number		
Four is *subtracted from* a number.		
Four *smaller than* a number	$x - 4$	
Four *fewer than* a number		
A number *diminished by* four		
A number *minus* 4		
The *difference between* a number and four		

English Phrases Describing Multiplication	Algebraic Expression	Diagram
Double a number		
Twice a number		
The *product* of two and a number	$2x$	
Two *of* a number		
Two *times* a number		

Since division is not commutative, the order is essential. A number divided by 3 is $\frac{x}{3}$. It is not correct to say $\frac{3}{x}$. Use extra care as you study each example.

English Phrases Describing Division	Algebraic Expression	Diagram

A number *divided by* five
One-*fifth* of a number $\dfrac{x}{5}$
The quotient of a number and five

Often other words are used in English instead of the word *number*. We can use a variable, such as x, here also.

EXAMPLE 1

English Phrase	Algebraic Expression
(a) A *quantity* is increased by five.	$x + 5$
(b) Double the *value*	$2x$
(c) One-third of the *weight*	$\dfrac{x}{3}$ or $\dfrac{1}{3}x$
(d) Twelve *more than* a number	$x + 12$
(e) Seven *less than* a number	$x - 7$

Note that the algebraic expression for "seven less than a number" does not follow the order of the words in the English phrase. The variable or expression that follows the words *less than* always comes first.

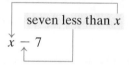

The variable or expression that follows the words *more than* technically comes before the plus sign. However, since addition is commutative, it also can be written after the plus sign.

Practice Problem 1   Write each English phrase as an algebraic expression.

(a) Four more than a number   **(b)** Triple a value

(c) Eight less than a number   **(d)** One-fourth of a height

NOTE TO STUDENT: *Fully worked-out solutions to all of the Practice Problems can be found at the back of the text starting at page SP-1*

More than one operation can be described in an English phrase. Sometimes parentheses must be used to make clear which operation is done first.

EXAMPLE 2

English Phrase	Algebraic Expression
(a) Seven more than double a number	$2x + 7$ *Note that these are **not** the same.*
(b) The value of the number is increased by seven and then doubled.	$2(x + 7)$ *Note that the word **then** tells us to add x and 7 before doubling.*
(c) One-half of the sum of a number and 3	$\dfrac{1}{2}(x + 3)$

Practice Problem 2 Write each English phrase as an algebraic expression.

(a) Eight more than triple a number

(b) A number is increased by eight and then it is tripled.

(c) One-third of the sum of a number and 4

② Writing an Algebraic Expression to Compare Two or More Quantities

Often in a word problem two or more quantities are described in terms of another. We will want to use a variable to represent one quantity and then write an algebraic expression using *the same variable* to represent the other quantity. Which quantity should we let the variable represent? We usually let the variable represent the quantity that is the basis of comparison: the quantity that the others are being *compared to*.

EXAMPLE 3 Use a variable and an algebraic expression to describe the two quantities in the English sentence "Mike's salary is $2000 more than Fred's salary."

Solution The two quantities that are being compared are Mike's salary and Fred's salary. Since Mike's salary is being *compared to* Fred's salary, we let the variable represent Fred's salary. The choice of the letter f helps us to remember that the variable represents Fred's salary.

$$\text{Let } f = \text{Fred's salary.}$$

Then $f + \$2000 = $ Mike's salary. *Since Mike's salary is $2000 more than Fred's.*

Practice Problem 3 Use a variable and an algebraic expression to describe the two quantities in the English sentence "Marie works 17 hours per week less than Ann."

NOTE TO STUDENT: Fully worked-out solutions to all of the Practice Problems can be found at the back of the text starting at page SP-1

EXAMPLE 4 The length of a rectangle is 3 meters shorter than twice the width. Use a variable and an algebraic expression to describe the length and the width. Draw a picture of the rectangle and label the length and width.

Solution The length of the rectangle is being *compared to* the width. Use the letter w for width.

$$\text{Let } w = \text{the width.}$$

$$\underbrace{\text{3 meters shorter than twice the width}}$$

$$\text{Then } 2w - 3 = \text{the length.}$$

A picture of the rectangle is shown.

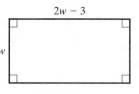

Practice Problem 4 The length of a rectangle is 5 meters longer than double the width. Use a variable and an algebraic expression to describe the length and the width. Draw a picture of the rectangle and label the length and width.

EXAMPLE 5   The first angle of a triangle is triple the second angle. The third angle of a triangle is 12° more than the second angle. Describe each angle algebraically. Draw a diagram of the triangle and label its parts.

Solution   Since the first and third angles are described in terms of the second angle, we let the variable represent the number of degrees in the second angle.

Let s = the number of degrees in the second angle.

Then $3s$ = the number of degrees in the first angle.

And $s + 12$ = the number of degrees in the third angle.

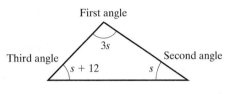

First angle

$3s$

Third angle

Second angle

$s + 12$

s

Practice Problem 5   The first angle of a triangle is 16° less than the second angle. The third angle is double the second angle. Describe each angle algebraically. Draw a diagram of the triangle and label its parts.

Some comparisons will involve fractions.

EXAMPLE 6   A theater manager was examining the records of attendance for last year. The number of people attending the theater in January was one-half of the number of people attending the theater in February. The number of people attending the theater in March was three-fifths of the number of people attending the theater in February. Use algebra to describe the attendance each month.

Solution   What are we looking for? The *number of people* who attended the theater *each month*. The basis of comparison is February. That is where we begin.

Let f = the number of people who attended in February.

Then $\dfrac{1}{2}f$ = the number of people who attended in January.

And $\dfrac{3}{5}f$ = the number of people who attended in March.

Practice Problem 6   The college dean noticed that in the spring the number of students on campus was two-thirds of the number of students on campus in the fall. She also noticed that in the summer the number of students on campus was one-fifth the number of students on campus in the fall. Use algebra to describe the number of students on campus in each of these three time periods.

Student Solutions Manual   CD/ Video   PH Math Tutor Center   MathXL®Tutorials on CD   MathXL®   MyMathLab®   Interactmath.com

Verbal and Writing Skills

Write an algebraic expression for each quantity. Let x represent the unknown value.

1. a quantity increased by 5

2. nine greater than a number

3. six fewer than a quantity

4. a value decreased by seven

5. one-eighth of a quantity

6. one-half of a quantity

7. twice a quantity

8. triple a number

9. three more than half of a number

10. five more than one-third of a number

11. double a quantity increased by nine

12. six times a number increased by eight

13. one-third of the sum of a number and seven

14. one-fourth of the sum of a number and 5

15. one-third of a number reduced by twice the same number

16. one-fifth of a number reduced by double the same number

17. seven less than triple a number

18. four less than seven times a number

Write an algebraic expression for each of the quantities being compared.

19. *Stock Value* The value of a share of IBM stock on that day was $74.50 more than the value of a share of AT&T stock.

20. *Investments* The annual income from Dr. Smith's mutual fund was $833 less than the annual income from her retirement fund.

▲ **21.** *Geometry* The length of the rectangle is 7 inches more than double the width.

▲ **22.** *Geometry* The length of the rectangle is 3 meters more than triple the width.

23. *Cookie Sales* The number of boxes of cookies sold by Sarah was 43 fewer than the number of boxes of cookies sold by Keiko. The number of boxes of cookies sold by Imelda was 53 more than the number sold by Keiko.

24. *Fish Catch* The number of pounds of fish caught by Captain Jack was 813 pounds more than the amount of fish caught by Captain Sally. The amount of fish caught by Captain Ben was 623 pounds less than the amount of fish caught by Captain Sally.

▲ **25.** *Geometry* The first angle of a triangle is 16 degrees less than the second angle. The third angle of a triangle is double the second angle.

▲ **26.** *Geometry* The first angle of a triangle is 19 degrees more than the third angle. The second angle is triple the third angle.

27. *Exports* The value of the exports of Japan was twice the value of the exports of Canada.

28. *Olympic Medals* Mark Spitz won two more Olympic medals than Carl Lewis did.

▲ **29. *Geometry*** The first angle of a triangle is triple the second angle. The third angle of a triangle is 14 degrees less than the second angle.

30. *Book Cost* The cost of Hiro's biology book was $13 more than the cost of his history book. The cost of his English book was $27 less than the cost of his history book.

Applications

Use algebra to describe the situation.

31. *Land Area* Kentucky has about half the land area of Minnesota. The land area of Maine is approximately two-fifths the land area of Minnesota. Describe the land area of each of these three states.

32. *Middle School Population* A census of El Cerrito Middle School found that the number of seventh graders was fifty more than the number of eighth graders. The number of sixth graders was three-fourths the number of eighth graders. Describe the population of each grade.

33. *Archery* In an archery tournament, the number of points awarded for an arrow in the gold circle (bull's eye) is six less than triple the points awarded for an arrow in the blue ring. Write an expression for each of these scores in an archery tournament.

34. *Orbital Times* The orbital time of Pluto is 82 years less than double the orbital time of Neptune.

To Think About

Kayak Rentals *The following bar graph depicts the number of people renting sea kayaks at Essex Boat Rental during July 2004. Use the bar graph to answer exercises 35 and 36.*

35. Write an expression for the number of men who rent Sea Kayaks at Essex Boat Rental in each age category. Start by using x for the number of men aged 16 to 24 who rented kayaks.

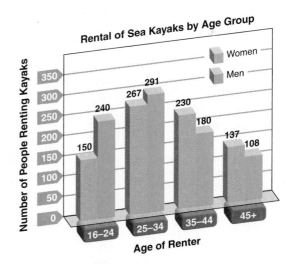

36. Write an expression for the number of women who rent Sea Kayaks at Essex Boat Rental. Start by using y for the number of women aged 35 to 44 who rented kayaks.

Cumulative Review

Solve for the variable.

37. $x + \dfrac{1}{2}(x - 3) = 9$

38. $\dfrac{3}{5}x - 3(x - 1) = 9$

39. $5(x - 8) = 13 + x - 5$

40. $6(w - 1) - 3(2 + w) = 9$

Student Learning Objectives

After studying this section, you will be able to:

1 Interpret inequality statements.

2 Graph an inequality on a number line.

3 Translate English phrases into algebraic statements

4 Solve and graph an inequality

1 Interpreting Inequality Statements

We frequently speak of one value being greater than or less than another value. We say that "5 is less than 7" or "9 is greater than 4." These relationships are called **inequalities.** We can write inequalities in mathematics by using symbols. We use the symbol < to represent the words "**is less than.**" We use the symbol > to represent the words "**is greater than.**"

Statement in Words	Statement in Algebra
5 is less than 7.	$5 < 7$
9 is greater than 4.	$9 > 4$

Note: "5 is less than 7" and "7 is greater than 5" have the same meaning. Similarly, $5 < 7$ and $7 > 5$ have the same meaning. They represent two equivalent ways of describing the same relationship between the two numbers 5 and 7.

We can better understand the concept of inequality if we examine a number line.

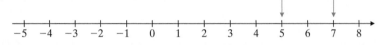

We say that one number is greater than another if it is to the right of the other on the number line. Thus $7 > 5$, since 7 is to the right of 5.

What about negative numbers? We can say "-1 is greater than -3" and write it in symbols as $-1 > -3$ because we know that -1 lies to the right of -3 on the number line.

EXAMPLE 1 In each statement, replace the question mark with the symbol < or >.

(a) $3 ? -1$ **(b)** $-2 ? 1$ **(c)** $-3 ? -4$ **(d)** $0 ? 3$ **(e)** $-3 ? 0$

Solution

(a) $3 > -1$ Use >, since 3 is to the right of -1 on the number line.

(b) $-2 < 1$ Use <, since -2 is to the left of 1. (Or equivalently, we could say that 1 is to the right of -2.)

(c) $-3 > -4$ Note that -3 is to the right of -4.

(d) $0 < 3$

(e) $-3 < 0$

Practice Problem 1 In each statement, replace the question mark with the symbol < or >.

(a) $7 ? 2$ **(b)** $-3 ? -4$ **(c)** $-1 ? 2$ **(d)** $-8 ? -5$ **(e)** $0 ? -2$ **(f)** $\dfrac{2}{5} ? \dfrac{3}{8}$

NOTE TO STUDENT: Fully worked-out solutions to all of the Practice Problems can be found at the back of the text starting at page SP-1

2 Graphing an Inequality on a Number Line

Sometimes we will use an inequality to express the relationship between a variable and a number. $x > 3$ means that x could have the value of *any number* greater than 3.

Any number that makes an inequality true is called a **solution** of the inequality. The set of all numbers that make the inequality true is called the **solution set.** A picture that represents all of the solutions of an inequality is called a **graph** of the inequality.

The inequality $x > 3$ can be graphed on the number line as follows:

Case 1

Note that all of the points to the right of 3 are shaded. The open circle at 3 indicates that we do not include the point for the number 3.

Sometimes a variable will be either less than or equal to a certain number. In the statement "x is less than or equal to -2," we are implying that x could have the value of -2 or any number less than -2. We write this as $x \leq -2$. We graph it as follows:

Case 2

The closed circle at -2 indicates that we *do* include the point for the number -2. *Note*: Be careful you do not confuse $\circ\!\!\longrightarrow$ with $\bullet\!\!\longrightarrow$. It is important to decide if you need an open circle or a closed one. Case 1 uses an open circle and Case 2 uses a closed circle.

EXAMPLE 2   State each mathematical relationship in words and then graph it.

(a) $x < -2$ **(b)** $x \geq -2$ **(c)** $-3 < x$ **(d)** $x \leq -6$

Solution

(a) We state that "x is less than -2."

$x < -2$

(b) We state that "x is greater than or equal to -2."

$x \geq -2$

(c) We can state that "-3 is less than x" or, equivalently, that "x is greater than -3." Be sure you see that $-3 < x$ is equivalent to $x > -3$. Although both statements are correct, we *usually write the variable first* in a simple inequality containing a variable and a numerical value.

$x > -3$

(d) We state that "x is less than or equal to -6."

$x \leq -6$

Practice Problem 2   State each mathematical relationship in words and then graph it on a number line in the margin.

(a) $x > 5$

(b) $x \leq -2$

(c) $3 > x$

(d) $x \geq -\dfrac{3}{2}$

NOTE TO STUDENT: Fully worked-out solutions to all of the Practice Problems can be found at the back of the text starting at page SP-1

TO THINK ABOUT: Comparing Results   What is the difference between the graphs in Example 2(a), 2(b), and Case 2 above? Why are these graphs different?

3 Translating English Phrases into Algebraic Statements

We can translate many everyday situations into algebraic statements with an unknown value and an inequality symbol. This is the first step in solving word problems using inequalities.

EXAMPLE 3   Translate each English statement into an algebraic statement.

(a) The police on the scene said that the car was traveling more than 80 miles per hour. (Use the variable s for speed.)

(b) The owner of the trucking company said that the payload of a truck must never exceed 4500 pounds. (Use the variable p for payload.)

Solution

(a) Since the speed must be greater than 80, we have $s > 80$.

(b) If the payload of the truck can never exceed 4500 pounds, then the payload must be always less than or equal to 4500 pounds. Thus we write $p \leq 4500$.

Practice Problem 3   Translate each English statement into an inequality.

(a) During the drying cycle, the temperature inside the clothes dryer must never exceed 180 degrees Fahrenheit. (Use the variable t for temperature.)

(b) The bank loan officer said that the total consumer debt incurred by Wally and Mary must be less than $15,000 if they want to qualify for a mortgage to buy their first home. (Use the variable d for debt.)

---

4 Solving and Graphing Inequalities on a Number Line

When we **solve an inequality,** we are finding *all* the values that make it true. To solve an inequality, we simplify it to the point where we can clearly see all possible values for the variable. We've solved equations by adding, subtracting, multiplying by, and dividing by a particular value on both sides of the equation. Here we perform similar operations with inequalities with one important exception. We'll show some examples so that you can see how these operations can be used with inequalities just as with equations.

We will first examine the pattern that occurs when we perform these operations *with a positive value* on both sides of an inequality.

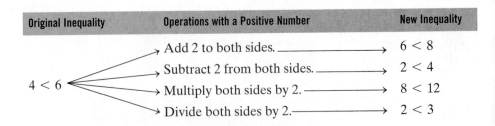

Original Inequality	Operations with a Positive Number	New Inequality
4 < 6	Add 2 to both sides.	6 < 8
	Subtract 2 from both sides.	2 < 4
	Multiply both sides by 2.	8 < 12
	Divide both sides by 2.	2 < 3

Notice that the inequality symbol remains the same when these operations are performed with a positive value.

Now let us examine what happens when we perform these operations *with a negative value.*

Original Inequality	Operations with a Negative Number	New Inequality
4 < 6	Add −2 to both sides.	2 < 4
	Subtract −2 from both sides.	6 < 8
	Multiply both sides by −2.	−8 ? −12
	Divide both sides by −2.	−2 ? −3

What happens to the inequality sign when we multiply both sides by a negative number? Since −8 is to the right of −12 on the number line, we know that the new inequality should be −8 > −12 if we want the statement to remain true. Notice how we reverse the direction of the inequality from < (less than) to > (greater than) when we multiply by a negative value. Thus we have the following.

$$4 < 6 \longrightarrow \text{ Multiply both sides by } -2. \longrightarrow -8 > -12$$

The same thing happens when we divide by a negative number. The inequality is reversed from < to >. We know this since −2 is to the right of −3 on the number line.

$$4 < 6 \longrightarrow \text{ Divide both sides by } -2. \longrightarrow -2 > -3$$

Similar reversals take place in the next example.

EXAMPLE 4 Perform the given operations and write the new inequalities.

Original Inequality		New Inequality
(a) −2 < −1 ⟶	Multiply both sides by −3. ⟶	6 > 3
(b) 0 > −4 ⟶	Divide both sides by −2. ⟶	0 < 2
(c) 8 ≥ 4 ⟶	Divide both sides by −4. ⟶	−2 ≤ −1

Notice that we perform the arithmetic with signed numbers just as we always do. But the new inequality signs reversed (from those of the original inequalities). *Whenever both sides of an inequality are multiplied or divided by a negative quantity, the direction of the inequality is reversed.*

Practice Problem 4 Perform the given operations and write the new inequalities.

(a) 7 > 2   Multiply each side by −2.
(b) −3 < −1   Multiply each side by −1.
(c) −10 ≥ −20   Divide each side by −10.
(d) −15 ≤ −5   Divide each side by −5.

NOTE TO STUDENT: Fully worked-out solutions to all of the Practice Problems can be found at the back of the text starting at page SP-1

PROCEDURE FOR SOLVING INEQUALITIES

You may use the same procedures to solve inequalities that you did to solve equations *except* that the direction of an inequality is *reversed* if you *multiply* or *divide* both sides *by a negative number.*

It may be helpful to think over quickly what we have discussed here. The inequalities remain the same when we add a number to both sides or subtract a number from both sides of the equation. The inequalities remain the same when we multiply both sides by a positive number or divide both sides by a positive number.

However, if we *multiply* both sides of an inequality by a *negative number* or if we *divide* both sides of an inequality by a *negative number,* then *the inequality is reversed.*

EXAMPLE 5 Solve and graph $3x + 7 \geq 13$.

Solution

$3x + 7 - 7 \geq 13 - 7$ Subtract 7 from both sides.

$\qquad 3x \geq 6$ Simplify.

$\qquad \dfrac{3x}{3} \geq \dfrac{6}{3}$ Divide both sides by 3.

$\qquad x \geq 2$ Simplify. Note that the direction of the inequality is not changed, since we have divided by a positive number.

The graph is as follows:

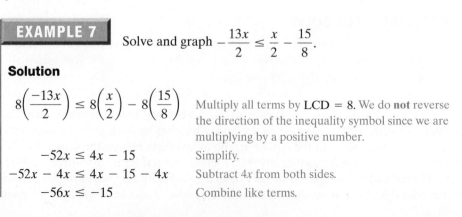

Practice Problem 5 Solve and graph $8x - 2 < 3$.

EXAMPLE 6 Solve and graph $5 - 3x > 7$.

Solution

$5 - 5 - 3x > 7 - 5$ Subtract 5 from both sides.

$\qquad -3x > 2$ Simplify.

$\qquad \dfrac{-3x}{-3} < \dfrac{2}{-3}$ Divide by -3 and **reverse the inequality** since you are dividing by a negative number.

$\qquad x < -\dfrac{2}{3}$ Note the direction of the inequality.

The graph is as follows:

Practice Problem 6 Solve and graph $4 - 5x > 7$.

Just like equations, some inequalities contain parentheses and fractions. The initial steps to solve these inequalities will be the same as those used to solve equations with parentheses and fractions. When the variable appears on both sides of the inequality, it is advisable to collect the x-terms on the left side of the inequality symbol.

EXAMPLE 7 Solve and graph $-\dfrac{13x}{2} \leq \dfrac{x}{2} - \dfrac{15}{8}$.

Solution

$8\left(\dfrac{-13x}{2}\right) \leq 8\left(\dfrac{x}{2}\right) - 8\left(\dfrac{15}{8}\right)$ Multiply all terms by LCD $= 8$. We do **not** reverse the direction of the inequality symbol since we are multiplying by a positive number.

$-52x \leq 4x - 15$ Simplify.

$-52x - 4x \leq 4x - 15 - 4x$ Subtract $4x$ from both sides.

$-56x \leq -15$ Combine like terms.

$$\frac{-56x}{-56} \geq \frac{-15}{-56}$$

Divide both sides by −56. We **reverse** the direction of the inequality when we divide both sides by a negative number.

$$x \geq \frac{15}{56}$$

The graph is as follows:

Practice Problem 7   Solve and graph $\frac{1}{2}x + 3 < \frac{2}{3}x$.

NOTE TO STUDENT: Fully worked-out solutions to all of the Practice Problems can be found at the back of the text starting at page SP-1

EXAMPLE 8   Solve and graph $\frac{1}{3}(3 - 2x) \leq -4(x + 1)$.

Solution

$$1 - \frac{2x}{3} \leq -4x - 4$$ Remove parentheses.

$$3(1) - 3\left(\frac{2x}{3}\right) \leq 3(-4x) - 3(4)$$ Multiply all terms by **LCD** = 3.

$$3 - 2x \leq -12x - 12$$ Simplify.

$$3 - 2x + 12x \leq -12x + 12x - 12$$ Add 12x to both sides.

$$3 + 10x \leq -12$$ Combine like terms.

$$3 - 3 + 10x \leq -12 - 3$$ Subtract 3 from both sides.

$$10x \leq -15$$ Simplify.

$$\frac{10x}{10} \leq \frac{-15}{10}$$ Divide both sides by 10. Since we are dividing by a **positive** number, the inequality is **not** reversed.

$$x \leq -\frac{3}{2}$$

The graph is as follows:

Practice Problem 8   Solve and graph $\frac{1}{2}(3 - x) \leq 2x + 5$.

CAUTION The most common error students make in solving inequalities is forgetting to reverse the direction of the inequality symbol when multiplying or dividing both sides of the inequality by a negative number.

Normally when you solve inequalities you solve for x by putting the variables on the left side. If you solve by placing the variables on the right side, you will end up with statements like $3 > x$. This is equivalent to $x < 3$. It is wise to express your answer with the variable on the left side.

EXAMPLE 9   A hospital director has determined that the costs of operating one floor of the hospital for an eight-hour shift must never exceed $2370. An expression for the cost of operating one floor of the hospital is $130n + 1200$, where n is the number of nurses. This expression is based on an estimate of $1200 in fixed costs and a cost of $130 per nurse for an eight-hour shift. Solve the inequality $130n + 1200 \leq 2370$ to determine the number of nurses that may be on duty on this floor during an eight-hour shift if the director's cost control measure is to be followed.

Solution

$$130n + 1200 \leq 2370 \qquad \text{The inequality we must solve.}$$

$$130n + 1200 - 1200 \leq 2370 - 1200 \qquad \text{Subtract 1200 from each side.}$$

$$130n \leq 1170 \qquad \text{Simplify.}$$

$$\frac{130n}{130} \leq \frac{1170}{130} \qquad \text{Divide each side by 130.}$$

$$n \leq 9$$

The number of nurses on duty on this floor during an eight-hour shift must always be less than or equal to nine.

Practice Problem 9   The company president of Staywell, Inc., wants the monthly profits never to be less than $2,500,000. He has determined that an expression for monthly profit for the company is $2000n - 700,000$. In the expression, n is the number of exercise machines manufactured each month. The profit on each machine is $2000, and the $-$700,000 in the expression represents the fixed costs of running the manufacturing division.

Solve the inequality $2000n - 700,000 \geq 2,500,000$ to find how many machines must be made and sold each month to satisfy these financial goals.

Developing Your Study Skills

Getting Organized for an Exam

Studying adequately for an exam requires careful preparation. Begin early so that you will be able to spread your review over several days. Even though you may still be learning new material at this time, you can be reviewing concepts previously learned in the chapter. Giving yourself plenty of time for review will take the pressure off. You need this time to process what you have learned and to tie concepts together.

Adequate preparation enables you to feel confident and to think clearly with less tension and anxiety.

3.6 EXERCISES

Student Solutions Manual | CD/Video | PH Math Tutor Center | MathXL®Tutorials on CD | MathXL® | MyMathLab® | Interactmath.com

Verbal and Writing Skills

1. Is the statement $5 > -6$ equivalent to the statement $-6 < 5$? Why?

2. Is the statement $-8 < -3$ equivalent to the statement $-3 > -8$? Why?

Replace the ? by $<$ or $>$.

3. $9 ? -3$

4. $-2 ? 5$

5. $0 ? -8$

6. $-9 ? 0$

7. $-4 ? -2$

8. $-3 ? -6$

9. (a) $-7 ? 2$
(b) $2 ? -7$

10. (a) $-5 ? 11$
(b) $11 ? -5$

11. (a) $15 ? -15$
(b) $-15 ? 15$

12. (a) $-17 ? 17$
(b) $17 ? -17$

13. $\dfrac{3}{5} ? \dfrac{4}{7}$

14. $\dfrac{4}{6} ? \dfrac{7}{9}$

15. $\dfrac{7}{8} ? \dfrac{25}{31}$

16. $\dfrac{9}{11} ? \dfrac{41}{53}$

17. $-6.6 ? -8.9$

18. $-4.2 ? -7.3$

19. $-4.2 ? 3.5$

20. $-2.6 ? 7.5$

21. $-\dfrac{13}{3} ? -4$

22. $-3 ? -\dfrac{15}{4}$

23. $-\dfrac{5}{8} ? -\dfrac{3}{5}$

24. $-\dfrac{2}{3} ? -\dfrac{3}{4}$

Graph each inequality on the number line.

25. $x > 7$

26. $x < 1$

27. $x \geq -6$

28. $x \leq -2$

29. $x > \dfrac{3}{4}$

30. $x \geq -\dfrac{5}{2}$

31. $x \leq -5.3$

32. $x > -3.5$

33. $25 < x$

34. $35 \geq x$

Translate each graph to an inequality using the variable x.

35.

36.

37.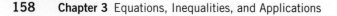

38.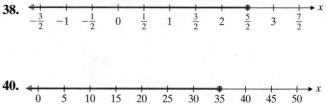

39.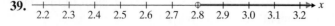

40.

Translate each English statement into an inequality.

41. *Weight Category* To box in the heavyweight category, your weight must be greater than 175 pounds. (Use the variable W for weight.)

42. *Cloud Formation* Cirrus clouds form more than 16,500 feet above the earth's surface. (Use the variable C for distance above the earth.)

43. *Full-Time Work* The number of hours for a full-time position at this company cannot be less than 37 in order to receive full-time benefits. (Use the variable h for hours.)

44. *Nurses on Duty* The number of nurses on duty on the floor can never exceed 6. (Use the variable n for the number of nurses.)

To Think About Exercises 45–46

45. Suppose that the variable x must satisfy *all* of these conditions.

$$x \le 2, \quad x > -3, \quad x < \frac{5}{2}, \quad x \ge -\frac{5}{2}$$

Graph on a number line the region that satisfies all of the conditions.

46. Suppose that the variable x must satisfy *all* of these conditions.

$$x < 4, \quad x > -4, \quad x \le \frac{7}{2}, \quad x \ge -\frac{9}{2}$$

Graph on a number line the region that satisfies all of the conditions.

Solve and graph the result.

47. $x + 7 \le 4$

48. $x - 5 < -3$

49. $5x \le 25$

50. $7x \ge -35$

51. $-2x < 18$

52. $-6x > 24$

53. $\frac{1}{2}x \ge 4$

54. $\frac{1}{3}x \le 2$

55. $-\dfrac{1}{4}x > 3$

56. $-\dfrac{1}{5}x < 10$

57. $5 - 2x \le 9$

58. $3 - 3x > 12$

59. $-4 + 5x < -3x + 8$

60. $-6 - 4x < 1 - 6x$

61. $\dfrac{5x}{6} - 5 > \dfrac{x}{6} - 9$

62. $\dfrac{x}{4} - 2 < \dfrac{3x}{4} + 5$

63. $2(3x + 4) > 3(x + 3)$

64. $5(x - 3) \le 2(x - 3)$

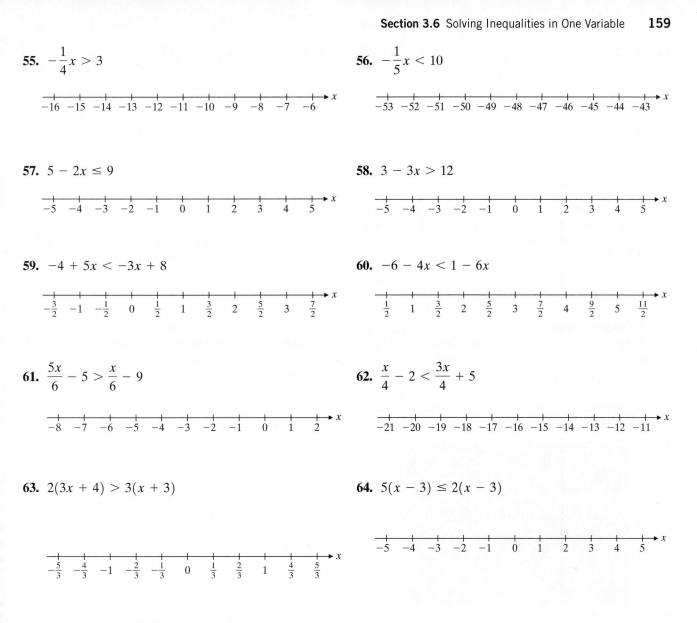

Verbal and Writing Skills

65. Add -2 to both sides of the inequality $5 > 3$. What is the result? Why is the direction of the inequality not reversed?

66. Divide -3 into both sides of the inequality $-21 > -29$. What is the result? Why is the direction of the inequality reversed?

Mixed Practice

Solve. Collect the variable terms on the left side of the inequality.

67. $3x + 8 < 7x - 4$ **68.** $7x + 3 > 9x - 5$ **69.** $6x - 2 \ge 4x + 6$ **70.** $5x - 5 \le 2x + 10$

71. $0.3(x - 1) < 0.1x - 0.5$ **72.** $0.2(3 - x) + 0.1 > 0.1(x - 2)$ **73.** $3 + 5(2 - x) \ge -3(x + 5)$

74. $7 - 2(x - 4) \leq 7(x - 3)$

75. $\dfrac{x + 6}{7} - \dfrac{6}{14} > \dfrac{x + 3}{2}$

76. $\dfrac{3x + 5}{4} + \dfrac{7}{12} > -\dfrac{x}{6}$

Applications

77. ***Course Average*** To pass a course with a B grade, a student must have an average of 80 or greater. A student's grades on three tests are 75, 83, and 86. Solve the inequality $\dfrac{75 + 83 + 86 + x}{4} \geq 80$ to find what score the student must get on the next test to get a B average or better.

78. ***Payment Options*** Sharon sells very expensive European sports cars. She may choose to receive $10,000.00 or 8% of her sales as payment for her work. Solve the inequality $0.08x > 10,000$ to find how much she needs to sell to make the 8% offer a better deal.

79. ***Elephant Weight*** The average African elephant weighs 268 pounds at birth. During the first three weeks of life the baby elephant will usually gain about 4 pounds per day. Assuming that growth rate, solve the inequality $268 + 4x \geq 300$ to find how many days it will be until a baby elephant weighs at least 300 pounds.

80. ***Car Loan*** Rennie is buying a used car that costs $4500. The deal called for a $600 down payment, and payments of $260 monthly. He wants to know whether he can pay off the car within a year. Solve the inequality $600 + 260x \geq 4500$ to find out the minimum number of months it will take to pay off the car.

Cumulative Review

81. Find 16% of 38.

82. 18 is what percent of 120?

83. ***Percent Accepted*** For the most coveted graduate study positions, only 16 out of 800 students are accepted. What percent are accepted?

84. Write the fraction $\frac{3}{8}$ as a percent.

▲ **85.** ***Tennis Court Fence*** A rectangular tennis court measures 36 feet wide and 78 feet long. Robert is building a fence to surround the tennis court. He wants the fence to be 4 feet from each side of the court. How many feet of fence will he need?

▲ **86.** ***Photo Enlargement*** Jemma has a job with the school newspaper. She has taken a picture with the dimensions 3" high by 5" wide. The editor likes the picture, but the available space is 30% wider and 20% higher than the picture Jemma took. What dimensions must Jemma enlarge the picture to?

Putting Your Skills to Work

Gasoline Consumption on a 27-Foot Outboard

Frank and his father have a 27-foot outboard sport fishing boat that they charter for part of the year. The boat can be equipped with either two 225-horsepower outboard motors or one 250-horsepower outboard motor. They tested the consumption of gasoline per hour at various speeds for each choice of motor and made the following chart.

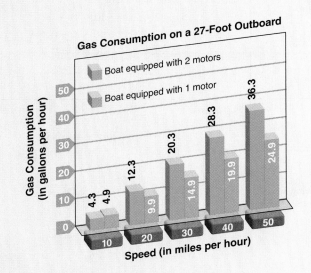

Problems for Individual Study and Analysis

1. How many more gallons per hour does the boat use at 40 miles per hour if it is equipped with two 225-horsepower outboard motors rather than one 250-horsepower motor?

2. If the boat is used for 30 hours of fishing per week and the usual cruising speed is 40 miles per hour, how many more gallons per week will be consumed if the boat is equipped with two 225-horsepower outboard motors rather than one 250-horsepower motor?

Problems for Group Investigation and Cooperative Learning

For the boat equipped with two 225-horsepower outboard motors the rate of gasoline consumption in gallons per hour (y) can be approximated from knowing the speed in miles per hour (x) using the equation $y = 0.8x - 3.7$. Use this equation for problems 3 and 4.

3. How many gallons per hour are consumed if the boat travels at 45 miles per hour?

4. If the boat is consuming 40.3 gallons per hour, how fast is the boat traveling?

For the boat equipped with one 250-horsepower outboard motor the rate of gasoline consumption in gallons per hour (y) can be approximated from knowing the speed in miles per hour (x) using the equation $y = 0.5x - 0.1$. Use this equation for problems 5 and 6.

5. Solve the above equation for x.

6. Use the result of problem 5 to find how many miles per hour the boat is traveling if it is consuming 17.4 gallons per hour.

Topic	Procedure	Examples
Solving equations without parentheses or fractions, p. 128.	1. On each side of the equation, combine like terms if possible. 2. Add or subtract terms on both sides of the equation in order to get all terms with the variable on one side of the equation. 3. Add or subtract a value on both sides of the equation to get all terms not containing the variable on the other side of the equation. 4. Divide both sides of the equation by the coefficient of the variable. 5. If possible, simplify the solution. 6. Check your solution by substituting the obtained value into the original equation.	Solve for x. $$5x + 2 + 2x = -10 + 4x + 3$$ $$7x + 2 = -7 + 4x$$ $$7x - 4x + 2 = -7 + 4x - 4x$$ $$3x + 2 = -7$$ $$3x + 2 - 2 = -7 - 2$$ $$3x = -9$$ $$\frac{3x}{3} = \frac{-9}{3}$$ $$x = -3$$ *Check:* Is -3 the solution of $$5x + 2 + 2x = -10 + 4x + 3?$$ $$5(-3) + 2 + 2(-3) \stackrel{?}{=} -10 + 4(-3) + 3$$ $$-15 + 2 - 6 \stackrel{?}{=} -10 + (-12) + 3$$ $$-13 - 6 \stackrel{?}{=} -22 + 3$$ $$-19 = -19 \ \checkmark$$
Solving equations with parentheses and/or fractions, p. 130 and p. 135.	1. Remove any parentheses. 2. Simplify, if possible. 3. If fractions exist, multiply all terms on both sides by the least common denominator of all the fractions. 4. Now follow the remaining steps for solving an equation without parentheses or fractions.	Solve for y. $$5(3y - 4) = \frac{1}{4}(6y + 4) - 48$$ $$15y - 20 = \frac{3}{2}y + 1 - 48$$ $$15y - 20 = \frac{3}{2}y - 47$$ $$2(15y) - 2(20) = 2\left(\frac{3}{2}y\right) - 2(47)$$ $$30y - 40 = 3y - 94$$ $$30y - 3y - 40 = 3y - 3y - 94$$ $$27y - 40 = -94$$ $$27y - 40 + 40 = -94 + 40$$ $$27y = -54$$ $$\frac{27y}{27} = \frac{-54}{27}$$ $$y = -2$$

Procedure for Solving Applied Problems

1. **Understand the problem.**
   (a) Read the word problem carefully to get an overview.
   (b) Determine what information you will need to solve the problem.
   (c) Draw a sketch. Label it with the known information. Determine what needs to be found.
   (d) Choose a variable to represent one unknown quantity.
   (e) If necessary, represent other unknown quantities in terms of that same variable.

2. **Write an equation.**
   (a) Look for key words to help you to translate the words into algebraic symbols.
   (b) Use a given relationship in the problem or an appropriate formula in order to write an equation.

3. **Solve and state the answer.**

4. **Check.**
   (a) Check the solution in the original equation. Is the answer reasonable?
   (b) Be sure the solution to the equation answers the question in the word problem. You may need to do some additional calculations if it does not.

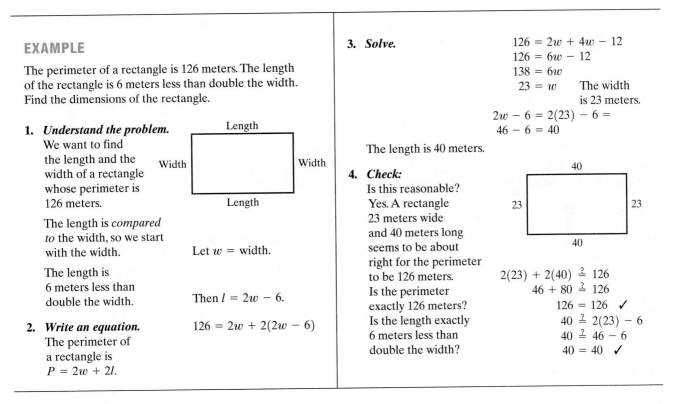

EXAMPLE

The perimeter of a rectangle is 126 meters. The length of the rectangle is 6 meters less than double the width. Find the dimensions of the rectangle.

1. **Understand the problem.**
   We want to find the length and the width of a rectangle whose perimeter is 126 meters.

   The length is *compared to* the width, so we start with the width.

   Let w = width.

   The length is 6 meters less than double the width.

   Then $l = 2w - 6$.

2. **Write an equation.**
   The perimeter of a rectangle is $P = 2w + 2l$.

   $126 = 2w + 2(2w - 6)$

3. **Solve.**

   $$126 = 2w + 4w - 12$$
   $$126 = 6w - 12$$
   $$138 = 6w$$
   $$23 = w \quad \text{The width is 23 meters.}$$

   $$2w - 6 = 2(23) - 6 =$$
   $$46 - 6 = 40$$

   The length is 40 meters.

4. **Check:**
   Is this reasonable?
   Yes. A rectangle 23 meters wide and 40 meters long seems to be about right for the perimeter to be 126 meters.
   Is the perimeter exactly 126 meters?
   Is the length exactly 6 meters less than double the width?

   $$2(23) + 2(40) \overset{?}{=} 126$$
   $$46 + 80 \overset{?}{=} 126$$
   $$126 = 126 \ \checkmark$$
   $$40 \overset{?}{=} 2(23) - 6$$
   $$40 \overset{?}{=} 46 - 6$$
   $$40 = 40 \ \checkmark$$

Topic	Procedure	Examples
Solving inequalities, p. 153.	1. Follow the steps for solving an equation. 2. If you divide or multiply both sides of the inequality by a *positive number*, the **direction** of the inequality **is not reversed.** 3. If you divide or multiply both sides of the inequality by a *negative number*, the **direction** of the inequality **is reversed.**	Solve for x and graph your solution. $$\frac{1}{2}(3x - 2) \le -5 + 5x - 3$$ First remove parentheses and simplify. $$\frac{3}{2}x - 1 \le -8 + 5x$$ Now multiply each term by 2. $$2\left(\frac{3}{2}x\right) - 2(1) \le 2(-8) + 2(5x)$$ $$3x - 2 \le -16 + 10x$$ $$3x - 10x - 2 \le -16 + 10x - 10x$$ $$-7x - 2 \le -16$$ $$-7x - 2 + 2 \le -16 + 2$$ $$-7x \le -14$$ When we divide both sides by a negative number, the inequality is reversed. $$\frac{-7x}{-7} \ge \frac{-14}{-7}$$ $$x \ge 2$$ Graphical solution:

Chapter 3 Review Problems

Sections 3.1–3.3

Solve for the variable. Noninteger answers may be left in fractional form or decimal form.

1. $5x = -35$

2. $x - 19 = -22$

3. $6 - 18x = 4 - 17x$

4. $18 - 10x = 63 + 5x$

5. $x - (0.5x + 2.6) = 17.6$

6. $-0.2(x + 1) = 0.3(x + 11)$

7. $3(x - 2) = -4(5 + x)$

8. $\frac{2}{3}x = -18$

9. $\frac{3}{4}x = 15$

10. $4(2x + 3) = 5(x - 3)$

11. $3(x - 3) = 13x + 21$

12. $0.9x + 1.0 = 0.3x + 0.4$

13. $2.4 - 0.3x = 0.4(x - 1)$

14. $12 - 5x = -7x - 2$

15. $2(3 - x) = 1 - (x - 2)$

16. $4(x + 5) - 7 = 2(x + 3)$

17. $3 = 2x + 5 - 3(x - 1)$

18. $2(5x - 1) - 7 = 3(x - 1) + 5 - 4x$

Section 3.4

Solve for the variable. Noninteger answers may be left in fractional form or decimal form.

19. $\dfrac{3}{4}x - 3 = \dfrac{1}{2}x + 2$

20. $1 = \dfrac{5x}{6} + \dfrac{2x}{3}$

21. $\dfrac{7x}{5} = 5 + \dfrac{2x}{5}$

22. $\dfrac{7x - 3}{2} - 4 = \dfrac{5x + 1}{3}$

23. $\dfrac{3x - 2}{2} + \dfrac{x}{4} = 2 + x$

24. $\dfrac{-3}{2}(x + 5) = 1 - x$

25. $\dfrac{-4}{3}(2x + 1) = -x - 2$

26. $\dfrac{1}{3}(x - 2) = \dfrac{x}{4} + 2$

27. $\dfrac{1}{5}(x - 3) = 2 - \dfrac{x}{2}$

28. $\dfrac{4}{5} + \dfrac{1}{2}x = \dfrac{1}{5}x + \dfrac{1}{2}$

29. $2x - \dfrac{3}{4} + \dfrac{7}{2}x = \dfrac{1}{2}x + \dfrac{1}{4}$

30. $\dfrac{3}{2}x - \dfrac{5}{6} + x = \dfrac{1}{2}x + \dfrac{2}{3}$

31. $-\dfrac{8}{3}x - 8 + 2x - 5 = -\dfrac{5}{3}$

32. $\dfrac{1}{6} + \dfrac{1}{3}(x - 3) = \dfrac{1}{2}(x + 9)$

33. $\dfrac{1}{7}(x + 5) - \dfrac{6}{14} = \dfrac{1}{2}(x + 3)$

34. $\dfrac{1}{6}(8x + 3) = \dfrac{1}{2}(2x + 7)$

Section 3.5

Write an algebraic expression. Use the variable x to represent the unknown value.

35. 19 more than a number

36. two-thirds of a number

37. triple the sum of a number and 4

38. twice a number decreased by three

Write an expression for each of the quantities compared. Use the letter specified.

39. *Workforce* The number of working people is four times the number of retired people. The number of unemployed people is one-half the number of retired people. (Use the letter *r*.)

▲ **40. *Geometry*** The length of the rectangle is 5 meters more than triple the width. (Use the letter *w*.)

▲ **41. *Geometry*** A triangle has three angles *A*, *B*, and *C*. The number of degrees in angle *A* is double the number of degrees in angle *B*. The number of degrees in angle *C* is 17 degrees less than the number in angle *B*. (Use the letter *b*.)

42. *Class Size* There are 29 more students in biology class than in algebra. There are one-half as many students in geology class as in algebra. (Use the letter *a*.)

Section 3.6

Solve each inequality and graph the result.

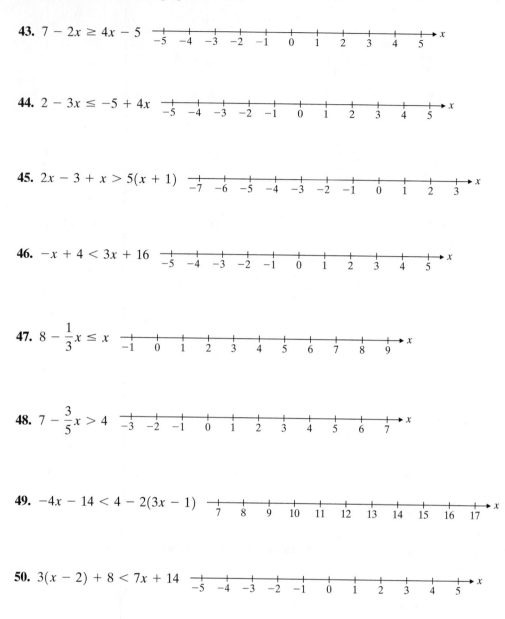

43. $7 - 2x \geq 4x - 5$

44. $2 - 3x \leq -5 + 4x$

45. $2x - 3 + x > 5(x + 1)$

46. $-x + 4 < 3x + 16$

47. $8 - \dfrac{1}{3}x \leq x$

48. $7 - \dfrac{3}{5}x > 4$

49. $-4x - 14 < 4 - 2(3x - 1)$

50. $3(x - 2) + 8 < 7x + 14$

Use an inequality to solve.

51. *Wages* Julian earns $15 per hour as a plasterer's assistant. His employer determines that the current job allows him to pay $480 in wages to Julian. What are the maximum number of hours that Julian can work on this job? (*Hint:* Use $15h \leq 480$.)

52. *Hiring a Temp* The cost of hiring a temporary secretary for a day is $85. Let $n =$ the number of temporary secretaries. Set up an inequality to determine how many times a temporary secretary may be hired if the company budget for temporary secretaries is $1445 per month. What is the maximum number of days a temporary secretary may be hired during the month? (*Hint:* Use $85n \leq 1445$.)

Mixed Practice

Solve for the variable. Noninteger answers may be left in fractional form or decimal form.

53. $8(3x + 5) - 10 = 9(x - 2) + 13$

54. $8 - 3x + 5 = 13 + 4x + 2$

55. $-2(x - 3) = -4x + 3(3x + 2)$

56. $\dfrac{1}{2} + \dfrac{5}{4}x = \dfrac{2}{5}x - \dfrac{1}{10} + 4$

57. $\dfrac{1}{6}x - \dfrac{2}{3} = \dfrac{1}{3}(x - 4)$

58. $\dfrac{1}{2}(x - 3) = \dfrac{1}{4}(3x - 1)$

Solve each inequality and graph the result.

59. $5 - \dfrac{1}{2}x > 4$

60. $2(x - 1) \geq 3(2 + x)$

61. $\dfrac{1}{3}(x + 2) \leq \dfrac{1}{2}(3x - 5)$

62. $4(2 - x) - (-5x + 1) \geq -8$

Solve for the variable. Noninteger answers may be left in fractional form or decimal form.

1.
2.
3.
4.
5.
6.
7.
8.
9.
10.
11.
12.
13.
14.
15.
16.
17.
18.
19.
20.
21.
22.
23.
24.

1. $3x + 5.6 = 11.6$

2. $9x - 8 = -6x - 3$

3. $2(2y - 3) = 4(2y + 2)$

4. $\frac{1}{7}y + 3 = \frac{1}{2}y$

5. $4(7 - 4x) = 3(6 - 2x)$

6. $0.8x + 0.18 - 0.4x = 0.3(x + 0.2)$

7. $\frac{2y}{3} + \frac{1}{5} - \frac{3y}{5} + \frac{1}{3} = 1$

8. $3 - 2y = 2(3y - 2) - 5y$

9. $5(20 - x) + 10x = 165$

10. $5(x + 40) - 6x = 9x$

11. $-2(2 - 3x) = 76 - 2x$

12. $20 - (2x + 6) = 5(2 - x) + 2x$

In questions 13–17, solve for x.

13. $2x - 3 = 12 - 6x + 3(2x + 3)$

14. $\frac{1}{3}x - \frac{3}{4}x = \frac{1}{12}$

15. $\frac{3}{5}x + \frac{7}{10} = \frac{1}{3}x + \frac{3}{2}$

16. $\frac{15x - 2}{28} = \frac{5x - 3}{7}$

17. $\frac{2}{3}(x + 8) + \frac{3}{5} = \frac{1}{5}(11 - 6x)$

Solve and graph the inequality.

18. $3(x - 2) \geq 5x$

19. $2 - 7(x + 1) - 5(x + 2) < 0$

20. $5 + 8x - 4 < 2x + 13$

21. $\frac{1}{4}x + \frac{1}{16} \leq \frac{1}{8}(7x - 2)$

Solve.

22. A number is doubled and then decreased by 11. The result is 59. What is the original number?

23. The sum of one-half of a number, one-ninth of the number, and one-twelfth of the number is twenty-five. Find the original number.

24. Double the sum of a number and 5 is the same as fourteen more than triple the same number. Find the number.

▲ **25.** A triangular region has a perimeter of 66 meters. The first side is two-thirds of the second side. The third side is 14 meters shorter than the second side. What are the lengths of the three sides of the triangular region?

25. _____

▲ **26.** A rectangle has a length 7 meters longer than double the width. The perimeter is 134 meters. Find the dimensions of the rectangle.

26. _____

▲ **27.** Find the circumference of a circle with radius 34 inches. Use $\pi = 3.14$ as an approximation.

27. _____

▲ **28.** Find the area of a trapezoid if the two bases are 10 inches and 14 inches and the altitude is 16 inches.

28. _____

▲ **29.** Find the volume of a sphere with radius 10 inches. Use $\pi = 3.14$ as an approximation and round your answer to the nearest cubic inch.

29. _____

▲ **30** Find the area of a parallelogram with a base of 12 centimeters and an altitude of 8 centimeters.

30. _____

▲ **31.** How much would it cost to carpet the area shown in the figure if carpeting costs $12 per square yard?

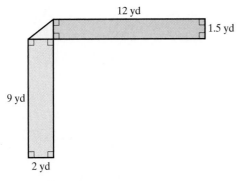

12 yd

1.5 yd

9 yd

2 yd

31. _____

A rainforest is one of the most amazing ecosystems in the entire world. It is a huge region with its own climate, an amazing variety of animals and plant life, and home to many species that do not exist anywhere else in the world. However, all is not well. The amount of land covered by rainforests is decreasing. Can you predict how rapidly this decrease is taking place? Turn to the Putting Your Skills to Work problems on page 211 to find out.

Graphing and Functions

4.1   THE RECTANGULAR COORDINATE SYSTEM   172

4.2   GRAPHING LINEAR EQUATIONS   184

4.3   THE SLOPE OF A LINE   194

        HOW AM I DOING? SECTIONS 4.1–4.3   205

4.4   WRITING THE EQUATION OF A LINE   207

        CHAPTER 4 ORGANIZER   212

        CHAPTER 4 REVIEW PROBLEMS   213

        HOW AM I DOING? CHAPTER 4 TEST   215

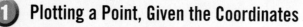

Student Learning Objectives

After studying this section, you will be able to:

 Plot a point, given the coordinates.

 Determine the coordinates of a plotted point.

3 Find ordered pairs for a given linear equation.

① Plotting a Point, Given the Coordinates

Oftentimes we can better understand an idea if we see a picture. This is the case with many mathematical concepts, including those relating to algebra. We can illustrate algebraic relationships with drawings called **graphs.** Before we can draw a graph, however, we need a frame of reference.

In Chapter 2 we showed that any real number can be represented on a number line. Look at the following number line. The arrow indicates the positive direction.

To form a **rectangular coordinate system,** we draw a second number line vertically. We construct it so that the 0 point on each number line is exactly at the same place. We refer to this location as the **origin.** The horizontal number line is often called the *x*-axis. The vertical number line is often called the *y*-axis. Arrows show the positive direction for each axis.

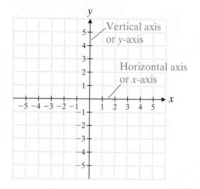

We can represent a point in this rectangular coordinate system by using an **ordered pair** of numbers. For example, (5, 2) is an ordered pair that represents a point in the rectangular coordinate system. The numbers in an ordered pair are often referred to as the **coordinates** of the point. The first number is called the *x*-**coordinate** and it represents the distance from the origin measured along the horizontal or *x*-axis. If the *x*-coordinate is positive, we count the proper number of squares to the right (that is, in the positive direction). If the *x*-coordinate is negative, we count to the left. The second number in the pair is called the *y*-**coordinate** and it represents the distance from the origin measured along the *y*-axis. If the *y*-coordinate is positive, we count the proper number of squares upward (that is, in the positive direction). If the *y*-coordinate is negative, we count downward.

$$(5, 2)$$
$$x\text{-coordinate} \quad \quad y\text{-coordinate}$$

Suppose the directory for the map on the left indicated that you would find a certain street in the region C3. To find the street you would first scan across the horizontal scale until you found section C; from there you would scan up the map until you hit Section 4 along the vertical scale. As we will see in the next example, plotting a point in the rectangular coordinate system is much like finding a street on a map with grids.

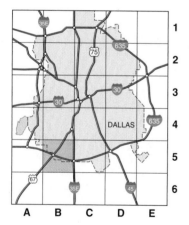

EXAMPLE 1 Plot the point (5, 2) on a rectangular coordinate system. Label this as point *A*.

Solution Since the *x*-coordinate is 5, we first count 5 units to the right on the *x*-axis. Then, because the *y*-coordinate is 2, we count 2 units up from the point where we stopped on the *x*-axis. This locates the point corresponding to (5, 2). We mark this point with a dot and label it *A*.

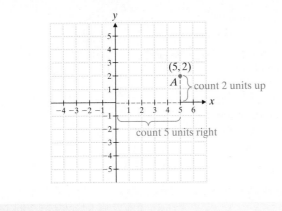

Practice Problem 1 Plot the point (3, 4) on the preceding coordinate system. Label this as point *B*.

NOTE TO STUDENT: Fully worked-out solutions to all of the Practice Problems can be found at the back of the text starting at page SP-1

It is important to remember that the first number in an ordered pair is the *x*-coordinate and the second number is the *y*-coordinate. The ordered pairs (5, 2) and (2, 5) represent different points.

EXAMPLE 2 Plot each point on the following coordinate system. Label the points *F*, *G*, and *H*, respectively.

(a) $(-5, 3)$ **(b)** $(2, -6)$ **(c)** $(-4, -5)$

Solution

(a) Notice that the *x*-coordinate, -5, is negative. On the coordinate grid, negative *x*-values appear to the left of the origin. Thus, we will begin by counting 5 squares to the left starting at the origin. Since the *y*-coordinate, 3, is positive, we will count 3 units up from the point where we stopped on the *x*-axis.

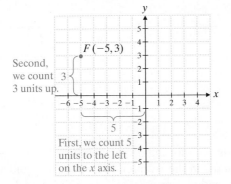

(b) The *x*-coordinate is positive. Begin by counting 2 squares to the right of the origin. Then count down because the *y*-coordinate is negative.

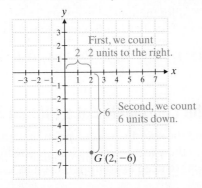

(c) The x-coordinate is negative. Begin by counting 4 squares to the left of the origin. Then count down because the y-coordinate is negative.

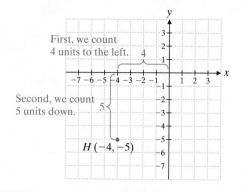

PRACTICE PROBLEM 2

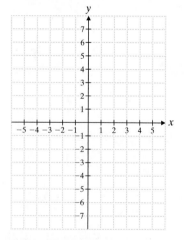

Practice Problem 2 Use the coordinate system in the margin to plot each point. Label the points I, J, and K, respectively.

(a) $(-2, -4)$　　　　**(b)** $(-4, 5)$　　　　**(c)** $(4, -2)$

EXAMPLE 3 Plot the following points.

$F: (0, 5)$　　　$G: \left(3, \frac{3}{2}\right)$　　　$H: (-6, 4)$　　　$I: (-3, -4)$

$J: (-4, 0)$　　　$K: (2, -3)$　　　$L: (6.5, -7.2)$

Solution These points are plotted in the figure.

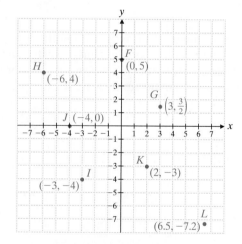

Note: When you are plotting decimal values like $(6.5, -7.2)$, plot the point halfway between 6 and 7 in the x-direction (for the 6.5) and at your best approximation of -7.2 in the y-direction.

PRACTICE PROBLEM 3

Practice Problem 3 Plot the following points. Label each point with both the letter and the ordered pair. Use the coordinate system provided in the margin.

$A: (3, 7)$　$B: (0, -6)$　$C: (3, -4.5)$　$D: \left(-\frac{7}{2}, 2\right)$

NOTE TO STUDENT: Fully worked-out solutions to all of the Practice Problems can be found at the back of the text starting at page SP-1

---

2 **Determining the Coordinates of a Plotted Point**

Sometimes we need to find the coordinates of a point that has been plotted. First, we count the units we need on the x-axis to get as close as possible to the point. Next we count the units up or down we need to go from the x-axis to reach the point.

EXAMPLE 4   What ordered pair of numbers represents point *A* in the graph below?

Solution   If we move along the *x*-axis until we get as close as possible to *A*, we end up at the number 5. Thus we obtain 5 as the first number of the ordered pair. Then we count 4 units upward on a line parallel to the *y*-axis to reach *A*. So we obtain 4 as the second number of the ordered pair. Thus point *A* is represented by the ordered pair $(5, 4)$.

Practice Problem 4   What ordered pair of numbers represents point *B* in the graph below?

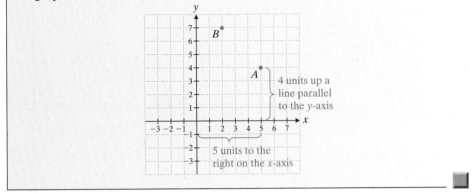

EXAMPLE 5   Write the coordinates of each point plotted in the following graph.

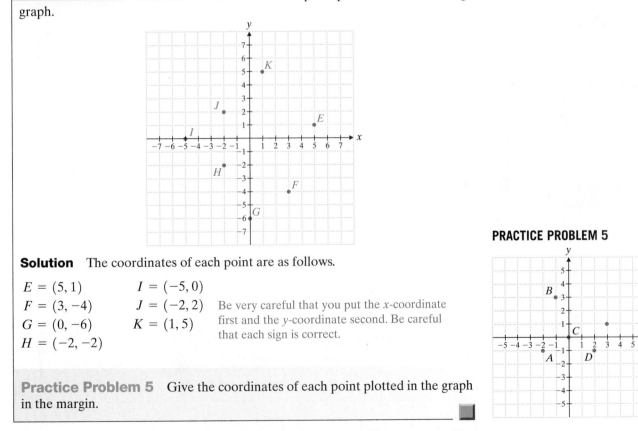

Solution   The coordinates of each point are as follows.

$E = (5, 1)$ $I = (-5, 0)$
$F = (3, -4)$ $J = (-2, 2)$ Be very careful that you put the *x*-coordinate
$G = (0, -6)$ $K = (1, 5)$ first and the *y*-coordinate second. Be careful
$H = (-2, -2)$ that each sign is correct.

PRACTICE PROBLEM 5

Practice Problem 5   Give the coordinates of each point plotted in the graph in the margin.

In examining data from real-world situations, we often find that plotting data points shows useful trends. In such cases, it is often necessary to use a different scale, one that displays only positive values.

EXAMPLE 6   The number of motor vehicle accidents in millions is recorded in the following table for the years 1980 to 2000.

(a) Plot points that represent this data on the given coordinate system.

(b) What trends are apparent from the plotted data?

Number of Years Since 1980	Number of Motor Vehicle Accidents (in Millions)
0	18
5	19
10	12
15	11
20	15

Source: U.S. National Highway Traffic Safety Administration

Solution

(a)

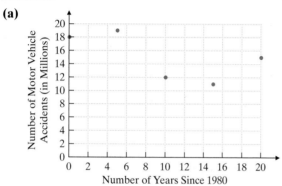

(b) From 1980 to 1985, there was a slight increase in the number of accidents. From 1985 to 1995, there was a significant decrease in the number of accidents. From 1995 to 2000, there was a moderate increase in the number of accidents.

Practice Problem 6   The number of motor vehicle deaths in thousands is recorded in the following table for the years 1980 to 2000.

(a) Plot points that represent this data on the given coordinate system.

(b) What trends are apparent from the plotted data?

Number of Years Since 1980	Number of Motor Vehicle Deaths (in Thousands)
0	51
5	44
10	45
15	42
20	43

Source: U.S. National Highway Traffic Safety Administration

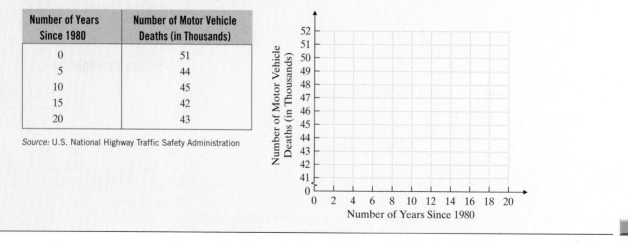

③ Finding Ordered Pairs for a Given Linear Equation

Equations such as $3x + 2y = 5$ and $6x + y = 3$ are called linear equations in two variables.

A **linear equation in two variables** is an equation that can be written in the form $Ax + By = C$ where A, B, and C are real numbers but A and B are not *both* zero.

Replacement values for x and y that make *true mathematical statements* of the equation are called *truth values,* and an ordered pair of these truth values is called a **solution.**

Consider the equation $3x + 2y = 5$. The ordered pair $(-1, 4)$ is a solution to the equation because when we replace x by -1 and y by 4 in the equation, we obtain a true statement.

$$3(-1) + 2(4) = 5 \quad \text{or} \quad -3 + 8 = 5 \quad \text{True statement.}$$

Likewise $(3, -2)$, $(5, -5)$, and $(7, -8)$ are also solutions to the equation. In fact, there are an infinite number of solutions for any given linear equation in two variables.

The linear equations that we work with are not always written in the form $Ax + By = C$, but are sometimes solved for y, as shown in Example 7.

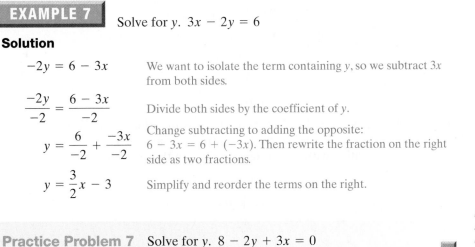

EXAMPLE 7   Solve for y. $3x - 2y = 6$

Solution

$-2y = 6 - 3x$ We want to isolate the term containing y, so we subtract $3x$ from both sides.

$\dfrac{-2y}{-2} = \dfrac{6 - 3x}{-2}$ Divide both sides by the coefficient of y.

$y = \dfrac{6}{-2} + \dfrac{-3x}{-2}$ Change subtracting to adding the opposite: $6 - 3x = 6 + (-3x)$. Then rewrite the fraction on the right side as two fractions.

$y = \dfrac{3}{2}x - 3$ Simplify and reorder the terms on the right.

Practice Problem 7   Solve for y. $8 - 2y + 3x = 0$

NOTE TO STUDENT: Fully worked-out solutions to all of the Practice Problems can be found at the back of the text starting at page SP-1

In general, there is a procedure for solving an equation for a specified variable.

PROCEDURE TO SOLVE AN EQUATION FOR A SPECIFIED VARIABLE

1. Remove any parentheses.
2. If fractions exist, multiply all terms on both sides by the LCD of all the fractions.
3. Combine like terms on each side if possible.
4. Add or subtract terms on both sides of the equation to get all terms with the desired variable on one side of the equation.
5. Add or subtract the appropriate quantities to get all terms that do *not* have the desired variable on the other side of the equation.
6. Divide both sides of the equation by the coefficient of the desired variable.
7. Simplify if possible.

Now consider the equation $y = \frac{3}{2}x - 3$ from Example 7. Notice that the ordered pair $(2, 0)$ is a *solution* to the equation because when we replace x by 2 and y by 0 we obtain a *true mathematical statement*:

$$(0) = \frac{3}{2}(2) - 3 \quad \text{or} \quad 0 = 3 - 3. \quad \text{True statement.}$$

If one value of an ordered-pair solution to a linear equation is known, the other can be quickly obtained. To do so, we replace the proper variable in the equation by the known value. Then using the methods learned in Chapter 3, we solve the resulting equation for the other variable.

EXAMPLE 8 Find the missing coordinate to complete the following ordered-pair solutions for the equation $2x + 3y = 15$.

(a) $(0, ?)$ **(b)** $(?, 1)$

Solution

(a) For the ordered pair $(0, ?)$ we know that $x = 0$. Replace x by 0 in the equation and solve for y.

$$2x + 3y = 15$$
$$2(0) + 3y = 15 \quad \text{Replace } x \text{ with 0.}$$
$$0 + 3y = 15 \quad \text{Simplify.}$$
$$y = 5 \quad \text{Divide both sides by 3.}$$

Thus we have the ordered pair $(0, 5)$.

(b) For the ordered pair $(?, 1)$, we *do not know* the value of x. However, we do know that $y = 1$. So we start by replacing the variable y by 1. We will end up with an equation with one variable, x. We can then solve for x.

$$2x + 3y = 15$$
$$2x + 3(1) = 15$$
$$2x + 3 = 15$$
$$2x = 12$$
$$x = 6$$

Thus we have the ordered pair $(6, 1)$.

NOTE TO STUDENT: Fully worked-out solutions to all of the Practice Problems can be found at the back of the text starting at page SP-1

Practice Problem 8 Find the missing coordinate to complete the following ordered-pair solutions for the equation $3x - 4y = 12$.

(a) $(0, ?)$ **(b)** $(?, 3)$ **(c)** $(?, -6)$

Verbal and Writing Skills

1. What is the *x*-coordinate of the origin?

2. What is the *y*-coordinate of the origin?

3. Explain why $(5, 1)$ is referred to as an *ordered* pair of numbers.

4. Explain how you would locate a point $(4, 3)$ on graph paper.

5. Plot the following points.
$J: (-4, 3.5)$ $K: (6, 0)$
$L: (5, -6)$ $M: (0, -4)$

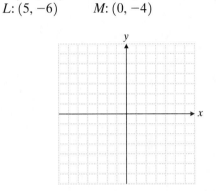

6. Plot the following points.
$R: (-3, 0)$ $S: (3.5, 4)$
$T: (-2, -2.5)$ $V: (0, 5)$

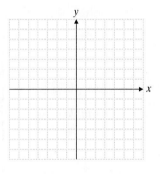

Consider the points plotted in the graph at right.

7. Give the coordinates for points R, S, X, and Y.

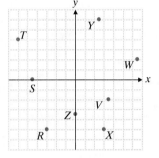

8. Give the coordinates for points T, V, W, and Z.

In exercises 9 and 10, 6 points are plotted in the figure. List all the ordered pairs needed to represent the points.

9.

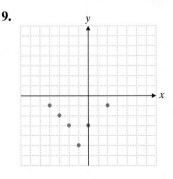

10.

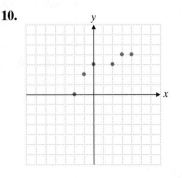

In each equation, solve for the indicated variable.

11. $x - y = -10$.   Solve for x.

12. $x - y = -2$.   Solve for x.

13. $y - 4 = -\dfrac{2}{3}x$.   Solve for y.

14. $y + 9 = \dfrac{3}{8}x$.   Solve for y.

15. $5x + y = 3$.   Solve for x.

16. $4x + y = 11$.   Solve for x.

17. $8x - 12y = 24$.   Solve for y.

18. $3y - 5x = 9$.   Solve for y.

To Think About Exercises 19–22

Solve for the indicated variable.

19. $S = \dfrac{1}{2}gt$.   Solve for g.

20. $S = \dfrac{1}{2}gt$.   Solve for t.

21. $A = P(1 + rt)$.   Solve for t.

▲ **22.** $A = \dfrac{1}{2}a(b_1 + b_2)$.   Solve for b_1.

Find the missing coordinate to complete the ordered-pair solution to the given linear equation.

23. $y = 4x + 7$
  (a) $(0, \ )$
  (b) $(2, \ )$

24. $y = 6x + 5$
  (a) $(0, \ )$
  (b) $(3, \ )$

25. $y = -4x + 2$
  (a) $(-5, \ )$
  (b) $(4, \ )$

26. $y = -2x + 3$
  (a) $(-6, \ )$
  (b) $(3, \ )$

27. $3x - 4y = 11$
  (a) $(-3, \ )$
  (b) $(\ , 1)$

28. $5x - 2y = 9$
  (a) $(7, \ )$
  (b) $(\ , -7)$

29. $2y + 3x = -6$
  (a) $(-2, \ )$
  (b) $(\ , 3)$

30. $-4x + 5y = -20$
  (a) $(10, \ )$
  (b) $(\ , -8)$

31. $2x + \dfrac{1}{5}y = 6$
  (a) $(\ , 20)$
  (b) $\left(\dfrac{9}{5}, \ \right)$

32. $3x + \dfrac{1}{4}y = 11$
  (a) $(\ , 8)$
  (b) $\left(\dfrac{13}{4}, \ \right)$

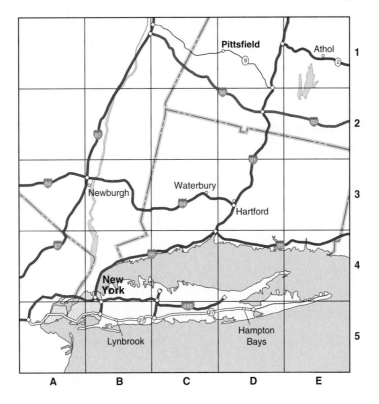

Using Road Maps *The preceding map shows a portion of New York, Connecticut, and Massachusetts. Like many maps used in driving or flying, it has horizontal and vertical grid markers for ease of use. For example, Newburgh, New York, is located in grid B3. Use the grid labels to indicate the locations of the following cities.*

33. Lynbrook, New York

34. Hampton Bays, New York

35. Athol, Massachusetts

36. Pittsfield, Massachusetts

37. Hartford, Connecticut

38. Waterbury, Connecticut

39. ***Number of Cellular Phones*** The number of cellular phones per thousand people in the United States from 1997 to 2002 is recorded in the following table. For example, 315 in the second column means that in that year, 315 out of every 1000 Americans owned cellular phones.
   (a) Plot points that represent this data on the given rectangular coordinate system.
   (b) What trends are obvious from the plotted data?

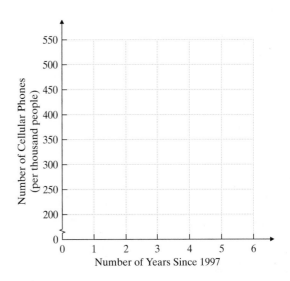

Number of Years Since 1997	Number of Cellular Phones (per 1000 People in U.S.)
0	200
1	250
2	315
3	400
4	450
5	485

Source: U.S. Federal Communications Commission

40. *Oil Production* The number of barrels of oil produced in the U.S. for selected years starting in 1940 is recorded in the following table. The number of barrels of oil is measured in hundred thousands. For example, 14 in the second column means 14 hundred thousand, or 1,400,000.

(a) Plot points on the given rectangular coordinate system that represent this data.

(b) What trends are apparent from the plotted data?

Number of Years Since 1940	Number of Barrels of Crude Oil (in Hundred Thousands)
0	14
10	20
20	26
30	35
40	31
50	27
60	21

Source: U.S. Department of Energy

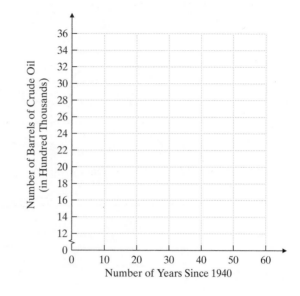

41. *Buying Books Online* The number of people buying books online continues to increase at an amazing rate. The following chart records the number of people for each of the years from 2000 to 2003.

Year	Number of People (in millions) Buying Books Online
2000	23
2001	32
2002	41
2003	49

Source: U.S. Department of Labor

(a) Plot points on the given rectangular coordinate system that represent this data.

(b) Based on your graph, what would you estimate would be the number of people buying books online for the year 2004?

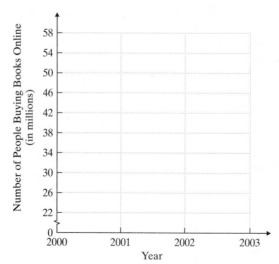

42. *Number of DVD Players* The number of households in the United States that have a DVD player continues to increase at a significant rate. The following chart records the number of households that have this device for each of the years from 2000 to 2003.

Year	Number of Households in Millions in U.S. That Have a DVD Player
2000	7
2001	19
2002	37
2003	48

Source: Federal Communications Commission

(a) Plot points on the given rectangular coordinate system that represents this data.

(b) Based on your graph, what would you estimate would be the number of households that have a DVD player in the year 2004?

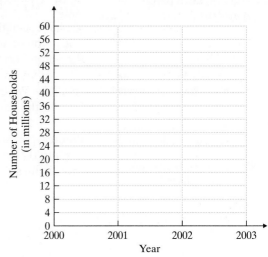

Cumulative Review

▲ 43. *Circular Swimming Pool* The circular pool at the hotel where Bob and Linda stayed in Orlando, Florida, has a radius of 19 yards. What is the area of the pool? (Use $\pi \approx 3.14$.)

44. A number is doubled and then decreased by three. The result is twenty-one. What is the original number?

45. *Circulation of a Newspaper* A major Russian newspaper called *Izvestia* had a circulation of 6,109,005 before the dissipation of the Soviet Union. This amount is approximately 17 times the current circulation. What is the current circulation of *Izvestia?* Round to the nearest whole number.

▲ 46. *Prices of Persian Rugs* An expensive Persian rug that measures 30 feet by 22 feet is priced at $44,020.00. A customer negotiates with the owner of the rug, and they agree upon a price of $36,300.

(a) What is the cost per square foot of the rug at the discounted price?

(b) The rug dealer has a smaller matching Persian rug measuring 14 feet by 8 feet. He says he will sell it to the customer at the same cost per square foot as the larger one. How much will the small rug cost?

Student Learning Objectives

After studying this section, you will be able to:

1 Graph a linear equation by plotting three ordered pairs.

2 Graph a straight line by plotting its intercepts.

3 Graph horizontal and vertical lines.

1 Graphing a Linear Equation by Plotting Three Ordered Pairs

We have seen that a solution to a linear equation in two variables is an ordered pair. The graph of an ordered pair is a point. Thus we can graph an equation by graphing the points corresponding to its ordered-pair solutions.

A linear equation in two variables has an infinite number of ordered-pair solutions. We can see that this is true by noting that we can substitute any number for x in the equation and solve it to obtain a y-value. For example, if we substitute $x = 0, 1, 2, 3, \ldots$ into the equation $y = -x + 3$ and solve for y, we obtain the ordered-pair solutions $(0, 3), (1, 2), (2, 1), (3, 0), \ldots$. (If desired, substitute these values into the equation to convince yourself.) If we plot these points on a rectangular coordinate system, we notice that they form a straight line.

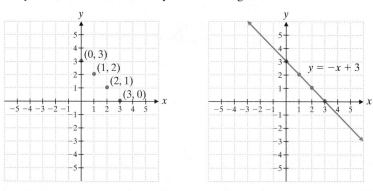

It turns out that all of the points corresponding to the ordered-pair solutions of $y = -x + 3$ lie on this line, and the line extends forever in both directions. A similar statement can be made about any linear equation in two variables.

> The graph of any linear equation in two variables is a straight line.

From geometry, we know that two points determine a line. Thus to graph a linear equation in two variables, we need only graph two ordered-pair solutions of the equation and then draw the line that passes through them. Having said this, we recommend that you use three points to graph a line. Two points will determine where the line is. The third point verifies that you have drawn the line correctly. For ease in plotting, it is better if the ordered pairs contain integers.

TO GRAPH A LINEAR EQUATION

1. Look for three ordered pairs that are solutions to the equation.
2. Plot the points.
3. Draw a line through the points.

EXAMPLE 1 Find three ordered pairs that satisfy $2x + y = 4$. Then graph the resulting straight line.

Solution Since we can choose any value for x, choose numbers that are convenient. To organize the results, we will make a table of values. We will let $x = 0$, $x = 1$, and $x = 3$, respectively. We write these numbers under x in our table of values. For each of these x-values, we find the corresponding y-value in the equation $2x + y = 4$.

Table of Values	
x	**y**
0	
1	
3	

$$2x + y = 4 \qquad\qquad 2x + y = 4 \qquad\qquad 2x + y = 4$$
$$2(0) + y = 4 \qquad\qquad 2(1) + y = 4 \qquad\qquad 2(3) + y = 4$$

$$0 + y = 4 \qquad\qquad 2 + y = 4 \qquad\qquad 6 + y = 4$$
$$y = 4 \qquad\qquad\qquad y = 2 \qquad\qquad\qquad y = -2$$

We record these results by placing each y-value in the table next to its corresponding x-value. Keep in mind that these values represent ordered pairs, each of which is a solution to the equation. To make calculating and graphing easier, we choose integer values whenever possible. If we plot these ordered pairs and connect the three points, we get a straight line that is the graph of the equation $2x + y = 4$. The graph of the equation is shown in the figure at the right.

Table of Values	
x	**y**
0	4
1	2
3	−2

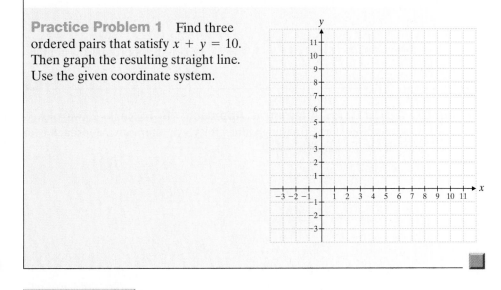

Practice Problem 1   Find three ordered pairs that satisfy $x + y = 10$. Then graph the resulting straight line. Use the given coordinate system.

NOTE TO STUDENT: Fully worked-out solutions to all of the Practice Problems can be found at the back of the text starting at page SP-1

EXAMPLE 2   Graph $5x - 4y + 2 = 2$.

Solution   First, we simplify the equation $5x - 4y + 2 = 2$ by adding -2 to each side.

$$5x - 4y + 2 - 2 = 2 - 2$$
$$5x - 4y = 0$$

Since we are free to choose any value of x, $x = 0$ is a natural choice. Calculate the value of y when $x = 0$.

$$5(0) - 4y = 0$$
$$-4y = 0 \qquad \text{Remember: Any number times 0 is 0.}$$
$$y = 0 \qquad \text{Since } -4y = 0, y \text{ must equal 0.}$$

Now let's see what happens when $x = 1$.

$$5(1) - 4y = 0$$
$$5 - 4y = 0$$
$$-4y = -5$$
$$y = \frac{-5}{-4} \quad \text{or} \quad \frac{5}{4} \qquad \text{This is not an easy number to graph.}$$

A better choice for a replacement of x is a number that is divisible by 4. Let's see why. Let $x = 4$ and let $x = -4$.

$$5(4) - 4y = 0 \qquad\qquad 5(-4) - 4y = 0$$
$$20 - 4y = 0 \qquad\qquad -20 - 4y = 0$$
$$-4y = -20 \qquad\qquad -4y = 20$$
$$y = \frac{-20}{-4} \quad \text{or} \quad 5 \qquad\qquad y = \frac{20}{-4} \quad \text{or} \quad -5$$

PRACTICE PROBLEM 2

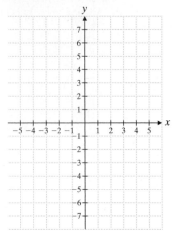

NOTE TO STUDENT: Fully worked-out solutions to all of the Practice Problems can be found at the back of the text starting at page SP-1

Now we can put these numbers into our table of values and graph the line.

Table of Values	
x	**y**
0	0
4	5
−4	−5

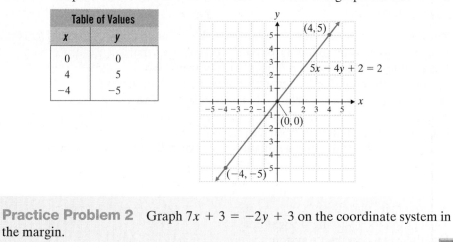

Practice Problem 2   Graph $7x + 3 = -2y + 3$ on the coordinate system in the margin.

TO THINK ABOUT: An Alternative Approach   In Example 2, we picked values of x and found the corresponding values for y. An alternative approach is to solve the equation for the variable y *first*.

$$5x - 4y = 0$$
$$-4y = -5x \qquad \text{Add } -5x \text{ to each side.}$$
$$\frac{-4y}{-4} = \frac{-5x}{-4} \qquad \text{Divide each side by } -4.$$
$$y = \frac{5}{4}x$$

Now let $x = -4$, $x = 0$, and $x = 4$, and find the corresponding values of y. Explain why you would choose multiples of 4 as replacements of x in this equation. Graph the equation and compare it to the graph in Example 2.

In the previous two examples we began by picking values for x. We could just as easily have chosen values for y.

② Graphing a Straight Line by Plotting Its Intercepts

What values should we pick for x and y? Which points should we use for plotting? For many straight lines it is easiest to pick the two *intercepts*. Some lines have only one intercept. We will discuss these separately.

> The **x-intercept** of a line is the point where the line crosses the x-axis; it has the form $(a, 0)$. The **y-intercept** of a line is the point where the line crosses the y-axis; it has the form $(0, b)$.

> **INTERCEPT METHOD OF GRAPHING**
>
> To graph an equation using intercepts, we:
>
> **1.** Find the x-intercept by letting $y = 0$ and solving for x.
> **2.** Find the y-intercept by letting $x = 0$ and solving for y.
> **3.** Find one additional ordered pair so that we have three points with which to plot the line.

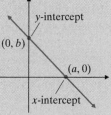

EXAMPLE 3   Use the intercept method to graph $5y - 3x = 15$.

Solution

$$\text{Let } y = 0. \qquad 5(0) - 3x = 15 \qquad \text{Replace } y \text{ by } 0.$$
$$-3x = 15 \qquad \text{Divide both sides by } -3.$$
$$x = -5$$

The ordered pair $(-5, 0)$ is the x-intercept.

$$\text{Let } x = 0. \qquad 5y - 3x = 15$$
$$5y - 3(0) = 15 \qquad \text{Replace } x \text{ by } 0.$$
$$5y = 15 \qquad \text{Divide both sides by } 5.$$
$$y = 3$$

The ordered pair $(0, 3)$ is the y-intercept.
    We find another ordered pair to have a third point.

$$\text{Let } y = 6. \qquad 5(6) - 3x = 15 \qquad\qquad \text{Replace } y \text{ by } 6.$$
$$30 - 3x = 15 \qquad\qquad \text{Simplify.}$$
$$-3x = -15 \qquad\qquad \text{Subtract } 30 \text{ from both sides.}$$
$$x = \frac{-15}{-3} \quad \text{or} \quad 5$$

The ordered pair is $(5, 6)$. Our table of values is

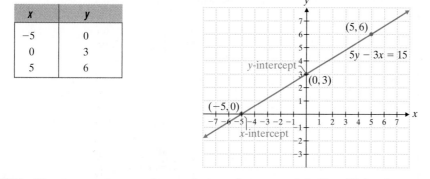

x	y
-5	0
0	3
5	6

CAUTION   The three points on the graph must form a straight line. If the three points do not form a straight line, you made a calculation error.

Practice Problem 3   Use the intercept method to graph $2y - x = 6$. Use the given coordinate system.

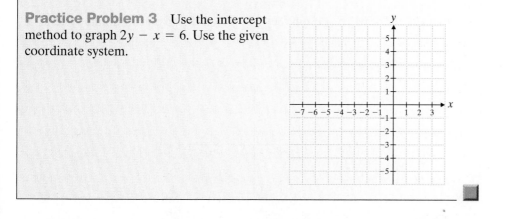

TO THINK ABOUT: Lines That Go Through the Origin   Can you draw all straight lines by the intercept method? Not really. Some straight lines may go through the origin and have only one intercept. If a line goes through the origin, it will have an equation of the form $Ax + By = 0$, where $A \neq 0$ or $B \neq 0$ or both. Examples are $3x + 4y = 0$ and $5x - 2y = 0$. In such cases you should plot two additional points besides the origin. Be sure to simplify each equation before attempting to graph it.

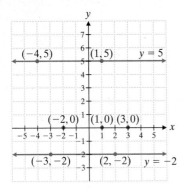

3 Graphing Horizontal and Vertical Lines

You will notice that the x-axis is a horizontal line. It is the line $y = 0$, since for any value of x, the value of y is 0. Try a few points. The points $(1, 0)$, $(3, 0)$, and $(-2, 0)$ all lie on the x-axis. Any horizontal line will be parallel to the x-axis. Lines such as $y = 5$ and $y = -2$ are horizontal lines. What does $y = 5$ mean? It means that for any value of x, y is 5. Likewise $y = -2$ means that for any value of x, $y = -2$.

How can we recognize the equation of a line that is horizontal, that is, parallel to the x-axis?

> If the graph of an equation is a straight line that is parallel to the x-axis (that is, a horizontal line), the equation will be of the form $y = b$, where b is some real number.

EXAMPLE 4 Graph $y = -3$.

Solution You could write the equation as $0x + y = -3$. Then it is clear that for any value of x that you substitute, you will always obtain $y = -3$. Thus, as shown in the figure, $(4, -3)$, $(0, -3)$, and $(-3, -3)$ are all ordered pairs that satisfy the equation $y = -3$. Since the y-coordinate of every point on this line is -3, it is easy to see that the horizontal line will be 3 units below the x-axis.

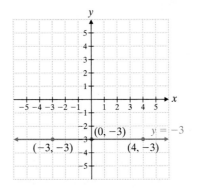

NOTE TO STUDENT: Fully worked-out solutions to all of the Practice Problems can be found at the back of the text starting at page SP-1

Practice Problem 4 Graph $2y - 3 = 0$ on the given coordinate system.

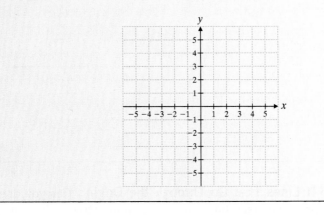

Notice that the y-axis is a vertical line. This is the line $x = 0$, since for any y, x is 0. Try a few points. The points $(0, 2)$, $(0, -3)$, and $\left(0, \frac{1}{2}\right)$ all lie on the y-axis. Any vertical line will be parallel to the y-axis. Lines such as $x = 2$ and $x = -3$ are vertical lines. Think of what $x = 2$ means. It means that for any value of y, x is 2. The graph of $x = 2$ is a vertical line two units to the right of the y-axis.

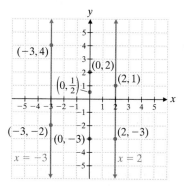

How can we recognize the equation of a line that is vertical, that is, parallel to the y-axis?

If the graph of an equation is a straight line that is parallel to the y-axis (that is, a vertical line), the equation will be of the form $x = a$, where a is some real number.

EXAMPLE 5   Graph $x = 5$.

Solution   This can be done immediately by drawing a vertical line 5 units to the right of the origin. The x-coordinate of every point on this line is 5.
The equation $x - 5 = 0$ can be rewritten as $x = 5$ and graphed as shown.

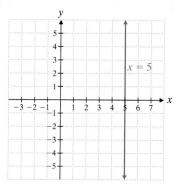

Practice Problem 5   Graph $x + 3 = 0$ on the following coordinate system.

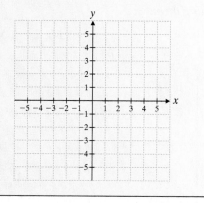

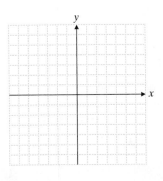

Student Solutions Manual   CD/Video   PH Math Tutor Center   MathXL®Tutorials on CD   MathXL®   MyMathLab®   Interactmath.com

Verbal and Writing Skills

1. Is the point $(-2, 5)$ a solution to the equation $2x + 5y = 0$? Why or why not?

2. The graph of a linear equation in two variables is a _____ _____.

3. The x-intercept of a line is the point where the line crosses the _____.

4. The graph of the equation $y = b$ is a _____ line.

Complete the ordered pairs so that each is a solution of the given linear equation. Then plot each solution and graph the equation by connecting the points by a straight line.

5. $y = -2x + 1$
   $(0, \ )$
   $(-2, \ )$
   $(1, \ )$

6. $y = -3x - 4$
   $(-2, \ )$
   $(-1, \ )$
   $(0, \ )$

7. $y = x - 4$
   $(0, \ )$
   $(2, \ )$
   $(4, \ )$

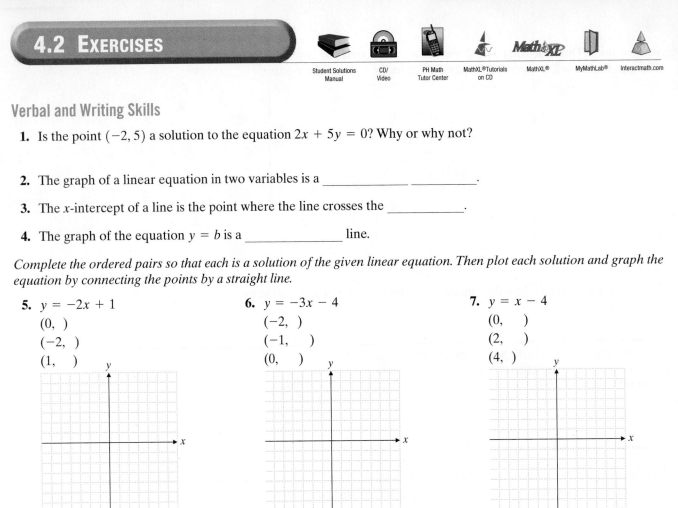

8. $y = 3x - 1$
   $(0, \ )$
   $(2, \ )$
   $(-2, \ )$

9. $y = -2x + 3$
   $(0, \ )$
   $(2, \ )$
   $(4, \ )$

10. $y = 2x - 5$
    $(0, \ )$
    $(2, \ )$
    $(4, \ )$

11. $y = 3x + 2$
    $(-1, \ )$
    $(0, \ )$
    $(1, \ )$

Graph each equation by plotting three points and connecting them.

12. $y = -3x + 2$

13. $3x - 2y = 0$

14. $2y - 5x = 0$

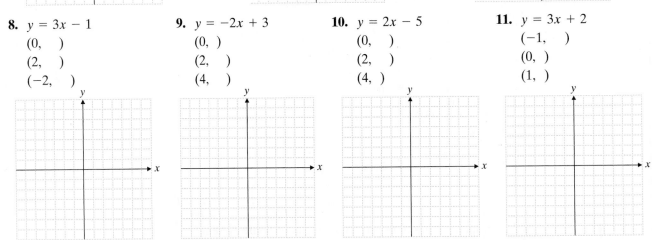

15. $y = -\dfrac{3}{4}x + 3$ **16.** $y = -\dfrac{2}{5}x - 2$ **17.** $4x + 3y = 12$ **18.** $3x + 2y = 6$

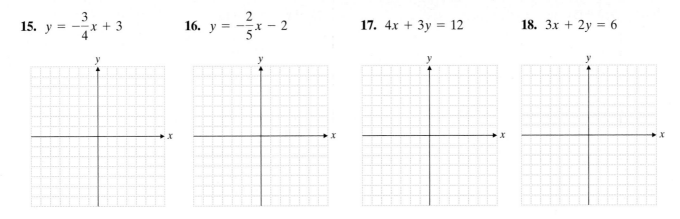

Graph each equation by plotting the intercepts and one other point.

19. $y = 6 - 2x$

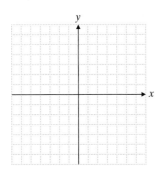

20. $y = 4 - 2x$

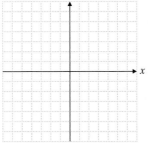

21. $x + 3 = 6y$

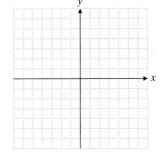

22. $x - 6 = 2y$

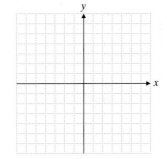

Mixed Practice

Graph the equation. Be sure to simplify the equation before graphing it.

23. $y - 2 = 3y$

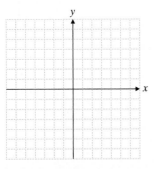

24. $3y + 1 = 7$

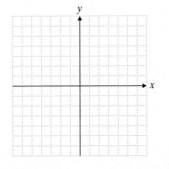

25. $2x + 9 = 5x$

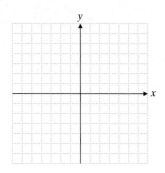

26. $3x - 4 = -13$

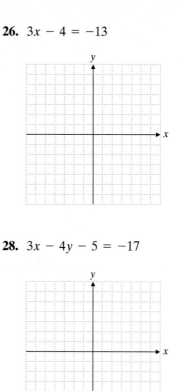

27. $2x + 5y - 2 = -12$

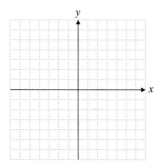

28. $3x - 4y - 5 = -17$

Applications

29. ***Cross-Country Skiing*** The number of calories burned by an average person while cross-country skiing is given by the equation $C = 8m$, where m is the number of minutes. (*Source:* National Center for Health Statistics.) Graph the equation for $m = 0, 15, 30, 45, 60$, and 75.

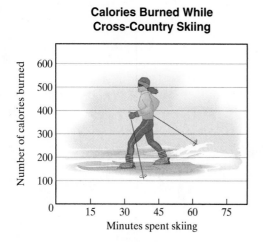

30. ***Calories Burned While Jogging*** The number of calories burned by an average person while jogging is given by the equation $C = \dfrac{28}{3}m$, where m is the number of minutes. (*Source:* National Center for Health Statistics.) Graph the equation for $m = 0, 15, 30, 45, 60$, and 75.

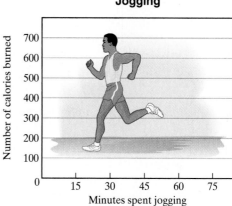

31. *Foreign Students in the United States* The number of foreign students enrolled in college in the United States is approximated by the equation $S = 12t + 280$, where t stands for the number of years since 1980, and S is the number of foreign students (in thousands). (*Source*: Statistical Abstract of the United States, 2002) Graph the equation for $t = 0, 6, 15, 21$.

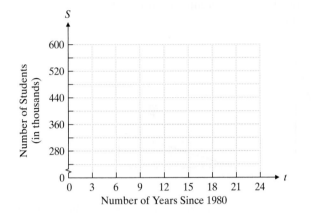

32. *Population of the United States* The approximate population of the United States is given by the equation $P = 2.3t + 179$ where P is the population in millions and t is the number of years since 1960. (*Source*: Bureau of the Census, U.S. Department of Commerce.) Graph the equation for $t = 0, 10, 30, 40$.

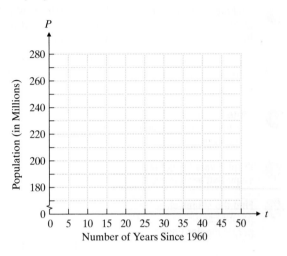

Cumulative Review

33. Solve. $2(x + 3) + 5x = 3x - 2$

34. Solve and graph on a number line. $4 - 3x \le 18$

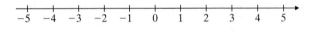

▲ **35.** *Geometry* A rectangle's width is 1 meter more than half of its length. Find the dimensions if the perimeter measures 53 meters.

36. *Education* Last semester there were 29 students for every 2 faculty members at Skyline University. At that time the school had 3074 students. How many faculty members were there last semester?

▲ **37.** *Geometry* One base of a trapezoid is 3 less than twice the length of the other base. The altitude of the trapezoid is 14 inches. If the area of the trapezoid is 63 square inches, find the length of each base.

TO THINK ABOUT: Verifying Your Answer Explain why you count down 1 unit and move to the right 2 units to represent the slope $-\frac{1}{2}$. Could you have done this in another way? Try it. Verify that this is the same line.

5 Finding the Slopes of Parallel and Perpendicular Lines

Parallel lines are two straight lines that never touch. Look at the parallel lines in the figure. Notice that the slope of line *a* is -3 and the slope of line *b* is also -3. Why do you think the slopes must be equal? What would happen if the slope of line *b* were -1? Graph it and see.

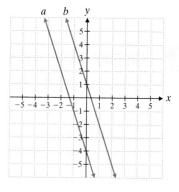

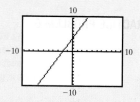

Graphing Calculator

Graphing Lines

You can graph a line given in the form $y = mx + b$ using a graphing calculator. For example, to graph $y = 2x + 4$, enter the right-hand side of the equation in the Y = editor of your calculator and graph. Choose an appropriate window to show all the intercepts. The following window is -10 to 10 by -10 to 10.
Display:

Try graphing other equations given in slope-intercept form.

PARALLEL LINES

Parallel lines are two straight lines that never touch.
Parallel lines have the same slope but different *y*-intercepts.

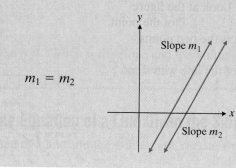

$$m_1 = m_2$$

Perpendicular lines are two lines that meet at a 90° angle. Look at the perpendicular lines in the figure at left. The slope of line *c* is -3. The slope of line *d* is $\frac{1}{3}$. Notice that

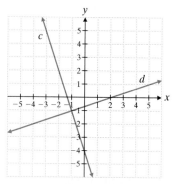

$$(-3)\left(\frac{1}{3}\right) = \left(-\frac{3}{1}\right)\left(\frac{1}{3}\right) = -1.$$

You may wish to draw several pairs of perpendicular lines to determine whether the product of their slopes is always -1.

PERPENDICULAR LINES

Perpendicular lines are two lines that meet at a 90° angle.
Perpendicular lines have slopes whose product is -1. If m_1 and m_2 are slopes of perpendicular lines, then

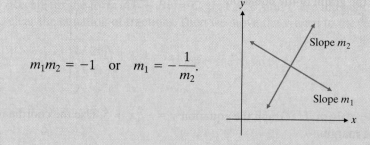

$$m_1 m_2 = -1 \quad \text{or} \quad m_1 = -\frac{1}{m_2}.$$

| **EXAMPLE 8** | Line h has a slope of $-\frac{2}{3}$. |

(a) If line f is parallel to line h, what is its slope?

(b) If line g is perpendicular to line h, what is its slope?

Solution

(a) Parallel lines have the same slope. Line f has a slope of $-\frac{2}{3}$.

(b) Perpendicular lines have slopes whose product is -1.

$$m_1 m_2 = -1$$

$$-\frac{2}{3} m_2 = -1 \qquad \text{Substitute } -\frac{2}{3} \text{ for } m_1.$$

$$\left(-\frac{3}{2}\right)\left(-\frac{2}{3}\right) m_2 = -1\left(-\frac{3}{2}\right) \qquad \text{Multiply both sides by } -\frac{3}{2}.$$

$$m_2 = \frac{3}{2}$$

Thus line g has a slope of $\frac{3}{2}$.

Practice Problem 8   Line h has a slope of $\frac{1}{4}$.

(a) If line j is parallel to line h, what is its slope?

(b) If line k is perpendicular to line h, what is its slope?

NOTE TO STUDENT: Fully worked-out solutions to all of the Practice Problems can be found at the back of the text starting at page SP-1

Graphing Calculator

Graphing Parallel Lines

If two equations are in the form $y = mx + b$, then it will be obvious that they are parallel because the slope will be the same. On a graphing calculator graph both of these equations:

$$y = -2x + 6$$
$$y = -2x - 4$$

Use the window of -10 to 10 for both x and y.
Display:

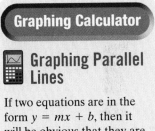

| **EXAMPLE 9** | The equation of line l is $y = -2x + 3$. |

(a) What is the slope of a line that is parallel to line l?

(b) What is the slope of a line that is perpendicular to line l?

Solution

(a) Looking at the equation, we can see that the slope of line l is -2.
The slope of a line that is parallel to line l is -2.

(b) Perpendicular lines have slopes whose product is -1.

$$m_1 m_2 = -1$$

$$(-2) m_2 = -1 \qquad \text{Substitute } -2 \text{ for } m_1.$$

$$m_2 = \frac{1}{2} \qquad \text{Because } (-2)\left(\frac{1}{2}\right) = -1.$$

The slope of a line that is perpendicular to line l is $\frac{1}{2}$.

Practice Problem 9   The equation of line n is $y = \frac{1}{4}x - 1$.

(a) What is the slope of a line that is parallel to line n?

(b) What is the slope of a line that is perpendicular to line n?

Verbal and Writing Skills

1. Can you find the slope of the line passing through $(5, -12)$ and $(5, -6)$? Why or why not?

2. Can you find the slope of the line passing through $(6, -2)$ and $(-8, -2)$? Why or why not?

Find the slope of a straight line that passes through the given pair of points.

3. $(4, 1)$ and $(6, 7)$ **4.** $(7, 5)$ and $(12, 10)$ **5.** $(6, 6)$ and $(9, 3)$

6. $(11, 2)$ and $(5, 14)$ **7.** $(-2, 1)$ and $(3, 4)$ **8.** $(5, 6)$ and $(-3, 1)$

9. $(-6, -5)$ and $(2, -7)$ **10.** $(-8, -3)$ and $(4, -9)$ **11.** $(-3, 0)$ and $(0, -4)$

12. $(0, 5)$ and $(5, 3)$ **13.** $\left(\frac{3}{4}, -4\right)$ and $(2, -8)$ **14.** $\left(\frac{5}{3}, -2\right)$ and $(3, 6)$

Find the slope and the y-intercept.

15. $y = 8x + 9$ **16.** $y = 2x + 10$ **17.** $y = -3x + 4$ **18.** $y = -8x - 7$

19. $y = -\frac{8}{7}x + \frac{3}{4}$ **20.** $y = \frac{5}{3}x - \frac{4}{5}$ **21.** $y = -6x$ **22.** $y = -2$

23. $6x + y = \frac{4}{5}$ **24.** $2x + y = -\frac{3}{4}$ **25.** $5x + 2y = 3$ **26.** $7x + 3y = 4$

27. $7x - 3y = 4$ **28.** $9x - 4y = 18$

Write the equation of the line in slope–intercept form.

29. $m = \frac{3}{5}$, y-intercept $(0, 3)$ **30.** $m = \frac{2}{3}$, y-intercept $(0, 5)$

31. $m = 6$, y-intercept $(0, -3)$ **32.** $m = 5$, y-intercept $(0, -6)$

33. $m = -\frac{5}{4}$, y-intercept $\left(0, -\frac{3}{4}\right)$ **34.** $m = -4$, y-intercept $\left(0, \frac{1}{2}\right)$

Graph the line $y = mx + b$ for the given values.

35. $m = \frac{3}{4}$, $b = -4$

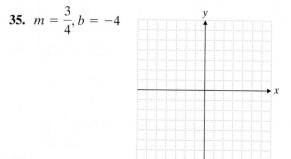

36. $m = \frac{1}{3}$, $b = -2$

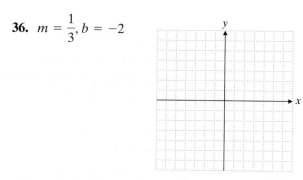

37. $m = -\dfrac{5}{3}, b = 2$

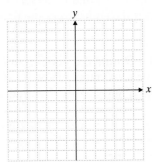

38. $m = -\dfrac{3}{2}, b = 4$

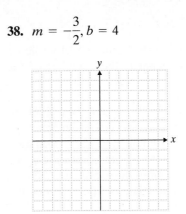

In exercises 39–44, graph the line.

39. $y = \dfrac{2}{3}x + 2$

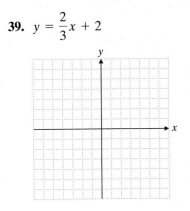

40. $y = \dfrac{3}{4}x + 1$

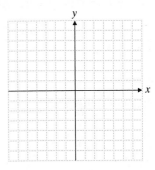

41. $y + 2x = 3$

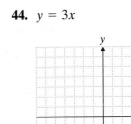

42. $y + 4x = 5$

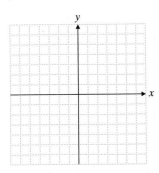

43. $y = 2x$

44. $y = 3x$

45. A line has a slope of $\dfrac{5}{6}$.
   (a) What is the slope of the line parallel to it?
   (b) What is the slope of the line perpendicular to it?

46. A line has a slope of $\dfrac{11}{4}$.
   (a) What is the slope of the line parallel to it?
   (b) What is the slope of the line perpendicular to it?

47. A line has a slope of 6.
   (a) What is the slope of the line parallel to it?
   (b) What is the slope of the line perpendicular to it?

48. A line has a slope of $-\dfrac{5}{8}$.
   (a) What is the slope of the line parallel to it?
   (b) What is the slope of the line perpendicular to it?

49. The equation of a line is $y = \dfrac{1}{3}x + 2$.
   (a) What is the slope of a line parallel to it?
   (b) What is the slope of a line perpendicular to it?

50. The equation of a line is $y = \dfrac{3}{5}x - 5$.
   (a) What is the slope of a line parallel to it?
   (b) What is the slope of a line perpendicular to it?

To Think About

51. Do the points $(3, -4)$, $(18, 6)$, and $(9, 0)$ all lie on the same line? If so, what is the equation of the line?

52. Do the points $(2, 1)$, $(-3, -2)$ and $(7, 4)$ lie on the same line? If so, what is the equation of the line?

53. *Federal Budget* During the years from 1980 to 2005, the total income for the U.S. federal budget can be approximated by the equation $y = 14(4x + 35)$, where x is the number of years since 1980 and y is the amount of money in billions of dollars. (*Source:* U.S. Office of Management and Budget)

(a) Write the equation in slope–intercept form.

(b) Find the slope and the y-intercept.

(c) In this specific equation, what is the meaning of the slope? What does it indicate?

54. *Civilian Employment* During the years from 1970 to 2005, the approximate number of civilians employed in the United States could be predicted by the equation $y = \frac{1}{10}(22x + 830)$, where x is the number of years since 1970 and y is the number of civilians employed, measured in millions. (*Source:* U.S. Bureau of Labor Statistics)

(a) Write the equation in slope–intercept form.

(b) Find the slope and the y-intercept.

(c) In this specific equation, what is the meaning of the slope? What does it indicate?

Cumulative Review

55. Add. $\dfrac{5}{12} + \dfrac{1}{3} + \dfrac{3}{5}$

56. Multiply. $\dfrac{25}{36} \times \dfrac{54}{45}$

Solve for x and graph the solution.

57. $3x + 8 > 2x + 12$

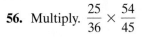

58. $\dfrac{1}{4}x + 3 > \dfrac{2}{3}x + 2$

59. $\dfrac{1}{2}(x + 2) \le \dfrac{1}{3}x + 5$

60. $7x - 2(x + 3) \le 4(x - 7)$

How are you doing with your homework assignments in Sections 4.1 to 4.3? Do you feel you have mastered the material so far? Do you understand the concepts you have covered? Before you go further in the textbook, take some time to do each of the following problems.

1. _____

4.1

1. Plot the following points.

E $(-6, 3)$
F $(5, -4)$
G $(-2, -8)$
H $(6.5, 3.5)$

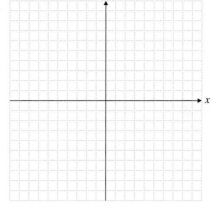

2. _____

2. Give the coordinates for points A, B, C, D.

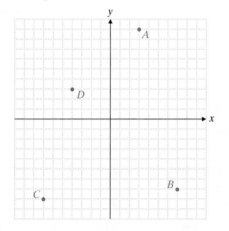

3. _____

3. Complete the ordered pairs for the equation $y = -7x + 3$.

(4,)
(0,)
(−2,)

4. Complete the table for the equation $6x - 5y = -30$.

x	y
0	
	0
	−6

4. _____

4.2

5. Graph $y = -4x - 3$.

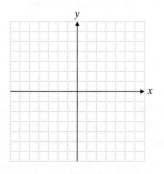

6. Graph $y = \dfrac{3}{4}x - 1$.

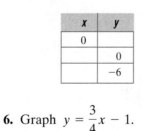

5. _____

6. _____

205

7. _____

7. Graph $3x - 5y = 0$.

8. _____

8. Graph $-5x + 2 = y + 3$.

9. _____

4.3

9. Find the slope of a straight line that passes through $(-6, -8)$ and $(2, -3)$.

10. _____

10. Find the slope and the y-intercept of $9x - 3y - 5 = 0$.

11. A line has a slope of $\dfrac{3}{4}$. What is the slope of a line perpendicular to it?

11. _____

12. A equation of a line is $3y + 11x + 7 = 0$. What is the slope of a line parallel to that line?

Now turn to page SA-9 and 10 for the answer to each of these problems. Each answer also includes a reference to the objective in which the problem is first taught. If you missed any of these problems, you should stop and review the Examples and Practice Problems in the referenced objective. A little review now will help you master the material in the upcoming sections of the text.

12. _____

4.4 WRITING THE EQUATION OF A LINE

 Writing the Equation of a Line Given a Point and a Slope

If we know the slope of a line and the *y*-intercept, we can write the equation of the line in slope–intercept form. Sometimes we are given the slope and a point on the line. We use the information to find the *y*-intercept. Then we can write the equation of the line.

It may be helpful to summarize our approach.

> **TO FIND THE EQUATION OF A LINE GIVEN A POINT AND A SLOPE**
>
> 1. Substitute the given values of *x*, *y*, and *m* into the equation $y = mx + b$.
> 2. Solve for *b*.
> 3. Use the values of *b* and *m* to write the equation in the form $y = mx + b$.

Student Learning Objectives

After studying this section, you will be able to:

1 Write the equation of a line given a point and a slope.

2 Write the equation of a line given two points.

3 Write the equation of a line given a graph of the line.

EXAMPLE 1 Find an equation of the line that passes through $(-3, 6)$ with slope $-\frac{2}{3}$.

Solution We are given the values $m = -\frac{2}{3}$, $x = -3$, and $y = 6$.

$$y = mx + b$$

$$6 = \left(-\frac{2}{3}\right)(-3) + b \quad \text{Substitute known values.}$$

$$6 = 2 + b$$

$$4 = b$$

The equation of the line is $y = -\frac{2}{3}x + 4$.

Practice Problem 1 Find an equation of the line that passes through $(-8, 12)$ with slope $-\frac{3}{4}$.

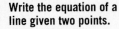

NOTE TO STUDENT: Fully worked-out solutions to all of the Practice Problems can be found at the back of the text starting at page SP-1

2 Writing the Equation of a Line Given Two Points

Our procedure can be extended to the case for which two points are given.

EXAMPLE 2 Find an equation of the line that passes through $(2, 5)$ and $(6, 3)$.

Solution We first find the slope of the line. Then we proceed as in Example 1.

$$m = \frac{y_2 - y_1}{x_2 - x_1}$$

$$m = \frac{3 - 5}{6 - 2} \quad \text{Substitute } (x_1, y_1) = (2, 5) \text{ and } (x_2, y_2) = (6, 3) \text{ into the formula.}$$

$$= \frac{-2}{4} = -\frac{1}{2}$$

Choose either point, say $(2, 5)$, to substitute into $y = mx + b$ as in Example 1.

$$5 = -\frac{1}{2}(2) + b$$

$$5 = -1 + b$$

$$6 = b$$

The equation of the line is $y = -\frac{1}{2}x + 6$.

Note: We could have substituted the slope and the other point, $(6, 3)$, into the slope–intercept form and arrived at the same answer. Try it.

NOTE TO STUDENT: *Fully worked-out solutions to all of the Practice Problems can be found at the back of the text starting at page SP-1*

Practice Problem 2   Find an equation of the line that passes through $(3, 5)$ and $(-1, 1)$.

③ Writing the Equation of a Line Given a Graph of the Line

EXAMPLE 3   What is the equation of the line in the figure at right?

Solution   First, look for the y-intercept. The line crosses the y-axis at $(0, 4)$. Thus $b = 4$.
    Second, find the slope.

$$m = \frac{\text{change in } y}{\text{change in } x}$$

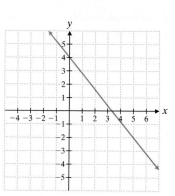

Look for another point on the line. We choose $(5, -2)$. Count the number of vertical units from 4 to -2 (rise). Count the number of horizontal units from 0 to 5 (run).

$$m = \frac{-6}{5}$$

Now, using $m = -\frac{6}{5}$ and $b = 4$, we can write the equation of the line.

$$y = mx + b$$

$$y = -\frac{6}{5}x + 4$$

PRACTICE PROBLEM 3

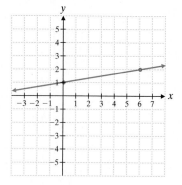

Practice Problem 3   What is the equation of the line in the figure at the left?

Find an equation of the line that has the given slope and passes through the given point.

1. $m = 4, (-3, 0)$

2. $m = 3, (2, -2)$

3. $m = -3, (2, 5)$

4. $m = -2, (3, 2)$

5. $m = -3, \left(\dfrac{1}{2}, 2\right)$

6. $m = -2, \left(3, \dfrac{1}{3}\right)$

7. $m = -\dfrac{2}{5}, (5, -3)$

8. $m = \dfrac{2}{3}, (3, -2)$

Write an equation of the line passing through the given points.

9. $(3, -12)$ and $(-4, 2)$

10. $(-3, 9)$ and $(2, -11)$

11. $(2, -6)$ and $(-1, 6)$

12. $(3, -11)$ and $(-2, 14)$

13. $(3, 5)$ and $(-1, -15)$

14. $(-1, -19)$ and $(2, 2)$

15. $\left(1, \dfrac{5}{6}\right)$ and $\left(3, \dfrac{3}{2}\right)$

16. $(2, 0)$ and $\left(\dfrac{3}{2}, \dfrac{1}{2}\right)$

Mixed Practice

17. Find the equation of a line with a slope of -2 that passes through the point $(4, 3)$.

18. Find the equation of a line with a slope of -4 that passes through the point $(5, 7)$.

19. Find the equation of a line that passes through $(2, -3)$ and $(-1, 6)$.

20. Find the equation of a line that passes through $(1, -8)$ and $(2, -14)$.

Write an equation of each line.

21. **22.** **23.** **24.**

25. **26.** **27.** **28.**

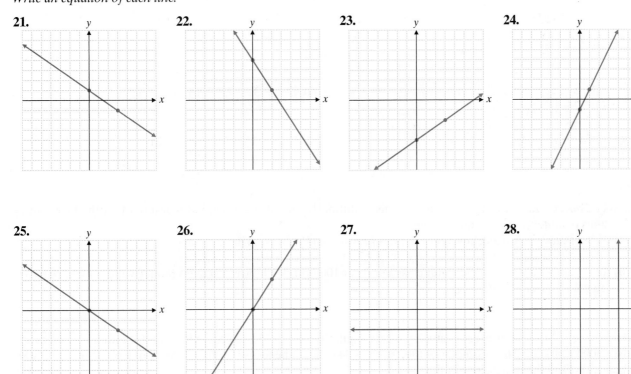

To Think About

Find an equation of the line that fits each description.

29. Passes through $(7, -2)$ and has zero slope

30. Passes through $(4, 6)$ and has undefined slope

31. Passes through $(4, -6)$ and is perpendicular to the x-axis.

32. Passes through $(-3, 5)$ and is perpendicular to the y-axis.

33. Passes through $(0, -4)$ and is parallel to $y = \frac{3}{4}x + 2$

34. Passes through $(0, -4)$ and is perpendicular to $y = \frac{3}{4}x + 2$

35. Passes through $(2, 3)$ and is perpendicular to $y = 2x - 9$

36. Passes through $(2, 9)$ and is parallel to $y = 5x - 3$

37. *Population Growth* The growth of the population of the United States during the period from 1980 to 2005 can be approximated by an equation of the form $y = mx + b$, where x is the number of years since 1980 and y is the population measured in millions. (*Source:* U.S. Census Bureau.) Find the equation if two ordered pairs that satisfy it are $(0, 227)$ and $(10, 251)$.

38. *Home Equity Loans* The amount of debt outstanding on home equity loans in the United States during the period from 1993 to 2005 can be approximated by an equation of the form $y = mx + b$, where x is the number of years since 1993 and y is the debt measured in billions of dollars. (*Source:* Board of Governors of the Federal Reserve System.) Find the equation if two ordered pairs that satisfy it are $(1, 280)$ and $(6, 500)$.

Cumulative Review

Solve.

39. $10 - 3x > 14 - 2x$

40. $2x - 3 \geq 7x - 18$

41. $30 - 2(x + 1) \leq 4x$

42. $2(x + 3) - 22 < 4(x - 2)$

43. *Leaky Faucet* Frank has a leaky faucet in his bathtub. He closed the drain and measured that the faucet drips 8 gallons of water in one 24-hour period.
(a) If the faucet isn't fixed, how many gallons of water will be wasted in one year?

(b) If the faucet isn't fixed and water costs $8.50 per 1000 gallons, how much extra money will Frank have to pay on his water bill for the year?

▲ **44.** *Archeology* Archeologists are searching a rectangular region in Mexico for evidence of a primitive civilization over 3000 years old. The perimeter of the region is 3440 feet. The length of the region is 70 feet longer than twice the width. Find the dimensions of the region.

Putting Your Skills to Work

Graphing the Size of Rainforests

Most of us are aware that the world's rainforests are disappearing, but do you realize how quickly? Rainforests cover only 2% of the Earth's surface, but are home to almost half of all life forms (plants and animals) on the planet. As deforestation continues, many species are becoming extinct and the world's climate is being negatively affected (a phenomenon known as the greenhouse effect).

In 1990, there were 1756 million hectares of rainforest on the planet. Since that time, rainforest destruction has occurred at 2.47 acres per second. (This area is about as large as two football fields.)

Problems for Individual Investigation and Analysis

1. How many acres of rainforest are destroyed each day? Each year? (Round to the nearest million.)

2. Approximately how many acres of rainforest were there in 1990? Round to the nearest million. (1 hectare = 2.47 acres)

3. Use your answers from questions 1 and 2 to determine how many acres of rainforest remained in 1992. How many acres of rainforest were there in 1995?

Problems for Group Investigation and Cooperative Learning

Suppose that the current rate of rainforest destruction continues without intervention. How many acres of rainforest will there be 20 years from now? 35 years

from now? In what year will there be no rainforests left in the world? Answer the following questions to find out.

4. Write a function that gives the number of acres of rainforest r (in millions of acres) that remain t years after 1990.

5. Complete the following table.

Number of Years after 1990	Amount of Rainforest Remaining on Earth (in Millions of Acres)
0	
5	
10	
15	
20	

6. Graph the information from question 5. What is the dependent variable? What is the independent variable? Be sure to use appropriate scales on the axes.

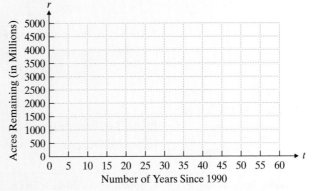

7. Using the graph, determine how many acres of rainforest will remain in the year 2035.

8. Using the graph, determine when there will be no rainforests left on Earth.

211

Topic	Procedure	Examples
Graphing straight lines, p. 184.	An equation of the form $$Ax + By = C$$ has a graph that is a straight line. To graph such an equation, plot any three points; two give the line and the third checks it. (Where possible, use the x- and y-intercepts.)	Graph $3x + 2y = 6$. | x	y
---	---
0	3
4	-3
2	0	
Finding the slope given two points, p. 194.	Nonvertical lines passing through distinct points (x_1, y_1) and (x_2, y_2) have slope $$m = \frac{y_2 - y_1}{x_2 - x_1}.$$ The slope of a horizontal line is 0. The slope of a vertical line is undefined.	What is the slope of the line through $(2, 8)$ and $(5, 1)$? $$m = \frac{1 - 8}{5 - 2} = -\frac{7}{3}$$
Finding the slope and y-intercept of a line given the equation, p. 198.	**1.** Rewrite the equation in the form $y = mx + b$. **2.** The slope is m. **3.** The y-intercept is $(0, b)$.	Find the slope and y-intercept. $$3x - 4y = 8$$ $$-4y = -3x + 8$$ $$y = \frac{3}{4}x - 2$$ The slope is $\frac{3}{4}$. The y-intercept is $(0, -2)$.
Finding the equation of a line given the slope and y-intercept, p. 198.	The slope–intercept form of the equation of a line is $$y = mx + b$$ The slope is m and the y-intercept is $(0, b)$.	Find the equation of the line with y-intercept $(0, 7)$ and with slope $m = 3$. $$y = 3x + 7$$
Graphing a line using slope and y-intercept, p. 199.	**1.** Plot the y-intercept. **2.** Starting from $(0, b)$, plot a second point using the slope. $$\text{slope} = \frac{\text{rise}}{\text{run}}$$ **3.** Draw a line that connects the two points.	Graph $y = -4x + 1$. First plot the y-intercept at $(0, 1)$. Slope $= -4$ or $\frac{-4}{1}$
Finding the slope of parallel and perpendicular lines, p. 200.	Parallel lines have the same slope. Perpendicular lines have slopes whose product is -1.	Line q has a slope of 2. The slope of a line parallel to q is 2. The slope of a line perpendicular to q is $-\frac{1}{2}$.
Finding the equation of a line through a point with a given slope, p. 207.	**1.** Substitute the known values in the equation $y = mx + b$. **2.** Solve for b. **3.** Use the values of m and b to write the general equation.	Find the equation of the line through $(3, 2)$ with slope $m = \frac{4}{5}$. $$y = mx + b \qquad 2 = \frac{4}{5}(3) + b$$ $$2 = \frac{12}{5} + b$$ $$-\frac{2}{5} = b$$ The equation is $y = \frac{4}{5}x - \frac{2}{5}$.

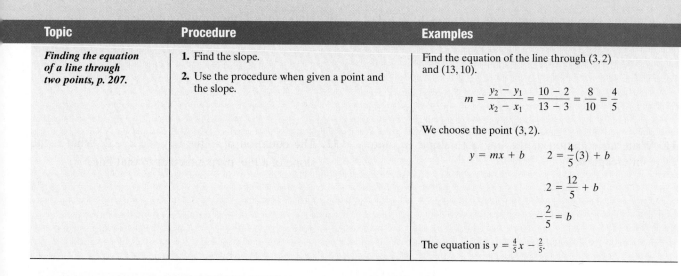

Topic	Procedure	Examples
Finding the equation of a line through two points, p. 207.	**1.** Find the slope. **2.** Use the procedure when given a point and the slope.	Find the equation of the line through $(3, 2)$ and $(13, 10)$. $$m = \frac{y_2 - y_1}{x_2 - x_1} = \frac{10 - 2}{13 - 3} = \frac{8}{10} = \frac{4}{5}$$ We choose the point $(3, 2)$. $$y = mx + b \qquad 2 = \frac{4}{5}(3) + b$$ $$2 = \frac{12}{5} + b$$ $$-\frac{2}{5} = b$$ The equation is $y = \frac{4}{5}x - \frac{2}{5}$.

Chapter 4 Review Problems

Section 4.1

1. Plot and label the following points.
   $A: (2, -3)$ $B: (-1, 0)$ $C: (3, 2)$ $D: (-2, -3)$

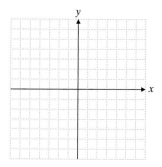

2. Give the coordinates of each point.

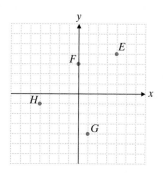

Complete the ordered pairs so that each is a solution to the given equation.

3. $y = 7 - 3x$
   (a) $(0, \ )$ **(b)** $(\ , 10)$

4. $2x + 5y = 12$
   (a) $(1, \ )$ **(b)** $(\ , 4)$

5. $x = 6$
   (a) $(\ , -1)$ **(b)** $(\ , 3)$

Section 4.2

6. Graph $3y = 2x + 6$.

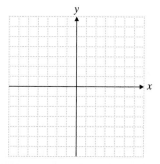

7. Graph $5y + x = -15$.

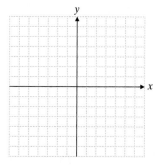

8. Graph $2y + 4x = -8 + 2y$.

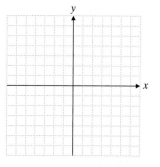

Section 4.3

9. Find the slope of the line passing through $(5, -3)$ and $\left(2, -\frac{1}{2}\right)$.

10. Find the slope and y-intercept of the line $9x - 11y + 15 = 0$.

11. Write an equation of the line with slope $-\frac{1}{2}$ and y-intercept $(0, 3)$.

12. The equation of a line is $y = \frac{3}{5}x - 2$. What is the slope of a line perpendicular to that line?

13. Graph $y = -\frac{1}{2}x + 3$.

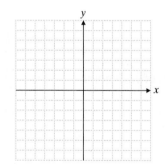

14. Graph $2x - 3y = -12$.

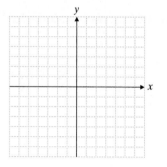

15. Graph $6x - 2y = 6 + 6x$.

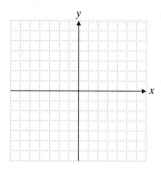

Section 4.4

16. Write an equation of the line passing through $(5, 6)$ having a slope of 2.

17. Write an equation of the line passing through $(3, -4)$ having a slope of -6.

18. Write an equation of the line passing through $(-4, 3)$ having a slope of $-\frac{3}{2}$.

19. Write an equation of the line passing through $(3, 7)$ and $(-6, 7)$.

20. What is the slope of a line parallel to a line whose equation is $y = -\frac{2}{3}x + 4$?

21. What is the slope of a line perpendicular to a line whose equation is $-3x + 4y = 8$?

Write an equation of the graph.

22.

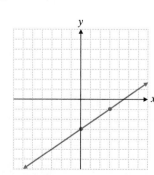

23.

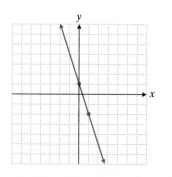

24.

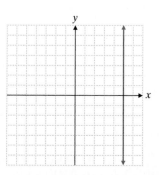

1. Plot and label the following points.
B: $(6, 1)$ C: $(-4, -3)$
D: $(-3, 0)$ E: $(5, -2)$

2. Graph the line $6x - 3 = 5x - 2y$.

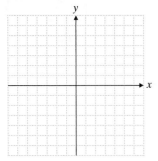

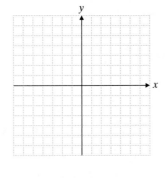

3. Graph the line $8x + 2y = -4$.

4. Graph $y = \frac{2}{3}x - 4$.

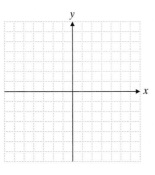

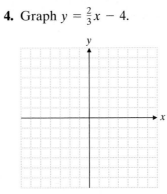

5. What is the slope and the y-intercept of the line $3x + 2y - 5 = 0$?

6. Find the slope of the line that passes through $(8, 6)$ and $(-3, -5)$.

7. Write an equation for the line that passes through $(4, -2)$ and has a slope of $\frac{1}{2}$.

8. Find the slope of the line through $(-3, 11)$ and $(6, 11)$.

9. Find an equation for the line passing through $(5, -4)$ and $(-3, 8)$.

10. Write an equation for the line through $(2, 7)$ and $(2, -2)$. What is the slope of this line?

1. _____

2. _____

3. _____

4. _____

5. _____

6. _____

7. _____

8. _____

9. _____

10. _____

11. _____

11. Graph the region described by $4y \leq 3x$.

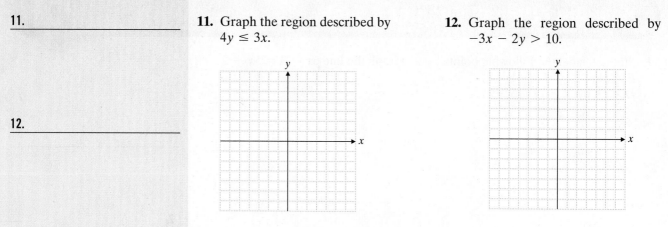

12. Graph the region described by $-3x - 2y > 10$.

12. _____

13. _____

13. Is this relation a function? $\{(2, -8)(3, -7)(2, 5)\}$ Why?

14. Look at the relation graphed below. Is this relation a function? Why?

14. _____

15. _____

15. Graph $y = 2x^2 - 3$.

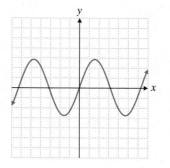

x	y
-2	
-1	
0	
1	
2	

16. (a) _____

    (b) _____

16. For $f(x) = -x^2 - 2x - 3$:

   (a) Find $f(0)$.

   (b) Find $f(-2)$.

17. (a) _____

    (b) _____

17. For $g(x) = \dfrac{3}{x - 4}$:

   (a) Find $g(3)$.

   (b) Find $g(-11)$.

Cell phones have become increasingly popular in recent years. You almost always see someone talking on his or her cell phone in public, even at the beach. For many of us, it is important that other people can contact us wherever we are. Having a cell phone available adds a sense of security in case an emergency should arise. However, choosing a cell phone plan can be confusing. Use your math skills to determine which phone plans are most economical in a variety of situations. Turn to page 233 to see if you can make wise mathematical decisions.

Systems of Linear Equations and Inequalities

5.1   SYSTEMS OF LINEAR EQUATIONS IN TWO VARIABLES   218

HOW AM I DOING? SECTION 5.1   232

CHAPTER 5 ORGANIZER   234

CHAPTER 5 REVIEW PROBLEMS   235

HOW AM I DOING? CHAPTER 5 TEST   240

Student Learning Objectives

After studying this section, you will be able to:

 Determine whether an ordered pair is a solution to a system of two linear equations.

 Solve a system of two linear equations by the graphing method.

③ Solve a system of two linear equations by the substitution method.

④ Solve a system of two linear equations by the addition (elimination) method.

⑤ Identify systems of linear equations that do not have a unique solution.

⑥ Choosing an appropriate method to solve a system of linear equations algebraically.

 ① Determining Whether an Ordered Pair Is a Solution to a System of Two Linear Equations

In Chapter 4 we found that a linear equation containing two variables, such as $4x + 3y = 12$, has an unlimited number of ordered pairs (x, y) that satisfy it. For example, $(3, 0)$, $(0, 4)$, and $(-3, 8)$ all satisfy the equation $4x + 3y = 12$. We call *two* linear equations in two unknowns a **system of two linear equations in two variables.** Many such systems have exactly one solution. A **solution to a system** of two linear equations in two variables is an *ordered pair* that is a solution to *each* equation.

EXAMPLE 1 Determine whether $(3, -2)$ is a solution to the following system.

$$x + 3y = -3$$
$$4x + 3y = 6$$

Solution We will begin by substituting $(3, -2)$ into the first equation to see whether the ordered pair is a solution to the first equation.

$$3 + 3(-2) \stackrel{?}{=} -3$$
$$3 - 6 \stackrel{?}{=} -3$$
$$-3 = -3 \quad \checkmark$$

Likewise, we will determine whether $(3, -2)$ is a solution to the second equation.

$$4(3) + 3(-2) \stackrel{?}{=} 6$$
$$12 - 6 \stackrel{?}{=} 6$$
$$6 = 6 \quad \checkmark$$

Since $(3, -2)$ is a solution to each equation in the system, it is a solution to the system itself.

It is important to remember that we cannot confirm that a particular ordered pair is in fact the solution to a system of two equations unless we have checked to see whether the solution satisfies both equations. Merely checking one equation is not sufficient. Determining whether an ordered pair is a solution to a system of equations requires that we verify that the solution satisfies *both* equations.

Practice Problem 1 Determine whether $(-3, 4)$ is a solution to the following system.

$$2x + 3y = 6$$
$$3x - 4y = 7$$

NOTE TO STUDENT: Fully worked-out solutions to all of the Practice Problems can be found at the back of the text starting at page SP-1

② Solving a System of Two Linear Equations by the Graphing Method

We can verify the solution to a system of linear equations by graphing each equation. If the lines intersect, the system has a unique solution. The point of intersection lies on both lines. Thus, it is a solution to each equation and the solution to the system. We will illustrate this by graphing the equations in Example 1. Notice that the coordinates of the point of intersection are $(3, -2)$. The solution to the system is $(3, -2)$.

This example shows that we can find the solution to a system of linear equations by graphing each line and determining the point of intersection.

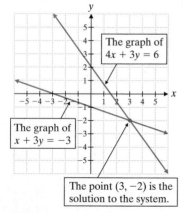

The graph of $4x + 3y = 6$

The graph of $x + 3y = -3$

The point $(3, -2)$ is the solution to the system.

EXAMPLE 2   Solve this system of equations by graphing.

$$2x + 3y = 12$$
$$x - y = 1$$

Solution   Using the methods that we developed in Chapter 4, we graph each line and determine the point at which the two lines intersect.

Finding the solution by the graphing method does not always lead to an accurate result, however, because it involves visual estimation of the point of intersection. Also, our plotting of one or more of the lines could be off slightly. Thus, we verify that our answer is correct by substituting $x = 3$ and $y = 2$ into the system of equations.

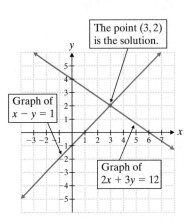

$$
\begin{array}{ll}
x - y = 1 & 2x + 3y = 12 \\
3 - 2 \overset{?}{=} 1 & 2(3) + 3(2) \overset{?}{=} 12 \\
1 = 1\ \checkmark & 12 = 12\ \checkmark
\end{array}
$$

Thus, we have verified that the solution to the system is $(3, 2)$.

Practice Problem 2   Solve this system of equations by graphing. Check your solution.

$$3x + 2y = 10$$
$$x - y = 5$$

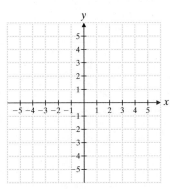

Many times when we graph a system, we find that the two straight lines intersect at one point. However, it is possible for a given system to have as its graph two parallel lines. In such a case there is no solution because there is no point that lies on both lines (i.e., no ordered pair that satisfies both equations). Such a system of equations is said to be **inconsistent.** Another possibility is that when we graph each equation in the system, we obtain one line. In such a case there are an infinite number of solutions. Any point that lies on the first line will also lie on the second line (i.e., any ordered pair). A system of equations in two variables is said to have **dependent equations** if it has infinitely many solutions. We will discuss these situations in more detail after we have developed algebraic methods for solving a system of equations.

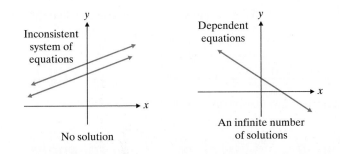

3 Solving a System of Two Linear Equations by the Substitution Method

An algebraic method of solving a system of linear equations in two variables is the **substitution method.** To use this method, we choose one equation and solve for one variable. It is usually best to solve for a variable that has a coefficient of $+1$ or -1. This will help us avoid introducing fractions. When we solve for one variable, we obtain an expression that contains the other variable. We *substitute* this expression into the second equation. Then we have one equation with one unknown, which we can easily solve. Once we know the value of this variable, we can substitute it into one of the original equations to find the value of the other variable.

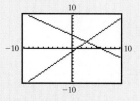
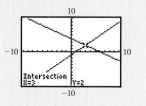
EXAMPLE 3   Find the solution to the following system of equations. Use the substitution method.

$$x + 3y = -7 \quad \textbf{(1)}$$
$$4x + 3y = -1 \quad \textbf{(2)}$$

Solution   We can work with equation **(1)** or equation **(2)**. Let's choose equation **(1)** because x has a coefficient of 1. Now let us solve for x. This gives us equation **(3)**.

$$x = -7 - 3y \quad \textbf{(3)} \qquad \text{Solve } x + 3y = -7 \text{ for } x.$$

Now we substitute this expression for x into equation **(2)** and solve the equation for y.

$$4x + 3y = -1 \quad \textbf{(2)}$$
$$4(-7 - 3y) + 3y = -1 \qquad \text{Replace } x \text{ with } -7 - 3y.$$
$$-28 - 12y + 3y = -1 \qquad \text{Simplify.}$$
$$-28 - 9y = -1 \qquad \text{Solve for } y.$$
$$-9y = -1 + 28$$
$$-9y = 27$$
$$y = -3$$

Now we substitute $y = -3$ into equation **(1)** or **(2)** to find x. Let's use **(1)**:

$$x + 3(-3) = -7 \qquad \textbf{(1)}$$
$$x - 9 = -7$$
$$x = -7 + 9$$
$$x = 2$$

Therefore, our solution is the ordered pair $(2, -3)$.
Check. We must verify the solution in both of the *original* equations.

$$
\begin{array}{ll}
x + 3y = -7 \quad \textbf{(1)} & 4x + 3y = -1 \quad \textbf{(2)} \\
2 + 3(-3) \overset{?}{=} -7 & 4(2) + 3(-3) \overset{?}{=} -1 \\
2 - 9 \overset{?}{=} -7 & 8 - 9 \overset{?}{=} -1 \\
-7 = -7 \ \checkmark & -1 = -1 \ \checkmark
\end{array}
$$

Practice Problem 3   Use the substitution method to solve this system.

$$2x - y = 7$$
$$3x + 4y = -6$$

We summarize the substitution method here.

HOW TO SOLVE A SYSTEM OF TWO LINEAR EQUATIONS BY THE SUBSTITUTION METHOD

1. Choose one of the two equations and solve for one variable in terms of the other variable.
2. Substitute this expression from step 1 into the *other* equation.
3. You now have one equation with one variable. Solve this equation for that variable.
4. Substitute this value for the variable into one of the original equations to obtain a value for the second variable.
5. Check the solution in both original equations.

If a system of equations contains fractions, clear the equations of fractions *before* performing any other steps.

EXAMPLE 4   Find the solution. $\dfrac{3}{2}x + y = \dfrac{5}{2}$ **(1)**

$$-y + 2x = -1 \quad \textbf{(2)}$$

Solution   We want to clear equation **(1)** of fractions. We observe that the LCD of the fractions is 2 .

$$2\left(\dfrac{3}{2}x\right) + 2\,(y) = 2\left(\dfrac{5}{2}\right) \quad \textbf{(1)} \quad \text{Multiply each term of the equation by the LCD.}$$

$$3x + 2y = 5 \qquad \textbf{(3)} \quad \text{This is equivalent to } \dfrac{3}{2}x + y = \dfrac{5}{2}.$$

Our new system is: $3x + 2y = 5$ **(3)**

$$-y + 2x = -1 \quad \textbf{(2)}$$

Now follow the five-step procedure.

Step 1   Solve for one variable. We will use equation **(2)**.

$$-y + 2x = -1$$
$$-y = -1 - 2x \qquad \text{(2)} \qquad \text{Add } -2x \text{ to both sides.}$$
$$y = 1 + 2x \qquad\qquad \text{Multiply each term by } -1.$$

Step 2   Substitute the resulting expression into equation **(3)**.

$$3x + 2(\,1 + 2x\,) = 5 \quad \textbf{(3)}$$

Step 3   Solve this equation for the variable.

$$3x + 2 + 4x = 5 \qquad \text{Remove parentheses.}$$
$$7x + 2 = 5$$
$$7x = 3$$
$$x = \dfrac{3}{7}$$

Step 4   Find the value of the second variable. We will use equation **(2)**.

$$-y + 2x = -1$$
$$-y + 2\left(\dfrac{3}{7}\right) = -1 \qquad \text{Replace } x \text{ with } \dfrac{3}{7}.$$
$$-y + \dfrac{6}{7} = -1$$
$$y - \dfrac{6}{7} = 1 \qquad \text{Multiply each term by } -1.$$
$$y = 1 + \dfrac{6}{7} = \dfrac{13}{7}$$

The solution to the system is $\left(\dfrac{3}{7}, \dfrac{13}{7}\right)$.

Step 5   Check. $\dfrac{3}{2}x + y = \dfrac{5}{2}$ **(1)** $-y + 2x = -1$ **(2)**

$$\dfrac{3}{2}\left(\dfrac{3}{7}\right) + \left(\dfrac{13}{7}\right) \overset{?}{=} \dfrac{5}{2} \qquad\qquad -\dfrac{13}{7} + 2\left(\dfrac{3}{7}\right) \overset{?}{=} -1$$

$$\dfrac{9}{14} + \dfrac{13}{7} \overset{?}{=} \dfrac{5}{2} \qquad\qquad -\dfrac{13}{7} + \dfrac{6}{7} \overset{?}{=} -\dfrac{7}{7}$$

$$\dfrac{9}{14} + \dfrac{26}{14} \overset{?}{=} \dfrac{35}{14} \qquad\qquad -\dfrac{7}{7} = -\dfrac{7}{7} \quad \checkmark$$

$$\dfrac{35}{14} = \dfrac{35}{14} \quad \checkmark$$

NOTE TO STUDENT: Fully worked-out solutions to all of the Practice Problems can be found at the back of the text starting at page SP-1

Practice Problem 4 Use the substitution method to solve this system. Be sure to check your answer.

$$\frac{1}{3}x - \frac{1}{2}y = 1$$
$$x + 4y = -8$$

4 Solving a System of Two Linear Equations by the Addition Method

Another way to solve a system of two linear equations in two variables is to add the two equations so that a variable is eliminated. This technique is called the **addition method** or the **elimination method.** We usually have to multiply one or both of the equations by suitable factors so that we obtain opposite coefficients on one variable (either x or y) in the equations.

EXAMPLE 5 Solve the following system by the addition method.

$$5x + 8y = -1 \quad (1)$$
$$3x + y = 7 \quad (2)$$

Solution We can eliminate either the x- or the y-variable. Let's choose y. We multiply equation **(2)** by -8 to obtain an equivalent equation **(3).**

$$-8(3x) + (-8)(y) = -8(7)$$
$$-24x - 8y = -56 \quad (3)$$

We now add equations **(1)** and **(3).**

$$
\begin{array}{rl}
5x + 8y = & -1 \quad (1) \\
\underline{-24x - 8y = -56} & \quad (3) \\
-19x \quad\;\; = -57 &
\end{array}
$$

We solve for x.

$$x = \frac{-57}{-19} = 3$$

Now we substitute $x = 3$ into equation **(2)** (we could also use equation **(1)**).

$$3(\,3\,) + y = 7 \quad (2)$$
$$9 + y = 7$$
$$y = -2$$

Our solution is $(3, -2)$.

Check.

$$5x + 8y = -1 \qquad\qquad 3x + y = 7$$
$$5(3) + 8(-2) \stackrel{?}{=} -1 \qquad\qquad 3(3) + (-2) \stackrel{?}{=} 7$$
$$15 + (-16) \stackrel{?}{=} -1 \qquad\qquad 9 + (-2) \stackrel{?}{=} 7$$
$$-1 = -1 \;\checkmark \qquad\qquad\qquad 7 = 7 \;\checkmark$$

Practice Problem 5   Use the addition method to solve this system.

$$-3x + y = 5$$
$$2x + 3y = 4$$

For convenience, we summarize the addition method here.

HOW TO SOLVE A SYSTEM OF TWO LINEAR EQUATIONS BY THE ADDITION (ELIMINATION) METHOD

1. Arrange each equation in the form $ax + by = c$. (Remember that a, b, and c can be any real numbers.)

2. Multiply one or both equations by appropriate numbers so that the coefficients of one of the variables are opposites.

3. Add the two equations from step 2 so that one variable is eliminated.

4. Solve the resulting equation for the remaining variable.

5. Substitute this value into one of the *original* equations and solve to find the value of the other variable.

6. Check the solution in both of the original equations.

EXAMPLE 6   Solve the following system by the addition method.

$$3x + 2y = -8 \quad \textbf{(1)}$$
$$2x + 5y = 2 \quad \textbf{(2)}$$

Solution   To eliminate the variable x, we multiply equation **(1)** by 2 and equation **(2)** by -3. We now have the following equivalent system.

$$6x + 4y = -16 \qquad \text{Multiply: } 2(3x + 2y) = 2(-8).$$
$$\underline{-6x - 15y = -6} \qquad \text{Multiply: } -3(2x + 5y) = -3(2).}$$
$$-11y = -22 \qquad \text{Add the equations.}$$
$$y = 2 \qquad \text{Solve for } y.$$

Substitute $y = 2$ into equation **(1).**

$$3x + 2(2) = -8$$
$$3x + 4 = -8 \qquad \text{Solve for } x.$$
$$3x = -12$$
$$x = -4$$

The solution to the system is $(-4, 2)$.

Check. Verify that this solution is correct.

Note. We could have easily eliminated the variable y in Example 6 by multiplying equation **(1)** by 5 and equation **(2)** by -2. Try it. Is the solution the same? Why?

Practice Problem 6   Use the addition (elimination) method to solve this system.

$$5x + 4y = 23$$
$$7x - 3y = 15$$

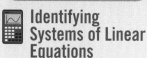
5 Identifying Systems of Linear Equations That Do Not Have a Unique Solution

So far we have examined only those systems that have one solution. But other systems must also be considered. These systems can best be illustrated with graphs. In general, the system of equations

$$ax + by = c$$
$$dx + ey = f$$

may have one solution, no solution, or an infinite number of solutions.

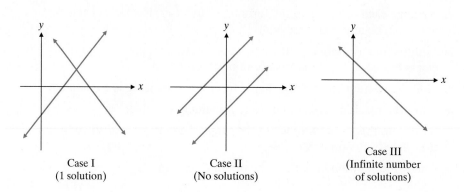

Case I	Case II	Case III
(1 solution)	(No solutions)	(Infinite number of solutions)

Case I: *One solution.* The two graphs intersect at one point, which is the solution. We say that the equations are **independent.** It is a **consistent system** of equations. There is a point (an ordered pair) *consistent* with both equations.

Case II: *No solution.* The two graphs are parallel and so do not intersect. We say that the system of equations is **inconsistent** because there is no point consistent with both equations.

Case III: *An infinite number of solutions.* The graphs of each equation yield the same line. Every ordered pair on this line is a solution to both of the equations. We say that the equations are **dependent.**

EXAMPLE 7 If possible, solve the system.

$$2x + 8y = 16 \quad \textbf{(1)}$$
$$4x + 16y = -8 \quad \textbf{(2)}$$

Solution To eliminate the variable y, we'll multiply equation **(1)** by -2.

$$-2(2x) + (-2)(8y) = (-2)(16)$$
$$-4x - 16y = -32 \quad \textbf{(3)}$$

We now have the following equivalent system.

$$-4x - 16y = -32 \quad \textbf{(3)}$$
$$4x + 16y = -8 \quad \textbf{(2)}$$

When we add equations **(3)** and **(2)**, we get

$$0 = -40,$$

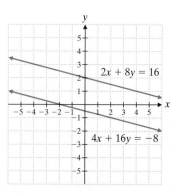

which, of course, is false. Thus, we conclude that this system of equations is inconsistent, and **there is no solution.** Therefore, equations **(1)** and **(2)** do not intersect, as we can see on the accompanying graph.

If we had used the substitution method to solve this system, we still would have obtained a false statement. When you try to solve an inconsistent system of linear equations by any method, you will always obtain a mathematical equation that is not true.

Practice Problem 7   If possible, solve the system.

$$4x - 2y = 6$$
$$-6x + 3y = 9$$

NOTE TO STUDENT: Fully worked-out solutions to all of the Practice Problems can be found at the back of the text starting at page SP-1

EXAMPLE 8   If possible, solve the system.

$$0.5x - 0.2y = \ \ \ 1.3 \quad \textbf{(1)}$$
$$-1.0x + 0.4y = -2.6 \quad \textbf{(2)}$$

Solution   Although we could work directly with the decimals, it is easier to multiply each equation by the appropriate power of 10 (10, 100, and so on) so that the coefficients of the new system are integers. Therefore, we will multiply equations **(1)** and **(2)** by 10 to obtain the following equivalent system.

$$5x - 2y = \ \ \ 13 \quad \textbf{(3)}$$
$$-10x + 4y = -26 \quad \textbf{(4)}$$

We can eliminate the variable y by multiplying each term of equation **(3)** by 2.

$$10x - 4y = \ \ \ 26 \quad \textbf{(3)}$$
$$\underline{-10x + 4y = -26} \quad \textbf{(4)}$$
$$0 = \ \ \ 0 \quad \text{Add the equations.}$$

This statement is always true; it is an **identity.** Hence, the two equations are dependent, and there are an infinite number of solutions. Any solution satisfying equation **(1)** will also satisfy equation **(2).** For example, (3, 1) is a solution to equation **(3).** (Prove this.) Hence, it must also be a solution to equation **(4).** (Prove it). Thus, the equations actually describe the same line, as you can see on the graph.

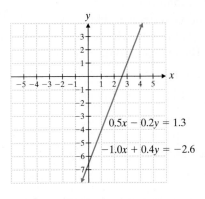

Practice Problem 8   If possible, solve the system.

$$0.3x - 0.9y = \ \ \ 1.8$$
$$-0.4x + 1.2y = -2.4$$

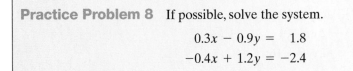

6   ## Choosing an Appropriate Method to Solve a System of Linear Equations Algebraically

At this point we will review the algebraic methods for solving systems of linear equations and discuss the advantages and disadvantages of each method.

Method	Advantage	Disadvantage
Substitution	Works well if one or more variables has a coefficient of 1 or −1.	Often becomes difficult to use if no variable has a coefficient of 1 or −1.
Addition	Works well if equations have fractional or decimal coefficients. Works well if no variable has a coefficient of 1 or −1.	None

EXAMPLE 9   Select a method and solve each system of equations.

(a) $\quad x + \ y = 3080$
$\quad\quad 2x + 3y = 8740$

(b) $\quad\quad 5x - 2y = 19$
$\quad\quad -3x + 7y = 35$

Solution

(a) Since there are x- and y-values that have coefficients of 1, we will select the substitution method.

$$y = 3080 - x \quad\quad \text{Solve the first equation for } y.$$
$$2x + 3(3080 - x) = 8740 \quad\quad \text{Substitute the expression into the second equation.}$$
$$2x + 9240 - 3x = 8740 \quad\quad \text{Remove parentheses.}$$
$$-1x = -500 \quad\quad \text{Simplify.}$$
$$x = 500 \quad\quad \text{Divide each side by } -1.$$

Substitute x = 500 into the equation obtained in step one.

$$y = 3080 - 500$$
$$y = 2580 \quad\quad \text{Simplify.}$$

The solution is $(500, 2580)$.

(b) Because none of the x- and y-variables have a coefficient of 1 or −1, we select the addition method. We choose to eliminate the y-variable. Thus, we would like the coefficients of y to be −14 and 14.

$$7(5x) - 7(2y) = 7(19) \quad\quad \text{Multiply each term of the first equation by 7.}$$
$$2(-3x) + 2(7y) = 2(35) \quad\quad \text{Multiply each term of the second equation by 2.}$$
$$35x - 14y = 133 \quad\quad \text{We now have an equivalent system of equations.}$$
$$\underline{-6x + 14y = \ \ 70}$$
$$29x \quad\quad = 203 \quad\quad \text{Add the two equations.}$$
$$x = 7 \quad\quad \text{Divide each side by 29.}$$

Substitute x = 7 into one of the original equations. We will use the first equation.

$$5(7) - 2y = 19$$
$$35 - 2y = 19 \quad\quad \text{Solve for } y.$$
$$-2y = -16$$
$$y = 8$$

The solution is $(7, 8)$.

Practice Problem 9   Select a method and solve each system of equations.

(a) $3x + 5y = 1485$
    $x + 2y = 564$

(b) $7x + 6y = 45$
    $6x - 5y = -2$

NOTE TO STUDENT: Fully worked-out solutions to all of the Practice Problems can be found at the back of the text starting at page SP-1

TO THINK ABOUT: Two Linear Equations with Two Variables   Now is a good time to look back over what we have learned. When you graph a system of two linear equations, what possible kinds of graphs will you obtain?

What will happen when you try to solve a system of two linear equations using algebraic methods? How many solutions are possible in each case? The following chart may help you to organize your answers to these questions.

Graph	Number of Solutions	Algebraic Interpretation
Two lines intersect at one point (6, −3)	**One unique solution**	You obtain one value for x and one value for y. For example, $x = 6, \ y = -3$.
Parallel lines	**No solution**	You obtain an equation that is inconsistent with known facts. For example, $0 = 6$. The system of equations is inconsistent.
Lines coincide	**Infinite number of solutions**	You obtain an equation that is always true. For example, $8 = 8$. The equations are dependent.

Verbal and Writing Skills

1. Explain what happens when a system of two linear equations is inconsistent. What effect does it have in obtaining a solution? What would the graph of such a system look like?

2. Explain what happens when a system of two linear equations has dependent equations. What effect does it have in obtaining a solution? What would the graph of such a system look like?

3. How many possible solutions can a system of two linear equations in two unknowns have?

4. When you have graphed a system of two linear equations in two unknowns, how do you determine the solution of the system?

Determine whether the given ordered pair is a solution to the system of equations.

5. $\left(\dfrac{3}{2}, -1\right)$ $4x + 1 = 6 - y$
$2x - 5y = 8$

6. $\left(-4, \dfrac{2}{3}\right)$ $2x - 3(y - 5) = 5$
$6y = x + 8$

Solve the system of equations by graphing. Check your solution.

7. $3x + y = 2$
$2x - y = 3$

8. $3x + y = 5$
$2x - y = 5$

9. $2x + 3y = 6$
$2x + y = -2$

10. $2x + 3y = -6$
$x - 3y = 6$

11. $y = -x + 3$
$x + y = -\dfrac{2}{3}$

12. $y = \dfrac{1}{3}x - 2$
$-x + 3y = 9$

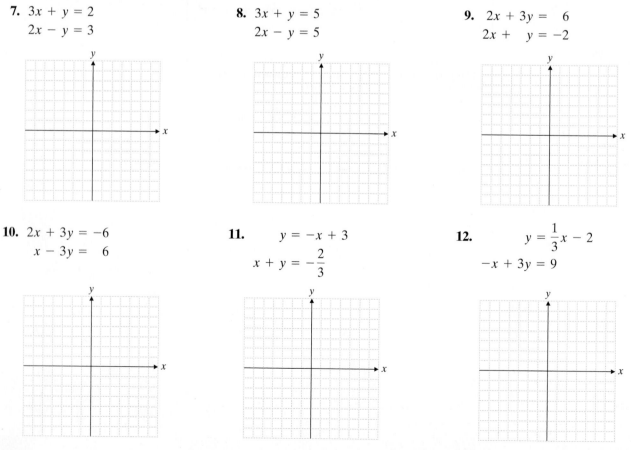

13. $y = -2x + 5$
$3y + 6x = 15$

14. $x - 3 = 2y + 1$
$y - \dfrac{x}{2} = -2$

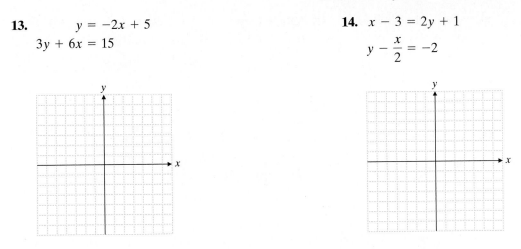

Find the solution to each system by the substitution method. Check your answers for Exercises 15–18.

15. $4x + 3y = 9$
$3y + 6 = x$

16. $4 - 4y = x$
$-x + 2y = 2$

17. $3x + 2y = -17$
$2x + \quad y = \quad 3$

18. $10x + 3y = 8$
$2x + \quad y = 2$

19. $5x + 2y = 5$
$3x + y = 4$

20. $4x + 2y = 4$
$3x + y = 4$

21. $\dfrac{5}{3}x + \dfrac{1}{3}y = -3$
$-2x + 3y = 24$

22. $\dfrac{4}{7}x + \dfrac{2}{7}y = \quad 2$
$3x + y = 13$

Find the solution to each system by the addition (elimination) method. Check your answers for Exercises 23–26.

23. $9x + 2y = 2$
$3x + 5y = 5$

24. $12x - 5y = -7$
$4x + 2y = \quad 5$

25. $6s - 3t = \quad 1$
$5s + 6t = 15$

26. $2s + 3t = \quad 5$
$3s - 6t = 18$

27. $\dfrac{7}{2}x + \dfrac{5}{2}y = -4$
$3x + \dfrac{2}{3}y = \quad 1$

28. $\dfrac{4}{3}x - y = 4$
$\dfrac{3}{4}x - y = \dfrac{1}{2}$

29. $1.6x + 1.5y = 1.8$
$0.4x + 0.3y = 0.6$

30. $2.5x + 0.6y = 0.2$
$0.5x - 1.2y = 0.7$

Mixed Practice

If possible, solve each system of equations. Use any method. If there is not a unique solution to a system, state a reason.

31. $7x - \quad y = \quad 6$
$3x + 2y = 22$

32. $8x - \quad y = 17$
$4x + 3y = 33$

33. $3x + 4y = \quad 8$
$5x + 6y = 10$

34. $7x + 5y = -25$
$3x + 7y = -\ 1$

35. $2x + \quad y = 4$
$\dfrac{2}{3}x + \dfrac{1}{4}y = 2$

36. $4x + 5y = \quad 2$
$\dfrac{1}{5}x + y = -\dfrac{7}{5}$

37. $0.2x = 0.1y - 1.2$
$2x - y = 6$

38. $0.1x - 0.6 = 0.3y$
$0.3x + 0.1y + 2.2 = 0$

39. $5x - 7y = 12$
$-10x + 14y = -24$

40. $3x - 11y = 9$
$-9x + 33y = 18$

41. $0.8x + 0.9y = 1.3$
$0.6x - 0.5y = 4.5$

42. $0.6y = 0.9x + 1$
$3x = 2y - 4$

43. $-a + \dfrac{4}{5}b = \dfrac{1}{5}$
$15a - 12b = 4$

44. $3a - 2b = \dfrac{3}{2}$
$\dfrac{3a}{2} - b = \dfrac{3}{4}$

45. $\dfrac{3}{8}x + y = 14$
$2x - \dfrac{7}{4}y = 18$

46. $\dfrac{4}{5}x - y = 7$
$x - \dfrac{4}{3}y = 8$

47. $3.2x - 1.5y = -3$
$0.7x + y = 2$

48. $3x - 0.2y = 1$
$1.1x + 0.4y = -2$

49. $3 - (2x + 1) = y + 6$
$x + y + 5 = 1 - x$

50. $2(y - 3) = x + 3y$
$x + 2 = 3 - y$

To Think About

51. *Bathroom Tile* Wayne Burton is having some tile replaced in his bathroom. He has obtained an estimate from two tile companies. Old World Tile gave an estimate of $200 to remove the old tile and $50 per hour to place new tile on the wall. Modern Bathroom Headquarters gave an estimate of $300 to remove the old tile and $30 per hour to place new tile on the wall.

(a) Create a cost equation for each company where y is the total cost of the tile work and x is the number of hours of labor. Write a system of equations.

(b) Graph the two equations using the values $x = 0, 4$, and 8.

(c) Determine from your graph how many hours of installing new tile will be required for the two companies to cost the same.

(d) Determine from your graph which company costs less to remove old tile and to install new tile if the time needed to install new tile is 6 hours.

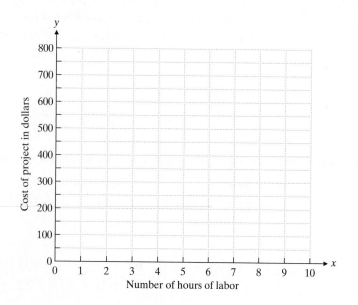

52. *Moving Furniture* Jeff and Shelley are planning to move some furniture to their daughter's house. Seaside Movers quoted a price of $100 for the truck and $40 per hour for the movers. Beverly Rapid Mover quoted a price of $50 for the truck and $50 per hour for the movers.
    (a) Create a cost equation for each company where y is the total cost of the move and x is the number of hours of labor. Write a system of equations.
    (b) Graph the two equations using the values $x = 0, 4,$ and 7.
    (c) Determine from your graph how many hours of moving would be required for the two companies to cost the same.
    (d) Determine from your graph which company costs less to conduct the move if the total number of hours needed for moving is 3 hours.

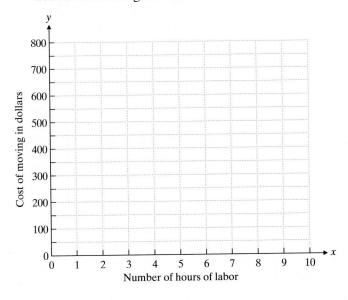

Cumulative Review

53. *Stained-Glass Table* Gina is covering the top of a rectangular table with a stained-glass mosaic. The stained glass she plans to use costs $8 per square foot. If the table top measures 18 inches by 27 inches, how much will Gina spend on the stained glass?

54. *City Parking Space* Eighty percent of the automobiles that enter the city of Boston during rush hour will have to park in private or municipal parking lots. If there are 273,511 private or municipal lot spaces filled by cars entering the city during rush hour every morning, how many cars enter the city during rush hour? Round your answer to the nearest car.

1. _____

2. _____

3. _____

4. _____

5. _____

6. _____

7. _____

How are you doing with your homework assignments in Section 5.1? Do you feel you have mastered the material so far? Do you understand the concepts you have covered? Before you go further in the textbook, take some time to do each of the following problems.

5.1

1. Solve by the substitution method.
$$4x - y = -1$$
$$3x + 2y = 13$$

2. Solve by the addition method.
$$3x + 2y = 9$$
$$5x + 4y = 13$$

Find the solution to each system of equations by any method. If there is no single solution to a system, state the reason.

3. $5x - 2y = 27$
$3x - 5y = -18$

4. $7x + 3y = 15$
$\frac{1}{3}x - \frac{1}{2}y = 2$

5. $2x - y = 3$
$-6x + 3y = -9$

6. $0.2x + 0.7y = -1$
$0.5x + 0.6y = -0.2$

7. $6x - 9y = 15$
$-4x + 6y = 8$

Now turn to page SA-14 for the answers to each of these problems. Each answer also includes a reference to the objective in which the problem is first taught. If you missed any of these problems, you should stop and review the Examples and Practice Problems in the referenced objective. A little review now will help you master the material in the upcoming sections of the text.

Putting Your Skills to Work

Analyzing Cell Phone Plans

Aaron and Gina are each interested in getting a cell phone, but their situations and the uses they will have for their cell phones are quite different.

Gina wants a cell phone to use in case of emergencies. Her job requires that she drive many miles each week, and she would like to have a cell phone available in case her car, which is far from new, breaks down. Aaron is self-employed and would use a cell phone to conduct business when he's occasionally away from his office during the week. He would probably use his cell phone for about 2 weekday hours each month.

Two of the cell phone plans available in their area are quite economical. Both plans offer a generous number of weekend minutes, but both Aaron and Gina plan to use their cell phones primarily during the week.

Plan A would cost $20 per month. It offers 30 free weekday minutes per month and charges $0.52/minute for any weekday minutes over 30. Plan B costs $30 per month. It also offers 30 free weekday minutes but charges $0.40 for any minutes used over 30.

Problems for Individual Investigation and Analysis

1. Write an equation that gives the monthly cost for each plan in terms of x, where x represents the number of weekday minutes more than 30 that are used.

2. Plot both equations on the axes.

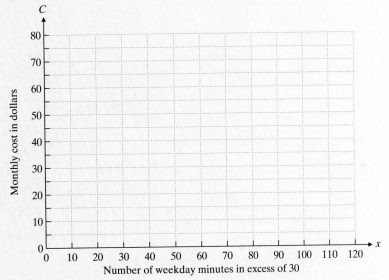

At what value of x do the equations appear to intersect? How many minutes of weekday cell phone use per month does this represent?

3. Solve the system of two equations for x algebraically. Does your answer agree with your answer to Exercise 2?

4. Which plan would be more economical for Gina? Which plan would be more economical for Aaron?

5. If Aaron uses his cell phone for 10 weekday hours during the month, what will his cell phone bill for that month be?

Problems for Group Investigation and Cooperative Study

Aaron investigates further and finds other cell phone plans that may be more economical for him. Plan C costs $40 per month. It offers 450 free weekday minutes per month and charges $0.30/minute for any weekday minutes over 450. Plan D costs $45 per month. It offers 600 free weekday minutes and charges $0.25 for additional minutes.

6. Of Plans B, C, or D, which is most economical for Aaron, given his estimated phone use?

7. If Aaron's business expands and he finds that he needs to use his phone about 8 weekday hours per month, which phone plan will be most economical?

Topic	Procedure	Examples
Finding a solution to a system of equations by the graphing method, p. 218.	**1.** Graph the first equation. **2.** Graph the second equation. **3.** Approximate from your graph where the two lines intersect, if they intersect at one point. **4.** If the lines are parallel, there is no solution. If the lines coincide, there are an infinite number of solutions.	Solve by graphing: $x + y = 6$ $\qquad\qquad\qquad\quad 2x - y = 6$ Graph each line. The solution is $(4, 2)$.
Solving a system of two linear equations by the substitution method, p. 220.	The substitution method is most appropriate when *at least one variable has a coefficient of 1 or −1.* **1.** Solve for one variable in one of the equations. **2.** In the other equation, replace that variable with the expression you obtained in step 1. **3.** Solve the resulting equation. **4.** Substitute the numerical value you obtain for a variable into one of the original equations and solve for the other variable. **5.** Check the solution in both original equations.	Solve: $\qquad 2x + y = 11 \qquad$ **(1)** $\qquad\qquad\quad x + 3y = 18 \qquad$ **(2)** $y = 11 - 2x$ from equation **(1)**. Substitute into **(2)**. $\qquad x + 3(11 - 2x) = 18$ $\qquad\quad x + 33 - 6x = 18$ $\qquad\qquad\qquad -5x = -15$ $\qquad\qquad\qquad\quad x = 3$ Substitute $x = 3$ into $2x + y = 11$. $\qquad\qquad 2(3) + y = 11$ $\qquad\qquad\qquad\quad y = 5$ The solution is $(3, 5)$.
Solving a system of two linear equations by the addition method, p. 223.	The addition method is most appropriate when the variables *all have coefficients other than 1 or −1.* **1.** Arrange each equation in the form $ax + by = c$. **2.** Multiply one or both equations by appropriate numerical values so that when the two resulting equations are added, one variable is eliminated. **3.** Solve the resulting equation. **4.** Substitute the numerical value you obtain for the variable into one of the original equations. **5.** Solve this equation to find the other variable.	Solve: $\qquad 2x + 3y = 5 \qquad$ **(1)** $\qquad\qquad\, -3x - 4y = -2 \qquad$ **(2)** Multiply equation **(1)** by 3 and **(2)** by 2. $\qquad\qquad 6x + 9y = 15$ $\qquad\qquad\underline{-6x - 8y = -4}$ $\qquad\qquad\qquad\quad y = 11$ Substitute $y = 11$ into equation **(1)**. $\qquad\qquad 2x + 3(11) = 5$ $\qquad\qquad\, 2x + 33 = 5$ $\qquad\qquad\qquad 2x = -28$ $\qquad\qquad\qquad\, x = -14$ The solution is $(-14, 11)$.
Inconsistent system of equations, p. 224.	If there is *no solution* to a system of linear equations, the system of equations is inconsistent. When you try to solve an inconsistent system, you obtain an equation that is not true, such as $0 = 5$.	Solve: $\qquad 4x + 3y = 10 \qquad$ **(1)** $\qquad\qquad\, -8x - 6y = 5 \qquad$ **(2)** Multiply equation **(1)** by 2 and add to **(2)**. $\qquad\qquad 8x + 6y = 20$ $\qquad\qquad\underline{-8x - 6y = 5}$ $\qquad\qquad\qquad\, 0 = 25$ But $0 \neq 25$. Thus, there is no solution. The system of equations is inconsistent.

Topic	Procedure	Examples
Dependent equations, p. 224.	If there are an *infinite number of solutions* to a system of linear equations, at least one pair of equations is dependent. When you try to solve a system that contains dependent equations, you will obtain an equation that is always true (such as $0 = 0$ or $3 = 3$). These equations are called *identities*.	Attempt to solve the system. $$x - 2y = -5 \quad \textbf{(1)}$$ $$-3x + 6y = 15 \quad \textbf{(2)}$$ Multiply equation **(1)** by 3 and add to **(2)**. $$3x - 6y = -15$$ $$\underline{-3x + 6y = 15}$$ $$0 = 0$$ There are an infinite number of solutions. The equations are dependent.

Chapter 5 Review Problems

Solve the following systems by graphing.

1. $x + 2y = 8$
$x - y = 2$

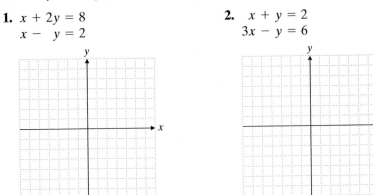

2. $x + y = 2$
$3x - y = 6$

3. $2x + y = 6$
$3x + 4y = 4$

Solve the following systems by substitution.

4. $3x - 2y = -9$
$2x + y = 1$

5. $-6x - y = 1$
$3x - 4y = 31$

6. $4x - 3y = 15$
$7x - y = 5$

7. $-7x + y = -4$
$5x + 2y = 11$

Solve the following systems by addition.

8. $-2x + 5y = -12$
$3x + y = 1$

9. $-3x + 4y = 9$
$5x + 3y = -15$

10. $7x - 4y = 2$
$6x - 5y = -3$

11. $5x + 2y = 3$
$7x + 5y = -20$

Solve by any appropriate method. If there is no unique solution, state why.

12. $x = 3 - 2y$
$3x + 6y = 8$

13. $x + 5y = 10$
$$y = 2 - \frac{1}{5}x$$

14. $7x + 6y = -10$
$2x + y = 0$

15. $3x + 4y = 1$
$9x - 2y = -4$

16. $x + \dfrac{1}{3}y = 1$
$\dfrac{1}{4}x - \dfrac{3}{4}y = -\dfrac{9}{4}$

17. $\dfrac{2}{3}x + y = 1$
$\dfrac{1}{3}x + y = \dfrac{5}{6}$

18. $3a + 8b = 0$
$9a + 2b = 11$

19. $3a + 5b = -2$
$10b = -6a - 4$

20. $x + 3 = 3y + 1$
$1 - 2(x - 2) = 6y + 1$

21. $10(x + 1) - 13 = -8y$
$4(2 - y) = 5(x + 1)$

22. $0.3x - 0.2y = 0.7$
$-0.6x + 0.4y = 0.3$

23. $0.2x - 0.1y = 0.8$
$0.1x + 0.3y = 1.1$

Solve by an appropriate method.

24. $3x - 2y - z = 3$
$2x + y + z = 1$
$-x - y + z = -4$

25. $-2x + y - z = -7$
$x - 2y - z = 2$
$6x + 4y + 2z = 4$

26. $2x + 5y + z = 3$
$x + y + 5z = 42$
$2x + y = 7$

27. $x + 2y + z = 5$
$3x - 8y = 17$
$2y + z = -2$

28. $2x - 4y + 3z = 0$
$x - 2y - 5z = 13$
$5x + 3y - 2z = 19$

29. $5x + 2y + 3z = 10$
$6x - 3y + 4z = 24$
$-2x + y + 2z = 2$

30. $\begin{aligned} 3x + 2y &= 7 \\ 2x \quad\;\; + 7z &= -26 \\ 5y + z &= 6 \end{aligned}$

31. $\begin{aligned} x - y &= 2 \\ 5x + 7y - 5z &= 2 \\ 3x - 5y + 2z &= -2 \end{aligned}$

Use a system of linear equations to solve each of the following exercises.

32. *Commercial Airline* A plane flies 720 miles against the wind in 3 hours. The return trip with the wind takes only $2\frac{1}{2}$ hours. Find the speed of the wind. Find the speed of the plane in still air.

33. *Football* Two football teams scored a total of 11 times during Saturday's game. They scored a number of touchdowns for 7 points each and several field goals at 3 points each. Altogether they scored 65 points. How many touchdowns and how many field goals did they score?

34. *Temporary Help Expenses* When the circus came to town last year, they hired general laborers at $70 per day and mechanics at $90 per day. They paid $1950 for this temporary help for one day. This year they hired exactly the same number of people of each type, but they paid $80 for general laborers and $100 for mechanics for the one day. This year they paid $2200 for temporary help. How many general laborers did they hire? How many mechanics did they hire?

35. *Circus Ticket Prices* A total of 590 tickets were sold for the circus matinee performance. Children's admission tickets were $6, and adult tickets were $11. The ticket receipts for the matinee performance were $4790. How many children's tickets were sold? How many adult tickets were sold?

36. *Baseball Equipment* A baseball coach bought two hats, five shirts, and four pairs of pants for $129. His assistant purchased one hat, one shirt, and two pairs of pants for $42. The next week the coach bought two hats, three shirts, and one pair of pants for $63. What was the cost of each item?

37. *Math Exam Scores* Jess, Chris, and Nick scored a total of 249 points on their last math exam. Jess's score was 20 points higher than Chris's score. Twice Nick's score was 6 more than the sum of Chris's and Jess's scores. What was each of their score on the exam?

38. *Food Costs* Four jars of jelly, three jars of peanut butter, and five jars of honey cost $9.80. Two jars of jelly, two jars of peanut butter, and one jar of honey cost $4.20. Three jars of jelly, four jars of peanut butter, and two jars of honey cost $7.70. Find the cost for one jar of jelly, one jar of peanut butter, and one jar of honey.

39. *Transportation Logistics* The church youth group is planning a trip to Mount Washington. A total of 127 people need rides. The church has available buses that hold forty passengers, and several parents have volunteered station wagons that hold eight passengers or sedans that hold five passengers. The youth leader is planning to use nine vehicles to transport the people. One parent said that if they didn't use any buses, tripled the number of station wagons, and doubled the number of sedans, they would be able to transport 126 people. How many buses, station wagons, and sedans are they planning to use if they use nine vehicles?

Mixed Practice Exercises 40–53

Solve by any appropriate method.

40. $-x - 5z = -5$
$\quad\ 13x + 2z = \quad 2$

41. $x - y = 1$
$\quad\ 5x + y = 7$

42. $2x + 5y = \quad 4$
$\quad\ 5x - 7y = -29$

43. $\dfrac{x}{2} - 3y = -6$

$\quad \dfrac{4}{3}x + 2y = \quad 4$

44. $\dfrac{3}{5}x - y = \quad 6$

$\qquad x + \dfrac{y}{3} = 10$

45. $\dfrac{x + 1}{5} = y + 2$

$\quad \dfrac{2y + 7}{3} = x - y$

46. $3(2 + x) = y + 1$
$\quad\ 5(x - y) = -7 - 3y$

47. $7(x + 3) = 2y + 25$
$\quad\ 3(x - 6) = -2(y + 1)$

48. $0.3x - 0.4y = 0.9$
$\quad\ 0.2x - 0.3y = 0.4$

49. $1.2x - y = 1.6$
$\quad\ x + 1.5y = 6$

50. $x - \dfrac{y}{2} + \dfrac{1}{2}z = -1$

$\quad 2x \qquad + \dfrac{5}{2}z = -1$

$\qquad\quad \dfrac{3}{2}y + 2z = \quad 1$

51. $2x - 3y + 2z = \quad 0$
$\quad\ x + 2y - \ z = \quad 2$
$\quad\ 2x + \ y + 3z = -1$

52. $x - 4y + 4z = -1$
$\quad\ 2x - \ y + 5z = -3$
$\quad\ x - 3y + \ z = \quad 4$

53. $x - 2y + z = \quad -5$
$\quad\ 2x + \qquad z = -10$
$\qquad\quad\ y - z = \quad 15$

Solve each of the following systems of linear inequalities by graphing.

54. $x - y \leq 3$

$y \leq -\dfrac{1}{4}x + 2$

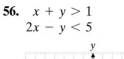

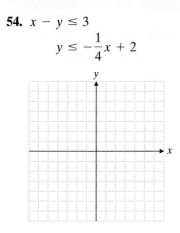

55. $-2x + 3y < 6$

$y > -2$

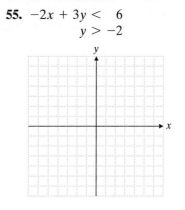

56. $x + y > 1$

$2x - y < 5$

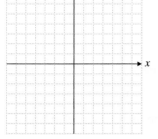

57. $x + y \geq 4$

$y \leq x$

$x \leq 6$

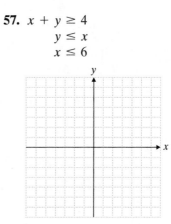

Solve each system of equations. If there is no solution to the system, give a reason.

1. _____

1. Solve using the substitution method:
$$x - y = 3$$
$$2x - 3y = -1$$

2. Solve using the addition method:
$$3x + 2y = 1$$
$$5x + 3y = 3$$

2. _____

In exercises 3–9, solve using any method.

3. _____

3. $5x - 3y = 3$
   $7x + y = 25$

4. $\frac{1}{4}a - \frac{3}{4}b = -1$

   $\frac{1}{3}a + b = \frac{5}{3}$

4. _____

5. $\frac{1}{3}x + \frac{5}{6}y = 2$

   $\frac{3}{5}x - y = -\frac{7}{5}$

6. $8x - 3y = 5$
   $-16x + 6y = 8$

5. _____

6. _____

7. $3x + 5y - 2z = -5$
   $2x + 3y - z = -2$
   $2x + 4y + 6z = 18$

8. $3x + 2y = 0$
   $2x - y + 3z = 8$
   $5x + 3y + z = 4$

9. $x + 5y + 4z = -3$
   $x - y - 2z = -3$
   $x + 2y + 3z = -5$

7. _____

Use a system of linear equations to solve the following exercises.

8. _____

10. A plane flew 1000 miles with a tailwind in 2 hours. The return trip against the wind took $2\frac{1}{2}$ hours. Find the speed of the wind and the speed of the plane in still air.

9. _____

11. The math club is selling items with the college logo to raise money. Sam bought 4 pens, a mug, and a T-shirt for $20.00. Alicia bought 2 pens and 2 mugs for $11.00. Ramon bought 6 pens, a mug, and 2 T-shirts for $33.00. What was the price of each pen, mug, and T-shirt?

12. Sue Miller had to move some supplies to Camp Cherith for the summer camp program. She rented a Portland Rent-A-Truck in April for 5 days and drove 150 miles. She paid $180 for the rental in April. Then in May she rented the same truck again for 7 days and drove 320 miles. She paid $274 for the rental in May. How much does Portland Rent-A-Truck charge for a daily rental of the truck? How much do they charge per mile?

10. _____

Solve the following systems of linear inequalities by graphing.

11. _____

13. $x + 2y \leq 6$
   $-2x + y \geq -2$

14. $3x + y > 8$
   $x - 2y > 5$

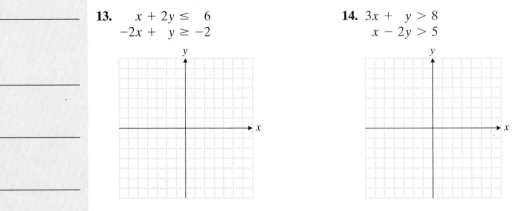

12. _____

13. _____

14. _____

Polynomials are an important tool of mathematics. They are used to create formulas that model many real-world phenomena. Let us take a simple example. Suppose you wanted to know how much more you might make over your lifetime if you obtain a bachelor's degree as opposed to just an associate's degree. Suppose you wanted to know what the expected annual income will be in the future if you obtain a bachelor's degree. Do you think you could use your mathematical skills to determine these values? Turn to the Putting Your Skills to Work problems on page 259 to find out.

Exponents and Polynomials

6.1   THE RULES OF EXPONENTS   242

6.2   NEGATIVE EXPONENTS AND SCIENTIFIC NOTATION   251

       HOW AM I DOING? SECTIONS 6.1–6.2   258

       CHAPTER 6 ORGANIZER   260

       CHAPTER 6 REVIEW PROBLEMS   260

       HOW AM I DOING? CHAPTER 6 TEST   262

6.1 THE RULES OF EXPONENTS

Student Learning Objectives

After studying this section, you will be able to:

1 Use the product rule to multiply exponential expressions with like bases.

2 Use the quotient rule to divide exponential expressions with like bases.

3 Raise exponential expressions to a power.

1 Using the Product Rule to Multiply Exponential Expressions with Like Bases

Recall that x^2 means $x \cdot x$. That is, x appears as a factor two times. The 2 is called the **exponent.** The **base** is the variable x. The expression x^2 is called an **exponential expression.** What happens when we multiply $x^2 \cdot x^2$? Is there a pattern that will help us form a general rule?

$$(2^2)(2^3) = \overbrace{(2 \cdot 2)(2 \cdot 2 \cdot 2)}^{5 \text{ twos}} = 2^5$$

The exponent means 2 occurs 5 times as a factor.

$$(3^3)(3^4) = \overbrace{(3 \cdot 3 \cdot 3)(3 \cdot 3 \cdot 3 \cdot 3)}^{7 \text{ threes}} = 3^7$$

Notice that $3 + 4 = 7$.

$$(x^3)(x^5) = \overbrace{(x \cdot x \cdot x)(x \cdot x \cdot x \cdot x \cdot x)}^{8 \ x\text{'s}} = x^8$$

The sum of the exponents is $3 + 5 = 8$.

$$(y^4)(y^2) = \overbrace{(y \cdot y \cdot y \cdot y)(y \cdot y)}^{6 \ y\text{'s}} = y^6$$

The sum of the exponents is $4 + 2 = 6$.

We can state the pattern in words and then use variables.

> ### THE PRODUCT RULE
>
> To multiply two exponential expressions that have the same base, keep the base and *add the exponents.*
> $$x^a \cdot x^b = x^{a+b}$$

Be sure to notice that this rule applies only to expressions that have the *same base*. Here x represents the base, while the letters a and b represent the exponents that are added.

It is important that you apply this rule even when an exponent is 1. Every variable that does not have a written exponent is understood to have an exponent of 1. Thus $x^1 = x$, $y^1 = y$, and so on.

EXAMPLE 1   Multiply.   (a) $x^3 \cdot x^6$ (b) $x \cdot x^5$

Solution

(a) $x^3 \cdot x^6 = x^{3+6} = x^9$

(b) $x \cdot x^5 = x^{1+5} = x^6$ Note that the exponent of the first x is 1.

Practice Problem 1   Multiply.   (a) $a^7 \cdot a^5$ (b) $w^{10} \cdot w$

NOTE TO STUDENT: Fully worked-out solutions to all of the Practice Problems can be found at the back of the text starting at page SP-1

EXAMPLE 2   Simplify.   (a) $y^5 \cdot y^{11}$ (b) $2^3 \cdot 2^5$ (c) $x^6 \cdot y^8$

Solution

(a) $y^5 \cdot y^{11} = y^{5+11} = y^{16}$

(b) $2^3 \cdot 2^5 = 2^{3+5} = 2^8$ Note that the base does not change! Only the exponent changes.

(c) $x^6 \cdot y^8$ The rule for multiplying exponential expressions does not apply since the bases are not the same. This cannot be simplified.

Practice Problem 2   Simplify, if possible.

(a) $x^3 \cdot x^9$ (b) $3^7 \cdot 3^4$ (c) $a^3 \cdot b^2$

We can now look at multiplying expressions such as $(2x^5)(3x^6)$.

The number 2 in $2x^5$ is called the **numerical coefficient.** Recall that a numerical coefficient is a number that is multiplied by a variable. When we multiply two expressions such as $2x^5$ and $3x^6$, we first multiply the numerical coefficients; we multiply the variables with exponents separately.

EXAMPLE 3   Multiply.   **(a)** $(2x^5)(3x^6)$ **(b)** $(5x^3)(x^6)$ **(c)** $(-6x)(-4x^5)$

Solution

(a) $(2x^5)(3x^6) = (2 \cdot 3)(x^5 \cdot x^6)$ Multiply the numerical coefficients.

$\qquad\qquad\quad\; = 6(x^5 \cdot x^6)$ Use the rule for multiplying expressions with exponents. Add the exponents.

$\qquad\qquad\quad\; = 6x^{11}$

(b) Every variable that does not have a visible numerical coefficient is understood to have a numerical coefficient of 1. Thus x^6 has a numerical coefficient of 1.

$$(5x^3)(x^6) = (5 \cdot 1)(x^3 \cdot x^6) = 5x^9$$

(c) $(-6x)(-4x^5) = (-6)(-4)(x^1 \cdot x^5) = 24x^6$ Remember that x has an exponent of 1.

Practice Problem 3   Multiply.

(a) $(-a^8)(a^4)$ **(b)** $(3y^2)(-2y^3)$ **(c)** $(-4x^3)(-5x^2)$

Problems of this type may involve more than one variable or more than two factors.

EXAMPLE 4   Multiply. $(5ab)\left(-\tfrac{1}{3}a\right)(9b^2)$

Solution $(5ab)\left(-\tfrac{1}{3}a\right)(9b^2) = (5)\left(-\tfrac{1}{3}\right)(9)(a \cdot a)(b \cdot b^2)$

$\qquad\qquad\qquad\qquad\qquad\;\; = -15a^2b^3$

As you do the following problems, keep in mind the rule for multiplying numbers with exponents and the rules for multiplying signed numbers.

Practice Problem 4   Multiply. $(2xy)\left(-\tfrac{1}{4}x^2y\right)(6xy^3)$

---

② Using the Quotient Rule to Divide Exponential Expressions with Like Bases

Frequently, we must divide exponential expressions. Since division by zero is undefined, in all problems in this chapter we assume that the denominator of any variable expression is not zero. We'll look at division in three separate parts.

Suppose that we want to simplify $x^5 \div x^2$. We could do the division the long way.

$$\frac{x^5}{x^2} = \frac{(x)(x)(x)\cancel{(x)}\cancel{(x)}}{\cancel{(x)}\cancel{(x)}} = x^3$$

Here we are using the arithmetical property of reducing fractions (see Section 0.1). When the same factor appears in both numerator and denominator, that factor can be removed.

A simpler way is to *subtract the exponents*. Notice that the base remains the same.

> ## THE QUOTIENT RULE (PART 1)
>
> $\dfrac{x^a}{x^b} = x^{a-b}$ Use this form if the larger exponent is in the numerator and $x \neq 0$.

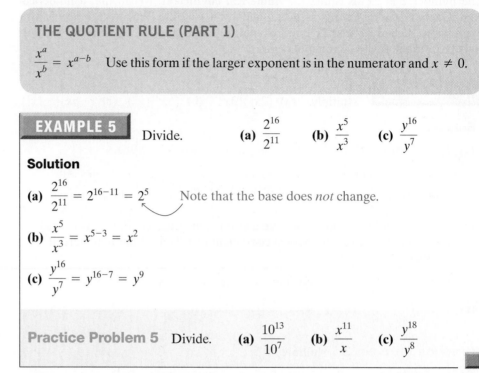

EXAMPLE 5   Divide.   **(a)** $\dfrac{2^{16}}{2^{11}}$ **(b)** $\dfrac{x^5}{x^3}$ **(c)** $\dfrac{y^{16}}{y^7}$

Solution

(a) $\dfrac{2^{16}}{2^{11}} = 2^{16-11} = 2^5$ Note that the base does *not* change.

(b) $\dfrac{x^5}{x^3} = x^{5-3} = x^2$

(c) $\dfrac{y^{16}}{y^7} = y^{16-7} = y^9$

NOTE TO STUDENT: *Fully worked-out solutions to all of the Practice Problems can be found at the back of the text starting at page SP-1*

Practice Problem 5   Divide.   **(a)** $\dfrac{10^{13}}{10^7}$ **(b)** $\dfrac{x^{11}}{x}$ **(c)** $\dfrac{y^{18}}{y^8}$

Now we consider the situation where the larger exponent is in the denominator. Suppose that we want to simplify $x^2 \div x^5$.

$$\frac{x^2}{x^5} = \frac{\cancel{(x)}\cancel{(x)}}{\cancel{(x)}\cancel{(x)}(x)(x)(x)} = \frac{1}{x^3}$$

> ## THE QUOTIENT RULE (PART 2)
>
> $\dfrac{x^a}{x^b} = \dfrac{1}{x^{b-a}}$ Use this form if the larger exponent is in the denominator and $x \neq 0$.

EXAMPLE 6   Divide.   **(a)** $\dfrac{12^{17}}{12^{20}}$ **(b)** $\dfrac{b^7}{b^9}$ **(c)** $\dfrac{x^{20}}{x^{24}}$

Solution

(a) $\dfrac{12^{17}}{12^{20}} = \dfrac{1}{12^{20-17}} = \dfrac{1}{12^3}$ Note that the base does *not* change.

(b) $\dfrac{b^7}{b^9} = \dfrac{1}{b^{9-7}} = \dfrac{1}{b^2}$

(c) $\dfrac{x^{20}}{x^{24}} = \dfrac{1}{x^{24-20}} = \dfrac{1}{x^4}$

Practice Problem 6   Divide.   **(a)** $\dfrac{c^3}{c^4}$ **(b)** $\dfrac{10^{31}}{10^{56}}$ **(c)** $\dfrac{z^{15}}{z^{21}}$

When there are numerical coefficients, use the rules for dividing signed numbers to reduce fractions to lowest terms.

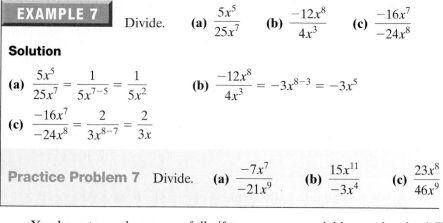

EXAMPLE 7   Divide.   (a) $\dfrac{5x^5}{25x^7}$ (b) $\dfrac{-12x^8}{4x^3}$ (c) $\dfrac{-16x^7}{-24x^8}$

Solution

(a) $\dfrac{5x^5}{25x^7} = \dfrac{1}{5x^{7-5}} = \dfrac{1}{5x^2}$ (b) $\dfrac{-12x^8}{4x^3} = -3x^{8-3} = -3x^5$

(c) $\dfrac{-16x^7}{-24x^8} = \dfrac{2}{3x^{8-7}} = \dfrac{2}{3x}$

Practice Problem 7   Divide.   (a) $\dfrac{-7x^7}{-21x^9}$ (b) $\dfrac{15x^{11}}{-3x^4}$ (c) $\dfrac{23x^8}{46x^9}$

You have to work very carefully if two or more variables are involved. Treat the coefficients and each variable separately.

EXAMPLE 8   Divide.   (a) $\dfrac{x^3y^2}{5xy^6}$ (b) $\dfrac{-3x^2y^5}{12x^6y^8}$

Solution

(a) $\dfrac{x^3y^2}{5xy^6} = \dfrac{x^2}{5y^4}$ (b) $\dfrac{-3x^2y^5}{12x^6y^8} = -\dfrac{1}{4x^4y^3}$

Practice Problem 8   Divide.   (a) $\dfrac{x^7y^9}{y^{10}}$ (b) $\dfrac{12x^5y^6}{-24x^3y^8}$

Suppose that a given base appears with the same exponent in the numerator and denominator of a fraction. In this case we can use the fact that *any nonzero number divided by itself is* 1.

EXAMPLE 9   Divide.   (a) $\dfrac{x^6}{x^6}$ (b) $\dfrac{3x^5}{x^5}$

Solution

(a) $\dfrac{x^6}{x^6} = 1$ (b) $\dfrac{3x^5}{x^5} = 3\left(\dfrac{x^5}{x^5}\right) = 3(1) = 3$

Practice Problem 9   Divide.   (a) $\dfrac{10^7}{10^7}$ (b) $\dfrac{12a^4}{15a^4}$

Do you see that if we had subtracted exponents when simplifying $\dfrac{x^6}{x^6}$ we would have obtained x^0 in Example 9? So we can surmise that any number (except 0) to the 0 power equals 1. We can write this fact as a separate rule.

THE QUOTIENT RULE (PART 3)

$$\dfrac{x^a}{x^a} = x^0 = 1 \quad \text{if } x \neq 0 \quad (0^0 \text{ remains undefined}).$$

TO THINK ABOUT: What Is 0 to the 0 Power?   What about 0^0? Why is it undefined? $0^0 = 0^{1-1}$. If we use the quotient rule, $0^{1-1} = \dfrac{0}{0}$. Since division by zero is undefined, we must agree that 0^0 is undefined.

EXAMPLE 10 Divide. (a) $\dfrac{4x^0 y^2}{8^0 y^5 z^3}$ (b) $\dfrac{5x^2 y}{10x^2 y^3}$

Solution

(a) $\dfrac{4x^0 y^2}{8^0 y^5 z^3} = \dfrac{4(1)y^2}{(1)y^5 z^3} = \dfrac{4y^2}{y^5 z^3} = \dfrac{4}{y^3 z^3}$ (b) $\dfrac{5x^2 y}{10x^2 y^3} = \dfrac{1x^0}{2y^2} = \dfrac{(1)(1)}{2y^2} = \dfrac{1}{2y^2}$

Practice Problem 10 Divide. (a) $\dfrac{-20a^3 b^8 c^4}{28a^3 b^7 c^5}$ (b) $\dfrac{5x^0 y^6}{10x^4 y^8}$

We can combine all three parts of the quotient rule we have developed.

THE QUOTIENT RULE

$\dfrac{x^a}{x^b} = x^{a-b}$ Use this form if the larger exponent is in the numerator and $x \neq 0$.

$\dfrac{x^a}{x^b} = \dfrac{1}{x^{b-a}}$ Use this form if the larger exponent is in the denominator and $x \neq 0$.

$\dfrac{x^a}{x^a} = x^0 = 1$ if $x \neq 0$.

We can combine the product rule and the quotient rule to simplify algebraic expressions that involve both multiplication and division.

EXAMPLE 11 Simplify. $\dfrac{(8x^2 y)(-3x^3 y^2)}{-6x^4 y^3}$

Solution $\dfrac{(8x^2 y)(-3x^3 y^2)}{-6x^4 y^3} = \dfrac{-24x^5 y^3}{-6x^4 y^3} = 4x$

NOTE TO STUDENT: Fully worked-out solutions to all of the Practice Problems can be found at the back of the text starting at page SP-1

Practice Problem 11 Simplify. $\dfrac{(-6ab^5)(3a^2 b^4)}{16a^5 b^7}$

❸ Raising Exponential Expressions to a Power

How do we simplify an expression such as $(x^4)^3$? $(x^4)^3$ is x^4 raised to the third power. For this type of problem we say that we are raising a power to a power. A problem such as $(x^4)^3$ could be done by writing the following.

$$(x^4)^3 = x^4 \cdot x^4 \cdot x^4 \quad \text{By definition}$$
$$= x^{12} \quad\quad\quad\; \text{By adding exponents}$$

Notice that when we add the exponents we get $4 + 4 + 4 = 12$. This is the same as multiplying 4 by 3. That is, $4 \cdot 3 = 12$. This process can be summarized by the following rule.

RAISING A POWER TO A POWER

To raise a power to a power, keep the same base and multiply the exponents.

$$(x^a)^b = x^{ab}$$

Recall what happens when you raise a negative number to a power. $(-1)^2 = 1$. $(-1)^3 = -1$. In general,

$$(-1)^n = \begin{cases} +1 & \text{if } n \text{ is even} \\ -1 & \text{if } n \text{ is odd.} \end{cases}$$

EXAMPLE 12   Simplify.   **(a)** $(x^3)^5$ **(b)** $(2^7)^3$ **(c)** $(-1)^8$

Solution

(a) $(x^3)^5 = x^{3 \cdot 5} = x^{15}$ **(b)** $(2^7)^3 = 2^{7 \cdot 3} = 2^{21}$ **(c)** $(-1)^8 = +1$

Note that in both parts (a) and (b) the base does not change.

Practice Problem 12   Simplify.   **(a)** $(a^4)^3$ **(b)** $(10^5)^2$ **(c)** $(-1)^{15}$

Here are two rules involving products and quotients that are very useful: the product raised to a power rule and the quotient raised to a power rule. We'll illustrate each with an example.

If a product in parentheses is raised to a power, the parentheses indicate that *each factor* must be raised to that power.

$$(xy)^2 = x^2y^2 \qquad (xy)^3 = x^3y^3$$

PRODUCT RAISED TO A POWER

$$(xy)^a = x^a y^a$$

EXAMPLE 13   Simplify.   **(a)** $(ab)^8$ **(b)** $(3x)^4$ **(c)** $(-2x^2)^3$

Solution

(a) $(ab)^8 = a^8 b^8$ **(b)** $(3x)^4 = (3)^4 x^4 = 81x^4$

(c) $(-2x^2)^3 = (-2)^3 \cdot (x^2)^3 = -8x^6$

Practice Problem 13   Simplify.   **(a)** $(3xy)^3$ **(b)** $(yz)^{37}$ **(c)** $(-3x^3)^2$

If a fractional expression within parentheses is raised to a power, the parentheses indicate that both numerator and denominator must be raised to that power.

$$\left(\frac{x}{y}\right)^5 = \frac{x^5}{y^5} \qquad \left(\frac{x}{y}\right)^2 = \frac{x^2}{y^2} \qquad \text{if } y \neq 0$$

QUOTIENT RAISED TO A POWER

$$\left(\frac{x}{y}\right)^a = \frac{x^a}{y^a} \qquad \text{if } y \neq 0$$

EXAMPLE 14   Simplify.   **(a)** $\left(\dfrac{x}{y}\right)^5$ **(b)** $\left(\dfrac{7}{w}\right)^4$

Solution

(a) $\left(\dfrac{x}{y}\right)^5 = \dfrac{x^5}{y^5}$ **(b)** $\left(\dfrac{7}{w}\right)^4 = \dfrac{7^4}{w^4} = \dfrac{2401}{w^4}$

Practice Problem 14   Simplify.   **(a)** $\left(\dfrac{x}{5}\right)^3$ **(b)** $\left(\dfrac{4a}{b}\right)^6$

Many expressions can be simplified by using the previous rules involving exponents. Be sure to take particular care to determine the correct sign, especially if there is a negative numerical coefficient.

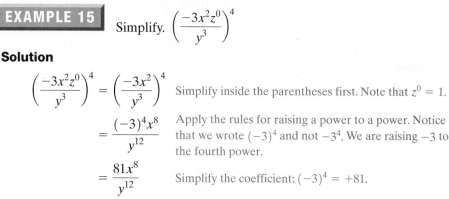

EXAMPLE 15 Simplify. $\left(\dfrac{-3x^2z^0}{y^3}\right)^4$

Solution

$$\left(\frac{-3x^2z^0}{y^3}\right)^4 = \left(\frac{-3x^2}{y^3}\right)^4 \qquad \text{Simplify inside the parentheses first. Note that } z^0 = 1.$$

$$= \frac{(-3)^4 x^8}{y^{12}} \qquad \begin{array}{l}\text{Apply the rules for raising a power to a power. Notice}\\ \text{that we wrote } (-3)^4 \text{ and not } -3^4. \text{ We are raising } -3 \text{ to}\\ \text{the fourth power.}\end{array}$$

$$= \frac{81x^8}{y^{12}} \qquad \text{Simplify the coefficient: } (-3)^4 = +81.$$

NOTE TO STUDENT: Fully worked-out solutions to all of the Practice Problems can be found at the back of the text starting at page SP-1

Practice Problem 15 Simplify. $\left(\dfrac{-2x^3y^0z}{4xz^2}\right)^5$

We list here the rules of exponents we have discussed in Section 6.1.

$$x^a \cdot x^b = x^{a+b}$$

$$\frac{x^a}{x^b} = \begin{cases} x^{a-b} & \text{if } a > b \\ \dfrac{1}{x^{b-a}} & \text{if } b > a \\ x^0 = 1 & \text{if } a = b \end{cases}$$

$$(x^a)^b = x^{ab}$$

$$(xy)^a = x^a y^a$$

$$\left(\frac{x}{y}\right)^a = \frac{x^a}{y^a} \quad y \neq 0$$

Developing Your Study Skills

Why Is Review Necessary?

You master a course in mathematics by learning the concepts one step at a time. Thus the study of mathematics is built step-by-step, with each step a supporting foundation for the next. The process is a carefully designed procedure, so no steps can be skipped. A student of mathematics needs to realize the importance of this building process to succeed.

Because new concepts depend on those previously learned, students often need to take time to review. The reviewing process will strengthen understanding and skills, which may be weak due to a lack of mastery or the passage of time. Review at the right time on the right concepts can strengthen previously learned skills and make progress possible.

Timely, periodic review of previously learned mathematical concepts is absolutely necessary for mastery of new concepts. You may have forgotten a concept or grown a bit rusty in applying it. Reviewing is the answer. Make use of the cumulative review problems in your textbook, whether they are assigned or not. Look back to previous chapters whenever you have forgotten how to do something. Review the chapter organizers from previous chapters. Study the examples and practice some exercises to refresh your understanding.

Be sure that you understand and can perform the computations of each new concept. This will enable you to move successfully on to the next one.

Remember, mathematics is a step-by-step building process. Learn each concept and reinforce and strengthen with review whenever necessary.

Verbal and Writing Skills

1. Write in your own words the product rule for exponents.

2. To be able to use the rules of exponents, what must be true of the bases?

3. If the larger exponent is in the denominator, the quotient rule states that $\dfrac{x^a}{x^b} = \dfrac{1}{x^{b-a}}$. Provide an example to show why this is true.

In exercises 4 and 5, identify the numerical coefficient, the base(s), and the exponent(s).

4. $-8x^5y^2$

5. $6x^{11}y$

6. Evaluate **(a)** $3x^0$ and **(b)** $(3x)^0$. **(c)** Why are the results different?

Write in simplest exponent form.

7. $2 \cdot 2 \cdot a \cdot a \cdot a \cdot b$

8. $5 \cdot x \cdot x \cdot x \cdot y \cdot y$

9. $(-3)(a)(a)(b)(c)(b)(c)(c)$

10. $(-7)(x)(y)(z)(y)(x)$

Multiply. Leave your answer in exponent form.

11. $(7^4)(7^6)$

12. $(4^3)(4^5)$

13. $(5^{10})(5^{16})$

14. $(6^5)(6^8)$

15. $x^4 \cdot x^8$

16. $x^9 \cdot x^6$

17. $w^{12} \cdot w^{20}$

18. $z^{16} \cdot z^{10}$

Multiply.

19. $-5x^4(4x^2)$

20. $6x^2(-9x^3)$

21. $(5x)(10x^2)$

22. $(-4x^2)(-3x)$

23. $(3x^2y)(8x^3y^3)$

24. $(6xy^3)(5x^4y)$

25. $\left(\dfrac{2}{5}xy^3\right)\left(\dfrac{1}{3}x^2y^2\right)$

26. $\left(\dfrac{4}{5}x^5y\right)\left(\dfrac{15}{16}x^2y^4\right)$

27. $(1.1x^2z)(-2.5xy)$

28. $(2.3x^4w)(-3.5xy^4)$

29. $(8a)(2a^3b)(0)$

30. $(5ab)(2a^2)(0)$

31. $(-16x^2y^4)(-5xy^3)$

32. $(-12x^4y)(-7x^5y^3)$

33. $(-8x^3y^2)(3xy^5)$

34. $(9x^2y^6)(-11x^3y^3)$

35. $(-2x^3y^2)(0)(-3x^4y)$

36. $(-4x^8y^2)(13y^3)(0)$

37. $(8a^4b^3)(-3x^2y^5)$

38. $(5x^3y)(-2w^4z)$

39. $(2x^2y)(-3y^3z^2)(5xz^4)$

40. $(3ab)(5a^2c)(-2b^2c^3)$

Divide. Leave your answer in exponent form. Assume that all variables in any denominator are nonzero.

41. $\dfrac{y^{12}}{y^5}$

42. $\dfrac{x^{13}}{x^3}$

43. $\dfrac{y^5}{y^8}$

44. $\dfrac{b^{20}}{b^{23}}$

45. $\dfrac{11^{18}}{11^{30}}$

46. $\dfrac{8^9}{8^{12}}$

47. $\dfrac{3^{18}}{3^{14}}$

48. $\dfrac{5^{16}}{5^{12}}$

49. $\dfrac{a^{13}}{4a^5}$

50. $\dfrac{b^{16}}{5b^{13}}$

51. $\dfrac{x^7}{y^9}$

52. $\dfrac{x^{20}}{y^3}$

53. $\dfrac{48x^5y^3}{24xy^3}$

54. $\dfrac{45a^4b^3}{15a^4b^2}$

55. $\dfrac{16x^5y}{-32x^2y^3}$

56. $\dfrac{-36x^3y^7}{72x^5y}$

57. $\dfrac{1.8f^4g^3}{54f^2g^8}$

58. $\dfrac{3.1s^5t^3}{62s^8t}$

59. $\dfrac{-51x^6y^8}{17x^3y^8}$

60. $\dfrac{-30x^5y^4}{5x^3y^4}$

61. $\dfrac{8^0x^2y^3}{16x^5y}$

62. $\dfrac{3^2x^3y^7}{3^0x^5y^2}$

63. $\dfrac{18a^6b^3c^0}{24a^5b^3}$

64. $\dfrac{12a^7b^8}{16a^3b^8c^0}$

65. $\dfrac{85a^2b}{45c^3}$

66. $\dfrac{28x}{63y^2z}$

To Think About

67. What expression can be multiplied by $(-3x^3yz)$ to obtain $81x^8y^2z^4$?

68. $63a^5b^6$ is divided by an expression and the result is $-9a^4b$. What is this expression?

Simplify.

69. $(x^2)^6$

70. $(w^5)^8$

71. $(xy^2)^7$

72. $(a^3b)^4$

73. $(rs^2)^6$

74. $(m^3n^2)^5$

75. $(3a^3b^2c)^3$

76. $(2x^4yz^3)^2$

77. $(-3a^4)^2$

78. $(-2a^5)^4$

79. $\left(\dfrac{x}{2m^4}\right)^7$

80. $\left(\dfrac{p^5}{6x}\right)^5$

81. $\left(\dfrac{5x}{7y^2}\right)^2$

82. $\left(\dfrac{2a^4}{3b^3}\right)^4$

83. $(-3a^2b^3c^0)^4$

84. $(-2a^5b^2c^0)^5$

85. $(-2x^3y^0z)^3$

86. $(-4xy^0z^4)^3$

87. $\dfrac{(3x)^5}{(3x^2)^3}$

88. $\dfrac{(6y^3)^4}{(6y)^2}$

Mixed Practice

89. $(3ab^2)^3(ab)$

90. $(-2a^2b^3)^3(ab^2)$

91. $\left(\dfrac{8}{y^5}\right)^2$

92. $\left(\dfrac{4}{x^6}\right)^3$

93. $\left(\dfrac{2x}{y^3}\right)^4$

94. $\left(\dfrac{3x^5}{y}\right)^3$

95. $\left(\dfrac{ab^2}{c^3d^4}\right)^4$

96. $\left(\dfrac{a^3b}{c^5d}\right)^5$

To Think About

97. What expression raised to the third power is $-27x^9y^{12}z^{21}$?

98. What expression raised to the fourth power is $16x^{20}y^{16}z^{28}$?

Cumulative Review

Simplify.

99. $-3 - 8$

100. $-17 + (-32) + (-24) + 27$

101. $\left(\dfrac{2}{3}\right)\left(-\dfrac{21}{8}\right)$

102. $\dfrac{-3}{4} \div \dfrac{-12}{80}$

Rain Forests Brazil, the largest country in South America, boasts a land area of approximately 8,511,960 sq km. Originally, 2,860,000 sq km in Brazil was covered by rain forest. As of 2002 the rain forest of that country only consists of 1,500,000 sq km. Round your answers to nearest tenth of a percent.

103. What percentage of Brazil's land area was covered by rain forest 2002?

104. If Brazil is said to lose 2.3% of its rain forest per year, how much rain forest was lost in the year after 2002?

(Information source: The Rain Forest Action Network)

1 Using Negative Exponents

If n is an integer, and $x \neq 0$, then x^{-n} is defined as follows:

DEFINITION OF A NEGATIVE EXPONENT

$$x^{-n} = \frac{1}{x^n}, \quad x \neq 0$$

Student Learning Objectives

After studying this section, you will be able to:

1 Use negative exponents.

2 Write numbers in scientific notation.

EXAMPLE 1 Write with positive exponents.

(a) y^{-3} **(b)** z^{-6} **(c)** w^{-1}

Solution

(a) $y^{-3} = \dfrac{1}{y^3}$ **(b)** $z^{-6} = \dfrac{1}{z^6}$ **(c)** $w^{-1} = \dfrac{1}{w^1} = \dfrac{1}{w}$

Practice Problem 1 Write with positive exponents.

(a) x^{-12} **(b)** w^{-5} **(c)** z^{-2}

NOTE TO STUDENT: Fully worked-out solutions to all of the Practice Problems can be found at the back of the text starting at page SP-1

To evaluate a numerical expression with a negative exponent, first write the expression with a positive exponent. Then simplify.

EXAMPLE 2 Evaluate. **(a)** 3^{-2} **(b)** 2^{-5}

Solution

(a) $3^{-2} = \dfrac{1}{3^2} = \dfrac{1}{9}$ **(b)** $2^{-5} = \dfrac{1}{2^5} = \dfrac{1}{32}$

Practice Problem 2 Evaluate. **(a)** 4^{-3} **(b)** 2^{-4}

All the previously studied laws of exponents are true for any integer exponent. These laws are summarized in the following box. Assume that $x, y \neq 0$.

LAWS OF EXPONENTS

The Product Rule

$$x^a \cdot x^b = x^{a+b}$$

The Quotient Rule

$$\frac{x^a}{x^b} = x^{a-b} \quad \text{Use if } a > b, \qquad \frac{x^a}{x^b} = \frac{1}{x^{b-a}} \quad \text{Use if } a < b.$$

Power Rules

$$(xy)^a = x^a y^a, \qquad (x^a)^b = x^{ab}, \qquad \left(\frac{x}{y}\right)^a = \frac{x^a}{y^a}$$

By using the definition of a negative exponent and the properties of fractions, we can derive two more helpful properties of exponents. Assume that $x, y \neq 0$.

PROPERTIES OF NEGATIVE EXPONENTS

$$\frac{1}{x^{-n}} = x^n \qquad\qquad \frac{x^{-m}}{y^{-n}} = \frac{y^n}{x^m}$$

EXAMPLE 3 Simplify. Write the expression with no negative exponents.

(a) $\dfrac{1}{x^{-6}}$ **(b)** $\dfrac{x^{-3}y^{-2}}{z^{-4}}$ **(c)** $x^{-2}y^3$

Solution

(a) $\dfrac{1}{x^{-6}} = x^6$ **(b)** $\dfrac{x^{-3}y^{-2}}{z^{-4}} = \dfrac{z^4}{x^3y^2}$ **(c)** $x^{-2}y^3 = \dfrac{y^3}{x^2}$

NOTE TO STUDENT: Fully worked-out solutions to all of the Practice Problems can be found at the back of the text starting at page SP-1

Practice Problem 3 Simplify. Write the expression with no negative exponents.

(a) $\dfrac{3}{w^{-4}}$ **(b)** $\dfrac{x^{-6}y^4}{z^{-2}}$ **(c)** $x^{-6}y^{-5}$

EXAMPLE 4 Simplify. Write the expression with no negative exponents.

(a) $(3x^{-4}y^2)^{-3}$ **(b)** $\dfrac{x^2y^{-4}}{x^{-5}y^3}$

Solution

(a) $(3x^{-4}y^2)^{-3} = 3^{-3}x^{12}y^{-6} = \dfrac{x^{12}}{3^3y^6} = \dfrac{x^{12}}{27y^6}$

(b) $\dfrac{x^2y^{-4}}{x^{-5}y^3} = \dfrac{x^2x^5}{y^4y^3} = \dfrac{x^7}{y^7}$ First rewrite the expression so that only positive exponents appear. Then simplify using the product rule.

Practice Problem 4 Simplify. Write the expression with no negative exponents.

(a) $(2x^4y^{-5})^{-2}$ **(b)** $\dfrac{y^{-3}z^{-4}}{y^2z^{-6}}$

② Writing Numbers in Scientific Notation

One common use of negative exponents is in writing numbers in scientific notation. Scientific notation is most useful in expressing very large and very small numbers.

SCIENTIFIC NOTATION

A positive number is written in **scientific notation** if it is in the form $a \times 10^n$, where $1 \leq a < 10$ and n is an integer.

EXAMPLE 5 Write in scientific notation. **(a)** 4567 **(b)** 157,000,000

Solution

(a) $4567 = 4.567 \times 1000$ To change 4567 to a number that is greater than 1 but less than 10, we move the decimal point three places to the left. We must then multiply the number by a power of 10 so that we do not change the value of the number. Use 1000.

$$= 4.567 \times 10^3$$

(b) $157,000,000 = 1.57000000 \times 100000000$

$$\underset{\text{8 places}}{\underbrace{}} \quad \underset{\text{8 zeros}}{\underbrace{}}$$

$$= 1.57 \times 10^8$$

Practice Problem 5 Write in scientific notation.

(a) 78,200 **(b)** 4,786,000

Numbers that are smaller than 1 will have a negative power of 10 if they are written in scientific notation.

EXAMPLE 6 Write in scientific notation. **(a)** 0.061 **(b)** 0.000052

Solution

(a) We need to write 0.061 as a number that is greater than 1 but less than 10. In which direction do we move the decimal point?

$0.061 = 6.1 \times 10^{-2}$ Move the decimal point 2 places to the right.

(b) $0.000052 = 5.2 \times 10^{-5}$ Why?

Practice Problem 6 Write in scientific notation.

(a) 0.98 **(b)** 0.000092

The reverse procedure transforms scientific notation into ordinary decimal notation.

EXAMPLE 7 Write in decimal notation.

(a) 1.568×10^2 **(b)** 7.432×10^{-3}

Solution

(a) $1.568 \times 10^2 = 1.568 \times 100$

$$= 156.8$$

Alternative Method

$1.568 \times 10^2 = 156.8$ The exponent 2 tells us to move the decimal point 2 places to the right.

(b) $7.432 \times 10^{-3} = 7.432 \times \dfrac{1}{1000}$

$$= 0.007432$$

Alternative Method

$7.432 \times 10^{-3} = 0.007432$ The exponent -3 tells us to move the decimal point 3 places to the left.

Practice Problem 7 Write in decimal notation.

(a) 1.93×10^6 **(b)** 8.562×10^{-5}

Calculator

Scientific Notation

Most calculators can display only eight digits at one time. Numbers with more than eight digits are usually shown in scientific notation. 1.12 E 08 or 1.12 8 means 1.12×10^8. You can use the calculator to compute with large numbers by entering the numbers using scientific notation. For example,

$$(7.48 \times 10^{24}) \times (3.5 \times 10^8)$$

is entered as follows.

7.48 $\boxed{\text{EXP}}$

24 $\boxed{\times}$ 3.5

$\boxed{\text{EXP}}$ 8 $\boxed{=}$

Display: $\boxed{\text{2.618 E 33}}$

or $\boxed{2.618 \quad 33}$

Note: Some calculators have an $\boxed{\text{EE}}$ key instead of $\boxed{\text{EXP}}$.

Compute on a calculator.

1. $35,000,000,000 + 77,000,000,000$

2. $(6.23 \times 10^{12}) \times (4.9 \times 10^5)$

3. $(2.5 \times 10^7)^5$

4. $3.3284 \times 10^{32} \div (6.28 \times 10^{24})$

5. How many seconds are there in 1000 years?

The distance light travels in one year is called a *light-year*. A light-year is a convenient unit of measure to use when investigating the distances between stars.

EXAMPLE 8   A light-year is a distance of 9,460,000,000,000,000 meters. Write this in scientific notation.

Solution $9,460,000,000,000,000 = 9.46 \times 10^{15}$ meters

Practice Problem 8   Astronomers measure distances to faraway galaxies in parsecs. A parsec is a distance of 30,900,000,000,000,000 meters. Write this in scientific notation.

To perform a calculation involving very large or very small numbers, it is usually helpful to write the numbers in scientific notation and then use the laws of exponents to do the calculation.

EXAMPLE 9   Use scientific notation and the laws of exponents to find the following. Leave your answer in scientific notation.

(a) $(32,000,000)(1,500,000,000,000)$ **(b)** $\dfrac{0.00063}{0.021}$

Solution

(a) $(32,000,000)(1,500,000,000,000)$

$= (3.2 \times 10^{7})(1.5 \times 10^{12})$ Write each number in scientific notation.

$= 3.2 \times 1.5 \times 10^{7} \times 10^{12}$ Rearrange the order. Remember that multiplication is commutative.

$= 4.8 \times 10^{19}$ Multiply 3.2×1.5. Multiply $10^{7} \times 10^{12}$.

(b) $\dfrac{0.00063}{0.021} = \dfrac{6.3 \times 10^{-4}}{2.1 \times 10^{-2}}$ Write each number in scientific notation.

$= \dfrac{6.3}{2.1} \times \dfrac{10^{-4}}{10^{-2}}$ Rearrange the order. We are actually using the definition of multiplication of fractions.

$= \dfrac{6.3}{2.1} \times \dfrac{10^{2}}{10^{4}}$ Rewrite with positive exponents.

$= 3.0 \times 10^{-2}$

NOTE TO STUDENT: Fully worked-out solutions to all of the Practice Problems can be found at the back of the text starting at page SP-1

Practice Problem 9   Use scientific notation and the laws of exponents to find the following. Leave your answer in scientific notation.

(a) $(56,000)(1,400,000,000)$ **(b)** $\dfrac{0.000111}{0.00000037}$

When we use scientific notation, we are writing approximate numbers. We must include some zeros so that the decimal point can be properly located. However, all other digits except for these zeros are considered **significant digits.** The number 34.56 has four significant digits. The number 0.0049 has two significant digits. The zeros are considered placeholders. The number 634,000 has three significant digits (unless we have specific knowledge to the contrary). The zeros are considered placeholders. We sometimes round numbers to a specific number of significant digits. For example, 0.08746 rounded to two significant digits is 0.087. When we round 1,348,593 to three significant digits, we obtain 1,350,000.

EXAMPLE 10   The approximate distance from Earth to the star Polaris is 208 parsecs. A parsec is a distance of approximately 3.09×10^{13} kilometers. How long would it take a space probe traveling at 40,000 kilometers per hour to reach the star? Round to three significant digits.

Solution

1. **Understand the problem.** Recall that the distance formula is

$$\text{distance} = \text{rate} \times \text{time}.$$

We are given the distance and the rate. We need to find the time. Let's take a look at the distance. The distance is given in parsecs, but the rate is given in kilometers per hour. We need to change the distance to kilometers. We are told that a parsec is approximately 3.09×10^{13} kilometers. That is, there are 3.09×10^{13} kilometers per parsec. We use this information to change 208 parsecs to kilometers.

$$208 \text{ parsecs} = \frac{(208 \text{ parsecs})(3.09 \times 10^{13} \text{ kilometers})}{1 \text{ parsec}} = 642.72 \times 10^{13} \text{ kilometers}$$

2. **Write an equation.** Use the distance formula.

$$d = r \times t$$

3. **Solve the equation and state the answer.** Substitute the known values into the formula and solve for the unknown, time.

$$642.72 \times 10^{13} \text{ km} = \frac{40{,}000 \text{ km}}{1 \text{ hr}} \times t$$

$$6.4272 \times 10^{15} \text{ km} = \frac{4 \times 10^4 \text{ km}}{1 \text{ hr}} \times t \qquad \text{Change the numbers to scientific notation.}$$

$$\frac{6.4272 \times 10^{15} \text{ km}}{\dfrac{4 \times 10^4 \text{ km}}{1 \text{ hr}}} = t \qquad \text{Divide both sides by } \dfrac{4 \times 10^4 \text{ km}}{1 \text{ hr}}.$$

$$\frac{(6.4272 \times 10^{15} \text{ km})(1 \text{ hr})}{4 \times 10^4 \text{ km}} = t$$

$$1.6068 \times 10^{11} \text{ hr} = t$$

1.6068×10^{11} is 160.68×10^9 or 160.68 billion hours. The space probe will take approximately 160.68 billion hours to reach the star.

Reread the problem. Are we finished? What is left to do? We need to round the answer to three significant digits. Rounding to three significant digits, we have

$$160.68 \times 10^9 \approx 161 \times 10^9.$$

This is approximately 161 billion hours or a little more than 18 million years.

4. **Check.** Unless you have had a great deal of experience working in astronomy, it would be difficult to determine whether this is a reasonable answer. You may wish to reread your analysis and redo your calculations as a check.

Practice Problem 10   The average distance from Earth to the distant star Betelgeuse is 159 parsecs. How many hours would it take a space probe to travel from Earth to Betelgeuse at a speed of 50,000 kilometers per hour? Round to three significant digits.

Simplify. Express your answer with positive exponents. Assume that all variables are nonzero.

1. x^{-4}

2. y^{-5}

3. 3^{-4}

4. 5^{-3}

5. $\dfrac{1}{y^{-8}}$

6. $\dfrac{1}{z^{-10}}$

7. $\dfrac{x^{-4}y^{-5}}{z^{-6}}$

8. $\dfrac{x^{-6}y^{-2}}{z^{-5}}$

9. $x^{-5}y^6$

10. $x^{-4}y^7$

11. $(2x^{-3})^{-3}$

12. $(4x^{-4})^{-2}$

13. $3x^{-2}$

14. $4y^{-4}$

15. $(4x^2y)^{-2}$

16. $(2x^3y^5)^{-3}$

Mixed Practice

17. $\dfrac{3xy^{-2}}{z^{-3}}$

18. $\dfrac{4x^{-2}y^{-3}}{y^4}$

19. $\dfrac{(3x)^{-2}}{(3x)^{-3}}$

20. $\dfrac{(2ab^2)^{-3}}{(2ab^2)^{-4}}$

21. $wx^{-5}y^3z^{-2}$

22. $a^5b^{-3}c^{-4}$

23. $(8^{-2})(2^3)$

24. $(9^2)(3^{-3})$

25. $\left(\dfrac{3x^0y^2}{z^4}\right)^{-2}$

26. $\left(\dfrac{2a^3b^0}{c^2}\right)^{-3}$

27. $\dfrac{x^{-2}y^{-3}}{x^4y^{-2}}$

28. $\dfrac{a^{-6}b^3}{a^{-2}b^{-5}}$

Write in scientific notation.

29. 123,780

30. 5,786,100

31. 0.063

32. 0.000742

33. 889,610,000,000

34. 7,652,000,000

35. 0.00000001963

36. 0.000007618

In exercises 37–42, write in decimal notation.

37. 3.02×10^5

38. 8.137×10^7

39. 4.7×10^{-4}

40. 6.53×10^{-3}

41. 9.83×10^5

42. 3.5×10^{-8}

43. *Bamboo Growth* The growth rate of some species of bamboo is 0.0000237 miles per hour. Write this in scientific notation.

44. *Neptune* Neptune is 2.793×10^9 miles from the sun. Write this in decimal notation.

45. *Red Blood Cell* A single human red blood cell is about 7×10^{-6} meters in diameter. Write this in decimal notation.

46. *Gold Atom* The average volume of an atom of gold is 0.00000000000000000000001695 cubic centimeters. Write this in scientific notation.

Evaluate by using scientific notation and the laws of exponents. Leave your answer in scientific notation.

47. $(56,000,000,000)(780,000,000)$

48. $(35,000,000)(84,000,000,000)$

49. $\dfrac{(5,000,000)(16,000)}{8,000,000,000}$

50. $(0.0075)(0.0000002)(0.001)$

51. $(0.003)^4$

52. $(500,000)^4$

53. $(150,000,000)(0.00005)(0.002)(30,000)$

54. $\dfrac{(1,600,000)(0.00003)}{2400}$

Applications

National Debt For fiscal year 2003, the national debt was determined to be approximately 6.816×10^{12} dollars. (*Source: Treasury Department of Public Debt.*)

55. The census bureau estimates that in 2003, the entire population of the United States was 2.92×10^8 people. If the national debt were evenly divided among every person in the country, how much debt would be assigned to each individual? Round to three significant digits.

56. The census bureau estimates that in 2003, the number of people in the United States who were over age 18 was approximately 2.28×10^8 people. If the national debt were evenly divided among every person over age 18 in the country, how much debt would be assigned to each individual? Round to three significant digits.

Space Travel   *A parsec is a distance of approximately* 3.09×10^{13} *kilometers.*

57. How long would it take a space probe to travel from Earth to the star Rigel, which is 276 parsecs from Earth? Assume that the space probe travels at 45,000 kilometers per hour. Round to three significant digits.

58. How long would it take a space probe to travel from Earth to the star Hadar, which is 150 parsecs from Earth? Assume that the space probe travels at 55,000 kilometers per hour. Round to three significant digits.

59. *Watch Hand* The tip of a $\frac{1}{3}$-inch-long hour hand on a watch travels at a speed of 0.00000275 miles per hour. How far has it traveled in a day?

60. *Neutron Mass* The mass of a neutron is approximately 1.675×10^{-27} kilogram. Find the mass of 180,000 neutrons.

61. *007 Films* The most profitable movie series made has been the James Bond series, which has grossed 3.2×10^9 over the 20 James Bond films. What is the average gross per film?

62. *Moles per Molecule* Avogadro's number says that there are approximately 6.02×10^{23} molecules/mole. How many molecules can one expect in 0.00483 mole?

63. *Construction Cost* In 1990 the cost for construction of new private buildings was estimated at 3.61×10^{11}. By 2010 the estimated cost for construction of new private buildings will be 9.36×10^{11}. What is the percent of increase from 1990 to 2010? Round to the nearest tenth of a percent. (*Source:* U.S. Census Bureau.)

64. *Construction Cost* In 1990 the cost for construction of new public buildings was estimated at 1.07×10^{11}. By 2010 the estimated cost for construction of new public buildings will be 3.06×10^{11}. What is the percent of increase from 1990 to 2010? Round to the nearest tenth of a percent. (*Source:* U.S. Census Bureau.)

Cumulative Review

Simplify.

65. $-2.7 - (-1.9)$

66. $(-1)^{33}$

67. $-\dfrac{3}{4} + \dfrac{5}{7}$

68. *Hand Shakes* A recent debate between two political candidates attracted 3540 people to a local gymnasium. At the conclusion of the debate, each person went to one side of the gymnasium to shake the hand of candidate #1 or to the other side of the room to shake the hand of candidate #2. Candidate #1 shook 524 less than triple the number of hands shaken by candidate #2. How many hands did each candidate shake?

69. *Salaries* Gina has a bachelor's degree. She earns $12,460 more a year than Mario, who holds an associate's degree. Alfonso, who has not yet been able to attend college, earns $8742 a year less than Mario. The combined annual salaries of the three people is $112,000. What is the annual salary of each person?

Horizontal parabolas Parabolas that open to the right or to the left. The following graphs represent horizontal parabolas.

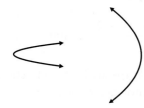

Hyperbola The set of points in a plane such that for each point in the set, the absolute value of the difference of its distances to two fixed points is constant. Each of these fixed points is called a *focus*. The following sketches represent graphs of hyperbolas.

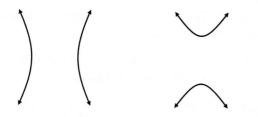

Hypotenuse of a right triangle The side opposite the right angle in any right triangle. The hypotenuse is always the longest side of a right triangle. In the following sketch the hypotenuse is side c.

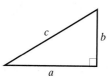

Imaginary number i, defined as $i = \sqrt{-1}$ and $i^2 = -1$.

Improper fraction A numerical fraction whose numerator is larger than or equal to its denominator. $\frac{8}{3}, \frac{5}{2}$, and $\frac{7}{7}$ are improper fractions.

Inconsistent system of equations A system of equations that does not have a solution.

Independent equations Two equations that are not dependent are said to be independent.

Index of a radical Indicates what type of a root is being taken. The index of a cube root is $\sqrt[3]{x}$, the 3 is the index of the radical. In $\sqrt[4]{y}$, the index is 4. The index of a square root is 2, but the index is not written in the square root symbol, as shown: $\sqrt{x}$.

Inequality A mathematical relationship between quantities that are not equal. $x \leq -3, w > 5$, and $x < 2y + 1$ are mathematical inequalities.

Integers The set of numbers $\ldots, -5, -4, -3, -2, -1, 0, 1, 2, 3, 4, 5, \ldots$.

Intercepts of an equation The point or points where the graph of the equation crosses the x-axis or the y-axis or both. (*See* x-intercept or y-intercept.)

Inverse function of a one-to-one function That function obtained by interchanging the first and second coordinates in each ordered pair of the function.

Inverse variation When a variable y varies inversely with x, written $y = \dfrac{k}{x}$, where k is the constant of variation.

Irrational number A real number that cannot be expressed in the form $\dfrac{a}{b}$, where a and b are integer and $b \neq 0$. $\sqrt{2}, \pi, 5 + 3\sqrt{2}$, and $-4\sqrt{7}$ are irrational numbers.

Isosceles triangle A triangle with two equal sides and two equal angles. Triangle ABC is an isosceles triangle. Angle BAC is equal to angle ACB. Side AB is equal in length to side BC.

Joint variation When a variable y varies jointly with x and z, written $y = kxz$, where k is the constant of variation.

Least common denominator of numerical fractions The smallest whole number that is exactly divisible by all denominators of a group of fractions. The least common denominator (LCD) of $\frac{1}{6}, \frac{2}{3}$, and $\frac{3}{5}$ is 30. The least common denominator is also called the lowest common denominator.

Leg of a right triangle One of the two shorter sides of a right triangle. In the following sketch, sides a and b are the legs of the right triangle.

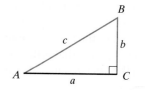

Like terms Terms that have identical variables and exponents. In the expression $5x^3 + 2xy^2 + 6x^2 - 3xy^2$, the term $2xy^2$ and the term $-3xy^2$ are like terms.

Linear equation in two variables An equation of the form $Ax + By = C$, where A, B, and C are real numbers. The graph of a linear equation in two variables is a straight line.

Logarithm For a positive number x, the power to which the base b must be raised to produce x. That is, $y = \log_b x$ is the same as $x = b^y$, where $b > 0$ and $b \neq 1$. A logarithm is an exponent.

Logarithmic equation An equation that contains at least one logarithm.

Magnitude of an earthquake The magnitude of an earthquake is measured by the formula $M = \log\left(\dfrac{I}{I_0}\right)$, where I is the intensity of the earthquake and I_0 is the minimum measurable intensity.

Matrix A rectangular array of numbers arranged in rows and columns. We use the symbol [ ] to indicate a matrix. The matrix $\begin{bmatrix} 3 & 4 & 5 \\ 6 & 7 & 8 \end{bmatrix}$ has two rows and three columns and is called a 2×3 *matrix*.

Minor of an element of a third-order determinant The second-order determinant that remains after we delete the row and column in which the element appears. The minor of the element 6 in the determinant $\begin{vmatrix} 1 & 2 & 3 \\ 7 & 6 & 8 \\ -3 & 5 & 9 \end{vmatrix}$ is the second-order determinant $\begin{vmatrix} 1 & 3 \\ -3 & 9 \end{vmatrix}$.

Mixed number A number that consists of an integer written next to a proper fraction. $2\frac{1}{3}$, $4\frac{6}{7}$, and $3\frac{3}{8}$ are all mixed numbers. Mixed numbers are sometimes called mixed fractions or mixed numerals.

Natural logarithm For a number x, $\ln x = \log_e x$ for all $x > 0$. A natural logarithm is a logarithm using base e.

Natural numbers the set of numbers $1, 2, 3, 4, 5, \ldots$. This set is also called the set of counting numbers.

Nonlinear system of equations A system of equations in which at least one equation is not a linear equation.

Numeral The symbol used to describe a number.

Numerator The top number or algebraic expression in a fraction. The numerator of

$$\frac{x + 3}{5x - 2}$$

is $x + 3$. The numerator of $\frac{12}{13}$ is 12.

Numerical coefficient The number that is multiplied by a variable or a group of variables. The numerical coefficient in $5x^3y^2$ is 5. The numerical coefficient in $-6abc$ is -6. The numerical coefficient in x^2y is 1. A numerical coefficient of 1 is not usually written.

Odd integers Integers that are not exactly divisible by 2, such as $\ldots, -3, -1, 1, 3, 5, 7, 9, \ldots$.

One-to-one function A function in which no two different ordered pairs have the same second coordinate.

Opposite of a number Two numbers that are the same distance from zero on the number line but lie on different sides of it are considered opposites. The opposite of -6 is 6. The opposite of $\frac{22}{7}$ is $-\frac{22}{7}$.

Ordered pair A pair of numbers presented in a specified order. An ordered pair is often used to specify a location on a graph. Every point in a rectangular coordinate system can be represented by an ordered pair (x, y).

Origin The point $(0, 0)$ in a rectangular coordinate system.

Parabola The set of points that is the same distance from some fixed line (called the *directrix*) and some fixed point (called the *focus*) that is not on the line. The graph of any equation of the form $y = ax^2 + bx + c$ or $x = ay^2 + by + c$, where $a, b,$ and c are real numbers and $a \neq 0$, is a parabola. Some examples of the graphs of parabolas are shown.

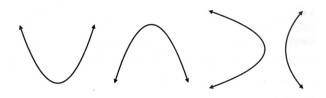

Parallel lines Two straight lines that never intersect. The graph of an inconsistent system of two linear equations in two variables will result in parallel lines.

Parallelogram A four-sided figure with opposite sides parallel. Figure $ABCD$ is a parallelogram.

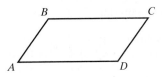

Percent Hundredths or "per one hundred"; indicated by the % symbol. Thirty-seven hundredths $\left(\dfrac{37}{100}\right) = 37\%$ (thirty-seven percent).

Perfect square number A number that is the square of an integer. The numbers $1, 4, 9, 16, 25, 36, 49, 64, 81, 100, 121, 144, \ldots$ are perfect square numbers.

Perfect-square trinomial A polynomial of the form $a^2 + 2ab + b^2$ or $a^2 - 2ab + b^2$ that may be factored using one of the following formulas:

$$a^2 + 2ab + b^2 = (a + b)^2$$

or

$$a^2 - 2ab + b^2 = (a - b)^2.$$

Perimeter The distance around any plane figure. The perimeter of this triangle is 13. The perimeter of this rectangle is 20.

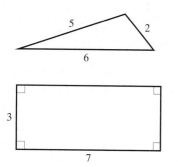

pH of a solution Defined by the equation $\text{pH} = -\log_{10}(\text{H}^+)$, where H^+ is the concentration of the hydrogen ion in the solution. The solution is an acid when the pH is less than 7 and a base when the pH is greater than 7.

Pi An irrational number, denoted by the symbol π, that is approximately equal to 3.141592654. In most cases 3.14 can be used as a sufficiently accurate approximation for π.

Point-slope form of the equation of a straight line For a straight line passing through the point (x_1, y_1) and having slope m, $y - y_1 = m(x - x_1)$.

Polynomial Expressions that contain terms with non-negative integer exponents. The expressions $5ab + 6$, $x^3 + 6x^2 + 3$, -12, and $x + 3y - 2$ are all polynomials. The expressions $x^{-2} + 2x^{-1}$, $2\sqrt{x} + 6$, and $\dfrac{5}{x} + 2x^2$ are not polynomials.

Prime number Any natural number greater than 1 whose only natural number factors are 1 and itself. The first eight prime numbers are 2, 3, 5, 7, 11, 13, 17, and 19.

Prime polynomial A prime polynomial is a polynomial that cannot be factored by the methods of elementary algebra. $x^2 + x + 1$ is a prime polynomial.

Principal square root The positive square root of a number. The symbol indicating the principal square root is $\sqrt{\ }$. Thus, $\sqrt{4}$ means to find the principal square root of 4, which is 2.

Proper fraction A numerical fraction whose numerator is less than its denominator; $\dfrac{3}{7}, \dfrac{2}{5}$, and $\dfrac{8}{9}$ are proper fractions.

Proportion A proportion is an equation stating that two ratios are equal.

$$\frac{a}{b} = \frac{c}{d} \qquad \text{where } b, d \neq 0$$

is a proportion.

Pythagorean theorem In any right triangle, if c is the length of the hypotenuse and a and b are the lengths of the two legs, then $c^2 = a^2 + b^2$.

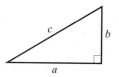

Quadratic equation in standard form An equation of the form $ax^2 + bx + c = 0$, where a, b, and c are real numbers and $a \neq 0$. A quadratic equation is classified as a second-degree equation.

Quadratic formula If $ax^2 + bx + c = 0$ and $a \neq 0$, then the roots to the equation are found by the formula

$$x = \frac{-b \pm \sqrt{b^2 - 4ac}}{2a}.$$

Quadratic inequalities An inequality written in the form $ax^2 + bx + c > 0$, where $a \neq 0$ and a, b, and c are real numbers. The $>$ symbol may be replaced by a $<, \geq$, or $\leq$ symbol.

Quotient The result of dividing one number or expression by another. In the problem $12 \div 4 = 3$, the quotient is 3.

Radical equation An equation that contains one or more radicals. The following are examples of radical equations.

$$\sqrt{9x - 20} = x \quad \text{and} \quad 4 = \sqrt{x - 3} + \sqrt{x + 5}$$

Radical sign The symbol $\sqrt{\ }$, which is used to indicate the root of a number.

Radicand The expression beneath the radical sign. The radicand of $\sqrt{7x}$ is $7x$.

Range of a relation In any relation, the set of values that represents the dependent variable is called its range. This is the set of all the second coordinates of the ordered pairs that define the relation.

Ratio The ratio of one number a to another number b is the quotient $a \div b$ or $\dfrac{a}{b}$.

Rational numbers A number that can be expressed in the form $\dfrac{a}{b}$, where a and b are integers and $b \neq 0$. $\dfrac{7}{3}, -\dfrac{2}{5}, \dfrac{7}{-8}, \dfrac{5}{1}$, 1.62, and 2.7156 are rational numbers.

Rationalizing the denominator The process of transforming a fraction that contains one or more radicals in the denominator to an equivalent fraction that does not contain any radicals in the denominator. When we rationalize the denominator of $\dfrac{5}{\sqrt{3}}$, we obtain $\dfrac{5\sqrt{3}}{3}$.

When we rationalize the denominator of $\dfrac{-2}{\sqrt{11} - \sqrt{7}}$, we obtain $-\dfrac{\sqrt{11} + \sqrt{7}}{2}$.

Rationalizing the numerator The process of transforming a fraction that contains one or more radicals in the numerator to an equivalent fraction that does not contain any radicals in the numerator. When we rationalize the numerator of $\dfrac{\sqrt{5}}{x}$, we obtain $\dfrac{5}{x\sqrt{5}}$.

Real number Any number that is rational or irrational. $2, 7, \sqrt{5}, \dfrac{3}{8}, \pi, -\dfrac{7}{5}$, and $-3\sqrt{5}$ are all real numbers.

Rectangle A four-sided figure with opposite sides parallel and all interior angles measuring 90°. The opposite sides of a rectangle are equal.

Reduced row echelon form In the reduced row echelon form of an augmented matrix, all the numbers to the left of the vertical line are 1s along the diagonal from the top left to the bottom right. If there are elements below or above the 1s, these elements are 0 s. Two examples of matrices in reduced row echelon form are

$$\left[\begin{array}{cc|c} 1 & 0 & 3 \\ 0 & 1 & 4 \end{array}\right] \quad \text{and} \quad \left[\begin{array}{ccc|c} 1 & 0 & 0 & 5 \\ 0 & 1 & 0 & 6 \\ 0 & 0 & 1 & 7 \end{array}\right].$$

Relation A relation is any set of ordered pairs.

Rhombus A parallelogram with four equal sides. Figure $ABCD$ is a rhombus.

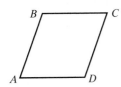

Right triangle A triangle that contains one right angle (an angle that measures exactly 90 degrees). It is indicated by a small rectangle at the corner of the angle.

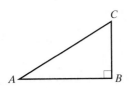

Root of an equation A value of the variable that makes an equation into a true statement. The root of an equation is also called the solution of an equation.

Scientific notation A positive number is written in scientific notation if it is in the form $a \times 10^n$, where $1 \le a < 10$ and n is an integer.

Similar radicals Two radicals that are simplified and have the same radicand and the same index. $2\sqrt[3]{7xy^2}$ and $-5\sqrt[3]{7xy^2}$ are similar radicals. Usually similar radicals are referred to as *like radicals*.

Simplifying a radical To simplify a radical when the root cannot be found exactly, we use the product rule for radicals, $\sqrt[n]{ab} = \sqrt[n]{a}\sqrt[n]{b}$ for $a \ge 0$ and $b \ge 0$. To simplify $\sqrt{20}$, we have $= \sqrt{4}\sqrt{5} = 2\sqrt{5}$. To simplify $\sqrt[3]{16x^4}$, we have $= \sqrt[3]{8x^3}\sqrt[3]{2x} = 2x\sqrt[3]{2x}$.

Simplifying imaginary numbers Using the property that states for all positive real numbers a, $\sqrt{-a} = \sqrt{-1}\sqrt{a} = i\sqrt{a}$. Thus, simplifying $\sqrt{-7}$, we have $\sqrt{-7} = \sqrt{-1}\sqrt{7} = i\sqrt{7}$.

Slope-intercept form The equation of a line that has slope m and the y-intercept at $(0, b)$ is given by $y = mx + b$.

Slope of a line The ratio of change in y over the change in x for any two different points on a nonvertical line. The slope m is determined by

$$m = \frac{y_2 - y_1}{x_2 - x_1},$$

where $x_2 \ne x_1$ for any two points (x_1, y_1) and (x_2, y_2) on a nonvertical line.

Solution of an equation A number that, when substituted into a given equation, yields an identity. The solution of an equation is also called the root of an equation.

Solution of a linear inequality The possible values that make a linear inequality true.

Solution of an inequality in two variables The set of all possible ordered pairs that when substituted into the inequality will yield a true statement.

Square A rectangle with four equal sides.

Square root If x is a real number and a is positive real number such that $a = x^2$, then x is a square root of a. One square root of 16 is 4 since $4^2 = 16$. Another square root of 16 is -4 since $(-4)^2 = 16$.

Standard form of the equation of a circle For a circle with center at (h, k) and a radius of r,

$$(x - h)^2 + (y - k)^2 = r^2.$$

Standard form of the equation of an ellipse For an ellipse with center at the origin,

$$\frac{x^2}{a^2} + \frac{y^2}{b^2} = 1, \qquad \text{where } a \text{ and } b > 0.$$

This ellipse has intercepts at $(a, 0)$, $(-a, 0)$, $(0, b)$, and $(0, -b)$.

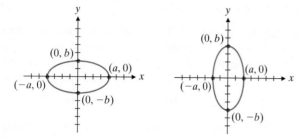

For an ellipse with center at (h, k),

$$\frac{(x - h)^2}{a^2} + \frac{(y - k)^2}{b^2} = 1, \qquad \text{where } a \text{ and } b > 0.$$

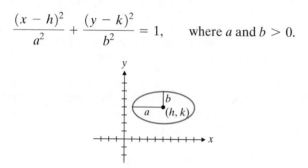

Standard form of the equation of a hyperbola with center at the origin For a horizontal hyperbola with center at the origin,

$$\frac{x^2}{a^2} - \frac{y^2}{b^2} = 1, \qquad \text{where } a \text{ and } b > 0.$$

The vertices are at $(-a, 0)$ and $(a, 0)$.

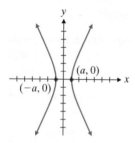

For a vertical hyperbola with center at the origin,

$$\frac{y^2}{b^2} - \frac{x^2}{a^2} = 1, \qquad \text{where } a \text{ and } b > 0.$$

The vertices are at $(0, b)$ and $(0, -b)$.

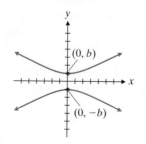

Standard form of the equation of a hyperbola with center at point (h, k) For a horizontal hyperbola with center at (h, k),

$$\frac{(x - h)^2}{a^2} - \frac{(y - k)^2}{b^2} = 1, \qquad \text{where } a \text{ and } b > 0.$$

The vertices are at $(h - a, k)$ and $(h + a, k)$.

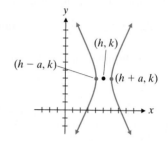

For a vertical hyperbola with center at (h, k),

$$\frac{(y - k)^2}{b^2} - \frac{(x - h)^2}{a^2} = 1, \qquad \text{where } a \text{ and } b > 0.$$

The vertices are at $(h, k + b)$ and $(h, k - b)$.

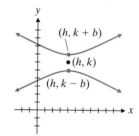

Standard form of the equation of a parabola For a vertical parabola with vertex at (h, k),

$$y = a(x - h)^2 + k, \qquad \text{where } a \neq 0.$$

For a horizontal parabola with vertex at (h, k),

$$x = a(y - k)^2 + h, \qquad \text{where } a \neq 0.$$

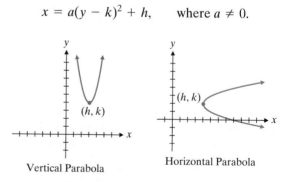

Vertical Parabola   Horizontal Parabola

Standard form of a quadratic equation A quadratic equation that is in the form $ax^2 + bx + c = 0$.

System of equations A set of two or more equations that must be considered together. The solution is the value for each variable of the system that satisfies each equation.

$$x + 3y = -7 \qquad 4x + 3y = -1$$

is a system of two equations in two unknowns. The solution is $(2, -3)$, or the values $x = 2, y = -3$.

System of inequalities Two or more inequalities in two variables that are considered at one time. The solution is the region that satisfies every inequality at one time. An example of a system of inequalities is

$$y > 2x + 1 \qquad y < \frac{1}{2}x + 2.$$

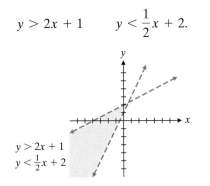

$$y > 2x + 1$$
$$y < \tfrac{1}{2}x + 2$$

Term A number, a variable, or a product of numbers and variables. For example, in the expression $a^3 - 3a^2b + 4ab^2 + 6b^3 + 8$, there are five terms. They are $a^3, -3a^2b, 4ab^2, 6b^3$, and 8. The terms of a polynomial are separated by plus and minus signs.

Trapezoid A four-sided figure with two sides parallel. The parallel sides are called the bases of the trapezoid. Figure $ABCD$ is a trapezoid.

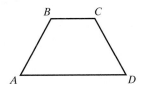

Trinomial A polynomial of three terms. The expressions $x^2 + 6x - 8$ and $a + 2b - 3c$ are trinomials.

Value of a second-order determinant For a second-order determinant $\begin{vmatrix} a & b \\ c & d \end{vmatrix}$, $ad - cb$.

Value of a third-order determinant For third-order determinant $\begin{vmatrix} a_1 & b_1 & c_1 \\ a_2 & b_2 & c_2 \\ a_3 & b_3 & c_3 \end{vmatrix}$,

$a_1b_2c_3 + b_1c_2a_3 + c_1a_2b_3 - a_3b_2c_1 - b_3c_2a_1 - c_3a_2b_1.$

Variable A letter that is used to represent a number or a set of numbers.

Variation An equation relating values of one variable to those of other variables. An equation of the form $y = kx$, where k is a constant, indicates *direct variation*. An equation of the form $y = \dfrac{k}{x}$, where k is a constant, indicates *inverse variation*. In both cases, k is called the *constant of variation*.

Vertex of a parabola In a vertical parabola, the lowest point on a parabola opening upward or the highest point on a parabola opening downward.

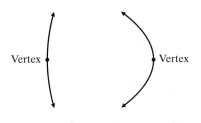

In a horizontal parabola, the leftmost point on a parabola opening to the right or the rightmost point on a parabola opening to the left.

Vertical line test If a vertical line can intersect the graph of a relation more than once, the relation is not a function.

Vertical parabolas Parabolas that open upward or downward. The following graphs represent vertical parabolas.

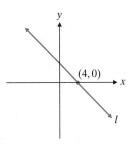

Whole numbers The set of numbers 0, 1, 2, 3, 4, 5, ...

x-intercept The ordered pair $(a, 0)$ is the x-intercept of a line if the line crosses the x-axis at $(a, 0)$. The x-intercept of line l on the following graph is $(4, 0)$.

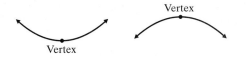

y-intercept The ordered pair $(0, b)$ is the y-intercept of a line if the line crosses the y-axis at $(0, b)$. The y-intercept of line p on the following graph is $(0, 3)$.

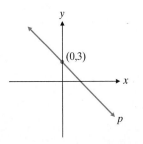

Appendix A Foundations for Intermediate Algebra

A.1 Integer Exponents, Square Roots, Order of Operations, and Scientific Notation

1 Raising a Number to a Power

Exponents or powers are used to indicate repeated multiplication. For example, we can write $6 \cdot 6 \cdot 6 \cdot 6$ as 6^4. In the expression 6^4, 4 is the **exponent** or **power** that tells us how many times the **base**, 6, appears as a factor. This is called **exponential notation**.

> **EXPONENTIAL NOTATION**
>
> If x is a real number and n is a positive integer, then
> $$x^n = \underbrace{x \cdot x \cdot x \cdot x \cdots}_{n \text{ factors}}$$

EXAMPLE 1 Evaluate.

(a) $(-2)^4$ **(b)** -2^4 **(c)** 3^5 **(d)** $(-5)^3$ **(e)** $\left(\dfrac{1}{3}\right)^3$

Solution

(a) $(-2)^4 = (-2)(-2)(-2)(-2) = (4)(-2)(-2) = (-8)(-2) = 16$

Notice that we are raising -2 to the fourth power. That is, the base is -2. We use parentheses to clearly indicate that the base is negative.

(b) $-2^4 = -(2 \cdot 2 \cdot 2 \cdot 2) = -16$

Here the base is 2. The base is not -2. We wish to find the negative of 2 raised to the fourth power.

(c) $3^5 = 3 \cdot 3 \cdot 3 \cdot 3 \cdot 3 = 243$

(d) $(-5)^3 = (-5)(-5)(-5) = (25)(-5) = -125$

(e) $\left(\dfrac{1}{3}\right)^3 = \left(\dfrac{1}{3}\right)\left(\dfrac{1}{3}\right)\left(\dfrac{1}{3}\right) = \dfrac{1}{27}$

Practice Problem 1 Evaluate.

(a) $(-3)^5$ **(b)** $(-3)^6$ **(c)** $(-4)^4$ **(d)** -4^4 **(e)** $\left(\dfrac{1}{5}\right)^2$

TO THINK ABOUT: Raising Negative Numbers to a Power Look at Practice Problem 1. What do you notice about raising a negative number to an even power? To an odd power? Will this always be true? Why?

2 Finding Square Roots

We say that a square root of 16 is 4 because $4 \cdot 4 = 16$. You will note that, since $(-4)(-4) = 16$, another square root of 16 is -4. For practical purposes, we are usually interested in the nonnegative square root. We call this the **principal square root.** $\sqrt{}$ is the principal square root symbol and is called a **radical.**

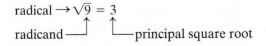

radical → $\sqrt{9} = 3$
radicand ——↑   ↑——principal square root

Student Learning Objectives

After studying this section, you will be able to:

1. Raise a number to a positive integer power.

2. Find square roots of numbers that are perfect squares.

3. Evaluate expressions by using the proper order of operations.

4. Rewrite expressions with negative exponents as expressions with positive exponents.

5. Use the product rule of exponents.

6. Use the quotient rule of exponents.

7. Use the power rules of exponents.

8. Express numbers in scientific notation.

The number or expression under the radical sign is called the **radicand.** Both 16 and 9 are called *perfect squares* because their square roots are integers.

> If x is an integer and a is a positive real number such that $a = x^2$, then x is a **square root** of a, and a is a **perfect square.**

EXAMPLE 2   Find the square roots of 25. What is the principal square root?

Solution   Since $(-5)^2 = 25$ and $5^2 = 25$, the square roots of 25 and 5 are -5. The principal square root is 5.

NOTE TO STUDENT: Fully worked-out solutions to all of the Practice Problems can be found at the back of the text starting at page SP-1

Practice Problem 2   What are the square roots of 49? What is the principal square root of 49?

We can find the square root of a positive number. However, there is no real number for $\sqrt{-4}$ or $\sqrt{-9}$. The square root of a negative number is not a real number.

EXAMPLE 3   Evaluate.   **(a)** $\sqrt{0.04}$ **(b)** $\sqrt{\dfrac{25}{36}}$ **(c)** $\sqrt{-16}$

Solution

(a) $(0.2)^2 = (0.2)(0.2) = 0.04$. Therefore, $\sqrt{0.04} = 0.2$.

(b) We can write $\sqrt{\dfrac{25}{36}}$ as $\dfrac{\sqrt{25}}{\sqrt{36}}$. $\dfrac{\sqrt{25}}{\sqrt{36}} = \dfrac{5}{6}$. Thus, $\sqrt{\dfrac{25}{36}} = \dfrac{5}{6}$.

(c) This is not a real number.

Practice Problem 3   Evaluate.   **(a)** $\sqrt{0.09}$ **(b)** $\sqrt{\dfrac{4}{81}}$ **(c)** $\sqrt{-25}$

The square roots of some numbers are irrational numbers. For example, $\sqrt{3}$ and $\sqrt{7}$ are irrational numbers. Thus, we often use rational numbers to *approximate* square roots that are irrational. They can be found on a calculator with a square root key. To find $\sqrt{3}$ on most calculators, we enter the 3 and then enter the $\boxed{\sqrt{}}$ key. Using a calculator, we might get 1.7320508 as our approximation. If you do not have a calculator, you can use the square root table at the back of the book. From the table we have $\sqrt{3} \approx 1.732$.

③ The Order of Operations of Real Numbers

Parentheses are used in numerical and algebraic expressions to group numbers and variables. When evaluating an expression containing parentheses, evaluate the numerical expressions inside the parentheses first. When we need more than one set of parentheses, we may also use brackets. To evaluate such an expression, work from the inside out.

When many arithmetic operations or grouping symbols are used, we use the following order of operations.

> **ORDER OF OPERATIONS FOR CALCULATIONS**
>
> 1. Combine numbers inside grouping symbols.
> 2. Raise numbers to their indicated powers and take any indicated roots.
> 3. Multiply and divide numbers from left to right.
> 4. Add and subtract numbers from left to right.

EXAMPLE 4 Evaluate. $12 - 3[7 + 5(6 - 9)]$

Solution

$$12 - 3[7 + 5(6 - 9)] = 12 - 3[7 + 5(-3)]$$ Begin with the innermost grouping symbol.

$$= 12 - 3[7 + (-15)]$$ Multiply inside the grouping symbol.

$$= 12 - 3[-8]$$ Add inside the grouping symbol.

$$= 12 + 24$$ Multiply.

$$= 36$$ Add.

Practice Problem 4 Evaluate.

(a) $6(12 - 8) + 4$ **(b)** $5[6 - 3(7 - 9)] - 8$

TO THINK ABOUT: Importance of Grouping Symbols Rewrite the expression in Example 4 without grouping symbols. Then evaluate the expression. Remember to first multiply from left to right and then add and subtract from left to right. Explain why the answers may differ.

A radical or absolute value symbol groups the quantities within it. Thus, we simplify the numerical expressions within the grouping symbol before we find the square root or the absolute value.

EXAMPLE 5 Evaluate. **(a)** $\sqrt{(-3)^2 + (4)^2}$ **(b)** $|5 - 8 + 7 - 13|$

Solution

(a) $\sqrt{(-3)^2 + (4)^2} = \sqrt{9 + 16} = \sqrt{25} = 5$

(b) $|5 - 8 + 7 - 13| = |-9| = 9$

Practice Problem 5 Evaluate.

(a) $\sqrt{(-5)^2 + 12^2}$ **(b)** $|-3 - 7 + 2 - (-4)|$

A fraction bar acts like a grouping symbol. We must evaluate the expressions above and below a fraction bar before we divide.

EXAMPLE 6 Evaluate. $\dfrac{2 \cdot 6^2 - 12 \div 3}{4 - 8}$

Solution We evaluate the numerator first.

$$2 \cdot 6^2 - 12 \div 3 = 2 \cdot 36 - 12 \div 3$$ Raise to a power.

$$= 72 - 4$$ Multiply and divide from left to right.

$$= 68$$ Subtract.

Next we evaluate the denominator.

$$4 - 8 = -4$$

Thus,

$$\frac{2 \cdot 6^2 - 12 \div 3}{4 - 8} = \frac{68}{-4} = -17$$

NOTE TO STUDENT: *Fully worked-out solutions to all of the Practice Problems can be found at the back of the text starting at page SP-1*

Practice Problem 6 Evaluate. $\dfrac{2(3) + 5(-2)}{1 + 2 \cdot 3^2 + 5(-3)}$

4 Rewriting Expressions with Negative Exponents as Expressions with Positive Exponents

Before we formally define the meaning of a negative exponent, let us look for a pattern.

On this side we decrease each exponent by 1 to obtain the expression on the next line.		On this side we divide each number by 3 to obtain the number on the next line.
	$3^4 = 81$	
	$3^3 = 27$	
	$3^2 = 9$	
	$3^1 = 3$	
	$3^0 = 1$	
	$3^{-1} = ?$	
	$3^{-2} = ?$	

What results would you expect on the last two lines? $3^{-1} = \dfrac{1}{3}$? Then $3^{-2} = \dfrac{1}{3^2} = \dfrac{1}{9}$. Do you see the pattern? Then we would have

$$3^{-3} = \dfrac{1}{3^3} = \dfrac{1}{27} \quad \text{and} \quad 3^{-4} = \dfrac{1}{3^4} = \dfrac{1}{81}.$$

Now we are ready to make a formal definition of a negative exponent.

> **DEFINITION OF NEGATIVE EXPONENTS**
>
> If x is any nonzero real number and n is an integer,
>
> $$x^{-n} = \dfrac{1}{x^n}.$$

EXAMPLE 7 Simplify. Do not leave negative exponents in your answers.

(a) 2^{-5} **(b)** w^{-6}

Solution

(a) $2^{-5} = \dfrac{1}{2^5} = \dfrac{1}{32}$ **(b)** $w^{-6} = \dfrac{1}{w^6}$

Practice Problem 7 Simplify. Do not leave negative exponents in your answers.

(a) 3^{-2} **(b)** z^{-8}

5 The Product Rule of Exponents

Numbers and variables with exponents can be multiplied quite simply if *the base is the same.* For example, we know that

$$(x^3)(x^2) = (x \cdot x \cdot x)(x \cdot x).$$

Since the factor x appears five times, it must be true that

$$x^3 \cdot x^2 = x^5.$$

Hence we can state a general rule.

PRODUCT RULE OF EXPONENTS

If x is a real number and n and m are integers, then

$$x^m \cdot x^n = x^{m+n}.$$

This rule says that the exponents are integers. Thus, they can be negative.

EXAMPLE 8   Multiply. **(a)** $(8a^{-3}b^{-8})(2a^5b^5)$ **(b)** $(a + b)^2(a + b)^3$

Solution   Simplify. Do not leave negative exponents in your answer.

(a) $(8a^{-3}b^{-8})(2a^5b^5) = 16a^{-3+5}b^{-8+5}$

$$= 16a^2b^{-3}$$

$$= 16a^2\left(\frac{1}{b^3}\right) = \frac{16a^2}{b^3}$$

(b) $(a + b)^2(a + b)^3 = (a + b)^{2+3} = (a + b)^5$ (The base is $a + b$.)

You may leave your answer in exponent form when the base is a binomial.

Practice Problem 8   Multiply. Then simplify. Do not leave negative exponents in your answers.

(a) $(7xy^{-2})(2x^{-5}y^{-6})$ **(b)** $(x + 2y)^4(x + 2y)^{10}$

---

6 The Quotient Rule of Exponents

We now develop the rule for dividing numbers with exponents. We know that

$$\frac{x^5}{x^3} = \frac{x \cdot x \cdot \cancel{x} \cdot \cancel{x} \cdot \cancel{x}}{\cancel{x} \cdot \cancel{x} \cdot \cancel{x}} = x \cdot x = x^2.$$

Note that $x^{5-3} = x^2$. This leads us to the following general rule.

QUOTIENT RULE OF EXPONENTS

If x is a nonzero real number and m and n are integers,

$$\frac{x^m}{x^n} = x^{m-n}.$$

EXAMPLE 9   Divide. $\dfrac{3x^{-5}y^{-6}}{27x^2y^{-8}}$

Solution   Simplify your answer so there are no negative exponents.

$$\frac{3x^{-5}y^{-6}}{27x^2y^{-8}} = \frac{1}{9}x^{-5-2}y^{-6-(-8)} = \frac{1}{9}x^{-5-2}y^{-6+8} = \frac{1}{9}x^{-7}y^2 = \frac{y^2}{9x^7}$$

Practice Problem 9   Divide. Then simplify your answer. $\dfrac{2x^{-3}y}{4x^{-2}y^5}$

Our quotient rule leads us to an interesting situation if $m = n$.

$$\frac{x^m}{x^m} = x^0$$

But what exactly is x^0? Whenever we divide any nonzero value by itself we always get 1, so we would therefore expect that $x^0 = 1$. But can we prove that? Yes.

$$\text{Since} \quad x^{-n} = \frac{1}{x^n},$$

$$\text{Then} \quad x^{-n} \cdot x^n = 1 \quad \text{Multiplying both sides by } x^n.$$
$$x^{-n+n} = 1 \quad \text{Using the product rule.}$$
$$x^0 = 1 \quad \text{Since } -n + n = 0.$$

RAISING A NUMBER TO THE ZERO POWER

For any nonzero real number x, $x^0 = 1$.

EXAMPLE 10   Divide. Then simplify your answers. Do not leave negative exponents in your answers.

(a) $(3x)^0$ **(b)** $\dfrac{-150a^3b^4c^2}{-300abc^2}$

Solution

(a) $(3x)^0 = 1$ Note that the entire expression is raised to the zero power.

Remember that we don't usually write an exponent of 1. Thus, $a = a^1$, and $b = b^1$.

(b) $\dfrac{-150a^3b^4c^2}{-300abc^2} = \dfrac{-150}{-300} \cdot \dfrac{a^3}{a^1} \cdot \dfrac{b^4}{b^1} \cdot \dfrac{c^2}{c^2} = \dfrac{1}{2} \cdot a^2 \cdot b^3 \cdot c^0 = \dfrac{a^2b^3}{2}$

Practice Problem 10   Divide. Then simplify your answers. Do not leave negative exponents in your answers.

(a) $\dfrac{30x^6y^5}{20x^3y^2}$ **(b)** $\dfrac{-15a^3b^4c^4}{3a^5b^4c^2}$ **(c)** $(5^{-3})(2a)^0$

NOTE TO STUDENT: Fully worked-out solutions to all of the Practice Problems can be found at the back of the text starting at page SP-1

For the remainder of this chapter, we will assume that for all exercises involving exponents, a simplified answer should not contain negative exponents.

7 The Power Rules of Exponents

Note that $(x^4)^3 = x^4 \cdot x^4 \cdot x^4 = x^{4+4+4} = x^{4 \cdot 3} = x^{12}$. In the same way we can show:

$$(xy)^3 = x^3y^3$$

$$\text{and} \left(\frac{x}{y}\right)^3 = \frac{x^3}{y^3} \quad (y \neq 0).$$

Therefore, we have the following rules.

POWER RULES OF EXPONENTS

If x and y are any real numbers and n and m are integers,

$$(x^m)^n = x^{mn}, \quad (xy)^n = x^ny^n, \text{ and}$$

$$\left(\frac{x}{y}\right)^n = \frac{x^n}{y^n}, \qquad \text{if } y \neq 0.$$

EXAMPLE 11 Use the power rules of exponents to simplify.

(a) $(x^6)^5$ **(b)** $(2^8)^4$ **(c)** $[(a + b)^2]^4$

Solution

(a) $(x^6)^5 = x^{6 \cdot 5} = x^{30}$

(b) $(2^8)^4 = 2^{32}$ Careful. Don't change the base of 2.

(c) $[(a + b)^2]^4 = (a + b)^8$ The base is $a + b$.

Practice Problem 11 Use the power rules of exponents to simplify.

(a) $(w^3)^8$ **(b)** $(5^2)^5$ **(c)** $[(x - 2y)^3]^3$

EXAMPLE 12 Simplify.

(a) $(3xy^2)^4$ **(b)** $\left(\dfrac{2a^2b^3}{3ab^4}\right)^3$ **(c)** $(2a^2b^{-3}c^0)^{-4}$

Solution

(a) $(3xy^2)^4 = 3^4 x^4 y^8 = 81 x^4 y^8$

(b) $\left(\dfrac{2a^2b^3}{3ab^4}\right)^3 = \dfrac{2^3 a^6 b^9}{3^3 a^3 b^{12}} = \dfrac{8a^3}{27b^3}$

(c) $(2a^2b^{-3}c^0)^{-4} = 2^{-4}a^{-8}b^{12} = \dfrac{b^{12}}{2^4 a^8} = \dfrac{b^{12}}{16a^8}$

Practice Problem 12 Simplify.

(a) $(4x^3y^4)^2$ **(b)** $\left(\dfrac{4xy}{3x^5y^6}\right)^3$ **(c)** $(3xy^2)^{-2}$

We need to derive one more rule. You should be able to follow the steps.

$$\frac{x^{-m}}{y^{-n}} = \frac{\dfrac{1}{x^m}}{\dfrac{1}{y^n}} = \frac{1}{x^m} \cdot \frac{y^n}{1} = \frac{y^n}{x^m}$$

RULE OF NEGATIVE EXPONENTS

If n and m are positive integers and x and y are nonzero real numbers, then

$$\frac{x^{-m}}{y^{-n}} = \frac{y^n}{x^m}.$$

For example, $\dfrac{x^{-5}}{y^{-6}} = \dfrac{y^6}{x^5}$ and $\dfrac{2^{-3}}{x^{-4}} = \dfrac{x^4}{2^3} = \dfrac{x^4}{8}$.

**Summary of Rules
of Exponents when $x, y \neq 0$**

1. $x^m \cdot x^n = x^{m+n}$

2. $\dfrac{x^m}{x^n} = x^{m-n}$

3. $x^{-n} = \dfrac{1}{x^n}$

4. $x^0 = 1$

5. $(x^m)^n = x^{mn}$

6. $(xy)^n = x^n y^n$

7. $\left(\dfrac{x}{y}\right)^n = \dfrac{x^n}{y^n}$

8. $\dfrac{x^{-m}}{y^{-n}} = \dfrac{y^n}{x^m}$

NOTE TO STUDENT: Fully worked-out solutions to all of the Practice Problems can be found at the back of the text starting at page SP-1

EXAMPLE 13   Simplify.   (a) $\dfrac{3x^{-2}y^3z^{-1}}{4x^3y^{-5}z^{-2}}$ (b) $\left(\dfrac{5xy^{-3}}{2x^{-4}yz^{-3}}\right)^{-2}$

Solution

(a) First remove all negative exponents.

$$\dfrac{3x^{-2}y^3z^{-1}}{4x^3y^{-5}z^{-2}} = \dfrac{3y^3y^5z^2}{4x^3x^2z^1}$$ Only variables with negative exponents will change their position.

$$= \dfrac{3y^8z^2}{4x^5z^1}$$

$$= \dfrac{3y^8z}{4x^5}$$

(b) First remove the parentheses by using the power rules of exponents.

$$\left(\dfrac{5xy^{-3}}{2x^{-4}yz^{-3}}\right)^{-2} = \dfrac{5^{-2}x^{-2}y^6}{2^{-2}x^8y^{-2}z^6}$$

$$= \dfrac{2^2y^6y^2}{5^2x^8x^2z^6}$$

$$= \dfrac{4y^8}{25x^{10}z^6}$$

Practice Problem 13   Simplify.

(a) $\dfrac{7x^2y^{-4}z^{-3}}{8x^{-5}y^{-6}z^2}$ (b) $\left(\dfrac{4x^2y^{-2}}{x^{-4}y^{-3}}\right)^{-3}$

⑧ Scientific Notation

Scientific notation is a convenient way to write very large or very small numbers. For example, we can write 50,000,000 as 5×10^7 since $10^7 = 10{,}000{,}000$, and we can write $0.0000000005 = 5 \times 10^{-10}$ since $10^{-10} = \dfrac{1}{10^{10}} = \dfrac{1}{10{,}000{,}000{,}000} = 0.0000000001$. In scientific notation, the first factor is a number between 1 and 10. The second factor is a power of 10.

> ### SCIENTIFIC NOTATION
>
> A positive number written in **scientific notation** has the form $a \times 10^n$, where $1 \leq a < 10$ and n is an integer.

The decimal notation and the scientific notation are just equivalent forms of the same number. To change a number from decimal notation to scientific notation, follow the steps below. Remember that the first factor must be a number between 1 and 10. This determines where to place the decimal point.

> ### CONVERT FROM DECIMAL NOTATION TO SCIENTIFIC NOTATION
>
> 1. Move the decimal point from its original position to the right of the first nonzero digit.
> 2. Count the number of places that you moved the decimal point. This number is the power of 10 (that is, the exponent).
> 3. If you moved the decimal point to the right, the exponent is negative; if you moved it to the left, the exponent is positive.

EXAMPLE 14   Write in scientific notation.

(a) 7816   **(b)** 15,200,000   **(c)** 0.0123   **(d)** 0.00046

Solution

(a) $7816 = 7.816 \times 10^3$ We moved the decimal point three places to the left, so the power of 10 is 3.

(b) $15,200,000 = 1.52 \times 10^7$

(c) $0.0123 = 1.23 \times 10^{-2}$ We moved the decimal point two places to the right, so the power of 10 is −2.

(d) $0.00046 = 4.6 \times 10^{-4}$

Practice Problem 14   Write in scientific notation.

(a) 128,320   **(b)** 476   **(c)** 0.0786   **(d)** 0.007

We can also change a number from scientific notation to decimal notation. We simply move the decimal point to the right or to the left the number of places indicated by the power of 10.

EXAMPLE 15   Write in decimal form.

(a) 8.8632×10^4 **(b)** 6.032×10^{-2} **(c)** 4.4861×10^{-5}

Solution

(a) $8.8632 \times 10^4 = 88,632$

                  —Move the decimal point two places to the left.

(b) $6.032 \times 10^{-2} = 0.06032$

(c) $4.4861 \times 10^{-5} = 0.000044861$

Practice Problem 15   Write in decimal form.

(a) 4.62×10^6 **(b)** 1.973×10^{-3} **(c)** 4.931×10^{-1}

Using scientific notation and the laws of exponents greatly simplifies calculations.

EXAMPLE 16   Evaluate using scientific notation $\dfrac{(0.000000036)(0.002)}{0.000012}$.

Solution   Rewrite the expression in scientific notation.

$$\frac{(3.6 \times 10^{-8})(2 \times 10^{-3})}{1.2 \times 10^{-5}}$$

Now rewrite using the commutative property.

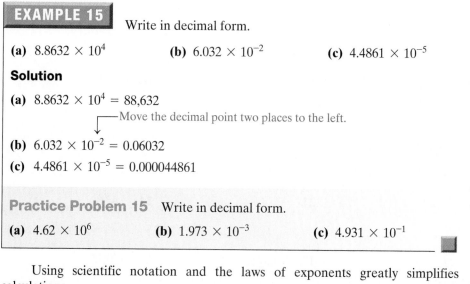

$$\frac{\overset{3}{\cancel{(3.6)}}(2)(10^{-8})(10^{-3})}{\underset{1}{\cancel{(1.2)}}(10^{-5})} = \frac{6.0}{1} \times \frac{10^{-11}}{10^{-5}}$$ Simplify and use the laws of exponents.

$$= 6.0 \times 10^{-11-(-5)}$$

$$= 6.0 \times 10^{-6}$$

Practice Problem 16   Evaluate using scientific notation $\dfrac{(55,000)(3,000,00\ldots)}{5,500,00\ldots}$

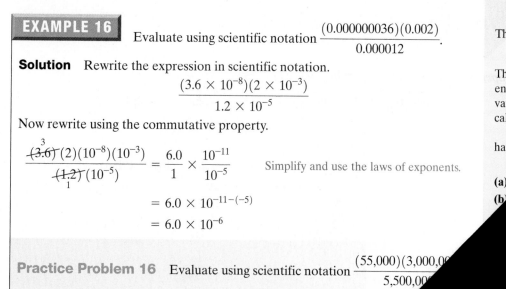

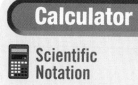

Calculator

Scientific Notation

Most scientific calculators can display only eight digits at one time. Numbers with more than eight digits are shown in scientific notation.

1.12 E 08 means 1.12×10^8. Note that the display on your calculator may be slightly different. You can use the calculator to compute large numbers by entering the numbers using scientific notation. For example, to compute

$$(7.48 \times 10^{24}) \times (3.5 \times 10^8)$$

on a scientific calculator, press these keys:

7.48 ⎡EE⎤ 24 ⎡×⎤

3.5 ⎡EE⎤ 8 ⎡=⎤

The display should read:

⎡ 2.618 E 33 ⎤

The label on the key used f... entering the power of 10... vary depending on th... calculator.

Some scienti... have an ⎡EX...

Try the...

(a) 3⁵...

(b)

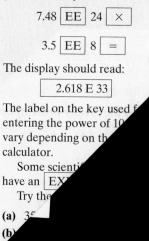

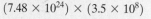

Verbal and Writing Skills

1. In the expression a^3, identify the base and the exponent.

2. When a negative number is raised to an odd power, is the result positive or negative?

3. When a negative number is raised to an even power, is the result positive or negative?

4. Will $-a^n$ always be negative? Why or why not?

5. What are the square roots of 121? Why are there two answers?

6. What is the principal square root?

Evaluate.

7. 2^5

8. 7^3

9. $(-5)^2$

10. $(-4)^3$

11. -6^2

12. -3^4

13. -1^4

14. -3^2

15. $\left(-\dfrac{1}{4}\right)^4$

16. $\left(-\dfrac{1}{5}\right)^3$

17. $(0.8)^2$

18. $(-0.5)^2$

19. $(0.04)^3$

20. $(0.05)^3$

Find each principal square root.

21. $\sqrt{81}$

22. $\sqrt{121}$

23. $-\sqrt{16}$

24. $-\sqrt{64}$

25. $\sqrt{\dfrac{4}{9}}$

26. $\sqrt{\dfrac{1}{36}}$

27. $\sqrt{0.09}$

28. $\sqrt{0.25}$

30. $\sqrt{\dfrac{1}{9} + \dfrac{3}{9}}$

31. $\sqrt{-36}$

32. $\sqrt{-49}$

39. *ons to evaluate each of the following.*

34. $16 \div (-8) - 6(-2)$

35. $-3^2 + 2(4 - 7)$

$ - 0.4) - 0.8]$

38. $-2[(3.6 + 0.3) - 0.9]$

$ - 2^3 + \sqrt{49}$

41. $\dfrac{|2^2 - 5| - 3^2}{-5 + 3}$

42. $\dfrac{|3 - 2^3| - 5}{2 + 3}$

43. $\dfrac{\sqrt{(-5)^2 - 3 + 14}}{|19 - 6 + 3 - 25|}$

44. $\dfrac{\sqrt{(-2)^2 - 3} + 3}{6 - |3 \cdot 2 - 8|}$

45. $\dfrac{\sqrt{6^2 - 3^2 - 2}}{(-3)^2 - 4}$

46. $\dfrac{\sqrt{4 \cdot 7 + 2^3}}{3^2 - 5}$

Simplify. Rewrite all expressions with positive exponents only.

47. 3^{-2}

48. 4^{-3}

49. x^{-5}

50. y^{-4}

Multiply. Leave your answer in exponential form.

51. $(3x)(-2x^5)$

52. $(5y^2)(3y)$

53. $(-12x^3y)(-3x^5y^2)$

54. $(-20a^3b^2)(5ab)$

55. $4x^0y$

56. $-6a^2b^0$

57. $(3xy)^0(7xy)$

58. $-8a^2b^3(-6a)^0$

59. $(2x^0y^5z)(-5xy^0z^8)$

60. $(4^0x^2y^3)(-3x^0y^6)$

61. $\left(-\dfrac{3}{5}m^{-2}n^4\right)(5m^2n^{-5})$

62. $\left(\dfrac{2}{3}m^2n^{-3}\right)(6m^{-5}n)$

Divide. Simplify your answers.

63. $\dfrac{2^8}{2^5}$

64. $\dfrac{3^{16}}{3^{18}}$

65. $\dfrac{2x^3}{x^8}$

66. $\dfrac{4y^3}{8y}$

67. $\dfrac{10ab^5c}{-2ab^2}$

68. $\dfrac{-64x^2y}{4x^2}$

69. $\dfrac{-20a^{-3}b^{-8}}{14a^{-5}b^{-12}}$

70. $\dfrac{-27x^7y^{10}}{-6x^{-2}y^{-3}}$

Use the power rules to simplify each expression.

71. $\left(\dfrac{x^2y^3}{z}\right)^6$

72. $\left(\dfrac{x^3}{y^5z^8}\right)^4$

73. $\left(\dfrac{3ab^{-2}}{4a^0b^4}\right)^2$

74. $\left(\dfrac{5a^3b}{-3a^{-2}b^0}\right)^3$

75. $\left(\dfrac{2xy^2}{x^{-3}y^{-4}}\right)^{-3}$

76. $\left(\dfrac{3x^{-4}y}{x^{-3}y^2}\right)^{-2}$

77. $(x^{-1}y^3)^{-2}(2x)^2$

78. $(x^3y^{-2})^{-2}(5x^{-5})^2$

79. $\dfrac{(-3m^5n^{-1})^3}{(mn)^2}$

80. $\dfrac{(m^4n^3)^{-1}}{(-5m^{-3}n^4)^2}$

Mixed Practice Exercises 81–92

Simplify. Express your answers with positive exponents only.

81. $\dfrac{2^{-3}a^2}{2^{-4}a^{-2}}$

82. $\dfrac{3^4a^{-3}}{3^3a^4}$

83. $\left(\dfrac{y^{-3}}{x}\right)^{-3}$

84. $\left(\dfrac{z}{y^{-5}}\right)^{-2}$

85. $\dfrac{a^{-2}b^0}{ab^{-5}}$

86. $\dfrac{b^{-2}d^0}{b^{-3}d^{-3}}$

87. $\left(\dfrac{14x^{-3}y^{-3}}{7x^{-4}y^{-3}}\right)^{-2}$

88. $\left(\dfrac{25x^{-1}y^{-6}}{5x^{-4}y^{-6}}\right)^{-2}$

89. $\dfrac{7^{-8}\cdot 5^{-6}}{7^{-9}\cdot 5^{-5}}$

90. $\dfrac{9^{-2}\cdot 8^{-10}}{9^{-1}\cdot 8^{-9}}$

91. $(9x^{-2}y)\left(-\dfrac{2}{3}x^3y^{-2}\right)$

92. $\left(\dfrac{4}{5}x^6y^{-1}\right)(-10x^{-8}y^2)$

Write in scientific notation.

93. 38

94. 759

95. 1,730,000

96. 5,318,000,000

97. 0.83

98. 0.0654

99. 0.0000529

100. 0.000007116

Write in decimal notation.

101. 7.13×10^5

102. 4.006×10^6

103. 3.07×10^{-1}

104. 7.07×10^{-3}

105. 9.01×10^{-7}

106. 6.668×10^{-9}

Perform the calculations indicated. Express your answers in scientific notation.

107. $(3.1 \times 10^{-4})(1.5 \times 10^{-2})$

108. $(3.1 \times 10^{-5})(2.0 \times 10^8)$

109. $\dfrac{3.6 \times 10^{-5}}{1.2 \times 10^{-6}}$

110. $\dfrac{4.6 \times 10^{-12}}{2.3 \times 10^5}$

Applications

111. *Oxygen Molecules* The weight of one oxygen molecule is 5.3×10^{-23} gram. How much would 2×10^4 molecules of oxygen weigh?

112. *Solar Probe* The average distance from Earth to the sun is 4.90×10^{11} feet. If a solar probe is launched from Earth and travels at 2×10^4 feet per second, how long would it take to reach the sun?

1 Identifying Types and Degrees of Polynomials

A **polynomial** is an algebraic expression of one or more terms. A **term** is a number, a variable raised to a nonnegative integer power, or a product of numbers and variables raised to nonnegative integer powers. There must be no division by a variable. Three types of polynomials that you will see often are **monomials, binomials,** and **trinomials.**

> 1. A **monomial** has *one* term.
> 2. A **binomial** has *two* terms.
> 3. A **trinomial** has *three* terms.

Here are some examples of polynomials.

Number of Variables	Monomials	Binomials	Trinomials	Other Polynomials
One Variable	$8x^3$	$2y^2 + 3y$	$5x^2 + 2x - 6$	$x^4 + 2x^3 - x^2 + 9$
Two Variables	$6x^2y$	$3x^2 - 5y^3$	$8x^2 + 5xy - 3y^2$	$x^3y + 5xy^2 + 3xy - 7y^5$
Three Variables	$12uvw^3$	$11a^2b + 5c^2$	$4a^2b^4 + 7c^4 - 2a^5$	$3c^2 + 4c - 8d + 2e - e^2$

The following are *not* polynomials.

$$2x^{-3} + 5x^2 - 3 \qquad 4ab^{\frac{1}{2}} \qquad \frac{2}{x} + \frac{3}{y}$$

TO THINK ABOUT: Understanding Polynomials Give a reason each expression above is not a polynomial.

Polynomials are also classified by degree. The **degree of a term** is the sum of the exponents of its variables. The **degree of a polynomial** is the degree of the highest-degree term in the polynomial. If the polynomial has no variable, then it has degree zero.

EXAMPLE 1 Name the type of polynomial and give its degree.

(a) $5x^6 + 3x^2 + 2$ **(b)** $7x + 6$
(c) $5x^2y + 3xy^3 + 6xy$ **(d)** $7x^4y^5$

Solution
(a) This is a trinomial of degree 6.
(b) This is a binomial of degree 1.   Remember that if a variable has no exponent,
(c) This is a trinomial of degree 4.   the exponent is understood to be 1.
(d) This is a monomial of degree 9.

Practice Problem 1 State the type of polynomial and give its degree.
(a) $3x^5 - 6x^4 + x^2$ **(b)** $5x^2 + 2$
(c) $3ab + 5a^2b^2 - 6a^4b$ **(d)** $16x^4y^6$

Student Learning Objectives

After studying this section, you will be able to:

1 Identify types and degrees of polynomials.

2 Evaluate polynomial functions.

3 Add and subtract polynomials.

4 Multiply two binomials by FOIL.

5 Multiply two binomials $(a + b)(a - b)$.

6 Multiply two binomials $(a - b)^2$ or $(a + b)^2$.

7 Multiply polynomials with more than two terms.

NOTE TO STUDENT: Fully worked-out solutions to all of the Practice Problems can be found at the back of the text starting at page SP-1

Some polynomials contain only one variable. A **polynomial in x** is an expression of the form

$$a_n x^n + a_{n-1} x^{n-1} + a_{n-2} x^{n-2} + \cdots + a_0$$

where n is a nonnegative integer and the constants $a_n, a_{n-1}, a_{n-2}, \ldots, a_0$ are real numbers. We usually write polynomials in **descending order** of the variable. That is, the exponents on the variables decrease from left to right. For example, the polynomial $4x^5 - 2x^3 + 6x^2 + 5x - 8$ is written in descending order.

2 Evaluating Polynomial Functions

A **polynomial function** is a function that is defined by a polynomial.
For example,

$$p(x) = 5x^2 - 3x + 6 \quad \text{and} \quad p(x) = 2x^5 - 3x^3 + 8x - 15$$

are both polynomial functions.
To evaluate a polynomial function, we use the skills developed in Section 3.6.

EXAMPLE 2 Evaluate the polynomial function $p(x) = -3x^3 + 2x^2 - 5x + 6$ for **(a)** $p(-3)$ and **(b)** $p(6)$.

Solution

(a) $p(-3) = -3(-3)^3 + 2(-3)^2 - 5(-3) + 6$
$ = -3(-27) + 2(9) - 5(-3) + 6$
$ = 81 + 18 + 15 + 6$
$ = 120$

(b) $p(6) = -3(6)^3 + 2(6)^2 - 5(6) + 6$
$ = -3(216) + 2(36) - 5(6) + 6$
$ = -648 + 72 - 30 + 6$
$ = -600$

Practice Problem 2 Evaluate the polynomial function
$p(x) = 2x^4 - 3x^3 + 6x - 8$ for **(a)** $p(-2)$ **(b)** $p(5)$.

NOTE TO STUDENT: Fully worked-out solutions to all of the Practice Problems can be found at the back of the text starting at page SP-1

---

3 Adding and Subtracting Polynomials

We can add and subtract polynomials by combining like terms as we learned in Sections 1.7 and 5.3.

EXAMPLE 3 Add: $(5x^2 - 3x - 8) + (-3x^2 - 7x + 9)$

Solution

$5x^2 - 3x - 8 - 3x^2 - 7x + 9$ We remove the parentheses and combine like terms.
$= 2x^2 - 10x + 1$

Practice Problem 3 Add: $(-7x^2 + 5x - 9) + (2x^2 - 3x + 5)$

To subtract real numbers, we add the opposite of the second number to the first. Thus, for real numbers a and b, we have $a - (+b) = a + (-b)$. Similarly for polynomials, to subtract polynomials we add the opposite of the second polynomial to the first.

EXAMPLE 4   Subtract: $(-5x^2 - 19x + 15) - (3x^2 - 4x + 13)$

Solution

$(-5x^2 - 19x + 15) + (-3x^2 + 4x - 13)$ We add the opposite of the second polynomial to the first polynomial.

$= -8x^2 - 15x + 2$

Practice Problem 4   Subtract: $(2x^2 - 14x + 9) - (-3x^2 + 10x + 7)$

4 Multiplying Two Binomials by FOIL

The FOIL method for multiplying two binomials has been developed to help you keep track of the order of the terms to be multiplied. The acronym FOIL means the following:

F	**F**irst
O	**O**uter
I	**I**nner
L	**L**ast

That is, we multiply the first terms, then the outer terms, then the inner terms, and finally, the last terms.

EXAMPLE 5   Multiply: $(5x + 2)(7x - 3)$

Solution

First + Outer + Inner + Last

$(5x + 2)(7x - 3) = 35x^2 - 15x + 14x - 6$

$= 35x^2 - x - 6$

Practice Problem 5   Multiply: $(7x + 3)(2x - 5)$

EXAMPLE 6   Multiply: $(7x^2 - 8)(2x - 3)$

Solution

$(7x^2 - 8)(2x - 3) = 14x^3 - 21x^2 - 16x + 24$

Note that in this case we were not able to combine the inner and outer products.

Practice Problem 6   Multiply: $(3x^2 - 2)(5x - 4)$

5 Multiplying $(a + b)(a - b)$

Products of the form $(a + b)(a - b)$ deserve special attention.

$$(a + b)(a - b) = a^2 - ab + ab - b^2 = a^2 - b^2$$

Notice that the middle terms, $-ab$ and $+ab$, when combined equal zero. The product is the difference of two squares, $a^2 - b^2$. This is always true when you multiply binomials of the form $(a + b)(a - b)$. You should memorize the following formula.

$$(a + b)(a - b) = a^2 - b^2$$

EXAMPLE 7 Multiply: $(2a - 9b)(2a + 9b)$

Solution $(2a - 9b)(2a + 9b) = (2a)^2 - (9b)^2 = 4a^2 - 81b^2$

Of course, we could have used the FOIL method, but recognizing the special product allowed us to save time.

NOTE TO STUDENT: Fully worked-out solutions to all of the Practice Problems can be found at the back of the text starting at page SP-1

Practice Problem 7   Multiply: $(7x - 2y)(7x + 2y)$

6 Multiplying $(a - b)^2$ or $(a + b)^2$

Another special product is the square of a binomial.

$$(a - b)^2 = (a - b)(a - b) = a^2 - ab - ab + b^2 = a^2 - 2ab + b^2$$

Once you understand the pattern, you should memorize these two formulas.

$$(a - b)^2 = a^2 - 2ab + b^2 \qquad (a + b)^2 = a^2 + 2ab + b^2$$

This procedure is also called **expanding a binomial.** *Note:* $(a - b)^2 \neq a^2 - b^2$ and $(a + b)^2 \neq a^2 + b^2$.

EXAMPLE 8 Multiply.   **(a)** $(5a - 8b)^2$ **(b)** $(3u + 11v^2)^2$

Solution

(a) $(5a - 8b)^2 = (5a)^2 - 2(5a)(8b) + (8b)^2 = 25a^2 - 80ab + 64b^2$

(b) Here $a = 3u$ and $b = 11v^2$.

$$(3u + 11v^2)^2 = (3u)^2 + 2(3u)(11v^2) + (11v^2)^2$$
$$= 9u^2 + 66uv^2 + 121v^4$$

Practice Problem 8   Multiply.   **(a)** $(4u + 5v)^2$ **(b)** $(7x^2 - 3y^2)^2$

7 Multiplying Polynomials with More Than Two Terms

The distributive property is the basis for multiplying polynomials. Recall that

$$a(b+c) = ab + ac.$$

We can use this property to multiply a polynomial by a monomial.

$$3xy(5x^3 + 2x^2 - 4x + 1) = 3xy(5x^3) + 3xy(2x^2) - 3xy(4x) + 3xy(1)$$
$$= 15x^4y + 6x^3y - 12x^2y + 3xy$$

A similar procedure can be used instead of FOIL to multiply two binomials.

$$(3x+5)(6x+7) = (3x+5)6x + (3x+5)7 \quad \text{We use the distributive}$$
$$\text{property again.}$$
$$= (3x)(6x) + (5)(6x) + (3x)(7) + (5)(7)$$
$$= 18x^2 + 30x + 21x + 35$$
$$= 18x^2 + 51x + 35$$

The multiplication of a binomial and a trinomial is more involved. One way to multiply two polynomials is to write them vertically, as we do when multiplying two- and three-digit numbers. We then multiply them in the usual way.

EXAMPLE 9   Multiply: $(4x^2 - 2x + 3)(-3x + 4)$

Solution

$$\begin{array}{r} 4x^2 - 2x + 3 \\ -3x + 4 \\ \hline 16x^2 - 8x + 12 \\ -12x^3 + 6x^2 - 9x \\ \hline -12x^3 + 22x^2 - 17x + 12 \end{array}$$

Multiply $(4x^2 - 2x + 3)(+4)$.
Multiply $(4x^2 - 2x + 3)(-3x)$.
Add the two products.

Practice Problem 9   Multiply: $(2x^2 - 3x + 1)(x^2 - 5x)$

Another way to multiply polynomials is to multiply horizontally. We redo Example 9 in the following example.

EXAMPLE 10   Multiply horizontally: $(4x^2 - 2x + 3)(-3x + 4)$

Solution   By the distributive law, we have the following:

$$(4x^2 - 2x + 3)(-3x + 4) = (4x^2 - 2x + 3)(-3x) + (4x^2 - 2x + 3)(4)$$
$$= -12x^3 + 6x^2 - 9x + 16x^2 - 8x + 12$$
$$= -12x^3 + 22x^2 - 17x + 12.$$

In actual practice you will find that you can do some of these steps mentally.

Practice Problem 10   Multiply horizontally: $(2x^2 - 3x + 1)(x^2 - 5x)$.

Name the type of polynomial and give its degree.

1. $2x^2 - 5x + 3$

2. $7x^3 + 6x^2 - 2$

3. $-3.2a^4bc^3$

4. $26.8a^3bc^2$

5. $\dfrac{3}{5}m^3n - \dfrac{2}{5}mn$

6. $\dfrac{2}{7}m^2n^2 + \dfrac{1}{2}mn^2$

For the polynomial function $p(x) = 5x^2 - 9x - 12$ evaluate the following:

7. $p(3)$

8. $p(-4)$

For the polynomial function $g(x) = -3x^3 - x^2 + 4x + 2$, evaluate the following:

9. $g(2)$

10. $g(-1)$

For the polynomial function $h(x) = 2x^4 - x^3 + 2x^2 - 4x - 3$ evaluate the following:

11. $h(-1)$

12. $h(3)$

Add or subtract the following polynomials as indicated.

13. $(x^2 + 3x - 2) + (-2x^2 - 5x + 1) + (x^2 - x - 5)$

14. $(2x^2 - 5x - 1) + (3x^2 - 7x + 3) + (-5x^2 + x + 1)$

15. $(7m^3 + 4m^2 - m + 2.5) - (-3m^3 + 5m + 3.8)$

16. $(3x^3 + 2x^2 - 8x - 9.2) - (-5x^3 + x^2 - x - 12.7)$

17. $(5a^3 - 2a^2 - 6a + 8) + (5a + 6) - (-a^2 - a + 2)$

18. $(a^5 + 3a^2) + (2a^4 - a^3 - 3a^2 + 2) - (a^4 + 3a^3 - 5)$

19. $\left(\dfrac{1}{2}x^2 - 7x\right) + \left(\dfrac{1}{3}x^2 + \dfrac{1}{4}x\right)$

20. $\left(\dfrac{1}{5}x^2 + 9x\right) + \left(\dfrac{4}{5}x^2 - \dfrac{1}{6}x\right)$

21. $(2.3x^3 - 5.6x^2 - 2) - (5.5x^3 - 7.4x^2 + 2)$

22. $(5.9x^3 + 3.4x^2 - 7) - (2.9x^3 - 9.6x^2 + 3)$

Multiply.

23. $(5x + 8)(2x + 9)$

24. $(6x + 7)(3x + 2)$

25. $(5w + 2d)(3a - 4b)$

26. $(7a + 8b)(5d - 8w)$

27. $(3x - 2y)(-4x + y)$

28. $(-9x - 5y)(3a + 2y)$

29. $(7r - s^2)(-4a - 11s^2)$

30. $(-3r - 2s^2)(5r - 6s^2)$

Multiply mentally. See Examples 7 and 8.

31. $(5x - 8y)(5x + 8y)$ **32.** $(2a - 7b)(2a + 7b)$ **33.** $(5a - 2b)^2$ **34.** $(6a + 5b)^2$

35. $(7m - 1)^2$ **36.** $(5r + 3)^2$ **37.** $(4 + 3x^2)(4 - 3x^2)$ **38.** $(7 - 5x^3)(7 + 5x^3)$

39. $(3m^3 + 1)^2$ **40.** $(4r^3 - 5)^2$

Multiply.

41. $2x(3x^2 - 5x + 1)$ **42.** $-5x(x^2 - 6x - 2)$

43. $-\dfrac{1}{3}xy(2x - 6y + 15)$ **44.** $\dfrac{3}{5}xy^3(x - 10y + 4)$

45. $(2x - 3)(x^2 - x + 1)$ **46.** $(4x + 1)(2x^2 + x + 1)$

47. $(3x^2 - 2xy - 6y^2)(2x - y)$ **48.** $(5x^2 + 3xy - 7y^2)(3x - 2y)$

49. $\left(\dfrac{3}{2}x^2 - x + 1\right)(x^2 + 2x - 6)$ **50.** $\left(\dfrac{2}{3}x^2 + 5x - 2\right)(2x^2 - 3x + 9)$

51. $(5a^3 - 3a^2 + 2a - 4)(a - 3)$ **52.** $(2b^3 - 5b^2 - 4b + 1)(2b - 1)$

First multiply any two binomials in the exercise; then multiply the result by the third binomial.

53. $(x + 2)(x - 3)(2x - 5)$ **54.** $(x - 6)(x + 2)(3x + 2)$

55. $(a + 3)(2 - a)(4 - 3a)$ **56.** $(6 - 5a)(a + 1)(2 - 3a)$

Applications

▲ **57.** *Geometry* The area of the base of a rectangular box measures $2x^2 + 5x + 8$ cm^2. The height of the box measures $3x + 5$ cm. Find the volume of the box.

▲ **58.** *Geometry* A rectangular garden has $3n^2 + 4n + 7$ flowers planted in each row. The garden has $2n + 5$ rows. Find the number of flowers in the garden.

Antimalaria Medication   *The concentration of a certain antimalaria medication, in parts per million after time t, in hours, is given by the polynomial* $p(t) = -0.03t^2 + 78.$

59. Find the concentration after 3 hours.   **60.** Find the concentration after 30 hours.

61. Find the concentration after 50 hours.   **62.** Find the concentration after 50.9 hours.

A.3 FACTORING POLYNOMIALS

Student Learning Objectives

After studying this section, you will be able to:

1 Factor out the greatest common factor from a polynomial.

2 Factor a polynomial by the grouping method.

3 Factor trinomials of the form $x^2 + bx + c$.

4 Factor trinomials of the form $ax^2 + bx + c$.

When two or more algebraic expressions (monomials, binomials, and so on) are multiplied, each expression is called a **factor.** We learned to multiply factors in Section 5.4 and Appendix A.2.

In this section, we will learn how to find the factors of a polynomial. **Factoring** is the opposite of multiplication and is an extremely important mathematical technique.

1 Factoring Out the Greatest Common Factor

To factor out a common factor, we make use of the distributive property.

$$ab + ac = a(b + c)$$

The **greatest common factor** is simply the largest factor that is common to all terms of the expression.

It must contain

1. The largest possible common factor of the numerical coefficients and
2. The largest possible common variable factor

EXAMPLE 1 Factor out the greatest common factor.

(a) $7x^2 - 14x$ **(b)** $40a^3 - 20a^2$

Solution

(a) $7x^2 - 14x = 7 \cdot x \cdot x - 7 \cdot 2 \cdot x = 7x(x - 2)$
Be careful. The greatest common factor is $7x$, not 7.

(b) $40a^3 - 20a^2 = 20a^2(2a - 1)$
The greatest common factor is $20a^2$.

Suppose we had written $10a(4a^2 - 2a)$ or $10a(2a)(2a - 1)$ as our answer. Although we have factored the expression, we have not found the *greatest* common factor.

Practice Problem 1 Factor out the greatest common factor.

(a) $19x^3 - 38x^2$ **(b)** $100a^4 - 50a^2$

NOTE TO STUDENT: *Fully worked-out solutions to all of the Practice Problems can be found at the back of the text starting at page SP-1*

How do you know whether you have factored correctly? You can do two things to verify your answer.

1. Examine the polynomial in the parentheses. Its terms should not have any remaining common factors.
2. Multiply the two factors. You should obtain the original expression.

In each of the remaining examples, you will be asked to **factor** a polynomial (i.e., to find the factors that, when multiplied, give the polynomial as a product). For each of these examples, this will require you to factor out the greatest common factor.

EXAMPLE 2   Factor $6x^3 - 9x^2y - 6x^2y^2$. Check your answer.

Solution $6x^3 - 9x^2y - 6x^2y^2 = 3x^2(2x - 3y - 2y^2)$

Check:

1. $(2x - 3y - 2y^2)$ has no common factors. If it did, we would know that we had not factored out the *greatest* common factor.

2. Multiply the two factors.

$$3x^2(2x - 3y - 2y^2) = 6x^3 - 9x^2y - 6x^2y^2$$

> Observe that we do obtain the original polynomial.

Practice Problem 2   Factor $9a^3 - 12a^2b^2 - 15a^4$. Check your answer.

The greatest common factor need not be a monomial. It may be a binomial or even a trinomial. For example, note the following:

$$5a(x + 3) + 2(x + 3) = (x + 3)(5a + 2)$$
$$5a(x + 4y) + 2(x + 4y) = (x + 4y)(5a + 2)$$

The common factors are binomials.

EXAMPLE 3   Factor.

(a) $2x(x + 5) - 3(x + 5)$
(b) $5a(a + b) - 2b(a + b) - (a + b)$

Solution

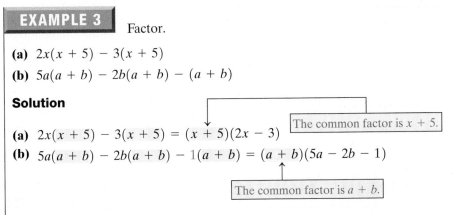

(a) $2x(x + 5) - 3(x + 5) = (x + 5)(2x - 3)$ The common factor is $x + 5$.
(b) $5a(a + b) - 2b(a + b) - 1(a + b) = (a + b)(5a - 2b - 1)$

> The common factor is $a + b$.

Note that if we place a 1 in front of the third term, it makes it easier to factor.

Practice Problem 3   Factor $7x(x + 2y) - 8y(x + 2y) - (x + 2y)$.

❷ Factoring by Grouping

Because the common factors in Example 3 were grouped inside parentheses, it was easy to pick them out. However, this rarely happens, so we have to learn how to manipulate expressions to find the greatest common factor.

Polynomials of four terms can often be factored by the method of Example 3(a). However, the parentheses are not always present in the original problem. When they are not present, we look for a way to remove a common factor from the first two terms. We then factor out a common factor from the first two terms and a common factor from the second two terms. Then we can find the greatest common factor of the original expression.

EXAMPLE 4   Factor $ax + 2ay + 2bx + 4by$.

Solution

Remove the greatest common factor (a) from the first two terms.

$$ax + 2ay + 2bx + 4by = a(x + 2y) + 2b(x + 2y)$$

Remove the greatest common factor $(2b)$ from the last two terms.

Now we can see that $(x + 2y)$ is a common factor.

$$a(x + 2y) + 2b(x + 2y) = (x + 2y)(a + 2b)$$

Practice Problem 4   Factor $bx + 5by + 2wx + 10wy$.

NOTE TO STUDENT: Fully worked-out solutions to all of the Practice Problems can be found at the back of the text starting at page SP-1

If a problem can be factored by this method, we must rearrange the order of the four terms whenever necessary so that the first two terms do have a common factor.

EXAMPLE 5   Factor $xy - 6 + 3x - 2y$.

Solution   Rearrange the terms so that the first two terms have a common factor and the last two terms have a common factor.

$xy + 3x - 2y - 6$ Factor out a common factor of x from the first two terms and -2 from the second two terms.

$= x(y + 3) - 2(y + 3)$ Since we factor out a negative number, we have: $-2y - 6 = -2(y + 3)$.

$= (y + 3)(x - 2)$ Factor out the common binomial factor $y + 3$.

Practice Problem 5   Factor $xy - 12 - 4x + 3y$.

TO THINK ABOUT: Example 5 Follow-Up   Notice that if you factored out a common factor of $+2$ from the last two terms, the resulting terms would not contain the same parenthetical expression: $x(y + 3) + 2(-y - 3)$. If the expressions inside the two sets of parentheses are not exactly the same, you cannot express the polynomial as a product of two factors!

EXAMPLE 6   Factor $2x^3 + 21 - 7x^2 - 6x$. Check your answer by multiplication.

Solution

$2x^3 - 7x^2 - 6x + 21$ Rearrange the terms.

$= x^2(2x - 7) - 3(2x - 7)$ Factor out a common factor from each group of two terms.

$= (2x - 7)(x^2 - 3)$ Factor out the common binomial factor $2x - 7$.

Check:

$$(2x - 7)(x^2 - 3) = 2x^3 - 6x - 7x^2 + 21 \quad \text{Multiply the two binomials.}$$

$$= 2x^3 + 21 - 7x^2 - 6x \quad \text{Rearrange the terms.}$$

The product is identical to the original expression.

Practice Problem 6 Factor $2x^3 - 15 - 10x + 3x^2$.

③ Factoring Trinomials of the Form $x^2 + bx + c$

If we multiply $(x + 4)(x + 5)$, we obtain $x^2 + 9x + 20$. But suppose that we already have the polynomial $x^2 + 9x + 20$ and need to factor it. In other words, suppose we need to find the expressions that, when multiplied, give us the polynomial. Let's use this example to find a general procedure.

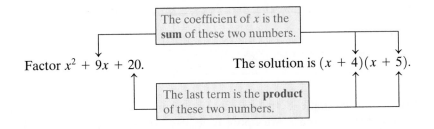

The coefficient of x is the **sum** of these two numbers.

Factor $x^2 + 9x + 20$.

The solution is $(x + 4)(x + 5)$.

The last term is the **product** of these two numbers.

FACTORING TRINOMIALS OF THE FORM $x^2 + bx + c$

1. The answer has the form $(x + m)(x + n)$, where m and n are real numbers.

2. The numbers m and n are chosen so that
   (a) $m \cdot n = c$ and
   (b) $m + n = b$.

If the last term of the trinomial is positive and the middle term is negative, the two numbers m and n will be negative numbers.

EXAMPLE 7 Factor $x^2 - 14x + 24$.

Solution We want to find two numbers whose product is 24 and whose sum is -14. They will both be negative numbers.

Factor Pairs of 24	Sum of the Factors
$(-24)(-1)$	$-24 - 1 = -25$
$(-12)(-2)$	$-12 - 2 = -14$ ✓
$(-6)(-4)$	$-6 - 4 = -10$
$(-8)(-3)$	$-8 - 3 = -11$

The numbers whose product is 24 and whose sum is -14 are -12 and -2. Thus,

$$x^2 - 14x + 24 = (x - 12)(x - 2).$$

Practice Problem 7 Factor $x^2 - 10x + 21$.

If the last term of the trinomial is negative, the two numbers m and n will be opposite in sign.

EXAMPLE 8   Factor $x^4 - 2x^2 - 24$.

Solution   Sometimes we can make a substitution that makes a polynomial easier to factor. We need to recognize that we can write this as $(x^2)^2 - 2(x^2) - 24$. We can make this polynomial easier to factor if we substitute y for x^2.
      Then we have

$$y^2 - 2y - 24.$$

The two numbers whose product is -24 and whose sum is -2 are -6 and 4.
      Therefore, we have

$$y^2 - 2y - 24 = (y - 6)(y + 4).$$

But $y = x^2$, so our answer is

$$x^4 - 2x^2 - 24 = (x^2 - 6)(x^2 + 4).$$

NOTE TO STUDENT: Fully worked-out solutions to all of the Practice Problems can be found at the back of the text starting at page SP-1

Practice Problem 8   Factor $x^4 + 9x^2 + 8$.

Note from Example 8 that c, the last term of the trinomial, is negative ($c = -24$) and that m and n are opposite in sign ($m = -6$ and $n = 4$). When we know the signs of both b and c, we then also know the signs of m and n as described in the box below.

FACTS ABOUT SIGNS

Suppose $x^2 + bx + c = (x + m)(x + n)$. We know certain facts about m and n.

1. m and n have the same sign if c is positive. (*Note:* We did *not* say that they will have the same sign as c.)
    (a) They are positive if b is positive.
    (b) They are negative if b is negative.

2. m and n have opposite signs if c is negative. The larger number is positive if b is positive and negative if b is negative.

If you understand these sign facts, continue on to Example 9. If not, review Examples 7 and 8.

EXAMPLE 9   Factor.   **(a)** $y^2 + 5y - 36$ **(b)** $x^4 - 4x^2 - 12$

Solution

(a) $y^2 + 5y - 36 = (y + 9)(y - 4)$ The larger number (9) is positive because $b = 5$ is positive.

(b) $x^4 - 4x^2 - 12 = (x^2 - 6)(x^2 + 2)$ The larger number (6) is negative because $b = -4$ is negative.

Practice Problem 9   Factor.

(a) $a^2 + 2a - 48$ **(b)** $x^4 + 2x^2 - 15$

Does the order in which we write the factors make any difference? In other words, is it true that $x^2 + bx + c = (x + n)(x + m)$? Since multiplication is commutative,

$$x^2 + bx + c = (x + n)(x + m) = (x + m)(x + n).$$

The order of the factors is not important.

We can also factor trinomials that have more than one variable.

EXAMPLE 10   Factor.

(a) $x^2 - 21xy + 20y^2$ **(b)** $x^2 + 4xy - 21y^2$

Solution   **(a)** $x^2 - 21xy + 20y^2 = (x - 20y)(x - y)$

The last terms in each factor contain the variable y.

(b) $x^2 + 4xy - 21y^2 = (x + 7y)(x - 3y)$

Practice Problem 10   Factor.

(a) $x^2 - 16xy + 15y^2$ **(b)** $x^2 + xy - 42y^2$

4 Factoring Trinomials of the Form $ax^2 + bx + c$

Using the Grouping Number Method. One way to factor a trinomial $ax^2 + bx + c$ is to write it as four terms and factor it by grouping as described earlier in this section (and also in Section 6.2). For example, the trinomial $2x^2 + 11x + 12$ can be written as $2x^2 + 3x + 8x + 12$.

$$2x^2 + 3x + 8x + 12 = x(2x + 3) + 4(2x + 3)$$
$$= (2x + 3)(x + 4)$$

We can factor all factorable trinomials of the form $ax^2 + bx + c$ in this way. Use the following procedure.

GROUPING NUMBER METHOD FOR FACTORING TRINOMIALS OF THE FORM $ax^2 + bx + c$

1. Obtain the grouping number ac.
2. Find the factor pair of the grouping number whose sum is b.
3. Use those two factors to write bx as the sum of two terms.
4. Factor by grouping.

EXAMPLE 11   Factor $6x^2 + 7x - 5$.

Solution

1. The grouping number is $(a)(c) = (6)(-5) = -30$.
2. Since $b = 7$, we want the factor pair of -30 whose sum is 7.

$$
\begin{aligned}
-30 &= (-30)(1) & -30 &= (5)(-6) \\
&= (30)(-1) & &= (-5)(6) \\
&= (15)(-2) & &= (3)(-10) \\
&= (-15)(2) & &= (-3)(10)
\end{aligned}
$$

3. Since $-3 + 10 = 7$, use -3 and 10 to write $6x^2 + 7x - 5$ with four terms.

$$6x^2 + 7x - 5 = 6x^2 - 3x + 10x - 5$$

4. Factor by grouping.

$$
\begin{aligned}
6x^2 - 3x + 10x - 5 &= 3x(2x - 1) + 5(2x - 1) \\
&= (2x - 1)(3x + 5)
\end{aligned}
$$

NOTE TO STUDENT: Fully worked-out solutions to all of the Practice Problems can be found at the back of the text starting at page SP-1

Practice Problem 11   Factor $10x^2 - 9x + 2$.

If the three terms have a common factor, then prior to using the four-step grouping number procedure, we first factor out the greatest common factor from the terms of the trinomial.

EXAMPLE 12   Factor $6x^3 - 26x^2 + 24x$.

Solution   First we factor out the greatest common factor $2x$ from each term.

$$6x^3 - 26x^2 + 24x = 2x(3x^2 - 13x + 12)$$

Next we follow the four steps to factor $3x^2 - 13x + 12$.

1. The grouping number is 36.
2. We want the factor pair of 36 whose sum is -13. The two factors are -4 and -9.
3. We use -4 and -9 to write $3x^2 - 13x + 12$ with four terms.

$$3x^2 - 13x + 12 = 3x^2 - 4x - 9x + 12$$

4. Factor by grouping. Remember that we first factored out the factor $2x$. This factor must be part of the answer.

$$
\begin{aligned}
2x(3x^2 - 4x - 9x + 12) &= 2x[x(3x - 4) - 3(3x - 4)] \\
&= 2x(3x - 4)(x - 3)
\end{aligned}
$$

Practice Problem 12   Factor $9x^3 - 15x^2 - 6x$.

Using the Trial-and-Error Method. Another way to factor trinomials of the form $ax^2 + bx + c$ is by trial and error. This method has an advantage if the grouping number is large and we would have to list many factors. In the trial-and-error method, we try different values and see which ones can be multiplied out to obtain the original expression.

If the last term is negative, there are many more sign possibilities.

EXAMPLE 13   Factor by trial and error $10x^2 - 49x - 5$.

Solution   The first terms in the factors could be $(10x)$ and (x) or $(5x)$ and $(2x)$. The second terms could be $(+1)$ and (-5) or (-1) and $(+5)$. We list all the possibilities and look for one that will yield a middle term of $-49x$.

Possible Factors	Middle Term of Product
$(2x - 1)(5x + 5)$	$+5x$
$(2x + 1)(5x - 5)$	$-5x$
$(2x + 5)(5x - 1)$	$+23x$
$(2x - 5)(5x + 1)$	$-23x$
$(10x - 5)(x + 1)$	$+5x$
$(10x + 5)(x - 1)$	$-5x$
$(10x - 1)(x + 5)$	$+49x$
$(10x + 1)(x - 5)$	$-49x$

Thus,

$$10x^2 - 49x - 5 = (10x + 1)(x - 5)$$

As a check, it is always a good idea to multiply the two binomials to see whether you obtain the original expression.

$$(10x + 1)(x - 5) = 10x^2 - 50x + 1x - 5$$
$$= 10x^2 - 49x - 5.$$

Practice Problem 13   Factor by trial and error $8x^2 - 6x - 5$.

EXAMPLE 14   Factor by trial and error $6x^4 + x^2 - 12$.

Solution   The first term of each factor must contain x^2. Suppose that we try the following:

Possible Factors	Middle Term of Product
$(2x^2 - 3)(3x^2 + 4)$	$-x^2$

The middle term we get is $-x^2$, but we need its opposite, $+x^2$. In this case, we just need to reverse the signs of -3 and 4. Do you see why? Therefore,

$$6x^4 + x^2 - 12 = (2x^2 + 3)(3x^2 - 4).$$

Practice Problem 14   Factor by trial and error $6x^4 + 13x^2 - 5$.

Factor. (Be sure to factor out the greatest common factor.) For additional review and practice, see Section 6.2.

1. $80 - 10y$

2. $16x - 16$

3. $5a^2 - 25a$

4. $7a^2 - 14a$

5. $3c^2x^3 - 9cx - 6c$

6. $5a^2b^4 + 15ab - 30a$

7. $30y^4 + 24y^3 + 18y^2$

8. $16y^5 - 24y^4 - 40y^3$

9. $15ab^2 + 5ab - 10a^3b$

10. $-12x^2y - 18xy + 6x$

11. $12xy^3 - 24x^3y^2 + 36x^2y^4 - 60x^4y^3$

12. $15a^3b^3 + 6a^4b^3 - 9a^2b^3 + 30a^5b^3$

13. $3x(x + y) - 2(x + y)$

14. $5a(a + 3b) - 4(a + 3b)$

Hint for Exercises 15 and 16: Is the expression in the first parentheses equal to the expression in the second parentheses?

15. $5b(a - 3b) + 8(-3b + a)$

16. $4y(x - 5y) - 3(-5y + x)$

17. $3x(a + 5b) + (a + 5b)$

18. $2w(s - 3t) - (s - 3t)$

19. $2a^2(3x - y) - 5b^3(3x - y)$

20. $7a^3(5a + 4) - 2(5a + 4)$

21. $3x(5x + y) - 8y(5x + y) - (5x + y)$

22. $4w(y - 8x) + 5z(y - 8x) + (y - 8x)$

23. $2a(a - 6b) - 3b(a - 6b) - 2(a - 6b)$

24. $3a(a + 4b) - 5b(a + 4b) - 9(a + 4b)$

Factor by grouping. For additional review and practice, see Section 6.2.

25. $x^3 + 5x^2 + 3x + 15$

26. $x^3 + 8x^2 + 2x + 16$

27. $2x + 6 - 3ax - 9a$

28. $2bc + 4b - 5c - 10$

29. $ab - 4a + 12 - 3b$

30. $2m^2 - 8mn - 5m + 20n$

31. $5x - 30 - 2xy + 12y$

32. $4x - 20 - 3xy + 15y$

33. $9y + 2x - 6 - 3xy$

34. $10y + 3x - 6 - 5xy$

Factor each polynomial. For additional review and practice, see Section 6.3.

35. $x^2 + 8x + 7$ **36.** $x^2 + 12x + 11$ **37.** $x^2 - 9x + 14$ **38.** $x^2 - 8x + 12$

39. $x^2 - 10x + 24$ **40.** $x^2 - 9x + 18$ **41.** $a^2 + 4a - 45$ **42.** $a^2 + 2a - 35$

43. $x^2 - xy - 42y^2$ **44.** $x^2 + xy - 30y^2$ **45.** $x^2 - 15xy + 14y^2$ **46.** $x^2 + 10xy + 9y^2$

47. $x^4 - 3x^2 - 40$ **48.** $x^4 + 6x^2 + 5$ **49.** $x^4 + 16x^2y^2 + 63y^4$ **50.** $x^4 - 6x^2 - 55$

Factor out the greatest common factor from the terms of the trinomial. Then factor the remaining trinomial.

51. $2x^2 + 26x + 44$ **52.** $2x^2 + 30x + 52$ **53.** $x^3 + x^2 - 20x$ **54.** $x^3 - 4x^2 - 45x$

Factor each polynomial. You may use the grouping number method or the trial-and-error method. For additional review and practice, see Section 6.4.

55. $2x^2 - x - 1$ **56.** $3x^2 + x - 2$ **57.** $6x^2 - 7x - 5$ **58.** $5x^2 - 13x - 28$

59. $3a^2 - 8a + 5$ **60.** $6a^2 + 11a + 3$ **61.** $8a^2 + 14a - 9$ **62.** $3a^2 - 20a + 12$

63. $2x^2 + 13x + 15$ **64.** $5x^2 - 8x - 4$ **65.** $3x^4 - 8x^2 - 3$ **66.** $6x^4 + 7x^2 - 5$

67. $6x^2 + 35xy + 11y^2$ **68.** $5x^2 + 12xy + 7y^2$ **69.** $7x^2 + 11xy - 6y^2$ **70.** $4x^2 - 13xy + 3y^2$

Factor out the greatest common factor from the terms of the trinomial. Then factor the remaining trinomial.

71. $4x^3 + 4x^2 - 15x$ **72.** $8x^3 + 6x^2 - 9x$ **73.** $10x^4 + 15x^3 + 5x^2$ **74.** $16x^4 + 48x^3 + 20x^2$

Student Learning Objectives

After studying this section, you will be able to:

1 Factor a binomial that is the difference of two squares.

2 Factor a perfect square trinomial.

3 Factor a binomial that is the sum or difference of two cubes.

1 Factoring the Difference of Two Squares

We learned in Appendix A.2 and Section 6.5 how to multiply binomials using the special product formula: $(a + b)(a - b) = a^2 - b^2$. We can use it now as a factoring formula.

FACTORING THE DIFFERENCE OF TWO SQUARES

$$a^2 - b^2 = (a + b)(a - b)$$

EXAMPLE 1 Factor $x^2 - 16$.

Solution In this case $a = x$ and $b = 4$ in the formula.

$$
\begin{array}{cccccc}
a^2 & - & b^2 & = & (a & + & b)(a & - & b) \\
\downarrow & & \downarrow & & \downarrow & & \downarrow\ \downarrow & & \downarrow \\
(x)^2 & - & (4)^2 & = & (x & + & 4)(x & - & 4)
\end{array}
$$

Practice Problem 1 Factor $x^2 - 9$.

EXAMPLE 2 Factor $25x^2 - 36$.

Solution We will use the formula $a^2 - b^2 = (a + b)(a - b)$.

$$25x^2 - 36 = (5x)^2 - (6)^2 = (5x + 6)(5x - 6)$$

Practice Problem 2 Factor $64x^2 - 121y^2$.

EXAMPLE 3 Factor $100w^4 - 9z^4$.

Solution $100w^4 - 9z^4 = (10w^2)^2 - (3z^2)^2 = (10w^2 + 3z^2)(10w^2 - 3z^2)$

Practice Problem 3 Factor $49x^2 - 25y^4$.

Whenever possible, a common factor should be factored out in the first step. Then the formula can be applied.

EXAMPLE 4 Factor $75x^2 - 3$.

Solution We factor out a common factor of 3 from each term.

$$
\begin{aligned}
75x^2 - 3 &= 3(25x^2 - 1) \\
&= 3(5x + 1)(5x - 1)
\end{aligned}
$$

Practice Problem 4 Factor $7x^2 - 28$.

NOTE TO STUDENT: Fully worked-out solutions to all of the Practice Problems can be found at the back of the text starting at page SP-1

② Factoring Perfect Square Trinomials

Recall the formulas for squaring a binomial from Appendix A.2 and Section 6.5.

$$(a - b)^2 = a^2 - 2ab + b^2$$
$$(a + b)^2 = a^2 + 2ab + b^2$$

We can use these formulas to factor a perfect square trinomial.

PERFECT SQUARE FACTORING FORMULAS

$$a^2 - 2ab + b^2 = (a - b)^2$$
$$a^2 + 2ab + b^2 = (a + b)^2$$

Recognizing these special cases will save you a lot of time when factoring. How can we recognize a perfect square trinomial?

1. The first and last terms are perfect squares. (The numerical values are $1, 4, 9, 16, 25, 36, \ldots$, and the variables have an exponent that is an even whole number.)
2. The middle term is twice the product of the values that, when squared, give the first and last terms.

EXAMPLE 5   Factor $25x^2 - 20x + 4$.

Solution   Is this trinomial a perfect square? Yes.

1. The first and last terms are perfect squares.

$$25x^2 - 20x + 4 = (5x)^2 - 20x + (2)^2$$

2. The middle term is twice the product of the value $5x$ and the value 2. In other words, $2(5x)(2) = 20x$.

$$(5x)^2 - 2(5x)(2) + (2)^2 = (5x - 2)^2$$

Therefore, we can use the formula $a^2 - 2ab + b^2 = (a - b)^2$. Thus,

$$25x^2 - 20x + 4 = (5x - 2)^2.$$

Practice Problem 5   Factor $9x^2 - 30x + 25$.

EXAMPLE 6   Factor $200x^2 + 360x + 162$.

Solution   First we factor out the common factor of 2.

$$200x^2 + 360x + 162 = 2(100x^2 + 180x + 81)$$
$$a^2 + 2ab + b^2 = (a + b)^2$$
$$2[100x^2 + 180x + 81] = 2[(10x)^2 + (2)(10x)(9) + (9)^2]$$
$$= 2(10x + 9)^2$$

Practice Problem 6   Factor $242x^2 + 88x + 8$.

EXAMPLE 7 Factor. **(a)** $x^4 + 14x^2 + 49$ **(b)** $9x^4 + 30x^2y^2 + 25y^4$

Solution

(a) $x^4 + 14x^2 + 49 = (x^2)^2 + 2(x^2)(7) + (7)^2$
$$= (x^2 + 7)^2$$

(b) $9x^4 + 30x^2y^2 + 25y^4 = (3x^2)^2 + 2(3x^2)(5y^2) + (5y^2)^2$
$$= (3x^2 + 5y^2)^2$$

Practice Problem 7 Factor.

(a) $49x^4 + 28x^2 + 4$ **(b)** $36x^4 + 84x^2y^2 + 49y^4$

NOTE TO STUDENT: Fully worked-out solutions to all of the Practice Problems can be found at the back of the text starting at page SP-1

③ Factoring the Sum or Difference of Two Cubes

There are also special formulas for factoring cubic binomials. We see that the factors of $x^3 + 27$ are $(x + 3)(x^2 - 3x + 9)$, and that the factors of $x^3 - 64$ are $(x - 4)(x^2 + 4x + 16)$. Therefore, we can generalize this pattern and derive the following factoring formulas.

> **SUM AND DIFFERENCE OF CUBES FACTORING FORMULAS**
> $$a^3 + b^3 = (a + b)(a^2 - ab + b^2)$$
> $$a^3 - b^3 = (a - b)(a^2 + ab + b^2)$$

EXAMPLE 8 Factor $125x^3 + y^3$.

Solution Here $a = 5x$ and $b = y$.

$$a^3 + b^3 = (a + b)(a^2 - ab + b^2)$$

$$125x^3 + y^3 = (5x)^3 + (y)^3 = (5x + y)(25x^2 - 5xy + y^2)$$

Practice Problem 8 Factor $8x^3 + 125y^3$.

EXAMPLE 9 Factor $64x^3 - 27$.

Solution Here $a = 4x$ and $b = 3$.

$$a^3 - b^3 = (a - b)(a^2 + ab + b^2)$$

$$64x^3 - 27 = (4x)^3 - (3)^3 = (4x - 3)(16x^2 + 12x + 9)$$

Practice Problem 9 Factor $64x^3 - 125y^3$.

EXAMPLE 10 Factor $125w^3 + 8z^6$.

Solution Here $a = 5w$ and $b = 2z^2$.

$$a^3 + b^3 = (a + b) \quad (a^2 - ab + b^2)$$
$$\downarrow \quad \downarrow \quad \downarrow \quad \downarrow \quad \downarrow$$
$$125w^3 + 8z^6 = (5w)^3 + (2z^2)^3 = (5w + 2z^2)(25w^2 - 10wz^2 + 4z^4)$$

Practice Problem 10 Factor $27w^3 + 125z^6$.

EXAMPLE 11 Factor $250x^3 - 2$.

Solution First we must factor out the common factor of 2.

$$250x^3 - 2 = 2(125x^3 - 1)$$
$$= 2(5x - 1)(25x^2 + 5x + 1)$$
$$\uparrow$$

Note that this trinomial cannot be factored.

Practice Problem 11 Factor $54x^3 - 16$.

What should you do if a polynomial is the difference of two cubes *and* the difference of two squares? Usually, it's easier to use the difference of two squares formula first. Then apply the difference of two cubes formula.

EXAMPLE 12 Factor $x^6 - y^6$.

Solution We can write this binomial as $(x^2)^3 - (y^2)^3$ or as $(x^3)^2 - (y^3)^2$. Therefore, we can use either the difference of two cubes formula or the difference of two squares formula. It's usually better to use the difference of two squares formula first, so we'll do that.

$$x^6 - y^6 = (x^3)^2 - (y^3)^2$$

Here $a = x^3$ and $b = y^3$. Therefore,

$$(x^3)^2 - (y^3)^2 = (x^3 + y^3)(x^3 - y^3).$$

Now we use the sum of two cubes formula for the first factor and the difference of two cubes formula for the second factor.

$$x^3 + y^3 = (x + y)(x^2 - xy + y^2)$$
$$x^3 - y^3 = (x - y)(x^2 + xy + y^2)$$

Hence,

$$x^6 - y^6 = (x + y)(x^2 - xy + y^2)(x - y)(x^2 + xy + y^2).$$

Practice Problem 12 Factor $64a^6 - 1$.

Often the various types of factoring problems are all mixed together. We need to be able to identify each type of polynomial quickly. The following table summarizes the information we have learned about factoring in Appendix A.3 and A.4.

Many polynomials require more than one factoring method. When you are asked to factor a polynomial, it is expected that you will factor it completely. Usually, the first step is factoring out a common factor; then the next step will become apparent.

Carefully go through each example in the following Factoring Organizer. Be sure you understand each step that is involved.

Factoring Organizer

Number of Terms in the Polynomial	Identifying Name and/or Formula	Example
A. Any number of terms	**Common factor** The terms have a common factor consisting of a number, a variable, or both.	$2x^2 - 16x = 2x(x - 8)$ $3x^2 + 9y - 12 = 3(x^2 + 3y - 4)$ $4x^2y + 2xy^2 - wxy + xyz = xy(4x + 2y - w + z)$
B. Two terms	**Difference of two squares** First and last terms are perfect squares. $a^2 - b^2 = (a + b)(a - b)$	$16x^2 - 1 = (4x + 1)(4x - 1)$ $25y^2 - 9x^2 = (5y + 3x)(5y - 3x)$
C. Two terms	**Sum and Difference of Cubes** First and last terms are perfect cubes. $a^3 + b^3 = (a + b)(a^2 - ab + b^2)$ $a^3 - b^3 = (a - b)(a^2 + ab + b^2)$	$8x^3 + 64 = (2x + 4)(4x^2 - 8x + 16)$ $8x^3 - 64 = (2x - 4)(4x^2 + 8x + 16)$
D. Three terms	**Perfect-square trinomial** First and last terms are perfect squares. $a^2 + 2ab + b^2 = (a + b)^2$ $a^2 - 2ab + b^2 = (a - b)^2$	$25x^2 - 10x + 1 = (5x - 1)^2$ $16x^2 + 24x + 9 = (4x + 3)^2$
E. Three terms	**Trinomial of the form $x^2 + bx + c$** It starts with x^2. The constants of the two factors are numbers whose product is c and whose sum is b.	$x^2 - 7x + 12 = (x - 3)(x - 4)$ $x^2 + 11x - 26 = (x + 13)(x - 2)$ $x^2 - 8x - 20 = (x - 10)(x + 2)$
F. Three terms	**Trinomial of the form $ax^2 + bx + c$** It starts with ax^2, where a is any number but 1.	Use trial-and-error or the grouping number method to factor $12x^2 - 5x - 2$. 1. The grouping number is -24. 2. The two numbers whose product is -24 and whose sum is -5 are -8 and 3. 3. $12x^2 - 5x - 2 = 12x^2 + 3x - 8x - 2$ $\qquad = 3x(4x + 1) - 2(4x + 1)$ $\qquad = (4x + 1)(3x - 2)$
G. Four terms	**Factor by grouping** Rearrange the order if the first two terms do not have a common factor.	$wx - 6yz + 2wy - 3xz = wx + 2wy - 3xz - 6yz$ $\qquad = w(x + 2y) - 3z(x + 2y)$ $\qquad = (x + 2y)(w - 3z)$

Verbal and Writing Skills

1. How do you determine if a factoring problem will use the difference of two squares?

2. How do you determine if a factoring problem will use the perfect square trinomial formula?

3. How do you determine if a factoring problem will use the sum of two cubes formula?

4. How do you determine if a factoring problem will use the difference of two cubes formula?

Use the difference of two squares formula to factor. Be sure to factor out any common factors.

5. $a^2 - 64$

6. $y^2 - 49$

7. $16x^2 - 81$

8. $4x^2 - 25$

9. $64x^2 - 1$

10. $81x^2 - 1$

11. $49m^2 - 9n^2$

12. $36x^2 - 25y^2$

13. $100y^2 - 81$

14. $49y^2 - 144$

15. $1 - 81x^2y^2$

16. $1 - 49x^2y^2$

17. $32x^2 - 18$

18. $50x^2 - 8$

19. $5x - 20x^3$

20. $49x^3 - 36x$

Use the perfect square trinomial formulas to factor. Be sure to factor out any common factors.

21. $9x^2 - 6x + 1$

22. $16y^2 - 8y + 1$

23. $49x^2 - 14x + 1$

24. $100y^2 - 20y + 1$

25. $81w^2 + 36wt + 4t^2$

26. $25w^2 + 20wt + 4t^2$

27. $36x^2 + 60xy + 25y^2$

28. $64x^2 + 48xy + 9y^2$

29. $8x^2 + 24x + 18$

30. $128x^2 + 32x + 2$

31. $3x^3 - 24x^2 + 48x$

32. $50x^3 - 20x^2 + 2x$

Use the sum and difference of cubes formulas to factor. Be sure to factor out any common factors.

33. $x^3 - 27$

34. $x^3 - 8$

35. $x^3 + 125$

36. $x^3 + 64$

37. $64x^3 - 1$

38. $125x^3 - 1$

39. $125x^3 - 8$

40. $27x^3 - 64$

41. $1 - 27x^3$

42. $1 - 8x^3$

43. $64x^3 + 125$

44. $27x^3 + 125$

45. $64s^6 + t^6$

46. $125s^6 + t^6$

47. $6y^3 - 6$

48. $80y^3 - 10$

49. $3x^3 - 24$ **50.** $54y^2 - 2$ **51.** $x^5 - 8x^2y^3$ **52.** $x^5 - 27x^2y^3$

Mixed Practice

Factor by the methods taught in both Appendix A.3 and A.4.

53. $x^2 - 2x - 63$ **54.** $x^2 + 6x - 40$ **55.** $6x^2 + x - 2$

56. $5x^2 + 17x + 6$ **57.** $25w^4 - 1$ **58.** $16m^4 - 25$

59. $b^4 + 6b^2 + 9$ **60.** $a^4 - 10a^2 + 25$ **61.** $yz^2 - 15 - 3z^2 + 5y$

62. $ad^4 - 4ab - d^4 + 4b$ **63.** $s^3r - t - s^2 + srt$ **64.** $28a^2x - 15b + 12bx - 35a^2$

65. $49m^6 - 81$ **66.** $4 - 9m^6$ **67.** $36y^6 - 60y^3 + 25$

68. $100n^6 - 140n^3 + 49$ **69.** $2a^8 - 50$ **70.** $12z^8 - 27$

71. $125m^3 + 8n^3$ **72.** $64z^3 - 27w^3$ **73.** $2x^2 + 4x - 96$

74. $3x^2 + 9x - 84$ **75.** $18x^2 + 21x + 6$ **76.** $24x^2 + 26x + 6$

77. $27ax^2 + 99ax - 36a$ **78.** $77bx^2 - 44bx - 33b$ **79.** $6x^3 + 26x^2 - 20x$

80. $12x^3 - 14x^2 + 4x$ **81.** $24a^3 - 3b^3$ **82.** $54w^3 + 250$

83. $4w^2 - 20wz + 25z^2$ **84.** $81x^4 - 36x^2 + 4$ **85.** $36a^2 - 81b^2$

86. $400x^4 - 36y^2$ **87.** $16x^4 - 81y^4$ **88.** $256x^4 - 1$

89. $125m^6 + 8$ **90.** $27n^6 + 125$

Try to factor the following four exercises by using the formulas for the perfect square trinomial. Why can't the formulas be used? Then factor each exercise correctly using an appropriate method.

91. $25x^2 + 25x + 4$

92. $16x^2 + 40x + 9$

93. $4x^2 - 15x + 9$

94. $36x^2 - 65x + 25$

Applications

▲ **95.** *Carpentry* Find the area of a maple cabinet surface that is constructed by a carpenter as a large square with sides of $4x$ feet and has a square cut out region whose sides are y feet. Factor the expression.

▲ **96.** *Base of a Lamp* A copper base for a lamp consists of a large circle of radius $2y$ inches with a cut out area in the center of radius x inches. Write an expression for the area of this copper base. Write your answer in factored form.

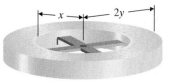

▲ **97.** *Tree Reforestation* A plan has been made in northern Maine to replace trees harvested by paper mills. The proposed planting zone is in the shape of a giant rectangle with an area of $30x^2 + 19x - 5$ square feet. Use your factoring skills to determine a possible configuration of the number of rows of trees and the number of trees to be placed in each row.

▲ **98.** *Tree Reforestation* A plan has been made in northern Washington to replace trees harvested by paper mills. The proposed planting zone is in the shape of a giant rectangle with an area of $12x^2 + 20x - 25$ square feet. Use your factoring skills to determine a possible configuration of the number of rows of trees and the number of trees to be placed in each row.

Student Learning Objectives

After studying this section, you will be able to:

 1 Use the point–slope form of the equation of a line.

2 Write the equation of the line passing through a given point that is parallel or perpendicular to a given line.

1 Using the Point–Slope Form of the Equation of a Line

Recall from Section 3.1 that we defined a line as an equation that can be written in the form $Ax + By = C$. This form is called the **standard form of the equation of a line** and although this form tells us that the graph is a straight line, it reveals little about the line. A more useful form of the equation was introduced in Section 3.3 called the **slope–intercept form,** $y = mx + b$. This form immediately reveals the slope and y-intercept of a line, and also allows us to easily write the equation of a line when we know its slope and y-intercept. But, what happens if we know the slope of a line and a point on the line that is not the y-intercept? Can we write the equation of the line? By the definition of slope, we have the following:

$$m = \frac{y - y_1}{x - x_1}$$

$$m(x - x_1) = y - y_1$$

That is, $y - y_1 = m(x - x_1)$.

This is the point–slope form of the equation of a line.

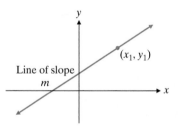

POINT–SLOPE FORM

The **point–slope form** of the equation of a line is $y - y_1 = m(x - x_1)$, where m is the slope and (x_1, y_1) are the coordinates of a known point on the line.

Write the Equation of a Line Given Its Slope and One Point on the Line.

EXAMPLE 1 Find an equation of the line that has slope $-\frac{3}{4}$ and passes through the point $(-6, 1)$. Express your answer in standard form.

Solution Since we don't know the y-intercept, we can't use the slope–intercept form easily. Therefore, we use the point–slope form.

$$y - y_1 = m(x - x_1)$$

$$y - 1 = -\frac{3}{4}[x - (-6)] \qquad \text{Substitute the given values.}$$

$$y - 1 = -\frac{3}{4}x - \frac{9}{2} \qquad \text{Simplify. (Do you see how we did this?)}$$

$$4y - 4(1) = 4\left(-\frac{3}{4}x\right) - 4\left(\frac{9}{2}\right) \qquad \text{Multiply each term by the LCD 4.}$$

$$4y - 4 = -3x - 18 \qquad \text{Simplify.}$$

$$3x + 4y = -18 + 4 \qquad \text{Add } 3x + 4 \text{ to each side.}$$

$$3x + 4y = -14 \qquad \text{Add like terms.}$$

The equation in standard form is $3x + 4y = -14$.

Practice Problem 1 Find an equation of the line that passes through $(5, -2)$ and has a slope of $\frac{3}{4}$. Express your answer in standard form.

Write the Equation of a Line Given Two Points on the Line. We can use the point–slope form to find the equation of a line if we are given two points. Carefully study the following example. Be sure you understand each step. You will encounter this type of problem frequently.

EXAMPLE 2   Find the equation of a line that passes through $(3, -2)$ and $(5, 1)$. Express your answer in slope–intercept form.

Solution   First we find the slope.

$$m = \frac{y_2 - y_1}{x_2 - x_1} = \frac{1 - (-2)}{5 - 3} = \frac{1 + 2}{2} = \frac{3}{2}$$

Now we substitute the value of the slope and the coordinates of either point into the point–slope equation. Let's use $(5, 1)$.

$$y - y_1 = m(x - x_1)$$

$$y - 1 = \frac{3}{2}(x - 5) \qquad \text{Substitute } m = \tfrac{3}{2} \text{ and } (x_1, y_1) = (5, 1).$$

$$y - 1 = \frac{3}{2}x - \frac{15}{2} \qquad \text{Remove parentheses.}$$

$$y = \frac{3}{2}x - \frac{15}{2} + 1 \qquad \text{Add 1 to each side of the equation.}$$

$$y = \frac{3}{2}x - \frac{15}{2} + \frac{2}{2} \qquad \text{Add the two fractions.}$$

$$y = \frac{3}{2}x - \frac{13}{2} \qquad \text{Simplify.}$$

Practice Problem 2 Find an equation of the line that passes through $(-4, 1)$ and $(-2, -3)$. Express your answer in slope–intercept form.

Before we go further, we want to point out that these various forms of the equation of a straight line are just that—*forms* for convenience. We are *not* using different equations each time, nor should you simply try to memorize the different variations without understanding when to use them. They can easily be derived from the definition of slope, as we have seen. And remember, you can *always* use the definition of slope to find the equation of a line. You will find it helpful to review Example 1 and Example 2 for a few minutes before going ahead to Example 3. It is important to see how each example is different.

2 Writing the Equation of Parallel and Perpendicular Lines

Let us now look at parallel and perpendicular lines. If we are given the equation of a line and a point not on the line, we can find the equation of a second line that passes through the given point and is parallel or perpendicular to the first line. We can do this because we know that the slopes of parallel lines are equal and that the slopes of perpendicular lines are negative reciprocals of each other.

Graphing Calculator

Using Linear Regression to Find an Equation

Many graphing calculators, such as the TI-83, will find the equation of a line in slope–intercept form if you enter the points as a collection of data and use the Regression feature. We would enter the data from Example 2 as follows:

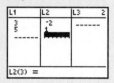

The output of the calculator uses the notation $y = ax + b$ instead of $y = mx + b$.

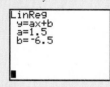

Thus, our answer to Example 2 using the graphing calculator would be $y = 1.5x - 6.5$.

NOTE TO STUDENT: Fully worked-out solutions to all of the Practice Problems can be found at the back of the text starting at page SP-1

We begin by finding the slope of the given line. Then we use the point–slope form to find the equation of the second line. Study carefully each step of the following example.

EXAMPLE 3 Find the equation of a line passing through the point $(-2, -4)$ and parallel to the line $2x + 5y = 8$. Express the answer in standard form.

Solution First we need to find the slope of the line $2x + 5y = 8$. We do this by writing the equation in slope–intercept form.

$$5y = -2x + 8$$

$$y = -\frac{2}{5}x + \frac{8}{5}$$

The slope of the given line is $-\frac{2}{5}$. Since parallel lines have the same slope, the slope of the unknown line is also $-\frac{2}{5}$. Now we substitute $m = -\frac{2}{5}$ and the coordinates of the point $(-2, -4)$ into the point–slope form of the equation of a line.

$$y - y_1 = m(x - x_1)$$

$$y - (-4) = -\frac{2}{5}[x - (-2)] \qquad \text{Substitute.}$$

$$y + 4 = -\frac{2}{5}(x + 2) \qquad \text{Simplify.}$$

$$y + 4 = -\frac{2}{5}x - \frac{4}{5} \qquad \text{Remove parentheses.}$$

$$5y + 5(4) = 5\left(-\frac{2}{5}x\right) - 5\left(\frac{4}{5}\right) \qquad \text{Multiply each term by the LCD 5.}$$

$$5y + 20 = -2x - 4 \qquad \text{Simplify.}$$

$$2x + 5y = -4 - 20 \qquad \text{Add } 2x - 20 \text{ to each side.}$$

$$2x + 5y = -24 \qquad \text{Simplify.}$$

$2x + 5y = -24$ is the equation of the line passing through the point $(-2, -4)$ and parallel to the line $2x + 5y = 8$.

NOTE TO STUDENT: Fully worked-out solutions to all of the Practice Problems can be found at the back of the text starting at page SP-1

Practice Problem 3 Find the equation of a line passing through $(4, -5)$ and parallel to the line $5x - 3y = 10$. Express the answer in standard form.

Some extra steps are needed if the desired line is to be perpendicular to the given line. Note carefully the approach in Example 4.

EXAMPLE 4   Find the equation of a line that passes through the point $(2, -3)$ and is perpendicular to the line $3x - y = -12$. Express the answer in standard form.

Solution   To find the slope of the line $3x - y = -12$, we rewrite it in slope–intercept form.

$$-y = -3x - 12$$
$$y = 3x + 12$$

This line has a slope of 3. Therefore, the slope of a line perpendicular to this line is the negative reciprocal $-\frac{1}{3}$.

Now substitute the slope $m = -\frac{1}{3}$ and the coordinates of the point $(2, -3)$ into the point–slope form of the equation.

$$y - y_1 = m(x - x_1)$$

$$y - (-3) = -\frac{1}{3}(x - 2) \qquad \text{Substitute.}$$

$$y + 3 = -\frac{1}{3}(x - 2) \qquad \text{Simplify.}$$

$$y + 3 = -\frac{1}{3}x + \frac{2}{3} \qquad \text{Remove parentheses.}$$

$$3y + 3(3) = 3\left(-\frac{1}{3}x\right) + 3\left(\frac{2}{3}\right) \qquad \text{Multiply each term by the LCD 3.}$$

$$3y + 9 = -x + 2 \qquad \text{Simplify.}$$
$$x + 3y = 2 - 9 \qquad \text{Add } x - 9 \text{ to each side.}$$
$$x + 3y = -7 \qquad \text{Simplify.}$$

$x + 3y = -7$ is the equation of a line that passes through the point $(2, -3)$ and is perpendicular to the line $3x - y = -12$.

Practice Problem 4   Find the equation of a line that passes through $(-4, 3)$ and is perpendicular to the line $6x + 3y = 7$. Express the answer in standard form.

Find the equation of the line that passes through the given point and has the given slope. Express your answer in slope–intercept form.

1. $(6, 4), m = -\dfrac{2}{3}$

2. $(4, 6), m = -\dfrac{1}{2}$

3. $(-7, -2), m = 5$

4. $(8, 0), m = -3$

5. $(6, 0), m = -\dfrac{1}{5}$

6. $(0, -1), m = -\dfrac{5}{3}$

Find the equation of a line passing through the pair of points. Write the equation in the slope–intercept form.

7. $(-4, -1)$ and $(3, 4)$

8. $(7, -2)$ and $(-1, -3)$

9. $\left(\dfrac{1}{2}, -3\right)$ and $\left(\dfrac{7}{2}, -5\right)$

10. $\left(\dfrac{7}{6}, 1\right)$ and $\left(-\dfrac{1}{3}, 0\right)$

11. $(12, -3)$ and $(7, -3)$

12. $(4, 8)$ and $(-3, 8)$

Find the equation of the line satisfying the conditions given. Express your answer in standard form.

13. Parallel to $5x - y = 4$ and passing through $(-2, 0)$

14. Parallel to $3x - y = -5$ and passing through $(-1, 0)$

15. Parallel to $x = 3y - 8$ and passing through $(5, -1)$

16. Parallel to $2y + x = 7$ and passing through $(-5, -4)$

17. Perpendicular to $2y = -3x$ and passing through $(6, -1)$

18. Perpendicular to $y = 5x$ and passing through $(4, -2)$

19. Perpendicular to $x + 7y = -12$ and passing through $(-4, -1)$

20. Perpendicular to $x - 4y = 2$ and passing through $(3, -1)$

To Think About

Without graphing determine whether the following pairs of lines are (a) parallel, (b) perpendicular, or (c) neither parallel nor perpendicular.

21. $-3x + 5y = 40$
$5y + 3x = 17$

22. $5x - 6y = 19$
$6x + 5y = -30$

23. $y = -\dfrac{3}{4}x - 2$
$6x + 8y = -5$

24. $y = \dfrac{2}{3}x + 6$
$-2x - 3y = -12$

25. $y = \dfrac{5}{6}x - \dfrac{1}{3}$
$6x + 5y = -12$

26. $y = \dfrac{3}{7}x - \dfrac{1}{14}$
$14y + 6x = 3$

Appendix B Using the Mathematics Blueprint for Problem Solving

① Using the Mathematics Blueprint to Solve Real-life Problems

When a builder constructs a new home or office building, he or she often has a blue-print. This accurate drawing shows the basic form of the building. It also shows the dimensions of the structure to be built. This blueprint serves as a useful reference throughout the construction process.

Similarly, when solving real-life problems, it is helpful to have a "mathematics blueprint." This is a simple way to organize the information provided in the word problem, in a chart, or in a graph. You can record the facts you need to use. You can determine what it is you are trying to find and how you can go about actually finding it. You can record other information that you think will be helpful as you work through the problem.

As we solve real-life problems, we will use three steps.

Step 1 *Understand the problem.* Here we will read through the problem. Draw a picture if it will help, and use the Mathematics Blueprint as a guide to assist us in thinking through the steps needed to solve the problem.

Step 2 *Solve and state the answer.* We will use arithmetic or algebraic procedures along with problem-solving strategies to find a solution.

Step 3 *Check.* We will use a variety of techniques to see if the answer in step 2 is the solution to the word problem. This will include estimating to see if the answer is reasonable, repeating our calculation, and working backward from the answer to see if we arrive at the original conditions of the problem.

▲ **EXAMPLE 1** Nancy and John want to install wall-to-wall carpeting in their living room. The floor of the rectangular living room is $11\frac{2}{3}$ feet wide and $19\frac{1}{2}$ feet long. How much will it cost if the carpet is $18.00 per square yard?

Solution

1. *Understand the problem.* First, read the problem carefully. Drawing a sketch of the living room may help you see what is required. The carpet will cover the floor of the living room, so we need to find the area. Now we fill in the Mathematics Blueprint.

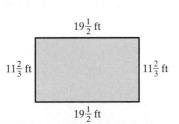

Mathematics Blueprint for Problem Solving

Gather the Facts	What Am I Solving For?	What Must I Calculate?	Key Points to Remember
The living room measures $11\frac{2}{3}$ ft by $19\frac{1}{2}$ ft. The carpet costs $18.00 per square yard.	**(a)** the area of the room in square feet **(b)** the area of the room in square yards **(c)** the cost of the carpet	**(a)** Multiply $11\frac{2}{3}$ ft by $19\frac{1}{2}$ ft to get area in square feet. **(b)** Divide the number of square feet by 9 to get the number of square yards. **(c)** Multiply the number of square yards by $18.00.	There are 9 square feet, 3 feet × 3 feet, in 1 square yard; therefore, we must divide the number of square feet by 9 to obtain square yards.

2. *Solve and state the answer.*

(a) To find the area of a rectangle, we multiply the length times the width.

$$11\frac{2}{3} \times 19\frac{1}{2} = \frac{35}{3} \times \frac{39}{2}$$

$$= \frac{455}{2} = 227\frac{1}{2} \text{ sq ft}$$

A minimum of $227\frac{1}{2}$ square feet of carpet will be needed. We say a minimum because some carpet may be wasted in cutting. Carpet is sold by the square yard. We will want to know the amount of carpet needed in square yards.

(b) To determine the area in square yards, we divide $227\frac{1}{2}$ by 9. (9 sq ft = 1 sq yd.)

$$227\frac{1}{2} \div 9 = \frac{455}{2} \div \frac{9}{1}$$

$$= \frac{455}{2} \times \frac{1}{9} = \frac{455}{18} = 25\frac{5}{18} \text{ sq yd}$$

A minimum of $25\frac{5}{18}$ square yards of carpet will be needed.

(c) Since the carpet costs $18.00 per square yard, we will multiply the number of square yards needed by $18.00.

$$25\frac{5}{18} \times 18 = \frac{455}{18} \times \frac{18}{1} = \$455$$

The carpet will cost a minimum of $455.00 for this room.

3. *Check.* We will estimate to see if our answers are reasonable.

(a) We will estimate by rounding each number to the nearest 10.

$$11\frac{2}{3} \times 19\frac{1}{2} \longrightarrow 10 \times 20 = 200 \text{ sq ft}$$

This is close to our answer of $227\frac{1}{2}$ sq ft. Our answer is reasonable. ✓

(b) We will estimate by rounding to one significant digit.

$$227\frac{1}{2} \div 9 \longrightarrow 200 \div 10 = 20 \text{ sq yd}$$

This is close to our answer of $25\frac{5}{18}$ sq yd. Our answer is reasonable. ✓

(c) We will estimate by rounding each number to the nearest 10.

$$25\frac{5}{18} \times 18 \longrightarrow 30 \times 20 = \$600$$

This is close to our answer of $455. Our answer seems reasonable. ✓

"Remember to estimate. It will save you time and money!"

NOTE TO STUDENT: *Fully worked-out solutions to all of the Practice Problems can be found at the back of the text starting at page SP-1*

▲ **Practice Problem 1** Jeff went to help Abby pick out wall-to-wall carpet for her new house. Her rectangular living room measures $16\frac{1}{2}$ feet by $10\frac{1}{2}$ feet. How much will it cost to carpet the room if the carpet costs $20 per square yard?

Mathematics Blueprint for Problem Solving

Gather the Facts	What Am I Solving For?	What Must I Calculate?	Key Points to Remember

TO THINK ABOUT: Example 1 Follow-Up Assume that the carpet in Example 1 comes in a standard width of 12 feet. How much carpet will be wasted if it is laid out on the living room floor in one strip that is $19\frac{1}{2}$ feet long? How much carpet will be wasted if it is laid in two sections side by side that are each $11\frac{2}{3}$ feet long? Assuming you have to pay for wasted carpet, what is the minimum cost to carpet the room?

EXAMPLE 2 The following chart shows the 2003 sales of Micropower Computer Software for each of the four regions of the United States. Use the chart to answer the following questions (round all answers to the nearest whole percent):

(a) What percent of the sales personnel are assigned to the Northeast?

(b) What percent of the volume of sales is attributed to the Northeast?

(c) What percent of the sales personnel are assigned to the Southeast?

(d) What percent of the volume of sales is attributed to the Southeast?

(e) Which of these two regions of the country has sales personnel that appear to be more effective in terms of the volume of sales?

Region of the U.S.	Number of Sales Personnel	Dollar Volume of Sales
Northeast	12	1,560,000
Southeast	18	4,300,000
Northwest	10	3,660,000
Southwest	15	3,720,000
Total	55	13,240,000

Solution

1. **Understand the problem.** We will only need to deal with figures from the Northeast region and the Southeast region.

Mathematics Blueprint for Problem Solving

Gather the Facts	What Am I Solving For?	What Must I Calculate?	Key Points to Remember
Personnel: 12 Northeast 18 Southeast 55 total Sales Volume: $1,560,000 NE $4,300,000 SE $13,240,000 Total	**(a)** the percent of the total personnel in the Northeast **(b)** the percent of the total sales in the Northeast **(c)** the percent of the total personnel in the Southeast **(d)** the percent of the total sales in the Southeast **(e)** compare the percentages from the two regions	**(a)** 12 of 55 is what percent? Divide. $12 \div 55$ **(b)** 1,560,000 of 13,240,000 is what percent? $1,560,000 \div 13,240,000$ **(c)** $18 \div 55$ **(d)** $4,300,000 \div 13,240,000$	We do not need to use the numbers for the Northwest or the Southwest.

2. Solve and state the answer.

(a) $\dfrac{12}{55} = 0.21818\ldots$

$\approx 22\%$

(b) $\dfrac{1,560,000}{13,240,000} = \dfrac{156}{1324} \approx 0.1178$

$\approx 12\%$

(c) $\dfrac{18}{55} = 0.32727\ldots$

$\approx 33\%$

(d) $\dfrac{4,300,000}{13,240,000} = \dfrac{430}{1324} \approx 0.3248$

$\approx 32\%$

(e) We notice that 22% of the sales force in the Northeast made 12% of the sales. The percent of the sales compared to the percent of the sales force is about half (12% of 24% would be half) or 50%. 33% of the sales force in the Southeast made 32% of the sales. The percent of sales compared to the percent of the sales force is close to 100%. We must be cautious here. *If there are no other significant factors,* it would appear that the Southeast sales force is more effective. (There may be other significant factors affecting sales, such as a recession in the Northeast, new and inexperienced sales personnel, or fewer competing companies in the Southeast.)

3. Check. You may want to use a calculator to check the division in step 2, or you may use estimation.

(a) $\dfrac{12}{55} \rightarrow \dfrac{10}{60} \approx 0.17$

$= 17\%$ ✓

(b) $\dfrac{1,560,000}{13,240,000} \rightarrow \dfrac{1,600,000}{13,000,000} \approx 0.12$

$= 12\%$ ✓

(c) $\dfrac{18}{55} \rightarrow \dfrac{20}{60} \approx 0.33$

$= 33\%$ ✓

(d) $\dfrac{4,300,000}{13,240,000} \rightarrow \dfrac{4,300,000}{13,000,000} \approx 0.33$

$= 33\%$ ✓

NOTE TO STUDENT: Fully worked-out solutions to all of the Practice Problems can be found at the back of the text starting at page SP-1

Practice Problem 2   Using the chart for Example 2, answer the following questions. (Round all answers to the nearest whole percent.)

(a) What percent of the sales personnel are assigned to the Northwest?

(b) What percent of the sales volume is attributed to the Northwest?

(c) What percent of the sales personnel are assigned to the Southwest?

(d) What percent of the sales volume is attributed to the Southwest?

(e) Which of these two regions of the country has sales personnel that appear to be more effective in terms of volume of sales?

Mathematics Blueprint for Problem Solving

Gather the Facts	What Am I Solving For?	What Must I Calculate?	Key Points to Remember

TO THINK ABOUT: Example 2 Follow-Up   Suppose in 2006 the number of sales personnel (55) increases by 60%. What would the new number of sales personnel be? Suppose in 2006 that the number of sales personnel decreases by 60% from the number of sales personnel in 2003. What would the new number be? Why is this number not 55, since we have increased the number by 60% and then decreased the result by 60%? Explain.

Applications

Use the Mathematics Blueprint for Problem Solving to help you solve each of the following exercises.

▲ 1. ***Vinyl Flooring*** Jocelyn wants to put new vinyl flooring in her kitchen. The kitchen measures $12\frac{3}{4}$ feet long by $9\frac{1}{2}$ feet wide. If the vinyl flooring she chose costs $20.00 per square yard, how much will the new flooring cost her? (Round your answer to the nearest cent.)

▲ 2. ***Decking Costs*** The Carters need to replace the deck floor off their kitchen door. The deck is $11\frac{1}{2}$ feet by $20\frac{1}{2}$ feet. If the new decking costs $4.50 per square foot, how much will it cost them to replace the deck? (Round your answer to the nearest cent.)

▲ 3. ***Garden Design*** Jenna White has room for a rectangular garden that can measure as much as $15\frac{1}{2}$ feet wide and $25\frac{2}{3}$ feet long.
   (a) She decides the garden should be as large as possible, but wants to fence it off to protect the vegetables from the neighborhood raccoons. How much fencing does she need?
   (b) She finds that she can buy a prepackaged 90 feet of fencing for $155.00 or she can get a cut-to-order length for $2.10 per foot. Which should she buy? How much money does she save?

▲ 4. ***Pond Design*** The Lee family is installing a backyard pond for their prize koi. (A koi is a kind of fish bred in Japan. They are noted for their large size and variety of color.)
   (a) If the pond measures $11\frac{1}{2}$ feet by 7 feet, and is $3\frac{1}{2}$ feet deep, how much water will it take to fill the pond?
   (b) If each cubic foot is 7.5 gallons, how many gallons of water will the pond hold?
   (c) If at least 200 gallons of water is recommended for each koi, how many koi can the Lee family place in their pond?

Exercise Training *The following directions are posted on the wall at the gym.*

Beginning exercise training schedule

On day 1, each athlete will begin the morning as follows:

Jog................. $1\frac{1}{2}$ miles

Walk.............. $1\frac{3}{4}$ miles

Rest............... $2\frac{1}{2}$ minutes

Walk.............. 1 mile

5. Betty's athletic trainer told her to follow the beginning exercise training schedule on day 1. On day 2, she is to increase all distances and times by $\frac{1}{3}$ that of day 1. On day 3, she is to increase all distances and times by $\frac{1}{3}$ that of day 2. What will be her training schedule on day 3?

6. Melinda's athletic trainer told her to follow the beginning exercise training schedule on day 1. On day 2, she is to increase all distances and times by $\frac{1}{3}$ that of day 1. On day 3, she is to once again increase all distances and times by $\frac{1}{3}$ that of day 1. What will be her training schedule on day 3?

To Think About

Refer to exercises 5 and 6 in working exercises 7–10.

7. Who will have a more demanding schedule on day 3, Betty or Melinda? Why?

8. If Betty kept up the same type of increase day after day, how many miles would she be jogging on day 5?

9. If Melinda kept up the same type of increase day after day, how many miles would she be jogging on day 7?

10. Which athletic trainer would appear to have the best plan for training athletes if they used this plan for 14 days? Why?

11. *House Prices* In 1985, the average selling price of an existing single-family home in Atlanta, Georgia, was $66,200. Between 1985 and 1990, the average price increased by 30%. Between 1990 and 2005 the average price increased again, this time by 15%. What was the median house price in Atlanta in 2005?

12. *Egg Weight* Chicken eggs are classified by weight per dozen eggs. Large eggs weigh 24 ounces per dozen and medium eggs weigh 21 ounces per dozen.
(a) If you do not include the shell, which is 12% of the total weight of an egg, how many ounces of eggs do you get from a dozen large eggs? From a dozen medium eggs?

(b) At a local market, large eggs sell for $1.79 a dozen, and medium eggs for $1.39 a dozen. If you do not include the shell, which is a better buy, large or medium eggs?

Family Budgets   *For the following problems, use the chart below.*

The Johnson family has created the following budget:

Rent	20%	Clothing	10%
Food	31%	Medical	12%
Utilities	5%	Savings	10%
Entertainment	6%	Miscellaneous	6%

13. The income for this family comes from Mrs. Johnson's annual salary of $50,000.
(a) If 28% of her salary is withheld for various taxes, how much money does the family have available for their budget?

(b) How much of Mrs. Johnson's take home pay is budgeted for food?

14. With one child ready to head off to college, Mrs. Johnson is looking for ways to save money.
(a) She figures out that if they plant a garden this year, the family can save 12% of their food costs. How much will she save in food costs? (This does not account for the cost of planting a garden.) What is the new food budget amount?

(b) What percentage of Mrs. Johnson's budget is the new food amount?

Paycheck Stub *Use the following information from a paycheck stub to solve exercises 15–18.*

TOBEY & SLATER INC. 5000 Stillwell Avenue Queens, NY 10001				Check Number 495885	Payroll Period		Pay Date 12-01-99
					From Date 10-30-99	To Date 11-30-99	
Name Fred J. Gilliani	Social Security No. 012-34-5678	I.D. Number 01	File Number 1379	Rate/Salary 1150.00	Department 0100	MS M	DEP 5 · Res NY

	Current	Year to Date		Current	Year to Date
GROSS	1,150.00	6,670.00	STATE	67.76	388.45
FEDERAL	138.97	781.07	LOCAL	5.18	30.04
FICA	87.98	510.28	DIS-SUI	.00	.00
W-2 GROSS		6,670.00	NET	790.47	4,960.16

Earnings					Deductions/Specials		
No.	Type	Hours	Rate	Amount	Dept/Job No.	No.	Description · Amount
96	REGULAR			1,150.00	0100	82	Retirement · 12.56
						75	Medical · 36.28
						56	Union Dues · 10.80

Gross pay is the pay an employee receives for his or her services before deductions. Net pay is the pay the employee actually gets to take home. You may round each amount to the nearest whole percent for exercises 15–18.

15. What percent of Fred's gross pay is deducted for federal, state, and local taxes?

16. What percent of Fred's gross pay is deducted for retirement and medical?

17. What percent of Fred's gross pay does he actually get to take home?

18. What percent of Fred's deductions are special deductions?

Appendix C Practice with Operations of Whole Numbers

Addition Practice

1. 23 +14	**2.** 42 +33	**3.** 50 +44	**4.** 83 +16	**5.** 51 +27

6. 16 +13	**7.** 32 +29	**8.** 64 +17	**9.** 327 + 42	**10.** 223 + 54

11. 463 + 28	**12.** 504 + 96	**13.** 739 +682	**14.** 567 +485

15. 840 + 60   **16.** 364 + 37   **17.** 915 + 796   **18.** 420 + 899

19. 213 + 46 + 30   **20.** 326 + 21 + 52   **21.** 132 + 441 + 16   **22.** 671 + 204 + 12

23. 139 + 61 + 222   **24.** 524 + 73 + 195   **25.** 701 + 166 + 24 + 11   **26.** 439 + 365 + 45 + 81

Subtraction Practice

1. 32 −11	**2.** 87 −25	**3.** 56 −34	**4.** 73 −30	**5.** 93 −25	**6.** 21 −16

7. 40 −11	**8.** 60 −15	**9.** 576 − 45	**10.** 294 − 71	**11.** 780 − 54	**12.** 208 − 17

13. 406 − 28	**14.** 100 − 34	**15.** 635 −126	**16.** 375 −147	**17.** 500 −244	**18.** 200 −137

19. 922 −739	**20.** 646 −377	**21.** 1729 − 856	**22.** 2382 − 490	**23.** 7806 − 327	**24.** 3024 − 156

25. 8200 −6134	**26.** 2004 −1326

Multiplication Practice

1. 23×3	**2.** 13×2	**3.** 54×7	**4.** 67×9	**5.** 74×21	**6.** 53×31

7. 92×40	**8.** 70×52	**9.** 82×95	**10.** 69×39	**11.** 212×43	**12.** 341×22

13. 295×41	**14.** 419×72	**15.** 304×68	**16.** 620×39	**17.** 261×144	**18.** 124×433

19. 545×522	**20.** 634×799	**21.** 391×609	**22.** 817×460	**23.** 3844×209	**24.** 7409×106

25. $72,499(683)$ **26.** $86,243(725)$

Division Practice

1. $8\overline{)128}$ **2.** $3\overline{)168}$ **3.** $7\overline{)415}$ **4.** $6\overline{)287}$

5. $9\overline{)1116}$ **6.** $4\overline{)1184}$ **7.** $6\overline{)1404}$ **8.** $3\overline{)1701}$

9. $8\overline{)4174}$ **10.** $5\overline{)3697}$ **11.** $17\overline{)5468}$ **12.** $13\overline{)9795}$

13. $146\overline{)12994}$ **14.** $163\overline{)14833}$ **15.** $1728 \div 54$ **16.** $3813 \div 93$

17. $3701 \div 34$ **18.** $6052 \div 49$ **19.** $15836 \div 74$ **20.** $23256 \div 68$

21. $30632 \div 27$ **22.** $85069 \div 79$ **23.** $30752 \div 248$ **24.** $49878 \div 326$

25. $271125 \div 241$ **26.** $546924 \div 357$

Appendix D Tables

Table D-1: Table of Square Roots

Square root values ending in 000 are exact. All other values are approximate and are rounded to the nearest thousandth.

x	$\sqrt{x}$	x	$\sqrt{x}$	x	$\sqrt{x}$	x	$\sqrt{x}$	x	$\sqrt{x}$
1	1.000	41	6.403	81	9.000	121	11.000	161	12.689
2	1.414	42	6.481	82	9.055	122	11.045	162	12.728
3	1.732	43	6.557	83	9.110	123	11.091	163	12.767
4	2.000	44	6.633	84	9.165	124	11.136	164	12.806
5	2.236	45	6.708	85	9.220	125	11.180	165	12.845
6	2.449	46	6.782	86	9.274	126	11.225	166	12.884
7	2.646	47	6.856	87	9.327	127	11.269	167	12.923
8	2.828	48	6.928	88	9.381	128	11.314	168	12.961
9	3.000	49	7.000	89	9.434	129	11.358	169	13.000
10	3.162	50	7.071	90	9.487	130	11.402	170	13.038
11	3.317	51	7.141	91	9.539	131	11.446	171	13.077
12	3.464	52	7.211	92	9.592	132	11.489	172	13.115
13	3.606	53	7.280	93	9.644	133	11.533	173	13.153
14	3.742	54	7.348	94	9.695	134	11.576	174	13.191
15	3.873	55	7.416	95	9.747	135	11.619	175	13.229
16	4.000	56	7.483	96	9.798	136	11.662	176	13.266
17	4.123	57	7.550	97	9.849	137	11.705	177	13.304
18	4.243	58	7.616	98	9.899	138	11.747	178	13.342
19	4.359	59	7.681	99	9.950	139	11.790	179	13.379
20	4.472	60	7.746	100	10.000	140	11.832	180	13.416
21	4.583	61	7.810	101	10.050	141	11.874	181	13.454
22	4.690	62	7.874	102	10.100	142	11.916	182	13.491
23	4.796	63	7.937	103	10.149	143	11.958	183	13.528
24	4.899	64	8.000	104	10.198	144	12.000	184	13.565
25	5.000	65	8.062	105	10.247	145	12.042	185	13.601
26	5.099	66	8.124	106	10.296	146	12.083	186	13.638
27	5.196	67	8.185	107	10.344	147	12.124	187	13.675
28	5.292	68	8.246	108	10.392	148	12.166	188	13.711
29	5.385	69	8.307	109	10.440	149	12.207	189	13.748
30	5.477	70	8.367	110	10.488	150	12.247	190	13.784
31	5.568	71	8.426	111	10.536	151	12.288	191	13.820
32	5.657	72	8.485	112	10.583	152	12.329	192	13.856
33	5.745	73	8.544	113	10.630	153	12.369	193	13.892
34	5.831	74	8.602	114	10.677	154	12.410	194	13.928
35	5.916	75	8.660	115	10.724	155	12.450	195	13.964
36	6.000	76	8.718	116	10.770	156	12.490	196	14.000
37	6.083	77	8.775	117	10.817	157	12.530	197	14.036
38	6.164	78	8.832	118	10.863	158	12.570	198	14.071
39	6.245	79	8.888	119	10.909	159	12.610	199	14.107
40	6.325	80	8.944	120	10.954	160	12.649	200	14.142

Table D-2: Exponential Values

x	e^x	e^{-x}	x	e^x	e^{-x}
0.00	1.0000	1.0000	1.6	4.9530	0.2019
0.01	1.0101	0.9900	1.7	5.4739	0.1827
0.02	1.0202	0.9802	1.8	6.0496	0.1653
0.03	1.0305	0.9704	1.9	6.6859	0.1496
0.04	1.0408	0.9608	2.0	7.3891	0.1353
0.05	1.0513	0.9512	2.1	8.1662	0.1225
0.06	1.0618	0.9418	2.2	9.0250	0.1108
0.07	1.0725	0.9324	2.3	9.9742	0.1003
0.08	1.0833	0.9231	2.4	11.023	0.0907
0.09	1.0942	0.9139	2.5	12.182	0.0821
0.10	1.1052	0.9048	2.6	13.464	0.0743
0.11	1.1163	0.8958	2.7	14.880	0.0672
0.12	1.1275	0.8869	2.8	16.445	0.0608
0.13	1.1388	0.8781	2.9	18.174	0.0550
0.14	1.1503	0.8694	3.0	20.086	0.0498
0.15	1.1618	0.8607	3.1	22.198	0.0450
0.16	1.1735	0.8521	3.2	24.533	0.0408
0.17	1.1853	0.8437	3.3	27.113	0.0369
0.18	1.1972	0.8353	3.4	29.964	0.0334
0.19	1.2092	0.8270	3.5	33.115	0.0302
0.20	1.2214	0.8187	3.6	36.598	0.0273
0.21	1.2337	0.8106	3.7	40.447	0.0247
0.22	1.2461	0.8025	3.8	44.701	0.0224
0.23	1.2586	0.7945	3.9	49.402	0.0202
0.24	1.2712	0.7866	4.0	54.598	0.0183
0.25	1.2840	0.7788	4.1	60.340	0.0166
0.26	1.2969	0.7711	4.2	66.686	0.0150
0.27	1.3100	0.7634	4.3	73.700	0.0136
0.28	1.3231	0.7558	4.4	81.451	0.0123
0.29	1.3364	0.7483	4.5	90.017	0.0111
0.30	1.3499	0.7408	4.6	99.484	0.0101
0.35	1.4191	0.7047	4.7	109.95	0.0091
0.40	1.4918	0.6703	4.8	121.51	0.0082
0.45	1.5683	0.6376	4.9	134.29	0.0074
0.50	1.6487	0.6065	5.0	148.41	0.0067
0.55	1.7333	0.5769	5.5	244.69	0.0041
0.60	1.8221	0.5488	6.0	403.43	0.0025
0.65	1.9155	0.5220	6.5	665.14	0.0015
0.70	2.0138	0.4966	7.0	1,096.6	0.00091
0.75	2.1170	0.4724	7.5	1,808.0	0.00055
0.80	2.2255	0.4493	8.0	2,981.0	0.00034
0.85	2.3396	0.4274	8.5	4,914.8	0.00020
0.90	2.4596	0.4066	9.0	8,103.1	0.00012
0.95	2.5857	0.3867	9.5	13,360	0.000075
1.0	2.7183	0.3679	10	22,026	0.000045
1.1	3.0042	0.3329	11	59,874	0.000017
1.2	3.3201	0.3012	12	162,755	0.0000061
1.3	3.6693	0.2725	13	442,413	0.0000023
1.4	4.0552	0.2466	14	1,202,604	0.0000008
1.5	4.4817	0.2231	15	3,269,017	0.0000003

Appendix E Determinants and Cramer's Rule

Student Learning Objectives

After studying this section, you will be able to:

1. Evaluate a second-order determinant.

2. Evaluate a third-order determinant.

3. Solve a system of two linear equations with two unknowns using Cramer's rule.

4. Solve a system of three linear equations with three unknowns using Cramer's rule.

1 Evaluating a Second-Order Determinant

Mathematicians have developed techniques to solve systems of linear equations by focusing on the coefficients of the variables and the constants in the equations. The computational techniques can be easily carried out by computers or calculators. We will learn to do them by hand so that you will have a better understanding of what is involved.

To begin, we need to define a matrix and a determinant. A **matrix** is any rectangular array of numbers that is arranged in rows and columns. We use the symbol [ ] to indicate a matrix.

$$\begin{bmatrix} 3 & 2 & 4 \\ -1 & 4 & 0 \end{bmatrix}, \quad \begin{bmatrix} 4 & -3 \\ 2 & \frac{1}{2} \\ 1 & 5 \end{bmatrix}, \quad [-4 \quad 1 \quad 6], \quad \text{and} \quad \begin{bmatrix} \frac{1}{4} \\ 3 \\ -2 \end{bmatrix}$$

are matrices. If you have a graphing calculator, you can enter the elements of a matrix and store them for future use. Let's examine two systems of equations.

$$\begin{aligned} 3x + 2y &= 16 \\ x + 4y &= 22 \end{aligned} \quad \text{and} \quad \begin{aligned} -6x &= 18 \\ x + 3y &= 9 \end{aligned}$$

We could write the coefficients of the variables in each of these systems as a matrix.

$$\begin{aligned} 3x + 2y \\ x + 4y \end{aligned} \Rightarrow \begin{bmatrix} 3 & 2 \\ 1 & 4 \end{bmatrix} \quad \text{and} \quad \begin{aligned} -6x \\ x + 3y \end{aligned} \Rightarrow \begin{bmatrix} -6 & 0 \\ 1 & 3 \end{bmatrix}$$

Now we define a determinant. A **determinant** is a *square* arrangement of numbers. We use the symbol | | to indicate a determinant.

$$\begin{vmatrix} 3 & 2 \\ 1 & 4 \end{vmatrix} \quad \text{and} \quad \begin{vmatrix} -6 & 0 \\ 1 & 3 \end{vmatrix}$$

are determinants. The value of a determinant is a *real number* and is defined as follows:

DEFINITION

The value of the second-order determinant $\begin{vmatrix} a & c \\ b & d \end{vmatrix}$ is $ad - bc$.

EXAMPLE 1 Find the value of each determinant.

(a) $\begin{vmatrix} -6 & 2 \\ -1 & 4 \end{vmatrix}$ (b) $\begin{vmatrix} 0 & -3 \\ -2 & 6 \end{vmatrix}$

Solution

(a) $\begin{vmatrix} -6 & 2 \\ -1 & 4 \end{vmatrix} = (-6)(4) - (-1)(2) = -24 - (-2) = -24 + 2 = -22$

(b) $\begin{vmatrix} 0 & -3 \\ -2 & 6 \end{vmatrix} = (0)(6) - (-2)(-3) = 0 - (+6) = -6$

NOTE TO STUDENT: Fully worked-out solutions to all of the Practice Problems can be found at the back of the text starting at page SP-1

Practice Problem 1 Find the value of each determinant.

(a) $\begin{vmatrix} -7 & 3 \\ -4 & -2 \end{vmatrix}$

(b) $\begin{vmatrix} 5 & 6 \\ 0 & -5 \end{vmatrix}$

2 Evaluating a Third-Order Determinant

Third-order determinants have three rows and three columns. Again, each determinant has exactly one value.

DEFINITION

The value of the third-order determinant

$$\begin{vmatrix} a_1 & b_1 & c_1 \\ a_2 & b_2 & c_2 \\ a_3 & b_3 & c_3 \end{vmatrix}$$

is

$$a_1 b_2 c_3 + b_1 c_2 a_3 + c_1 a_2 b_3 - a_3 b_2 c_1 - b_3 c_2 a_1 - c_3 a_2 b_1.$$

Because this definition is difficult to memorize and cumbersome to use, we evaluate third-order determinants by a simpler method called **expansion by minors.** The **minor** of an element (number or variable) of a third-order determinant is the second-order determinant that remains after we delete the row and column in which the element appears.

EXAMPLE 2 Find (a) the minor of 6 and (b) the minor of -3 in the determinant.

$$\begin{vmatrix} 6 & 1 & 2 \\ -3 & 4 & 5 \\ -2 & 7 & 8 \end{vmatrix}$$

Solution

(a) Since the element 6 appears in the first row and the first column, we delete them.

$$\begin{vmatrix} \cancel{6} & \cancel{1} & \cancel{2} \\ -\cancel{3} & 4 & 5 \\ -\cancel{2} & 7 & 8 \end{vmatrix}$$

Therefore, the minor of 6 is $\begin{vmatrix} 4 & 5 \\ 7 & 8 \end{vmatrix}$

(b) Since -3 appears in the first column and the second row, we delete them.

$$\begin{vmatrix} \cancel{6} & 1 & 2 \\ -\cancel{3} & \cancel{4} & \cancel{5} \\ -\cancel{2} & 7 & 8 \end{vmatrix}$$

The minor of -3 is $\begin{vmatrix} 1 & 2 \\ 7 & 8 \end{vmatrix}.$

Practice Problem 2 Find (a) the minor of 3 and (b) the minor of -6 in the determinant.

$$\begin{vmatrix} 1 & 2 & 7 \\ -4 & -5 & -6 \\ 3 & 4 & -9 \end{vmatrix}$$

To evaluate a third-order determinant, we use expansion by minors of elements in the first column; for example, we have

$$\begin{vmatrix} a_1 & b_1 & c_1 \\ a_2 & b_2 & c_2 \\ a_3 & b_3 & c_3 \end{vmatrix} = a_1 \begin{vmatrix} b_2 & c_2 \\ b_3 & c_3 \end{vmatrix} - a_2 \begin{vmatrix} b_1 & c_1 \\ b_3 & c_3 \end{vmatrix} + a_3 \begin{vmatrix} b_1 & c_1 \\ b_2 & c_2 \end{vmatrix}$$

Note that the signs alternate. We then evaluate the second-order determinant according to our definition.

EXAMPLE 3   Evaluate the determinant $\begin{vmatrix} 2 & 3 & 6 \\ 4 & -2 & 0 \\ 1 & -5 & -3 \end{vmatrix}$ by expanding it by minors of elements in the first column.

Solution

$$\begin{vmatrix} 2 & 3 & 6 \\ 4 & -2 & 0 \\ 1 & -5 & -3 \end{vmatrix} = 2 \begin{vmatrix} -2 & 0 \\ -5 & -3 \end{vmatrix} - 4 \begin{vmatrix} 3 & 6 \\ -5 & -3 \end{vmatrix} + 1 \begin{vmatrix} 3 & 6 \\ -2 & 0 \end{vmatrix}$$

$$= 2[(-2)(-3) - (-5)(0)] - 4[(3)(-3) - (-5)(6)] + 1[(3)(0) - (-2)(6)]$$

$$= 2[6 - 0] - 4[-9 - (-30)] + 1[0 - (-12)]$$

$$= 2(6) - 4(21) + 1(12)$$

$$= 12 - 84 + 12$$

$$= -60$$

NOTE TO STUDENT: Fully worked-out solutions to all of the Practice Problems can be found at the back of the text starting at page SP-1

Practice Problem 3   Evaluate the determinant $\begin{vmatrix} 1 & 2 & -3 \\ 2 & -1 & 2 \\ 3 & 1 & 4 \end{vmatrix}$.

---

③ Solving a System of Two Linear Equations with Two Unknowns Using Cramer's Rule

We can solve a linear system of two equations with two unknowns by Cramer's rule. The rule is named for Gabriel Cramer, a Swiss mathematician who lived from 1704 to 1752. Cramer's rule expresses the solution to each variable of a linear system as the quotient of two determinants. Computer programs are available to solve a system of equations by Cramer's rule.

CRAMER'S RULE

The solution to

$$a_1 x + b_1 y = c_1$$

$$a_2 x + b_2 y = c_2$$

is $x = \dfrac{D_x}{D}$ and $y = \dfrac{D_y}{D}$, $D \neq 0$,

where $D_x = \begin{vmatrix} c_1 & b_1 \\ c_2 & b_2 \end{vmatrix}$, $D_y = \begin{vmatrix} a_1 & c_1 \\ a_2 & c_2 \end{vmatrix}$,   and $D = \begin{vmatrix} a_1 & b_1 \\ a_2 & b_2 \end{vmatrix}$.

EXAMPLE 4   Solve by Cramer's rule.

$$-3x + y = 7$$
$$-4x - 3y = 5$$

Solution

$$D = \begin{vmatrix} -3 & 1 \\ -4 & -3 \end{vmatrix} \qquad D_x = \begin{vmatrix} 7 & 1 \\ 5 & -3 \end{vmatrix} \qquad D_y = \begin{vmatrix} -3 & 7 \\ -4 & 5 \end{vmatrix}$$

$$\begin{aligned} &= (-3)(-3) - (-4)(1) & &= (7)(-3) - (5)(1) & &= (-3)(5) - (-4)(7) \\ &= 9 - (-4) & &= -21 - 5 & &= -15 - (-28) \\ &= 9 + 4 & &= -26 & &= -15 + 28 \\ &= 13 & & & &= 13 \end{aligned}$$

Hence,

$$x = \frac{D_x}{D} = \frac{-26}{13} = -2$$

$$y = \frac{D_y}{D} = \frac{13}{13} = 1.$$

The solution to the system is $x = -2$ and $y = 1$. Verify this.

Practice Problem 4   Solve by Cramer's rule.

$$5x + 3y = 17$$
$$2x - 5y = 13$$

Solving a System of Three Linear Equations with Three Unknowns Using Cramer's Rule

It is quite easy to extend Cramer's rule to three linear equations.

CRAMER'S RULE

The solution to the system

$$a_1x + b_1y + c_1z = d_1$$
$$a_2x + b_2y + c_2z = d_2$$
$$a_3x + b_3y + c_3z = d_3$$

is $$x = \frac{D_x}{D}, \qquad y = \frac{D_y}{D}, \quad \text{and} \quad z = \frac{D_z}{D}, \qquad D \neq 0,$$

$$D = \begin{vmatrix} a_1 & b_1 & c_1 \\ a_2 & b_2 & c_2 \\ a_3 & b_3 & c_3 \end{vmatrix}, \qquad D_x = \begin{vmatrix} d_1 & b_1 & c_1 \\ d_2 & b_2 & c_2 \\ d_3 & b_3 & c_3 \end{vmatrix},$$

where

$$D_y = \begin{vmatrix} a_1 & d_1 & c_1 \\ a_2 & d_2 & c_2 \\ a_3 & d_3 & c_3 \end{vmatrix}, \quad \text{and} \quad D_z = \begin{vmatrix} a_1 & b_1 & d_1 \\ a_2 & b_2 & d_2 \\ a_3 & b_3 & d_3 \end{vmatrix}.$$

EXAMPLE 5   Use Cramer's rule to solve the system.

$$2x - y + z = 6$$
$$3x + 2y - z = 5$$
$$2x + 3y - 2z = 1$$

Solution

We will expand each determinant by the first column.

$$D = \begin{vmatrix} 2 & -1 & 1 \\ 3 & 2 & -1 \\ 2 & 3 & -2 \end{vmatrix}$$

$$= 2 \begin{vmatrix} 2 & -1 \\ 3 & -2 \end{vmatrix} - 3 \begin{vmatrix} -1 & 1 \\ 3 & -2 \end{vmatrix} + 2 \begin{vmatrix} -1 & 1 \\ 2 & -1 \end{vmatrix}$$

$$= 2[-4 - (-3)] - 3[2 - 3] + 2[1 - 2]$$

$$= 2[-1] - 3[-1] + 2[-1]$$

$$= -2 + 3 - 2$$

$$= -1$$

$$D_x = \begin{vmatrix} 6 & -1 & 1 \\ 5 & 2 & -1 \\ 1 & 3 & -2 \end{vmatrix}$$

$$= 6 \begin{vmatrix} 2 & -1 \\ 3 & -2 \end{vmatrix} - 5 \begin{vmatrix} -1 & 1 \\ 3 & -2 \end{vmatrix} + 1 \begin{vmatrix} -1 & 1 \\ 2 & -1 \end{vmatrix}$$

$$= 6[-4 - (-3)] - 5[2 - 3] + 1[1 - 2]$$

$$= 6[-1] - 5[-1] + 1[-1]$$

$$= -6 + 5 - 1$$

$$= -2$$

Graphing Calculator

Copying Matrices

If you are using a graphing calculator to evaluate the four determinants in Example 5 or similar exercises, first enter matrix D into the calculator. Then copy the matrix using the copy function to three additional locations. Usually we store matrix D as matrix A. Then store a copy of it as matrix B, C, and D. Finally, use the Edit function and modify one column of each of matrices B, C, and D so that they become D_x, D_y, and D_z. This allows you to evaluate all four determinants in a minimum amount of time.

$$D_y = \begin{vmatrix} 2 & 6 & 1 \\ 3 & 5 & -1 \\ 2 & 1 & -2 \end{vmatrix}$$

$$= 2 \begin{vmatrix} 5 & -1 \\ 1 & -2 \end{vmatrix} - 3 \begin{vmatrix} 6 & 1 \\ 1 & -2 \end{vmatrix} + 2 \begin{vmatrix} 6 & 1 \\ 5 & -1 \end{vmatrix}$$

$$= 2[-10 - (-1)] - 3[-12 - 1] + 2[-6 - 5]$$

$$= 2[-9] - 3[-13] + 2[-11]$$

$$= -18 + 39 - 22$$

$$= -1$$

$$D_z = \begin{vmatrix} 2 & -1 & 6 \\ 3 & 2 & 5 \\ 2 & 3 & 1 \end{vmatrix}$$

$$= 2 \begin{vmatrix} 2 & 5 \\ 3 & 1 \end{vmatrix} - 3 \begin{vmatrix} -1 & 6 \\ 3 & 1 \end{vmatrix} + 2 \begin{vmatrix} -1 & 6 \\ 2 & 5 \end{vmatrix}$$

$$= 2[2 - 15] - 3[-1 - 18] + 2[-5 - 12]$$

$$= 2[-13] - 3[-19] + 2[-17]$$

$$= -26 + 57 - 34$$

$$= -3$$

$$x = \frac{D_x}{D} = \frac{-2}{-1} = 2; \qquad y = \frac{D_y}{D} = \frac{-1}{-1} = 1; \qquad z = \frac{D_z}{D} = \frac{-3}{-1} = 3$$

Practice Problem 5   Find the solution to the system by Cramer's rule.

$$2x + 3y - z = -1$$
$$3x + 5y - 2z = -3$$
$$x + 2y + 3z = 2$$

NOTE TO STUDENT: Fully worked-out solutions to all of the Practice Problems can be found at the back of the text starting at page SP-1

Cramer's rule cannot be used for every system of linear equations. If the equations are dependent or if the system of equations is inconsistent, the determinant of coefficients will be zero. Division by zero is not defined. In such a situation the system will not have a unique answer.

If $D = 0$, then the following are true:

1. If $D_x = 0$ and $D_y = 0$ (and $D_z = 0$, if there are three equations), then the equations are *dependent*. Such a system will have an infinite number of solutions.

2. If at least one of D_x or D_y (or D_z if there are three equations) is nonzero, then the system of equations is *inconsistent*. Such a system will have no solution.

Evaluate each determinant.

1. $\begin{vmatrix} 5 & 6 \\ 2 & 1 \end{vmatrix}$

2. $\begin{vmatrix} 3 & 4 \\ 1 & 8 \end{vmatrix}$

3. $\begin{vmatrix} 2 & -1 \\ 3 & 6 \end{vmatrix}$

4. $\begin{vmatrix} -4 & 2 \\ 1 & 5 \end{vmatrix}$

5. $\begin{vmatrix} -\frac{1}{2} & -\frac{2}{3} \\ 9 & 8 \end{vmatrix}$

6. $\begin{vmatrix} 10 & 4 \\ -\frac{3}{2} & -\frac{2}{5} \end{vmatrix}$

7. $\begin{vmatrix} -5 & 3 \\ -4 & -7 \end{vmatrix}$

8. $\begin{vmatrix} 2 & -3 \\ -4 & -6 \end{vmatrix}$

9. $\begin{vmatrix} 0 & -6 \\ 3 & -4 \end{vmatrix}$

10. $\begin{vmatrix} -5 & 0 \\ 2 & -7 \end{vmatrix}$

11. $\begin{vmatrix} 2 & -5 \\ -4 & 10 \end{vmatrix}$

12. $\begin{vmatrix} -3 & 6 \\ 7 & -14 \end{vmatrix}$

13. $\begin{vmatrix} 0 & 0 \\ -2 & 6 \end{vmatrix}$

14. $\begin{vmatrix} -4 & 0 \\ -3 & 0 \end{vmatrix}$

15. $\begin{vmatrix} 0.3 & 0.6 \\ 1.2 & 0.4 \end{vmatrix}$

16. $\begin{vmatrix} 0.1 & 0.7 \\ 0.5 & 0.8 \end{vmatrix}$

17. $\begin{vmatrix} 7 & 4 \\ b & -a \end{vmatrix}$

18. $\begin{vmatrix} \frac{1}{4} & \frac{3}{5} \\ \frac{2}{3} & \frac{1}{5} \end{vmatrix}$

19. $\begin{vmatrix} \frac{3}{7} & -\frac{1}{3} \\ -\frac{1}{4} & \frac{1}{2} \end{vmatrix}$

20. $\begin{vmatrix} -3 & y \\ -2 & x \end{vmatrix}$

In the following determinant $\begin{vmatrix} 3 & -4 & 7 \\ -2 & 6 & 10 \\ 1 & -5 & 9 \end{vmatrix}$,

21. Find the minor of 3.

22. Find the minor of -2.

23. Find the minor of 10.

24. Find the minor of 9.

Evaluate each of the following determinants.

25. $\begin{vmatrix} 4 & 1 & 2 \\ 3 & -1 & 0 \\ 1 & 2 & 3 \end{vmatrix}$

26. $\begin{vmatrix} 2 & 3 & 1 \\ -3 & 1 & 0 \\ 2 & 1 & 4 \end{vmatrix}$

27. $\begin{vmatrix} -4 & 0 & -1 \\ 2 & 1 & -1 \\ 0 & 3 & 2 \end{vmatrix}$

28. $\begin{vmatrix} 3 & -4 & -1 \\ -2 & 1 & 3 \\ 0 & 1 & 4 \end{vmatrix}$

29. $\begin{vmatrix} \frac{1}{2} & 1 & -1 \\ \frac{3}{2} & 1 & 2 \\ 3 & 0 & -2 \end{vmatrix}$

30. $\begin{vmatrix} 1 & 2 & 3 \\ 4 & -2 & -1 \\ 5 & -3 & 2 \end{vmatrix}$

31. $\begin{vmatrix} 4 & 1 & 2 \\ -1 & -2 & -3 \\ 4 & -1 & 3 \end{vmatrix}$

32. $\begin{vmatrix} -\frac{1}{2} & 2 & 3 \\ \frac{5}{2} & -2 & -1 \\ \frac{3}{4} & -3 & 2 \end{vmatrix}$

33. $\begin{vmatrix} 2 & 0 & -2 \\ -1 & 0 & 2 \\ 3 & 4 & 3 \end{vmatrix}$

34. $\begin{vmatrix} 7 & 0 & 2 \\ 1 & 0 & -5 \\ 3 & 0 & 6 \end{vmatrix}$

35. $\begin{vmatrix} 6 & -4 & 3 \\ 1 & 2 & 4 \\ 0 & 0 & 0 \end{vmatrix}$

36. $\begin{vmatrix} 7 & 0 & 3 \\ 1 & 2 & 4 \\ 3 & 0 & -7 \end{vmatrix}$

Optional Graphing Calculator Problems

If you have a graphing calculator, use the determinant function to evaluate the following:

37. $\begin{vmatrix} 1.3 & 1.8 & 2.5 \\ 7.9 & 5.3 & 6.0 \\ 1.7 & 1.8 & 2.8 \end{vmatrix}$

38. $\begin{vmatrix} 0.7 & 5.3 & 0.4 \\ 1.6 & 0.3 & 3.7 \\ 0.8 & 6.7 & 4.2 \end{vmatrix}$

39. $\begin{vmatrix} -55 & 17 & 19 \\ -62 & 23 & 31 \\ 81 & 51 & 74 \end{vmatrix}$

40. $\begin{vmatrix} 82 & -20 & 56 \\ 93 & -18 & 39 \\ 65 & -27 & 72 \end{vmatrix}$

Solve each system by Cramer's rule.

41. $x + 2y = 8$
$2x + y = 7$

42. $x + 3y = 6$
$2x + y = 7$

43. $5x + 4y = 10$
$-x + 2y = 12$

44. $3x + 5y = 11$
$2x + y = -2$

45. $x - 5y = 0$
$x + 6y = 22$

46. $x - 3y = 4$
$-3x + 4y = -12$

47. $0.3x + 0.5y = 0.2$
$0.1x + 0.2y = 0.0$

48. $0.5x + 0.3y = -0.7$
$0.4x + 0.5y = -0.3$

Solve by Cramer's rule. Round your answers to four decimal places.

49. $52.9634x - 27.3715y = 86.1239$
$31.9872x + 61.4598y = 44.9812$

50. $0.0076x + 0.0092y = 0.01237$
$-0.5628x - 0.2374y = -0.7635$

Solve each system by Cramer's rule.

51. $2x + y + z = 4$
$x - y - 2z = -2$
$x + y - z = 1$

52. $x + 2y - z = -4$
$x + 4y - 2z = -6$
$2x + 3y + z = 3$

53. $2x + 2y + 3z = 6$
$x - y + z = 1$
$3x + y + z = 1$

54. $4x + y + 2z = 6$
$x + y + z = 1$
$-x + 3y - z = -5$

55. $x + 2y + z = 1$
$3x - 4z = 8$
$3y + 5z = -1$

56. $3x + y + z = 2$
$2y + 3z = -6$
$2x - y = -1$

Optional Graphing Calculator Problems

Round your answers to the nearest thousandth.

57. $10x + 20y + 10z = -2$
$-24x - 31y - 11z = -12$
$61x + 39y + 28z = -45$

58. $121x + 134y + 101z = 146$
$315x - 112y - 108z = 426$
$148x + 503y + 516z = -127$

59. $28w + 35x - 18y + 40z = 60$
$60w + 32x + 28y = 400$
$30w + 15x + 18y + 66z = 720$
$26w - 18x - 15y + 75z = 125$

Appendix F Solving Systems of Linear Equations Using Matrices

 Solving a System of Linear Equations Using Matrices

In Appendix B we defined a matrix as any rectangular array of numbers that is arranged in rows and columns.

$$\begin{bmatrix} 2 & 3 \\ 5 & 6 \end{bmatrix}$$

This is a 2×2 matrix with two rows and two columns.

$$\begin{bmatrix} 1 & -5 & -6 & 2 \\ 3 & 4 & -8 & -2 \\ 2 & 7 & 9 & -4 \end{bmatrix}$$

This is a 3×4 matrix with three rows and four columns.

A matrix that is derived from a linear system of equations is called the **augmented matrix** of the system. This augmented matrix is made up of two smaller matrices separated by a vertical line. The coefficients of each variable in a linear system are placed to the left of the vertical line. The constants are placed to the right of the vertical line.

The augmented matrix for the system of equations

$$-3x + 5y = -22$$
$$2x - y = 10$$

is the 2×3 matrix

$$\left[\begin{array}{rr|r} -3 & 5 & -22 \\ 2 & -1 & 10 \end{array}\right].$$

The augmented matrix for the system of equations

$$3x - 5y + 2z = 8$$
$$x + y + z = 3$$
$$3x - 2y + 4z = 10$$

is the 3×4 matrix

$$\left[\begin{array}{rrr|r} 3 & -5 & 2 & 8 \\ 1 & 1 & 1 & 3 \\ 3 & -2 & 4 & 10 \end{array}\right].$$

EXAMPLE 1 Write the solution to the system of linear equations represented by the following matrix.

$$\left[\begin{array}{rr|r} 1 & -3 & -7 \\ 0 & 1 & 4 \end{array}\right]$$

Solution This system is represented by the equations

$$x - 3y = -7 \quad \text{and}$$
$$0x + y = 4.$$

Since we know that $y = 4$, we can find x by substitution.

$$x - 3y = -7$$
$$x - 3(4) = -7$$
$$x - 12 = -7$$
$$x = 5$$

Thus, the solution to the system is $x = 5$; $y = 4$. We can also write the solution as $(5, 4)$.

NOTE TO STUDENT: Fully worked-out solutions to all of the Practice Problems can be found at the back of the text starting at page SP-1

Practice Problem 1 Write the solution to the system of linear equations represented by the following matrix.

$$\begin{bmatrix} 1 & 9 & | & 33 \\ 0 & 1 & | & 3 \end{bmatrix}$$

To solve a system of linear equations in matrix form, we use three row operations of the matrix.

MATRIX ROW OPERATIONS

1. Any two rows of a matrix may be interchanged.

2. All the numbers in a row may be multiplied or divided by any nonzero number.

3. All the numbers in any row or any multiple of a row may be added to the corresponding numbers of any other row.

To obtain the values for x and y in a system of two linear equations, we use row operations to obtain an augmented matrix in a form similar to the form of the matrix in Example 1.

The desired form is

$$\begin{bmatrix} 1 & a & | & b \\ 0 & 1 & | & c \end{bmatrix} \quad \text{or} \quad \begin{bmatrix} 1 & a & b & | & d \\ 0 & 1 & c & | & e \\ 0 & 0 & 1 & | & f \end{bmatrix}.$$

The last row of the matrix will allow us to find the value of one of the variables. We can then use substitution to find the other variables.

EXAMPLE 2 Use matrices to solve the system.

$$4x - 3y = -13$$
$$x + 2y = 5$$

Solution The augmented matrix for this system of linear equations is

$$\begin{bmatrix} 4 & -3 & | & -13 \\ 1 & 2 & | & 5 \end{bmatrix}.$$

First we want to obtain a 1 as the first element in the first row. We can obtain this by interchanging rows one and two.

$$\begin{bmatrix} 1 & 2 & | & 5 \\ 4 & -3 & | & -13 \end{bmatrix} \quad R_1 \longleftrightarrow R_2$$

Next we wish to obtain a 0 as the first element of the second row. To obtain this we multiply -4 by all the elements of row one and add this to row two.

$$\begin{bmatrix} 1 & 2 & | & 5 \\ 0 & -11 & | & -33 \end{bmatrix} \quad -4R_1 + R_2$$

Next, to obtain a 1 as the second element of the second row, we multiply each element of row two by $\left(-\frac{1}{11}\right)$.

$$\begin{bmatrix} 1 & 2 & | & 5 \\ 0 & 1 & | & 3 \end{bmatrix} \quad -\frac{1}{11}R_2$$

This final matrix is in the desired form. It represents the linear system

$$x + 2y = 5$$
$$y = 3.$$

Since we know that $y = 3$, we substitute this value into the first equation.

$$x + 2(3) = 5$$
$$x + 6 = 5$$
$$x = -1$$

Thus, the solution to the system is $(-1, 3)$.

*NOTE TO STUDENT: Fully worked-out
solutions to all of the Practice Problems
can be found at the back of the text
starting at page SP-1*

Practice Problem 2   Use matrices to solve the system.

$$3x - 2y = -6$$
$$x - 3y = 5$$

Now we continue with a similar example involving three equations and three unknowns.

EXAMPLE 3   Use matrices to solve the system.

$$2x + 3y - z = 11$$
$$x + 2y + z = 12$$
$$3x - y + 2z = 5$$

Solution   The augmented matrix that represents this system of linear equations is

$$\left[\begin{array}{ccc|c} 2 & 3 & -1 & 11 \\ 1 & 2 & 1 & 12 \\ 3 & -1 & 2 & 5 \end{array}\right].$$

To obtain a one as the first element of the first row, we first need to interchange the first and second rows.

$$\left[\begin{array}{ccc|c} 1 & 2 & 1 & 12 \\ 2 & 3 & -1 & 11 \\ 3 & -1 & 2 & 5 \end{array}\right] \quad R_1 \longleftrightarrow R_2$$

Now, in order to obtain a 0 as the first element of the second row, we multiply row one by -2 and add the result to row two. In order to obtain a 0 as the first element of the third row, we multiply row one by -3 and add the result to row three.

$$\left[\begin{array}{ccc|c} 1 & 2 & 1 & 12 \\ 0 & -1 & -3 & -13 \\ 0 & -7 & -1 & -31 \end{array}\right] \quad \begin{array}{c} -2R_1 + R_2 \\ -3R_1 + R_3 \end{array}$$

To obtain a 1 as the second element of row two, we multiply all the elements of row two by -1.

$$\left[\begin{array}{ccc|c} 1 & 2 & 1 & 12 \\ 0 & 1 & 3 & 13 \\ 0 & -7 & -1 & -31 \end{array}\right] \quad -1R_2$$

Next, in order to obtain a 0 as the second element of row three, we add 7 times row two to row three.

$$\left[\begin{array}{ccc|c} 1 & 2 & 1 & 12 \\ 0 & 1 & 3 & 13 \\ 0 & 0 & 20 & 60 \end{array}\right] \quad 7R_2 + R_3$$

Finally, we multiply all the elements of row three by $\frac{1}{20}$. Thus, we have the following:

$$\left[\begin{array}{ccc|c} 1 & 2 & 1 & 12 \\ 0 & 1 & 3 & 13 \\ 0 & 0 & 1 & 3 \end{array}\right] \quad \frac{1}{20}R_3$$

From the final line of the matrix, we see that $z = 3$. If we substitute this value into the equation represented by the second line, we have

$$y + 3z = 13$$
$$y + 3(3) = 13$$
$$y + 9 = 13$$
$$y = 4.$$

Now we substitute the values obtained for y and for z into the equation represented by first line of the matrix.

$$x + 2y + z = 12$$
$$x + 2(4) + 3 = 12$$
$$x + 8 + 3 = 12$$
$$x + 11 = 12$$
$$x = 1$$

Thus, the solution to this linear system of three equations is $(1, 4, 3)$.

Practice Problem 3   Use matrices to solve the system.

$$2x + y - 2z = -15$$
$$4x - 2y + z = 15$$
$$x + 3y + 2z = -5$$

We could continue to use these row operations to obtain an augmented matrix of the form

$$\begin{bmatrix} 1 & 0 & a \\ 0 & 1 & b \end{bmatrix} \quad \text{or} \quad \begin{bmatrix} 1 & 0 & 0 & a \\ 0 & 1 & 0 & b \\ 0 & 0 & 1 & c \end{bmatrix}.$$

This form of the augmented matrix is given a special name. It is known as the **reduced row echelon form.** If the augmented matrix of a system of linear equations is placed in this form, we would immediately know the solution to the system. Thus, if a system of linear equations in the variables x, y, and z had an augmented matrix that could be placed in the form

$$\begin{bmatrix} 1 & 0 & 0 & 7 \\ 0 & 1 & 0 & 32 \\ 0 & 0 & 1 & 18 \end{bmatrix},$$

we could determine directly that $x = 7$, $y = 32$, and $z = 18$. A similar pattern is obtained for a system of four equations in four unknowns, and so on. Thus, if a system of linear equations in the variables w, x, y, and z had an augmented matrix that could be placed in the form

$$\begin{bmatrix} 1 & 0 & 0 & 0 & 23.4 \\ 0 & 1 & 0 & 0 & 48.6 \\ 0 & 0 & 1 & 0 & 0.73 \\ 0 & 0 & 0 & 1 & 5.97 \end{bmatrix},$$

we could directly conclude that $w = 23.4$, $x = 48.6$, $y = 0.73$, and $z = 5.97$. Reducing a matrix to reduced row echelon form is readily done on computers. Many mathematical software packages contain matrix operations that will obtain the reduced row echelon form of an augmented matrix. A number of the newer graphing calculators such as the TI-83 can be used to obtain the reduced row echelon form by using the **rref** command on a given matrix.

Graphing Calculator

Obtaining a Reduced Row Echelon Form of an Augmented Matrix

If your graphing calculator has a routine to obtain the **reduced row echelon form** of a matrix **(rref)**, then this routine will allow you to quickly obtain the solution of a system of linear equations if one exists. If your calculator has this capability, solve the following system.

$$5w + 2x + 3y + 4z = -8.3$$
$$-4w + 3x + 2y + 7z = -70.1$$
$$6w + x + 4y + 5z = -13.3$$
$$7w + 4x + y + 2z = 14.1$$

Answer:
$$w = 3.1, x = 2.2,$$
$$y = 4.6, z = -10.5$$

Solve each system of equations by the matrix method. Round your answers to the nearest tenth.

1. $2x + 3y = 5$
$5x + y = 19$

2. $3x + 5y = -15$
$2x + 7y = -10$

3. $2x + y = -3$
$5x - y = 24$

4. $x + 5y = -9$
$4x - 3y = -13$

5. $5x + 2y = 6$
$3x + 4y = 12$

6. $-5x + y = 24$
$x + 5y = 10$

7. $3x - 2y + 3 = 5$
$x + 4y - 1 = 9$

8. $3x + y - 4 = 12$
$-2x + 3y + 2 = -5$

9. $-7x + 3y = 2.7$
$6x + 5y = 25.7$

10. $x - 2y - 3z = 4$
$2x + 3y + z = 1$
$-3x + y - 2z = 5$

11. $x + y - z = -2$
$2x - y + 3z = 19$
$4x + 3y - z = 5$

12. $5x - y + 4z = 5$
$6x + y - 5z = 17$
$2x - 3y + z = -11$

13. $x + y - z = -3$
$x + y + z = 3$
$3x - y + z = 7$

14. $2x - y + z = 5$
$x + 2y - z = -2$
$x + y - 2z = -5$

15. $2x - 3y + z = 11$
$x + y + 2z = 8$
$x + 3y - z = -11$

16. $4x + 3y + 5z = 2$
$2y + 7z = 16$
$2x - y = 6$

17. $6x - y + z = 9$
$2x + 3z = 16$
$4x + 7y + 5z = 20$

18. $3x + 2y = 44$
$4y + 3z = 19$
$2x + 3z = -5$

Optional Graphing Calculator Problems

If your graphing calculator has the necessary capability, solve the following exercises. Round your answers to the nearest tenth.

19. $5x + 6y + 7z = 45.6$
$1.4x - 3.2y + 1.6z = 3.12$
$9x - 8y + 22z = 70.8$

20. $2x + 12y + 9z = 37.9$
$1.6x + 1.8y - 2.5z = -20.53$
$7x + 8y + 4z = 39.6$

21. $6w + 5x + 3y + 1.5z = 41.7$
$2w + 6.7x - 5y + 7z = -21.92$
$12w + x + 5y - 6z = 58.4$
$3w + 8x - 15y + z = -142.8$

22. $2w + 3x + 11y - 14z = 6.7$
$5w + 8x + 7y + 3z = 25.3$
$-4w + x + 1.5y - 9z = -53.4$
$9w + 7x - 2.5y + 6z = 22.9$

Appendix G Sets

① Roster Form

Set theory is the basis of several mathematical topics. Sorting and classifying objects into categories is something we do every day. You may organize your closet so all your sweaters are together. When you go through your mail, you may separate bills from junk mail.

A **set** is a collection of objects called **elements.** Numbers can be classified into several different sets. The natural numbers, for example, are the set of whole numbers excluding 0. Prime numbers make up another set. They are the set of natural numbers greater than 1 whose only natural number factors are 1 and itself. We can write these sets the following way.

$$N = \{1, 2, 3, 4, 5, \dots\}$$
$$P = \{2, 3, 5, 7, 11, 13, \dots\}$$

There are several things to notice. Capital letters are usually used to represent sets. When elements of a set are listed, they are separated by commas and enclosed by braces. When we list the elements of a set this way, we say the set is in **roster form.** The three dots in sets N and P indicate that the pattern of numbers continues.

To indicate an element is part of a set, we use the symbol $\in$. Since 17 is a prime number, we can write $17 \in P$. This is read "17 is an element of set P".

Student Learning Objectives

After studying this section, you will be able to:

① Write a set in roster form.

② Write a set in set-builder notation.

③ Find the union and intersection of sets.

④ Identify subsets.

EXAMPLE 1 Write in roster form.

(a) Set D is the set of Beatles.

(b) Set X is the set of natural numbers between 2 and 7.

(c) Set Y is the set of natural numbers between 2 and 7, inclusive.

Solution

(a) Writing set D in roster form, we have

$$D = \{John\ Lennon,\ Paul\ McCartney,\ George\ Harrison,\ Ringo\ Starr\}.$$

(b) $X = \{3, 4, 5, 6\}$.

(c) The word inclusive means the numbers 2 and 7 are included.

$$Y = \{2, 3, 4, 5, 6, 7\}$$

Practice Problem 1 Write in roster form.

(a) Set A is the set of continents on Earth.

(b) Set C is the set of natural numbers between 35 and 42.

(c) Set D is the set of natural numbers between 35 and 42, inclusive.

NOTE TO STUDENT: Fully worked-out solutions to all of the Practice Problems can be found at the back of the text starting at page SP-1

The sets in Example 1 are **finite sets;** we can count the number of elements. Set D in part (a) contains four elements and set Y in part (c) has six elements. The set of natural numbers $N = \{1, 2, 3, \dots\}$ is an example of an **infinite set.** The list of numbers continues without bound; there are infinitely many elements. Some sets contain no elements and are called **empty sets.** The empty set is denoted by the symbol $\{\ \}$ or $\varnothing$. The set of students in your class that are 11 feet tall is an empty set.

② Set-Builder Notation

All the sets we have seen so far have been in roster form or have been described in words. Another way to write a set is **set-builder notation,** used often in higher mathematics. An example of a set written in set-builder notation is

$$A = \{x \mid x \text{ is a natural number greater than } 10\}.$$

We read this as "Set A is the set of all elements x such that x is a natural number greater than 10." We also could have written $A = \{x \mid x \in N \text{ and } x > 10\}$. $x \in N$ means x is an element of the natural numbers.

Let's look at each part of set-builder notation and its meaning.

{	x	|	criteria }
↓	↓	↓	↓
The set of	all elements x	such that	x meets these criteria

EXAMPLE 2   Write set B in set-builder notation. $B = \{a, e, i, o, u\}$

Solution   For an element to be in set B, it must be a vowel of the alphabet. We write $B = \{x \mid x \text{ is a vowel}\}$. Notice what is written to the right of the bar. We don't describe the set in words here. We simply indicate what criteria an element must meet to be in the set. $B = \{x \mid x \text{ is the set of vowels}\}$ is *not* correct.

Practice Problem 2   Write set C in set-builder notation. $C = \{4, 6, 8, 10, 12\}$ (*Hint:* There is more than one acceptable answer.)

NOTE TO STUDENT: Fully worked-out solutions to all of the Practice Problems can be found at the back of the text starting at page SP-1

③ The Union and Intersection of Sets

Addition, subtraction, multiplication, and division are operations used on numbers. There are other operations used on sets. The two most common operations are union and intersection.

The **union** of two sets A and B, written $A \cup B$, is the set of elements that are in set A, *or* set B.

EXAMPLE 3   Find $A \cup B$ if $A = \{a, b, c, d, e\}$ and $B = \{a, c, d, g\}$.

Solution   To find the set $A \cup B$, we combine the elements of A with those of B. We have $A \cup B = \{a, b, c, d, e, g\}$.

Practice Problem 3   Find $G \cup H$ if $G = \{!, *, \%, \$\}$ and $H = \{\$, ?, \wedge, +\}$.

The **intersection** of sets A and B, written $A \cap B$, is the set of elements in set A *and* set B.

EXAMPLE 4   Find $A \cap B$ if $A = \{a, b, c, d, e\}$ and $B = \{a, c, d, g\}$.

Solution   The elements that are common to sets A and B are a, c, and d. Thus $A \cap B = \{a, c, d\}$.

Practice Problem 4   Find $G \cap H$ if $G = \{!, *, \%, \$\}$ and $H = \{\$, ?, \wedge, +\}$.

We have talked about one important set of numbers, the natural numbers. There are several other sets of numbers that we summarize below.

Sets of Numbers	
Real number	$\{x \mid x$ can be placed on the number line$\}$
Natural numbers	$\{1, 2, 3, 4, 5, \dots\}$
Whole numbers	$\{0, 1, 2, 3, 4, 5, \dots\}$
Integers	$\{\dots, -2, -1, 0, 1, 2, \dots\}$
Rational numbers	$\{x \mid x$ can be written as $\dfrac{p}{q}$ where p and q are integers, and $q \neq 0\}$
Irrational numbers	$\{x \mid x$ is a real number that is not rational$\}$

You are probably more familiar with the terms natural numbers, whole numbers, and integer than the others. Let's look at rational, irrational, and real numbers in more detail.

A **rational number** is a number that can be written as a fraction (with a denominator not equal to 0). Here are some examples of rational numbers:

$$-5, \quad 3.54, \quad \sqrt{9}, \quad \frac{1}{4}$$

The first three numbers can be written as $\dfrac{-5}{1}, \dfrac{354}{100},$ and $\dfrac{3}{1}$, respectively, and so are considered rational numbers. Every integer is rational since it can be written with 1 in the denominator. When a number is written in decimal form, we can easily determine whether or not it is a rational number. If the decimal repeats or terminates, it is a rational number.

$\dfrac{1}{3} = 0.3333\dots = 0.\overline{3}$ and $\dfrac{13}{22} = 0.5909090\dots = 0.5\overline{90}$ are repeating decimals

$\dfrac{3}{10} = 0.3$ and $-1\dfrac{9}{16} = -0.5625$ are terminating decimals   } rational numbers

There are some numbers whose decimal representation is not a repeating or terminating decimal. For example, if we looked at the decimal forms of $\sqrt{2}, \sqrt{6},$ and $\sqrt{7}$, we would see that the decimal does not end and does not contain digits that repeat. These are **irrational numbers.** Pi (π) is another irrational number. When these numbers are used in calculations, we use approximations: $\sqrt{6} \approx 2.449$ and $\pi \approx 3.14$.

All the numbers we have discussed above can be placed on the number line. Some of them are shown below.

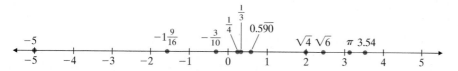

Any number that can be placed on the number line is a **real number.** The set of real numbers is the union of the rational and irrational numbers.

④ Subsets

We have seen that all integers are rational numbers and all rational numbers are real numbers. When all the elements of one set are contained in another set, we say that it is a **subset.** Here is a more formal definition.

Set A is a subset of set B, written $A \subseteq B$, if all elements in A are also in B.

Consider the sets $A = \{$Amy, Jack, Ron$\}$ and $B = \{$Amy, Harry, Lena, Jack, Ron$\}$. All three elements of set A are also in set B. Therefore, set A is a subset of set B, and we can write $A \subseteq B$.

EXAMPLE 5 Determine if the statement is true or false. If false, state the reason.

(a) $A = \{t, v\}$ and $B = \{r, s, t, u, v, w\}$, so $A \subseteq B$.

(b) The set of integers is a subset of the natural numbers.

Solution

(a) True. All the elements of A are also in B.

(b) False. To see why, consider the number -3. -3 is an element of the set of integers, but -3 is not a natural number. So the integers is not a subset of the natural numbers.

The natural numbers, however, is a subset of the set of integers. Do you see why?

NOTE TO STUDENT: Fully worked-out solutions to all of the Practice Problems can be found at the back of the text starting at page SP-1

Practice Problem 5 Determine if the statement is true or false. If false, state the reason.

(a) $C = \{a, b, c, d, e, f\}$ and $D = \{c, f\}$ so $C \subseteq D$.

(b) The set of whole numbers is a subset of the rational numbers.

The table below shows the relationship among the sets of numbers we have discussed.

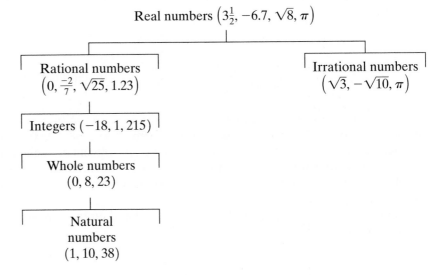

Real numbers $\left(3\frac{1}{2}, -6.7, \sqrt{8}, \pi\right)$

Rational numbers $\left(0, \frac{-2}{7}, \sqrt{25}, 1.23\right)$

Irrational numbers $\left(\sqrt{3}, -\sqrt{10}, \pi\right)$

Integers $(-18, 1, 215)$

Whole numbers $(0, 8, 23)$

Natural numbers $(1, 10, 38)$

Fill in the blank with appropriate word or words.

1. The objects of a set are called _____.

2. When the elements of a set are listed in braces, the set is in _____.

3. The _____ of two sets is the elements the sets have in common.

4. The symbol _____ means 'intersection'.

5. A set that contains no elements is called the _____.

6. If a set is _____, we can count the number of elements it contains.

In exercises 7–14, write the set in roster form.

7. The set of states in the United States that begin with the letter C.

8. $A = \{x \mid x \in N \text{ and } 4 < x < 10\}$

9. $C = \{x \mid x \text{ is odd}\}$

10. $M = \{x \mid x \in P \text{ and } 2 < x < 23\}$

11. $F = \{x \mid x \in N \text{ and } x \text{ is a multiple of 5 between 10 and 50}\}$

12. $B = \{x \mid x \text{ is an integer between } -3 \text{ and } 2, \text{ inclusive}\}$

13. A is the set of integers less than 0.

14. The set of the last five months of the year

Exercises 15–20, write the set in set-builder notation.

15. $O = \{\text{Atlantic, Pacific, Indian, Arctic}\}$

16. $B = \{3, 6, 9, 12, 15\}$

17. $G = \{2, 4, 6, 8\}$

18. $K = \{31, 37, 41, 43\}$

19. $T = \{\text{scalene, isosceles, equilateral}\}$

20. C is the set of planets in our solar system

21. If $A = \{-1, 2, 3, 5, 8\}$ and $B = \{-2, -1, 3, 5\}$, find
    (a) $A \cup B$ (b) $A \cap B$

22. If $C = \{d, e, f, g, h, i, j\}$ and $D = \{x, z\}$, find
    (a) $C \cup D$ (b) $C \cap D$

Given sets A, B, and C, decide if the statements in exercises 23–34 are true or false. If it is false, give the reason.
$A = \{1, 2, 3, 4, 5, \dots\}$, $B = \{10, 20, 30, 40, \dots\}$, $C = \{1, 2, 3, 4, 5\}$

23. B is a finite set

24. $A \subseteq C$

25. $68 \in A$

26. $120 \in B$

27. $B \subseteq A$

28. $B \cap C = \{10, 20, 30, 40\}$

29. $A \cap C = \{ \}$

30. $A \cup B = \{1, 2, 3, 4, 5, \dots\}$

31. *A* is the set of whole numbers

32. *B* = {*x* | *x* ∈ *N* and *x* is a multiple of 10 greater than 5}

33. *A* ∪ *C* is the set of natural numbers

34. *B* ∩ *C* = { }

35. Give an example of a subset of *A*. *A* = {Joe, Ann, Nina, Doug}

36. Give an example of a set of which *B* is a subset. *B* = {poodle, Irish setter, dachshund}

Below is a table of the top 10 most popular boy and girl names for 1980 and 2000. Use the table to answer exercises 37 and 38. Source: www.cherishedmoments.com

	1980		2000	
	Boy	**Girl**	**Boy**	**Girl**
1.	Michael	Jennifer	Jacob	Emily
2.	Jason	Jessica	Michael	Hannah
3.	Christopher	Amanda	Matthew	Madison
4.	David	Melissa	Joshua	Ashley
5.	James	Sarah	Christopher	Sarah
6.	Matthew	Nicole	Nicholas	Alexis
7.	John	Heather	Andrew	Samantha
8.	Joshua	Amy	Joseph	Jessica
9.	Robert	Michelle	Daniel	Taylor
10.	Daniel	Elizabeth	Tyler	Elizabeth

37. (a) Write set *B* in roster form. *B* is the set of the most popular boys' names in 1980 or 2000.

(b) Your answer to part (a) represents a(n) _____ of two sets.

38. (a) Write set *G* in roster form. *G* is the set of the most popular girls' names in 1980 and 2000.

(b) Your answer to part (a) represents a(n) _____ of two sets.

39. Decide which elements of the following set are whole numbers, natural numbers, integers, rational numbers, irrational numbers, or real numbers.

$$\left\{ 3.62, \sqrt{20}, \frac{-3}{11}, 15, \frac{22}{3}, 0, \sqrt{81}, -17 \right\}$$

40. Is the set of whole numbers a subset of the real numbers? Explain.

41. Is the set of integers a subset of the whole numbers? Explain.

42. Which sets of numbers are subsets of the rational numbers?

43. List all sets of numbers of which the whole numbers are a subset.

Solutions to Practice Problems

Chapter 1

1.1 Practice Problems

1. (a) $\dfrac{10}{16} = \dfrac{2 \times 5}{2 \times 8} = \dfrac{5}{8}$ **(b)** $\dfrac{24}{36} = \dfrac{12 \times 2}{12 \times 3} = \dfrac{2}{3}$

(c) $\dfrac{36}{42} = \dfrac{6 \times 6}{6 \times 7} = \dfrac{6}{7}$

2. (a) $\dfrac{4}{12} = \dfrac{2 \times 2 \times 1}{2 \times 2 \times 3} = \dfrac{1}{3}$ **(b)** $\dfrac{25}{125} = \dfrac{5 \times 5 \times 1}{5 \times 5 \times 5} = \dfrac{1}{5}$

(c) $\dfrac{73}{146} = \dfrac{73 \times 1}{73 \times 2} = \dfrac{1}{2}$

3. (a) $\dfrac{18}{6} = \dfrac{3 \times 6}{6} = 3$ **(b)** $\dfrac{146}{73} = \dfrac{73 \times 2}{73} = 2$

(c) $\dfrac{28}{7} = \dfrac{7 \times 4}{7} = 4$

4. 56 out of $154 = \dfrac{56}{154} = \dfrac{2 \times 7 \times 4}{2 \times 7 \times 11} = \dfrac{4}{11}$

5. (a) $\dfrac{12}{7} = 12 \div 7 = 7\overline{)12} = 1\dfrac{5}{7}$

$\dfrac{7}{5}$ Remainder

(b) $\dfrac{20}{5} = 20 \div 5 = 5\overline{)20} = 4$

$\dfrac{20}{0}$ Remainder

6. (a) $3\dfrac{2}{5} = \dfrac{(3 \times 5) + 2}{5} = \dfrac{15 + 2}{5} = \dfrac{17}{5}$

(b) $1\dfrac{3}{7} = \dfrac{(1 \times 7) + 3}{7} = \dfrac{7 + 3}{7} = \dfrac{10}{7}$

(c) $2\dfrac{6}{11} = \dfrac{(2 \times 11) + 6}{11} = \dfrac{22 + 6}{11} = \dfrac{28}{11}$

(d) $4\dfrac{2}{3} = \dfrac{(4 \times 3) + 2}{3} = \dfrac{12 + 2}{3} = \dfrac{14}{3}$

7. (a) $\dfrac{3}{8} = \dfrac{?}{24}$ Observe $8 \times 3 = 24$ **(b)** $\dfrac{5}{6} = \dfrac{?}{30}$

$\dfrac{3 \times 3}{8 \times 3} = \dfrac{9}{24}$ $\dfrac{5 \times 5}{6 \times 5} = \dfrac{25}{30}$

(c) $\dfrac{2}{7} = \dfrac{?}{56}$

$\dfrac{2 \times 8}{7 \times 8} = \dfrac{16}{56}$

1.2 Practice Problems

1. (a) $\dfrac{3}{6} + \dfrac{2}{6} = \dfrac{3 + 2}{6} = \dfrac{5}{6}$ **(b)** $\dfrac{3}{11} + \dfrac{8}{11} = \dfrac{11}{11} = 1$

(c) $\dfrac{1}{8} + \dfrac{2}{8} + \dfrac{1}{8} = \dfrac{1 + 2 + 1}{8} = \dfrac{4}{8} = \dfrac{1}{2}$

(d) $\dfrac{5}{9} + \dfrac{8}{9} = \dfrac{5 + 8}{9} = \dfrac{13}{9} = 1\dfrac{4}{9}$

2. (a) $\dfrac{11}{13} - \dfrac{6}{13} = \dfrac{11 - 6}{13} = \dfrac{5}{13}$

(b) $\dfrac{8}{9} - \dfrac{2}{9} = \dfrac{8 - 2}{9} = \dfrac{6}{9} = \dfrac{2}{3}$

3. Find LCD of $\dfrac{1}{8}$ and $\dfrac{5}{12}$.

$8 = 2 \cdot 2 \cdot 2$
$12 = \Big\downarrow 2 \cdot 2 \cdot 3$
$2 \cdot 2 \cdot 2 \cdot 3 = 24$ LCD $= 24$

4. Find the LCD using prime factors.

$\dfrac{8}{35}$ and $\dfrac{6}{15}$

$35 = 7 \cdot 5$
$15 = \Big| 5 \cdot 3$
$\downarrow \downarrow \downarrow$
$7 \cdot 5 \cdot 3$ LCD $= 105$

5. Find LCD of $\dfrac{5}{12}$ and $\dfrac{7}{30}$.

$12 = 3 \cdot 2 \cdot 2$
$30 = 3 \Big| 2 \cdot 5$
$\downarrow \downarrow \downarrow \downarrow$
$3 \cdot 2 \cdot 2 \cdot 5$ LCD $= 60$

6. Find LCD of $\dfrac{1}{18}, \dfrac{2}{27}$ and $\dfrac{5}{12}$.

$12 = 2 \cdot 2 \cdot 3$
$18 = 2 \Big| 3 \cdot 3$
$27 = \Big| 3 \cdot 3 \cdot 3$
$\downarrow \downarrow \downarrow \downarrow \downarrow$
$2 \cdot 2 \cdot 3 \cdot 3 \cdot 3$ LCD $= 108$

7. Add $\dfrac{1}{8} + \dfrac{5}{12}$

First find the LCD.
$8 = 2 \cdot 2 \cdot 2$
$12 = 2 \cdot 2 \Big| \cdot 3$
$\downarrow \downarrow \downarrow \downarrow$
$2 \cdot 2 \cdot 2 \cdot 3$ LCD $= 24$

Then change to equivalent fractions and add.
$\dfrac{1}{8} \times \dfrac{3}{3} + \dfrac{5}{12} \times \dfrac{2}{2} = \dfrac{3}{24} + \dfrac{10}{24} = \dfrac{3 + 10}{24} = \dfrac{13}{24}$

8. $\dfrac{3}{5} + \dfrac{4}{25} + \dfrac{1}{10}$

First find the LCD.
$5 = 5$
$10 = 2 \cdot 5$
$25 = \Big| 5 \cdot 5$
$\downarrow \downarrow \downarrow$
$2 \cdot 5 \cdot 5$ LCD $= 50$

Then change to equivalent fractions and add.
$\dfrac{3}{5} \times \dfrac{10}{10} + \dfrac{4}{25} \times \dfrac{2}{2} + \dfrac{1}{10} \times \dfrac{5}{5} = \dfrac{30}{50} + \dfrac{8}{50} + \dfrac{5}{50}$

$ = \dfrac{30 + 8 + 5}{50} = \dfrac{43}{50}$

9. Add $\dfrac{1}{49} + \dfrac{3}{14}$

First find the LCD.
$14 = 2 \cdot 7$
$49 = \Big| 7 \cdot 7$
$\downarrow \downarrow \downarrow$
$2 \cdot 7 \cdot 7$ LCD $= 98$

Then change to equivalent fractions and add.
$\dfrac{1}{49} \times \dfrac{2}{2} + \dfrac{3}{14} \times \dfrac{7}{7} = \dfrac{2}{98} + \dfrac{21}{98} = \dfrac{2 + 21}{98} = \dfrac{23}{98}$

10. $\dfrac{1}{12} - \dfrac{1}{30}$

First find the LCD.

$12 = 2 \cdot 2 \cdot 3$

$30 = \quad 2 \cdot 3 \cdot 5$

$\qquad\qquad 2 \cdot 2 \cdot 3 \cdot 5 \qquad$ LCD = 60

Then change to equivalent fractions and subtract.

$\dfrac{1}{12} \times \dfrac{5}{5} - \dfrac{1}{30} \times \dfrac{2}{2} = \dfrac{5}{60} - \dfrac{2}{60} = \dfrac{5-2}{60} = \dfrac{3}{60} = \dfrac{1}{20}$

11. $\dfrac{2}{3} + \dfrac{3}{4} - \dfrac{3}{8}$

First find the LCD.

$3 = \qquad\qquad 3$

$4 = \quad 2 \cdot 2$

$8 = \quad 2 \cdot 2 \cdot 2$

$\qquad 2 \cdot 2 \cdot 2 \cdot 3 \qquad$ LCD = 24

Then change to equivalent fractions and add and subtract.

$\dfrac{2}{3} \times \dfrac{8}{8} + \dfrac{3}{4} \times \dfrac{6}{6} - \dfrac{3}{8} \times \dfrac{3}{3}$

$\qquad = \dfrac{16}{24} + \dfrac{18}{24} - \dfrac{9}{24} = \dfrac{16 + 18 - 9}{24} = \dfrac{25}{24} = 1\dfrac{1}{24}$

12. (a) $1\dfrac{2}{3} + 2\dfrac{4}{5} = \dfrac{5}{3} + \dfrac{14}{5} = \dfrac{5}{3} \times \dfrac{5}{5} + \dfrac{14}{5} \times \dfrac{3}{3} = \dfrac{25}{15} + \dfrac{42}{15}$

$\qquad\qquad = \dfrac{25 + 42}{15} = \dfrac{67}{15} = 4\dfrac{7}{15}$

(b) $5\dfrac{1}{4} - 2\dfrac{2}{3} = \dfrac{21}{4} - \dfrac{8}{3} = \dfrac{21}{4} \times \dfrac{3}{3} - \dfrac{8}{3} \times \dfrac{4}{4} = \dfrac{63}{12} - \dfrac{32}{12}$

$\qquad\qquad = \dfrac{63 - 32}{12} = \dfrac{31}{12} = 2\dfrac{7}{12}$

13.

$4\dfrac{1}{5} + 4\dfrac{1}{5} + 6\dfrac{1}{2} + 6\dfrac{1}{2}$

$= \dfrac{21}{5} + \dfrac{21}{5} + \dfrac{13}{2} + \dfrac{13}{2}$

LCD = 10

$\dfrac{21}{5} \times \dfrac{2}{2} + \dfrac{21}{5} \times \dfrac{2}{2} + \dfrac{13}{2} \times \dfrac{5}{5} + \dfrac{13}{2} \times \dfrac{5}{5}$

$= \dfrac{42}{10} + \dfrac{42}{10} + \dfrac{65}{10} + \dfrac{65}{10} = \dfrac{42 + 42 + 65 + 65}{10} = \dfrac{214}{10} = 21\dfrac{2}{5}$

The perimeter is $21\dfrac{2}{5}$ cm.

1.3 Practice Problems

1. (a) $\dfrac{2}{7} \times \dfrac{5}{11} = \dfrac{2 \cdot 5}{7 \cdot 11} = \dfrac{10}{77}$

(b) $\dfrac{1}{5} \times \dfrac{7}{10} = \dfrac{1 \times 7}{5 \times 10} = \dfrac{7}{50}$

(c) $\dfrac{9}{5} \times \dfrac{1}{4} = \dfrac{9 \times 1}{5 \times 4} = \dfrac{9}{20}$

(d) $\dfrac{8}{9} \times \dfrac{3}{10} = \dfrac{8 \times 3}{9 \times 10} = \dfrac{24}{90} = \dfrac{4}{15}$

2. (a) $\dfrac{3}{5} \times \dfrac{4}{3} = \dfrac{3 \cdot 4}{5 \cdot 3} = \dfrac{4}{5}$

(b) $\dfrac{9}{10} \times \dfrac{5}{12} = \dfrac{3 \cdot 3}{2 \cdot 5} \times \dfrac{5}{2 \cdot 2 \cdot 3} = \dfrac{3}{8}$

3. (a) $4 \times \dfrac{2}{7} = \dfrac{4}{1} \times \dfrac{2}{7} = \dfrac{4 \cdot 2}{1 \cdot 7} = \dfrac{8}{7} = 1\dfrac{1}{7}$

(b) $12 \times \dfrac{3}{4} = \dfrac{12}{1} \times \dfrac{3}{4} = \dfrac{2 \cdot 2 \cdot 3}{1} \times \dfrac{3}{2 \cdot 2} = 9$

4. Multiply. $5\dfrac{3}{5}$ times $3\dfrac{3}{4}$

$5\dfrac{3}{5} \times 3\dfrac{3}{4} = \dfrac{28}{5} \times \dfrac{15}{4} = \dfrac{2 \cdot 2 \cdot 7}{5} \times \dfrac{3 \cdot 5}{2 \cdot 2} = \dfrac{21}{1} = 21$

21 square miles

5. $3\dfrac{1}{2} \times \dfrac{1}{14} \times 4 = \dfrac{7}{2} \times \dfrac{1}{14} \times \dfrac{4}{1} = \dfrac{7}{2} \times \dfrac{1}{2 \cdot 7} \times \dfrac{2 \cdot 2}{1} = 1$

6. (a) $\dfrac{2}{5} \div \dfrac{1}{3} = \dfrac{2}{5} \times \dfrac{3}{1} = \dfrac{6}{5}$

(b) $\dfrac{12}{13} \div \dfrac{4}{3} = \dfrac{2 \cdot 2 \cdot 3}{13} \times \dfrac{3}{2 \cdot 2} = \dfrac{9}{13}$

7. (a) $\dfrac{3}{7} \div 6 = \dfrac{3}{7} \div \dfrac{6}{1} = \dfrac{3}{7} \times \dfrac{1}{6} = \dfrac{3}{42} = \dfrac{1}{14}$

(b) $8 \div \dfrac{2}{3} = \dfrac{8}{1} \times \dfrac{3}{2} = 12$

8. (a) $\dfrac{\frac{3}{11}}{\frac{5}{7}} = \dfrac{3}{11} \div \dfrac{5}{7} = \dfrac{3}{11} \times \dfrac{7}{5} = \dfrac{21}{55}$

(b) $\dfrac{\frac{12}{5}}{\frac{8}{15}} = \dfrac{12}{5} \div \dfrac{8}{15} = \dfrac{2 \cdot 2 \cdot 3}{5} \times \dfrac{3 \cdot 5}{2 \cdot 2 \cdot 2} = \dfrac{9}{2} = 4\dfrac{1}{2}$

9. (a) $1\dfrac{2}{5} \div 2\dfrac{1}{3} = \dfrac{7}{5} \div \dfrac{7}{3} = \dfrac{7}{5} \times \dfrac{3}{7} = \dfrac{3}{5}$

(b) $4\dfrac{2}{3} \div 7 = \dfrac{14}{3} \times \dfrac{1}{7} = \dfrac{2 \cdot 7}{3} \times \dfrac{1}{7} = \dfrac{2}{3}$

(c) $\dfrac{1\frac{1}{5}}{1\frac{2}{7}} = 1\dfrac{1}{5} \div 1\dfrac{2}{7} = \dfrac{6}{5} \div \dfrac{9}{7} = \dfrac{6}{5} \times \dfrac{7}{9} = \dfrac{2 \cdot 3}{5} \times \dfrac{7}{3 \cdot 3} = \dfrac{14}{15}$

10. $64 \div 5\dfrac{1}{3} = 64 \div \dfrac{16}{3} = 64 \times \dfrac{3}{16} = 12$ jars

11. $25\dfrac{1}{2} \times 5\dfrac{1}{4} = \dfrac{51}{2} \times \dfrac{21}{4} = \dfrac{1071}{8} = 133\dfrac{7}{8}$ miles

1.4 Practice Problems

1. (a) $0.9 = \dfrac{9}{10} =$ nine tenths   **(b)** $\dfrac{9}{100} =$ nine hundredths.

(c) $0.731 = \dfrac{731}{1000} =$ seven hundred thirty-one thousandths

(d) $1.371 = 1\dfrac{371}{1000} =$ one and three hundred seventy-one thousandths

(e) $0.0005 = \dfrac{5}{10,000} =$ five ten-thousandths

2. (a) $\dfrac{3}{8}$

$\begin{array}{r} 0.375 \\ 8\overline{)3.000} \\ \underline{2\ 4} \\ 60 \\ \underline{56} \\ 40 \\ \underline{40} \\ 0 \end{array}$

(b) $\dfrac{7}{200}$

$\begin{array}{r} 0.035 \\ 200\overline{)7.000} \\ \underline{6\ 00} \\ 1\ 000 \\ \underline{1\ 000} \\ 0 \end{array}$

(c) $\dfrac{33}{20}$

$\begin{array}{r} 1.65 \\ 20\overline{)33.00} \\ \underline{20} \\ 13\ 0 \\ \underline{12\ 0} \\ 1\ 00 \\ \underline{1\ 00} \\ 0 \end{array}$

3. (a) $\dfrac{1}{6}$ $6\overline{)1.000}$ $0.166 = 0.1\overline{6}$

$$\underline{6}$$
$$40$$
$$\underline{36}$$
$$40$$
$$\underline{36}$$
$$4$$

(b) $\dfrac{5}{11}$ $11\overline{)5.0000}$ $0.4545 = .\overline{45}$

$$\underline{4\;4}$$
$$60$$
$$\underline{55}$$
$$50$$
$$\underline{44}$$
$$60$$
$$\underline{55}$$
$$5$$

4. (a) 0.8 $\dfrac{8}{10} = \dfrac{2 \cdot 2 \cdot 2}{2 \cdot 5} = \dfrac{4}{5}$

(b) 0.88 $\dfrac{88}{100} = \dfrac{11 \cdot 2 \cdot 2}{5 \cdot 5 \cdot 2 \cdot 2} = \dfrac{22}{25}$

(c) 0.45 $\dfrac{45}{100} = \dfrac{5 \cdot 3 \cdot 3}{5 \cdot 5 \cdot 2 \cdot 2} = \dfrac{9}{20}$

(d) 0.148 $\dfrac{148}{1000} = \dfrac{2 \cdot 2 \cdot 37}{5 \cdot 5 \cdot 5 \cdot 2 \cdot 2 \cdot 2} = \dfrac{37}{250}$

(e) 0.612 $\dfrac{612}{1000} = \dfrac{17 \cdot 3 \cdot 3 \cdot 2 \cdot 2}{5 \cdot 5 \cdot 5 \cdot 2 \cdot 2 \cdot 2} = \dfrac{153}{250}$

(f) 0.016 $\dfrac{16}{1000} = \dfrac{2 \cdot 2 \cdot 2 \cdot 2}{5 \cdot 5 \cdot 5 \cdot 2 \cdot 2 \cdot 2} = \dfrac{2}{125}$

5. (a) $\begin{array}{r} 3.12 \\ 5.08 \\ 1.42 \\ \hline 9.62 \end{array}$ (b) $\begin{array}{r} 152.003 \\ -136.118 \\ \hline 15.885 \end{array}$ (c) $\begin{array}{r} 1.1 \\ 3.16 \\ 5.123 \\ \hline 9.383 \end{array}$ (d) $\begin{array}{r} 1.0052 \\ -0.1234 \\ \hline 0.8818 \end{array}$

6. (a) $\begin{array}{r} 0.061 \\ 5.0008 \\ 1.3 \\ \hline 6.3618 \end{array}$ (b) $\begin{array}{r} 18.000 \\ -\;0.126 \\ \hline 17.874 \end{array}$

7. $\begin{array}{r} 0.5 \\ \times\;0.3 \\ \hline 0.15 \end{array}$

8. $\begin{array}{r} 0.12 \\ \times\;\;0.4 \\ \hline 0.048 \end{array}$

9. (a) $\begin{array}{r} 1.23 \\ \times\;0.005 \\ \hline 0.00615 \end{array}$ (b) $\begin{array}{r} 0.00002 \\ \times\;\;0.003 \\ \hline 0.00000006 \end{array}$

10. $6\overline{)31.56}$ $\$5.26$

$$\underline{30}$$
$$15$$
$$\underline{12}$$
$$36$$
$$\underline{36}$$
$$0$$

$\$5.26$ for each box of paper

11. $.06.\overline{)1800.00.}$ $30{,}000.$

12. $4.9.\overline{)0.0.1764}$

$$49\overline{)0.1764} \qquad 0.0036$$
$$\underline{147}$$
$$294$$
$$\underline{294}$$
$$0$$

13. (a) $0.0016 \times 100 = 0.16$
Move decimal point 2 places to the right.
  (b) $2.34 \times 1000 = 2340$
Move decimal point 3 places to the right.
  (c) $56.75 \times 10{,}000 = 567{,}500$
Move decimal point 4 places to the right.

14. (a) $\dfrac{5.82}{10}$ (Move decimal point 1 place to the left.) 0.582

  (b) $\dfrac{123.4}{1000}$ (Move decimal point 3 places to the left.) 0.1234

  (c) $\dfrac{0.00614}{10{,}000}$ (Move decimal point 4 places to the left.)
0.000000614

Chapter 2

2.1 Practice Problems

1.

Number	Integer	Rational Number	Irrational Number	Real Number
(a) $-\dfrac{2}{5}$		X		X
(b) $1.515151\ldots$		X		X
(c) -8	X	X		X
(d) π			X	X

2. (a) Population growth of 1,259 is $+1{,}259$.
  (b) Depreciation of 763 is -763.00.
  (c) Wind chill factor of minus 10 is -10.

3. (a) The additive inverse of $+\dfrac{2}{5}$ is $-\dfrac{2}{5}$.

  (b) The additive inverse of -1.92 is $+1.92$.
  (c) The opposite of a loss of 12 yards on a football play is a gain of 12 yards on the play.

4. (a) $|-7.34| = 7.34$

  (b) $\left|\dfrac{5}{8}\right| = \dfrac{5}{8}$ (c) $\left|\dfrac{0}{2}\right| = \dfrac{0}{2} = 0$

5. (a) $37 + 19$
$37 + 19 = 56$
$37 + 19 = +56$
  (b) $-23 + (-35)$
$23 + 35 = 58$
$-23 + (-35) = -58$

6. $-\dfrac{3}{5} + \left(-\dfrac{4}{7}\right)$

$$-\dfrac{21}{35} + \left(-\dfrac{20}{35}\right)$$

$$-\dfrac{21}{35} + \left(-\dfrac{20}{35}\right) = -\dfrac{41}{35}$$

7. $-12.7 + (-9.38)$
$12.7 + 9.38 = 22.08$
$-12.7 + (-9.38) = -22.08$

8. $-7 + (-11) + (-33)$
$= -18 + (-33)$
$= -51$

9. $-9 + 15$
$15 - 9 = 6$
$-9 + 15 = 6$

10. $-\dfrac{5}{12} + \dfrac{7}{12} + \left(-\dfrac{11}{12}\right)$

$$= \dfrac{2}{12} + \left(-\dfrac{11}{12}\right) = -\dfrac{9}{12} = -\dfrac{3}{4}$$

11. $-6.3 + (-8.0) + 3.5$
$= -14.3 + 3.5$
$= -10.8$

12. $\begin{array}{ll} -6 & \quad +5 + (-7) + (-2) + 5 + 3 \\ -6 & \quad +5 \\ -7 & \quad +5 \\ \underline{-2} & \quad \underline{+3} \\ -15 & \quad 13 \end{array}$

$-15 + 13 = -2$

13. (a) $-2.9 + (-5.7) = -8.6$ **(b)** $\dfrac{2}{3} + \left(-\dfrac{1}{4}\right)$

$= \dfrac{8}{12} + \left(-\dfrac{3}{12}\right) = \dfrac{5}{12}$

2.2 Practice Problems

1. $9 - (-3) = 9 + (+3) = 12$

2. $-12 - (-5) = -12 + (+5) = -7$

3. (a) $\dfrac{5}{9} - \dfrac{7}{9} = \dfrac{5}{9} + \left(-\dfrac{7}{9}\right) = -\dfrac{2}{9}$

(b) $-\dfrac{5}{21} - \left(-\dfrac{3}{7}\right) = -\dfrac{5}{21} + \left(+\dfrac{3}{7}\right) = -\dfrac{5}{21} + \left(+\dfrac{9}{21}\right) = +\dfrac{4}{21}$

4. $-17.3 - (-17.3)$
$= -17.3 + 17.3$
$= 0$

5. (a) $-21 - 9$ **(b)** $17 - 36$
$\quad = -21 + (-9)$ $\quad = 17 + (-36)$
$\quad = -30$ $\quad = -19$

(c) $12 - (-15)$ **(d)** $\dfrac{3}{5} - 2$
$\quad = 12 + (+15)$ $\quad = \dfrac{3}{5} + (-2)$
$\quad = 27$
$\quad\quad = \dfrac{3}{5} + \left(-\dfrac{10}{5}\right) = -\dfrac{7}{5}$ or $-1\dfrac{2}{5}$

6. $350 - (-186)$
$= 350 + 186$
$= 536$ The helicopter is 536 feet from the sunken vessel.

2.3 Practice Problems

1. (a) $(-6)(-2) = 12$

(b) $(7)(9) = 63$

(c) $\left(-\dfrac{3}{5}\right)\left(\dfrac{2}{7}\right) = -\dfrac{6}{35}$

(d) $\left(\dfrac{5}{6}\right)(-7) = \left(\dfrac{5}{6}\right)\left(-\dfrac{7}{1}\right) = -\dfrac{35}{6}$

2. $(-5)(-2)(-6)$
$= (+10)(-6) = -60$

3. (a) positive; $-2(-3) = 6$ **(b)** negative; $(-1)(-3)(-2)$
$= 3(-2)$
$= -6$

(c) positive; $-4\left(-\dfrac{1}{4}\right)(-2)(-6)$
$= 1(-2)(-6)$
$= -2(-6)$
$= +12$ or 12

4. (a) $-36 \div (-2) = 18$

(b) $-49 \div 7 = -7$

(c) $\dfrac{50}{-10} = -5$

(d) $\dfrac{-39}{13} = -3$

5. (a) $-12.6 \div (-1.8) = 7$

(b) $0.45 \div (-0.9) = -0.5$

6. $-\dfrac{5}{16} \div \left(-\dfrac{10}{13}\right) = \left(-\dfrac{5}{16}\right)\left(-\dfrac{13}{10}\right) = \left(-\dfrac{\overset{1}{\cancel{5}}}{16}\right)\left(-\dfrac{13}{\underset{2}{\cancel{10}}}\right) = \dfrac{13}{32}$

7. (a) $\dfrac{-12}{-\dfrac{4}{5}} = -12 \div \left(-\dfrac{4}{5}\right) = -12\left(-\dfrac{5}{4}\right) = \left(-\dfrac{\overset{3}{\cancel{12}}}{1}\right)\left(-\dfrac{5}{\underset{1}{\cancel{4}}}\right) = 15$

(b) $\dfrac{-\dfrac{2}{9}}{\dfrac{8}{13}} = -\dfrac{2}{9} \div \dfrac{8}{13} = -\dfrac{\overset{1}{\cancel{2}}}{9}\left(\dfrac{13}{\underset{4}{\cancel{8}}}\right) = -\dfrac{13}{36}$

8. (a) $6(-10) = -60$ yards

(b) $7(15) = 105$ yards

(c) $-60 + 105 = 45$ yards

2.4 Practice Problems

1. (a) $6(6)(6)(6) = 6^4$

(b) $-2(-2)(-2)(-2)(-2) = (-2)^5$

(c) $108(108)(108) = 108^3$

(d) $-11(-11)(-11)(-11)(-11)(-11) = (-11)^6$

(e) $(w)(w)(w) = w^3$

(f) $(z)(z)(z)(z) = z^4$

2. (a) $3^5 = (3)(3)(3)(3)(3) = 243$

(b) $2^2 + 3^3$
$2^2 = (2)(2) = 4$
$3^3 = (3)(3)(3) = 27$
$4 + 27 = 31$

3. (a) $(-3)^3 = -27$

(b) $(-2)^6 = 64$

(c) $-2^4 = -(2^4) = -16$

(d) $-(3^6) = -729$

4. (a) $\left(\dfrac{1}{3}\right)^3 = \left(\dfrac{1}{3}\right)\left(\dfrac{1}{3}\right)\left(\dfrac{1}{3}\right) = \dfrac{1}{27}$

(b) $(0.3)^4 = (0.3)(0.3)(0.3)(0.3) = 0.0081$

(c) $\left(\dfrac{3}{2}\right)^4 = \left(\dfrac{3}{2}\right)\left(\dfrac{3}{2}\right)\left(\dfrac{3}{2}\right)\left(\dfrac{3}{2}\right) = \dfrac{81}{16}$

(d) $(3)^4(4)^2$
$3^4 = (3)(3)(3)(3) = 81$
$4^2 = (4)(4) = 16$
$(81)(16) = 1296$

(e) $4^2 - 2^4 = 16 - 16 = 0$

2.5 Practice Problems

1. $25 \div 5 \cdot 6 + 2^3$
$= 25 \div 5 \cdot 6 + 8$
$= 5 \cdot 6 + 8$
$= 30 + 8$
$= 38$

2. $(-4)^3 - 2^6$
$= -64 - 64$
$= -128$

3. $6 - (8 - 12)^2 + 8 \div 2$
$= 6 - (-4)^2 + 8 \div 2$
$= 6 - (16) + 8 \div 2$
$= 6 - 16 + 4$
$= -10 + 4$
$= -6$

4. $\left(-\dfrac{1}{7}\right)\left(-\dfrac{14}{5}\right) + \left(-\dfrac{1}{2}\right) \div \left(\dfrac{3}{4}\right)$

$= \left(-\dfrac{1}{7}\right)\left(-\dfrac{14}{5}\right) + \left(-\dfrac{1}{2}\right) \times \left(\dfrac{4}{3}\right)$

$= \dfrac{2}{5} + \left(-\dfrac{2}{3}\right)$

$= \dfrac{2 \cdot 3}{5 \cdot 3} + \left(-\dfrac{2 \cdot 5}{3 \cdot 5}\right)$

$= \dfrac{6}{15} + \left(-\dfrac{10}{15}\right) = -\dfrac{4}{15}$

2.6 Practice Problems

1. (a) $3(x + 2y) = 3x + 6y$

(b) $-a(a - 3b) = -a(a) + (-a)(-3b) = -a^2 + 3ab$

2. (a) $-(-3x + y) = (-1)(-3x + y) = (-1)(-3x) + (-1)(y)$

$= 3x - y$

3. (a) $\dfrac{3}{5}(a^2 - 5a + 25) = \left(\dfrac{3}{5}\right)(a^2) + \left(\dfrac{3}{5}\right)(-5a) + \left(\dfrac{3}{5}\right)(25)$

$= \dfrac{3}{5}a^2 - 3a + 15$

(b) $2.5(x^2 - 3.5x + 1.2)$

$= (2.5)(x^2) + (2.5)(-3.5x) + (2.5)(1.2)$

$= 2.5x^2 - 8.75x + 3$

4. $-4x(x - 2y + 3) = (-4)(x)(x) - (-4)(x)(2)(y)$

$\qquad\qquad\qquad\qquad + (-4)(x)(3)$

$= -4x^2 + 8xy - 12x$

5. $(3x^2 - 2x)(-4) = (3x^2)(-4) - (2x)(-4) = -12x^2 + 8x$

6. $400(6x + 9y) = 400(6x) + 400(9y)$

$= 2400x + 3600y$

2.7 Practice Problems

1. (a) $5a$ and $8a$ are like terms.

$2b$ and $-4b$ are like terms.

(b) y^2 and $-7y^2$ are like terms. These are the only like terms.

2. (a) $16y^3 + 9y^3 = (16 + 9)y^3 = 25y^3$

(b) $5a + 7a + 4a = (5 + 7 + 4)a = 16a$

3. $-8y^2 - 9y^2 + 4y^2 = (-8 - 9 + 4)y^2 = -13y^2$

4. (a) $1.3x + 3a - 9.6x + 2a = -8.3x + 5a$

(b) $5ab - 2ab^2 - 3a^2b + 6ab = 5ab + 6ab - 2ab^2 - 3a^2b$

$= 11ab - 2ab^2 - 3a^2b$

(c) $7x^2y - 2xy^2 - 3x^2y - 4xy^2 + 5x^2y$

$= 7x^2y - 3x^2y + 5x^2y - 2xy^2 - 4xy^2 = 9x^2y - 6xy^2$

5. $5xy - 2x^2y + 6xy^2 - xy - 3xy^2 - 7x^2y$

$= 5xy - xy - 2x^2y - 7x^2y + 6xy^2 - 3xy^2$

$= 4xy - 9x^2y + 3xy^2$

6. $\dfrac{1}{7}a^2 + 2a^2 = \dfrac{1}{7}a^2 + \dfrac{2}{1}a^2 = \dfrac{1}{7}a^2 + \dfrac{2 \cdot 7}{1 \cdot 7}a^2$

$= \dfrac{1}{7}a^2 + \dfrac{14}{7}a^2 = \dfrac{15}{7}a^2$

$-\dfrac{5}{12}b - \dfrac{1}{3}b = -\dfrac{5}{12}b - \dfrac{1 \cdot 4}{3 \cdot 4}b = -\dfrac{5}{12}b - \dfrac{4}{12}b$

$= -\dfrac{9}{12}b = -\dfrac{3}{4}b$

Thus, our solution is $\dfrac{15}{7}a^2 - \dfrac{3}{4}b$

7. $5a(2 - 3b) - 4(6a + 2ab) = 10a - 15ab - 24a - 8ab$

$= -14a - 23ab$

2.8 Practice Problems

1. $4 - \dfrac{1}{2}x = 4 - \dfrac{1}{2}(-8)$

$= 4 + 4$

$= 8$

2. (a) $4x^2 = 4(-3)^2 = 4(9) = 36$

(b) $(4x)^2 = [4(-3)]^2 = [-12]^2 = 144$

3. $2x^2 - 3x = 2(-2)^2 - 3(-2)$

$= 2(4) - 3(-2)$

$= 8 + 6$

$= 14$

4. Area of a triangle is

$A = \dfrac{1}{2}ba$

altitude $= 3$ meters (m)

base $= 7$ meters (m)

$A = \dfrac{1}{2}(7 \text{ m})(3 \text{ m})$

$= \dfrac{1}{2}(7)(3)(m)(m)$

$= \left(\dfrac{7}{2}\right)(3)(m)^2$

$= \dfrac{21}{2}(m)^2$

$= 10.5$ square meters

5. Area of a circle is

$A = \pi r^2$

$r = 3$ meters

$A \approx 3.14(3 \text{ m})^2$

$= 3.14(9)(m)^2$

$= 28.26$ square meters

6. Formula $\quad C = \dfrac{5}{9}(F - 32)$

$= \dfrac{5}{9}(68 - 32)$

$= \dfrac{5}{9}(36)$

$= 5(4)$

$= 20°$ Celsius

7. Use the formula.

$k = 1.61 \ (r) \qquad$ Replace r by 35.

$k = 1.61 \ (35)$

$k = 56.35 \qquad$ The truck is violating the minimum speed limit.

2.9 Practice Problems

1. $5[4x - 3(y - 2)]$

$= 5[4x - 3y + 6]$

$= 20x - 15y + 30$

2. $-3[2a - (3b - c) + 4a]$

$= -3[2a - 3b + c + 4a]$

$= -3[6a - 3b + c]$

$= -18a + 9b - 3c$

3. $3[4x - 2(1 - x)] - [3x + (x - 2)]$

$= 3[4x - 2 + 2x] - [3x + x - 2]$

$= 12x - 6 + 6x - 3x - x + 2$

$= 14x - 4$

4. $-2\{5x - 3x[2x - (x^2 - 4x)]\}$

$= -2\{5x - 3x[2x - x^2 + 4x]\}$

$= -2\{5x - 3x[6x - x^2]\}$

$= -2\{5x - 18x^2 + 3x^3\}$

$= -10x + 36x^2 - 6x^3$

$= -6x^3 + 36x^2 - 10x$

Chapter 3

3.1 Practice Problems

1. $x + 14 = 23$
$x + 14 + (-14) = 23 + (-14)$
$x + 0 = 9$
$x = 9$
Check. $9 + 14 = 23$
$23 = 23$

2. $17 = x - 5$
$\underline{+\ 5\qquad\ +\ 5}$ **Check.** $17 \overset{?}{=} 22 - 5$
$22 = x$ $17 = 17$

3. $0.5 - 1.2 = x - 0.3$
$-0.7 = x - 0.3$
$\underline{+0.3\qquad\ +\ 0.3}$ **Check.** $0.5 - 1.2 \overset{?}{=} -0.4 - 0.3$
$-0.4 = x$ $-0.7 = -0.7$

4. $x + 8 = -22 + 6$
$x = -2$
Check. $-2 + 8 \overset{?}{=} -22 + 6$
$6 \neq -16$ This is not true.
Thus $x = -2$ is not a solution. Solve to find the solution.
$x + 8 = -22 + 6 = -16$
$x = -16 - 8$
$x = -24$

5. $\dfrac{1}{20} - \dfrac{1}{2} = x + \dfrac{3}{5}$ **Check.**

$\dfrac{1}{20} - \dfrac{1 \cdot 10}{2 \cdot 10} = x + \dfrac{3 \cdot 4}{5 \cdot 4}$ $\dfrac{1}{20} - \dfrac{1}{2} \overset{?}{=} -1\dfrac{1}{20} + \dfrac{3}{5}$

$\dfrac{1}{20} - \dfrac{10}{20} = x + \dfrac{12}{20}$ $\dfrac{1}{20} - \dfrac{10}{20} \overset{?}{=} -\dfrac{21}{20} + \dfrac{12}{20}$

$-\dfrac{9}{20} = x + \dfrac{12}{20}$ $-\dfrac{9}{20} = -\dfrac{9}{20}$ ✓

$-\dfrac{9}{20} - \dfrac{12}{20} = x + \dfrac{12}{20} - \dfrac{12}{20}$

$-\dfrac{21}{20} = -1\dfrac{1}{20} = x$

3.2 Practice Problems

1. $\cancel{(8)}\dfrac{1}{\cancel{8}}x = -2(8)$ **2.** $\dfrac{\cancel{9}x}{\cancel{9}} = \dfrac{72}{9}$ **3.** $\dfrac{\cancel{6}x}{\cancel{6}} = \dfrac{50}{6}$

$x = -16$ $x = 8$ $x = \dfrac{25}{3}$

4. $\dfrac{-\cancel{27}x}{-\cancel{27}} = \dfrac{54}{-27}$ **5.** $\dfrac{-x}{-1} = \dfrac{36}{-1}$ **6.** $\dfrac{-51}{-6} = \dfrac{-6x}{-6}$

$x = -2$ $x = -36$ $\dfrac{17}{2} = x$

7. $16.2 = 5.2x - 3.4x$
$16.2 = 1.8x$
$\dfrac{16.2}{1.8} = \dfrac{1.8x}{1.8}$
$9 = x$

3.3 Practice Problems

1. $9x + 2 = 38$ **Check.** $9(4) + 2 \overset{?}{=} 38$
$\underline{-\ 2\quad -2}$ $36 + 2 \overset{?}{=} 38$
$\dfrac{9x}{9} = \dfrac{36}{9}$ $38 = 38$ ✓
$x = 4$

2. $13x = 2x - 66$ **Check.** $13(-6) \overset{?}{=} 2(-6) - 66$
$\underline{-\ 2x\quad -2x}$ $-78 \overset{?}{=} -12 - 66$
$\dfrac{11x}{11} = \dfrac{-66}{11}$ $-78 = -78$
$x = -6$

3. $3x + 2 = 5x + 2$ **Check.** $3(0) + 2 \overset{?}{=} 5(0) + 2$
$\underline{-\ 2\qquad\ -\ 2}$ $2 = 2$
$3x = 5x$
$\underline{-5x\quad\ -5x}$
$-2x = 0$
$x = 0$

4. $-z + 8 - z = 3z + 10 - 3$
$-2z + 8 = 3z + 7$
$\underline{-3z\qquad\ -3z}$
$-5z + 8 = 7$
$\underline{-\ 8\quad = -8}$
$\dfrac{-5z}{-5} = \dfrac{-1}{-5}$
$z = \dfrac{1}{5}$

5. $4x - (x + 3) = 12 - 3(x - 2)$
$4x - x - 3 = 12 - 3x + 6$
$3x - 3 = -3x + 18$
$\underline{+3x\qquad\ +\ 3x}$
$6x - 3 = 18$
$\underline{+3\qquad +3}$
$\dfrac{6x}{6} = \dfrac{21}{6}$
$x = \dfrac{21}{6} = \dfrac{7}{2}$ or $3\dfrac{1}{2}$

Check. $4\left(\dfrac{7}{2}\right) - \left(\dfrac{7}{2} + 3\right) \overset{?}{=} 12 - 3\left(\dfrac{7}{2} - 2\right)$

$14 - \dfrac{13}{2} \overset{?}{=} 12 - 3\left(\dfrac{3}{2}\right)$

$\dfrac{28}{2} - \dfrac{13}{2} \overset{?}{=} \dfrac{24}{2} - \dfrac{9}{2};\quad \dfrac{15}{2} = \dfrac{15}{2}$ ✓

6. $4(-2x - 3) = -5(x - 2) + 2$
$-8x - 12 = -5x + 10 + 2$
$-8x - 12 = -5x + 12$
$\underline{+5x\qquad\ +5x}$
$-3x - 12 = 12$
$\underline{+12 = +12}$
$\dfrac{-3x}{-3} = \dfrac{24}{-3}$ ✓
$x = -8$

7. $0.3x - 2(x + 0.1) = 0.4(x - 3) - 1.1$
$0.3x - 2x - 0.2 = 0.4x - 1.2 - 1.1$
$-1.7x - 0.2 = 0.4x - 2.3$
$\underline{-0.4x\qquad\ -0.4x}$
$-2.1x - 0.2 = -2.3$ ✓
$\underline{+\ 0.2\quad +0.2}$
$\dfrac{-2.1x}{-2.1} = \dfrac{-2.1}{-2.1}$
$x = 1$

8. $5(2z - 1) + 7 = 7z - 4(z + 3)$
$10z - 5 + 7 = 7z - 4z - 12$
$10z + 2 = 3z - 12$
$\underline{-3z\qquad\ -\ 3z}$
$7z + 2 = -12$
$\underline{-2\qquad\ -\ 2}$
$\dfrac{7z}{7} = -\dfrac{14}{7}$
$z = -2$

Check. $5[2(-2) - 1] + 7 \overset{?}{=} 7(-2) - 4[-2 + 3]$

$5(-5) + 7 \overset{?}{=} -14 - 4(1)$

$-25 + 7 \overset{?}{=} -18$

$-18 = -18$ ✓

3.4 Practice Problems

1. $\dfrac{3}{8}x - \dfrac{3}{2} = \dfrac{1}{4}x$

$3x - 12 = \quad 2x$

$\dfrac{-2x \qquad\qquad -2x}{x - 12 = \quad 0}$

$\dfrac{+12 \quad +12}{x = \quad 12}$

2. $\dfrac{5x}{4} - 1 = \dfrac{3x}{4} + \dfrac{1}{2}$

$5x - 4 = 3x + 2$

$\dfrac{-3x \qquad -3x}{2x - 4 = \quad +2}$

$\dfrac{+4 = \qquad +4}{\dfrac{2x}{2} = \dfrac{6}{2}}$

$x = 3$

Check. $\dfrac{5(3)}{4} - 1 \overset{?}{=} \dfrac{3(3)}{4} + \dfrac{1}{2}$

$\dfrac{15}{4} - 1 \overset{?}{=} \dfrac{9}{4} + \dfrac{1}{2}$

$\dfrac{15}{4} - \dfrac{4}{4} \overset{?}{=} \dfrac{9}{4} + \dfrac{2}{4}$

$\dfrac{11}{4} = \dfrac{11}{4}$ ✓

3. $\dfrac{x + 6}{9} = \dfrac{x}{6} + \dfrac{1}{2}$

$\dfrac{x}{9} + \dfrac{6}{9} = \dfrac{x}{6} + \dfrac{1}{2}$

$18\left(\dfrac{x}{9}\right) + 18\left(\dfrac{6}{9}\right) = 18\left(\dfrac{x}{6}\right) + 18\left(\dfrac{1}{2}\right)$

$2x + 12 = 3x + 9$

$\dfrac{-2x \qquad\quad -2x}{12 = x + 9}$

$\dfrac{-9 \qquad - 9}{3 = x}$

4. $\dfrac{1}{3}(x - 2) = \dfrac{1}{4}(x + 5) - \dfrac{5}{3}$

$\dfrac{1}{3}x - \dfrac{2}{3} = \dfrac{1}{4}x + \dfrac{5}{4} - \dfrac{5}{3}$

$4x - 8 = \quad 3x + 15 - 20$

$4x - 8 = \quad 3x - 5$

$\dfrac{-3x \qquad = -3x}{x - 8 = \qquad -5}$

$\dfrac{+8 \qquad\qquad +8}{x = \qquad 3}$

Check. $\dfrac{1}{3}(3 - 2) \overset{?}{=} \dfrac{1}{4}(3 + 5) - \dfrac{5}{3}$

$\dfrac{1}{3}(1) \overset{?}{=} \dfrac{1}{4}(8) - \dfrac{5}{3}$

$\dfrac{1}{3} \overset{?}{=} 2 - \dfrac{5}{3}$

$\dfrac{1}{3} \overset{?}{=} \dfrac{6}{3} - \dfrac{5}{3}$

$\dfrac{1}{3} = \dfrac{1}{3}$ ✓

5. $\quad 2.8 = 0.3(x - 2) + 2(0.1x - 0.3)$

$2.8 = 0.3x - 0.6 + 0.2x - 0.6$

$10(2.8) = 10(0.3x) - 10(0.6) + 10(0.2x) - 10(0.6)$

$28 = 3x - 6 + 2x - 6$

$28 = 5x - 12$

$\dfrac{+12 \qquad\quad + 12}{40 = 5x}$

$8 = x$

3.5 Practice Problems

1. (a) $x + 4$ **(b)** $3x$ **(c)** $x - 8$ **(d)** $\dfrac{1}{4}x$

2. (a) $3x + 8$ **(b)** $3(x + 8)$ **(c)** $\dfrac{1}{3}(x + 4)$

3. Let a = Ann's hours per week.
Then $a - 17$ = Marie's hours per week.

4. $l = 2w + 5$ width = w

length = $2w + 5$

w

5. 1st angle = $s - 16$
2nd angle = s
3rd angle = $2s$

$2s$

s $s - 16$

6. Let x = the number of students in the fall.

$\dfrac{2}{3}x$ = the number of students in the spring.

$\dfrac{1}{5}x$ = the number of students in the summer.

3.6 Practice Problems

1. (a) $7 > 2$ **(b)** $-3 > -4$ **(c)** $-1 < 2$

(d) $-8 < -5$ **(e)** $0 > -2$ **(f)** $\dfrac{2}{5} > \dfrac{3}{8}$

2. (a) $x > 5$; x is greater than 5

(b) $x \le -2$; x is less than or equal to -2

(c) $3 > x$; 3 is greater than x (or x is less than 3)

(d) $x \ge -\dfrac{3}{2}$; x is greater than or equal to $-\dfrac{3}{2}$

3. (a) $t \le 180$ **(b)** $d < 15{,}000$

4. (a) $\quad 7 > 2$ **(b)** $-3 < -1$

$-14 < -4$ $3 > 1$

(c) $-10 \ge -20$ **(d)** $-15 \le -5$

$1 \le 2$ $3 \ge 1$

5. $8x - 2 \ < 3$

$\dfrac{+2 \qquad +2}{\dfrac{8x}{8} < \dfrac{5}{8}}$

$x < \dfrac{5}{8}$

6. $\quad 4 - 5x > \ 7$

$\dfrac{-4 \qquad\qquad -4}{\dfrac{-5x}{-5} < \dfrac{3}{-5}}$

$x < \dfrac{-3}{5}$

7. $\dfrac{1}{2}x + 3 < \dfrac{2}{3}x$

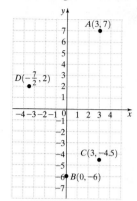

$$3x + 18 < 4x$$
$$\underline{-4x \qquad\quad -4x}$$
$$-x + 18 < 0$$
$$\underline{-18 \quad -18}$$
$$\dfrac{-x}{-1} > \dfrac{-18}{-1}$$
$$x > 18$$

8. $\dfrac{1}{2}(3 - x) \le 2x + 5$

$$\dfrac{3}{2} - \dfrac{1}{2}x \le 2x + 5$$
$$3 - x \le 4x + 10$$
$$-5x \le 7$$
$$x \ge -\dfrac{7}{5}$$

9. $2000n - 700{,}000 \ge 2{,}500{,}000$
$$2{,}000n \ge 3{,}200{,}000$$
$$n \ge 1{,}600$$

Chapter 4

4.1 Practice Problems

1. Point B is 3 units to the right on the x-axis and 4 units up from the point where we stopped on the x-axis.

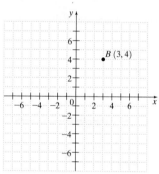

2. (a) Begin by counting 2 squares to the left starting at the origin. Since the y-coordinate is negative, count 4 units down from the point where we stopped on the x-axis. Label the point I.

(b) Begin by counting 4 squares to the left of the origin. Then count 5 units up because the y-coordinate is positive. Label the point J.

(c) Begin by counting 4 units to the right of the origin. Then count 2 units down because the y-coordinate is negative. Label the point K.

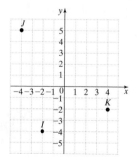

3. The points are plotted in the figure.

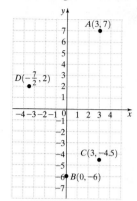

4. Move along the x-axis to get as close as possible to B. We end up at 2. Thus the first number of the ordered pair is 2. Then count 7 units upward on a line parallel to the y-axis to reach B. So the second number of the ordered pair is 7. Thus, $B = (2, 7)$.

5. $A = (-2, -1); B = (-1, 3); C = (0, 0); D = (2, -1); E = (3, 1)$

6. (a)

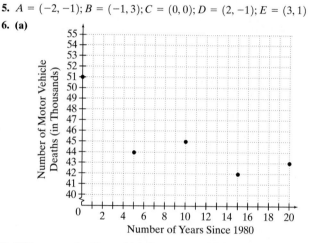

(b) 1980 was a significant high in motor vehicle deaths. During 1985–2000, the number of motor vehicle deaths was relatively stable.

7. Solve for y. $8 - 2y + 3x = 0$

$$8 - 2y = -3x \qquad \text{Subtract } 3x \text{ from both sides.}$$
$$-2y = -3x - 8 \quad \text{Subtract 8 from both sides.}$$
$$\dfrac{-2y}{-2} = \dfrac{-3x + (-8)}{-2} \quad \begin{array}{l}\text{Write } -3x - 8 \text{ as}\\ -3x + (-8) \text{ and}\\ \text{divide both sides}\\ \text{by } -2.\end{array}$$

$$y = \dfrac{-3x}{-2} + \dfrac{(-8)}{-2} \quad or \quad y = \dfrac{3}{2}x + 4$$

8. (a) Replace x by 0 in the equation. $3(0) - 4y = 12$
$$0 - 4y = 12$$
$$y = -3 \qquad (0, -3)$$

(b) Replace the variable y by 3. $3x - 4(3) = 12$
$$3x - 12 = 12$$
$$3x = 24$$
$$x = 8 \qquad (8, 3)$$

(c) Replace the variable y by -6.
$$3x - 4(-6) = 12$$
$$3x + 24 = 12$$
$$3x = -12$$
$$x = -4 \qquad (-4, -6)$$

4.2 Practice Problems

1. Graph $x + y = 10$.
Let $x = 0$.
$0 + y = 10$
$y = 10$

Let $x = 5$.
$5 + y = 10$
$y = 5$

Let $x = 2$.
$2 + y = 10$
$y = 8$

Plot the ordered pairs.
$(0, 10), (5, 5),$ and $(2, 8)$

2. $7x + 3 = -2y + 3$
$7x + 3 - 3 = -2y + 3 - 3$
$7x = -2y$
$7x + 2y = -2y + 2y$
$7x + 2y = 0$

Let $x = 0$.
$7(0) + 2y = 0$
$2y = 0$
$y = 0$

Let $x = -2$.
$7(-2) + 2y = 0$
$-14 + 2y = 0$
$2y = 14$
$y = 7$

Let $x = 2$.
$7(2) + 2y = 0$
$14 + 2y = 0$
$2y = -14$
$y = -7$

Graph the ordered pairs. $(0, 0), (2, -7),$ and $(-2, 7)$

3. $2y - x = 6$
Find the two intercepts.

Let $x = 0$. 　　Let $y = 0$.
$2y - 0 = 6$　　$2(0) - x = 6$
$2y = 6$　　　$-x = 6$
$y = 3$　　　　$x = -6$

Find the third point.
Let $y = 1$.
$2(1) - x = 6$
$2 - x = 6$
$-x = 4$
$x = -4$

Graph the ordered pairs.
$(0, 3), (-6, 0),$ and $(-4, 1)$

4. $2y - 3 = 0$
Solve for y.
$2y = 3$
$y = \dfrac{3}{2}$

This line is parallel to the x-axis.
It is a horizontal line $1\frac{1}{2}$ units
above the x-axis.

5. $x + 3 = 0$
Solve for x.
$x = -3$
This line is parallel to the y-axis.
It is a vertical line 3 units
to the left of the y-axis.

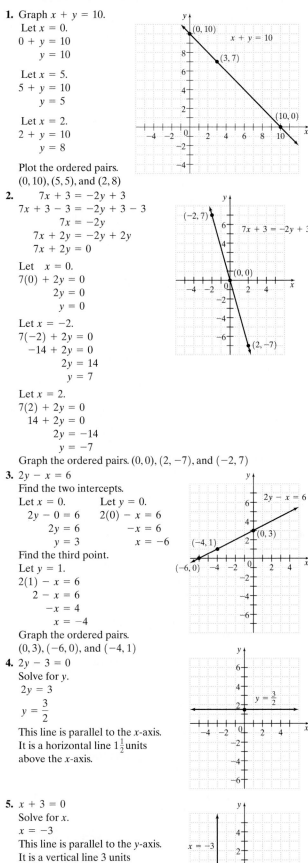

4.3 Practice Problems

1. $m = \dfrac{y_2 - y_1}{x_2 - x_1} = \dfrac{-1 - 1}{-4 - 6} = \dfrac{-2}{-10} = \dfrac{1}{5}$

2. $m = \dfrac{y_2 - y_1}{x_2 - x_1} = \dfrac{1 - 0}{-1 - 2} = \dfrac{1}{-3} = -\dfrac{1}{3}$

3. (a) $m = \dfrac{4 - 0}{-4 - (-4)} = \dfrac{4}{0}$

$\dfrac{4}{0}$ is undefined. Therefore there is no slope and the line is a vertical line through $x = -4$.

(b) $m = \dfrac{-11 - (-11)}{3 - (-7)} = \dfrac{0}{10} = 0$

$m = 0$. The line is a horizontal line through $y = -11$.

4. Solve for y.
$4x - 2y = -5$
$-2y = -4x - 5$
$y = \dfrac{-4x - 5}{-2}$

$y = 2x + \dfrac{5}{2}$ Slope $= 2$ y-intercept $= \left(0, \dfrac{5}{2}\right)$

5. (a) $y = mx + b$

$m = -\dfrac{3}{7}$ y-intercept $= \left(0, \dfrac{2}{7}\right)$

$y = -\dfrac{3}{7}x + \dfrac{2}{7}$

(b) $y = -\dfrac{3}{7}x + \dfrac{2}{7}$

$7(y) = 7\left(-\dfrac{3}{7}x\right) + 7\left(\dfrac{2}{7}\right)$

$7y = -3x + 2$
$3x + 7y = 2$

6. y-intercept $= (0, -1)$. Thus the coordinates of the y-intercept for this line are $(0, -1)$. Plot the point. Slope is $\dfrac{\text{rise}}{\text{run}}$. Since the slope for this line is $\dfrac{3}{4}$, we will go up (rise) 3 units and go over (run) 4 units to the right from the point $(0, -1)$. This is the point $(4, 2)$.

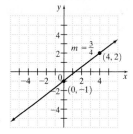

7. $y = -\dfrac{2}{3}x + 5$

The y-intercept is $(0, 5)$ since $b = 5$. Plot the point $(0, 5)$. The slope is $-\dfrac{2}{3} = \dfrac{-2}{3}$. Begin at $(0, 5)$, go down 2 units and to the right 3 units. This is the point $(3, 3)$. Draw a line that connects the points $(0, 5)$ and $(3, 3)$.

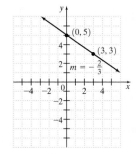

8. (a) Parallel lines have the same slope. Line j has a slope of $\dfrac{1}{4}$.

(b) Perpendicular lines have slopes whose product is -1.

$$m_1 m_2 = -1$$
$$\frac{1}{4} m_2 = -1$$
$$4\left(\frac{1}{4}\right) m_2 = -1(4)$$
$$m_2 = -4$$

Thus line k has a slope of -4.

9. (a) The slope of line n is $\frac{1}{4}$. The slope of a line that is parallel to line n is $\frac{1}{4}$.

(b) $m_1 m_2 = -1$
$$\frac{1}{4} m_2 = -1$$
$$m_2 = -4$$

The slope of a line that is perpendicular to n is -4.

4.4 Practice Problems

1. $y = mx + b$
$$12 = -\frac{3}{4}(-8) + b$$
$$12 = 6 + b$$
$$6 = b$$

The equation of the line is $y = -\frac{3}{4}x + 6$.

2. Find the slope.
$$m = \frac{y_2 - y_1}{x_2 - x_1} = \frac{1 - 5}{-1 - 3} = \frac{-4}{-4} = 1$$

Using either of the two points given, substitute x and y values into the equation $y = mx + b$.
$m = 1 \quad x = 3 \quad$ and $\quad y = 5$.
$$y = mx + b$$
$$5 = 1(3) + b$$
$$5 = 3 + b$$
$$2 = b$$

The equation of the line is $y = x + 2$.

3. The y-intercept is $(0, 1)$. Thus $b = 1$. Look for another point in the line. We choose $(6, 2)$. Count the number of vertical units from 1 to 2 (rise). Count the number of horizontal units from 0 to 6 (run).

$m = \frac{1}{6}$ Now we can write the equation of the line.
$$y = mx + b$$
$$y = \frac{1}{6}x + 1$$

Chapter 5

5.1 Practice Problems

1. Substitute $(-3, 4)$ into the first equation to see if the ordered pair is a solution.
$$2x + 3y = 6$$
$$2(-3) + 3(4) \stackrel{?}{=} 6$$
$$-6 + 12 \stackrel{?}{=} 6$$
$$6 = 6 \checkmark$$

Likewise, we will determine if $(-3, 4)$ is a solution to the second equation.
$$3x - 4y = 7$$
$$3(-3) - 4(4) \stackrel{?}{=} 7$$
$$-9 - 16 \stackrel{?}{=} 7$$
$$-25 \neq 7$$

Since $(-3, 4)$ is not a solution to each equation in the system, it is not a solution to the system itself.

2. You can use any method we developed in Chapter 3 to graph each line. We will change each equation to slope-intercept form to graph.
$$3x + 2y = 10$$
$$2y = -3x + 10$$

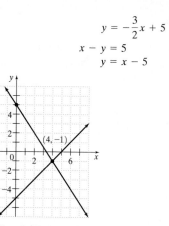

$$y = -\frac{3}{2}x + 5$$
$$x - y = 5$$
$$y = x - 5$$

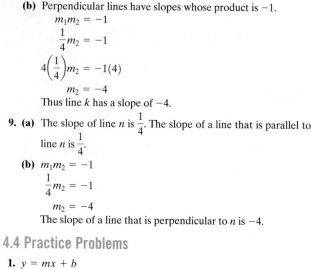

The lines intersect at the point $(4, -1)$. Thus $(4, -1)$ is a solution. We verify this by substituting $x = 4$ and $y = -1$ into the system of equations.

$$3x + 2y = 10 \qquad\qquad x - y = 5$$
$$3(4) + 2(-1) \stackrel{?}{=} 10 \qquad 4 - (-1) \stackrel{?}{=} 5$$
$$12 - 2 \stackrel{?}{=} 10 \qquad\qquad 5 = 5 \checkmark$$
$$10 = 10 \checkmark$$

3.
$$2x - y = 7 \quad [1]$$
$$3x + 4y = -6 \quad [2]$$

Solve equation [1] for y.
$$-y = 7 - 2x$$
$$y = -7 + 2x \quad [3]$$

Substitute $-7 + 2x$ for y in equation [2].
$$3x + 4(-7 + 2x) = -6$$
$$3x - 28 + 8x = -6$$
$$11x - 28 = -6$$
$$11x = 22$$
$$x = 2$$

Substitute $x = 2$ into equation [3].
$$y = -7 + 2(2)$$
$$y = -7 + 4$$
$$y = -3$$

The solution is $(2, -3)$.

4. $\dfrac{x}{3} - \dfrac{y}{2} = 1$
$x + 4y = -8$

Clear the first equation of fractions. We observe that the LCD is 6.
$$6\left(\frac{x}{3}\right) - 6\left(\frac{y}{2}\right) = 6(1)$$
$$2x - 3y = 6$$

Step 1   Solve the second equation for x.
$$x + 4y = -8$$
$$x = -4y - 8$$

Step 2   Substitute $x = -4y - 8$ into the equation $2x - 3y = 6$.
$$2(-4y - 8) - 3y = 6$$

Step 3   Solve this equation.
$$-8y - 16 - 3y = 6$$
$$-11y - 16 = 6$$
$$-11y = 22$$
$$y = -2$$

Step 4   Obtain the value of the second variable.
$$x + 4y = -8$$
$$x + 4(-2) = -8$$
$$x - 8 = -8$$
$$x = 0$$

The solution is $(0, -2)$.

Step 5   Check.
$$\frac{x}{3} - \frac{y}{2} = 1 \qquad\qquad x + 4y = -8$$
$$\frac{0}{3} - \frac{(-2)}{2} \stackrel{?}{=} 1 \qquad 0 + 4(-2) \stackrel{?}{=} -8$$
$$0 + 1 \stackrel{?}{=} 1 \qquad\qquad -8 = -8 \checkmark$$
$$1 = 1 \quad \checkmark$$

5. $-3x + y = 5$ [1]
$\quad 2x + 3y = 4$ [2]
Multiply equation [1] by -3 and add to equation [2].

$$9x - 3y = -15$$
$$\underline{2x + 3y = 4}$$
$$11x = -11$$
$$x = -1$$

Now substitute $x = -1$ into equation [1].

$$-3(-1) + y = 5$$
$$3 + y = 5$$
$$y = 2$$

The solution is $(-1, 2)$.

6. $5x + 4y = 23$ [1]
$\quad 7x - 3y = 15$ [2]
Multiply equation [1] by 3 and equation [2] by 4.

$$15x + 12y = 69$$
$$\underline{28x - 12y = 60}$$
$$43x = 129$$
$$x = 3$$

Now substitute $x = 3$ into equation [1].

$$5(3) + 4y = 23$$
$$15 + 4y = 23$$
$$4y = 8$$
$$y = 2$$

The solution is $(3, 2)$.

7. $4x - 2y = 6$ [1]
$\quad -6x + 3y = 9$ [2]
Multiply equation [1] by 3 and equation [2] by 2 and add together.

$$12x - 6y = 18$$
$$\underline{-12x + 6y = 18}$$
$$0 = 36$$

This statement is of course false. Thus, we conclude that this system of equations is inconsistent, so there is **no solution.**

8. $0.3x - 0.9y = 1.8$ [1]
$\quad -0.4x + 1.2y = -2.4$ [2]
Multiply both equations by 10 to obtain a more convenient form.

$$3x - 9y = 18 \quad [3]$$
$$-4x + 12y = -24 \quad [4]$$

Multiply equation [3] by 4 and equation [4] by 3.

$$12x - 36y = 72$$
$$\underline{-12x + 36y = -72}$$
$$0 = 0$$

This statement is always true. Hence these are dependent equations. There are an infinite number of solutions.

9. (a) $3x + 5y = 1485$
$\quadx + 2y = 564$

Solve for x in the second equation and solve using the substitution method.

$$x = -2y + 564$$
$$3(-2y + 564) + 5y = 1485$$
$$-6y + 1692 + 5y = 1485$$
$$-y = -207$$
$$y = 207$$

Substitute $y = 207$ into the second equation and solve for x.

$$x + 2(207) = 564$$
$$x + 414 = 564$$
$$x = 150 \qquad \text{The solution is } (150, 207).$$

(b) $7x + 6y = 45$
$\quad 6x - 5y = -2$

Using the addition method, multiply the first equation by -6 and the second equation by 7.

$$-6(7x) + (-6)(6y) = (-6)(45)$$
$$7(6x) - 7(5y) = 7(-2)$$
$$-42x - 36y = -270$$
$$\underline{42x - 35y = -14}$$
$$-71y = -284$$
$$y = 4$$

Substitute $y = 4$ into the first equation and solve for x.

$$7x + 6(4) = 45$$
$$7x + 24 = 45$$
$$7x = 21$$
$$x = 3 \qquad \text{The solution is } (3, 4).$$

Chapter 6

6.1 Practice Problems

1. (a) $a^7 \cdot a^5 = a^{7+5} = a^{12}$ **(b)** $w^{10} \cdot w = w^{10+1} = w^{11}$
2. (a) $x^3 \cdot x^9 = x^{3+9} = x^{12}$ **(b)** $3^7 \cdot 3^4 = 3^{7+4} = 3^{11}$
    (c) $a^3 \cdot b^2 = a^3 \cdot b^2$ (cannot be simplified)
3. (a) $(-a^8)(a^4) = (-1 \cdot 1)(a^8 \cdot a^4)$
$$= -1(a^8 \cdot a^4)$$
$$= -1a^{12} = -a^{12}$$

   (b) $(3y^2)(-2y^3) = (3)(-2)(y^2 \cdot y^3) = -6y^5$
   (c) $(-4x^3)(-5x^2) = (-4)(-5)(x^3 \cdot x^2) = 20x^5$

4. $(2xy)\left(-\dfrac{1}{4}x^2y\right)(6xy^3) = (2)\left(-\dfrac{1}{4}\right)(6)(x \cdot x^2 \cdot x)(y \cdot y \cdot y^3)$
$$= -3x^4y^5$$

5. (a) $\dfrac{10^{13}}{10^7} = 10^{13-7} = 10^6$ **(b)** $\dfrac{x^{11}}{x} = x^{11-1} = x^{10}$

   (c) $\dfrac{y^{18}}{y^8} = y^{18-8} = y^{10}$

6. (a) $\dfrac{c^3}{c^4} = \dfrac{1}{c^{4-3}} = \dfrac{1}{c}$ **(b)** $\dfrac{10^{31}}{10^{56}} = \dfrac{1}{10^{56-31}} = \dfrac{1}{10^{25}}$

   (c) $\dfrac{z^{15}}{z^{21}} = \dfrac{1}{z^{21-15}} = \dfrac{1}{z^6}$

7. (a) $\dfrac{-7x^7}{-21x^9} = \dfrac{1}{3x^{9-7}} = \dfrac{1}{3x^2}$ **(b)** $\dfrac{15x^{11}}{-3x^4} = -5x^{11-4} = -5x^7$

   (c) $\dfrac{23x^8}{46x^9} = \dfrac{1}{2x^{9-8}} = \dfrac{1}{2x}$

8. (a) $\dfrac{x^7y^9}{y^{10}} = \dfrac{x^7}{y}$ **(b)** $\dfrac{12x^5y^6}{-24x^3y^8} = -\dfrac{x^2}{2y^2}$

9. (a) $\dfrac{10^7}{10^7} = 1$ **(b)** $\dfrac{12a^4}{15a^4} = \dfrac{4}{5}\left(\dfrac{a^4}{a^4}\right) = \dfrac{4}{5}(1) = \dfrac{4}{5}$

10. (a) $\dfrac{-20a^3b^8c^4}{28a^3b^7c^5} = -\dfrac{5a^0b}{7c} = -\dfrac{5(1)b}{7c} = -\dfrac{5b}{7c}$

   (b) $\dfrac{5x^0y^6}{10x^4y^8} = \dfrac{5(1)y^6}{10x^4y^8} = \dfrac{1}{2x^4y^2}$

11. $\dfrac{(-6ab^5)(3a^2b^4)}{16a^5b^7} = \dfrac{-18a^3b^9}{16a^5b^7} = -\dfrac{9b^2}{8a^2}$

12. (a) $(a^4)^3 = a^{4 \cdot 3} = a^{12}$
   (b) $(10^5)^2 = 10^{5 \cdot 2} = 10^{10}$ **(c)** $(-1)^{15} = -1$

13. (a) $(3xy)^3 = (3)^3x^3y^3 = 27x^3y^3$
   (b) $(yz)^{37} = y^{37}z^{37}$ **(c)** $(-3x^3)^2 = (-3)^2(x^3)^2 = 9x^6$

14. (a) $\left(\dfrac{x}{5}\right)^3 = \dfrac{x^3}{5^3} = \dfrac{x^3}{125}$ **(b)** $\left(\dfrac{4a}{b}\right)^6 = \dfrac{4^6a^6}{b^6} = \dfrac{4096a^6}{b^6}$

15. $\left(\dfrac{-2x^3y^0z}{4xz^2}\right)^5 = \left(\dfrac{-x^2}{2z}\right)^5 = \dfrac{(-1)^5(x^2)^5}{2^5z^5} = -\dfrac{x^{10}}{32z^5}$

6.2 Practice Problems

1. (a) $x^{-12} = \dfrac{1}{x^{12}}$ **(b)** $w^{-5} = \dfrac{1}{w^5}$ **(c)** $z^{-2} = \dfrac{1}{z^2}$

2. (a) $4^{-3} = \dfrac{1}{4^3} = \dfrac{1}{64}$ **(b)** $2^{-4} = \dfrac{1}{2^4} = \dfrac{1}{16}$

3. (a) $\dfrac{3}{w^{-4}} = 3w^4$ **(b)** $\dfrac{x^{-6}y^4}{z^{-2}} = \dfrac{y^4z^2}{x^6}$ **(c)** $x^{-6}y^{-5} = \dfrac{1}{x^6y^5}$

4. (a) $(2x^4y^{-5})^{-2} = 2^{-2}x^{-8}y^{10} = \dfrac{y^{10}}{2^2x^8} = \dfrac{y^{10}}{4x^8}$

(b) $\dfrac{y^{-3}z^{-4}}{y^2z^{-6}} = \dfrac{z^6}{y^2y^3z^4} = \dfrac{z^6}{y^5z^4} = \dfrac{z^2}{y^5}$

5. (a) $78,200 = 7.82 \times 10,000 = 7.82 \times 10^4$

(b) $4,786,000 = 4.786 \times 1,000,000 = 4.786 \times 10^6$

6. (a) $0.98 = 9.8 \times 10^{-1}$ **(b)** $0.000092 = 9.2 \times 10^{-5}$

7. (a) $1.93 \times 10^6 = 1.93 \times 1,000,000 = 1,930,000.0$

(b) $8.562 \times 10^{-5} = 8.562 \times \dfrac{1}{100,000} = 0.00008562$

8. $30,900,000,000,000,000 = 3.09 \times 10^{16}$ meters

9. (a) $(56,000)(1,400,000,000) = (5.6 \times 10^4)(1.4 \times 10^9)$

$= (5.6)(1.4)(10^4)(10^9)$

$= 7.84 \times 10^{13}$

(b) $\dfrac{0.000111}{0.00000037} = \dfrac{1.11 \times 10^{-4}}{3.7 \times 10^{-7}} = \dfrac{1.11}{3.7} \times \dfrac{10^{-4}}{10^{-7}}$

$= \dfrac{1.11}{3.7} \times \dfrac{10^7}{10^4} = 0.3 \times 10^3 = 3.0 \times 10^2$

10. 159 parsecs $= (159 \text{ parsecs}) \dfrac{(3.09 \times 10^{13} \text{ kilometers})}{1 \text{ parsec}}$

$= 491.31 \times 10^{13}$ kilometers

$d = r \times t$

$491.31 \times 10^{13} \text{ km} = \dfrac{50,000 \text{ km}}{1 \text{ hr}} \times t$

$4.9131 \times 10^{15} \text{ km} = \dfrac{5 \times 10^4 \text{ km}}{1 \text{ hr}} \times t$

$\dfrac{4.9131 \times 10^{15} \text{ km}}{\dfrac{5 \times 10^4 \text{ km}}{1 \text{ hr}}} = t$

$\dfrac{4.9131 \times 10^{15} \text{ km } (1 \text{ hr})}{5.0 \times 10^4 \text{ km}} = t$

$0.98262 \times 10^{11} \text{ hr} = t$

9.83×10^{10} hours

Appendix A

A.1 Practice Problems

1. (a) $(-3)^5 = (-3)(-3)(-3)(-3)(-3) = -243$

(b) $(-3)^6 = (-3)(-3)(-3)(-3)(-3)(-3) = 729$

(c) $(-4)^4 = (-4)(-4)(-4)(-4) = 256$

(d) $-4^4 = -(4 \cdot 4 \cdot 4 \cdot 4) = -256$

(e) $\left(\dfrac{1}{5}\right)^2 = \left(\dfrac{1}{5}\right)\left(\dfrac{1}{5}\right) = \dfrac{1}{25}$

2. Since $(-7)^2 = 49$ and $7^2 = 49$ the square roots of 49 are -7 and 7. The principal square root is 7.

3. (a) $(0.3)^2 = (0.3)(0.3) = 0.09$, therefore, $\sqrt{0.09} = 0.3$.

(b) $\sqrt{\dfrac{4}{81}} = \dfrac{\sqrt{4}}{\sqrt{81}} = \dfrac{2}{9}$

(c) This is not a real number.

4. (a) $6(12 - 8) + 4 = 6(4) + 4$

$= 24 + 4 = 28$

(b) $5[6 - 3(7 - 9)] - 8 = 5[6 - 3(-2)] - 8$

$= 5[6 + 6] - 8$

$= 5[12] - 8 = 60 - 8 = 52$

5. (a) $\sqrt{(-5)^2 + 12^2} = \sqrt{25 + 144} = \sqrt{169} = 13$

(b) $|-3 - 7 + 2 - (-4)| = |-3 - 7 + 2 + 4|$

$= |-10 + 6| = |-4| = 4$

6. $\dfrac{2(3) + 5(-2)}{1 + 2 \cdot 3^2 + 5(-3)} = \dfrac{6 - 10}{1 + 2 \cdot 9 + 5(-3)}$

$= \dfrac{-4}{1 + 18 + (-15)} = \dfrac{-4}{4} = -1$

7. (a) $3^{-2} = \dfrac{1}{3^2} = \dfrac{1}{9}$

(b) $z^{-8} = \dfrac{1}{z^8}$

8. (a) $(7xy^{-2})(2x^{-5}y^{-6}) = 14x^{-4}y^{-8} = \dfrac{14}{x^4y^8}$

(b) $(x + 2y)^4(x + 2y)^{10} = (x + 2y)^{14}$

9. $\dfrac{2x^{-3}y}{4x^{-2}y^5} = \dfrac{1}{2}x^{-3-(-2)}y^{1-5} = \dfrac{1}{2}x^{-1}y^{-4} = \dfrac{1}{2xy^4}$

10. (a) $\dfrac{30x^6y^5}{20x^3y^2} = \dfrac{30}{20} \cdot \dfrac{x^6}{x^3} \cdot \dfrac{y^5}{y^2} = \dfrac{3}{2}x^3y^3$ or $\dfrac{3x^3y^3}{2}$

(b) $\dfrac{-15a^3b^4c^4}{3a^5b^4c^2} = \dfrac{-15}{3} \cdot \dfrac{a^3}{a^5} \cdot \dfrac{b^4}{b^4} \cdot \dfrac{c^4}{c^2} = -5a^{-2}c^2 = -\dfrac{5c^2}{a^2}$

(c) $(5^{-3})(2a)^0 = (5^{-3})(1) = \dfrac{1}{5^3} = \dfrac{1}{125}$

11. (a) $(w^3)^8 = w^{3 \cdot 8} = w^{24}$

(b) $(5^2)^5 = 5^{2 \cdot 5} = 5^{10}$

(c) $[(x - 2y)^3]^3 = (x - 2y)^{3 \cdot 3} = (x - 2y)^9$

12. (a) $(4x^3y^4)^2 = 4^2x^6y^8 = 16x^6y^8$

(b) $\left(\dfrac{4xy}{3x^5y^6}\right)^3 = \dfrac{4^3x^3y^3}{3^3x^{15}y^{18}} = \dfrac{64x^3y^3}{27x^{15}y^{18}} = \dfrac{64}{27x^{12}y^{15}}$

(c) $(3xy^2)^{-2} = 3^{-2}x^{-2}y^{-4} = \dfrac{1}{9x^2y^4}$

13. (a) $\dfrac{7x^2y^{-4}z^{-3}}{8x^{-5}y^{-6}z^2} = \dfrac{7x^2 \cdot x^5 \cdot y^6}{8 \cdot y^4 \cdot z^3 \cdot z^2} = \dfrac{7x^7y^2}{8z^5}$

(b) $\left(\dfrac{4x^2y^{-2}}{x^{-4}y^{-3}}\right)^{-3} = \dfrac{4^{-3}x^{-6}y^6}{x^{12}y^9} = \dfrac{y^6}{4^3x^{12} \cdot x^6y^9} = \dfrac{1}{64x^{18}y^3}$

14. (a) $128,320 = 1.2832 \times 10^5$ **(b)** $476 = 4.76 \times 10^2$

(c) $0.0786 = 7.86 \times 10^{-2}$ **(d)** $0.007 = 7 \times 10^{-3}$

15. (a) $4.62 \times 10^6 = 4,620,000$ **(b)** $1.973 \times 10^{-3} = 0.001973$

(c) $4.931 \times 10^{-1} = 0.4931$

16. $\dfrac{(55,000)(3,000,000)}{5,500,000} = \dfrac{(5.5 \times 10^4)(3.0 \times 10^6)}{5.5 \times 10^6}$

$= \dfrac{3.0}{1} \times \dfrac{10^{10}}{10^6}$

$= 3.0 \times 10^{10-6} = 3.0 \times 10^4$

A.2 Practice Problems

1. (a) $3x^5 - 6x^4 + x^2$

This is a trinomial of degree 5.

(b) $5x^2 + 2$

This is a binomial of degree 2.

(c) $3ab + 5a^2b^2 - 6a^4b$

This is a trinomial of degree 5.

(d) $16x^4y^6$

This is a monomial of degree 10.

2. $p(x) = 2x^4 - 3x^3 + 6x - 8$

(a) $p(-2) = 2(-2)^4 - 3(-2)^3 + 6(-2) - 8$

$= 2(16) - 3(-8) + 6(-2) - 8$

$= 32 + 24 - 12 - 8$

$= 36$

(b) $p(5) = 2(5)^4 - 3(5)^3 + 6(5) - 8$

$= 2(625) - 3(125) + 6(5) - 8$

$= 1250 - 375 + 30 - 8$

$= 897$

3. $(-7x^2 + 5x - 9) + (2x^2 - 3x + 5)$

We remove the parentheses and combine like terms.

$= -7x^2 + 2x^2 + 5x - 3x - 9 + 5$

$= -5x^2 + 2x - 4$

4. $(2x^2 - 14x + 9) - (-3x^2 + 10x + 7)$

We add the opposite of the second polynomial to the first polynomial.

$$= (2x^2 - 14x + 9) + (3x^2 - 10x - 7)$$
$$= 2x^2 + 3x^2 - 14x - 10x + 9 - 7 = 5x^2 - 24x + 2$$

5.

$$(7x + 3)(2x - 5)$$

$$14x^2 - 35x + 6x - 15 = 14x^2 - 29x - 15$$

6.

$$(3x^2 - 2)(5x - 4)$$

$$15x^3 - 12x^2 - 10x + 8$$

7. (a) $(7x - 2y)(7x + 2y) = (7x)^2 - (2y)^2$
$$= 49x^2 - 4y^2$$

8. (a) $(4u + 5v)^2 = (4u)^2 + 2(4u)(5v) + (5v)^2$
$$= 16u^2 + 40uv + 25v^2$$

(b) $(7x^2 - 3y^2)^2 = (7x^2)^2 - 2(7x^2)(3y^2) + (3y^2)^2$
$$= 49x^4 - 42x^2y^2 + 9y^4$$

9.

$$
\begin{array}{r}
2x^2 - 3x + 1 \\
\underline{x^2 - 5x} \\
-10x^3 + 15x^2 - 5x \\
\underline{2x^4 - 3x^3 + x^2} \\
2x^4 - 13x^3 + 16x^2 - 5x
\end{array}
$$

10. $(2x^2 - 3x + 1)(x^2 - 5x)$
$$= (2x^2 - 3x + 1)(x^2) + (2x^2 - 3x + 1)(-5x)$$
$$= 2x^4 - 3x^3 + x^2 - 10x^3 + 15x^2 - 5x$$
$$= 2x^4 - 3x^3 - 10x^3 + x^2 + 15x^2 - 5x$$
$$= 2x^4 - 13x^3 + 16x^2 - 5x$$

A.3 Practice Problems

1. (a) $19x^3 - 38x^2 = 19x^2(x - 2)$
(b) $100a^4 - 50a^2 = 50a^2(2a^2 - 1)$
2. $9a^3 - 12a^2b^2 - 15a^4 = 3a^2(3a - 4b^2 - 5a^2)$
To check, we multiply.
$$3a^2(3a - 4b^2 - 5a^2) = 9a^3 - 12a^2b^2 - 15a^4$$
This is the original polynomial. It checks.
3. $7x(x + 2y) - 8y(x + 2y) - (x + 2y)$
$$= (x + 2y)(7x - 8y - 1)$$
4. $bx + 5by + 2wx + 10wy = b(x + 5y) + 2w(x + 5y)$
$$= (x + 5y)(b + 2w)$$
5. To factor $xy - 12 - 4x + 3y$, rearrange the terms. Then factor.
$$xy - 4x + 3y - 12$$
$$= x(y - 4) + 3(y - 4)$$
$$= (y - 4)(x + 3)$$
6. To factor $2x^3 - 15 - 10x + 3x^2$, rearrange the terms. Then factor.
$$2x^3 - 10x + 3x^2 - 15$$
$$= 2x(x^2 - 5) + 3(x^2 - 5)$$
$$= (x^2 - 5)(2x + 3)$$
7. $x^2 - 10x + 21 = (x - 7)(x - 3)$
8. $x^4 + 9x^2 + 8 = (x^2 + 8)(x^2 + 1)$
9. (a) $a^2 + 2a - 48 = (a + 8)(a - 6)$
(b) $x^4 + 2x^2 - 15 = (x^2 + 5)(x^2 - 3)$
10. (a) $x^2 - 16xy + 15y^2 = (x - 15y)(x - y)$
(b) $x^2 + xy - 42y^2 = (x + 7y)(x - 6y)$
11. Factor $10x^2 - 9x + 2$.
The grouping number is 20. Two numbers whose product is 20 and whose sum is -9 are -5 and -4.
$$10x^2 - 5x - 4x + 2$$
$$= 5x(2x - 1) - 2(2x - 1)$$
$$= (2x - 1)(5x - 2)$$
12. $9x^3 - 15x^2 - 6x = 3x(3x^2 - 5x - 2)$
$$= 3x(3x^2 - 6x + x - 2)$$
$$= 3x[3x(x - 2) + 1(x - 2)]$$
$$= 3x(x - 2)(3x + 1)$$

13. $8x^2 - 6x - 5 = (4x - 5)(2x + 1)$
14. $6x^4 + 13x^2 - 5 = (2x^2 + 5)(3x^2 - 1)$

A.4 Practice Problems

1. $x^2 - 9 = (x + 3)(x - 3)$
2. $64x^2 - 121y^2 = (8x + 11y)(8x - 11y)$
3. $49x^2 - 25y^4 = (7x + 5y^2)(7x - 5y^2)$
4. $7x^2 - 28 = 7(x^2 - 4) = 7(x + 2)(x - 2)$
5. $9x^2 - 30x + 25 = (3x - 5)^2$
6. $242x^2 + 88x + 8 = 2(121x^2 + 44x + 4)$
$$= 2(11x + 2)^2$$
7. (a) $49x^4 + 28x^2 + 4 = (7x^2 + 2)^2$
(b) $36x^4 + 84x^2y^2 + 49y^4 = (6x^2 + 7y^2)^2$
8. $8x^3 + 125y^3 = (2x + 5y)(4x^2 - 10xy + 25y^2)$
9. $64x^3 - 125y^3 = (4x - 5y)(16x^2 + 20xy + 25y^2)$
10. $27w^3 + 125z^6 = (3w + 5z^2)(9w^2 - 15wz^2 + 25z^4)$
11. $54x^3 - 16 = 2(27x^3 - 8)$
$$= 2(3x - 2)(9x^2 + 6x + 4)$$
12. $64a^6 - 1$
Use the difference of two squares first.
$$(8a^3 + 1)(8a^3 - 1)$$
Now use the formula for the sum and difference of two cubes.
$$(2a + 1)(4a^2 - 2a + 1)(2a - 1)(4a^2 + 2a + 1)$$

A.5 Practice Problems

1.
$$y - y_1 = m(x - x_1)$$
$$y - (-2) = \frac{3}{4}(x - 5)$$
$$y + 2 = \frac{3}{4}x - \frac{15}{4}$$
$$4y + 4(2) = 4\left(\frac{3}{4}x\right) - 4\left(\frac{15}{4}\right)$$
$$4y + 8 = 3x - 15$$
$$-3x + 4y = -15 - 8$$
$$3x - 4y = 23$$

2. $(-4, 1)$ and $(-2, -3)$
$$m = \frac{y_2 - y_1}{x_2 - x_1} = \frac{-3 - 1}{-2 - (-4)} = \frac{-4}{-2 + 4} = \frac{-4}{2} = -2$$
Substitute $m = -2$ and $(x_1, y_1) = (-4, 1)$ into the point–slope equation.
$$y - y_1 = m(x - x_1)$$
$$y - 1 = -2[x - (-4)]$$
$$y - 1 = -2(x + 4)$$
$$y - 1 = -2x - 8$$
$$y = -2x - 7$$

3. First, we need to find the slope of the line $5x - 3y = 10$. We do this by writing the equation in slope–intercept form
$$5x - 3y = 10$$
$$-3y = -5x + 10$$
$$y = \frac{5}{3}x - \frac{10}{3}$$
The slope is $\frac{5}{3}$. A line parallel to this passing through $(4, -5)$ would have an equation
$$y - (-5) = \frac{5}{3}(x - 4)$$
$$y + 5 = \frac{5}{3}x - \frac{20}{3}$$
$$3y + 3(5) = 3\left(\frac{5}{3}x\right) - 3\left(\frac{20}{3}\right)$$
$$3y + 15 = 5x - 20$$
$$-5x + 3y = -35$$
$$5x - 3y = 35$$

4. Find the slope of the line $6x + 3y = 7$ by rewriting it in slope–intercept form.

$$6x + 3y = 7$$
$$3y = -6x + 7$$
$$y = -2x + \frac{7}{3}$$

The slope is -2. A line perpendicular to this passing through $(-4, 3)$ would have a slope of $\frac{1}{2}$, and would have the equation

$$y - 3 = \frac{1}{2}[x - (-4)]$$

$$y - 3 = \frac{1}{2}(x + 4)$$
$$y - 3 = \frac{1}{2}x + 2$$
$$2y - 2(3) = 2\left(\frac{1}{2}x\right) + 2(2)$$
$$2y - 6 = x + 4$$
$$-x + 2y = 10$$
$$x - 2y = -10$$

Appendix B Practice Problems

1.

Mathematics Blueprint for Problem Solving

Gather the Facts	What Am I Solving for?	What Must I Calculate?	Key Points to Remember
Living Room measures $16\frac{1}{2}$ ft $\times$ $10\frac{1}{2}$ ft.	Area of room in square feet.	Multiply $16\frac{1}{2}$ ft by $10\frac{1}{2}$ ft to get the area in square feet.	9 sq feet = 1 square yard
The carpet costs $20.00 per square yard.	Area of room in square yards. Cost of the carpet.	Divide the number of square feet by 9 to get the number of square yards. Multiply the number of square yards by $20.00.	

$$16\frac{1}{2} \times 10\frac{1}{2} = 173\frac{1}{4} \text{ square feet}$$

$$173\frac{1}{4} \div 9 = 19\frac{1}{4} \text{ square yards}$$

$$19\frac{1}{4} \times 20 = \$385.00 \text{ total cost of carpet}$$

Check:

Estimate area of room $16 \times 10 = 160$ square feet
Estimate area in square yards $160 \div 10 = 16$
Estimate the cost $16 \times 20 = \$320.00$

This is close to our answer of $385.00. Our answer seems reasonable.

2. (a) $\dfrac{10}{55} \approx 0.181 \approx 18\%$ **(b)** $\dfrac{3,660,000}{13,240,000} \approx 0.276 \approx 28\%$

(c) $\dfrac{15}{55} \approx 0.273 \approx 27\%$ **(d)** $\dfrac{3,720,000}{13,240,000} \approx 0.281 \approx 28\%$

(e) We notice that 18% of the company's sales force is located in the Northwest, and they were responsible for 28% of the sales volume. The percent of sales compared to the percent of sales force is about 150%. 27% of the company's sales force is located in the Southwest, and they were responsible for 28% of the sales volume. The percent of sales compared to the per-cent of sales force is approximately 100%. It would appear that the Northwest sales force is more effective.

Appendix E

Practice Problems

1. (a) $(-7)(-2) - (-4)(3) = 14 - (-12) = 26$

(b) $(5)(-5) - (0)(6) = -25 - 0 = -25$

2. (a) Since 3 appears in the first column and third row, we delete them.

$$\begin{vmatrix} 1 & 2 & 7 \\ -4 & -5 & -6 \\ 3 & 4 & -9 \end{vmatrix}$$

The minor of 3 is $\begin{vmatrix} 2 & 7 \\ -5 & -6 \end{vmatrix}$.

(b) Since -6 appears in second row and third column, we delete them.

$$\begin{vmatrix} 1 & 2 & 7 \\ -4 & -5 & -6 \\ 3 & 4 & -9 \end{vmatrix}$$

The minor of -6 is $\begin{vmatrix} 1 & 2 \\ 3 & 4 \end{vmatrix}$.

3. We can find the determinant by expanding it by minors of elements in the first column.

$$\begin{vmatrix} 1 & 2 & -3 \\ 2 & -1 & 2 \\ 3 & 1 & 4 \end{vmatrix} = 1\begin{vmatrix} -1 & 2 \\ 1 & 4 \end{vmatrix} - 2\begin{vmatrix} 2 & -3 \\ 1 & 4 \end{vmatrix} + 3\begin{vmatrix} 2 & -3 \\ -1 & 2 \end{vmatrix}$$

$$= 1[(-1)(4) - (1)(2)] - 2[(2)(4) - (1)(-3)]$$
$$+ 3[(2)(2) - (-1)(-3)]$$
$$= 1[-4 - 2] - 2[8 - (-3)] + 3[4 - 3]$$
$$= 1(-6) - 2(11) + 3(1)$$
$$= -6 - 22 + 3$$
$$= -25$$

4. $D = \begin{vmatrix} 5 & 3 \\ 2 & -5 \end{vmatrix}$ $D_x = \begin{vmatrix} 17 & 3 \\ 13 & -5 \end{vmatrix}$

$$= (5)(-5) - (2)(3) \qquad = (17)(-5) - (13)(3)$$
$$= -25 - 6 \qquad\qquad = -85 - 39$$
$$= -31 \qquad\qquad\quad = -124$$

$$D_y = \begin{vmatrix} 5 & 17 \\ 2 & 13 \end{vmatrix}$$

$$= (5)(13) - (2)(17)$$
$$= 65 - 34$$
$$= 31$$

$$x = \frac{D_x}{D} = \frac{-124}{-31} = 4, \qquad y = \frac{D_y}{D} = \frac{31}{-31} = -1$$

5. We will expand each determinant by the first column.

$$D = \begin{vmatrix} 2 & 3 & -1 \\ 3 & 5 & -2 \\ 1 & 2 & 3 \end{vmatrix} = 2\begin{vmatrix} 5 & -2 \\ 2 & 3 \end{vmatrix} - 3\begin{vmatrix} 3 & -1 \\ 2 & 3 \end{vmatrix} + 1\begin{vmatrix} 3 & -1 \\ 5 & -2 \end{vmatrix}$$

$$= 2[15 - (-4)] - 3[9 - (-2)] + 1[-6 - (-5)]$$
$$= 2(19) - 3(11) + 1(-1)$$
$$= 4$$

$$D_x = \begin{vmatrix} -1 & 3 & -1 \\ -3 & 5 & -2 \\ 2 & 2 & 3 \end{vmatrix} = -1\begin{vmatrix} 5 & -2 \\ 2 & 3 \end{vmatrix} - (-3)\begin{vmatrix} 3 & -1 \\ 2 & 3 \end{vmatrix} + 2\begin{vmatrix} 3 & -1 \\ 5 & -2 \end{vmatrix}$$

$$= -1[15 - (-4)] + 3[9 - (-2)]$$
$$+ 2[-6 - (-5)]$$
$$= -1(19) + 3(11) + 2(-1)$$
$$= 12$$

$$D_y = \begin{vmatrix} 2 & -1 & -1 \\ 3 & -3 & -2 \\ 1 & 2 & 3 \end{vmatrix} = 2\begin{vmatrix} -3 & -2 \\ 2 & 3 \end{vmatrix} - 3\begin{vmatrix} -1 & -1 \\ 2 & 3 \end{vmatrix} + 1\begin{vmatrix} -1 & -1 \\ -3 & -2 \end{vmatrix}$$

$$= 2[-9 - (-4)] - 3[-3 - (-2)] + 1[2 - 3]$$
$$= 2(-5) - 3(-1) + 1(-1)$$
$$= -8$$

$$D_z = \begin{vmatrix} 2 & 3 & -1 \\ 3 & 5 & -3 \\ 1 & 2 & 2 \end{vmatrix} = 2\begin{vmatrix} 5 & -3 \\ 2 & 2 \end{vmatrix} - 3\begin{vmatrix} 3 & -1 \\ 2 & 2 \end{vmatrix} + 1\begin{vmatrix} 3 & -1 \\ 5 & -3 \end{vmatrix}$$

$$= 2[10 - (-6)] - 3[6 - (-2)]$$
$$+ 1[-9 - (-5)]$$
$$= 2(16) - 3(8) + 1(-4)$$
$$= 4$$

$$x = \frac{D_x}{D} = \frac{12}{4} = 3; \quad y = \frac{D_y}{D} = \frac{-8}{4} = -2; \quad z = \frac{D_z}{D} = \frac{4}{4} = 1$$

Appendix F

Practice Problems

1. The system is represented by the equations $x + 9y = 33$ and $0x + y = 3$.

Since we know that $y = 3$, we can find x by substitution.

$$x + 9y = 33$$
$$x + 9(3) = 33$$
$$x + 27 = 33$$
$$x = 6$$

The solution to the system is $(6, 3)$.

2. The augmented matrix for this system of equations is

$$\begin{bmatrix} 3 & -2 & | & -6 \\ 1 & -3 & | & 5 \end{bmatrix}.$$

Interchange rows one and two so there is a 1 as the first element in the first row.

$$\begin{bmatrix} 1 & -3 & | & 5 \\ 3 & -2 & | & -6 \end{bmatrix} \qquad R_1 \leftrightarrow R_2$$

We want a 0 as the first element in the second row. Multiply row one by -3 and add this to row two.

$$\begin{bmatrix} 1 & -3 & | & 5 \\ 0 & 7 & | & -21 \end{bmatrix} \qquad -3R_1 + R_2$$

Now, to obtain a 1 as the second element of row two, multiply each element of row two by $\frac{1}{7}$.

$$\begin{bmatrix} 1 & -3 & | & 5 \\ 0 & 1 & | & -3 \end{bmatrix}. \qquad \frac{1}{7}R_2$$

This represents the linear system $\quad x - 3y = 5$
$$\hspace{6.5cm} y = -3.$$

We know $y = -3$. Substitute this value into the first equation.
$$x - 3(-3) = 5$$
$$x + 9 = 5$$
$$x = -4$$

The solution to the system is $(-4, -3)$.

3. The augmented matrix is

$$\begin{bmatrix} 2 & 1 & -2 & | & -15 \\ 4 & -2 & 1 & | & 15 \\ 1 & 3 & 2 & | & -5 \end{bmatrix}$$

$$\begin{bmatrix} 1 & 3 & 2 & | & -5 \\ 4 & -2 & 1 & | & 15 \\ 2 & 1 & -2 & | & -15 \end{bmatrix} \qquad R_1 \leftrightarrow R_3$$

$$\begin{bmatrix} 1 & 3 & 2 & | & -5 \\ 0 & -14 & -7 & | & 35 \\ 0 & -5 & -6 & | & -5 \end{bmatrix} \qquad \begin{matrix} -4R_1 + R_2 \\ -2R_1 + R_3 \end{matrix}$$

$$\begin{bmatrix} 1 & 3 & 2 & | & -5 \\ 0 & 1 & \frac{1}{2} & | & -\frac{5}{2} \\ 0 & -5 & -6 & | & -5 \end{bmatrix} \qquad -\frac{1}{14}R_2$$

$$\begin{bmatrix} 1 & 3 & 2 & | & -5 \\ 0 & 1 & \frac{1}{2} & | & -\frac{5}{2} \\ 0 & 0 & -\frac{7}{2} & | & -\frac{35}{2} \end{bmatrix} \qquad 5R_2 + R_3$$

$$\begin{bmatrix} 1 & 3 & 2 & | & -5 \\ 0 & 1 & \frac{1}{2} & | & -\frac{5}{2} \\ 0 & 0 & 1 & | & 5 \end{bmatrix} \qquad -\frac{2}{7}R_3$$

We now know that $z = 5$. Substitute this value into the second equation to find y.

$$y + \tfrac{1}{2}(5) = -\tfrac{5}{2}$$
$$y + \tfrac{5}{2} = -\tfrac{5}{2}$$
$$y = -5$$

Now substitute $y = -5$ and $z = 5$ into the first equation.

$$x + 3y + 2z = -5$$
$$x + 3(-5) + 2(5) = -5$$
$$x - 15 + 10 = -5$$
$$x - 5 = -5$$
$$x = 0$$

The solution to this system is $(0, -5, 5)$.

Appendix G

Practice Problems

1. (a) $A = \{$Africa, Antarctica, Asia, Australia, Europe, North America, South America$\}$

   (b) $C = \{36, 37, 38, 39, 40, 41\}$

   (c) $D = \{35, 36, 37, 38, 39, 40, 41, 42\}$

2. Some possible answers:

   $C = \{x | x$ is an even number between 2 and 14$\}$
   $C = \{x | x$ is an even number between 4 and 12, inclusive$\}$
   $C = \{x | x$ is even and $2 < x < 14\}$
   $C = \{x | x$ is even and $4 \leq x \leq 12\}$
   $C = \{x | x = 2n$, where $n = 2, 3, 4, 5, 6\}$

3. Combining elements of G and H, we have

   $$G \cup H = \{!, *, \%, \$, ?, \wedge, +\}.$$

4. The only element common to both G and H is $, thus

   $$G \cap H = \{\$\}.$$

5. (a) True. All elements of D are in C.
   (b) True. Whole numbers are also rational numbers.

Answers to Selected Exercises

Chapter 1

1.1 Exercises

1. 12   **3.** When two or more numbers are multiplied, each number that is multiplied is called a factor. In 2×3, 2 and 3 are factors.

5.   **7.** $\frac{3}{4}$ **9.** $\frac{1}{3}$ **11.** 5   **13.** $\frac{2}{3}$ **15.** $\frac{6}{17}$ **17.** $\frac{7}{9}$ **19.** $2\frac{5}{6}$ **21.** $12\frac{1}{3}$ **23.** $5\frac{3}{7}$

25. $20\frac{1}{2}$ **27.** $6\frac{2}{5}$ **29.** $9\frac{2}{5}$ **31.** $\frac{16}{5}$ **33.** $\frac{33}{5}$ **35.** 8   **37.** $\frac{59}{7}$ **39.** $\frac{97}{4}$ **41.** $\frac{47}{3}$ **43.** 12   **45.** 21   **47.** 12   **49.** 21

51. 15   **53.** 70   **55.** $22\frac{16}{17}$ **57.** $\frac{33}{160}$ **59.** $\frac{1}{4}$ **61.** $\frac{1}{2}$ **63.** Aaron Dunsay $\frac{3}{5}$, Paul Banks $\frac{2}{5}$, Tom Re $\frac{4}{5}$ **65.** $\frac{13}{16}$

1.2 Exercises

1. Answers may vary. A sample answer is: 8 is exactly divisible by 4.   **3.** 105   **5.** 20   **7.** 54   **9.** 105   **11.** 120

13. 120   **15.** 70   **17.** 90   **19.** $\frac{5}{8}$ **21.** $\frac{2}{7}$ **23.** $\frac{29}{24}$ or $1\frac{5}{24}$ **25.** $\frac{31}{63}$ **27.** $\frac{11}{15}$ **29.** $\frac{17}{36}$ **31.** $\frac{2}{45}$ **33.** $\frac{1}{2}$ **35.** $\frac{53}{56}$

37. $\frac{3}{2}$ or $1\frac{1}{2}$ **39.** $\frac{11}{30}$ **41.** $\frac{1}{4}$ **43.** $\frac{1}{2}$ **45.** $7\frac{11}{15}$ **47.** $1\frac{35}{72}$ **49.** $4\frac{11}{12}$ **51.** $6\frac{13}{28}$ **53.** $5\frac{19}{24}$ **55.** $4\frac{3}{7}$ **57.** $8\frac{7}{8}$

59. $\frac{29}{18}$ or $1\frac{11}{18}$ **61.** $\frac{83}{14}$ or $5\frac{13}{14}$ **63.** $\frac{10}{21}$ **65.** $\frac{27}{10}$ or $2\frac{7}{10}$ **67.** $19\frac{11}{21}$ **69.** $1\frac{13}{24}$ **71.** $12\frac{1}{12}$ **73.** $30\frac{7}{9}$ **75.** $10\frac{7}{24}$ miles

77. $4\frac{1}{12}$ hours   **79.** $A = 12$ inches, $B = 15\frac{7}{8}$ inches   **81.** $1\frac{5}{8}$ inches   **83.** $\frac{9}{11}$ **84.** $\frac{133}{5}$

1.3 Exercises

1. First, change each number to an improper fraction. Look for a common factor in the numerator and denominator to divide by, and, if one is found, peform the division. Multiply the numerators. Multiply the denominators.

3. $\frac{20}{7}$ or $2\frac{6}{7}$ **5.** $\frac{17}{30}$ **7.** $\frac{6}{25}$ **9.** $\frac{12}{5}$ or $2\frac{2}{5}$ **11.** $\frac{1}{6}$ **13.** $\frac{6}{7}$ **15.** $\frac{18}{5}$ or $3\frac{3}{5}$ **17.** $\frac{3}{5}$ **19.** $\frac{1}{7}$ **21.** 14   **23.** $\frac{8}{7}$ or $1\frac{1}{7}$ **25.** $\frac{7}{27}$

27. $\frac{7}{6}$ or $1\frac{1}{6}$ **29.** $\frac{15}{14}$ or $1\frac{1}{14}$ **31.** $\frac{8}{35}$ **33.** $\frac{4}{3}$ or $1\frac{1}{3}$ **35.** $\frac{26}{3}$ or $8\frac{2}{3}$ **37.** $\frac{7}{12}$ **39.** $\frac{8}{15}$ **41.** 1   **43.** $\frac{5}{4}$ or $1\frac{1}{4}$ **45.** $\frac{219}{4}$ or $54\frac{3}{4}$

47. $\frac{17}{2}$ or $8\frac{1}{2}$ **49.** 28   **51.** $\frac{3}{16}$ **53.** (a) $\frac{5}{63}$ (b) $\frac{7}{125}$ **55.** (a) $\frac{7}{6}$ (b) $\frac{8}{21}$ **57.** $71\frac{1}{2}$ yards   **59.** $2\frac{4}{5}$ miles   **61.** $\frac{29}{31}$ **62.** $\frac{3}{7}$

63. $3\frac{1}{7}$ **64.** $3\frac{3}{5}$ **65.** $\frac{37}{3}$ **66.** $\frac{79}{8}$

How Am I Doing? Sections 1.1–1.3

1. $\frac{3}{11}$ (obj. 0.1.2)   **2.** $\frac{2}{5}$ (obj. 0.1.2)   **3.** $3\frac{3}{4}$ (obj. 0.1.3)   **4.** $\frac{33}{7}$ (obj. 0.1.3)   **5.** 6 (obj. 0.1.4)   **6.** 35 (obj. 0.1.4)

7. $120 = $ LCD (obj. 0.2.2)   **8.** $\frac{5}{7}$ (obj. 0.2.1)   **9.** $\frac{19}{42}$ (obj. 0.2.3)   **10.** $8\frac{5}{12}$ (obj. 0.2.4)   **11.** $\frac{7}{18}$ (obj. 0.2.3)

12. $\frac{4}{21}$ (obj. 0.2.3)   **13.** $1\frac{33}{40}$ (obj. 0.2.4)   **14.** $\frac{10}{9}$ or $1\frac{1}{9}$ (obj. 0.3.1)   **15.** $\frac{21}{2}$ or $10\frac{1}{2}$ (obj. 0.3.1)   **16.** $\frac{7}{2}$ or $3\frac{1}{2}$ (obj. 0.3.2)

17. $\frac{28}{39}$ (obj. 0.3.2)   **18.** $\frac{4}{15}$ (obj. 0.3.2)   **19.** 20 square miles (obj. 0.3.1)

1.4 Exercises

1. 10; 100; 10,000; and so on   **3.** three, left   **5.** 0.625   **7.** 0.2   **9.** $0.\overline{63}$ **11.** $\frac{4}{5}$ **13.** $\frac{1}{4}$ **15.** $\frac{5}{8}$ **17.** $\frac{3}{50}$ **19.** $\frac{13}{5}$ or $2\frac{3}{5}$

21. $\frac{11}{2}$ or $5\frac{1}{2}$ **23.** 2.09   **25.** 10.82   **27.** 261.208   **29.** 131.79   **31.** 51.443   **33.** 122.63   **35.** 30.282   **37.** 0.0032

39. 0.10575   **41.** 219.7   **43.** 0.0565   **45.** 2.64   **47.** 261.5   **49.** 0.257   **51.** 3450   **53.** 0.0076   **55.** 73,600   **57.** 0.73892
59. 14.98   **61.** 855,400   **63.** 1.425   **65.** 11.7257   **67.** 2.12   **69.** 768.3   **71.** 23.65   **73.** 1.537   **75.** 24.13 cm   **77.** $212.75

79. No, there were 0.3 milligrams of copper in excess.   **81.** $\frac{2}{3}$ **82.** $\frac{1}{6}$ **83.** $\frac{93}{100}$ **84.** $\frac{11}{10}$ or $1\frac{1}{10}$

Putting Your Skills to Work

1. 12,700 sq mi   **2.** 9400 sq mi   **3.** About 4 times   **4.** About 319 times

Chapter 1 Review Problems

1. $\frac{3}{4}$ **2.** $\frac{3}{10}$ **3.** $\frac{18}{41}$ **4.** $\frac{3}{5}$ **5.** $\frac{23}{5}$ **6.** $6\frac{4}{5}$ **7.** $6\frac{1}{2}$ **8.** 15   **9.** 5   **10.** 40   **11.** 22   **12.** $\frac{17}{20}$ **13.** $\frac{29}{24}$ or $1\frac{5}{24}$

14. $\frac{4}{15}$ **15.** $\frac{13}{30}$ **16.** $\frac{173}{30}$ or $5\frac{23}{30}$ **17.** $\frac{79}{20}$ or $3\frac{19}{20}$ **18.** $2\frac{29}{36}$ **19.** $\frac{23}{12}$ or $1\frac{11}{12}$ **20.** $\frac{30}{11}$ or $2\frac{8}{11}$ **21.** $\frac{21}{2}$ or $10\frac{1}{2}$ **22.** $\frac{19}{8}$ or $2\frac{3}{8}$

23. $\frac{20}{7}$ or $2\frac{6}{7}$ **24.** $\frac{1}{16}$ **25.** $\frac{24}{5}$ or $4\frac{4}{5}$ **26.** $\frac{3}{20}$ **27.** 6   **28.** 7.201   **29.** 7.737   **30.** 29.561   **31.** 4.436   **32.** 0.03745

33. 362,341   **34.** 0.07956   **35.** 10.368   **36.** 0.00186   **37.** 0.07132   **38.** 1.3075   **39.** 90   **40.** 1.82   **41.** 0.5   **42.** 0.375

How Am I Doing? Chapter 1 Test

1. $\frac{8}{9}$ (obj. 0.1.2)   **2.** $\frac{4}{3}$ (obj. 0.1.2)   **3.** $\frac{45}{7}$ (obj. 0.1.3)   **4.** $11\frac{2}{3}$ (obj. 0.1.3)   **5.** $\frac{15}{8}$ or $1\frac{7}{8}$ (obj. 0.2.3)   **6.** $\frac{39}{8}$ or $4\frac{7}{8}$ (obj. 0.2.4)

7. $\frac{5}{6}$ (obj. 0.2.4)   **8.** $\frac{4}{3}$ or $1\frac{1}{3}$ (obj. 0.3.1)   **9.** $\frac{5}{24}$ (obj. 0.3.1)   **10.** $\frac{43}{22}$ or $1\frac{21}{22}$ (obj. 0.3.2)   **11.** $\frac{65}{8}$ or $8\frac{1}{8}$ (obj. 0.3.1)

12. $\frac{7}{2}$ or $3\frac{1}{2}$ (obj. 0.3.2)   **13.** 14.64 (obj. 0.4.4)   **14.** 3.9897 (obj. 0.4.4)   **15.** 1.312 (obj. 0.4.5)   **16.** 73.85 (obj. 0.4.5)

17. 230 (obj. 0.4.6)   **18.** 263,259 (obj. 0.4.7)   **19.** 7.3% (obj. 0.5.1)   **20.** 1.965 (obj. 0.5.2)   **21.** 6.3 (obj. 0.5.3)

22. 0.336 (obj. 0.5.3)   **23.** 6% (obj. 0.5.4)   **24.** 30% (obj. 0.5.4)   **25.** 18 (obj. 0.3.2)   **26.** 100 (obj. 0.5.5)   **27.** 700 (obj. 0.5.5)

Chapter 2

2.1 Exercises

1. Whole number, rational number, real number   **3.** Irrational number, real number   **5.** Rational number, real number

7. Rational number, real number   **9.** Irrational number, real number   **11.** $-20,000$ **13.** $-37\frac{1}{2}$ **15.** $+7$ **17.** -8 **19.** 2.73

21. 1.3   **23.** $\frac{5}{6}$ **25.** -11 **27.** -31 **29.** $\frac{1}{4}$ **31.** $-\frac{7}{13}$ **33.** $\frac{1}{35}$ **35.** -3.8 **37.** 0.4   **39.** -14.16 **41.** -6 **43.** -5

45. $-\frac{4}{15}$ **47.** -8 **49.** -3 **51.** 59   **53.** $\frac{7}{18}$ **55.** $\frac{2}{5}$ **57.** 0.76   **59.** 12   **61.** 0   **63.** 15.94   **65.** \$167 profit

67. $-\$3800$ **69.** 3 yard gain   **71.** 3500   **73.** \$32,000,000   **75.** 18   **77.** 6 yards   **79.** $\frac{2}{3}$ **80.** $\frac{8}{27}$ **81.** $\frac{1}{12}$ **82.** $\frac{25}{34}$

83. 1.52   **84.** 0.65   **85.** 1.141   **86.** 0.26

2.2 Exercises

1. First change subtracting -3 to adding a positive three. Then use the rules for addition of two real numbers with different signs.
Thus, $-8 - (-3) = -8 + 3 = -5$.   **3.** -17 **5.** -5 **7.** -11 **9.** 8   **11.** 5   **13.** 0   **15.** -3 **17.** $-\frac{2}{5}$ **19.** $\frac{27}{20}$ or $1\frac{7}{20}$

21. $-\frac{19}{12}$ or $-1\frac{7}{12}$ **23.** -0.9 **25.** 4.47   **27.** $-\frac{17}{5}$ or $-3\frac{2}{5}$ **29.** $\frac{40}{7}$ or $5\frac{5}{7}$ **31.** -53 **33.** -73 **35.** 7.1   **37.** $8\frac{3}{4}$ **39.** $-6\frac{1}{6}$

41. $-\frac{21}{20}$ or $-1\frac{1}{20}$ **43.** -8.5 **45.** $-5\frac{4}{5}$ **47.** 8.162   **49.** -5.047 **51.** 7   **53.** -48 **55.** -2 **57.** 11   **59.** -62

61. 1.6   **63.** 38   **65.** \$149   **67.** 6051 meters   **69.** -21 **70.** -51 **71.** -19 **72.** $-8°C$ **73.** $6\frac{2}{3}$ miles were snow covered

2.3 Exercises

1. To multiply two real numbers, multiply the absolute values. The sign of the result is positive if both numbers have the same sign, but negative if the two numbers have opposite signs.   **3.** -20 **5.** 0   **7.** 24   **9.** 0.264   **11.** -1.75 **13.** $-\frac{3}{2}$ or $-1\frac{1}{2}$ **15.** $\frac{9}{11}$ **17.** $-\frac{5}{26}$

19. 4   **21.** 6   **23.** 20   **25.** -12 **27.** -130 **29.** -0.6 **31.** -0.9 **33.** $-\frac{3}{10}$ **35.** $\frac{20}{3}$ or $6\frac{2}{3}$ **37.** $\frac{7}{10}$ **39.** 14

41. $-\frac{5}{4}$ or $-1\frac{1}{4}$ **43.** $\frac{15}{16}$ **45.** -24 **47.** 24   **49.** -16 **51.** -0.00018 **53.** $-\frac{8}{35}$ **55.** $\frac{2}{27}$ **57.** 9   **59.** -2 **61.** 17

63. -72 **65.** -1 **67.** He gave \$4.40 to each boy and to himself.   **69.** \$328.50   **71.** 20 yards   **73.** 70 yards

75. The Panthers gained 20 yards   **77.** The Panthers would have gained 105 fewer yards.   **78.** -6.69 **79.** $-\frac{11}{6}$ or $-1\frac{5}{6}$

80. -15 **81.** -88 **82.** 266 square yards

2.4 Exercises

1. The base is 4 and the exponent is 4. Thus you multiply $(4)(4)(4)(4) = 256$.
3. The answer is negative. When you raise a negative number to an odd power the result is always negative.
5. If you have parentheses surrounding the -2, then the base is -2 and the exponent is 4. The result is 16. If you do not have parentheses, then the base is 2. You evaluate to obtain 16 and then take the negative of 16, which is -16. Thus $(-2)^4 = 16$ but $-2^4 = -16$.   **7.** 5^7 **9.** w^2

11. p^4 **13.** $(3q)^3$ or $3^3 q^3$ **15.** 27   **17.** 81   **19.** 216   **21.** -27 **23.** 16   **25.** -25 **27.** $\frac{1}{16}$ **29.** $\frac{8}{125}$ **31.** 1.21

33. 0.0016   **35.** 256   **37.** -256 **39.** 161   **41.** 116   **43.** -91 **45.** 23   **47.** -576 **49.** -512 **51.** 16,777,216

53. -7 **55.** -19 **56.** $-\frac{5}{3}$ or $-1\frac{2}{3}$ **57.** -8 **58.** 2.52   **59.** \$1696

2.5 Exercises

1. $3(4) + 6(5)$ **3.** (a) 90 (b) 42   **5.** 12   **7.** 13   **9.** -29 **11.** 24   **13.** 21   **15.** 13   **17.** -6 **19.** 42   **21.** $\frac{9}{4}$ or $2\frac{1}{4}$

23. 0.848   **25.** $\frac{3}{10}$ **27.** 5   **29.** $-\frac{23}{2}$ or $-11\frac{1}{2}$ **31.** 7.56   **33.** $\frac{1}{4}$ **35.** $3(-2) + 9(-1) + 5(0) + 1(1)$ **37.** 1 above par

39. 0.125   **40.** $-\frac{19}{12}$ or $-1\frac{7}{12}$ **41.** -1 **42.** $\frac{72}{125}$ **43.** 45 ounces   **44.** 0.684   **45.** 0.54

How Am I Doing? Sections 2.1–2.5

1. -9 (obj. 1.1.4)   **2.** $-\frac{41}{24}$ or $-1\frac{17}{24}$ (obj. 1.1.3)   **3.** 1.24 (obj. 1.1.3)   **4.** -7.1 (obj. 1.1.4)   **5.** 11 (obj. 1.2.1)

6. $-\frac{17}{15}$ or $-1\frac{2}{15}$ (obj. 1.2.1)   **7.** 12.3 (obj. 1.2.1)   **8.** 10 (obj. 1.2.1)   **9.** -96 (obj. 1.3.1)   **10.** $\frac{10}{11}$ (obj. 1.3.1)

11. -0.9 (obj. 1.3.3)   **12.** $-\frac{10}{17}$ (obj. 1.3.3)   **13.** 0.343 (obj. 1.4.2)   **14.** 256 (obj. 1.4.2)   **15.** -256 (obj. 1.4.2)

16. $\frac{8}{27}$ (obj. 1.4.2)   **17.** 141 (obj. 1.4.2)   **18.** 7 (obj. 1.5.1)   **19.** 10 (obj. 1.5.1)   **20.** 11 (obj. 1.5.1)

21. -3.3 (obj. 1.5.1)   **22.** $-\frac{9}{20}$ (obj. 1.5.1)

2.6 Exercises

1. variable   **3.** Here we are multiplying 4 by x by x. Since we know from the definition of exponents that x multiplied by x is x^2, this gives us an answer of $4x^2$.
5. Yes, $a(b - c)$ can be written as $a[b + (-c)]$
$$3(10 - 2) = (3 \times 10) - (3 \times 2)$$
$$3 \times 8 = 30 - 6$$
$$24 = 24$$
7. $3x - 6y$ **9.** $-8a + 6b$ **11.** $9x + 3y$ **13.** $-10a - 15b$ **15.** $-x + 3y$ **17.** $-81x + 45y - 72$ **19.** $-10x + 2y - 12$

21. $10x^2 - 20x + 15$ **23.** $\frac{x^2}{5} + 2xy - \frac{4x}{5}$ **25.** $5x^2 + 10xy + 5xz$ **27.** $-4x + 6$ **29.** $18x^2 + 3xy - 3x$

31. $-3x^2 y - 2xy^2 + xy$ **33.** $6x^2 y + 9xy^2 - 6xy$ **35.** $9.43x^2 - 5.29x + 0.92$ **37.** $0.36x^3 + 0.09x^2 - 0.15x$
39. $0.3x^2 + 0.4xy - 2.5x$ **41.** $800(5x + 14y) = 4000x + 11{,}200y$ square feet   **43.** $8xy - 20y$ dollars
45. $4x(3000 - 2y) = 12{,}000 - 8xy$ square feet   **46.** -16 **47.** 64   **48.** 14   **49.** 4   **50.** 10   **51.** 56%   **52.** 14 days

2.7 Exercises

1. A term is a number, a variable, or a product of numbers and variables.
3. The two terms $5x$ and $-8x$ are like terms because they both have the variable x with the exponent of one.
5. The only like terms are $7xy$ and $-14xy$ because the other two have different exponents even though they have the same variables.
7. $-25b^2$ **9.** $18x^4 + 7x^2$ **11.** $-5x - 5y$ **13.** $7.1x - 3.5y$ **15.** $-2x - 8.7y$ **17.** $5p + q - 18$ **19.** $5bc - 6ac$

21. $x^2 - 10x + 3$ **23.** $-10y^2 - 16y + 12$ **25.** $-\frac{1}{15}x - \frac{2}{21}y$ **27.** $\frac{11}{20}a^2 - \frac{5}{6}b$ **29.** $-8ab - 3a - 6b$ **31.** $28a - 20b$

33. $-27ab - 11b^2$ **35.** $-8x^2 - 39y$ **37.** $32x + 23$ **39.** $7a + 9b$ **41.** $7a + 7b + 3$ centimeters   **43.** $36x - 20$ inches

45. $-\frac{2}{15}$ **46.** $-\frac{5}{6}$ **47.** $\frac{23}{50}$ **48.** $-\frac{15}{98}$ **49.** 0.2 liter

2.8 Exercises

1. -5 **3.** -11 **5.** $\frac{25}{2}$ or $12\frac{1}{2}$ **7.** -26 **9.** -1.3 **11.** $\frac{25}{4}$ or $6\frac{1}{4}$ **13.** 10   **15.** 3   **17.** -24 **19.** -20 **21.** 9   **23.** 39

25. -2 **27.** 15   **29.** 42   **31.** -9 **33.** 29   **35.** 49   **37.** 32   **39.** $-\frac{1}{2}$ **41.** 352 square feet   **43.** 1.24 square centimeters

45. 32 square inches   **47.** 56,000 square feet   **49.** 50.24 square centimeters   **51.** $-78.5°C$ **53.** \$2340.00   **55.** $-58°F$ to $140°F$

57. 1.4 miles; air is thin, oxygen is lacking   **59.** 16   **60.** $-x^2 + 2x - 4y$ **61.** 6.2 minutes/song
62. $53.5 = 54$ papers each approximately

2.9 Exercises

1. $-(3x + 2y)$ **3.** distributive   **5.** $3x + 6y$ **7.** $5a + 3b$ **9.** $x - 7y$ **11.** $8x^3 - 4x^2 + 12x$ **13.** $-2x + 26y$
15. $4x - 6y - 3$ **17.** $15a - 60ab$ **19.** $12a^3 - 19a^2 - 22a$ **21.** $3a^2 + 16b + 12b^2$ **23.** $-7a + 8b$ **25.** $9b^2 + 36b - 12$
27. $12a^2 - 8b$ **29.** 219 unsuccessful; 8541 successful   **31.** 97.52°F   **32.** 453,416 square feet   **33.** 300,000 sq feet; $16,500.00
34. 11.375 sq ft   **35.** Great Danes weigh 264.4 to 330.75 kg on average.   **36.** Miniature Pinschers weigh on average 19.845 to 30.87 kg.
    $1387.75

Putting Your Skills to Work

1. about 21,190,964   **2.** about 9,518,000   **3.** 846,622,338 people   **4.** 76,598,250 people   **5.** 92,190,000   **6.** 105,690,000

Chapter 2 Review Problems

1. -8 **2.** -4.2 **3.** -9 **4.** 1.9   **5.** $-\dfrac{1}{3}$ **6.** $-\dfrac{7}{22}$ **7.** $\dfrac{1}{6}$ **8.** $\dfrac{22}{15}$ or $1\dfrac{7}{15}$ **9.** 8   **10.** 13   **11.** -33 **12.** 9.2

13. $-\dfrac{13}{8}$ or $-1\dfrac{5}{8}$ **14.** $\dfrac{1}{2}$ **15.** -22.7 **16.** -88 **17.** -3 **18.** 18   **19.** 32   **20.** $-\dfrac{2}{3}$ **21.** $-\dfrac{25}{7}$ or $-3\dfrac{4}{7}$ **22.** -72

23. 30   **24.** -30 **25.** -4 **26.** 16   **27.** -29 **28.** 1   **29.** $-\dfrac{1}{2}$ **30.** $-\dfrac{4}{7}$ **31.** -30 **32.** -5 **33.** -9.1 **34.** 0.9

35. 10.1   **36.** -1.2 **37.** 1.9   **38.** -1.3 **39.** 24 yards   **40.** -22°F   **41.** 7363 feet   **42.** $2\dfrac{1}{4}$ point loss   **43.** -243

44. -128 **45.** 625   **46.** $\dfrac{8}{27}$ **47.** -81 **48.** 0.36   **49.** $\dfrac{25}{36}$ **50.** $\dfrac{27}{64}$ **51.** -44 **52.** 30   **53.** 1   **54.** $15x - 35y$

55. $6x^2 - 14xy + 8x$ **56.** $-7x^2 + 3x - 11$ **57.** $-6xy^2 - 3xy + 3y^2$ **58.** $-5a^2b + 3bc$ **59.** $-3x - 4y$ **60.** $-5x^2 - 35x - 9$

61. $10x^2 - 8x - \dfrac{1}{2}$ **62.** -55 **63.** 1   **64.** -4 **65.** -15 **66.** 10   **67.** -16 **68.** $\dfrac{32}{5}$ **69.** $810   **70.** 86°F

71. $2119.50   **72.** $8580.00   **73.** 100,000 sq ft   **74.** 10.45 sq feet $689.70   **75.** $-2x + 42$ **76.** $-17x - 18$ **77.** $-2 + 10x$
    $200,000
78. $-12x^2 + 63x$ **79.** $5xy^3 - 6x^3y - 13x^2y^2 - 6x^2y$ **80.** $x - 10y + 35 - 15xy$ **81.** $10x - 22y - 36$
82. $-10a + 25ab - 15b^2 - 10ab^2$ **83.** $-3x - 9xy + 18y^2$ **84.** $10x + 8xy - 32y$ **85.** -2.3 **86.** 8   **87.** $-\dfrac{22}{15}$ or $-1\dfrac{7}{15}$
88. $-\dfrac{1}{8}$ **89.** -1 **90.** -0.5 **91.** $\dfrac{3}{2}$ or $1\dfrac{1}{2}$ **92.** 6   **93.** 240   **94.** -25.42 **95.** $600   **96.** 0.0081

97. -0.0625 **98.** 10   **99.** $-4.9x + 4.1y$ **100.** $-\dfrac{1}{9}$ **101.** $-\dfrac{2}{3}$ **102.** The dog doesn't have a fever. 101.48° is below normal.
103. $3y^2 + 12y - 7x - 28$ **104.** $-12x + 6y + 12xy$

How Am I Doing? Chapter 2 Test

1. -0.3 (obj. 1.1.4)   **2.** 2 (obj. 1.2.1)   **3.** $-\dfrac{14}{3}$ or $-4\dfrac{2}{3}$ (obj. 1.3.1)   **4.** -70 (obj. 1.3.1)   **5.** 4 (obj. 1.3.3)   **6.** -3 (obj. 1.3.3)

7. -64 (obj. 1.4.2)   **8.** 2.56 (obj. 1.4.2)   **9.** $\dfrac{16}{81}$ (obj. 1.4.2)   **10.** 6.8 (obj. 1.5.1)   **11.** -25 (obj. 1.5.1)

12. $-5x^2 - 10xy + 35x$ (obj. 1.6.1)   **13.** $6a^2b^2 + 4ab^3 - 14a^2b^3$ (obj. 1.6.1)   **14.** $2a^2b + \dfrac{15}{2}ab$ (obj. 1.7.2)
15. $-1.8x^2y - 4.7xy^2$ (obj. 1.7.2)   **16.** $5a + 30$ (obj. 1.7.2)   **17.** $14x - 16y$ (obj. 1.7.2)   **18.** 122 (obj. 1.8.1)   **19.** 37 (obj. 1.8.1)
20. $\dfrac{13}{6}$ or $2\dfrac{1}{6}$ (obj. 1.8.1)   **21.** 96.6 kilometers/hr (obj. 1.8.2)   **22.** 22,800 sq ft (obj. 1.8.2)   **23.** $23.12 (obj. 1.8.2)   **24.** 3 cans (obj. 1.8.2)
25. $3x - 6xy - 21y^2$ (obj. 1.9.1)   **26.** $-3a - 9ab + 3b^2 - 3ab^2$ (obj. 1.9.1)

Chapter 3

3.1 Exercises

1. equals, equal   **3.** solution   **5.** answers vary   **7.** $x = 4$ **9.** $x = 12$ **11.** $x = 17$ **13.** $x = -5$ **15.** $x = -13$ **17.** $x = 62$
19. $x = 15$ **21.** $x = 21$ **23.** $x = 0$ **25.** $x = -7$ **27.** $x = 21$ **29.** no, $x = 9$ **31.** no, $x = -13$ **33.** yes   **35.** yes

37. $x = -1.8$ **39.** $x = 2.5$ **41.** $x = 1$ **43.** $x = -\dfrac{1}{4}$ **45.** $x = -7$ **47.** $x = \dfrac{17}{6}$ or $2\dfrac{5}{6}$ **49.** $x = \dfrac{13}{12}$ or $1\dfrac{1}{12}$ **51.** $x = 7.2$

53. $x = 1.4906$ **55.** $-2x - 4y$ **56.** $-2y^2 - 4y + 4$ **57.** yes, this was $1.9\% < 3\%$ **58.** $14.92   **59.** 117 feet

3.2 Exercises

1. 6 **3.** 7 **5.** $x = 36$ **7.** $x = -27$ **9.** $x = 80$ **11.** $x = -15$ **13.** $x = 4$ **15.** $x = 8$ **17.** $x = -\frac{8}{3}$ or $-2\frac{2}{3}$

19. $x = 50$ **21.** $x = 15$ **23.** $x = -7$ **25.** $x = 0.2$ or $\frac{1}{5}$ **27.** $x = 4$ **29.** no, $x = -7$ **31.** yes **33.** $y = -0.03$

35. $t = \frac{8}{3}$ or $2\frac{2}{3}$ **37.** $y = -0.7$ **39.** $x = 3$ **41.** $x = -4$ **43.** $x = \frac{7}{9}$ **45.** $x = 1$ **47.** $x = 3$ **49.** $x = 27$

51. $x = -5.26$ **53.** To solve an equation, we are performing steps to get an equivalent equation that has the same solution. Now $a = b$ and $a(0) = b(0)$ are not equivalent equations because they do not have the same solution. So we must have the requirement that when we multiply both sides of the equation by c, it is absolutely essential that c is nonzero.

55. $48 - 6 = 42$ **56.** $-27 - 10 = -37$ **57.** $5 + 16 = 21$ **58.** $93\frac{1}{3}\%$ **59.** \$632 **60.** 104 calves **61.** 27 earthquakes

3.3 Exercises

1. $x = 2$ **3.** $x = 6$ **5.** $x = -4$ **7.** $x = 13$ **9.** $x = 3.1$ **11.** $x = 40$ **13.** $x = -27$ **15.** $x = 8$ **17.** $x = 3$ **19.** $x = 7$
21. $x = -9$ **23.** yes **25.** no, $x = -11$ **27.** $x = -1$ **29.** $x = 7$ **31.** $y = 1$ **33.** $x = 16$ **35.** $y = 3$ **37.** $x = 4$

39. $x = -\frac{1}{3}$ **41.** $x = 2.5$ or $2\frac{1}{2}$ **43.** $x = 6.5$ or $6\frac{1}{2}$ **45.** $x = 8$ **47.** $x = -3.2$ or $-3\frac{1}{5}$ **49.** $y = 2$ **51.** $x = -4$ **53.** $z = 5$

55. $a = -6.5$ **57.** $x = -\frac{2}{3}$ **59.** $x = -0.25$ or $-\frac{1}{4}$ **61.** $x = 8$ **63.** $x = -4.5$ **65.** $x = \frac{7}{6}$ or $1\frac{1}{6}$ **67.** $x = -4.23$

69. $14x^2 - 14xy$ **70.** $-10x - 60$ **71.** $\$844\frac{1}{4}$ or \$844.25 **72.** (a) \$91.00 (b) \$94.50

3.4 Exercises

1. $x = -1$ **3.** $x = 1$ **5.** $x = 1$ **7.** $x = 24$ **9.** $y = 20$ **11.** $x = 3$ **13.** $x = \frac{7}{3}$ or $2\frac{1}{3}$ **15.** $x = -3.5$ **17.** yes **19.** no

21. $x = 1$ **23.** $x = 8$ **25.** $x = 2$ **27.** $x = -3$ **29.** $y = 4$ **31.** $x = -22$ **33.** $x = 2$ **35.** $x = -12$ **37.** $x = -\frac{5}{3}$ or $-1\frac{2}{3}$

39. $x = 0.4$ **41.** no solution **43.** infinite number of solutions **45.** $x = 0$ **47.** no solution **49.** $\frac{27}{14}$ or $1\frac{13}{14}$ **50.** $\frac{19}{20}$

51. $-\frac{52}{3}$ or $-17\frac{1}{3}$ **52.** $\frac{22}{5}$ or $4\frac{2}{5}$ **53.** 264 pairs **54.** 3173 seats **55.** \$226.08 **56.** \$108

How Am I Doing? Sections 3.1–3.4

1. $x = -9$ (obj. 2.1.1) **2.** $x = -10.9$ (obj. 2.1.1) **3.** $x = 9$ (obj. 2.2.2) **4.** $x = -8$ (obj. 2.2.2) **5.** $x = \frac{2}{3}$ (obj. 2.3.1)

6. $x = \frac{7}{26}$ (obj. 2.3.2) **7.** $x = \frac{3}{5}$ (obj. 2.3.3) **8.** $x = 3.75$ (obj. 2.3.3) **9.** $x = -1.6$ or $-1\frac{3}{5}$ (obj. 2.3.3) **10.** $x = \frac{8}{9}$ (obj. 2.4.1)

11. $x = -3$ (obj. 2.4.1) **12.** $x = \frac{9}{11}$ (obj. 2.4.1) **13.** $x = 5$ (obj. 2.4.1) **14.** $x = -\frac{1}{3}$ (obj. 2.4.1)

3.5 Exercises

1. $x + 5$ **3.** $x - 6$ **5.** $\frac{1}{8}x$ or $\frac{x}{8}$ **7.** $2x$ **9.** $3 + \frac{1}{2}x$ **11.** $2x + 9$ **13.** $\frac{1}{3}(x + 7)$ **15.** $\frac{1}{3}x - 2x$ **17.** $3x - 7$

19. x = value of a share of AT&T stock **21.** $2w + 7$ = length **23.** x = number of boxes sold by Keiko
$x + 74.50$ = value of a share of IBM stock w = width $x - 43$ = number of boxes sold by Sarah
$x + 53$ = number of boxes sold by Imelda

25. 1st angle = $s - 16$ **27.** v = value of exports of Canada **29.** 1st angle = $3x$
2nd angle = s $2v$ = value of exports of Japan 2nd angle = x
3rd angle = $2s$ 3rd angle = $x - 14$

31. A = area of Minnesota

$\frac{1}{2}A$ = area of Kentucky

$\frac{2}{5}A$ = area of Maine

33. x = points for an arrow in the blue ring. **35.** x = men aged 16–24 **37.** $x = 7$ **38.** $x = -\frac{5}{2}$ or $-2\frac{1}{2}$
$3x - 6$ = points awarded for an arrow in the gold ring. $x + 51$ = men aged 25–34
$x - 60$ = men aged 35–44
$x - 132$ = men aged 45 and above

39. $x = 12$ **40.** $w = 7$

3.6 Exercises

1. Yes, both statements imply 5 is to the right of -6 on the number line.   **3.** >   **5.** >   **7.** <   **9. (a)** <   **(b)** >
11. (a) >   **(b)** <   **13.** >   **15.** >   **17.** >   **19.** <   **21.** <   **23.** <   **25.**
$$\underset{5 \quad 6 \quad 7 \quad 8 \quad 9}{\vdash\!\!+\!\!-\!\!+\!\!-\!\!+\!\!-\!\!+\!\!\rightarrow}$$

27.
$$\underset{-7 \quad -6 \quad -5 \quad -4 \quad -3}{\longleftarrow\!\!-\!\!\bullet\!\!=\!\!=\!\!=\!\!-\!\!\rightarrow}$$
29.
$$\underset{\frac{1}{4} \quad \frac{1}{2} \quad \frac{3}{4} \quad 1 \quad \frac{5}{4}}{\vdash\!\!+\!\!-\!\!\circ\!\!=\!\!=\!\!\rightarrow}$$
31.
$$\underset{-5.6 \ -5.5 \ -5.4 \ -5.3 \ -5.2 \ -5.1}{\longleftarrow\!\!=\!\!=\!\!\bullet\!\!-\!\!+\!\!-\!\!+\!\!\rightarrow}$$
33.
$$\underset{10 \quad 15 \quad 20 \quad 25 \quad 30}{\vdash\!\!+\!\!-\!\!+\!\!-\!\!\circ\!\!=\!\!\rightarrow}$$

35. $x \geq -\dfrac{2}{3}$ **37.** $x < -20$ **39.** $x > 2.8$ **41.** $W > 175$ **43.** $h \geq 37$ **45.**
$$\overset{-\frac{5}{2}}{\underset{-3 \ -2 \ -1 \ 0 \ 1 \ 2}{\vdash\!\!\bullet\!\!=\!\!=\!\!=\!\!\bullet\!\!\rightarrow}}$$

47. $x \leq -3$
$$\underset{-5 \ -4 \ -3 \ -2 \ -1 \ 0}{\longleftarrow\!\!=\!\!\bullet\!\!-\!\!+\!\!-\!\!+\!\!\rightarrow}$$
49. $x \leq 5$
$$\underset{-2 \ -1 \ 0 \ 1 \ 2 \ 3 \ 4 \ 5 \ 6 \ 7 \ 8}{\longleftarrow\!\!=\!\!=\!\!=\!\!=\!\!=\!\!=\!\!\bullet\!\!-\!\!+\!\!-\!\!+\!\!\rightarrow}$$

51. $x > -9$
$$\underset{-11 \ -10 \ -9 \ -8 \ -7}{\vdash\!\!+\!\!-\!\!\circ\!\!=\!\!=\!\!\rightarrow}$$
53. $x \geq 8$
$$\underset{5 \ 6 \ 7 \ 8 \ 9 \ 10 \ 11}{\vdash\!\!+\!\!-\!\!\bullet\!\!=\!\!=\!\!=\!\!\rightarrow}$$
55. $x < -12$
$$\underset{-14 \ -13 \ -12 \ -11 \ -10}{\longleftarrow\!\!=\!\!\circ\!\!-\!\!+\!\!-\!\!+\!\!}$$

57. $x \geq -2$
$$\underset{-3 \ -2 \ -1 \ 0 \ 1 \ 2}{\vdash\!\!-\!\!\bullet\!\!=\!\!=\!\!=\!\!\rightarrow}$$
59. $x < \dfrac{3}{2}$
$$\underset{\frac{1}{2} \ 1 \ \frac{3}{2} \ 2 \ \frac{5}{2}}{\longleftarrow\!\!=\!\!\circ\!\!-\!\!+\!\!-\!\!}$$
61. $x > -6$
$$\underset{-10 \ -9 \ -8 \ -7 \ -6 \ -5 \ -4}{\vdash\!\!+\!\!-\!\!+\!\!-\!\!\circ\!\!=\!\!=\!\!\rightarrow}$$

63. $x > \dfrac{1}{3}$
$$\underset{0 \ \frac{1}{3} \ \frac{2}{3} \ 1 \ \frac{4}{3}}{\vdash\!\!\circ\!\!=\!\!=\!\!=\!\!\rightarrow}$$
65. $3 > 1$ Adding any number to both sides of an inequality doesn't reverse the direction.

67. $x > 3$ **69.** $x \geq 4$ **71.** $x < -1$ **73.** $x \leq 14$ **75.** $x < -3$ **77.** 76 or greater   **79.** 8 days or more   **81.** 6.08   **82.** 15%
83. 2%   **84.** 37.5%   **85.** 260 feet   **86.** width = 6.5 inches
height = 3.6 inches

Putting Your Skills to Work

1. 8.4 gallons per hour   **2.** 252 gallons   **3.** 32.3 gallons per hour   **4.** 55 miles per hour   **5.** $x = \dfrac{y + 0.1}{0.5}$ or $2y + 0.2 = x$ **6.** 35 mph

Chapter 3 Review Problems

1. -7 **2.** -3 **3.** 2   **4.** -3 **5.** 40.4   **6.** -7 **7.** -2 **8.** -27 **9.** 20   **10.** -9 **11.** -3 **12.** -1 **13.** 4
14. -7 **15.** 3   **16.** $-\dfrac{7}{2}$ or $-3\dfrac{1}{2}$ or -3.5 **17.** 5   **18.** 1   **19.** 20   **20.** $\dfrac{2}{3}$ **21.** 5   **22.** $\dfrac{35}{11}$ or $3\dfrac{2}{11}$ **23.** 4   **24.** -17
25. $\dfrac{2}{5}$ or 0.4   **26.** 32   **27.** $\dfrac{26}{7}$ or $3\dfrac{5}{7}$ **28.** -1 **29.** $\dfrac{1}{5}$ **30.** $\dfrac{3}{4}$ **31.** -17 **32.** -32 **33.** $-3\dfrac{2}{5}$ or $-\dfrac{17}{5}$ or -3.4 **34.** 9

35. $x + 19$ **36.** $\dfrac{2}{3}x$ **37.** $3(x + 4)$ **38.** $2x - 3$ **39.** r = the number of retired people; $4r$ = the number of working people; $0.5r$ = the
number of unemployed people   **40.** $3w + 5$ = the length; w = the width
41. b = the number of degrees in angle B; $2b$ = the number of degrees in angle A; $b - 17$ = the number of degrees in angle C
42. a = the number of students in algebra; $a + 29$ = the number of students in biology; $0.5a$ = the number of students in geology
43. $x \leq 2$
$$\underset{-2 \ -1 \ 0 \ 1 \ 2 \ 3}{\longleftarrow\!\!=\!\!=\!\!=\!\!\bullet\!\!-\!\!+\!\!\rightarrow}$$
44. $x \geq 1$
$$\underset{-2 \ -1 \ 0 \ 1 \ 2 \ 3}{\vdash\!\!+\!\!-\!\!\bullet\!\!=\!\!=\!\!\rightarrow}$$
45. $x < -4$
$$\underset{-5 \ -4 \ -3 \ -2 \ -1 \ 0}{\longleftarrow\!\!=\!\!\circ\!\!-\!\!+\!\!-\!\!+\!\!\rightarrow}$$

46. $x > -3$
$$\underset{-5 \ -4 \ -3 \ -2 \ -1 \ 0}{\vdash\!\!+\!\!-\!\!\circ\!\!=\!\!=\!\!\rightarrow}$$
47. $x \geq 6$
$$\underset{5 \ 6 \ 7}{\vdash\!\!-\!\!\bullet\!\!=\!\!\rightarrow}$$
48. $x < 5$
$$\underset{3 \ 4 \ 5 \ 6 \ 7}{\longleftarrow\!\!=\!\!\circ\!\!-\!\!+\!\!-\!\!}$$

49. $x < 10$
$$\underset{7 \ 8 \ 9 \ 10 \ 11 \ 12}{\longleftarrow\!\!=\!\!\circ\!\!-\!\!+\!\!-\!\!+\!\!}$$
50. $x > -3$
$$\underset{-5 \ -4 \ -3 \ -2 \ -1 \ 0}{\vdash\!\!+\!\!-\!\!\circ\!\!=\!\!=\!\!\rightarrow}$$
51. $h \leq 32$ hours   **52.** $n \leq 17$

53. $-\dfrac{7}{3}$ or $-2\dfrac{1}{3}$ **54.** $-\dfrac{2}{7}$ **55.** 0   **56.** 4   **57.** 4   **58.** -5 **59.** $x < 2$
$$\underset{-1 \ 0 \ 1 \ 2 \ 3 \ 4}{\longleftarrow\!\!=\!\!\circ\!\!-\!\!+\!\!-\!\!}$$

60. $x \leq -8$
$$\underset{-10 \ -9 \ -8 \ -7 \ -6 \ -5}{\longleftarrow\!\!=\!\!\bullet\!\!-\!\!+\!\!-\!\!+\!\!\rightarrow}$$
61. $x \geq \dfrac{19}{7}$
$$\underset{\frac{15}{7} \ \frac{17}{7} \ \frac{19}{7}}{\vdash\!\!-\!\!+\!\!\bullet\!\!=\!\!\rightarrow}$$
62. $x \geq -15$
$$\underset{-15 \ -13 \ -11}{\vdash\!\!\bullet\!\!=\!\!=\!\!=\!\!\rightarrow}$$

How Am I Doing? Chapter 3 Test

1. $x = 2$ (obj. 2.3.1)   **2.** $x = \dfrac{1}{3}$ (obj. 2.3.2)   **3.** $y = -\dfrac{7}{2}$ or $-3\dfrac{1}{2}$ or -3.5 (obj. 2.3.3)   **4.** $y = 8.4$ or $\dfrac{42}{5}$ or $8\dfrac{2}{5}$ (obj. 2.4.1)

5. $x = 1$ (obj. 2.3.3)   **6.** $x = -1.2$ (obj. 2.3.3)   **7.** $y = 7$ (obj. 2.4.1)   **8.** $y = \dfrac{7}{3}$ or $2\dfrac{1}{3}$ (obj. 2.3.3)   **9.** $x = 13$ (obj. 2.3.3)

10. $x = 20$ (obj. 2.3.3)   **11.** $x = 10$ (obj. 2.3.3)   **12.** $x = -4$ (obj. 2.3.3)   **13.** $x = 12$ (obj. 2.3.3)   **14.** $x = -\dfrac{1}{5}$ or -0.2 (obj. 2.4.1)

15. $x = 3$ (obj. 2.4.1)   **16.** $x = 2$ (obj. 2.4.1)   **17.** $x = -2$ (obj. 2.4.1)   **18.** $x \leq -3$ (obj. 2.8.4)
$$\underset{-5 \ -4 \ -3 \ -2 \ -1 \ 0}{\longleftarrow\!\!=\!\!\bullet\!\!-\!\!+\!\!-\!\!+\!\!\rightarrow}$$
19. $x > -\dfrac{5}{4}$ (obj. 2.8.4)
$$\underset{-\frac{7}{4} \ -\frac{5}{4} \ -\frac{3}{4}}{\vdash\!\!-\!\!\circ\!\!=\!\!\rightarrow}$$
20. $x < 2$ (obj. 2.8.4)
$$\underset{0 \ 1 \ 2 \ 3 \ 4}{\longleftarrow\!\!=\!\!\circ\!\!-\!\!+\!\!-\!\!}$$

21. $x \geq \dfrac{1}{2}$ (obj. 2.8.4)
$$\underset{-\frac{1}{2} \ 0 \ \frac{1}{2} \ 1 \ \frac{3}{2}}{\vdash\!\!-\!\!+\!\!\bullet\!\!=\!\!=\!\!\rightarrow}$$
22. 35 (obj. 2.6.1)   **23.** 36 (obj. 2.6.1)   **24.** -4 (obj. 2.6.1)

25. first side = 20 m; second side = 30 m; third side = 16 m (obj. 2.6.2)   **26.** width = 20 m; length = 47 m (obj. 2.6.2)
27. 213.52 in. (obj. 2.7.1)   **28.** 192 square inches (obj. 2.7.1)   **29.** 4187 in.^{3} (obj. 2.7.2)   **30.** 96 cm^2 (obj. 2.7.1)   **31.** \$450 (obj. 2.7.3)

Chapter 4

4.1 Exercises

1. 0   **3.** The order in which you write the numbers matters. The graph of $(5, 1)$ is not the same as the graph of $(1, 5)$.

5.

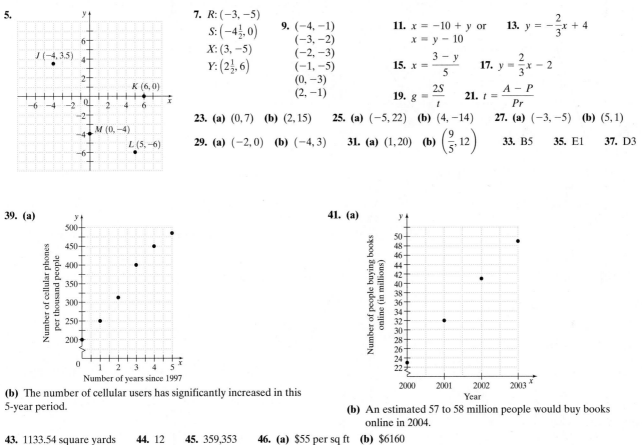

7. $R: (-3, -5)$
$S: \left(-4\frac{1}{2}, 0\right)$
$X: (3, -5)$
$Y: \left(2\frac{1}{2}, 6\right)$

9. $(-4, -1)$
$(-3, -2)$
$(-2, -3)$
$(-1, -5)$
$(0, -3)$
$(2, -1)$

11. $x = -10 + y$ or
$x = y - 10$

13. $y = -\dfrac{2}{3}x + 4$

15. $x = \dfrac{3 - y}{5}$ **17.** $y = \dfrac{2}{3}x - 2$

19. $g = \dfrac{2S}{t}$ **21.** $t = \dfrac{A - P}{Pr}$

23. (a) $(0, 7)$ **(b)** $(2, 15)$ **25. (a)** $(-5, 22)$ **(b)** $(4, -14)$ **27. (a)** $(-3, -5)$ **(b)** $(5, 1)$

29. (a) $(-2, 0)$ **(b)** $(-4, 3)$ **31. (a)** $(1, 20)$ **(b)** $\left(\dfrac{9}{5}, 12\right)$ **33.** B5   **35.** E1   **37.** D3

39. (a)

41. (a)

(b) The number of cellular users has significantly increased in this 5-year period.

(b) An estimated 57 to 58 million people would buy books online in 2004.

43. 1133.54 square yards   **44.** 12   **45.** 359,353   **46. (a)** $55 per sq ft   **(b)** $6160

4.2 Exercises

1. No, replacing x by -2 and y by 5 in the equation does not result in a true statement.   **3.** x-axis

5. $y = -2x + 1$
$(0, 1)$
$(-2, 5)$
$(1, -1)$

7. $y = x - 4$
$(0, -4)$
$(2, -2)$
$(4, 0)$

9. $y = -2x + 3$
$(0, 3)$
$(2, -1)$
$(4, -5)$

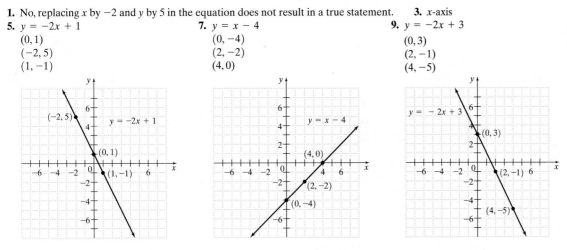

11. $y = 3x + 2$
$(-1, -1)$
$(0, 2)$
$(1, 5)$

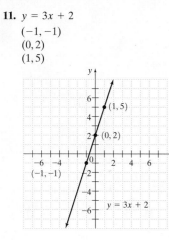

13. $3x - 2y = 0$

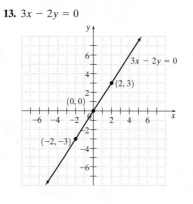

15. $y = -\frac{3}{4}x + 3$

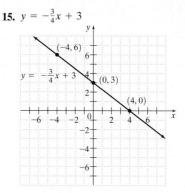

17. $4x + 3y = 12$

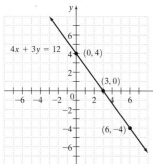

19. $y = 6 - 2x$

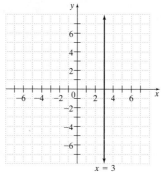

21. $x + 3 = 6y$

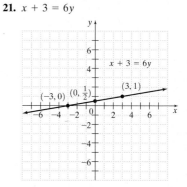

23. $y - 2 = 3y$

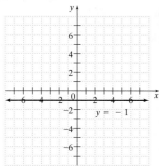

25. $2x + 9 = 5x$

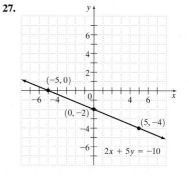

27.

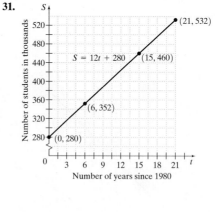

29. $C = 0; C = 120; C = 240; C = 360;$
$C = 480; C = 600$

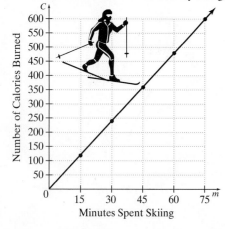

31.

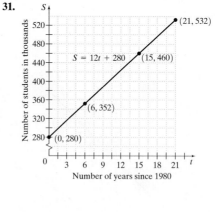

33. -2 **34.** $x \geq -\dfrac{14}{3}$

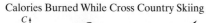

35. $W = 9.5$ meters
$L = 17$ meters

36. 212

37. one base $= 4$ in.
other base $= 5$ in.

4.3 Exercises

1. No, division by zero is impossible, so the slope is undefined. **3.** 3 **5.** -1 **7.** $\frac{3}{5}$ **9.** $-\frac{1}{4}$ **11.** $-\frac{4}{3}$ **13.** $-\frac{16}{5}$

15. $m = 8; (0, 9)$ **17.** $m = -3; (0, 4)$ **19.** $m = -\frac{8}{7}\left(0, \frac{3}{4}\right)$ **21.** $m = -6; (0, 0)$ **23.** $m = -6; \left(0, \frac{4}{5}\right)$ **25.** $m = -\frac{5}{2}; \left(0, \frac{3}{2}\right)$

27. $m = \frac{7}{3}; \left(0, -\frac{4}{3}\right)$ **29.** $y = \frac{3}{5}x + 3$ **31.** $y = 6x - 3$ **33.** $y = -\frac{5}{4}x - \frac{3}{4}$

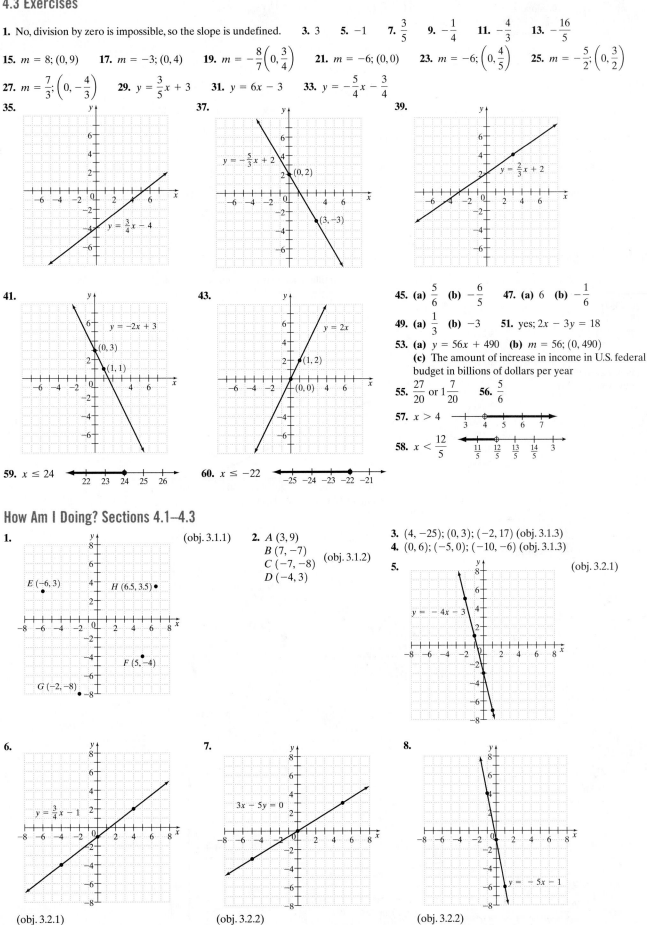

35. $y = \frac{3}{4}x - 4$

37. $y = -\frac{5}{3}x + 2$ $(0, 2)$ $(3, -3)$

39. $y = \frac{2}{3}x + 2$

41. $y = -2x + 3$ $(0, 3)$ $(1, 1)$

43. $y = 2x$ $(1, 2)$ $(0, 0)$

45. (a) $\frac{5}{6}$ (b) $-\frac{6}{5}$ **47.** (a) 6 (b) $-\frac{1}{6}$

49. (a) $\frac{1}{3}$ (b) -3 **51.** yes; $2x - 3y = 18$

53. (a) $y = 56x + 490$ (b) $m = 56; (0, 490)$
(c) The amount of increase in income in U.S. federal budget in billions of dollars per year

55. $\frac{27}{20}$ or $1\frac{7}{20}$ **56.** $\frac{5}{6}$

57. $x > 4$

58. $x < \frac{12}{5}$

59. $x \le 24$ **60.** $x \le -22$

How Am I Doing? Sections 4.1–4.3

1. (obj. 3.1.1)
$E (-6, 3)$ $H (6.5, 3.5)$ $F (5, -4)$ $G (-2, -8)$

2. $A (3, 9)$
$B (7, -7)$
$C (-7, -8)$ (obj. 3.1.2)
$D (-4, 3)$

3. $(4, -25); (0, 3); (-2, 17)$ (obj. 3.1.3)
4. $(0, 6); (-5, 0); (-10, -6)$ (obj. 3.1.3)

5. (obj. 3.2.1)
$y = -4x - 3$

6. $y = \frac{3}{4}x - 1$
(obj. 3.2.1)

7. $3x - 5y = 0$
(obj. 3.2.2)

8. $y = -5x - 1$
(obj. 3.2.2)

9. $\frac{5}{8}$ (obj. 3.3.1)   **10.** slope = 3   **11.** $-\frac{4}{3}$ (obj. 3.3.5)   **12.** $-\frac{11}{3}$ (obj. 3.3.5)

y-intercept = $\left(0, -\frac{5}{3}\right)$

(obj. 3.3.2)

4.4 Exercises

1. $y = 4x + 12$ **3.** $y = -3x + 11$ **5.** $y = -3x + \frac{7}{2}$ **7.** $y = -\frac{2}{5}x - 1$ **9.** $y = -2x - 6$ **11.** $y = -4x + 2$

13. $y = 5x - 10$ **15.** $y = \frac{1}{3}x + \frac{1}{2}$ **17.** $y = -2x + 11$ **19.** $y = -3x + 3$ **21.** $y = -\frac{2}{3}x + 1$ **23.** $y = \frac{2}{3}x - 4$

25. $y = -\frac{2}{3}x$ **27.** $y = -2$ **29.** $y = -2$ **31.** $x = 4$ **33.** $y = \frac{3}{4}x - 4$ **35.** $y = -\frac{1}{2}x + 4$ **37.** $y = 2.4x + 227$

39. $x < -4$ **40.** $x \le 3$ **41.** $x \ge 4\frac{2}{3}$ **42.** $x > -4$ **43. (a)** 2920 gallons **(b)** \$24.82   **44.** width = 550 feet
length = 1170 feet

Putting Your Skills to Work

1. 213, 408 acres; 78,000,000 acres   **2.** 4337 million acres   **3.** 4181 million acres, 3947 million acres   **4.** $r(t) = 4337 - 78t$

5. $(0, 4337)$
$(5, 3947)$
$(10, 3557)$
$(15, 3167)$
$(20, 2777)$
7. about 827 million acres
8. approximately 2045

6. $r(t) = 4337 - 78t$

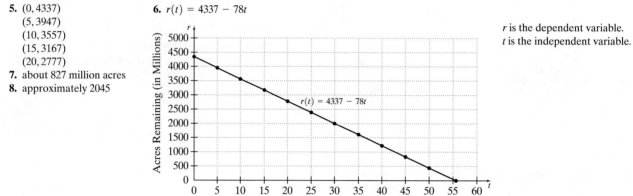

r is the dependent variable.
t is the independent variable.

Chapter 4 Review Problems

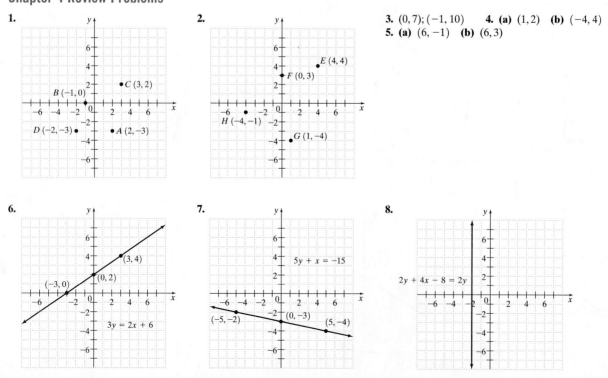

3. $(0, 7); (-1, 10)$ **4. (a)** $(1, 2)$ **(b)** $(-4, 4)$
5. (a) $(6, -1)$ **(b)** $(6, 3)$

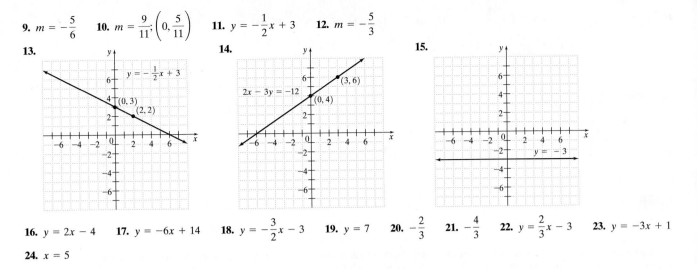

9. $m = -\dfrac{5}{6}$ **10.** $m = \dfrac{9}{11}$; $\left(0, \dfrac{5}{11}\right)$ **11.** $y = -\dfrac{1}{2}x + 3$ **12.** $m = -\dfrac{5}{3}$

13.   **14.**   **15.**

16. $y = 2x - 4$ **17.** $y = -6x + 14$ **18.** $y = -\dfrac{3}{2}x - 3$ **19.** $y = 7$ **20.** $-\dfrac{2}{3}$ **21.** $-\dfrac{4}{3}$ **22.** $y = \dfrac{2}{3}x - 3$ **23.** $y = -3x + 1$

24. $x = 5$

How Am I Doing? Chapter 4 Test

1.   (obj. 3.1.1)   **2.**   (obj. 3.2.1)

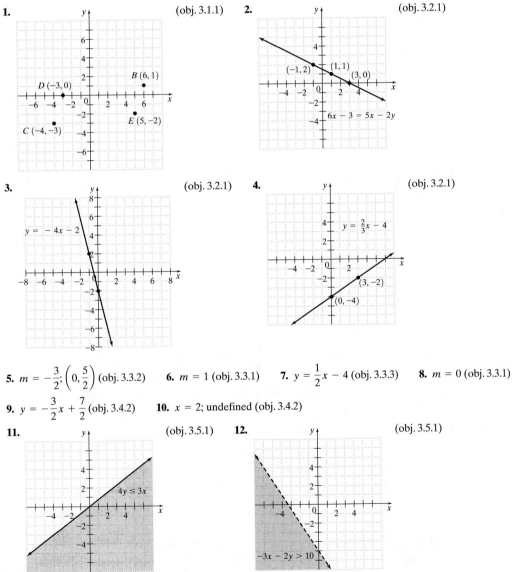

3.   (obj. 3.2.1)   **4.**   (obj. 3.2.1)

5. $m = -\dfrac{3}{2}$; $\left(0, \dfrac{5}{2}\right)$ (obj. 3.3.2)   **6.** $m = 1$ (obj. 3.3.1)   **7.** $y = \dfrac{1}{2}x - 4$ (obj. 3.3.3)   **8.** $m = 0$ (obj. 3.3.1)

9. $y = -\dfrac{3}{2}x + \dfrac{7}{2}$ (obj. 3.4.2)   **10.** $x = 2$; undefined (obj. 3.4.2)

11.   (obj. 3.5.1)   **12.**   (obj. 3.5.1)

13. No, two different ordered pairs have the same first coordinate. (obj. 3.6.1)

14. Yes, any vertical line passes through no more than one point on the graph. (obj. 3.6.3)

15.

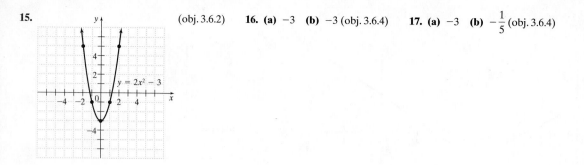

(obj. 3.6.2)   **16. (a)** -3 **(b)** -3 (obj. 3.6.4)   **17. (a)** -3 **(b)** $-\dfrac{1}{5}$ (obj. 3.6.4)

Chapter 5

5.1 Exercises

1. There is no solution. There is no point (x, y) that satisfies both equations. The graph of such a system yields two parallel lines.
3. It may have one solution, it may have no solution, or it may have an infinite number of solutions.

5. $\left(\dfrac{3}{2}, -1\right)$ is a solution to the system.

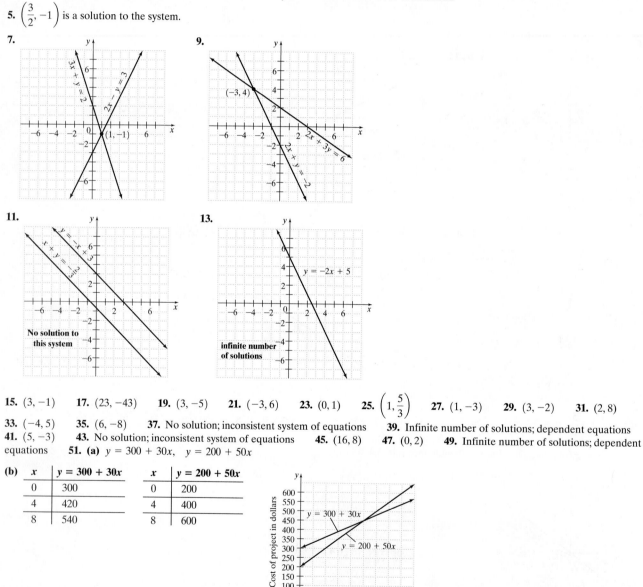

7.

9.

11.

13.

15. $(3, -1)$ **17.** $(23, -43)$ **19.** $(3, -5)$ **21.** $(-3, 6)$ **23.** $(0, 1)$ **25.** $\left(1, \dfrac{5}{3}\right)$ **27.** $(1, -3)$ **29.** $(3, -2)$ **31.** $(2, 8)$

33. $(-4, 5)$ **35.** $(6, -8)$ **37.** No solution; inconsistent system of equations   **39.** Infinite number of solutions; dependent equations
41. $(5, -3)$ **43.** No solution; inconsistent system of equations   **45.** $(16, 8)$ **47.** $(0, 2)$ **49.** Infinite number of solutions; dependent
equations   **51. (a)** $y = 300 + 30x$, $y = 200 + 50x$

(b)

x	$y = 300 + 30x$
0	300
4	420
8	540

x	$y = 200 + 50x$
0	200
4	400
8	600

(c) The cost will be the same for 5 hours of installing new tile.   **(d)** The cost will be less for Modern Bathroom Headquarters.
53. $27   **54.** 341,889 cars

Putting Your Skills to Work

1. Plan A: $C = 20 + 0.52x$ Plan B: $C = 30 + 0.4x$

2.

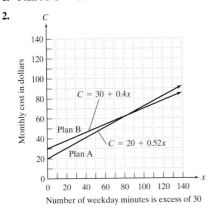

The graphs seem to intersect when x is about 83. This represents 113 weekday minutes of cell phone use per month.
3. $x = 83.3$, yes   **4.** Plan A would be more economical for Gina. Plan B would be more economical for Aaron.
5. $258   **6.** Plan C   **7.** Plan D

Chapter 5 Review Problems

1.   **2.**   **3.**

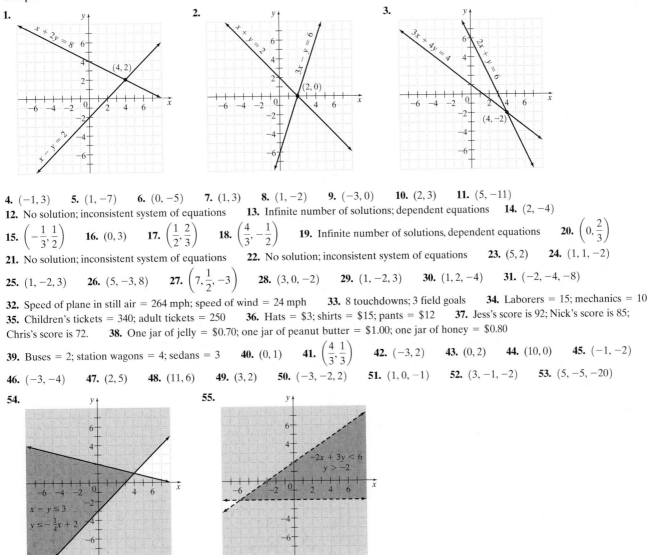

4. $(-1, 3)$ **5.** $(1, -7)$ **6.** $(0, -5)$ **7.** $(1, 3)$ **8.** $(1, -2)$ **9.** $(-3, 0)$ **10.** $(2, 3)$ **11.** $(5, -11)$
12. No solution; inconsistent system of equations   **13.** Infinite number of solutions; dependent equations   **14.** $(2, -4)$
15. $\left(-\frac{1}{3}, \frac{1}{2}\right)$ **16.** $(0, 3)$ **17.** $\left(\frac{1}{2}, \frac{2}{3}\right)$ **18.** $\left(\frac{4}{3}, -\frac{1}{2}\right)$ **19.** Infinite number of solutions, dependent equations   **20.** $\left(0, \frac{2}{3}\right)$
21. No solution; inconsistent system of equations   **22.** No solution; inconsistent system of equations   **23.** $(5, 2)$ **24.** $(1, 1, -2)$
25. $(1, -2, 3)$ **26.** $(5, -3, 8)$ **27.** $\left(7, \frac{1}{2}, -3\right)$ **28.** $(3, 0, -2)$ **29.** $(1, -2, 3)$ **30.** $(1, 2, -4)$ **31.** $(-2, -4, -8)$
32. Speed of plane in still air $= 264$ mph; speed of wind $= 24$ mph   **33.** 8 touchdowns; 3 field goals   **34.** Laborers $= 15$; mechanics $= 10$
35. Children's tickets $= 340$; adult tickets $= 250$ **36.** Hats $= 3; shirts $= 15; pants $= 12 **37.** Jess's score is 92; Nick's score is 85;
Chris's score is 72.   **38.** One jar of jelly $= 0.70; one jar of peanut butter $= 1.00; one jar of honey $= 0.80
39. Buses $= 2$; station wagons $= 4$; sedans $= 3$ **40.** $(0, 1)$ **41.** $\left(\frac{4}{3}, \frac{1}{3}\right)$ **42.** $(-3, 2)$ **43.** $(0, 2)$ **44.** $(10, 0)$ **45.** $(-1, -2)$
46. $(-3, -4)$ **47.** $(2, 5)$ **48.** $(11, 6)$ **49.** $(3, 2)$ **50.** $(-3, -2, 2)$ **51.** $(1, 0, -1)$ **52.** $(3, -1, -2)$ **53.** $(5, -5, -20)$
54.   **55.**

56.   **57.**

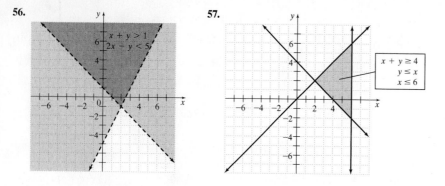

How Am I Doing? Chapter 5 Test

1. $(10, 7)$ (obj. 4.1.3)   **2.** $(3, -4)$ (obj. 4.1.4)   **3.** $(3, 4)$ (obj. 4.1.3)   **4.** $\left(\frac{1}{2}, \frac{3}{2}\right)$ (obj. 4.1.4)   **5.** $(1, 2)$ (obj. 4.1.4)

6. No solution; inconsistent system of equations (obj. 4.1.5)   **7.** $(2, -1, 3)$ (obj. 4.2.2)

Chapter 6

6.1 Exercises

1. When multiplying exponential expressions with the same base, keep the base the same and add the exponents.

3. $\frac{2^2}{2^3} = \frac{2 \cdot 2}{2 \cdot 2 \cdot 2} = \frac{1}{2} = \frac{1}{2^{3-2}}$ **5.** $6; x; y$: 11 and 1   **7.** $2^2 a^3 b$ **9.** $-3a^2 b^2 c^3$ **11.** 7^{10} **13.** 5^{26} **15.** x^{12} **17.** w^{32} **19.** $-20x^6$

21. $50x^3$ **23.** $24x^5 y^4$ **25.** $\frac{2}{15} x^3 y^5$ **27.** $-2.75 x^3 yz$ **29.** 0 **31.** $80x^3 y^7$ **33.** $-24x^4 y^7$ **35.** 0 **37.** $-24a^4 b^3 x^2 y^5$

39. $-30x^3 y^4 z^6$ **41.** y^7 **43.** $\frac{1}{y^3}$ **45.** $\frac{1}{11^{12}}$ **47.** 3^4 **49.** $\frac{a^8}{4}$ **51.** $\frac{x^7}{y^6}$ **53.** $2x^4$ **55.** $-\frac{x^3}{2y^2}$ **57.** $\frac{f^2}{30g^5}$ **59.** $-3x^3$ **61.** $\frac{y^2}{16x^3}$

63. $\frac{3a}{4}$ **65.** $\frac{17a^2 b}{9c^3}$ **67.** $-27x^5 yz^3$ **69.** x^{12} **71.** $x^7 y^{14}$ **73.** $r^6 s^{12}$ **75.** $27a^9 b^6 c^3$ **77.** $9a^8$ **79.** $\frac{x^7}{128m^{28}}$ **81.** $\frac{25x^2}{49y^4}$

83. $81a^8 b^{12}$ **85.** $-8x^9 z^3$ **87.** $\frac{9}{x}$ **89.** $27a^4 b^7$ **91.** $\frac{64}{y^{10}}$ **93.** $\frac{16x^4}{y^{12}}$ **95.** $\frac{a^4 b^8}{c^{12} d^{16}}$ **97.** $-3x^3 y^4 z^7$ **99.** -11 **100.** -46

101. $-\frac{7}{4}$ **102.** 5 **103.** approximately 17.6%   **104.** 34,500 sq km of rain forest lost

6.2 Exercises

1. $\frac{1}{x^4}$ **3.** $\frac{1}{81}$ **5.** y^8 **7.** $\frac{z^6}{x^4 y^5}$ **9.** $\frac{y^6}{x^5}$ **11.** $\frac{x^9}{8}$ **13.** $\frac{3}{x^2}$ **15.** $\frac{1}{16x^4 y^2}$ **17.** $\frac{3xz^3}{y^2}$ **19.** $3x$ **21.** $\frac{wy^3}{x^5 z^2}$ **23.** $\frac{1}{8}$ **25.** $\frac{z^8}{9y^4}$

27. $\frac{1}{x^6 y}$ **29.** 1.2378×10^5 **31.** 6.3×10^{-2} **33.** 8.8961×10^{11} **35.** 1.963×10^{-8} **37.** $302{,}000$ **39.** 0.00047 **41.** $983{,}000$

43. 2.37×10^{-5} mph   **45.** 0.000007 meters   **47.** 4.368×10^{19} **49.** 1.0×10^1 **51.** 8.1×10^{-11} **53.** 4.5×10^5

55. 2.33×10^4 dollars   **57.** 1.90×10^{11} hours   **59.** 6.6×10^{-5} miles   **61.** $\$1.6 \times 10^8$ **63.** 159.3% **65.** -0.8 **66.** -1 **67.** $-\frac{1}{28}$

68. Candidate 1 shook 2524 hands.
Candidate 2 shook 1016 hands.
69.   Mario $= \$36{,}094$
Alfonso $= \$27{,}352$
Gina $= \$48{,}554$

Putting Your Skills to Work

1. $\$13{,}526$ **2.** $\$568{,}082$ **3.** 35.4% **4.** $\$136{,}777$ **5.** $\$45{,}272$ **6.** $\$43{,}912$

Chapter 6 Review Problems

1. $-18a^7$ **2.** 5^{23} **3.** $6x^4 y^6$ **4.** $-14x^4 y^9$ **5.** $\frac{1}{7^{12}}$ **6.** $\frac{1}{x^5}$ **7.** y^{14} **8.** $\frac{1}{9^{11}}$ **9.** $-\frac{3}{5x^5 y^4}$ **10.** $-\frac{2a}{3b^6}$ **11.** x^{24} **12.** b^{30}

13. $9a^6 b^4$ **14.** $81x^{12} y^4$ **15.** $\frac{25a^2 b^4}{c^6}$ **16.** $\frac{y^9}{64w^{15} z^6}$ **17.** $\frac{b^5}{a^3}$ **18.** $\frac{m^8}{p^5}$ **19.** $\frac{2y^3}{x^6}$ **20.** $\frac{x^8}{9y^6}$ **21.** $\frac{y^8}{25x^4}$ **22.** $\frac{3y^2}{x^3}$ **23.** $\frac{4w^2}{x^5 y^6 z^8}$

24. $\dfrac{b^5c^3d^4}{27a^2}$ **25.** 1.563402×10^{11} **26.** 1.79632×10^5 **27.** 7.8×10^{-3} **28.** 6.173×10^{-5} **29.** 120,000   **30.** 6,034,000
31. 3,000,000   **32.** 0.25   **33.** 0.0000432   **34.** 0.000000006   **35.** 2.0×10^{13} **36.** 9.36×10^{19} **37.** 9.6×10^{-10} **38.** 7.8×10^{-11}
39. 3.504×10^8 kilometers   **40.** 7.94×10^{14} cycles   **41.** 6×10^9

How Am I Doing? Chapter 6 Test

1. 3^{34} (obj. 5.1.1)   **2.** $\dfrac{1}{25^{16}}$ (obj. 5.1.7)   **3.** 8^{24} (obj. 5.1.3)   **4.** $12x^4y^{10}$ (obj. 5.1.1)   **5.** $-\dfrac{7x^3}{5}$ (obj. 5.1.2)   **6.** $-125x^3y^{18}$ (obj. 5.1.3)

7. $\dfrac{49a^{14}b^4}{9}$ (obj. 5.1.3)   **8.** $\dfrac{3x^4}{4}$ (obj. 5.1.3)   **9.** $\dfrac{1}{64}$ (obj. 5.2.1)   **10.** $\dfrac{6c^5}{a^4b^3}$ (obj. 5.2.1)   **11.** $3xy^7$ (obj. 5.2.1)

12. 5.482×10^{-4} (obj. 5.2.2)   **13.** 582,000,000 (obj. 5.2.2)   **14.** 2.4×10^{-6} (obj. 5.2.2)   **15.** $-2x^2 + 5x$ (obj. 5.3.2)
16. $-11x^3 - 4x^2 + 7x - 8$ (obj. 5.3.3)   **17.** $-21x^5 + 28x^4 - 42x^3 + 14x^2$ (obj. 5.4.1)   **18.** $15x^4y^3 - 18x^3y^2 + 6x^2y$ (obj. 5.4.1)
19. $10a^2 + 7ab - 12b^2$ (obj. 5.4.2)   **20.** $6x^3 - 11x^2 - 19x - 6$ (obj. 5.5.3)   **21.** $49x^4 + 28x^2y^2 + 4y^4$ (obj. 5.5.2)
22. $25s^2 - 121t^2$ (obj. 5.5.1)   **23.** $12x^4 - 14x^3 + 25x^2 - 29x + 10$ (obj. 5.5.3)   **24.** $3x^4 + 4x^3y - 15x^2y^2$ (obj. 5.5.1)
25. $3x^3 - x + 5$ (obj. 5.6.1)   **26.** $2x^2 - 7x + 4$ (obj. 5.6.2)   **27.** $2x^2 + 6x + 12$ (obj. 5.6.2)   **28.** 3.044×10^9 barrels per year (obj. 5.2.2)
29. 4.18×10^6 miles (obj. 5.2.2)

Appendix A

A.1 Exercises

1. The base is a. The exponent is 3.   **3.** Positive   **5.** $+11$ and -11; $(+11)(+11) = 121$ and $(-11)(-11) = 121$ **7.** 32   **9.** 25

11. -36 **13.** -1 **15.** $\dfrac{1}{256}$ **17.** 0.64   **19.** 0.000064   **21.** 9   **23.** -4 **25.** $\dfrac{2}{3}$ **27.** 0.3   **29.** 1   **31.** Not a real number

33. -27 **35.** -15 **37.** 0   **39.** -28 **41.** 4   **43.** $\dfrac{2}{3}$ **45.** 1   **47.** $\dfrac{1}{9}$ **49.** $\dfrac{1}{x^5}$ **51.** $-6x^6$ **53.** $36x^8y^3$ **55.** $4y$

57. $7xy$ **59.** $-10xy^5z^9$ **61.** $-\dfrac{3}{n}$ **63.** 8   **65.** $\dfrac{2}{x^5}$ **67.** $-5b^3c$ **69.** $-\dfrac{10}{7}a^2b^4$ **71.** $\dfrac{x^{12}y^{18}}{z^6}$ **73.** $\dfrac{9a^2}{16b^{12}}$ **75.** $\dfrac{1}{8x^{12}y^{18}}$

77. $\dfrac{4x^4}{y^6}$ **79.** $-\dfrac{27m^{13}}{n^5}$ **81.** $2a^4$ **83.** x^3y^9 **85.** $\dfrac{b^5}{a^3}$ **87.** $\dfrac{1}{4x^2}$ **89.** $\dfrac{7}{5}$ **91.** $-\dfrac{6x}{y}$ **93.** 3.8×10^1 **95.** 1.73×10^6
97. 8.3×10^{-1} **99.** 5.29×10^{-5} **101.** 713,000   **103.** 0.307   **105.** 0.000000901   **107.** 4.65×10^{-6} **109.** 3×10^1
111. 1.06×10^{-18} gram

A.2 Exercises

1. Trinomial, 2nd degree   **3.** Monomial, 8th degree   **5.** Binomial, 4th degree   **7.** 6   **9.** -18 **11.** 6   **13.** $-3x - 6$

15. $10m^3 + 4m^2 - 6m - 1.3$ **17.** $5a^3 - a^2 + 12$ **19.** $\dfrac{5}{6}x^2 - 6\dfrac{3}{4}x$ **21.** $-3.2x^3 + 1.8x^2 - 4$ **23.** $10x^2 + 61x + 72$

25. $15aw + 6ad - 20bw - 8bd$ **27.** $-12x^2 + 11xy - 2y^2$ **29.** $-28ar - 77rs^2 + 4as^2 + 11s^4$ **31.** $25x^2 - 64y^2$
33. $25a^2 - 20ab + 4b^2$ **35.** $49m^2 - 14m + 1$ **37.** $16 - 9x^4$ **39.** $9m^6 + 6m^3 + 1$ **41.** $6x^3 - 10x^2 + 2x$
43. $-\dfrac{2}{3}x^2y + 2xy^2 - 5xy$ **45.** $2x^3 - 5x^2 + 5x - 3$ **47.** $6x^3 - 7x^2y - 10xy^2 + 6y^3$ **49.** $\dfrac{3}{2}x^4 + 2x^3 - 10x^2 + 8x - 6$
51. $5a^4 - 18a^3 + 11a^2 - 10a + 12$ **53.** $2x^3 - 7x^2 - 7x + 30$ **55.** $3a^3 - a^2 - 22a + 24$ **57.** $6x^3 + 25x^2 + 49x + 40$ cm³
59. 77.73 parts per million   **61.** 3 parts per million

A.3 Exercises

1. $10(8 - y)$ **3.** $5a(a - 5)$ **5.** $3c(cx^3 - 3x - 2)$ **7.** $6y^2(5y^2 + 4y + 3)$ **9.** $5ab(3b + 1 - 2a^2)$
11. $12xy^2(y - 2x^2 + 3xy^2 - 5x^3y)$ **13.** $(x + y)(3x - 2)$ **15.** $(a - 3b)(5b + 8)$ **17.** $(a + 5b)(3x + 1)$ **19.** $(3x - y)(2a^2 - 5b^3)$
21. $(5x + y)(3x - 8y - 1)$ **23.** $(a - 6b)(2a - 3b - 2)$ **25.** $(x + 5)(x^2 + 3)$ **27.** $(x + 3)(2 - 3a)$ **29.** $(b - 4)(a - 3)$
31. $(x - 6)(5 - 2y)$ **33.** $(x - 3)(2 - 3y)$ **35.** $(x + 7)(x + 1)$ **37.** $(x - 7)(x - 2)$ **39.** $(x - 6)(x - 4)$
41. $(a + 9)(a - 5)$ **43.** $(x - 7y)(x + 6y)$ **45.** $(x - 14y)(x - y)$ **47.** $(x^2 - 8)(x^2 + 5)$ **49.** $(x^2 + 7y^2)(x^2 + 9y^2)$
51. $2(x + 11)(x + 2)$ **53.** $x(x + 5)(x - 4)$ **55.** $(2x + 1)(x - 1)$ **57.** $(3x - 5)(2x + 1)$ **59.** $(3a - 5)(a - 1)$
61. $(4a + 9)(2a - 1)$ **63.** $(2x + 3)(x + 5)$ **65.** $(3x^2 + 1)(x^2 - 3)$ **67.** $(3x + y)(2x + 11y)$ **69.** $(7x - 3y)(x + 2y)$
71. $x(2x + 5)(2x - 3)$ **73.** $5x^2(2x + 1)(x + 1)$

A.4 Exercises

1. The problem will have two terms. It will be in the form $a^2 - b^2$. One term is positive and one term is negative. The values and variables for the first and second terms are both perfect squares. So each one will be of the form 1, 4, 9, 16, 25, 36, and/or x^2, x^4, x^6, etc.
3. There will be two terms added together. It will be of the form $a^3 + b^3$. Each term will contain a number or variable cubed or both. They will be of the form 1, 8, 27, 64, 125, and/or x^3, x^6, x^9, etc.   **5.** $(a + 8)(a - 8)$ **7.** $(4x - 9)(4x + 9)$ **9.** $(8x - 1)(8x + 1)$
11. $(7m - 3n)(7m + 3n)$ **13.** $(10y - 9)(10y + 9)$ **15.** $(1 - 9xy)(1 + 9xy)$ **17.** $2(4x + 3)(4x - 3)$ **19.** $5x(1 + 2x)(1 - 2x)$
21. $(3x - 1)^2$ **23.** $(7x - 1)^2$ **25.** $(9w + 2t)^2$ **27.** $(6x + 5y)^2$ **29.** $2(2x + 3)^2$ **31.** $3x(x - 4)^2$ **33.** $(x - 3)(x^2 + 3x + 9)$
35. $(x + 5)(x^2 - 5x + 25)$ **37.** $(4x - 1)(16x^2 + 4x + 1)$ **39.** $(5x - 2)(25x^2 + 10x + 4)$ **41.** $(1 - 3x)(1 + 3x + 9x^2)$
43. $(4x + 5)(16x^2 - 20x + 25)$ **45.** $(4s^2 + t^2)(16s^4 - 4s^2t^2 + t^4)$ **47.** $6(y - 1)(y^2 + y + 1)$ **49.** $3(x - 2)(x^2 + 2x + 4)$

51. $x^2(x - 2y)(x^2 + 2xy + 4y^2)$ **53.** $(x - 9)(x + 7)$ **55.** $(3x + 2)(2x - 1)$ **57.** $(5w^2 + 1)(5w^2 - 1)$ **59.** $(b^2 + 3)^2$
61. $(z^2 + 5)(y - 3)$ **63.** $(sr - 1)(s^2 + t)$ **65.** $(7m^3 - 9)(7m^3 + 9)$ **67.** $(6y^3 - 5)^2$ **69.** $2(a^4 - 5)(a^4 + 5)$
71. $(5m + 2n)(25m^2 - 10mn + 4n^2)$ **73.** $2(x + 8)(x - 6)$ **75.** $3(3x + 2)(2x + 1)$ **77.** $9a(3x - 1)(x + 4)$
79. $2x(3x - 2)(x + 5)$ **81.** $3(2a - b)(4a^2 + 2ab + b^2)$ **83.** $(2w - 5z)^2$ **85.** $9(2a - 3b)(2a + 3b)$
87. $(4x^2 + 9y^2)(2x - 3y)(2x + 3y)$ **89.** $(5m^2 + 2)(25m^4 - 10m^2 + 4)$ **91.** $(5x + 4)(5x + 1)$ **93.** $(4x - 3)(x - 3)$
95. $A = (4x + y)(4x - y)$ square feet   **97.** One possibility is to have $6x + 5$ rows with $5x - 1$ trees in each row. Another possibility is to have $5x - 1$ rows with $6x + 5$ trees in each row.

A.5 Exercises

1. $y = -\frac{2}{3}x + 8$ **3.** $y = 5x + 33$ **5.** $y = -\frac{1}{5}x + \frac{6}{5}$ **7.** $y = \frac{5}{7}x + \frac{13}{7}$ **9.** $y = -\frac{2}{3}x - \frac{8}{3}$ **11.** $y = -3$
13. $5x - y = -10$ **15.** $x - 3y = 8$ **17.** $2x - 3y = 15$ **19.** $7x - y = -27$ **21.** neither   **23.** parallel   **25.** perpendicular

Appendix B
Exercises

1. $269.17   **3. (a)** $82\frac{1}{3}$ feet **(b)** 90 feet; $17.90   **5.** jog, $2\frac{2}{3}$ miles; walk $3\frac{1}{9}$ miles rest, $4\frac{4}{9}$ minutes; walk, $1\frac{7}{9}$ miles

7. Betty; Melinda increases each activity by $\frac{2}{3}$ by day 3 but Betty increases each activity by $\frac{7}{9}$ by day 3.   **9.** $4\frac{1}{2}$ miles
11. $98,969.00   **13. (a)** $36,000 **(b)** $11,160   **15.** 18%   **17.** 69%

Appendix C
Exercises
Addition Practice

1. 37   **2.** 75   **3.** 94   **4.** 99   **5.** 78   **6.** 29   **7.** 61   **8.** 81   **9.** 369   **10.** 277   **11.** 491   **12.** 600   **13.** 1421
14. 1052   **15.** 900   **16.** 401   **17.** 1711   **18.** 1319   **19.** 289   **20.** 399   **21.** 589   **22.** 887   **23.** 422   **24.** 792   **25.** 902
26. 930

Subtraction Practice

1. 21   **2.** 62   **3.** 22   **4.** 43   **5.** 68   **6.** 5   **7.** 29   **8.** 45   **9.** 531   **10.** 223   **11.** 726   **12.** 191   **13.** 378
14. 66   **15.** 509   **16.** 228   **17.** 256   **18.** 63   **19.** 183   **20.** 269   **21.** 873   **22.** 1892   **23.** 7479   **24.** 2868   **25.** 2066
26. 678

Multiplication Practice

1. 69   **2.** 26   **3.** 378   **4.** 603   **5.** 1554   **6.** 1643   **7.** 3680   **8.** 3640   **9.** 7790   **10.** 2691   **11.** 9116   **12.** 7502
13. 12,095   **14.** 30,168   **15.** 20,672   **16.** 24,180   **17.** 37,584   **18.** 53,692   **19.** 284,490   **20.** 506,566   **21.** 238,119
22. 375,820   **23.** 803,396   **24.** 785,354   **25.** 49,516,817   **26.** 62,526,175

Division Practice

1. 16   **2.** 56   **3.** 59 R2   **4.** 47 R5   **5.** 124   **6.** 296   **7.** 234   **8.** 567   **9.** 521 R6   **10.** 739 R2   **11.** 321 R11
12. 753 R6   **13.** 89   **14.** 91   **15.** 32   **16.** 41   **17.** 108 R29   **18.** 123 R25   **19.** 214   **20.** 342   **21.** 1134 R14
22. 1076 R65   **23.** 124   **24.** 153   **25.** 1125   **26.** 1532

Appendix E
Exercises

1. -7 **3.** 15   **5.** 2   **7.** 47   **9.** 18   **11.** 0   **13.** 0   **15.** -0.6 **17.** $-7a - 4b$ **19.** $\frac{11}{84}$ **21.** $\begin{vmatrix} 6 & 10 \\ -5 & 9 \end{vmatrix}$ **23.** $\begin{vmatrix} 3 & -4 \\ 1 & -5 \end{vmatrix}$
25. -7 **27.** -26 **29.** 11   **31.** -27 **33.** -8 **35.** 0   **37.** -3.179 **39.** 18,553   **41.** $x = 2; y = 3$ **43.** $x = -2; y = 5$
45. $x = 10; y = 2$ **47.** $x = 4; y = -2$ **49.** $x = 1.5795; y = -0.0902$ **51.** $x = 1; y = 1; z = 1$ **53.** $x = -\frac{1}{2}; y = \frac{1}{2}; z = 2$
55. $x = 4; y = -2; z = 1$ **57.** $x = -0.219; y = 1.893; z = -3.768$ **59.** $w = -3.105; x = 4.402; y = 15.909; z = 6.981$

Appendix F
Exercises

1. $(4, -1)$ **3.** $(3, -9)$ **5.** $(0, 3)$ **7.** $(2, 2)$ **9.** $(1.2, 3.7)$ **11.** $(3, -1, 4)$ **13.** $(1, -1, 3)$ **15.** $(0, -2, 5)$ **17.** $(0.5, -1, 5)$
19. $(3.6, 1.8, 2.4)$ **21.** $(4.2, -3.6, 8.8, 5.4)$

Appendix G

Exercises

1. elements   **3.** intersection   **5.** empty set   **7.** {California, Colorado, Connecticut}   **9.** {1, 3, 5, 7, . . .}   **11.** {15, 20, 25, 30, 35, 40, 45}
13. {. . . , −3, −2, −1}   **15.** $O = \{x \mid x$ is an ocean$\}$ **17.** $G = \{x$ is even and $2 \le x \le 8\}$ **19.** $T = \{x \mid x$ is a type of triangle$\}$
21. (a) {−2, −1, 2, 3, 5, 8} **(b)** {−1, 3, 5}   **23.** False. B is an infinite set.   **25.** True   **27.** True   **29.** False; $A \cap C = \{1, 2, 3, 4, 5\}$
31. False; the set of whole numbers includes 0.   **33.** True   **35.** Answers will vary. One possible answer is {Ann, Nina}.
37. (a) {Andrew, Christopher, Daniel, David, Jacob, James, Jason, John, Joseph, Joshua, Matthew, Michael, Nicholas, Robert, Tyler} **(b)** union
39. whole numbers: 15, 0, $\sqrt{81}$; natural numbers: 15, $\sqrt{81}$; integers: 15, 0, $\sqrt{81}$, −17; rational numbers: 3.62, $\frac{-3}{11}$, 15, $\frac{22}{3}$, 0, $\sqrt{81}$, −17; irrational
numbers: $\sqrt{20}$; real numbers: 3.62, $\sqrt{20}$, $\frac{-3}{11}$, 15, $\frac{22}{3}$, 0, $\sqrt{81}$, −17   **41.** No. The set of integers contains negative numbers. Negative numbers
are not part of the set of whole numbers.   **43.** The set of whole numbers is a subset of the integers, the rational numbers, and the real
numbers.

Applications Index

A

Astronomy/space science applications:
  Neptune, distance from the sun, 256
  planetary orbital times, 149
  space travel, 257, 261
Automobile/other vehicles applications:
  car loan, 160
  car payments, 74, 160
  hybrid cars, 41
  rental truck costs, 240
Aviation applications:
  air speed, 237, 240
  airport runway, 89

B

Banking applications, *See also* Finance
      applications
  car payments, 74, 160
  checking account balance, 65, 121
  home equity loans, 210
  simple interest, 111
Business applications:
  cell phone sales, 89
  equal contributions, 74
  full-time work, 158
  profit/loss, 59, 60
  salary, *See* wages/salary
  temporary employment help:
    expenses, 237
    hiring, 166
  wages/salary, 41, 166, 257
  workforce, 165

C

Computer/electronics/Internet
      applications:
  books, buying online, 182
  computer chips, 101
  computer speed, 261
  computer usage, 107
Construction applications, *See* Home
      improvement/construction
      applications
Cooking applications, *See* Food/cooking
      applications

D

Demographic applications:
  U.S. population, 193
    growth in, 210

E

Education applications:
  athletic field, 89
  book cost, 149
  class size, 165
  college logo item sale, 240
  course average, 160
  faculty members, 193

foreign students in the U.S., 193
homework grading, 102
math exam scores, 237
measurement, 41
middle school population, 149
mural painting, 89
percent of graduate students
      accepted, 160
school fees, 59
student loans, 74
student transfers, 9
value of an education, 259
vent grill, 142
Entertainment applications:
  Jeopardy quiz show, 112
  MTV video, 21
  tips, 106
Environmental applications:
  butterfly population, 59
  drinking water safety, 41
  earthquakes, 127
  falcon population, 142
  fish catch statistics, 10, 148
  land area, 149
  rainforests:
    size, 211, 250
  whale calf population, 127
  world's largest lakes, 42

F

Finance applications, *See also* Banking
      applications; Stock market
      applications
  car payments, 74
  credit card balance, 59
  federal taxes, 65
  income tax, 9
Food/cooking applications:
  fish catch statistics, 10, 148
  food costs, 237
  health drink, 83
  serving size, 94
  trail mix recipe, 9
  turkey weight, 41

G

Geometric/measurement applications:
  circle, circumference, 169
  circular irrigation system area, 106
  circumference, 169
  field dimensions, 89
  number sum, 168
  parallelogram area, 169
  rectangle:
    length, 148, 165, 169
    width, 193
  sign area, 101
  sphere volume, 169

trapezoid:
    area, 169
    base, 193
  triangle:
    angles, 148–149, 165
    perimeter, 94, 148–149, 169

H

Health care applications:
  calories burned while
      jogging, 192
Hobby/craft applications:
  aquariums, 21
  stained-glass table, 231
Home improvement/construction
      applications:
  bathroom tile, 230
  carpentry, 21, 101
  carpeting length, 169
  construction cost, 257
  curtain material, 41
  home equity line of credit, 59
  leaky faucet, 210
  marble flooring, 106
  pool fencing, 94
  roofing, 101
  window coating, 102
Home life applications:
  triangular roof support beam, 114
Hospital applications:
  nurses on duty, 158

M

Manufacturing applications:
  CD recording, 102
  exports, 148
  profit, 111
  pullovers, 29
  quality control, 121
  shirts, 29
  sneaker production, 75
Map applications:
  road maps, 181
Measurement applications, *See*
      Geometric/measurement
      applications
Miscellaneous applications:
  007 films, 257
  archeology, 210
  auditorium seating, 142
  bamboo growth, 256
  cell phones, 181
    plan analysis, 233
  circus ticket prices, 237
  city parking space, 231
  civilian employment, 204
  cookie sales, 148
  dog body temperature, 112

dog weight, 106
driveway blacktop sealer, 114
DVD players, 183
elephant weight, 160
elevation difference, 65
elevation levels, 110
exports, 148
framing a masterpiece, 94
hand shakes, 257
Jeopardy quiz show, 112
moving furniture, 231
national debt, 256
newspaper circulation, 183
oil production, 182
parking lot sealer, 111
Persian rug prices, 183
photo enlargement, 160
radar picture, 121
robot, 106
sea level, 102
sea rescue, 65
sign painting, 111
signal paint, 106, 111
signal tower frame, 101
time change, 59
TV parts, 101
U.S. federal budget, 204
watch hand, 257

R

Retail applications:
    discount merchandise, 127
    discount store markdown
        policy, 60
    employee discount, 134
    kayak rentals, 149

S

Sales applications:
    cell phone sales, 89
    college logo item sale, 240
    cookie sales, 148
Science applications:
    atomic clock, 261
    gold atom, 256
    moles per molecule, 257
    neutron mass, 257
    red blood cells, 256
Space travel applications, *See*
        Astronomy/space science
        applications
Sports/recreation/leisure applications:
    archery, 149
    baseball, 10
        equipment, 237
    basketball, 9
    bicycle travel, 102
    boxing weight, 158
    cross-country racing, 29
    cross-country skiing, 192
    fairway care, 21
    fishing boat, gas consumption, 161
    football, 59, 60, 72, 74–75, 110, 237
    golf, 83
    hiking, 65
    inline skating, 20
    jogging, 192
    kayak rentals, 149
    Kentucky Derby, 9
    marathon training, 20
    mountain biking, 29
    Olympic medals, 148
    putting green care, 21

    sail dimensions, 102
    sail material, 142
    soccer practice, 89
    swimming pool, circular, 183
    tennis court fence, 160
    trapezoidal field, 114
Stock market applications:
    investments, 127, 134, 148
    stocks:
        prices, 110
        trading, 74
        value, 148

T

Tax applications:
    federal taxes, 65
    income tax, 9
Time and distance applications, *See also*
        Automobile/other vehicles
        applications
    miles per hour, 114
Travel applications, *See also* Automobile/
        other vehicles applications;
        Aviation applications
    road maps, 181
    transportation logistics, 237

W

Weather applications:
    cloud formation, 158
    temperature, 59, 65, 101,
        106, 111
        change, 65, 110
        tolerance, 102
Wildlife management applications, *See*
        Environmental applications

Subject Index

A

Absolute value, 52, 108
Accuracy problems, 99
Addition:
  of decimals, 34–35, 44
  of fractions:
    common denominator, 43
    with different denominators, 13–16
  of mixed numbers, 16–18, 43
  of real numbers, 50–60, 108
    with opposite signs, 54–55, 108
    with the same sign, 52–54, 108
Addition method:
  solving systems of linear equations
    by, 222–223, 226
Addition principle, 116–119
  using with the multiplication
    principle, 128–131
Additive inverse, 51–52, 117
Additive inverse property, 62
Algebraic expressions:
  defined, 85
  evaluating for a specified value,
    95–96
  simplifying:
    by removing grouping symbols,
      103–104
    using the distributive property,
      85–87
  translating English phrases into,
    144–146
  using substitution to evaluate, 95–99,
    109
  writing to compare two or more
    quantities, 146–147
Algebraic statements:
  English phrases, translating into, 152
Altitude, 96
Area, 96

B

Base, 76
  cubed, 76
  exponents, 242
  negative, 77
  positive, 77
  raised to the (exponent)-th power, 76
  squared, 76
  of a trapezoid, 97
Basic mathematical definitions,
  understanding, 2

C

Calculator, *See also* Graphing calculator
  exponents, 77
  fraction to decimal, 32
  negative numbers, 55
  order of operations, 81
Center, circle, 97

Circle, 97
Circumference, 97
Class:
  attendance, 18
  making a friend in, 39
  participation, 18
  taking notes in, 139
Coefficient, 124
Combining like terms, 90–92, 109
Common factors, dividing out, 22
Commutative property of
  multiplication, 23–24
Complex fractions, 25–26, *See also*
  Fractions
Consistent system of equations, 224
Coordinates, 172
Counting numbers, 2–3
Cubed base, 76

D

Decimal places, 31, 37
  counting the number of, 36
Decimal point, 31
Decimals, 37
  adding, 34–35, 44
  adding zeros to the right-hand side
    of, 34–35
  changing fractions to, 32–33, 44
  changing to fractions, 33–34, 44
  changing to percents, 41
  defined, 31
  dividing, 36–37, 44
    by a multiple of 10, 39
  multiplying, 35–36, 44
    by a multiple of 10, 38–39
  subtracting, 34–35, 44
Denominator, 2–3
Dependent equations, 219, 224
Distributive property:
  defined, 85
  using to simplify algebraic
    expressions, 85–87
Dividend, 36
Division:
  of decimals, 36–39, 44
    by a multiple of 10, 38–39
  dividend, 36
  divisor, 36
  of fractions, 24–25, 44
  of mixed numbers, 26–27, 44
  of real numbers, 66, 69–72,
    108
  by zero, 71
Division principle, 123–124
Divisor, 36

E

Elimination method, solving systems of
  linear equations by, 222–223

English phrases:
  algebraic expressions, writing to
    compare two or more quantities,
    146–147
  describing addition, 144
  describing division, 145
  describing multiplication, 144
  describing subtraction, 144
  translating algebraic expressions,
    146–147
  translating into algebraic
    statements, 152
Equation of a line, 207–208
  writing:
    given a graph of the line, 208
    given a point and a slope, 207, 212
    given two points, 207–208, 212
Equations, 116
  of the form $ax + b = c$, 128
  with fractions, solving, 135–139, 162
  with infinite number of solutions, 139
  with no solution, 139
  with parentheses, solving, 130–131, 162
  procedure for solving, for a specified
    variable, 177
  solving, procedure for, 137
  with the variable on both sides,
    solving, 128–130, 162
Equivalent equations, 116
Examination:
  getting organized for, 156
  night before, 104
  studying for, 156
Exponential expressions, 242
  with like bases, using the quotient
    rule to divide, 243–246
  raising to a power, 246–248
Exponential notation, parts of, 76
Exponents, 76–79, 108
  calculator, 77
  defined, 242
  exponent of zero, 245, 260
  laws of, 251
  negative, 251–255, 260
  numerical coefficient, 243
  power rules, 251
  product rule, 251
  quotient rule, 251
  raising a power to a power,
    246–247, 260
  rules of, 242–248
  sign rule for, 77

F

Factors, 2–3, 76, 85
  common, dividing out, 22
  prime, using to find the least common
    denominator of two or more
    fractions, 12–13

Formulas:
  geometric, 96–97
  using substitution to evaluate, 95–99,
      109
Fraction bars, 103
Fractions, 2, 23–24
  adding:
    common denominator, 11, 43
    different denominators, 13–16
    mixed numbers, 16–18
  changing decimals to, 33–34
  changing to an equivalent fraction
      with a given denominator, 7, 43
  changing to decimals, 44
  with a common denominator,
      adding/subtracting, 11
  complex, 25–26
  dividing, 24–25, 44
  equations with, solving, 135–139
  improper, converting between mixed
      numbers and, 4–5, 43
  invert and multiply method, 26
  multiplying, 21–23, 43
    by a whole number, 23
  proper, 4
  reducing, 2–4
  simplifying, 2–4, 43
  subtracting:
    common denominator, 11, 43
    different denominators, 13–16

G
Geometric formulas, 162
Graphing:
  horizontal lines, 188–189
  intercept method of, 186–187
  linear equations, 184–193
    by plotting three ordered pairs,
        184–186
  parallel lines, 201
  straight lines, 184, 212
    by plotting its intercepts, 186–187
  vertical lines, 188–189
Graphing calculator, See also
    Calculator
  parallel lines, graphing, 201
  systems of linear equations:
    identifying, 224
    solving, 220
Graphs, 172
  inequalities, 150
Grouping symbols, 103–104, 109

H
Help resources, 125
Homework, 24–25
  how to do, 87
Horizontal lines, graphing, 188–189

I
Identity, 225
Improper fractions:
  converting between mixed numbers
      and, 4–5

defined, 4
Inconsistent system of equations,
    219, 224
Independent equations, 224
Inequalities:
  defined, 150
  on a number line, graphing with,
      150–151
  solving, 164
Inequality statements, interpreting, 150
Integers, 50
Intercept method of graphing,
    186–187
Invert and multiply method, 26
Irrational numbers, 50
Is greater than, 150
Is less than, 150

L
LCD, See Least common denominator
    (LCD)
Least common denominator
    (LCD), 135
  defined, 12
  finding, 12–13, 43
    using prime factors, 12
Light-year, 254
Like terms:
  combining, 90–92, 109
  defined, 90
Linear equations, See also Systems of
    linear equations
  graphing, 184–193
    by plotting three ordered pairs,
        184–186
  with two variables, 227
Linear equations in two variables:
  defined, 176–177
  finding ordered pairs for,
      176–178
Lowest common denominator, See
    Least common denominator
    (LCD)
Lowest terms, 3

M
Mathematics:
  reasons for studying, 119
  review, need for, 248
  steps toward success in, 75
Mixed numbers:
  adding, 16–18, 43
  changing improper fractions to, 5–6
  changing to improper fractions, 6–7, 43
  defined, 5
  dividing, 26–27, 44
  multiplying, 23–24, 44
  subtracting, 16–18, 43
Monomials
  dividing, 244, 260
  multiplying, 242, 260
Multiplication:
  of decimals, 35–36, 44
    by a multiple of 10, 38–39

of fractions, 21–23, 43
  of mixed numbers, 23–24, 44
  of monomials, 260
  of real numbers, 66–68, 108
Multiplication principle, 122–125
  using with the addition principle,
      128–131
Multiplicative identity, 4
Multiplicative inverse, 125

N
Natural numbers, 2–3
Negative exponents, 251–255, 260
  defined, 251
  properties of, 252
  scientific notation, writing numbers
      in, 252–253, 260
Negative numbers, 50
  calculator, 55
  raising to a power, 77, 108
Negative slope, 197
New material, previewing, 81
Note taking, 139
Number line, 50
  inequalities on, graphing with,
      150–151
  solving and graphing inequalities on,
      152–156
Numbers:
  irrational, 50
  mixed, 5–7, 16–18, 23–24, 26–27,
      43–44
  natural, 2–3
  negative, 50, 55, 77
  prime, 2–3
  real, 50–63, 66–75, 76, 108
  types of, 50
  whole, 2, 50
Numerals, 2
Numerator, 2–3

O
Opposite numbers (opposite in sign),
    51–52, 117
Order of operations, 80–83, 108
  calculator, 81
  defined, 80
Ordered pairs, 172, 218
  finding for a given linear equation,
      177–178
Organizer, 43–44
Origin, 172
  lines that go through, 187

P
Parallel lines:
  defined, 200
  finding the slopes of, 200–201, 212
  graphing, 201
Parallelogram, 96
Percents:
  defined, 41
  of a given number, finding, 44
Perimeter, 96

Period (.), in decimal points, 31
Periodic review, need for, 248
Perpendicular lines:
    defined, 200
    finding the slopes of, 200–201, 212
Plotted point, determining the
        coordinates of, 174–176
Plotting a point, 172–174
Positive numbers, 50
Positive slope, 197
Previewing new material, 81
Prime factors, using to find the least
        common denominator of two or
        more fractions, 12–13
Prime numbers, 2–3
Product raised to a power, 247
Product rule, for exponents, 242

Q
Quotient, 36
Quotient raised to a power, 247
Quotient rule, 246–247

R
Raising a power to a power, 246–247,
        260
Rational numbers, 50
Real numbers, 50
    adding, 50–60, 108
    dividing, 69–72, 108
    division by zero, 71
    with like or unlike signs, subtracting,
        61–63
    multiplication properties for,
        using, 68
    multiplying, 66–75, 108
    negative, 76
    with opposite signs, adding, 54–55, 108
    positive, 76
    with the same sign, adding, 52–54, 108
    subtracting, 61–65, 108
    using in real-life situations, 51–52
    using the addition properties for,
        56–57
Rectangle, 96
Rectangular coordinate systems,
        172–183
Reduced form, 2
Reducing a fraction, 2

Removing parentheses, 85–87, 91,
        103–104, 108
    innermost, order of removal, 103–104
Review, need for, 248
Right angles, 96

S
Scientific notation:
    calculator, 252–253
    significant digits, 254
    writing numbers in, 252–253, 260
Significant digits, 254
Simplest form, 2
Simplifying a fraction, 2
Slope of a line, 194–201
    defined, 194
    finding given two points on a line,
        194–197, 212
    finding y-intercept and, given its
        equation, 197–198, 212
    slope of a straight line, 197
    undefined slope, 197
    using to describe a line, 196
    and y-intercept:
        graphing a line using, 199–200,
            212
        writing the equation of a line
            given, 198–199, 212
    zero slope, 197
Slope–intercept form of a line, 198
Solution set, 150
Solutions, 116, 177
    inequalities, 150–151
    to a system of two linear equations in
        two variables, 218
Solving an equation, 116
Square, 97
Square units, 96
Squared base, 76
Straight lines:
    graphing, 184, 212
        by plotting its intercepts, 186–187
    slope of, 197
Substitution method:
    solving systems of linear equations
        by, 219–220, 226
Substitution, using to evaluate algebraic
        expressions and formulas,
        95–99, 109

Subtraction:
    of decimals, 34–35, 44
    of fractions:
        common denominator, 43
        with different denominators, 13–16
    of mixed numbers, 16–18, 43
    of real numbers, 61–65, 108
        with like or unlike signs, 61–63
Systems of linear equations:
    choosing a method to solve
        algebraically, 226–227
    solving by addition method, 222–223
    solving by graphing method, 218–219
    solving by substitution method,
        219–220
    in two variables, 218–227

T
Term, 85
Textbook, reading, 63
Trapezoid, 97
Triangle formula, 97
Truth values, 177
Two-dimensional figures, geometric
        formulas, 96–97

U
Undefined slope, 197

V
Variables, 76, 85–87
Vertical lines, graphing, 188–189

W
Whole numbers, 2, 50

X
x-axis, 172
x-coordinates, 172
x-intercept, 186

Y
y-axis, 172
y-coordinates, 172
y-intercept, 186

Z
Zero slope, 197
Zero to the zero power, 245–246